Psychology from the Standpoint of an Interbehaviorist

N. H. Pronko

Professor of Psychology Emeritus
Wichita State University

Brooks/Cole Publishing Company
Monterey, California

A Division of Wadsworth, Inc.

To J. R. Kantor

Inspiring teacher, indefatigable scholar,
and theoretician par excellence

Consulting Editor: *Edward L. Walker, New Mexico State University*

Printed in the United States of America

10 9 8 7 6 5 4 3 2 1

Library of Congress Cataloging in Publication Data

Pronko, Nicholas Henry, 1908–
    Psychology from the standpoint of an interbehaviorist.

    Bibliography: p. 503
    Includes index.
    1. Psychology. 2. Behaviorism. 3. Social
interaction. I. Title.
BF121.P74   150.19′43   80-10247
ISBN 0-8185-0397-1

Acquisition Editor: *C. Deborah Laughton*
Production Coordinator: *Marilu Uland*
Book Design and Production: *Greg Hubit Bookworks, Larkspur, California*
Typesetting: *Graphic Typesetting Service, Los Angeles, California*

Preface

What This Book Is About

This book is about interbehavioral psychology, a nontraditional system somewhat akin to Skinner's behaviorism, with ecological psychology, and other similar approaches. These systems have at least one feature in common: they look beyond the skin and contents of the individual organism in their attempt to interpret behavior.

By contrast, much of contemporary psychology adopts a self-actional approach. Self-actional views look *within* the organism (chiefly to the mind or brain) in explaining behavior. Such approaches serve as a point of departure for this book, which looks on behavior as a *joint function* of an organism *and* stimulus object in the richness of their mutual context. Some investigators have called such a broad view a "transactional," "event" or "field" approach, a convenient example of which is furnished by Kantor's interbehavioral framework. Therefore, one of my aims is to present interbehavioral theory as such. Beyond that, I apply Kantorian theory to a diversity of data generally available in scattered literature. However, I feel that my most important job is to compare and contrast organism-centered or self-actional approaches with the broader event, or field, views such as those of Kantor, Skinner, Barker, Kimble, Kuo, Noel Smith, Bijou, Baer, Verplanck, Bandura, Day, and others. Throughout the book, the reader can compare self-actional versus field or event interpretations of a great variety of behaviors. Such comparisons offer the reader a choice of alternative interpretations.

Psychology does not suffer from a scarcity of data. On the contrary, there is a rich storehouse of fascinating material but much of it is approached from a variety of narrow, theoretical orientations that emphasize either the physiology of the brain, "powers of the mind," or heredity versus environment (or vice versa). Interbehavioral theory provides an enriched perspective that can assimilate the facts and that can emancipate us from the folklore and narrow approaches in which the facts are embedded.

There are fashions in intellectual trends just as there are in dress. For example, people are attracted to Zen and other Eastern religions and to such popular movements as transcendental meditation, transactional analysis, and *est*. Such trends may be symptomatic of dissatisfaction with scientifically rigorous—but narrow—traditional viewpoints in psychology. For this reason, I have chosen to reexamine traditional assumptions with the aim of providing a broader approach, one that meets the criteria of science but that is more inclusive.

As for my own position, I rejected from the outset a neutral eclecticism that attempts to organize incompatible or contradictory theories into a seemingly coherent system Instead, I have consistently assumed an interbehavioral stand, in the hope of providing my readers with a strategic perspective for working out their own eventual orientation.

The title of this book *(Psychology from the Standpoint of an Interbehaviorist)* should be read with emphasis on the word *an*. It is *not* a book by *interbehaviorists* or by *the* interbehaviorist (J. R. Kantor), but by *one* member of that class of psychologists. It is about interbehaviorism as *I* have come to understand it. Therefore I alone am responsible for any inevitable deviations from the original theoretical formulation.

One final point concerns the present status of interbehavioral psychology. Recent developments in psychology, biology (with the recent explosive growth of one subdiscipline, ecology), and other disciplines have given interbehavioral psychology special prominence and distinction. Its time seems to have come. Support for such a suggestion comes from a variety of fields whose workers are looking for a broader foundation than that provided by traditional, self-actional systems. The following bibliography furnishes a scanty sampling of the ferment in various areas that are experimenting with the broader approaches I examine here:

Sample Bibliography

Canter, D. *The psychology of place.* New York: St. Martin's Press, 1977.

Emery, F. E., and Trist, E. L. *Towards a social ecology.* New York: Plenum Press, 1973.

Hawley, A. H. *Roderick D. McKenzie: On human ecology.* Chicago: University of Chicago Press, 1968.

Holahan, C. J. *Environment and behavior.* New York: Plenum Press, 1978.

McGurk, H. (Ed.). *Ecological factors in human development.* New York: North Holland, 1977.

Moos, R. H. *The human context: Environmental determinants of behavior.* New York: Wiley, 1976.

Moos, R., and Brownstein, R. *Environment and Utopia.* New York: Plenum Press, 1977.

Stokols, D. (Ed.). *Perspectives on environment and behavior.* New York: Plenum Press, 1977.

Williams, E. P., and Raush, H. L. (Eds.). *Naturalistic viewpoints in psychological research.* New York: Holt, Rinehart & Winston, 1969.

How This Book Is Organized

There are roughly four major parts to this book, although the book is not formally divided. Chapter 1 "The Nature of Psychological Events from an Interbehavioral Viewpoint," suggests a procedure for analyzing psychological events or occurrences.

Chapter 2, "The Reactional Biography," essentially deals with the manner in which events become related to other events of the reactional biography or psychological history of the individual.

A *developmental view* connects the next three chapters. Chapter 3 deals with behavior origins. Chapter 4 discusses basic or enduring phases of the reactional biography. Chapter 5 considers the mature or societal phase of development, stressing the role of social factors.

Chapter 6, "Personality," takes a synthetic view of behavior as it is organized in relation to a given individual. In Chapter 7, what is conventionally referred to as "abnormal personality" is considered from a social psychological (nonmedical) approach as problems in living. Chapter 8, on intelligence, is included because there is a close connection between intelligence and personality and because there is widespread interest in the topic.

The rest of the book (Chapters 9 through 12) works from a *cross-sectional* approach, with the aim of learning something about the behaving organism via an analysis of different classes of behaviors such as attending, perceiving, remembering, forgetting, feeling, and emoting.

Acknowledgments

This book would never have seen the light of day but for an invitation to write it, and for continued encouragement and prompting to do so, from Terry Hendrix, former executive editor of Brooks/Cole. My appreciation is also due Ed Walker for his careful reading of the entire manuscript and for his many helpful suggestions. Two colleagues of mine deserve special recognition for their assistance. Grant Kenyon read Chapters 1 through 9 with a fine-tooth comb, and David Herman matched him in his perusal and criticism of Chapter 12. Many and lengthy discussions with both led to a clarification of my own ideas.

The book also benefited from extensive critical reviews by the following individuals: Benjamin A. Fairbank, Jr., New Mexico State University; Frank Ireland, Ferris State College; Gerald Mertens, St. Cloud State University; Joseph Rubinstein, Purdue University; and Leigh Shaffer, Nebraska Wesleyan University.

Special mention is due the able and dedicated staff of Brooks/Cole, particularly to C. Deborah Laughton and Marilu Uland for initiating and guiding the book's production. I am grateful to Greg Hubit for his fastidious attention in designing the book and in his final preparation of the manuscript for the printer. I extend my sincere thanks to Linda Purrington, who took extensive pains in ferreting out errors in construction and documentation, in her determination to achieve as error-proof a product as possible.

In the preparation of the manuscript, I owe special thanks to Tybel Elizabeth Edwards for transforming my seemingly inscrutable, arthritic scrawl into a correctly and becomingly typed manuscript. Paul Magelli and Martin Reif of the Fairmount College of Liberal Arts and Sciences rendered much-appreciated help as I needed it. Above all, I must express my deep appreciation to my wife, Gary, for her unstinting encouragement from the very initiation of this project and for her continuous, varied assistance during its progress.

N. H. Pronko

Contents

**Chapter 7
"Abnormal Personality," "Psychopathology," "Mental Illness,"
or "Problems in Living"?   244**

**Chapter 8
"Intelligence" and Intelligent Testing   281**

1

The Nature of Psychological Events from an Interbehavioral Point of View

An Initial Statement in a Nutshell

Interbehavioral psychology is a philosophically advanced approach to psychology which provides an account of human behavior strictly in empirical and scientifically verifiable terms. In so doing it avoids numerous philosophical pitfalls which plague much of popular psychology. The philosophical base of interbehavioral psychology has some features in common with Skinner's form of behaviorism and ecological psychology among others. Such psychologies look to the environment, and thus beyond the skin and the contents of the organism, in their attempts to interpret behavior.

[Walker, personal communication, 1979]

Walker's statement provides a broad preliminary sketch of the interbehavioral and related investigatory frameworks. Let us note certain additional features of these recent psychological viewpoints.

Psychologists who have adopted these newer approaches recognize the fact that behavior does not occur in a vacuum, because behavior also takes place in the surroundings of the organism. Therefore, these psychologists require a broad observational base, one that takes into account not only the organism but also the relevant environmental variables. To varying degrees,

1

these workers view all of the relevant factors as participants in their joint and mutual interaction. There are differences among these approaches, but they all assign the same role to the organism. Orientations that view psychological data as events instead of as intraorganismic happenings no longer give the organism a position at center stage. Instead of the organism carrying practically all of the explanatory burden, as formerly, it now shares that function with the other participating factors. Instead of dealing in generalities, however, we can more profitably move on to an examination of psychological action in the following case history, one that begs for interpretation.

A Case History

For 13 years—from the age of 7 to the age of 20—a young woman suffered from a severe phobia of running water (case cited in Young, 1936). She (we shall call her Diane) could not recall, no matter how hard she tried, when or under what circumstance her irrational, but nonetheless real, phobia had started. It dominated her life throughout much of her childhood and her entire teenage years.

Splashing sounds of water distressed her most. During her early years, her bathtub had to be filled while she was in a distant part of the house. After that was accomplished, it took three members of Diane's family to hold her in the tub while she was satisfactorily washed, to the accompaniment of her struggling and screaming. In school, even children drinking at the water fountain upset her and made her fearful if they were too noisy. On one such occasion, she even fainted.

Traveling by train was also hazardous and was avoided as much as possible. However, if she had to travel by railroad, her window curtain had to be pulled down to prevent her from panicking at the sight of a body of water. Her life was severely restricted.

The climax to the story coincided with the visit of an aunt from a distant city, whom Diane and her mother had not seen for 13 years. The mother, alone, met Diane's aunt at the station and told her about Diane's troublesome phobia of running water. When she met Diane, the aunt immediately declared "I have never told." The ensuing conversation provoked Diane to recall the circumstances surrounding the origin of her phobia.

As reconstructed, the story goes that, 13 years before, Diane and her mother had visited this aunt. One day, they went on a picnic. The mother decided to leave the group early, but Diane begged to be allowed to stay on with the aunt. The mother agreed, on the strength of Diane's promise to obey the aunt and to stay close to her. But on a later walk in the woods, Diane forgot her promise and ran off alone. A search was organized, and soon Diane was found lying wedged among the rocks of a small stream with a waterfall pouring down over her head. She was crying hysterically. The child was terrified over the punishment she might suffer at her mother's hands on account of her disobedience. While drying Diane's clothes at a nearby farmhouse, the aunt reassured Diane with the promise that she would never tell, and she did not. The next morning the little girl and her aunt parted; they did not see each other until 13 years later. Not having anyone in whom to confide, and to talk things out with, and with whom she could ventilate her feelings, she repressed the memory of the incident, as we say. Later, when she tried to recall how her phobia originated, she was unable to do so, even with the help of supportive parents and therapists.

Diane's story has a happy ending (Young, 1936, p. 11): "After the memory had been reinstated, the young woman found it possible to approach running water without discomfort and gradually the special adjustment of conduct, which the phobia had necessitated, disappeared."

Diane's case history is interesting, but we are not yet prepared to do much beyond merely enjoying it. Her phobia extended over a long period and involved an immense number of episodes related not only to her own activities but also to the activities of her mother, schoolmates, teachers, railroad personnel, and so forth.

If we are to come to grips, in a psychological sense, with histories such as that of Diane's phobia, we first need to acquire some analytic tools. In subsequent sections of this book, we will learn how to dissect large chunks of behavior into small, understandable units and to relate them to each other so as to understand the whole. Our job will be similar to the task of the biology student who learns how to dissect a frog or an embryo pig in order to understand the whole organism.

Unfortunately, natural phenomena are not packaged with a printed set of instructions detailing how they must be understood. Throughout history, scientists have not always agreed on how to understand gravity, light, magnetism, the universe, plant and animal life, and thinking, remembering, fearing, hating, loving, and so on. They disagreed because they were reared in different historical periods, with different perspectives and differing assumptions about the phenomena that they chose to study.

For example, I am going to assume that the things that we shall study, such activities as seeing, hearing, learning, remembering, forgetting, and talking, are not at all supernatural. I am going to work under the assumption that all of these psychological happenings are as natural as rocks rolling down a mountain, as lightning, and as plants and animals being born, growing, and dying. But we should examine the validity of such assumptions (which are sometimes hidden). Are they justified? Do they color our results? For example, one assumption under which psychologists conduct inquiry is that a human being consists of a body and a mind. Other psychologists refuse to acknowledge the existence of mind; they explain seeing, hearing, learning, remembering, and forgetting in physiological terms. It is worthwhile to consider such questions if we are to do a thorough, solidly based inquiry into our subject matter.

But first let me say a word about the aim and focus of this book in relation to recent developments, not only in psychology but also in other disciplines.

Ecology as a Stepping Stone

Humanity's concern about air, water, land, and even noise pollution calls attention to the importance of our environment. The recent expansion of the branch of biology known as *ecology* has sensitized us to our surroundings. Ecology focuses on *the relationship of organisms to their environment and to each other.* The ecologist investigates not organisms alone, or environments alone but their reciprocal, joint activity. The ecologist observes and interprets events or a field of occurrences in which *both* organisms and their surroundings—or, better still, organisms *in* their surroundings—are of focal interest. The *context* in which an organism is viewed is just as important as the organism. It is the totality or the entire happening that is under inspection.

Ecological terms, such as *ecosystem,* force one to adopt a broader perspective than preceding views that centered on the organism as existing in a vacuum. According to the *New Columbia Encyclopedia* (Harris & Levey, 1975), an ecosystem is the basic ecological unit of study. An ecosystem may be as small as a rusty tin can full of mosquito larvae, or a rotting log, or it may be as large as Lake Erie or even the entire planet Earth. In any case, the ecologist studies a community of plants and animals in relation to each other and to the chemical and physical conditions in their surroundings. The raw materials for life processes—climate, altitude, temperature—all must be taken into account in a comprehensive event or field approach, which extends beyond the solitary organism. In fact, we may say that the ecologist does not study organisms at all; he or she focuses on whatever transpires *between* the organisms and the conditions in their surroundings. This field approach of the ecologist can serve as a model, or paradigm, for our study.

The Viewpoint of This Book

The position that I shall consistently hold in this book is closely akin to the field[1] approach of the ecologist. Our key term, *field,* may be defined as the

---

[1] My use of the term *field* should not be confused with an earlier use of that term by Lewin (1931) in a behavioral framework; he interpreted *field* as a phenomenological field of psychic forces.

complex or totality of interdependent factors that constitute or participate in a psychological event. Our job is to discern the pattern of the related variables that account for the behavioral occurrence.

In order to understand our data, we must also take into account the order or sequence of events. For example, Diane's phobia made no sense until we pieced together the relevant events, some of which had occurred 13 years earlier. Applying a field approach to Diane's problem requires an ecological type of analysis in which we view her as an organism interacting with people and things under very specific conditions applicable only to Diane. These interactions are seen as totalities, wholes, or fields, rather than as responses localized somewhere within the organism (conventionally, in the organism's head). We gain understanding by studying the series of events specific to a given individual.

A viewpoint that works along these lines was elaborated by J. R. Kantor in his *Principles of Psychology* (Kantor, 1924, 1926) and, more recently, by Kantor and Smith (1975) in a framework known as "interbehavioral psychology."

After clearing up fundamental matters, I will expound Kantor's system and apply it to a variety of psychological data. Because interbehavioral psychology stresses total events and the relationship between those events, it stands out as a distinctive approach, one that calls for constant comparison and contrast with other systematic viewpoints. Noting such resemblances and differences enriches our way of thinking about behavior and permits us to make our own choices about the way we understand human behavior.

In a growing research discipline, inquiry is directed not to rearranging old facts and explanations into more elegant formal patterns, but rather to the discovery of new patterns of explanation.

[Hanson, 1958, p. 2]

The Subject Matter of the Sciences

To be a scientist, one must have something to study. Certainly, there are countless "goings-on" in and on this planet and in the sky above. From these occurrences each of the sciences carves out a distinctive set of events for its own study. Thus, astronomers investigate such celestial bodies as stars, planets, and galaxies and, more generally, matter and energy in the universe at large. In addition to their interest in matter and energy and the relationship between them, physicists also study mechanics, light, sound, heat, electricity, and magnetism. Biologists concern themselves with the myriad varieties of living things on this earth. How plants and animals assimilate materials from their surroundings and grow fat and breathe, excrete, reproduce, and die constitute the subject matter of biology.

The Subject Matter of Psychology

As extensive as this list is, we have not yet exhausted all that happens on the earth. Imagine that you are a Martian coming to Earth for the first time. It is early morning, and you can see human beings rising, hurrying through their toileting and breakfast and scurrying to work. They travel by buses, streetcars, subways, trains, and automobiles, operated by themselves or other humans. You can also observe people operating machines in factories, buying and selling, cooking, praying, cleaning, building, tearing down, crying, laughing, fighting, loving, hating, making love, killing each other in war or murder, slaughtering animals for food, farming, fishing, carpentering, painting, composing, teaching, studying, and so on. If you, as the visitor from Mars, delve further into these events, you might become a psychologist. These human activities, as well as those of infrahuman animals, set the stage for the psychologist's study.

Note that there are certain characteristics common to all the sciences: Each starts with certain facts in the world of reality. These facts are the crude data or events that were observed and that are the starting points for further analysis, classification, and theorizing. The important point here is that scientists start by observing certain things happening around them. These observations become their subject matter; the divisions of the sciences are only divisions of specialized interests. Some events can be taken into the laboratory for more accurate observation, control, and analysis. But, as Sidman (1960, p. 9) points out, "Behavior is a rich subject matter, and thus far we have observed only a small sample in the laboratory." Although the laboratory offers ideal conditions for scientific inquiry, field observations must not be scorned. All progress in astronomy has been made without laboratories, being limited to observatories that permit the study of celestial bodies *as they occur* and not as the astronomer might like to make them occur. Geology is another science that is restricted to field study or naturalistic observation. Psychology relies on both laboratory and/or naturalistic observation. Still other methods are discussed later.

The Aim of Psychology

We have already considered the aims of science. In psychology, our aim is to describe psychological subject matter so thoroughly and comprehensively that we can "make sense of it." If, following our study, we find that it falls into a certain order or pattern—if it shows "rhyme and reason"—we are on our way to reaching our goal. If we are able to analyze psychological events and assess the role of the relevant variables, we may even know how to *make* events happen. In other words, if we attain that high level of success, we have achieved the ability to make predictions. In sum, our aim is the same as that of the other sciences; that is, foresight and understanding.

Scientific Procedure in Psychology

In harmony with procedures in the other sciences and following the lead of Kantor and Smith (1975), I propose the adoption of the following three steps in our inquiry: definition, analysis, and interpretation. Not only these three measures but also the general approach to psychological events, the analytic procedures, and the resulting constructs will be expounded in the tradition of J. R. Kantor's interbehavioral psychology. His system will be explained in the following pages in an attempt to discover "new patterns of explanation." (See Figure 1-1.)

Distinguishing Between Biological and Psychological Subject Matter

To achieve clear-cut results in any inquiry, we must distinguish between what we are going to study and other, closely related things. For example, we must draw boundaries between our subject matter and the subject matter of biology. If we confuse the two areas, our understanding may also be confused.

For an illustration of a biological event, all we need is a frog's leg muscle and the attached nerve. By attaching a weight to the leg end and administering a series of electric shocks via the nerve, we can learn a great deal about muscle fatigue. Apparently, then, in the biological branch of study known as *physiology*, we can investigate dissected parts of organisms. But whole organisms are necessary in psychological investigation.

The reflex reaction of the frog's muscle and nerve is a tissue-excitation reaction. This fact points up another distinction between biology and psychology. The muscle–nerve preparation is highly limited in what it can do. Given the same conditions, the leg muscle can do only one thing when it is electrically stimulated. Because of its structure and because it is contractile tissue, it must jerk the way it does when it is adequately stimulated. Furthermore, learning does not enter the picture at all. From the very first occasion, the organismic fragment does the only thing it will always do under the same conditions. It is a simple tissue-excitation response, assigned to the province of biological inquiry.

Now, in contrast to the biological example just described, let us consider a fairly typical psychological datum—a small child, Anna, is asking her mother for milk. We prick up our ears when we hear Anna say *"Leche!"*

Figure 1-1   J. R. Kantor, professor emeritus, Indiana University; presently research associate, University of Chicago. Founder of interbehavioral psychology. (Photo by Jean Grant.)

And we are surprised when her verbal command works, for she gets her milk. However, the incident makes sense to us when we learn that Anna has been reared in Spain and has used the Spanish word for milk. But another Anna, reared in Czechoslovakia, demands *mleko* and obtains milk. In Turkey, children use the word *syoot*, which is equally effective. In comparing the responses of our different Annas and the biologist's muscle–nerve preparation, we find a number of distinguishing characteristics:

1. If we were to examine each of the Annas *at birth*, we would find a total absence of the verbal response in every one of them. Not so with the muscle–nerve preparation. It works the way it does as soon as it is structurally developed.

2. As for the verbal response, it makes its appearance at some point in the child's development, but only as the result of *learning*, a procedure no muscle–nerve preparation has to undergo. Furthermore, if one of the Annas were reared isolated in an attic with a minimum of human contact, the absence of a verbal response noted at birth might persist over a lifetime.

3. Another great difference between the two samples under comparison lies in the fact that, for psychological purposes, our Annas should be intact. No lung and vocal cords in a head severed from the organism can ask for milk. The whole organism is necessary, but for studying the muscle and nerve the rest of the frog can be discarded.

4. Returning to the muscle–nerve preparation, it does not matter whether the specimen was obtained from frogs raised in Spain, Czechoslovakia, or Turkey. As long as the frogs are all of the same species, we get the same results. But where Anna is reared determines (a) the presence or absence of any response or (b) the particular configuration of her response. The history of organisms and their specific social conditions are critical in psychological inquiry. For part reactions, such as the muscle–nerve preparation, social learning factors are of no consequence.

To emphasize the differences between biological and psychological events, I have intentionally taken extreme examples. But biologists are not restricted to studying pieces of organisms. They are also interested in the *total* organism, as when they study respiration, circulation, digestion, assimilation, excretion, and reproduction. Can we still find any distinguishing characteristics between the two disciplines on an organismic basis? I think so. It happens that the same organisms may be involved in events studied by both scientists but in the following different ways: instead of being interested in respiration, digestion, and so on, the psychologist is interested, as previously stated, in organisms loving, fearing, hating, buying and selling, voting, praying, and so on.

Respiration and digestion seem radically different from voting and praying, yet the boundaries between the data and procedures of biology and of psychology are sometimes not respected. Is there any way of clearly defining the data of psychology from those of biology? The answer is an unambiguous yes. Kantor has always insisted on a clear separation between the two fields. He has achieved such a delineation, not on some a priori or logical basis, but empirically, as the result of a firsthand inspection of the data of the two fields. Here are his criteria:

1. *Psychological events are historical.*   One must learn how to hate, love, speak, walk, pray, and vote. One does not have to learn how to breathe, circulate blood, digest food, or sneeze. The former have their own space/time framework or developmental history (which we will come to know

later as the "reactional biography" or "interactional history"). The examples, given earlier, of Anna's learning to pronounce the word for "milk" under different conditions illustrate the point.

2. *Psychological events show a specificity not apparent in biological data.* Any foreign substance can cause the eye to secrete tears, but a German novel does not elicit universal reading responses from all humans. Even Germans who can read the book may react differently to it. Specific circumstances have much to do with their reactions. They may use it as a paperweight, to throw at some one as in anger, to read for enjoyment, or to burn. Such specificity, for example, is lacking in the physiological gag reflex, which is the same whether one uses a finger, tongue depresser, table knife, or fountain pen to elicit vomiting.

In this respect, psychology is more complex than biology. The same object can be reacted to differently, or different objects can be responded to similarly. A young mother proudly displays her baby to a visitor and declares "He's on solids now. Pencils, keys, rubber bands, cigarette butts, bugs, and soap." The baby has not yet learned to react differentially to those diverse objects. In time, he will evolve highly specific reactions to them.

3. *Psychological events show integration.* The infant's reaching response for a toy can be combined with a mouthing reaction. Self-feeding requires grasping a spoon, holding it upright, filling it with food, and moving it toward and into the mouth—a highly integrated act. Similarly, the beginning dancer practices separate foot movements and eventually fuses them into one uniform action.

4. *Psychological events show variability.* "If at first you don't succeed, try, try again." But this proverb does not imply that you should go at solving a problem in the same stereotyped fashion until your head is "bloody but unbowed." You must show some diversity in your plan of attack. Assume that you are working at a crossword puzzle that requires a three-letter word in a certain position. You try *b-i-t*, but it doesn't work. You don't erase it and write in once more the letters *b-i-t*. That would be idiotic. This time you try *b-a-t*, and, if that doesn't work, *b-u-t*, and so on. Reflexes, however, show a monotonous repetitiveness under constant conditions. A blink reflex or a knee jerk always operates in the same way. Humans vary their behavior, thereby manifesting a flexibility and, possibly, a higher level of "adaptation" than is apparent in biological events.

5. *Psychological events are modifiable.* Through successive contacts with things in its surroundings, the organism's response toward them changes. For a baby, a spoon, in addition to its function for transporting food, becomes an object to bang against the tray of the high chair, to poke the family cat, or to throw on the floor. People fall in love, but they also fall out of love. They acquire skills they did not formerly have, and they also lose them. Schools

are really agents of change or modifiability. The college graduate undergoes many behavioral changes during his or her conventional four-year residence. Change also occurs in a biological framework, as in the wrinkling of skin or loss of elasticity in bone, but such data are not readily confused with the child's first utterance of "Da-da," of a college student's facile use of a "foreign" language, or of an individual's certification as a jet airplane pilot.

6. *Psychological events manifest inhibition.*   The hostess at a children's party enters the room with a dish of candy. Billy's "impulse" is to run for it and to help himself. But his mother has trained him to sit still until the dish is brought to him. He spots a large piece of candy on the side of the plate away from him. However, he takes a smaller piece from the side of the plate closer to him. Billy's training resulted in his substituting the responses that he did show for others that he might have shown. This substitution of one reaction for another is what Kantor means by *inhibition.* Situations demanding choice require the substitution of one response for another.

The child who must decide between strawberry and vanilla ice cream can't have it both ways. It does not matter which, but the child must choose one *or* the other. According to William James, when you have a choice to make and do not take either alternative, that in itself is a choice. In such a case, one takes the consequences of refusing either alternative whatever that might be.

Inhibition as a property of psychological events is illustrated in some of our social habits. Williams and Degenhardt (1954, p. 20) did a study of paruresis, which they define as "a difficulty (or impossibility) of initiating the flow of urine in the presence of others, a difficulty that is immediately relieved when the social conditions are changed." Their survey of this problem in 1419 college students revealed that 14.4% complained about urinating in the presence of others, even when there were stall separations. Others required solo occupation of a bathroom with locked door. And we are sometimes careful not to let our friends hear us urinate when we use their bathroom. And people have many other inhibition hangups in sexual, affectional, moral, ethical, and anger areas. The presence of other people does not have a similar effect on the operation of knee jerks, swallowing, and sneezing as tissue-excitation reactions. However, reflexes can become involved in psychological events through conditioning.

7. *Psychological events show delayability.*   Knee jerks go into operation immediately on stimulation. But I could make a date with you for next week, and although my reaction would be initiated by our conversation *now* it would not be completed until the arranged time and place *next week.*

Let's take a simpler illustration. We are experimenting with a raccoon, which we are training to approach one of three compartments facing it. We do so by briefly illuminating one compartment at random and feeding the animal when it selects the proper one. After the raccoon has mastered the task, we interpose a clear, plastic barrier between it and the food compartments.

Now we try the delayed response part of our experiment. We light up the compartment, on and off, but do not remove the barrier until 5 seconds have passed. We find that, as soon as we raise it, the raccoon still picks the proper compartment. Even intervals of 30 to 45 seconds do not prevent a correct response.

Both the human and the animal situation show that psychological events show a certain flexibility in their temporal aspects. That is, a time interval can elapse between stimulus and response without interfering with the event. The boxer can *anticipate* a punch to the jaw and duck appropriately, thus preventing a fractured jaw. And one can also respond to memories of situations that happened last week, last year, or even 30 or 40 years ago.

Properties of psychological events. We have completed our characterization of psychological events with the stricture that not every event must show all of the eight attributes just listed. However, we may be certain that where two or more properties are apparent we are dealing with an occurrence that belongs in the psychological domain.

The significance of Kantor's definition of psychological events. If we inquire about the procedure of the chemist, for example, we find that he or she defines liquids, solids, and gases on the basis of their properties. He or she does the same with gases, separating each one on the basis of its distinct properties. The student of living things uses the same procedure, defining life by its distinctive properties such as irritability and metabolism.

Kantor has done a similar service for psychology. He did not isolate the data of psychology on the basis of philosophical conceptions derived from traditional hand-me-downs He simply noted the properties of the data he observed, found that psychological events possessed certain attributes that physiological and anatomical data do not possess, and, on the basis of those properties, successfully drew a boundary between biology and psychology. In this respect, his procedure is consistent with that of other sciences.

The Role of Analysis in Scientific Inquiry

Having pinpointed a psychological event, our next job is to dissect it or "take it apart" and to assess the role of each of the interrelated parts, factors, or variables. Suppose we are administering a shock to the foot of a dog in a conditioning laboratory in an effort to train the dog to raise its paw to a buzzer. Some of the conditions we must control and evaluate are the dog's experience, the strength of the shock, the number of repetitions of buzzer and shock, the time interval between buzzer and shock, and the presence of other dogs or humans in the lab. Careful records should allow us to tease out the role of each variable in relationship to the role of the other variables. If we have done our job properly, we have arrived at the third step in our procedure—interpretation.

The Place of Interpretation in Scientific Inquiry

After a proper dissection of events, we should be able to understand them. As stated earlier, the aim of all the sciences is to grasp "what's going on," to make sense of events, to look for uniformities, invariant sequences, to try to find order, regularity, and pattern. All of the foregoing phrases are different ways of defining *theory*. But remember that all the sciences start with data or facts. The following quotation from Einstein's *Essays in Science* (1934, p. 14) underscores this point: "Pure logical thinking cannot yield us any knowledge of the empirical world; *all knowledge of reality starts from experience and ends in it*" (emphasis added). But a mere collection of data cannot build up to a science. The illustrious physicist and mathematician, Poincaré (1946, p. 127) observed that an accumulation of facts is no more a science than a pile of bricks is a house. Our laboratory study of conditioning a dog was an analysis of events involving dogs, shocks, buzzers, and other relevant factors that resulted in the elaboration of the principles of conditioning theory. The soundness of the established theory has been confirmed countless times by the fact of prediction and control. If you were to go into a conditioning laboratory and were to apply the principles of conditioning, you would get the same results, a confirmation of the fact that you *understood* conditioning. Theory or interpretation may be compared to fitting together all the bits and pieces of a jigsaw puzzle to make a meaningful picture.

The Unit of Behavior Study

Having delimited our special field of study, we are ready to probe more deeply in order to achieve a finer analysis of psychological events. Our first problem concerns the proper unit of study, a problem not limited to psychology. The astronomical day, month, and year are readily recognized as some of the astronomer's units of study, based on rotation and revolution of astronomical bodies. Respiration and the heartbeat are familiar examples from physiology. The former involves the point at which the breath is drawn in to the point where it is completely expired, after which moment another respiratory unit begins. They are continuous but divisible.

The Behavior Segment

Attempts to place the "major" source of human action either within the organism or in the external environment are both

*unjustified. There is no behavioral "prime mover." Humanists
and behaviorists alike are mistaken in their efforts to find a
first cause either inside or outside the organism. Man and his
environment are in continual and intimate reciprocity—each
controls the other—and we would spend our time much more
productively if we were to focus on the nature of their
interdependence rather than defending claims to priority.*

[Mahoney, 1975, p. 865]

The most outstanding feature of psychological events is their continuity. Our psychological life can be compared to a stream with an uninterrupted flow. We are, in one way or another, perpetually busy psychologically, for even in our sleep we are thinking (dreaming, we call it), and we "respect" the edge of the bed when we get there, and we respond to "nature's calls," ringing phones, and smoke alarms.

At first glance, the nonstop ongoingness of behavior would appear to give us trouble. But let me point out that astronomical bodies and heartbeats during their existence also show the same continuous busyness. Apparently, we must follow the lead of the other sciences and carve out a unit of study for ourselves. Because observation of events is the proper starting point for a science, let us set up observation on campus. By good fortune, we observe a student saying "Hi!" Our immediate question is "How did that happen? Is the student in the habit of going around saying "Hi!" repeatedly for no reason at all?" No. His "Hi!" occurred at the moment he spotted a fellow student and friend. As an initial step, let us agree to call the appearance of the fellow student a stimulus and our first student's "Hi!" a response, and we have the focal aspect of our fundamental unit, a behavior segment. A single stimulus and its correlated response (in context) constitute a behavior segment or a single irreducible slice of psychological happening carved out of the continuing flow. Isolating a behavior segment might be compared to stopping a motion picture film and "freezing" the action at a single frame (see Figure 1-2). "Unfractured observation" is desirable as an *initial* approach to one's data, but we must seek out the relevant variables or aspects of events if we expect to make any headway. Analysis calls for "fracturing" or dissecting observations.

Having established the behavior segment as a unit of study, let us examine it for its other components. What needs to be emphasized next is the mutual and reciprocal nature of stimulus and response. We may assume that there is never a response without a stimulus and never a stimulus without a response. Each is indispensable to the other, much as it takes two to tango. While it is true that the stimulus "does something" to the organism, it is equally true that the organism "does something" with respect to the stimulus. Their action is, therefore, joint, shared, or equal in the total field. Neith-

FIELD

Setting Factors

Stimulus   Response

Preceding segment

Stimulus object   Organism

Succeeding segment

function   ↑   function

Medium of "contact"

Behavior segment

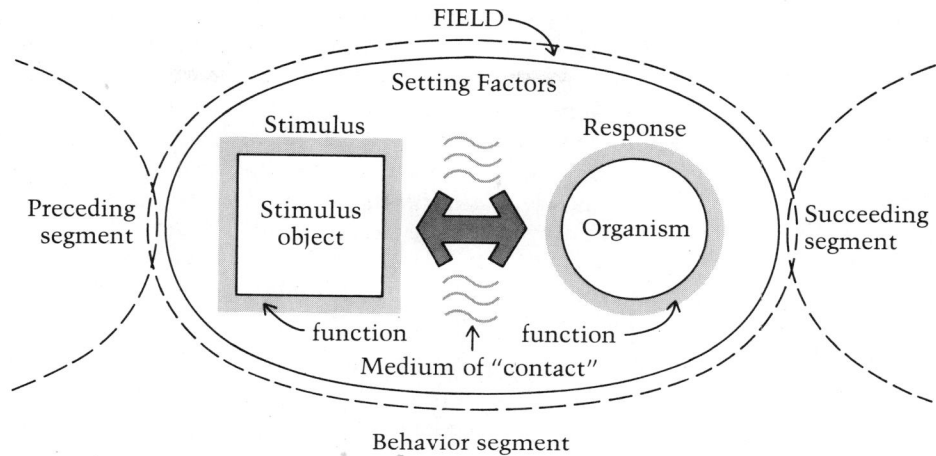

Figure 1-2 A single behavioral unit or behavior segment isolated from the behavioral stream. By analogy with a motion-picture film, the behavior segment may be compared with the film stopped for examination at a single frame. (From Smith and Shaw, 1979.)

er has priority over the other, because both are *essential*. Kantor (1933, p. 22) long ago represented the mutual and coordinate relationship of stimulus and response with a double-headed arrow, thus:

$$S \longleftarrow - - - - - - - - - - \longrightarrow R$$

Earlier in his theoretical development, Kantor used the term *interaction* to refer to the conjoint action of stimulus and response. More recently, he has shown a preference for the term *interbehavior*. In his *Contingencies of Reinforcement* (1969), Skinner also uses the term *interaction* to denote a *field* type of orientation. We shall use either term to refer to a field or event orientation in opposition to a self-actional view (Bentley, 1954; Dewey and Bentley, 1949). Popular psychology, with its emphasis on "capacity," drive," "giftedness," "IQ," and such, is self-actional. Self-actional explanations view behavior as *originating* within the organism or the organism's mind. In an older terminology, this would be an effect without a cause. Self-actional concepts are not congenial with the approach developed here.

Behavior Situations

The example of one student greeting another with "Hi!" was deliberately picked for its simplicity, but much of our behavior does not come in such single, separate units. Consider a card game, a phone conversation, writing a letter, constructing a wall, or playing a concerto. None of these situations can be compared to a now-you-see-it, now-you-don't friend greeting a friend with "Hi!" They are more complex by far. But the important point is that, if we need to, we can dissect the complex behavior situations into their component, sequential behavior segments. For example, pretend that you and I meet, and you say "Hi!"

Your greeting, which is a response to the sight of me, becomes a stimulus that in turn evokes the response "Hi!" from me.
My "Hi!" stimulates you to respond with the conventional form, "How are you?" Your response, in turn, stimulates me to respond with an equally conventional phrase, "Fine." And so on.

Thus the apparent complexity has been reduced to a manageable, simple structure. I propose that a behavior situation be defined as a series or sequence of related behavior segments or stimulus–response units.

Types of Behavior Segments

Operation behavior segments.   One type of conditioning calls for presenting, let us say, a metronome to a dog, followed by an electric shock to its paw. One can actually record and measure the extent of the lift of the paw. With the aid of a time line on the recording apparatus, it is possible to indicate the very beginning and end of the response. It is a clear-cut reaction and, for that reason, experimentally desirable. This kind of definite, specific, simple response meets the criterion of what we shall label as an *operation* behavior segment. Here are further illustrations: I enter a phone booth and insert a dime into the coin slot. Inserting the dime is an operation behavior segment. I push the doorbell at a friend's home—another operation behavior segment. I am walking along on a rainy day. In the street next to the curb, I detect a wet, folded $5 bill. My stooping and picking it up constitutes another operation behavior segment.

Process behavior segments.   Not all behavior segments are as simple and as easily circumscribed as are operation behavior segments. For example, stirring a cake, drilling a tooth, or removing an appendix do not belong in this same category as our responses to "What's 2 times 2?" or "Strike middle 'C' on the piano." The complexity of the former contrasts with the simplicity of the latter. To take another illustration, a student is at a study desk confronted by a calculus problem, the stimulus. His or her response is not as clear-cut and definite as striking a match. The calculus situation calls for a process response system or a chain-of-reaction system.

Witting behavior segments.   Cameron's (1947) treatment of the self-reaction is most relevant here. Cameron speaks about reacting to one's biological features or to one's own behavior. Such factors can stimulate reactions similar to the reactions to the biological features (obesity, big nose, baldness) of others or to the behavior (aggressiveness, shyness) of others. Now, witting behavior involves the monitoring of one's own behavior. The beauty contestant studies him- or herself in the mirror, checking every nuance of walk and posture, in preparation for the beauty parade. The self-monitoring may result in straightening the shoulders or sucking in the abdomen. The person is very much aware of *what* is involved in the activity, which brings us to witting behavior segments. When stimulus–response units involve monitoring one's own appearance, posture, breathing, or voice quality, we are concerned with witting behavior segments. This strongly suggests that the overly shy are too preoccupied with their appearance and/or behavior. They monitor themselves too strictly.

Unwitting behavior segments. These stimulus–response units are the direct opposite of witting types of events. Self-monitoring certainly enters into a recent amputee's training in walking again but most of us don't "give a thought" to how we put each foot forward in turn as we walk and converse with a friend. It would be a different matter if we had to cross a swollen stream via a narrow plank. Careful monitoring would be called for. What had been unwitting before now would become witting.

Here are further examples of unwitting action: While studying, students may "play" with their hair, twisting it constantly, unaware of what they're doing. One student confessed that she had denuded her arm hair, eyebrows, and eyelashes by unwittingly plucking the hairs out while studying. The habit of shifting spectacles upward by wrinkling the nose is also unwitting when carried out "unaware." One's gestures may also be carried out quite unwittingly. Jason (1976) reports the case of a client who squeezed his nose compulsively, to the point of causing pain and soreness. The same client complained about excessive daydreaming. Both problems were greatly alleviated through the practice of careful self-monitoring—by making the unwitting witting. In a taped psychiatric interview with a prisoner, Wilmer (1969) discovered that the prisoner had "punctuated" his portion of the interview with 144 repetitions of the meaningless, unwitting phrase "You know."

An older psychological framework interpreted the behaviors just described as manifestations of the subconscious or unconscious "mind." This approach is not useful, for two reasons: (1) such a construct is phrased in terms of hypothetical entities, and (2) the construct is useless in any practical sense because there is no way to apply it, for how can one work with an imaginary "unconscious mind?" The advantage of the witting–unwitting construct is that it is phrased in terms of relationships between a given individual's behavior and his or her own behavior. Only the presence or absence of a self-reaction is involved. By manipulating that relationship, as by self-monitoring compulsive nose squeezing, one can modify behavior, thus validating the construct.

Types of Responses

Setting aside our analysis of the behavior segment for the time being, we now concentrate on the organism's side of the picture. Our immediate question is "What is the organism's role in the event? What does the organism do with reference to the stimulus? What can we learn about its responses?"

Simple response.   It would be a serious mistake to think that all responses are alike. Take the following example: You grasp a hot pan handle and let go of it in a split second. Only one thing occurs; it is not possible to interpret your action as anything but a simple response. It contains one act unit. Why don't we relegate it to the biologist's reflex reaction? The answer is that, particularly in the adult, the response has been overlaid with psychological attributes. For example, we may find the word "Ouch!" incorporated into the act in one culture, while a person from another culture yells "Oi!" Or, if a mother has hold of that hot pan handle and her baby is below it, she may manifest inhibition of that reflex, burning her hand rather than the baby. So, although it is simple, it is nevertheless psychological insofar as it manifests any of the properties of the psychological events discussed earlier. If it does not show any of those properties, then it is only a biological reflex.

Complex responses.   It would be fairly safe to assume that not much of our behavior fits the model of the simple response. It is more likely to be classed as complex responses, consisting of at least three act units, as follows. Obviously if someone in an auditorium is waving at me and I am looking in a different direction, I cannot respond. But, if I shift the direction of my gaze, this is the attentional phase of my response. The next thing that happens is that I "spot" the person waving; this act of discrimination is labeled *perception*. The last part of this particular response under examination is the final act unit; that is, my waving back to the person. The final act unit terminates the particular behavior segment, and the show goes on. Continuity guarantees that another behavior segment will follow. (See Figure 1-3.)

Response function.   A thorough analysis of psychological action along interbehavioral lines demands the concept of response function. The response function is correlative with stimulus function and calls attention to the need for going beyond the configuration of the response itself. "No" can mean "yes" and "yes" can mean "no," depending on how a question is phrased. Kneeling as a worshipful posture in church and kneeling to crack open a safe may look alike, but they serve different functions. People around

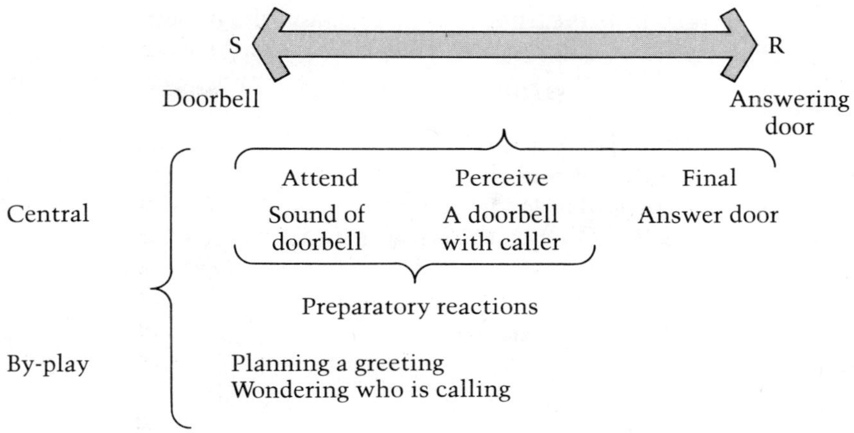

Figure 1-3 A complex response illustrating the central response pattern (the "main show") along with the accompanying or by-play action. (From Smith and Shaw, 1979.)

the Mediterranean wave goodbye in a way similar to the way we might signal "Come here." The same act has different response functions. To obtain a pellet of food, a rat may depress a bar with snout, right paw, left paw, or both paws. The response function may be served with different anatomical configurations. Thus we must not adhere too strictly to anatomy—there are different ways to skin a cat. Polio patients may type or paint using their mouths, while others use their hands. Very different anatomical configurations can serve the same or similar response functions.

By-play action. But our analytic job is not yet over. When the doorbell rings, as you make your way to the door you are also behaving in ways we describe in everyday terms: "I wonder who would be ringing the door at 2:30 A.M. I had better be on guard," and so on. All such accompanying or incidental responses are lumped together as by-play action. The interrelationships between simple and complex responses and by-play action are illustrated in Figure 1-3.

The prevailing self-actional approach in psychology has stressed the role of the organism. Behavior was believed to transpire in a sort of theater somewhere inside the person, most likely in the head. Because the person was considered the source of all things psychological, it is easy to see how any other relevant factors were overlooked. In my opinion, psychology began to make its greatest advances when it widened its observational base to include, in addition to the organism, the other main variable, crudely labeled as the *stimulus*. Our analysis now takes us in that direction.

Imagine that a film of your life is being shown. Your joys, sorrows, griefs, postures, and movements of all sorts, facial expressions—there they are, all of them. The odd thing about that film is that all the factors or conditions that elicited the rich variety of reactions displayed have been blotted out. It should be apparent that, under such conditions, your behavior would not make any sense. What you were crying or laughing *about* or what a particular gesture signifies would be incomprehensible without the missing link; that is, the stimulus.

Objects, Stimulus Objects, and Stimulus Functions

The Role of Objects in Psychological Investigation

The layperson is often very much puzzled by the fact that all the children in a given family are exposed to the "same" piano but only one may turn out to be an excellent pianist, while the rest are indifferent to it. Another child in the same family may "take to" Mom's books and turn out to be an "egghead," while the rest may not. The question implied is "Why don't the same objects produce uniform results in all the children?" The answer is that the orientation that prompts such a question is physical, not psychological. An inventory of all the objects, persons, and conditions surrounding an organism constitutes only a *possible* setting for psychological occurrences. A metaphor from the theater may help to make the point. Imagine a beautiful Victorian stage setting, and properly illuminated, with drapes and heavy furniture but no actors. How long would the audience look on the spectacle? Similarly, the objects, persons, and conditions in the environment of an organism provide only a "stage setting" for psychological occurrences. Only when the organism and some other variable confront one another and do something in relation to each other does a psychological event come into being. Before that time, there are indeed only "objects." Thus, to talk about objects is nonpsychological. And so, in a psychological sense, a piano is not "the same thing" for every member of a family. For one person, it is a piece of furniture to be dusted every Friday. For another person, it is a source of great satisfaction as a musical instrument. But now the piano is no longer simply an object. It has become a stimulus object.

Stimulus Objects

When an object participates in a psychological event, it becomes a stimulus object. This will be our technical term to designate any object (book, shoe, fork, hammer, scalpel), another organism (human, dog, cat, bear, elephant, mosquito), or situation (fire, flood, explosion, riot, tornado) in a reciprocal relationship with an organism (human, fly, spider). Note that the term *stimulus object* doesn't tell very much, it only points to some thing or organism as playing a role in a psychological event; it doesn't specify what the role is. For example, suppose I merely tell you that a Korean peasant woman and an eel confront each other. The eel has become a stimulus object, you know that. But that is all you know until I indicate that eels in Korea are typically caught for food. Immediately on capture, they are popped into the mouth, their heads are bitten off in one clean bite, and they are stored in a basket. Now, we are ready to consider *stimulus function.*

Stimulus Function

In our analysis of the behavior segment, stress was on the mutual, reciprocal action of the stimulus variable as well as the organismic variable. Again, while the organism does something with respect to the stimulus object, the stimulus object does something with respect to the organism. Prove it! Well, note that Korean peasant women do not go around catching eels and biting off their heads if there are no eels. Nor do they respond in that way when someone hands them a piece of clothing or a transistor set. Only eels in the stream act in the specific way described. We have now stumbled on the construct of stimulus function, or the role that a stimulus object plays in a psychological event, which we define as the action or function of the stimulus object or the particular way the stimulus object acts on the organism. For example, a pair of pliers may function as a tool, a paperweight, or a weapon, depending on the situation.

How stimulus functions originate.   I think you will readily agree that eels in streams do not have the same stimulus function the world over. Some people would be repulsed at the sight of an eel, and some of this same group might eat an eel with gusto and might consider it a delicacy if it were identified simply as a fish. Apparently, culture may have something to do with shaping the stimulus function of eels (and perhaps many other things as well).

When the child first comes into this world, it enters on a psychologically bare stage consisting only of objects—humans, cats, dogs, toys, and food in all its varieties. As the child participates in its contacts with those objects, they become stimulus objects. Applesauce is devoured from the start, but carrots, accepted at first, are later consistently spat out energetically, no matter how carefully disguised. In turn, baby rattles, milk bottles, dolls, tricycles, bicycles, skateboards, motorcycles, and pianos take on stimulus functions through the organism's successive contacts with such, and other, stimulus objects. Again we are reminded of the importance of the dimension previously labeled as *historical;* foresight and understanding lie in this direction. With that noble incentive, we next examine different classes of stimulus function.

Classes of stimulus function   There are three classes of stimulus function.

Direct and substitute stimulus functions.   Imagine that you look at the clock in the tower and note that the time is 10:15. Because your response is directly to the tower clock as a clock, it serves a direct stimulus function. So do knife and fork you pick up and use in eating, as well as a key you take out of your pocket and insert into a lock to open a door. All illustrate a direct stimulus function.

Now return to the example of the clock. Suppose that when you look at the clock you do not even read the time indicated; instead, you recall looking up and hearing Big Ben in the clock tower of the House of Parliament in London. The first clock tower serves an indirect or substitute stimulus function, an incidental or subordinate role in the behavior segment now under scrutiny. In a sense, it only "pinch hits" or substitutes for the Big Ben clock tower. In another sense, it only "triggers" the whole affair—your adjustment is to Big Ben as you saw and heard it on a previous occasion on your London visit. As such, the clock in the tower serves a substitute stimulus function.

Endogenous and exogenous stimulus function.   Our discussion of witting and unwitting behavior may help us now to distinguish between endogenous and exogenous stimulus function. There, we were interested in knowing whether people were "aware" of carrying out certain acts of their own. Now, without regard to that distinction, we stress the locus of the stimulus function. It is based on (1) one's own biological conditions (headache or stomach cramp) and (2) one's own behavior (guilt, shame, or pride over one's own act)?

All such self-reactions elicited by factors "localizable" in or on the organism's own biological conditions or own behavior constitute endogenous stimulus functions. A hypochondriac, then, is one whose bodily functioning or organs lie within normal limits. If disease or a bodily defect is present, then these conditions elicit habitual preoccupation or *over*concern. Such conditions illustrate endogenous stimulus function. But one's own behavior can also call forth exaggerated reaction, even enough to cause loss of sleep. My precipitate stock-market purchase can cause *me* much anxiety. Here is another endogenous stimulus function connected with my behavior. Now if *I* begin to worry about the unwise financial investment that *you* made, then your behavior comprises for me an exogenous stimulus function. However, if *you* begin to lose sleep over *your* own high-risk adventure, then your action constitutes an endogenous stimulus function in the behavior segment that involves you.

Summing up then, the distinction between endogenous and exogenous stimulus functions is made on the basis of the relationship between the organism's response and the locus of the stimulus object. When that relationship involves an individual's own biological or behavioral factors, an endogenous stimulus function is indicated. When the locus is anywhere else, we have exogenous stimulus function.

Apparent and inapparent stimulus function.   Every science studies phenomena that range from the gross to the very subtle. In physics, for example, thunder and lightning or an avalanche are at the opposite extreme from highly subtle radio waves or cosmic rays. In biology, reflex movements contrast with subtle glandular secretions or nervous-system activity. For example, it is impossible to detect visually if an isolated nerve fiber is "active." The same holds true in psychology. First, some stimulus functions are crude or gross. A brick hurtling through the air at you elicits avoidance responses. But the following rhyme calls forth a response the stimulus function of which is so delicate in its operation that the author of the rhyme cannot "put his finger on it."

> I do not like thee, Dr. Fell.
> The reason why I cannot tell.
> But this I know and know full well.
> I do not like thee, Dr. Fell.

Note that the rhyme's author is certain of a dislike for Dr. Fell—only the reason for it is inapparent. Could it be the resemblance between Dr. Fell and a feared relative in the author's childhood? Who knows? We assume that in that individual's past history something happened that is connected with the present dislike of Dr. Fell. The important point is that the individual concerned cannot identify or pinpoint the subtle stimulus function that elicited the response.

> "There's something about him that makes me want to cut the cards."
> "What?"
> "I don't know; I just don't trust him."

Psychology, then, like the other sciences, studies phenomena that range from crude to very subtle. In passing, let me point out that the same is true of responses, which range from the gross action in acts of violence to the subtle glaring or approving look or a slight nod of the head.

Medium of Contact

Suppose that, as we enter an art museum, the lights go out just as I've asked you your opinion of a painting. You cannot express an opinion because you didn't have a chance to "take it in." Note that an object is physically present before an organism who is ready to respond but nothing happens because a key factor—light—is missing. A moment later, the lights go on; you now can discriminate the painting and express your evaluation of it. Clearly, the light played an important role in the event. One might want to ask "Well, isn't the painting important?" The answer is that it is, for without the painting no seeing of the painting can occur. But the point *here* is that even with the painting present, but no light, no seeing of the painting takes place. Light, then, is a facilitating factor that makes it possible for the stimulus object and the organism to enter into a psychological relationship with one another. The special term *medium of contact* refers to the facilitating role of light in mediating visual kinds of events.

Light is not the only medium of contact. For example, most organisms hear—this reaction is mediated by air or water. One can easily prove that water will "carry" sounds by ducking under water as a distant gun is fired and hearing it under water. But air is the medium par excellence for mediating auditory behaviors for most land animals. Figure 1-4 illustrates a physics experiment that many students have done. First, a bell jar is inverted over a tight-fitting base. The air within the bell jar can be pumped out, creating a near-vacuum. Inside the bell jar is a door bell connected to a switch outside that can be opened and closed as needed. Now, when the switch is closed

Figure 1-4   Inverted bell jar illustrates both visual and auditory media of contact. Under normal conditions, the switch outside the bell jar is closed; the door bell inside the bell jar can be "seen" to be ringing and can be heard, simultaneously. But if the air is exhausted and the switch is closed, the door bell can be seen vibrating but cannot be heard, because the air medium of contact has been interrupted

before the air is exhausted, one can both see the bell's hammer doing its job and also hear the bell. When the interior of the bell jar is a near-vacuum, one can *see* the bell ringing but one *cannot hear it*. The medium of contact between the organism and stimulus object has been interrupted. Thus, air is another medium of contact.

Imagine that someone has left a gasoline can open—we can smell the gas 10 feet away. Bug spray, room deodorants, perfume, and the roast in the oven can similarly be detected at a distance. On my desk lie a silver letter opener and a glass paperweight and, even though they are right under my nose, they do not smell—or, better, I cannot smell them. What's the difference? The difference lies in the fact that substances that give off a gaseous form facilitate contact between that substance and the organism. An interesting, incidental sidelight is offered by the event labeled as *adaptation*. When one first starts to paint a room, the odor of the paint cannot be ignored but after some 30 minutes or so of continued painting, one no longer notices the smell of the paint. The occurrence suggests that the relationship between the responding organism and the stimulus object is neither static nor constant; it changes over time. We may have the "same" paint and the "same" organism, but the succession of smell events is *not* the same.

When Helen Keller was 19 months old, an illness left her deaf and blind. The chief medium of contact left to her was touch. It took Annie Sullivan, "the miracle worker," to tame the "wild beast" of a child by using touch in such an ingenious way that it substituted for the loss of sight and hearing. Eventually, Helen Keller graduated *cum laude* from Radcliffe, wrote a series of books, and became an international leader of the blind. She developed into a very accomplished person mainly through touch and, in a lesser way, through smell and vibration. We can get an insight into the utility of touch when a blackout knocks out our dominating visual medium of contact by plunging us into darkness and forces us to navigate and to try to recognize objects in pitch darkness. The children's game of Blind Man's Bluff is a fun way of forcing dependence on touch media of contact via a temporary and artificial "blindness."

When we take into our mouths an apple, an orange, or a potato, each goes into a chemical solution with the aid of saliva, which then makes it possible for us to discriminate the distinctive taste of each of the objects. A parlor game can prove the point to any doubting Thomas. Blindfold a volunteer subject and put a clothes pin on the subject's nose or pinch his or her nostrils closed so as to exclude cues that might be introduced via smell. Next, wipe the subject's tongue dry with a gauze. Now briefly touch the tip of the volunteer's tongue with pieces of apple, carrot, and potato and ask the volunteer to identify the food substance. With visual and smell cues eliminated, the identification is difficult to make, simply because the chemical solution or medium of contact was wiped out by keeping the tongue dry. Of course, once the tongue is drawn back into the mouth and a bit of the food substance goes into solution, the identification can be made. This game also illustrates the role of smell in our day-to-day recognition of food substances; that is why the nose has to be closed in the demonstration. Even touch inside the mouth makes its contribution, because we normally recognize differences among the textures of apples, oranges, and potatoes.

The medium of contact for pain is closely bound up with the anatomical and physiological properties of the organism. When the constituent tissues of the organism are crushed, scalded, cut, stretched, lacerated, swollen, or frozen, they mediate pain responses. If you should object by claiming that it is your *tooth* that aches, then the answer from the standpoint tentatively adopted here is that the infected tooth is simultaneously the stimulus object and the medium of contact. Traditionally, the aching tooth incident has been explained by saying that "messages" are sent to the brain via nerves and *there*, or in the mind, are being experienced as pain. An alternative description is in terms of an *event* involving an organism's encounter with an inflamed, swollen tissue that happens to be an intimate part of that organism (endogenous stimulus function). The encounter could involve my sympathetic involvement with your toothache (exogenous stimulus function).

Interbehavioral Setting

It is an obvious proposition that things do not happen in a vacuum. The conditions under which they occur also have some effect on the outcome. For example, in physics, the pressure of a given gas depends on the temperature under which it is found. In biology, plant and animal growth and adaptation are a function of such ecological conditions as soil nutrients, water, prey and predator balance, climate, and still other physicochemical conditions.

If one grants the assumption that behavioral events are more complex than biological or physicochemical happenings, then one might expect that events on the psychological level are determined by more and different variables than biological and physicochemical events. Suppose you are in the chemistry lab combining nitric acid and iron in a test tube. You may be telling risqué stories to your lab partner, laughing, and even dancing a jig while you carry out your experiment. You need not worry because your action will have no effect on the outcome of your chemistry experiment. But you had better not "carry on" like that in the psychology laboratory while your experimental subject is trying to learn the way through a finger maze, or your experiment will be ruined.

A striking illustration of the crucial role that background factors play in human situations is provided in the following quotation from Hudson (1975, p. 69) on the ritual of the medical gynecological examination.

Every day, throughout the Western world, staid women of all ages allow men they do not know, often accompanied by groups of young students of both sexes, to examine and discuss parts of their body that they normally shelter even from their husbands or lovers—parts of their bodies around which center the elaborate gradations of self-disclosure and self-expression that go to make up their sense of themselves as women. Yet, *if the situation is defined as "medical,"* they bare themselves on the instant to the probing hands and by no means entirely impersonal gaze of complete strangers. [Emphasis added]

Apparently other factors in addition to the organism and stimulus object and medium of contact must be considered in understanding psychological events.

A mother has finished icing a cake in the presence of her 2-year-old Johnnie. A telephone ring forces her to leave the room. On her return, she finds the cake hopelessly ruined. Johnnie was the culprit. Moral: whether mother is in the kitchen or out of the kitchen makes a great difference in events involving a cake and a child. Similarly, whether the teacher is in the classroom or out of the classroom makes a great difference in Tommy's reaction to Mary's pigtail before him and the finger paints on his desk top. Parents in the room or out of the room can have a tremendous effect on the range, duration, and content of a phone conversation carried on by a teen-ager. Soft music, candlelight, spotless silverware on a spotless tablecloth provide a setting of elegance and culinary enjoyment. Contrast such a setting with that of a cheap café with well-worn, heavy plates and cups, smudged water glasses, greasy-looking grill, and an occasional cockroach. It should be obvious that the same gourmet delight served under the two different settings would not be approached with the same gusto.

Summary up to This Point

A great number of topics have been covered in this chapter so far. Our first problem concerned a convenient unit of study abstracted from the ongoing flow of behavior. I proposed the construct of behavior segment containing a single stimulus–response unit. I suggested its further usefulness in embracing larger behavioral chunks (behavior situations) that could be handled as a series of behavior segments. I next examined and discriminated four different kinds of behavior segments (operation, process, witting, and unwitting). Briefly focusing on the organism's participation in the event, I discerned both simple and complex responses. I next differentiated between objects, stimulus objects, and stimulus functions. The main point here was that objects as objects in the organism's surroundings were meaningless in psychological inquiry. But as soon as an object became part and parcel of a psychological event involving an organism, it became a *stimulus* object, playing a specific role or stimulus *function* as defined by the organism's response. This led us to a consideration of different classes of stimulus function, each of which should teach us something more about psychological events, or at least that is my hope. The fact that responses also serve different functions concerned us next. We recognized the part played by light, air, and so on in facilitating (but not guaranteeing) the occurrence of psychological events. Finally, I noted the importance of factors found in the setting under which stimulus object and reacting organism come together.

Even this recapitulation of the variety of aspects of psychological events included in this chapter shows the great complexity of our subject matter. The following quotation from Alfred North Whitehead (1957, p. 163) is intended to reinforce the point:

> I agree that the view of nature which I have maintained . . . is not a simple one. Nature appears as a complex system whose factors are dimly discerned by us. But, as I ask you, Is not this the very truth? Should we not distrust the jaunty assurance with which every age prides itself that it at last has hit upon the ultimate concepts in which all that happens can be formulated? The aim of science is to seek the simplest explanations of complex facts. We are apt to fall into the error of thinking that the facts are simple because simplicity is the goal of our quest. The guiding motto in the life of every natural philosopher [or scientist] should be, Seek simplicity and distrust it.

Approaches to the Study of Psychological Data

The time has come to choose a general orientation or framework that will be compatible with the type of analysis that we have followed thus far. The choice we make should also benefit from the issues and problems raised in our previous consideration of a number of fundamentals. Because the oldest theoretical framework is mentalism, we consider it first.

Mentalism

Mentalism is not difficult to explain—it is the same as popular psychology. "Everyone knows" that we "have" a "body" and a "mind" or "consciousness." How one affects the other no one knows, but that has not discouraged adoption of the mind theory. If such a theory were restricted to the psychological views of nonscientists, we would not need to consider it any more than we would need to consider the idea that the earth is flat. However, the mind theory is adopted by some psychologists and some scientific workers in related fields, so we are obligated to examine it carefully. The following sample will serve our present purpose.

The author of the following quotation is a distinguished scientist (Kety, 1969, p. 334) in the area of biochemistry called psychopharmacology.

There are more rigorous disciplines in the hierarchy of the neurosciences than psychopharmacology, which has as its ultimate goal an understanding of the interaction between chemical substances and the mind. In that very statement I label myself a dualist, an appellation I shall not eschew. I am quite content with reducing the universe to two types of entities—mental and material. A further reduction at the present time I would feel to be an unnecessary oversimplification. I cannot conceive any more than Leibniz was able to do, how a vortex of events in one world can effect a change in the other, yet it is our common experience that they do.

Note, first, that according to this opening statement Kety is a dualist, a term that is defined in his subsequent statements. He postulates that the universe is made up of two different entities—mental (hence the term *mentalism)* and material. He also assumes that chemical substances somehow affect the mind. How? He has no more conception of how events in "one world" can influence events in the other any more than did Leibniz. Leibniz was a philosopher who worked about 300 years ago. According to him, God simply created the two radically different substances, the soul and the body, with a kind of built-in nature by which each, following its own peculiar laws, resulted in a harmony between the two. Essentially, what Leibniz did was to declare absolute parallelism between the body and the soul, much as two clocks that keep absolutely the same time, without direct influence on each other but simply because they had both been created perfectly and started off together at "the beginning of time." Here is the important question at this point: Assuming that psychology should have made some advance in the last 200 years, why would a 20th-century scientist work under the postulational system of a 17th-century philosopher? Note that Kety accepts Leibniz's parallelistic assumption of mind (the recent version of soul) without question and without any need for justification.

Objections to mentalism

1. First and foremost, neither Kety nor Leibniz made any observations of mind. It is almost impossible to emphasize too much that "mind" is a hypothetical *construct,* and *not* an observable. No one ever saw a mind. It is a verbally imposed explanation for an event.
2. Mentalism violates certain points of caution raised earlier. Let me just mention two of them: first, mind is self-actional, and, second, it illustrates a static conception and an insensitivity to the origin and nature of the assumptions under which one operates.
3. It is interesting, from a psychological standpoint, that Kety not once questions the validity of his dualistic approach or examines its origin. He simply *assumes* that a person consists of a visible portion (body) and an invisible one (mind).

4. Which brings us to the next point, that the body–mind theory did not come about as the result of scientific investigation. It was a prescientific belief handed down for centuries by tradition and forced on the data. On this point, I quote from Harvey Cushing (1940, p. 11), a celebrated American brain surgeon who commented some time ago, after many hundreds of operations on the brain: "Being obliged because of his hazardous tasks to keep his feet on the ground, the neuro-surgeon is very much puzzled about the mind, which in all his exploring he has never been able satisfactorily to locate, much less feel or see even in the left hemisphere, where it is reported to abide."

5. Despite the fact that Kety is stumped as to how chemicals can affect minds, he nevertheless proceeds in his inquiry with that seemingly frustrating handicap.

6. A further objection to constructs of "mind," "psychic states," "consciousness," and such is their transpatial character; that is, they do not share the same space as natural objects occupy because they cannot be localized. They are, in that sense, nonnatural, antinatural, or supernatural.

7. Finally, Kety acts as if his dualistic approach to the area of his interest were the only way to go about the job. But that is not so; there are other frameworks for scientific investigation into the whole range of psychological activities. We will discuss them later.

These criticisms are not to be interpreted as a personal attack on Kety. His position simply happens to be a convenient target for evaluating the mentalistic or dualistic framework and for indicating some of the problems it raises.

Behaviorism

Historically, classical behaviorism arose as a revolt against dualism. The theory is far more complicated than here presented; the most extensive account of behaviorist development is available in Kantor's *Aim and Progress of Psychology* (1971). The central figure of the revolutionary movement was John B. Watson, who about 1913 declared himself opposed to the mentalistic postulate of invisible minds, sensations, psychic states, consciousness, and the method of introspection (looking within the mind). He advocated the *elimination* of all such transpatial entities. In that sense, his position was negativistic. According to Kantor, if mentalism may be represented by the formula

$$Psychology = Body + Mind$$

then the Watsonian behavioristic formula is

$$Psychology \; = \; Body \; - \; Mind$$

With one of the "two worlds" that Kety talked about denied or ignored, a mindless psychology concentrated on the bodily. In its classical "theory," behaviorism stressed such organic factors as drives, genes, needs, glands, and other bodily structures.

Objections to classical behaviorism

1. While classical behaviorism's attempt to abolish supernatural entities was laudable, it had certain undesirable consequences. It distorted psychological data, as described in the previous chapter, by transforming them into mere movements of an anatomical and physiological sort. Behaviorist psychologists studied such data as learning and thinking as if they were merely physiological.

2. Another result of this negative approach was to load the organism with an overbearing theoretical burden. In the kind of analysis I have proposed, a constellation of factors, in addition to those localizable on the side of the organism and stimulus object, share in the explanation. Medium of contact, setting factors, and the historical dimension all contribute. When the focus is entirely on the body, one must ascribe imaginary or fictitious powers to such structures as the brain and genes. To use Kety's (1969) position once more as an example, consider this statement of his: "I adopt a fundamental working *assumption*—that chemical substances may affect the mind by acting on the brain" (p. 334, emphasis added). Eliminate the "mind" in that sentence and you have a traditional behavioristic stance. The brain, then—not the mind at the behest of brain, as under mentalism—becomes (verbally) a computer. It alone "carries the ball," theoretically, that mind does under the dualistic approach.

3. Emphasis on the organic led to a specialization in the simpler types of data such as animal experiments and conditioned reflexes, thus restricting psychology to a focus on simpler behaviors.

4. Watsonian behaviorism relied on cause–effect thinking, the stimulus being considered a trigger for the response as effect. The other event variables considered earlier were largely neglected.

Other criticisms can be and have been made incisively by Kantor (1971, 1977) but the preceding ones are the most relevant here.

Interbehaviorism

As early as 1924, Kantor developed a systematic viewpoint for behavioral inquiry in his *Principles of Psychology* (1924). Even at that early date he parted company with the behaviorists as well as the mentalists, because both were trapped by their dualistic view. The behaviorists differed only by denying one aspect of the duality that mentalists espoused. However, inter-behaviorism (as Kantor's viewpoint has come to be known) also denies any unobservable, transpatial phenomena such as consciousness, but not merely because it disavows the mind part of the body–mind postulate. It detaches itself entirely from the hoary dualistic tradition and declares, like the child in the story of "The Emperor's New Clothes," that observation simply does not reveal any body *and* mind or body *minus* mind, consciousness, psychic processes, and so on. The data of psychology are naturalistic and differ only in detail from the data of the other sciences. It is important to stress that the interbehaviorist considers the subject matter of psychology to be natural, not unnatural, antinatural, or supernatural. That is to say, dreaming, speaking, learning, remembering, loving, fearing, and hating are as lawful as digestion, circulation, respiration and light, heat, gravity, and electromagnetic phenomena. Kantor (1971, p. 528) refers to this view as a homogeneity formulation of the sciences. His view implies that all the sciences are "natural" sciences because they observe the "interactions between objects and processes (particles, molecules, planets, organisms, radiations, energies) on the basis of specific conditions."

Interbehavioral views select for study the interactions of organisms (human or infrahuman) and other organisms, objects, or situations having the psychological properties we considered earlier. As I have already pointed out, consonant with the procedures of chemists in characterizing their data, and biologists theirs, interbehaviorists isolate events involving an organism and another variable. These events are historical, differential, integrative, variable, delayable, inhibitable, and modifiable.

Another distinctive feature of the interbehavioral approach is its insistence on field. Simple or crude cause–effect thinking is ruled out. It is true that organism and stimulus object are of central interest, but neither is glorified above the other. Their role with respect to each other is coordinate, reciprocal, mutual, and symmetrical. They are not equal to each other, but they "hang in there together"—each depends on the other. Without an organism to read a book, no book can be read, and, without a book to be read, no organism will read a book.

Although organism and stimulus object are of central importance, we note again the necessary role played by the medium of contact and setting factors. All of these together, in relation to each other or the event or field, are the fundamental unit of study. In my opinion, "event psychology" or "field theory" are appropriate synonyms for interbehaviorism. Thus, starting with "unfractured observation" of events as they occur, analysis involves the evaluation of as many factors as can be discovered in the field. Once the variables of an event can be identified, that event can be repeated by bringing together the same constellation of relevant variables. For example, if I succeed in conditioning a dog to lift its paw by pairing shock and metronome, you should be able to do the same by duplicating my procedure.

Now, which of the three frameworks, mentalism, behaviorism, or interbehaviorism, shall we adopt for our own inquiry into psychological data? Ideally, we should use all three every step of the way, comparing and contrasting their respective contributions to our own foresight and understanding. But that would be a colossal task. Let us guardedly adopt a field or event approach and see where it gets us. At various points, we will match a field or event construction with a dualistic or behavioristic theoretical proposition and try to evaluate each. As an inducement to such an adventure, let me point out how a framework oriented toward events fares with respect to the following points.

1. It is extensional in orientation in that it favors observations free of linguistic hindrances imposed by an intensional or word-centered orientation, as in dualism's mind, traditional behaviorism's brain powers, and so on.
2. It rejects such reifications as mind, talent, and consciousness.
3. It is nonelementalist, as indicated by its refusal to split wholes or events; analysis is always in terms of the total field.
4. It honors indexing by its insistence on studying specific organisms and specific stimulus objects in specific situations.
5. It respects the "to-be-is-to-be-related" injunction by studying organism and stimulus object, medium of contact, and setting factors in relation to one another in the whole field.
6. It spurns self-action and the mechanical type of interaction and is more at home with the interbehavioral view or field approach.
7. It is a dynamic or process point of view by contrast with the static, mentalistic mind or the mind's surrogate, the brain, as a storage room. By contrast, stress is on the constant flow of events.
8. It is antireductionistic, subscribing to the assumption that the hierarchy of phenomena (as sociological, psychological, biological) should be studied each at its own level instead of being forced into the data or theory of facts at some lower level.
9. It assumes that behavior is as natural as rolling stones, energy transformations, or movement and reproduction in the animal kingdom. Behavior is considered *a part of* nature instead of *apart from* it.
10. In the free will–determinism controversy, it is determinist in the sense of Einstein's (1954, p. 262) "conviction . . . of the rationality or intelligibility of the world [that] lies behind all scientific work of a higher order."
11. It shares in physics' recent developments (through the work of Einstein) of its relativistic and field concepts by stressing behavioral fields in place of older fictional, concentrated power spots within an alleged mind, brain, or gene.

Related Developments

In the decades from 1930 to 1960, psychology was in a state of relative stability. But, according to Segal and Lachman (1976), since 1960 psychological research and theory have been in a state of flux. Developments in computer science, linguistic theory, and mathematics, among other factors, have heavily influenced psychology. In addition to those recent movements, there were some less conspicuous or older trends, all of which share a rejection of a self-actional and reductionistic approach to the subject matter of psychology. To some degree or other, proponents of such views favor a field or event approach to psychological inquiry. To the extent that they meet a field or event criterion, they are consonant with interbehavioral theory as expounded in this book. In addition to those writers whose work is mentioned elsewhere in this book, the following deserve special, but brief, regard: Skinner 1939, 1953), Kimble (1967), Kuo (1967), Barker (1968), Bandura (1969, 1974), Willems and Rausch (1969), Rogers-Warren and Warren (1977), Frederiksen (1972), Moos (1973), Craik (1973), and Sommer (1977).

B. F. Skinner

One behaviorist who stands apart from the general trend is B. F. Skinner of Harvard University. As a matter of fact, Skinner's approach to psychological inquiry comes much closer to event psychology than to the self-actional type of behaviorism criticized earlier.

Early in his career, Skinner (See Figure 1-5) was considered to be "anti-theory." He explains why in his book *Contingencies of Reinforcement: A Theoretical Analysis* (Skinner, 1969). If by *theory* you mean "any explanation of an observed fact which appeals to events taking place somewhere else, at some other level of observation, described in different terms, and measured, if at all, in different dimensions—events, for example, in the real nervous system, the conceptual [nervous] system, or the mind" (Skinner, 1969, p. vii), then Skinner is not interested in that kind of theory. Actually, what Skinner is opposed to is *hypothetical* constructs, whether of the reductionistic or dualistic sort, because he states further on (p. viii) that "theory is essential to the scientific understanding of behavior as a subject matter." Skinner's basic formulation is phrased in terms of an "interaction between an organism and its environment" (p. 7) always involving (1) the occasion connected with a response (2) the response itself, and (3) the reinforcing consequences. That he takes a broader view than a simple interactional view is revealed in the following statement: "The interrelationships are much more complex than those between a stimulus and a response, and they are much more productive in both theoretical and experimental analyses" (pp. 7–8). Further evidence that Skinner's approach is near to field theory is indicated in his *The Behavior of Organisms* (1938), when he applies the term

Figure 1-5   B. F. Skinner, founder of the experimental analysis of operant behavior. He developed laboratory methods and extended operant principles to verbal behavior, instruction, psychotherapy, and the design of cultures.

system to behavior analysis. Here *system* refers to what one arrives at "only through an experimental analysis . . . in which the parts or aspects of behavior are identified and their mutual relations established" (1938, p. 435).

Still another difference between orthodox behaviorists and Skinner's radical behaviorism involves his stand on statistics. He is critical of the statistical approach as depending on "unrefined methods of measurement and a general neglect of the problem of direct description" (Skinner, 1938, p. 443). And so he throws in his lot with the "nonstatistical investigation of *the individual*" (1938, p. 444, emphasis added), depending on developing techniques of measurement and control toward achieving reliability or reproducibility of events. Skinner's stress on the individual organism is confirmed by the following statement: "Instead of studying a thousand rats for one hour each, or a hundred rats for ten hours each, the investigator is likely to study one rat for a thousand hours" (1969, p. 112). In the same publication, Skinner emphasizes the need for controlling "the past history of the organism . . . possibly from birth" (p. 94). For Skinner, as for Kantor, analyzing the flow of events will yield prediction and control.

Another point of resemblance between Skinner's position and the field approach that I am expounding here lies in his stand on the nervous system. He sees psychology and neurology as "two independent subject matters (behavior and the nervous system) which must have their own techniques and methods and yield their own respective data" (Skinner, 1938, p. 423). He does not consider behavior chaotic and sees no need to reduce it by appealing to a hypothetical agent residing in the nervous system.

Gregory Kimble

In his article "Basic Tenets of Behaviorism," Gregory Kimble (1967) points out that when Pavlov and his associates studied conditioning in dogs they made a serious error in their construction. They actually observed dogs trained to lift a paw to a bell by delivering an electric shock to the paw. But, when they explained that event in terms of such hypothetical brain processes as *irradiation*, the concept of irradiation was not physiology but only an *inference* drawn from observing a behavioral fact. Therefore, says Kimble, (p. 76), one must recognize "a distinction between fact and inference from fact," a distinction that is often ignored.

Kimble goes on to consider the basic facts of psychology: "descriptions of behavior and accounts of the circumstances under which behavior occurs" (Kimble, 1967, p. 76). Pushed a bit further, the facts are what we call *responses* (descriptions of behavior) and *stimuli* (the circumstances under which behavior occurs), which give us the S–R formula.

This formulation is simplicity itself. Yet it has not been universally accepted. As stated, the S–R formula only points out that behavior is connected with surrounding conditions but, according to Kimble, it has often taken on a stronger form that converts S–R into S ⟶ R. The latter expression suggests a clearly identifiable single stimulus as the *cause* of a response. Kimble's behaviorism does not consider that a tiny mouse *alone* would cause a woman to stand on a chair and scream. Hasn't the past history of that woman, and of women in general, also played a part in the scene? Still other variables, such as antecedent conditions, play a role. Kimble thinks that if psychologists stick to facts instead of inferences from facts, they will be able to embrace the expanded S–R approach that he advocates instead of dealing with materials "that are basic to neuroanatomy, poetry or religion" (1967, p. 80). Kimble's rejection of strict cause–effect type of thinking in favor of a broader approach that sticks to facts, not inferences, places him among the field theorists.

Z. Y. Kuo

Three years before he died, Kuo published a book entitled *The Dynamics of Behavior Development: An Epigenetic View* (1967). Because his systematic stand harmonizes with the field event I am developing, I here set down some of the fundamentals of his approach, beginning with his admonition that "no scientific theory should last for more than two or three decades without being greatly modified or entirely supplanted" (Kuo, 1967, p. xi).

Kuo's epigenetic viewpoint. With the term "epigenetic," Kuo describes a continuous, dynamic, ever-changing developmental process that begins with fertilization and ends with death. He agrees with the ancient Greek philosopher Heraclitus (600–500 B.C.) that change is the only constant thing. The most important point about epigenesis is that at every point of development a new relationship is established between the organism and the environment (viewed from a biological standpoint) or between the organism's behavioral response and its correlated stimulus object (viewed psychologically). Things are never the same. Both variables are in a state of flux or, stated otherwise, the succession of events changes. Each change sets the stage for the next change in a lawful, orderly way.

Kuo's view differs from that of many psychologists, as indicated by his key term *bidirectional*, which is applied to the interaction of the organism and stimulating condition. The organism, in his view, is not a passive "thing" pulled and pushed by environmental forces. Every organismic response is "a functional product of the dynamic relationship between the organism and its environment." Through continued interaction, not only the organism changes but also the way the environment affects the organism changes. Kuo comes very close to a field or event type of construction.

Other important points

1. Kuo's objective is to study the behavioral repertoire of the individual. He is, therefore, antistatistical, preferring the same kind of precision that comes by studying a single organism over an extended time interval that appeals to Skinner.
2. Kuo *prefers* the laboratory to the often inadequate observation of animals in the wild, especially when such observations are too short to observe variability that may occur.
3. "The developmental history of the animal is of utmost importance" (Kuo, 1967, p. 18). Where some ethologists assume a self-actional,

static instinct of aggression, Kuo points out how acts that look like uniform responses are often more apparent than real.

When Kuo studied fighting in one specific dog, Bobby, he found that the extreme variability in the dog's behavior was a function of the following factors:

a. Whether or not the other dog offered resistance
b. Whether or not the other dog fell on his back
c. Whether or not other friendly dogs attacked the other dog
d. Whether or not the other dog had defeated Bobby as a pup
e. Whether or not the other dog was a female or a female in heat
f. Whether or not Bobby was well fed
g. Whether the temperature was hot or cold
h. Whether Bobby had already had a fight

Kuo found similar variation in Bobby's reactions to other stimulus variables presented repeatedly under different conditions. Even when Bobby attacked the same dog on different occasions, he "never attacked the same dog twice in the same manner" (Kuo, 1967, p. 17). Therefore, Kuo asks, how can you talk about any genetically determined instinct? For Kuo, nothing is predetermined; there are only shifts in the *natural sequence* of events under observation.

It would be an easy guess that Kuo does not subscribe to any internal (neural) principles to explain behavior, because behavior and its correlated conditions are observable. For example, most people believe that cats are born with a natural instinct to kill mice or rats. But, by manipulating conditions in the laboratory, Kuo found that he could train kittens to love, fear, hate, or kill and eat rats or mice. He achieved the same results with kittens and birds, and with dogs and birds. Furthermore, he proved that "there is no genetic basis in the neural organization that determines the kinds of food which the young of a given species . . . will eat. . . . Animals eat what they eat not because of what they are born with but because of what they are fed with" (Kuo, 1967, p. 71). For Kuo, any behavior is as "natural" as any other, for all develop under certain specifiable conditions. Nothing is preordained.

Roger Barker

Roger Barker acknowledges the fact that psychology has been mostly an experimental science, one that has relegated second place to descriptive or naturalistic methods of investigation. Yet he feels that behaviors that occur frequently in everyday life have been left out of account because they are too difficult to create in the experimental laboratory. Consequently, he has become a kind of natural historian by moving himself and his staff to Oskaloosa, Kansas, a town of 830 inhabitants. Here, for the past twenty years, he has been recording and analyzing behavior as it occurs in its natural setting.

As a consequence, he has evolved a broader-than-average viewpoint, which he expounds in his book, *Ecological Psychology* (Barker, 1968).

Our interest in ecological psychology lies less in Barker's theoretical formulation than in his procedure or method. In trying to understand the behavior of individuals, Barker found little help in trying to ferret out the individual's "motives," "drives," or "experience." What helped most was his discovery of the importance of behavior settings. Just as the biologist makes sense of the adaptation of the biological organism by relating adaptation to its environment, so Barker found that the behavior of individuals, when correlated with its behavioral settings, was not nonsensical. As he states it, (1968, p. 164),

> While it is possible to smoke at a Worship Service, to dance during a Court Session, and to recite a Latin lesson in a Machine Shop, such matchings of behavior and behavior settings almost never occur in Midwest [Oskaloosa], although they would not be infrequent if these kinds of behavior were distributed among behavior settings by chance.

In fact, Barker found that he could predict the behavior of individuals better by noting whether they were in a drugstore, tavern, post office, or mortuary than by investigating their "behavior tendencies" and other self-actional agents. Barker's procedure involved field observations of an individual child's behavior stream analyzed into segments labeled *behavior episodes* connected with "ecological inputs" (Barker, 1968, p. 150). He looked for lawfulness between the "inputs" and behavior episodes, and he found it. The 119 children that Barker and his staff were most concerned with were involved in a total of about 100,000 episodes each day—36 million in a year! Yet out of this mass of data he found a dramatic change in the children's behavior correlated with a change in situation from "classroom, to hall, to playground; from drugstore to street; from baseball game to shower room" (p. 152). Another finding showed a greater uniformity of different children in the same behavioral situation than the same child in different situations (for example, Joe Doakes in Sunday School and in a Boy Scout meeting). What impressed Barker among his findings was the flexibility and versatility of people as they shifted from "a Band Concert to a Prayer Service, a Football Game, a Spelling Bee, a Dance, an X-Ray Laboratory, a Horse Show, a Piano Recital, a Telephone Booth, a Wedding" (p. 164). With his discovery of the significance of the behavior setting, Barker also discovered "law and order."

While it is true that Barker's ecological psychology does not cover all of an individual's behavior (according to *his* postulates), the work that he reports does not fit a self-actional approach. Indeed, he sees behavior as a joint function of organismic action and the particular locale in which it occurs. His view, therefore, comes close to a field theory as confirmed in Barker's quotation from Egon Brunswich (1957, p. 5): "Both organism and environment will have to be seen as systems, each with properties of its own, yet both hewn from basically the same block." The statement appears to be an appropriate metaphor to close an account of Barker's ecological psychology.

Albert Bandura

Albert Bandura and his social learning theory belong in the tradition of ecological psychology for two reasons: (1) he extends the laboratory and its methods to the school, hospital, and community, and (2) he rejects "theories that tend to assign causal properties to hypothetical internal forces" (1969, p. 62). He works with observable variables in which the person is seen "neither as an internally impelled system nor a passive reactor to external stimulation. Rather, psychological functioning involves a reciprocal interaction between behavior and its controlling environment" (p. 63). His program includes not only the validation of the principles involved in social learning but also their application toward the amelioration of developmental and clinical problems and toward effecting broader cultural and social change.

Etc., Etc., Etc.

The literature in the area of naturalistic observation of human behavior or ecological psychology is rapidly expanding. It would take us too far afield to do more than mention some representative, random samplings. The sample includes the following two books: *Naturalistic Viewpoints in Psychological Research*, edited by E. P. Willems and H. L. Raush (1969), and *Ecological Perspectives in Behavior Analysis*, edited by A. Rogers-Warren and S. F. Warren (1977). N. Frederiksen (1972) has published "Toward a Taxonomy of Situations," and in a related paper Moos (1973) deals with "Conceptualizations of Human Environments." Craik (1973) reviews publications in the area in a review article, "Environmental Psychology," in the *Annual Review of Psychology*, 1973. His summary of publications in the area of "man –environment relations" embraces a bibliography of 280 items. The January 1977 issue of the *APA Monitor* has a lead article by Robert Sommer entitled "Toward a Psychology of Natural Behavior" pleading for an extension of research in extralaboratory behavior.

Such recent developments as those cited may well presage a movement in the direction of field studies. If so, then "internal causes" and "inferences from facts"—all self-actional agents and forces—may well have to take a back seat. Why? Because, as Barker (1968, p. 195) discovered, "All inhabitants of a setting of the genotype Drugstore behave drugstore, and all inhabitants of a Tavern behave tavern." In other words, a field type of observation forces the observer to give full recognition to the circumstances so prominently connected with the observed behavior so that, if a drugstore setting explains why people act the way they do when they are in a drugstore and a tavern setting explains why people behave the way they do when they are in a tavern, "inferences from facts" as to what's going on inside the skin or the genes are superfluous. Certainly, if such a movement continues to grow, then field theory may well prevail. But, until such a day should come to pass, at least we are in good company. Certainly we are not alone.

Chapter Summary

This chapter delimits the subject matter of psychology in order to distinguish it from possible confusion with the subject matter of biology. In common with the other sciences, psychology relies on the procedures of definition, analysis, and interpretation to arrive at the basic unit of study, the behavior segment, and then more complex chain reactions or behavior situations. Further analysis yielded types of behavior segments, types of responses, the central response pattern, and by-play action. Sharp distinctions are drawn among object, stimulus object, and stimulus function, and the various classes of stimulus function. Certain conditions (media of contact) make it possible for organism and stimulus object to interact, and the surroundings or setting in which behavior interactions are embedded also influence behavioral events. There are three very different approaches to the study of psychological events—mentalism or dualism, behaviorism, and interbehaviorism.

2 The Reactional Biography: The Individual's Psychological History

We make some progress toward understanding anything when we discover how it is related to other things, especially to antecedent events.

[Skinner, 1959, p. 229, emphasis added]

In the preceding chapter, I examined modes of explaining, describing, or interpreting psychological events via reductionistic and mentalistic constructs, and I rejected both. What's the alternative? My analysis of the subject matter of psychology up to this point has emphasized total fields, events, or systems. Therefore, it seems an attractive, easy, logical step to look for some regularity or "ideal of natural order" in the flow of those events. The question "Can we find any lawfulness in the way successive events are related to each other? If we find "rhyme and reason" with such an analysis and gain foresight and understanding, why resort to an imaginary nervous system or an equally fictitious mind type of explanation?" I propose that we test out a construct such as is suggested by Skinner in the quotation that opens this chapter. More specifically, if we want to understand a particular event in the present, let us try relating it to an antecedent event or events. If our attempt works, it would seem that we have a simpler and therefore more desirable construct than the *hypothetical* theories stated in terms of a conceptual nervous system or mind that cannot be verified. As Hanson (1958, p. 95) puts it, "If that to which I refer when accounting for events needs more explaining than that to which you refer, then your explanation is better than mine." As a convenient model for such an approach, let us try Kantor and Smith's (1975) construct of the reactional biography.

The Nature of the Reactional Biography

Earlier, Kantor (1933, p. 44) defined the reactional biography as "the complete behavioral experience of the individual." In their recent formulation, Kantor and Smith (1975) have adopted the term *interbehavioral history*, because it sounds more inclusive than *reactional biography*. With the latter term, they stress the organism's acquisition of responses and functions, while another term, *stimulus evolution*, refers to the other side of the picture, the evolution of stimulus functions. Interbehavioral history covers both. I propose to use the terms *reactional biography* and *interbehavioral history* interchangeably. Both terms will refer implicitly to the series of events of a given individual—his or her psychological or interbehavioral history. More specifically, we are here involved in a dimension requiring an expansion of the field beyond the organism, a field that involves the organism and stimulus object(s) in their successive contacts. The series of their joint interactions will be distinguished from mere biological events by those properties of psychological events discussed in the preceding chapter.

The Complexity of the Reactional Biography

The totality of the behavioral events connected with a single individual indicates the immensity and complexity of the reactional biography. If we were to attain a complete reactional biography of any individual, we would have to include every back scratch, nose blow, every "ahem," every sight, smell, touch, and so on—a quite impossible feat. But in this respect, we are no worse off than the astronomer who has no notion of how many astronomical bodies remain to be counted. The biologist, too, realizes that many species of plants and animals are yet to be discovered, identified, and catalogued. Nevertheless, both astronomy and biology are recognized sciences, and both have made great headway by working with the incomplete data that they do have. Likewise, in psychology, it is surprising how much insight a psychologist may gain from a sporadic but connected series of related behaviors that can explain delinquency, crime, "neurosis," or "psychosis."

The Beginning of the Reactional Biography

Imagine that we have a complete motion-picture record of your psychological development. But instead of viewing the film from the beginning, we are going to run it in a reverse direction, starting with the present moment. At

first, we see you displaying all the accomplishments, skills (musical, mathematical, mechanical), language attainments (native and foreign), knowledge
of the sciences, arts, and philosophy. You can anticipate that viewing the
film backward will reveal simpler stages of your current excellences until
eventually we reach a point in your development at which none of what you
do so well now is there to be seen at all. We have reached the zero point of
your interbehavioral history, in the sense that no behavior has yet made its
appearance.

According to this reactional-biography conception, all behavioral happenings have a zero point at some stage in the life history of the organism.
For every person, there was a time in the life span when that individual did
not carry out the acts performed so well now. But, with that individual's
first crude attempt at uttering the word *Mama*, reaching for the milk bottle,
and grasping the baby rattle, the zero point was left behind. Those attempts,
no matter how feeble, were the start of a reactional biography that launched
that person on a program of definite behavioral acquisition. The zero points
of some acts are easily observable; for example, the first step in walking, the
first spoken word, the first solution of an arithmetic problem. But some
behaviors are not as easily observable and may originate even in the fetal life
of the individual.

The Zero Point of the Reactional Biography

The possibility of locating a psychological zero point in the fetal stage
strongly implies a close connection between the organism's biological condition and opportunities for psychological development. With the help of
Figure 2-1, we now examine that relationship.

Development of the Biological Organism

The life history of the biological organism (represented by the solid line in
Figure 2-1) obviously begins at conception, with the fertilization of the egg
cell by the sperm cell. From this point on, we have an organism—an organism because it is organized as a living system—that, under proper conditions, will eventuate in the "normal" boy or girl infant 9 months later.
During the organism's uterine development, both its biological immaturity
and its sheltered existence permit few opportunities for behavior development. What few there are will be considered in greater detail in the following chapter. But even at birth, when the child has been described as an
alimentary canal with a loud clamor at one end and a total lack of responsibility at the other end, it is still helpless and limited for psychological
purposes. But to continue with the organism's biological development, we
note, on that solid line, infancy, childhood, adolescence, youth, an apex
during early adulthood, and a slow decline into old age, senility, and death.

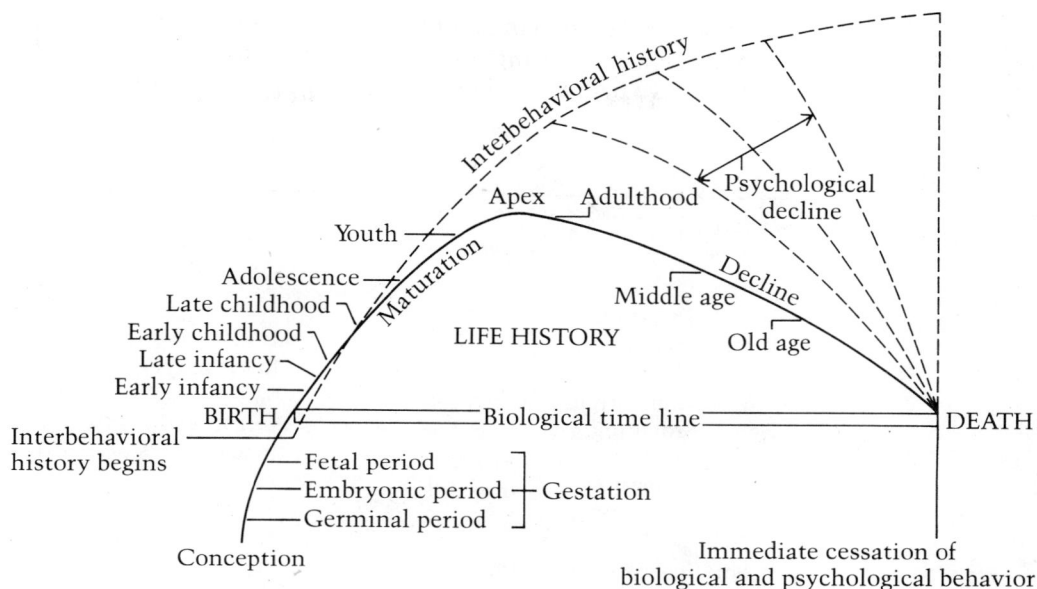

Figure 2-1   Diagram suggesting development of reactional biography in relation to biological life history. Note the possible divergent course of the two developments.

All the stages of the growth and deterioration of the living organism are defined in terms of the structure and function of the constituent cells, organs, and organ systems. Here is another criterion that can help distinguish between the organism's life history and reactional biography. The same organism may participate in both histories but they are, nevertheless, two different histories.

Development of the Reactional Biogrphy

How does a representation of the reactional-biography development fit in with the organism's biological growth? In our Figure 2-1, Kantor and Smith (1975) indicate that with the dashed line. The reactional biography is shown as originating during the fetal period, a point to be taken up in the next chapter. But if we proceed beyond birth we note a close parallel between the two lines. This simply means that such behaviors as running, hopping, and skipping must wait for legs to elongate in order to permit proper biological structures for those behaviors. At this point, the two developments parallel each other, after which there are a number of possibilities.

   An interesting fact appears in the separation of the two lines after adolescence and youth. The interbehavioral history line may continue to rise, with a psychological decline at any of the later ages, but not necessarily so. For some, psychological deterioration does not occur until extreme old age, or all of a sudden, with the death of the individual. The following short list of creative people, still creative in old age, illustrates the point.

ARTIST	AGE	PRODUCTION AT AGE GIVEN
Titian (Tiziano Vecellio), 1477–1576 (Italian painter)	98	*Battle of Lepanto* (painting)
Washington Irving, 1783–1859 (American author)	76	*Life of George Washington* (biography)
Robert Browning, 1812–1889 (English poet)	76	*Parleyings with Certain People* (book)
William C. Bryant, 1794–1878 (American poet and editor)	76-77	Translations of the *Iliad* and the *Odyssey* (ancient Greek epics)
	84	Editor-in-Chief, *N.Y. Evening Post*
Oliver Wendell Holmes, 1841–1935 (American jurist and author)	79	*Over the Teacups* (book)
Jean Baptiste Lamarck, 1744–1829 (French naturalist)	86	*Natural History* (scientific treatise)
Johann Wolfang von Goethe 1749–1832 (German poet, novelist, and dramatist)	82	*Faust* (dramatic poem, later used as source of several operas)

A Conversation with a 100-Year-old Man

Barnard Collier interviewed a man just over 100 years old. This is how Collier describes his subject (1973, p. 12):

> He told me that his legs are nearly gone, his back is weak, his hands shake so much it makes him mad as a hornet when he turns a page or writes down some idea. He can't smell anything, he can't hear without a hearing aid, he forgets some words entirely, and forgets how to spell others . . . and his eyes work now in peculiar ways.

The description of Collier's interviewee reads like that of a man in extreme senility. Certainly one can easily infer a deteriorated anatomical and physiological status. While this man was driving to church one Sunday morning, he was troubled with double vision when looking at trees or houses. He must be far down on the declining slope of the biological life history.

It is a different matter when we read about the same man's reactional-biography status. Collier's interviewee, Charles Greeley Abbot, was a world-famous astrophysicist and former secretary of the Smithsonian Institution. He had won recognition for his work on sunspots and the weather, for standardized instruments used in measuring the sun's heat, and at the time of the interview working on solar engines. According to the *New Columbia Encyclopedia* (Harris and Levey, 1975, p. 3), "he was the oldest person ever to receive a U.S. patent when his last was issued to him at the age of 99." At the time of the interview and for a year longer, he was still working on improvements for his solar engines, trying to find ways of converting solar energy directly into electrical current. According to Collier, Abbott still answers his phone but he may hang up abruptly if the caller takes too long. "If you apologize for taking the time of a man one hundred years old, he snaps, 'I'm very jealous of my time'" (Collier, 1973, p. 12). He visits the Smithsonian every other Monday morning to pick up his mail and "watch young women" (p. 13). Dr. Abbot is a very busy man intellectually and otherwise, too—insofar as his enfeebled biological condition will permit.

The Divergence of the Biological Life History and the Reactional Biography

The case of Dr. Abbot accentuates the possible separation of the biological life history and the reactional biography. "With one foot in the grave," Abbot could nevertheless function at top level in the area of his long-time, specialized area of scientific interest. What is the meaning of the fact that the two lines in Figure 2-1 can go their separate ways?

Psychological Reactions Are More Than the Operation of Biological Structures

As Kantor (1933, p. 49) long ago pointed out, "in spite of the exceedingly intimate relationship between the biological and psychological developments, psychological reactions are not merely the operation of biological mechanisms." The *mere* possession of tongue, teeth, lips, vocal chords, and lungs will never explain why one child speaks Spanish and another, Polish. In fact, even with those structures present and in good working order there may be no speech whatsoever. To speak, the *organism* with these structures intact must undergo a reactional biography of a certain type, under certain conditions. It must have contact with others—parents, usually—who speak a certain language; living *exclusively* with deaf-mute parents (despite the necessary anatomical structures) would result in a speechless child. Also, the parents must not anticipate the child's every need, or the child may not speak. The parents must reinforce the child's approximations to standard speech. These conditions hint at some of the variables, in addition to the requisite anatomical "organs of speech," that are essential in a person's acquisition of speech during the reactional biography. This analysis should help to explain the implications of the divergence between the biological life history and the reactional-biography lines in Figure 2-1. Again, the two developments, even when they involve "the *same* organism" (as identified by a photograph, for example), are not the same. They involve two *different* stories, with different ends, procedures, and different results. They concentrate on different sets of variables—the biologist on structures and their functions and the psychologist on the flow of events, with a main focus on organism–stimulus-object interactions within a specific context.

Biological Structures as Participating Factors

We must do full justice to the place of the biological conditions in the interbehavioral history. Let us use the "organs of speech" just referred to as an illustration. No one can deny that they do play a role in the psychological event of speaking. Those structures can be considered as an instrument of speech; it is *by their means* that the organism, let us say, greets another person. Without them, speech might never develop, but, once acquired, speech can be managed without vocal chords or tongue if and when amputation of either is required. With an event or field type of orientation, the *organs* of speech are viewed as "participating factors" (Kantor, 1933, p. 50). In self-actional theories, the organs of speech (aided and abetted by the mind or brain) are more likely to be considered as "the cause" of speech. There is a radical difference in the two views, a difference that can be stated as "necessary conditions" versus "causal conditions." The former considers the anatomical structures as *facilitating* conditions, those that *make it possible* for the organism to speak. The latter considers the same organs as the very source and origin of speech (with the aid of the brain, of course).

Biological Limitations on the Reactional Biography

Suppose that Beethoven had been *born* deaf. His musical career would never have begun. But he was not born deaf. His "normal" ears *facilitated* his development of the necessary discriminations, but these must be viewed within the context of a complex reactional biography, which is also indispensable to a musical career. In the past, it was easy to overlook a musician's interbehavioral history and give all the credit to his "sharp ears" or a "musical gene."

Another point regarding Beethoven's "ears." He became deaf at the age of 32, yet he composed the bulk of his work after that period (Marek, 1969).

Thus, the relationship between "ears" and creativity is not the same early in interbehavioral history as it is *after* one's establishment in a musical career.

We have already considered the case of Helen Keller and need only to relate it briefly to the present discussion. Helen's early deafness and blindness shut off two important media of contact for reactional-biography development. There is no way of knowing how many similar cases spent their lives in institutions—a possibility that was once considered for Helen Keller. But heroic attempts to compensate for that handicap produced an accomplished person. These are some of the facts that need to be seriously weighed in unraveling the relationship between anatomical factors and the reactional biography.

There are many ways in which anatomical conditions limit reactional-biography development. Because humans are born without wings, they cannot acquire flying behavior the way birds do. Because of their different hand structures, chimps and gorillas cannot perform delicate manual operations. A child born without arms or hands cannot write in the conventional manner but, as the news media occasionally report, such a child can produce "foot writing," feeding, and dressing behavior. The National Foundation March of Dimes has recorded the remarkable case of "Little Marty," a "Thalidomide baby" without arms or hands, dressing himself, and, with the aid of prostheses, writing, painting, typing, eating, and even playing soccer. Marty even achieved limited swimming (without prostheses). But an abused child chained to a bed, in solitary confinement, and with normal arms, hands, and legs may be unable to do what Little Marty accomplishes *without* the requisite appendages. Our conclusion is that an intact organism is desirable. Absence of organs handicaps the organism's interbehavioral history in a way that may or may not be compensated or substituted for. Yet presence of a given structure—"good ears," for example—will not guarantee "sharp auditory discriminations" unless and until that organism is involved in a series of events involving stimulus objects (such as pianos) under certain conditions to be elaborated in the following chapter.

How to Analyze the Flow of Events

We have already established the continuity of events in our discussion of the succession of behavioral units (behavior segments) and in our treatment of the reactional biography. Our next question is how to analyze and understand the behavioral stream. Several decades ago, Herman and Kenyon (1956) argued that there is no way to understand a particular behavioral occurrence without taking the historical dimension into account. For example, suppose you introduce a rat to a maze and restrict yourself to gathering data exclusively in terms of errors per trial or the time per trial. According to Herman and Kenyon, you are committing a grievous error if you do not consider that rat's previous history. Is the rat a so-called naive rat, or has it had previous experience in running a maze? These facts out of the rat's past must be known and specified, along with the variables in the *present* situation. In other words, Herman and Kenyon are alerting us to the need for carving out, to analyze, a larger "chunk" or slice of behavioral continuity than that under our nose at a given moment.

Another example involves a frequent laboratory observation referred to as *spontaneous recovery.*[1] It would be best to consider an actual, well-controlled laboratory experiment. Because of the extended time interval involved, we select a study conducted by Murphy, Miller, and Finocchio (1956). Just enough of the experimental procedure is given to clarify the meaning of the term *spontaneous recovery.*

Conditioning and Extinguishing a Response

Essentially, the experimenters conditioned a group of eight rats as follows. They presented each rat with a red-light stimulus for 2 seconds. At the end of 2 seconds, they delivered a shock to the rat via the cage floor made of stainless-steel strips. A bar protruding from the wall would terminate or prevent the shock when the rat pressed it. With that setup, Murphy and his coworkers proceeded to condition their animal subjects until they reached a criterion of 90% response (nine conditioned responses out of 10 trials). At this point, they proceeded to extinguish the bar-pressing response by eliminating reinforcement. Naturally, conditioned responses occurred with ever-decreasing frequency, as shown in Figure 2-2, for the last three days of the extinction series. During the third from the last day the conditioned re-

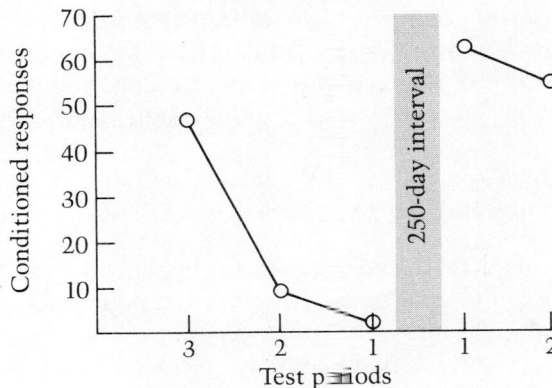

Figure 2-2   Conditioned responses for the last three test periods of extinction and the first two periods of spontaneous recovery.

[1] For this example and others, I am indebted to my colleague, David Herman. Both the example and my discussion of it grew out of rap sessions with him.

sponse occurred about 47 times or about 50% of the time. During the next to the last day, it dropped to 9 times or about 10% and on the last extinction day to 0 in six animals and 10% in two animals. At this point, the experiment was terminated for the time being.

Spontaneous Recovery

In testing for spontaneous recovery, previous investigators had used extremely short time intervals, ranging anywhere from 1 minute, the shortest, to 48 hours, the longest. Murphy and his colleagues arbitrarily decided on an interval of 205 days (about 7 months). During that period, the rats had had no contact with the red light. But on the 206th day they were confronted with red light alone, no shock. What would happen? The bar-pressing response had largely been eliminated 205 days ago. What actually happened was that the eight rat subjects together gave a total of 60 conditioned responses on the very first test period (red light alone *without any shock reinforcement*)! Three of the subjects performed at the criterion level!

Now, *here is the crucial point.* Suppose we should walk in for the first time, just as Murphy and Company are carrying out their tests on the 206th day. Suppose we observe the rats busily engaged in their bar-pressing activity to a red light. Ordinary rats do not do such things. How can we understand their action if that's all we know? There is *no way* to interpret why rats should press a bar when they discriminate a red light *unless* we are told what happened 205 days before. Explanation demands that we join together the chunk of behavioral events spanning 206 days, if we are to make sense of what is going on. Again, to state it in other terms, spontaneous behavior is really not "spontaneous" after all, because it is a function of what happened 206 days before. As Herman and Kenyon (1956, p. 34) put it, "Recognizing the continuous character of behavior is imperative for adequate descriptive constructs."

Ebbinghaus' Classic Work on Learning and Memory

For further help in getting at the rhyme and reason of the behavioral stream, we turn to examples from Hermann Ebbinghaus. Ebbinghaus (1850–1909) was ahead of his time in developing quantitative experimental methods for studying learning and remembering at a time when introspection was the accepted method. He was criticized for using only one subject, himself, but today the intensive study of the single organism is a respectable procedure, if done with care.

To homogenize his materials as much as possible, Ebbinghaus (1964) invented the nonsense syllable, which is simply a vowel between two consonants. By noting the number of repetitions required to recite a given list of nonsense syllables, he could study "forgetting" as a function of time, length of list, and, later, length of nonsense syllables, meaningfulness, and so on.

What is of immediate importance to us is his ingenious discovery of comparing the original learning time or number of repetitions with the same criteria after various time intervals following the original learning.

The relearning and saving method.   What Ebbinghaus did in one series of studies was to learn eight series of 12 syllables each to the point of one perfect recall. To do this took him an average of 1081 seconds. Then, he engaged in some other activities and after 19 minutes returned to the list to find that he had forgotten some of the nonsense syllables. He therefore relearned them and found that this time it took him an average of only 498 seconds. Thus, the second learning was achieved at a saving of about 54%.

A more striking illustration of "the relearning and saving method," as it has been called, is referred to in Hilgard's introduction to the Ebbinghaus book (1964). Hilgard points out that Ebbinghaus also worked with meaningful materials that also produced orderly results. While Ebbinghaus was in his thirties, he had memorized some cantos from Byron's poem *Don Juan*. In time, he had "forgotten" them "completely." After 22 years, when he was in his fifties, he relearned them. "There was still evidence of saving in the time required to relearn them" (Hilgard, in Ebbinghaus, 1964, p. ix). Thus, one way we can be certain that some act has been "completely forgotten" is to check out the time it takes to relearn it and compare it with the original learning time.

Implications of the relearning and saving method.   The most important point about relearning something is that the particular behavior under scrutiny at the moment cannot (or should not) be separated from its relevant predecessor in the behavioral stream. One cannot demonstrate saving time in learning a poem unless one has *previously* learned it. Or, if one learns a poem *now* it will be easier to relearn it *later* even when it seems to have been "completely forgotten." Similarly, it makes no sense to amputate spontaneous recovery from the foregoing sequence of behavioral events and studied as such, because spontaneous recovery is indissolubly linked with the preceding conditioning and extinction. The two events must be held together in analysis. As the quotation at the beginning of the present chapter says "We make some progress toward understanding anything when we discover how it is related to antecedent events" (Skinner, 1959, p. 229).

On the Propriety of Inference

Question: When is an inference a proper inference? *Answer:* When it can be tested and verified. Suppose you come home and find that your home has been thoroughly vandalized. You may infer that a certain neighborhood gang has struck or you may infer that the destruction was wrought by gremlins (imaginary malicious gnomes). It may be possible to verify the first theory, for a neighborhood gang is a potentially observ*able* entity. It is possible and even probable that a neighbor saw the gang enter your home and even identified them. This is not possible with the nonobservable gremlins.

If we carry over this analogy to (1) spontaneous recovery and (2) learning and relearning nonsense syllables, we are free to go either of two routes. We may, from an instance of spontaneous recovery, either infer that conditioning and extinction events had occurred previously (a test*able* hypothesis), or we may make inferences about some fictitious happenings in brains or minds. Similarly, for Ebbinghaus' results. We have the option of explaining the original learning situation or we may imagine certain "traces" in Ebbinghaus' brain that made it easier for him to relearn nonsense lists. But it is important to point out that, while both types of inferences are speculative, one type makes an inference from one observable phenomenon to another observable phenomenon, while the other type makes an inferential leap from an observable phenomenon (for example, the time Ebbinghaus saved in relearning Byron's *Don Juan* cantos after 22 years) to *unobservable* phenomena, namely fictitious happenings in Ebbinghaus' brain or mind. Rachlin (1977, p. 373) reinforces this point in the following quotation:

> If a subject in an experiment is instructed on Day 1 to make response X on Day 2, the cause of response X when it is observed, need not be attributed to anything inside the subject's head, but directly to events on the previous day. There is nothing logically wrong with supposing that events on Day 1 directly cause events on Day 2 without supposing a chain of intermediary events (in the mind or the nervous system or elsewhere).

But Rachlin's statement will not satisfy people who are accustomed to rely on internal principles. Some people require a *continuity* between events on Day 1 and those on Day 2 even if they are purely imaginary brain-or-mind goings-on. Rachlin describes a parallel in this regard, with the physicist of the 19th century. In his words (Rachlin, 1977, pp. 373–374),

> When Faraday first suggested that physical forces could act at a distance, the response of other physicists was to infer a series of imaginary hooks bridging the gap between a magnet and an iron filing. But, as time has gone on, the notion of action at a spatial distance has come to be generally accepted without the intermediary hooks. Similarly, action at a temporal distance ought to be accepted without the intermediary . . . neural circuits or cognitions that are usually invoked to bridge the gap.

Rachlin is comfortable with the "action at a distance" view implied in the explanation of his hypothetical subject's Response X on Day 2 simply "because" of the instructions received on Day 1. Others require "intermediary hooks" in the form of imaginary neural traces in the brain. On this point, let us follow in Rachlin's footsteps and see if it advances our study. If not, we are free to drop it and try another approach.

A Small Sampling of Experimentation from an Interbehavioral Approach

The question before us right now is "Can a field or interbehavioral theory provide a paradigm or guide for experimental investigation?" Consider the following examples.

Rats and Killer Whales

Ray, Upson, and Henderson (1977) have adopted an interbehavioral type of orientation, first, in their study of the effect of changes in environmental settings on the behavioral-flow dynamics in laboratory rats. Secondly, they studied the rhythms in the respiratory dynamics of killer whales in relation to temporal and spatial factors. Their "flow diagrams" (p. 649) do not fragment behaviors but view them intact in their ongoing sequence. Behavioral events are fully appreciated for what they are—highly complex, dynamic situations moving on in a space–time framework. Ray and his colleagues have only begun their experimental and naturalistic observation from a field or interbehavioral viewpoint. Their work is promising.

Drugs and Behavior

James McKearney is senior scientist at the Worcester Foundation for Experimental Biology, at Shrewsbury, Massachusetts. As such, he is deeply engrossed in the study of drug effects. But the viewpoint he adopts for his drug studies sets him apart from traditional researchers with their more limited approaches. Here is the way in which he discusses the effect of drugs on behavior after numerous studies (McKearney, 1976a, p. 611):

> From the behavioral standpoint, we now know that the effects of most drugs *depend*,[2] among other things, on the individual's past experience, on characteristics of presently ongoing behaviors, and on the total environmental context in which behavior occurs. The effects of a given drug can be very different depending on different characteristics of behaviors that occur only seconds apart, and this is not parsimoniously explained by assuming moment to moment fluctuations in the anatomy, physiology, or chemistry of the nervous system. Many of the behavioral effects of drugs probably will not be explained on any other level of analysis simply because behavior itself does not exist on these levels. This is a hard pill to swallow for many behavioral pharmacologists, if you will excuse the

---

[2] Emphasis added. I called attention to *depend* because most people think of drugs as having an absolute effect, but this investigator says drug effects depend on a number of factors.

pun. Behavior is not simply a convenient index of the state of the nervous system; as Dews pointed out, for behavioral pharmacology, behavior is *the* thing, and this must not be forgotten.

A field orientation is obvious in this series of statements. Simple cause–effect thinking is out, the kind of thinking in which a given drug (cause) was believed to *always* produce an energizing or tranquilizing result (effect). McKearney's acknowledged approach is frankly interbehavioral (McKearney, 1977, 1978). The quotation provides a convenient exercise for picking out such interbehavioral constructs as reactional biography, participating biological factors, the biologically interrelated but independent status of behavioral events, the nonworkableness of reductionistic explanations, the importance of setting factors, of ongoing behaviors, and possibly still others.

In another recent paper (Morse, McKearney, and Kelleher, 1977, p. 177) McKearney and his colleagues similarly assess the role of the numerous factors that are involved in observing and interpreting drug effects, and they warn "Neglecting these important factors, or overemphasis on any one to the exclusion of others, will produce conclusions of only limited generality." So far, drug studies by the McKearney group have emphasized the multiple and complex determination of behavior. Other experiments (McKearney, 1973, 1976b) indicate that the behavioral effects of drugs can completely depend on the *context* in which behavior is studied. Still other laboratory investigations (McKearney, 1968, 1969, 1970, 1972; McKearney and Barrett, 1975) permit the conclusion that noxious stimuli do not have invariant behavioral effects; for example, the same intense electric shock can have either reinforcing or punishing effects, depending on a subject's past experience and on the current situation in which it is studied.

Outside the Laboratory

At this point, we leave the laboratory and reenter the outside world in an effort to examine a number of everyday behavioral situations far too complex for direct experimental analysis at our present state of development. However, we must do the best we can, even though there is no way of controlling all of the variables that enter into the events. Our job is comparable to that of the seismologist studying earthquakes *as they occur*, the meteorologist studying tornadoes, or the ecologist analyzing the complex interrelationship of organisms and their environments *in nature*, much as Barker (1968) did in his analysis of behavior settings in Midtown.

For one thing, we can be as fastidious in our postulation as we were in the laboratory, and we can see to it that our constructs are derived exclusively from our observations, not out of importations from cultural traditions or out of borrowings from other sciences. Our guiding questions in examining and thinking about the following data will be "Do they fit or support the reactional-biography hypothesis? Can the behaviors under inspection be understood as developments out of antecedent events, or do they require antinatural or supernatural constructs? Are they *a part* of nature or *apart* from nature?"

"Are Geniuses Born or Made?"

If we are governed by strict semantic principles in analyzing genius, our first duty is to look to the origin and usage of the word *genius*. The *Oxford Dictionary of English Etymology* (Onions, 1966) informs us that *genius* and *genie* are related and that the earlier term *genie* refers to a disembodied spirit or "sprite of Arabian demonology" (p. 393). The first recorded usage of the term *genius* to mean "native capacity" or to a person possessing such capacity occurred in the 17th century. In the 18th century, it was used to mean "extraordinary native intellectual power" (p. 393). The oldest recorded Latin usage of the term (up to A.D. 200) was with reference to "attendant spirit, inclination or appetite, (rarely) intellectual capacity" (p. 393). Thus, our term has had an old, if not honorable, history. Its most prevalent usage has subsistential or fictitious reference (such as genies, gremlins, and other nonobservables). Above all, it is certainly not a scientific term, but one that has come down to us in the cultural stream with a heavy accretion of mysticism and a transpatial (ghostly) aura.

Ernest Jones on Genius

Our next job is to determine what data, if any, in the everyday world, we can pick out as a starting point for dealing with the problem so vaguely defined for us by the hoary term *genius*. In an article, "How to Tell Your Friends from Geniuses," Ernest Jones (1957, p. 9) questions "whether there really is such a thing as genius—that is to say, any attribute that differs essentially in its very nature from those present in all human beings." He answers the question with a very firm no and holds to the view that "the manifold differences between various individuals, and indeed between the various races of mankind are quantitative rather than qualitative." He further notes that sometimes a quantitative difference may be so remarkable as to suggest "something qualitative and absolute" (p. 9). He appears to reject self-actional, supernatural theories of genius, and, by narrowing the field down to *scientific production* of the highest order, he proposes certain characteristics of genius so defined—among them "intuitive flashes," spontaneity, periodicity of productivity, originality or seeing things from a different perspective from that of most people, power of concentration, and skepticism. All of the foregoing terms can be translated into terms with objective referents. Essentially, what Jones seems to be saying is that the behavior of people that we call *geniuses* is different only in degree but not in kind from the behavior of ordinary people. There is nothing "out of this world" about their performance. So we should be able to arrange the performances of a group of people, even geniuses, on a continuum or gradient. At the left, we would put the performer who is rated poorest, the next one to the right would be better, and so on until the one at the extreme right would be rated *the best*. Actually, judges at musical competitions and dog shows engage in this kind of rating all the time. They may be involved in ranking all degrees of performance from "very poor" to "superb."

The crucial question is "At which point along the continuum do we draw a line and declare that from this point on the performers are geniuses?" If the performances vary only by small degrees, any cutoff point must be arbitrary. But, if we overlook that argument and simply state that the superior performers have been endowed with a "talent" or genie to the degree to which they excel, we are putting forth an untestable hypothesis. There are still other questions: *"How* did the best performers come to be endowed with such a quality? What are the principles governing its distribution? And *how* has the alleged "talent" made them better performers?" To these questions, the response is usually deep silence. However, there is another option. We may choose to interpret the performance of the best 10 artists, let us say, as a rarely achieved reactional excellence, which varies as a function of differences in the varying aspects of the reactional biographies of the individuals involved. It is with this redefinition of *genius* that we continue.

A Reactional-Biography View of Genius

If we were allowed to experiment at will with people, we could soon put the reactional-biography construct of genius to the test. But the geniuses are found only in the extralaboratory world and are studied *in retrospect*, from autobiographies or biographies, snatchy reconstructions, remnants, diaries, and such behavioral products as poems, short stories, or musical compositions.

The Childhood Pattern of Genius

With full awareness of the complexity of the problem, McCurdy (1957) nevertheless decided to look for possible uniformities in the early life of geniuses. From the biographies of the 20 geniuses that he selected for study, he did find a certain pattern or uniformity in their early rearing. Here are some of the factors:

1. Favorable parental attention toward the young child, both in the form of affection and intellectual stimulation
2. A closely knit family with discouragement of outside contacts, sometimes even isolation

3. Domination of the child by an adult world, including the world of adult books, with its consequent increase of knowledge and excitement of imagination

McCurdy's study is more historical than psychological; it is global (takes in social, economic and other variables), is highly inferential, and is based on (nonpsychological) data that are largely literary and slanted. But it does suggest the operation of objective factors in his subjects that, from an early age, stimulated the acquisition of cumulative reactions that eventuated in behavior labeled as *genius*. Thus, genius or reactional excellence appears to bloom with an early start. The earlier the better.

Other Variables

Lili Kraus.   Lili Kraus, the Hungarian pianist, is revered around the globe. Although advanced in years, in a recent concert season in America she performed all 25 of Mozart's piano concertos in a series of nine concerts, and in five recitals she played all of the Mozart sonatas. As for her heredity, her Czech father ran a cutlery shop in Budapest. But she had an early start in piano, and by the age of 8 she was enrolled at the Hungarian Royal Academy of Music where she had such magnificent teachers as Kodaly and Bartok. In preparation for her American concert tour, she practiced 8 hours a day for 2 years! In fact, according to Marion Stone (1968, p. 22) she has continued "putting in at least eight hours of practice every day, often begun well before breakfast." As an aside, if genius were guaranteed by some internal entity, why is such extended and laborious practice necessary? And if such pianistic excellence as Lili Kraus is admired for is acquired behavior, then it makes sense that, to obtain such high levels of performance, much shaping and improvement of every portion of a piece is demanded. On this point, *Time* (October 14, 1966, p. 50) quotes her as saying

A work of art must be broken into a thousand pieces if it is to survive in the eternal. I eat, I talk, I clean my teeth, but always in the back of my head I can hear the music going on. This concert series is a life-consuming event, but also a life-crowning one.

Mozart.   In her psychological study *Mozart the Dramatist*, Brigid Brophy (1964) brings out some elements of the pattern that McCurdy found in the lives of geniuses. For an early start in the area of his excellence, how could one begin much sooner than Mozart's parents did with their son? We read that his "training at the piano began almost as early as his training at the lavatory" (Brophy, 1964, p. 253). Young Mozart's father was a musician in his own right, but he sacrificed his own musical career in order to advance that of his son. On this point, Brophy (1964, p. 262) comments "Greater love hath no artist than to lay down his own artistic ambitions to take up his son's." Mozart's life in an adult world with adult objects and domination by parents, in line with McCurdy's findings, are much in evidence. And, according to Donald Brook (1947), a similar pattern is apparent in the lives of Bach, Chopin, Liszt, Clara Schumann, Busoni, Rachmaninoff (who practiced 12 hours a day and expected his students to do the same), and Paderewski, who "worked like a slave to make doubly certain of every single phrase in the pieces he had to play, for he found it was the only way to allay nervousness. If even the briefest passage remained uncertain he would spend hours in mastering it so that it could be played almost subconsciously" (Brook, 1947, pp. 129–130). In explaining genius, we must choose between internal "genie" or the shaping and refining of responses to stimulus objects.

Margaret Mitchell's Gone with the Wind

When *Gone with the Wind* was published in 1936, it sold a million copies by the end of the year. And, according to Richard Corliss (1976), since then it has sold over 20 million more, in 27 languages. Soon after Margaret Mitchell married an advertising executive, she settled down to writing her famous novel, writing most of it between 1926 and 1929, when arthritis imprisoned her in her home. According to Corlis (p. 7),

> She would spend a month refining a single chapter, "substituting Anglo-Saxon derivatives for Latin ones, simple sentence constructions for the more cumbersome Latin constructions." Some chapters she rewrote as many as thirty times; one chapter she rewrote seventy times! Later, she frequently referred to the novel as "lousy," but this captious judgment didn't bother her while she was working on it, for she had no intention of submitting it to a publisher. She must have been as astonished as her friends when *Publishers Weekly,* in an early review, said that *"Gone with the Wind* is very possibly the greatest American novel."

When one further recalls that Truman Capote worked 5 years on his book *In Cold Blood* and that Alex Haley's research and writing of *Roots* consumed 12 years of his life, one tends to agree with Carlyle's dictum to the effect that genius is first of all a transcendent capacity for taking trouble.

Bernstein on Beethoven

According to a common notion, a work of art simply pours out of the genius in one steady gush. But what are the facts? Our finest example comes from that giant of composers, Beethoven. In this case, we have reliable evidence by a reputable musician, Leonard Bernstein, who has made a prodigious study and analysis of Beethoven's sketchbooks and notebooks. In a Columbia LP record, "Leonard Bernstein on Beethoven," he analyzes Beethoven's rejected sketches for the first movement of his *Fifth Symphony* and demonstrates, with orchestral help, how the first movement would have sounded had Beethoven not rejected them. Photographic reproductions of Beethoven's manuscript score negate the common theory that all a genius has to do is to put pen to paper. Here are a few excerpts from Bernstein's revealing analysis. According to Bernstein, Beethoven went through

> . . . a gigantic struggle to achieve the rightness as we know his Fifth Symphony today. . . . We know from his notebooks that he wrote down fourteen versions of the melody that opens the second movement of this symphony. Fourteen versions over a period of eight years. . . . Beethoven struggled with all his force. The man rejected, rewrote, scratched out, tore up, and sometimes altered a passage as many as twenty times. Look at those agonized changes, those feverish scrawls. Beethoven's manuscript looks like a bloody record of a tremendous inner battle. And yet before he had begun to write this wild-looking score, Beethoven had for three years been filling notebooks with sketches.

Bernstein summarizes, "Imagine a whole lifetime of this struggle, movement after movement, symphony after symphony, sonata after quartet after concerto. Always probing and rejecting in his dedication to perfection." Bernstein's comments are somewhat poetic and dramatic, but they do not portray a genius at work as a placid, tranquil being; the picture is closer to the pangs of childbirth.

The Talking Typewriter

Can children 2½ to 3 years of age be expected to read, spell, punctuate, and use the touch method in typewriting? Yes, they can. Documentary evidence of such attainments has been available since O. K. Moore and A. R. Anderson (1960) made motion-picture recordings of children doing just that even when technological facilities were at their most primitive stage of development. An introductory film shows their first subjects, ranging in age from 3 to 5 years, already reading and writing without formal instruction. A second film sketches their methods, and the third in the series gives an indication of how quickly such learning takes place. A little girl—then 2 years, 11 months old—is shown reading a first-grade story. At 3 years, 4 months, she is pictured reading a second-grade story. Her rapid progress in writing and in typing is also recorded.

How the Talking Typewriter Works

Since those early beginnings with simple apparatus, Moore's talking-typewriter project has undergone tremendous expansion. The machine now has been completely computerized, and Moore's procedure has spread far and wide beyond his own center at the University of Pittsburgh. For example, Gloria Bronsema is directing one such center at Waterloo, Iowa. A 5-year-old subject with whom Gloria has worked is shown at the basic unit in Figure 2-3.

The computerized typewriter has a plastic, overall shield that keeps the moving parts "child-proof" but still permits visibility of the child's typing, which is rendered jumbo size. The automatic carriage return offers obvious advantages, such as hurt-free fingers. The keyboard, which is all the child needs, is jam-proof, once a key has been depressed no other key of the total keyboard can be depressed until the built-in cycle is completed.

The keys are colored, and the child's fingernails are colored to correspond, so that proper placement of fingers is accomplished as a basis for later acquiring touch typing. Each child works alone in a cubicle for an assigned time of not over 30 minutes a day, but is permitted to leave earlier if it so desires. The machine is the only teacher, although an attendant is nearby if needed.

Figure 2-3 Five-year-old Toya working at a talking typewriter. As a "graduate" of the program, she will be one of the "guide children" to introduce and explain the lab to new students. (Courtesy of Gloria Bronsema.)

The arrangements up to this point are fun enough, but the game has hardly begun. The total situation invites exploration. As the child depresses a key, a corresponding figure, letter, or punctuation mark appears on the paper in the machine, and a voice over the loudspeaker says the mark's name. Now another key can be depressed, and so on. But the game can be varied, as when a red arrow points to a certain letter displayed on the exhibitor. Now the child is required to depress the corresponding letter on the keyboard, which will permit only that key to operate. Once this routine has been mastered, the child is ready for other games.

From Letters to Words

The next operation may involve a display of words, for example "DOG," with the red arrow of the exhibitor pointing to "D." Should the child try to depress the "G" or "O" keys, they will not operate. In this case, the computer requires that "D" should be depressed first. If the child "catches on" and depresses "D," that letter appears on the paper in the machine and a soft voice over the microphone says "D." The red arrow moves on the "O," and as the child responds in proper sequence the machine repeats each of the steps and, after naming "G" says "DOG." Continuing to work with series of words, one fine day the child recognizes joyfully that the letters that have been learned so well build up into words. All that learning "self-taught," without the continued instruction and at such a tender age! One set of factors that assures such fantastic results has been labeled *multi sensorial*. Note that the child is involved in the engaging enterprise via sound, sight, and touch. Another factor that whets the appetite for learning is what Moore calls the *responsive environment*. Moore (1969) considers the following features essential for an environment to qualify as responsive.

1. It must permit exploration, which facilitates discovery on different levels of integration.
2. It provides immediate consequences for the child's actions. (See discussion of Skinner's operant conditioning in a subsequent chapter.)
3. The pace or rate of learning is *largely* in the hands of the learner.
4. Instead of having things explained, interconnected discoveries and inferences are left to the learner.
5. The activity in which the child engages in response to the talking typewriter must be *autotelic*, or as close to play activity as possible. In such children's games as skipping rope or playing jacks, certain features stand out. The children are engaged in games freely— voluntarily. Social pressures are ruled out as in assigned homework that a child is hassled about or as in an enforced 30 minutes' practice at the piano. When the musical "prodigy" arises at 5:00 A.M. to practice *voluntarily* the practice has become "play." This means that the activity engaged in has acquired its own reinforcing prop-

erties. Another way to say it is that the rewards have become intrinsic, not extrinsic. Children at the talking typewriter get no extrinsic rewards—no gold stars, no candy, no badges, no honor rolls—just the fun that is theirs from doing their thing.

The Proof of the Pudding

One line of evidence for the success of the responsive environment is that children do not get bored with the talking typewriter after a short time. According to Moore (1969, p. 600), "children will come to it for an indefinitely long period of time." Furthermore, they develop high-level skills and take pride in their accomplishments. Confidence in future explorations and growth follows naturally. According to a brochure issued by the Responsive Environments Corporation,

> In the last 5 years, several hundred students between the ages of 2 and 19 years have learned to read, write, typewrite, and take dictation. The group was made up mostly of children of average intelligence but included a few with very high IQ's and some with scores as low as 45, from disadvantaged to affluent environments. Students at all levels showed a marked increase in IQ scores while all of them learned these skills. [p. 3]

Moore gives favorable results of studies that he has carried out with others. In one carefully designed field experiment in laboratories in Chicago's inner-city Black ghetto, the question was whether Moore's methods would prepare preschool children for successful work in the later formal program of education. Results suggest that "exposure of very young children of severely deprived populations to a clarifying environments laboratory can prevent premature mental-age stabilization" (Moore, 1977, p. 7).

According to Moore (1969, p. 10), his outstanding success with the talking-typewriter laboratory has been achieved in "the most economically impoverished portion of Pittsburgh's inner city." In a 5-year plan, Moore took children from "the most academically inept school in the greater Pittsburgh area" (p. 10). He gathered all the nursery-school children into the laboratory program. The following year, he continued with them as kindergarteners and added the new nursery-school enrollees. He continued with this procedure until all children from nursery school through third grade had been put through the laboratory program. Says Moore (1969, p. 10) "What we sought to demonstrate was that the basic learning potential of impoverished ghetto blacks was of very high quality and that a suitably designed learning environment would give this potential a chance to show itself." Moore (1974) has produced films of his Pittsburgh study, "Black Excellence" and "Reaction to Black Excellence." These furnish "vivid examples of black excellence, and they gainsay propositions about intrinsic genetic, social, or cultural inferiority on the part of blacks" (Moore, 1977, p. 11).

The Language Arts Typing Program

A typewriter program has been conducted at the Boyd Elementary School in Jackson, Mississippi. Their laboratory houses 30 IBM Selectric typewriters (noncomputerized) with multiple listening stations and tape recorders for individualized instruction. Teachers require use of the touch system from the beginning, starting at a dictation rate of one letter per second. The initial slow rate maintains enthusiasm and prevents frustration.

An Integrated Plan

Spelling. According to a release from Boyd's principal, Betty Hollingsworth (personal communication, no date), a number of other subject matters can be integrated into the typing program. For example, spelling words assigned for a given week are dictated to the pupils. The words on tapes are seen and pronounced with sufficient time allowed for each word to be typed several times. Figure 2-4 shows a pupil in such a situation. The children favor this exercise because it gives them a chance to learn how to spell the words and, simultaneously, to increase their typing speed. Note that sight, sound, and touch are involved, as in O. K. Moore's program.

Creative writing. Once a week, creative writing lessons are held. Tapes introduce topics to pupils and spur motivation to write typed short stories, letters, interviews, reports, and news articles.

School newspaper. A school newspaper offers opportunities to write articles of student interest. The best short stories and other items done in the creative-writing class may also appear in it. The stencils are typed by students, and work is done even after school hours. So is practice.

Speed tests. Although speed typing is not stressed in a language arts typing program, during the last semester pupils are encouraged to speed up their rates. Once a week, a 1-minute speed test is given, and the names of pupils who attain 40 words per minute are posted. As they improve beyond the rate, the better scores are added. At the end of the year, certificates are awarded to all those who can type 40 words per minute. All this happens in the sixth grade!

The Boyd program has certain similarities to Moore's talking-typewriter program. There are also differences. The important point is that improvement in the present conventional procedures in teaching can permit pupils to make great strides in behavior acquisition. In my opinion, a new era in education is only in its initial stage. The studies reviewed here offer a preview of things to come.

Figure 2-4 Janis Knight, typing teacher, and her sixth-grade pupil at Boyd Elementary School, Jackson, Mississippi. (Courtesy of IBM.)

Suzuki's Fantastic Child Violinists

A little over 100 years ago, violins had neither been seen nor heard in Japan. Along with Western music and other Western musical instruments, they were unknown. Furthermore, Western musicologists believed that the "Oriental ear" was simply incapable of even appreciating, let alone mastering, Occidental music.

Today, every spring, 2000 children, ranging in age from 3 to 15 years, come from all parts of Japan and assemble at the Olympic Sports Palace in

Tokyo, much as shown in Figure 2-5, to give an incredible mass violin concert. Their program, played in unison, includes such numbers as all three movements of Bach's *Concerto in A Minor*, Bach's *Concerto for Two Violins*, Vivaldi's *Concerto in A Minor*, Handel's *Sonata in D Major*, Mozart's *Concerto in D Major*, and "Twinkle, Twinkle, Little Star," the beginning specialty of the 3-year-olds.

How can the two apparently contradictory statements be reconciled? The phenomenal development was initiated by a master teacher of violin, Shinichi Suzuki. It all started about 30 years ago when a Japanese father brought his 4-year-old son to Suzuki for violin lessons. Reacting conventionally, Suzuki remarked, "He's too young!" Afterward, as he reflected on the incident, he realized that the boy understood and spoke the difficult Japanese *language* very well. Why? Because he was born with an "ability" to speak Japanese? Obviously not, because if that same child had been transported at birth to the Soviet Union or Spain, he would just as easily have spoken Russian or Spanish.

Figure 2-5 A recent spring concert given at the Budokan in Tokyo, at which 3000 young violinists from all over Japan gathered and played in unison. (Courtesy of Shinichi Suzuki.)

Suzuki carried over the "mother-tongue" analogy into music, recalled the father whose son he had rejected as a pupil, and started the 4-year-old on a career that carried him to an instructorship in violin at the Curtis Institute of Music in Philadelphia and then to the world concert stage. This was Toshiya Eto. Another distinguished pupil, Koji Toyoda, won Geneva's celebrated Concours International d'Execution Musicale, and is currently concertmaster of the Cologne Chamber Orchestra. But Suzuki has no diabolical plan to gain a monopoly of this planet's violin concert stage. His only wish is to provide enrichment, beauty, and poetry to children's lives.

Suzuki's Program

When should one *start* learning the violin? Says Suzuki (1969) "the sooner, the better." Since he is of the opinion that learning begins with birth, start then. How? By playing high-fidelity records to the infant in the cradle over and over and over again, so that in a few years the child has a sizable *recognition* repertoire of classical pieces. According to Suzuki, violin recordings by Isaac Stern, Fritz Kreisler, and Arthur Grumiaux provide the child with "the best teachers in the world;" that is, as models. Three years after their birth, when the infant music listeners take violin in hand, they will use the same "teachers" to come to the high tonal standards set for them. "Of course," says Suzuki, "if you want to, you can assume that 'Any Child Can be Tone Deaf.'" How? Suzuki's answer (Suzuki, no date, p. 1): "Any human being in the world will grow up to be tone-deaf if he [or she] is brought up from the day of birth for twelve or thirteen years hearing everyday only records of music played out of tune."

The specifics of musical training (or, better, *education* of talent) with games and play (as shown in Figure 2-6) and no forcing or coaxing is described in Cook (1970) and Suzuki (1969). I need only add that Suzuki holds to the bold notion that he can take *any* presumably biologically normal child from *any* continent, *any* racial group or *any* nationality, that can speak its mother tongue, and he will bring it up to the level attained by his past and present students. According to him, there is no inherited talent for music, just as there is not for speaking the Japanese language, and children the world over are equipotential. If large numbers prove anything, according to Suzuki (1969, p. 112), in Japan alone, when one totals all the children registered in the branch studios for the past 30 years, "over 200,000 children have already taken this course." And now there are "Suzuki teachers" in the United States.

Evaluation of the Japanese Children's Mastery of the Violin

In relating Suzuki's achievements to the conception of the reactional biography, it is important to assess the performance of the Japanese child violin-

Figure 2-6   Suzuki's young violinists at a summer recital at Matsumoto Castle, Matsumoto, Japan. (Courtesy of Shinichi Suzuki.)

ists. We must make certain that their musical behavior is "genuine"; that is, that their performance is comparable in some manner to that of students taught elsewhere and by other systems of teaching. According to some critics, those in the minority, Suzuki's child violinists are said to "play mechanically," "without feeling"—"like trained seals." What do the "pros" say? In evaluating the performance of a group of Suzuki's protégés at Wichita State University, James Ceaser, professor of music performance and concertmaster of the Wichita Symphony Orchestra, made the following comments:

> They showed their beautiful discipline and previous hard work in making a memorable thirty-minute tape. Besides that, they presented afternoon and evening programs to packed houses at the University. This group, ages 4 to 16, played solos and ensemble pieces in an astounding manner. They were beautiful to watch and hear; their technique on the violin left no room for doubt as to intonation and a full lovely sound or tone. These young violinists played the classics flawlessly, with warmth and love. To one who has spent a lifetime in music, it was an incredible unforgettable experience.

Joseph Szigeti, violinist of international fame, wrote me (personal communication) that as early as 1948 he wrote a letter to the *New York Times* extolling Suzuki's methods and accomplishments but that his letter was never published! Clifford Cook, professor of string instruments at the Oberlin College Conservatory, writes "Mr. Suzuki's Talent Education Program appears to me to be the most significant and promising development in string education today" (Cook, 1970, p. 101). And following a performance by 10 of Suzuki's children in America in 1964, *Newsweek* of March 23, 1964, quoted master violin teacher Ivan Gamalian of the Juilliard School as saying (p. 64) "This is amazing. They showed remarkable training, a wonderful feeling for the rhythm and flow of the music."

During a visit to Tokyo, 20th-century's greatest cellist, Pablo Casals, attended a concert given by 400 Suzuki violinists. By the time the children finished playing the Bach *Concerto for Two Violins*, "the maestro was weeping" (Suzuki, 1969, p. 114), and he embraced Suzuki and a number of the young performers. Finally, the New England Conservatory, the Eastman School and the Oberlin College Conservatory have initiated Suzuki-type programs for which he is a frequent consultant.

These commendations should help illuminate the question whether Suzuki's young violinists are "trained seals" or whether they show genuine musical achievement. In my opinion, only traditional conceptions of a fixed, inherited potential prevent a worldwide achievement of the high-level skill attained by almost a quarter of a million Japanese children, an attainment that a different set of cultural conditions made utterly impossible a century ago.

"Australia's Water Babies"

> ### Child, 4, Drowns in Family Pool
>
> Mary Lee Smith, 4, daughter of Mr. and Mrs. John Smith, drowned Sunday in the family swimming pool.
>
> Authorities say she was found face down in the pool about 9:15 A.M. by her mother and older sister.

This kind of item frequently appears in newspapers. It is representative of a recurring family tragedy. According to the *Australasian Post* of October 27, 1966, in California alone more than 2300 youngsters under 14 years old drowned, 850 of them toddlers. And yet, if swimming teacher Claire Timmermans of Melbourne, Australia, could have her way, she would have prevented every one of those tragedies by "drown-proofing" each of the victims when they were babies. That babies have actually been saved from drowning is corroborated by the following story with a happy ending (Claire Timmermans, personal communication):

> One of our little babies fell into a pool last week. She is twelve months old. She didn't panic but just floated on her back until her mother fished her out. Not all our babies are this good but I am so thrilled that our efforts are beginning to pay off. Many of our Melbourne socialites are bringing their babies to our baby classes. This is not just snob appeal but being practical. These people move in a class of people many of whom have backyard pools. So baby swimming is now the *in thing.*

Claire Timmermans is the world's leading authority on swimming instruction for babies. She and her husband, who is also a professional swimming teacher and coach, have, for 20 years, been teaching babies to swim. They operate their school in a swimming pool maintained at a constant temperature of 95° F. More recently, they have been teaching mothers how to teach their own babies to swim. The technique that the Timmermans use is described in Claire Timmermans' book, *How to Teach Your Baby to Swim* (1975). Another book by an American exponent of swimming instruction for babies has been written by Lucile Cowle entitled *Teaching Your Tot to Swim* (1970). It is not the techniques that are important to our purpose but the results and certain features of Claire Timmermans' experiences, to which subject we now proceed.

Claire Timmermans' Experiences

An interesting point that touches on our consideration of the reactional biography comes out in Claire Timmermans' (1975) disclosure that her father was an internationally famous water-polo player, with whom she and her four sisters spent much time in water play. When Claire's first child, Andrea, came along, she initiated her into a bathtub filled with warm water, on the recommendation of a nurse. Of course, she supported the child so that the water level was no higher than the ears when the child was on her back. This, Andrea's first experience with "a large body of water," occurred when she was 16 days old.

Claire felt that the experience was so relaxing and beneficial to Andrea that she was encouraged to take her into the pool. From here on, through a steady progression of steps, the child learned to swim. At 17 weeks, Andrea could paddle about 2 yards on her stomach and could float indefinitely on her back. At 3 years of age as shown in Figure 2-7, she "towed" a child to the side of the pool in an enacted "rescue." Also, at 3 years of age, as demonstrated in Figure 2-8, she repeated the act with her mother "in tow." This time she passed both preliminary and official exams for the Royal Life Saving Certificate.

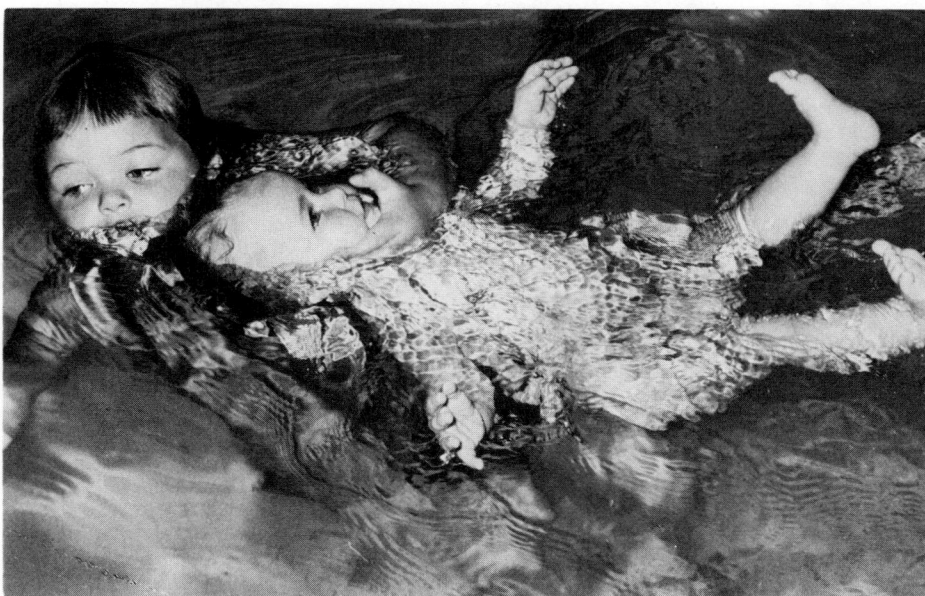

Figure 2-7 "To the rescue": 3-year-old Andrea Timmermans of Mentone, Australia, shown "saving" 12-month-old Christine. (Courtesy of Claire Timmermans, author of *How to Teach Your Baby to Swim.* New York: Stein and Day, 1975.)

When the Timmermans' second baby, Mark, came along, his parents were determined to begin his swimming lessons earlier than they had with Andrea. In fact, they aimed for his day of birth as the most appropriate day. Why? Because the water would simply continue his "free-floating" uterine existence of the previous 9 months.[3] Mark made great gains in a gradual buildup of coordinations that evolved into complex swimming movements.

Violin Playing and Swimming

We have been considering the child violinists of Japan and the baby swimmers of Australia (and today of the United States, Germany, and the Soviet Union). What could they possibly have in common? Much, from a psychological standpoint.

[3] In this respect, Claire Timmermans was anticipating the findings and procedures of Frederick Leboyer, whose work will be considered later.

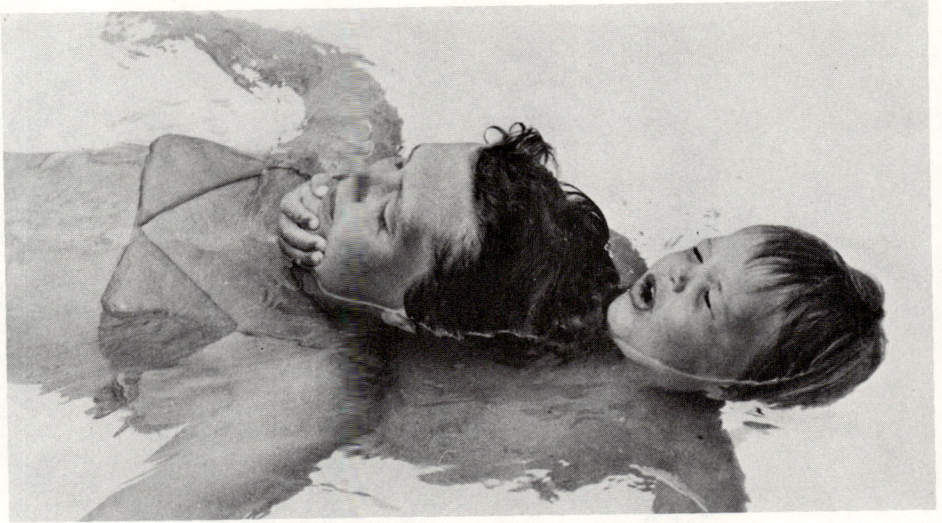

Figure 2-8 Three-year-old Andrea Timmermans of Australia demonstrates her life-saving technique with her mother in tow after she (Andrea) passed both preliminary and official practical examinations for her certificate from the Royal Life Saving Society (Courtesy of Claire Timmermans, author of *How to Teach Your Baby to Swim.* New York: Stein and Day, 1975.)

1. Both kinds of training were initiated on the principle, "the earlier, the better." Why? Because possible contradictory or negative factors have not yet had a chance to work, such as stinging soap in the eyes from having one's hair shampooed. In other words, there are no prior reactions to compete with those to be shaped in the water.
2. Both kinds of training were based on a gradual shaping of responses through a reinforcement of a gradual approximation toward the achievement of the desired end result.
3. In neither case were the children selected on the basis of any anatomical criterion or study of the child's hereditary past. *Any* biologically normal child was an acceptable candidate.

Albert Maori Kiki: Ten Thousand Years in a Lifetime

Out of the "Stone Age"

There are a few spots in the world in which people live under very primitive conditions. One such area is an island divided into two territories, New Guinea and Papua, both administered by Australia. Suppose we should arbitrarily select Papua and ask this question: "What would one dare predict about a Black boy growing up in the 'Stone Age' in Papua?" One's forecast would be made in the light of the following life conditions of an actual boy, Albert Maori Kiki.

Kiki's tribe lived by hunting. His people were constantly on the move, because game in a given area was exhausted after 6 months to a year. Their lack of stable homes determined their whole existence. For example, permanent housing was discouraged. Instead, they contrived lean-tos by arranging a few sticks or limbs covered with leaves. Even pots would have been a nuisance on moving day. For the same reason, they did not raise pigs, but they kept hunting dogs. For utensils, they depended on gourds, string bags, stone axes, and bows and arrows. Meat was roasted over a fire made by rubbing two sticks together.

One of these Papuans, Kiki, wrote an autobiography from which we quote (1968, p. 13): "Our only clothing was a piece of barkcloth which covered the head like a cap and hung down the back nearly to the ankles. . . . We relied on a few quick-growing crops like sweet potatoes and bananas, but mainly we lived on game; wild pigs, cassowary birds, birds' eggs, snakes, lizards."

Instead of watching Saturday and Sunday football or baseball games on television, the chief excitement of the men was derived from war with neighboring tribes. War called for such associated functions as continuous alert for enemy activity, preparation of weapons, and "payback" expeditions. The last was governed by the "eye for eye, tooth for tooth" principle. Kiki (1968, p. 15) describes how it was carried out in practice:

> When the enemy had killed a man and left his body untouched, we also would not touch the one we killed in revenge. If his head had been cut off, we too had to cut off the head of our victim. *If they had eaten our relative it became our duty to eat the one we had killed for his sake.* [Emphasis added]

Into the White Civilization

From this point on, the picture of Kiki's life can be painted in broad strokes. Had Kiki continued the life he so eloquently describes, he would have lived all his days as a "Stone-Age man." However, forced contacts with Whites changed the direction of his reactional biography. At the age of 10, Kiki was compelled to go to school against his wishes. He says "At first I went to school stark naked because even at that age most children in Orokolo did not wear any clothes; only the girls came in their grass skirts" (Kiki, 1968, p. 58). Kiki escaped from the mission school on numerous occasions, which made for very irregular schooling.

From now on, the tempo of his story can be speeded up. At the age of 16, Kiki got a job in a hospital as a medical orderly or "doctor boy" (p. 62). In addition to learning how to dress wounds and to look after patients, the medical assistant for whom he worked pushed him into office work that included typing. A White Australian at the hospital, Albert Speer, took an interest in Kiki, inspiring him with an ambition to acquire more learning so he could lead his people out of the "Stone Age." He attended another school for 2 years and learned to "speak English properly" (p. 68), which in turn opened up an opportunity to attend a medical school for Blacks in Fiji. Because his English was still inadequate, medical school was very hard for him, and he failed the medical course. But he reentered the laboratory course and in 3 years qualified as a certified pathologist.

Side by side with his academic learning, he was developing strong social and political interests and became an activist in behalf of his people. Kiki characterizes this period as his "Fighting Years" (pp. 86–103). He became more and more interested in the welfare of his people, agitating against discrimination by Australia toward Papua and New Guinea. Later he worked for home rule for the two countries, and more recently he resigned his government job so as to devote full time to organizing the Pangu Party, whose main objective was to unify the two countries, Papua and New Guinea, and to push for independence.

In reviewing his life, Kiki (1968, p. 186) says "As I look back at my early childhood in my mother's village . . . I feel I have come a very long way." Within four decades, Kiki has spanned, on the one hand, a simple culture of stone axes, bows and arrows, gourds for pots, of making fire by rubbing two sticks together and of cannibalism, and, on the other hand, high intellectual accomplishment, professional attainment, keen social and political sensitivities, and recognition as a strong and effective political leader—or "ten thousand years in a lifetime"

The Diary of a Mongoloid

Imagine the anguish of parents who discover that their newborn child is mongoloid. The usual reaction is to consign the infant to an institution. As for the infant, his development is aborted, for how can much growth be expected even in a normal child in the light of results obtained from institutionalized children reared in physical and psychological sterility?

When Grace and Douglas Hunt heard the ominous diagnosis of mongolism for their new son, they experienced the usual grief and tragedy of other parents of deformed children. However, their reaction differed from that of most other parents. About 2 weeks after Nigel's birth, the prediction was made (Hunt, 1967, p. 22) that "No matter how much love and care we gave Nigel, he would be an idiot and that nothing we could do would alter the fact. If we had accepted this, it would have become true." Another self-fulfilling prophecy would have to come to pass. The child would have been institutionalized and destined to attain a state of profound retardation after a number of years' residence with other retarded children and adults. The Hunts, particularly Grace Hunt, refused to accept the dire prediction. Instead, she treated her deformed baby as if it were normal.

Mongoloids Can Learn to Read

With infinite patience, as a game, Grace Hunt spelled out words phonetically for her baby as soon as he could talk. In fact, we are told that "no child in his primary school could read better" (Hunt, 1967, p. 23)! Grace's devotion to her son was rewarded, for in time he became the first mongoloid to write a book, *The World of Nigel Hunt,* on which this report is based.

Two possible objections are important here: (1) Do the Hunts, like most parents, exaggerate their child's performance? (2) Perhaps Nigel is not a "genuine" mongoloid. Both points are covered in a foreword to the Hunt book written by the distinguished English neurologist and student of mental retardation, L. S. Penrose. Penrose refers to Nigel's "autobiographical essay, written spontaneously" (Hunt, 1967, p. 9). He speaks of "Nigel's astonishing knowledge of words," of his "acute powers of observation," and his extremely good memory of separate events (p. 10). On the debit side, Penrose reports Nigel's limitation to concrete thinking, being unable to make any generalization. But, he also tells (p. 12) about Nigel's "vivid powers of description" and "Often an unexpected phrase which shows a charming blend of childishness and sophistication. . . . Punctuation and spelling are surprisingly good throughout the typescript, and very few corrections were necessary."

Penrose addresses himself to the doubting Thomases who question if Nigel really wrote the manuscript himself. On this point, he adds, "Anyone who had met him, however, would find any such doubts quickly dispelled" (Hunt, 1967, p. 12). When we learn that Penrose knew the boy since Nigel was 3 years old, that he considers him "remarkably well adjusted" (p. 12), and that he believes that "his mental development has been phenomenal" (p. 12), we can accept the characterizations in the context of Penrose's scientific training and work. The genuineness of Nigel's diagnosis as a mongoloid is covered in Penrose's disclosure of an "extra chromosome" in the boy's cellular structure (p. 13), notwithstanding which, he predicts that young Nigel "will go on learning . . . and will no doubt proceed to further triumphs" (pp. 12–13).

"No Mongol Has Ever Written a Book Before"

In Douglas Hunt's preface to the book written by his 17-year-old son, he says (p. 15) "No mongol has ever written a book before." The following excerpt is a further elaboration (p. 16):

All but the most enlightened of the medical profession would hoot with laughter at the very idea that a Mongoloid could write much more than his name, even after years of training. They will say that this book is just a stunt.

Figure 2-9   Nigel Hunt, a medically certified mongoloid, at the typewriter where he typed the manuscript for his book, *The World of Nigel Hunt* (1967). (Courtesy of Thames Television's *This Week* program.)

It is not.

This book was actually written by Nigel Hunt, who, as he says in the first chapter, taught himself to type. [See Figure 2-9.] I showed him how to use the shift key for capital letters and that is all.

And a final word from Nigel's father (Hunt, 1967, pp. 125–126):

May I conclude by telling you one more true story to illustrate the fallibility of the experts and to encourage you if you have a child like Nigel?

Before Nigel was 5, I was summoned to the senior officer concerned with mental affairs (in a certain country). My wife and Nigel and I went to see this "expert," who was to help decide our child's fate.

The first thing the good lady said to us—in Nigel's hearing, of course—was, "Oh, yes, a little Mongoloid. Quite ineducable. Do you want him put away?"

Had we been more easily impressed by "experts," we might have said "Yes."

But, because what Nigel has to say may be much more interesting to us than his father's remarks, here is a brief excerpt from Nigel's diary during a trip to Switzerland (Hunt, 1967, p. 75):

This time we flew to Zürich and were met again by Fraulein Glaser, a Swiss friend of ours, then we took the train to Innsbruck. We were met at Innsbruck by Herbert with the hotel bus and we rode past the Olympic ski-jump which we saw on telly and we saw the Europabrücke. We saw the beginning of it when we went over the Brenner in 1960.

The next day we went shopping at Innsbruck, where we saw a restaurant. My father said, "Let's go and have a snack," so we did. We both had würstel and drinks galore, and after went over to the little alley-ways to the Goldenes Dachl (Golden Roof) in the song "Das Lied Vom Goldenen Dachl," Gewsichter Winkler, which explains the beauty of the roof.

What a difference a particular reactional biography can make! Suppose the Hunts had institutionalized their mongoloid son. His reactional biography in a psychologically barren institution would have been shallow and simple. It is questionable whether he would have learned to read and write. Contrast those bleak possibilities with the rich and complex reactional biography that Nigel developed in the stimulating circumstances provided by his family, despite his mongoloid condition. Can the reactional biography compensate for a biological defect? That seems to be the strong implication of Nigel Hunt's story.

An Autistic Child Is Reached

The following quotation is from an extraordinary and beautiful book, *Son-Rise*, written by Raun Kahlil's father, Barry Neil Kaufman (1976, p. 2). It reports on Raun's profoundly autistic condition at 17 months of age.

A little boy set adrift on the circulation of his own system. Encapsulated behind an invisible and seemingly impenetrable wall. Soon he would be labeled. A tragedy. Unreachable. Bizarre. Statistically, he would fall into a category reserved for all those we see as hopeless . . . unapproachable . . . irreversible.

But the story begins at the point at which the Kaufmans were anticipating the birth of a boy as an addition to their two children, girls, aged 7 and 3.

And they got a boy! But from the start, not all went well. The new child cried day and night. After ⸗ weeks, a serious ear infection surfaced and continued despite heavy medication. The medication produced a severe state of dehydration, and the end result was a critical condition that confined the baby to isolation within a hospital. The crisis passed, and all seemed well again.

Tragedy

What ensued was a tragedy from the standpoint of the ordinary person, but the Kaufmans are not ordinary people. After a year, new disturbing symptoms gradually began to appear—audio insensitivity, aloofness, extreme passivity, periods of staring, solitariness, avoiding and withdrawing from human contact, and, in place of language growth, muteness. Stereotyped activity such as spinning plates and other objects, finger play, and body rocking were Raun's obsessive and sole occupations.

Gradually, the term *autism*, dreaded by most people, intruded itself into the parents' thinking. Confirmation from a variety of professionals followed. Doctor after doctor declared the condition "irreversible and incurable. The professionals offered no real hope or help, but in our love for our son and his beauty we had found a determination to persist" (Kaufman, 1976, p. 19).

A Program

The program that the Kaufmans instituted must be read in toto to be really appreciated. But here are the highlights. Basically, out of a deep love for the child, they chose to thoroughly accept the child *as he was* and might always be. They chose this option instead of bemoaning their bad luck. Secondly, they determined to get through to the child, and they carried out that determination tenaciously and persistently. Thirdly, Barry and Suzi (Raun's mother) got down to Raun's level and imitated his spinning of plates and pans by the hour, in an attempt to show their acceptance and approval of his activity. This phase of their program permeated every contact, every approach, every movement toward Raun.

The second phase of the Kaufman program was conceived as a motivational-therapy experiment. Because of Raun's cognitive and perceptual difficulties, the plan was to draw him out of his "self-imposed solitary confinement" by offering him increased awareness and opportunities. Their hope was that, by motivating him adequately, the little boy would find satisfying experiences beyond his safe, ritualized world.

The third phase of their projected plan for Raun was an instructional procedure for breaking every activity into assimilable little bits and pieces. In actual execution, this is how their total plan worked out (Kaufman, 1976, p. 3): "Eight or nine hours each day she [Suzi] would sit with him. Feed him. Talk with him. Touch him. Sing to him. Mimic him. Eight or nine hours each day with him oblivious all the time, except for a very few minutes. Precious minutes."

The Results

The 75 hours a week by Suzi alone, let alone the additional devoted hours by Barry and Raun's two caring sisters eventually had an effect. The food, music, and persistent eye contact got Raun involved with people. But progress was slow and as erratic as the stock market—hopeful advances one week, regressions the next. But movement and change, although gradual and uphill, were definite. Even Raun's before and after photographs (Figures 2-10a and b) show it.

Figure 2-10a Before, Raun is seen in an episode of solitary preoccupation with an object, sometimes maintained for hours on end.

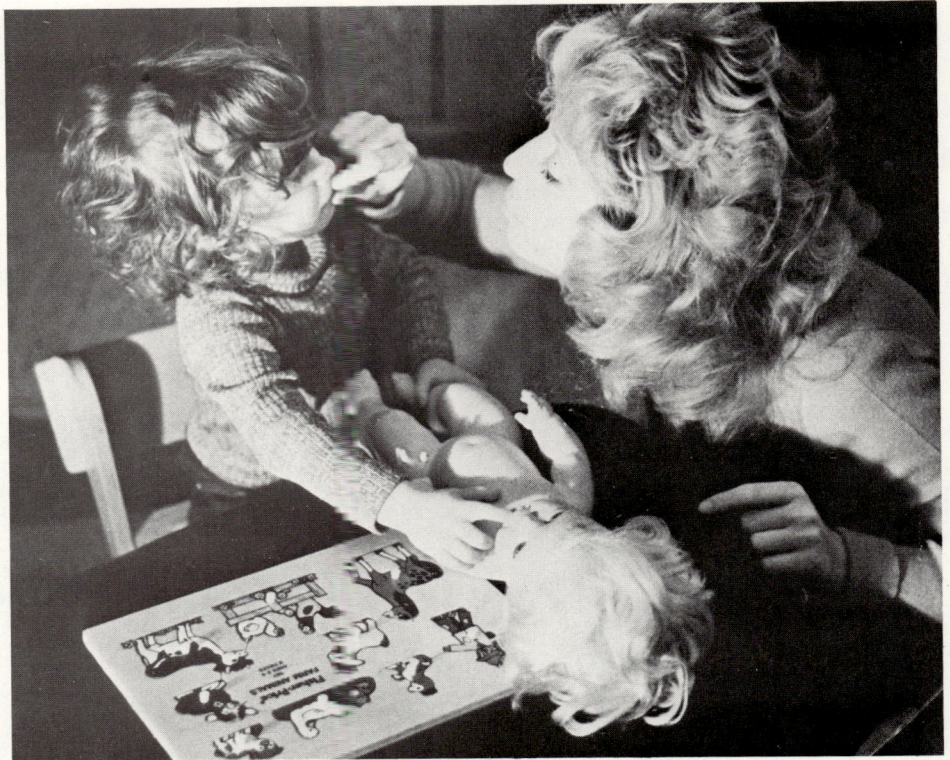

Figure 2-10b   After, Raun is seen after he reentered the human world. In this episode, with much physical contact, praise, and affection, his mother is teaching him to say *mouth* as part of body identification and language training. (Courtesy of Barry Neil Kaufman, author of *So-Rise,* 1976, and *To Love Is to Be Happy with,* 1977.)

Imagine the excitement in the Kaufman family when Raun uttered his first word, "Wa," (for "water") and in quick succession three additional words, all in only one day. Interest in the piano followed, and then, miracle of miracles, in one week Raun's vocabulary expanded from a mere 7 words to 75! During the same day, Raun took his mother by the hand, said "Come," and led her into their "work room" for games and puzzles. With this act, he seemed to declare his intention to reenter the world held out to him by his loving family. Subsequently, Raun showed increasing affection toward others and contact with them, acts from which he had withdrawn only 4 months before. We read (p. 152):

Raun Kahlil is two and a half years old and continues to soar. He is loving, happy, creative. And communicative. Each day he gives birth to a new sunrise.

Raun loves life and life loves him back. His enjoyment of people remains intense; he can speak in sentences up to fourteen words.

Raun did have one relapse, but today, at 2½ years of age, Raun Kahlil (Kaufman, Personal communication, 1977)

> has entered a "regular" kindergarten in a "regular" school—one full year ahead of the normal schedule for children his age. The teachers observe that he is more socially and verbally sophisticated than his peers, exhibiting talents in elementary reading, math and music. Most significant for us (which we celebrate) is Raun's obvious happiness, his gentle and loving attitude toward himself and others . . . a little man who easily shares his joy and lust for living with all those who cross his path. For those who are not aware of his journey, a meeting with Raun is simply an encounter with a very bright, out-going and engaging human being.

This record describes the status quo of a little boy obviously making great strides toward a promising adulthood. His parents are full of hope and confidence in his enormous potential for human development and change. However, the change in his behavior was achieved only as the result of a radical intervention in the reactional biography. A certain kind of institutional interbehavioral history could have perpetuated the earlier, profound autistic behavior.

A Remarkable Black Family

Surely, if you were told that in a family with six girls, *all* had graduated from college with honors, four with master's degrees and two with doctorates, you would ungrudgingly admit that such a record was unique. But if you were further informed that that family was Black and that their momentous achievement was won in the South during the worst days of segregation, before the civil-rights movement, you would be tempted to dismiss the Guinness-Book-type of report as extravagant fiction. Yet it is a fact. The following data, secured from Ernest Dunbar (1969) and Irene Dobbs Jackson (personal communication, 1978), reads like a series of *Who's Who* listings. (The six sisters are shown in Figure 2-11.)

1. *Irene Dobbs Jackson.*   The eldest daughter. Valedictorian of her 1925 high-school class and of her Spellman College graduating class. Master's degree in French at Toulouse University in France; back to Spellman College to teach. Back to Toulouse with three children (after her husband's death) to obtain her doctorate. For a bit over 20 years since then, she has served as professor of French and chairperson of the department of modern languages at North Carolina Central University at Durham, North Carolina. Her son, Maynard Jackson, distinguished himself when he became the first

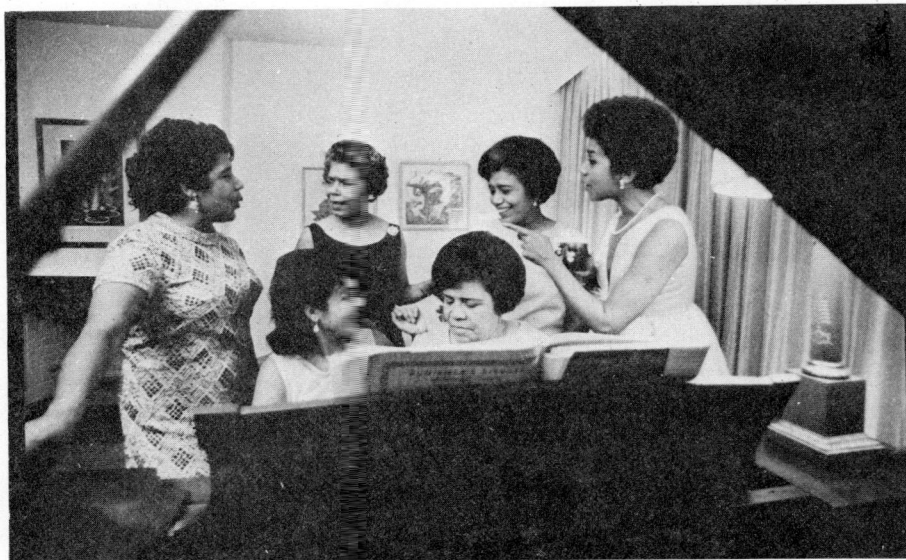

Figure 2-11 A remarkable family. From left to right, back row: Millicent Jordan, Willie Blackburn, Josephine Clement, June Butts (pointing at Millicent). Seated at piano, left to right: Mattiwilda Janzon, Irene Jackson. Four of them are professors, one an international opera singer (Janzon), and one a teacher of emotionally disturbed children (Clement). (Courtesy of Mrs. Maynard Jackson, Sr.)

Black vice mayor of Atlanta at 31 years of age. Since then, he has twice won the mayoralty.

2. *Millicent Dobbs Jordan.*   Bachelor's degree with honors, and master's degree. Currently professor of English and Afro-American literature at Spellman College. She, like all the rest, had 10 years of piano instruction beginning at the age of 7. Millicent is married to Dr. Robert Jordan, an Atlanta dentist who earned his master's degree from the University of Kansas.

3. *Willie Dobbs Blackburn*   Bachelor's degree with honors and master's degree. Presently chairperson of the language division of Jackson State College in Jackson, Mississippi. Married Benjamin Blackburn, exteacher and football coach, now an official of the department of education of the state of Mississippi. A son, Dr. Benjamin Blackburn, is on the faculty of a dental school at Nashville.

4. *Josephine Dobbs Clement.*   Bachelor's degree with honors and master's degree. She has put in a stint as college professor at North Carolina College at Durham. Married William A. Clement, vice president of North Carolina

Mutual Insurance Company, the largest Black-managed life-insurance company in the United States. Josephine has many community interests but *also* finds time to work with emotionally disturbed children in the county school system.

5. *Mattiwilda Dobbs Janzon.*   The celebrity in the family; like the rest, she had 10 years of piano lessons. Bachelor's degree with honors at Spellman (graduating first in her class), followed by 4 years of voice study in New York and master's in Spanish from Columbia University. Scholarships and prizes followed: first a Marian Anderson singing scholarship, then a John Hay Whitney fellowship for further voice study in Paris and in Spain. Winning the International Music Competition in Switzerland really boosted her career. After that, she sang at La Scala, at the Metropolitan Opera in New York many times, and in most of the world's great opera houses. Married since 1957 to Bengt Janzon, public relations director of Sweden's National Board of Health and Welfare, she sings at the Royal Swedish Opera and elsewhere and conducts voice workshops at universities and colleges.

6. *June Dobbs Butts.*   Bachelor's degree with honors and a doctorate in education from Columbia University. Has taught at such schools as Tennessee State University and Fisk University. She teaches a course in psychology of childhood and adolescence in the urban context at Baruch College in New York. She is married to Dr. Hugh Butts. She is not only a homemaker and teacher but as a good citizen is involved in activities too numerous to mention.

What Is the Explanation for Such High Achievement?

Irene Dobbs Jackson (personal communication, 1978) lists such factors in her family's achievement as stability of the parental marriage and of a close family life. "Pleasant, loving disciplined home—piano, books, travel, fun and games, parties, work, study." In place of bitterness at the injustices stemming from segregation, there were understanding of the system and the discovery of ways to circumvent those barriers. Self-respect and self-esteem were maintained through genuine achievement.

John Wesley Dobbs, the father, was a rare individual. As a child, after the breakup of his parents' marriage, his mother took him from rural Georgia to Savannah. He started school at the late age of 9, skipping grades because of his superior performance. At 11, he started work by selling newspapers, and he worked hard the rest of his days, sometimes holding down three jobs in order to provide the advantages for his family that he wanted it to have. He started college but had to drop out in his second year in order to support his mother and sister. But he did not drop out from educating himself. After he obtained a job as railway mail clerk (in which he rose to be a supervisor) he visited Fisk University Library at the end of his "run" in Nashville and brought back loads of books. At that time, Blacks were not allowed to draw books from the Atlanta public library. In fact, it was not until 1959 that his daughter, Irene Jackson, demanded and got a card there, the first Black to do so.

With those books on history, government, and economics, John Dobbs opened up new worlds for himself, his wife, and his six daughters. Meals at the table were adorned with philosophical and other profound discussions that would go on for days. Other advantages came to the family in their summer travels to the north, to such cities as New York, Boston, and Chicago. He discouraged his girls from going to "Jim Crow" places. Above all, he had great expectations for his girls. Says Irene Jackson, "He wanted us to be more than was humanly possible. But we tried. We broke our necks trying to preserve the image he had of us" (Dunbar, 1969, p. 33).

Conclusion

All in all, the observations that we have considered are in harmony with the reactional-biography hypothesis. Because they are not highly controlled experimental data, we cannot claim that they *prove* the validity of that hypothesis, but they do offer strong support for it. Something else that the data reveal is that, often, practice outstrips theory. Outside of O. K. Moore, most of the individuals involved in the programs we have considered had little or no theory to guide their practice, only flashes of insight and intuition. Why? Because the traditional science of behavior is mostly self-actional. With an adequate theory to guide practice, we can

> create a world in which people will achieve far more than they have ever achieved before in art, music, literature, science, technology, and above all, the enjoyment of life. It would be a world in which people feel freer than they have ever felt before. . . . In building such a world, we shall need all the help a science of behavior can give us. [Skinner, 1976, p. 532]

Chapter Summary

According to the construct of the reactional biography or interbehavioral history, present events are a function of antecedent events. The lawfulness of psychological events is found in a dimension in which one traces out the succession of behavior segments or organism–stimulus-object interactions as distinct from the organism in its life activities in biological inquiry. Divergence between the individual's biological and psychological evolution is possible and has certain implications.

More specifically, even in an experimental situation prior events must be taken into account in attempting to understand the immediate situation.

Extinction and spontaneous recovery, and learning and relearning, illustrate the need to include a sufficiently large chunk of related behaviors to attain understanding.

At this point, we left the laboratory and looked at the various faces of life in the everyday world. A wide variety of crude data abosrbed our attention: the full range of genius behavior; pre-school children learning to type, spell, write, and create stories and poems, and sixth-graders writing news articles and stories and typing at 40 words per minute or better; thousands of Japanese children playing the violin with excellence appropriate to adults; babies learning to swim. A Black "Stone-Age" Papuan could become a contemporary pathologist and political leader; a mongoloid, apparently as the first in history, wrote an autobiography; an autistic child was "recalled to life" after a spell of "solitary existence"; and a Black family achieved surpassing excellence despite all manner of social handicaps. All of these data fit the reactional-biography hypothesis, dispensing with nonnatural, or supernatural, self-actional theories and thus encouraging further exploration and testing of the construct of interbehavioral history or reactional biography, which will be our next quest.

3 Origins and Sequences of the Reactional Biography

"He who sees things from their beginnings will have the most advantageous view of them." So said Aristotle, who wrote the first great compendium of embryology, and who looked upon living nature with a breadth of vision far in advance of his time.

[Gesell, 1945, p. 1]

The Greek philosopher Aristotle was far ahead of his time (384–322 B.C.) in his realization that present events are a function of antecedent events, each of which is to be traced back to the point where the whole sequence originates. This is the way to foresight and understanding, which are our goals in this chapter. Therefore, we shall try to track down the earliest manifestations of behaviors to their very source. When and in what form are they nascent (come into existence), and what is the nature of their sequence? No sooner do we start on our adventure than we encounter the theory of maturation, according to which some reactions are believed to have an origin, not in antecedent psychological events but in certain anatomical conditions of the organism. Apparently we have encountered a roadblock in our pursuit of the zero point of the inter-behavioral history and are compelled to inquire into the validity of the construct of maturation.

Maturation and the Reactional Biography

We cannot expect the term *maturation* to have the same precision as the chemist's "H_2O" or "CO_2." Maturation is an import from the language of common sense and is used in psychology to refer to reactions that are inherited but that are not capable of performance until the appropriate organs and neural connections have reached a certain stage of growth or development. McNeil (1966, p. 19) states that a "distinction is usually made between those changes that take place as a consequence of learning and those produced by growth and maturation." He further explains (p. 19) that the term *maturation* "describes that part of development that takes place in the absence of specific experience or practice."

According to some psychologists, then, certain behaviors develop as the result of a series of interactions between organism and stimulus object, while others simply result from a maturing or ripening of a biological structure or structures. When the appropriate maturational stage of the particular portion of the biological organism has been reached, the structure is said to be ready to respond by an adequate "trigger." The metaphor that maturation theory has adopted comes from biological terminology derived from the growth process referred to as *ripening* or *maturing*. Thus it is only a metaphor.

Another feature of maturation theory, as applied to psychological data, is that it is self-actional; it explains nothing. It only says that certain behaviors simply come into being, like Venus arising out of the waves. The maturation construct is reminiscent of the ancient theory of the spontaneous generation of life. In my opinion, this is unsatisfactory.

Pronko on Maturation

If one makes no distinction between biological and psychological events, then one can easily apply the same construct (such as maturation) to both sets of data. But all of our analysis up to this point has stressed the distinct properties of psychological events by comparison with biological functioning. Perhaps, we can help to clear up the problem with a semantic analysis of the term *maturation*. A dictionary definition refers to a state of complete growth or development. Embryology is the primary science dealing with the elaboration of the organism from conception to developmental completeness. Granted that the most dramatic growth phase precedes birth, nevertheless elongation of legs and such continue after birth. I would suggest that the term *maturation* be limited to refer to the changes in growth and differentiation of the biological organism toward full development.

The Proper Role of Maturation

Our next logical question is "What is the relationship between the developing biological organism and behavior development?" First, is there any evidence that behaviors simply ripen or "mature"? Some people think that walking, for example, one fine day, pops out, so to speak; the child, lo and behold, just up and walks. Later on, I hope to show that legs do not just up and walk; that, in fact, children interact with variables that, through their histories, build up into creeping, crawling, walking, running, skipping, jumping, skating, and dancing. Obviously, skating and jumping cannot precede creeping and crawling. As pointed out in our discussion of the early phases of the interactional history, the acquisition of such complex psychological activities must wait on the maturation of the infant. Only after certain anatomical structures (for example, elongation of legs) have made their appearance can the more complex behaviors develop. But both require an interactional history.

And now we are led into a clear formulation of the relationship between maturation and the reactional biography. We may say that the biological conditions labeled as *maturational* make possible the acquisition of behaviors that involve the participation of those factors. They are *facilitating*, but not *causal*, conditions. For example, the knowledge that an infant has normal vocal structures will not enable us to predict (1) whether it will speak or not speak, or (2) if it does speak, what the language will be. And, if we refer to Little Marty in the previous chapter, it would be hazardous, knowing that he was born without arms or hands, to predict that he would not swim, for he did learn to swim. At best, then, biological maturation facilitates the buildup of related psychological activities, but, even in the absence of some biological factors, special measures can apparently overcome what would normally be considered handicaps. Under ordinary conditions, biologically defective or undeveloped organisms are somewhat limited in the evolution of their reactional biographies.

Conclusion on Maturation

We may at least tentatively conclude that, both before and after birth, organisms are not completely developed. It is also granted that certain stages of structural growth must be reached before an organism can start building up a reactional biography requiring such structures. But a series of contacts with stimulus objects is likewise indispensable. As a final example, persons with "normal" sex structures may become heterosexual, homosexual, and so on, or they may not perform any sexual behavior. But, *if* they do, we may rest assured that a reactional biography will be necessary. The implication is that organisms mature, and we may sensibly talk about such organs as sex structures and breasts maturing, but we cannot sensibly talk about behaviors maturing or ripening. The very construct of maturation incorporated into psychology has, perhaps, prevented us from seeing walking, sexual reactions, and so on as behavior acquisitions occurring right under our very noses.

We Enter the Womb

Having considered the problem of maturation, we are ready once more to resume our search for the beginnings of psychological kinds of action. To make sure that we get to the bottom of things, we shall have to enter the womb. If we were biologists, we would want to start even with the nature of the egg cell and sperm cell that participate in the conception, or starting point, of every individual. However, our special interest will have to wait until later stages of the elaboration of the organism.

As background, we might review some of the events that lead into our study. The infant emerges from the uterus after about 9 months of development. During its residence there, it increases in size and complexity, elaborating structures and functions that are further integrated into systems and eventually coordinated as a functional unit, the organism. The upshot is that, after about 7 months of development, a level of organization is attained that permits ingestion and digestion of food, circulation, respiration, and other functions that enable a relatively independent existence of what is at last a fairly complete organism with "all systems go" (see Figure 3-1).

A Few "Snapshots of Life in the Uterus"

It is easy to think that our encounter with gravity begins only when we start to stand and walk. However, according to Gesell (1945, p. 32), an early student of fetal behavior, "man begins his life-long contest with gravity even before he is born . . . most of the basic organization of this distinctly human posture is laid down during the fetal period" (p. 32). The trouble comes from our thinking of the fetus as an inert passenger within the pregnant mother, whereas the truth is that there is never a dull moment. In fact, that is where all the action is. The fetus frequently moves and changes position, propelling itself by feet and legs, rolling over, and so on (Liley, 1972, p. 100).

At 12 to 16 weeks from conception,[1] the following activities have been noted: moving the lips in unison, opening and closing the mouth, opening and closing the hands, synchronized movement of arms and legs suggestive of locomotion (Gesell, 1945, pp. 68–70). We learn even more from Liley (1972, p. 100) who has observed that changes in the position of the mother elicit shifts in the position of the fetus *as if* to restore its previous "comfort" (p. 100). Swallowing the amniotic fluid and fetal hiccups are common, and "it is not uncommon in obstetric radiology to detect the fetus sucking thumbs, fingers or toes, and *thumbsucking has been photographed in the 9-week abortus*" (Liley, 1972, p. 103, emphasis added). Audition is also functional, and, according to Liley, "from at least 25 weeks the fetus will

---

[1] Pregnancy usually lasts 40 weeks, 10 lunar months, or 9 calendar months.

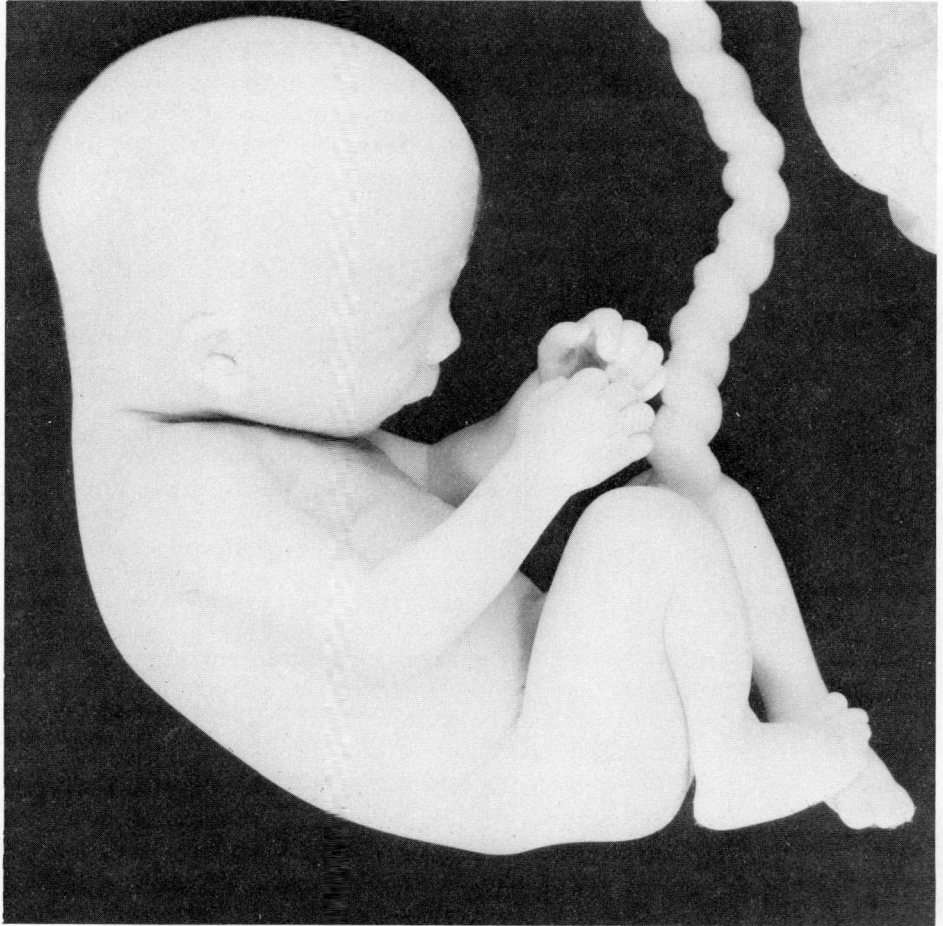

Figure 3-1   Photograph of 7-month-old fetus, at this stage capable of surviving outside the uterus. (From Jan Langman, *Medical Embryology (3rd ed.).* Baltimore, Md.: The Williams & Wilkins Co., 1975.)

jump in synchrony with the tympanist's contribution to an orchestral performance" (p. 103). We can only speculate how the fetus would react at a rock concert.

An Experiment to Test for Hearing in the Fetus

But we have better evidence for audition in the fetus, specifically in the work of Sakabe, Arayama and Suzuki (1969) carried out at Shinshu University at Matsumoto, Japan. They worked with six mothers at their 32nd to

38th week of pregnancy and recorded fetal evoked responses to auditory stimuli. First, they located the position of the top of the fetus' head by feeling through the abdominal wall of their pregnant subjects. As shown in Figure 3-2, they attached an active electrode at the nearest place to the fetus' head and a reference electrode at about the fetus' neck region. The acoustic stimulus was a 1000-Hz tone burst presented through a bone-conduction vibrator attached to the abdominal wall at a point judged to be nearest to the fetal ear. Via the active electrode, they were able to record and measure the electroencephalographic (EEG) response. This way, they could note the relationship between the brain waves as an index of fetal response in relation to presence or absence of the auditory stimulus.

The results. The results as revealed by the recorded EEG waves were clear-cut. The difference between the EEG recordings when an acoustic stimulus was given compared with EEG recordings when no stimulus was given left no doubt that the fetuses had reacted in an auditory fashion.[2] Further validation was obtained by comparing the EEGs of fetuses responding to an auditory stimulus to the EEGs obtained from the top of the head of a newborn baby responding to the same auditory stimulus. Comparison of the two showed a close match. And, as a final check, they took a recording from the abdominal wall of a nonpregnant woman, which produced only a

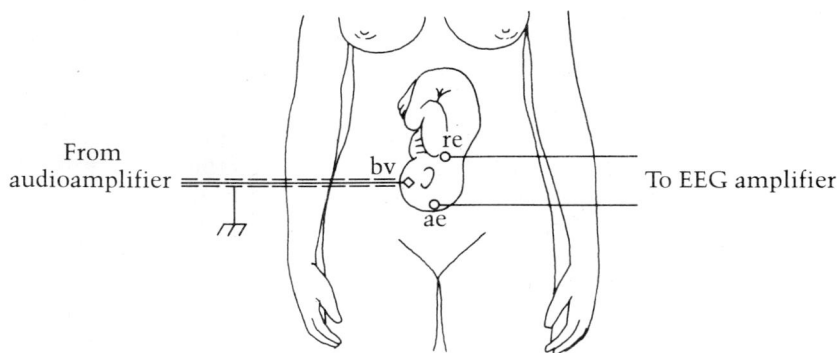

Figure 3-2 Schematic representation of electrodes and bone conduction vibrator in an experiment to study the human fetal response to acoustic stimuli. re = reference electrode; ae = active electrode; bv = bone conduction vibrator. (From N. Sakabe, T. Arayama, and T. Suzuki, "Human Fetal Evoked Response to Acoustic Stimulation." *Acta Oto-Laryngolica, Supplementum 252,* 1969, 31. Reproduced by permission.)

---

[2] The fact that Speit (in a subsequent experiment, 1948) got no fetal response to a vibratory stimulus may be a function of Sakabe's finer instrumentation (Sakabe, 1969). However, it is clear that Spelt established a conditioned response (CR) to the vibratory stimulus.

flat wave, adding further support to the notion that the fetus at about the 36th week from conception can respond auditorially.

Other evidence.   So far, we have dealt with auditory stimuli that impinge on the fetus from the external world. Are there any internal sounds that the fetus can react to? According to Liley, there is a veritable gastrointestinal symphony orchestration of sounds to engage the attention of the uterine resident. "The loudest sounds to reach the foetus or an intrauterine phono-catheter are maternal borborygmi peaking to 85 decibels" (Liley, 1972, p. 103). (Borborygmi are the rumblings and gurglings and splashing of the stomach and bowel.) The intermittent voice of the mother, gentle or scream-ing at the other kids (as the case might be), provides another source of stimu-lation. But above all is the dominating beat of the mother's heart, pulsing in synchrony with the great arteries supplying the uterus and the placental bed. Our traditional conceptions about "the dark, silent womb" make it hard to believe that it could be the noisy place described above. But we can be convinced by listening to an actual recording of the sounds produced by the main artery and veins and other areas of the womb. Such a recording was made by Hajime Murooka, head of the department of obstetrics and gynecol-ogy at Nippon Medical University at Yokohama, Japan. It is obtainable as a cassette tape under the title "Lullaby from the Womb" (Capitol 4XT-11421).

Significance of the Maternal Heart Sounds

Salk's studies.   Is it of any significance that the fetus may have heard the perpetual rhythm of the mother's heart and uterine artery and veins from about the 25th week? After considerable naturalistic observation and ex-perimentation, Salk (1961) is convinced that an auditory imprinting (or early learning) of the fetus occurs in relation to the maternal heartbeat.

In one study (1962), he submitted two groups of newborn infants to heartbeat sounds of 72 and 128 beats per minute, respectively. He found an increase in restlessness and crying to the heartbeat at 128 beats per minute. Another study used 102 subjects in an experimental group and 112 subjects in the control group. This time the experimental groups heard the tape-recorded heartbeat at 72 beats per minute; the control group heard nothing. As far as crying went, it occurred 38.4% of the time in the experimental group compared with a figure of 59.8% for the control group. The results favored Salk's imprinting hypothesis. Salk also found a significant difference in weight gain for the experimental group with an equivalent food intake for both groups (1962, pp. 755–760).

In still another experiment with foundlings in a hospital, Salk tested the time it took babies to fall asleep. With the normal rate of heartbeat sound, it took an average of 23.00 minutes. With no sound, that average was 46.04 minutes. A metronome set at 72 beats per minute gave an average going-to-sleep time of 49.25 minutes and recorded lullabies took 48.69 minutes (Salk, 1969, p. 6). The Murooka cassette tape of the maternal heartbeat and uterine artery sound referred to earlier is being marketed with the express purpose of soothing babies or putting them to sleep.

Liley's queries. Concerning the powerful, pervasive, and continuous maternal heartbeat to which the fetus is subjected, Liley (1972) poses some far-reaching questions for possible hypothesis testing.

> Does this long exposure explain why a baby is comforted by holding him to your chest or is lulled to sleep by the old wives' alarm clock, or the modern magnetic tape of a heart beat? Does this experience explain why the tick of a grandfather clock in a quiet study or library can be a reassurance rather than a distraction, why people asked to set a metronome to a rate which 'satisfies' them will usually choose a rate in the 50–90 beat per minute range—and twins show a strong concordance in independent choice? Elias Carnetti points out that all the drum rhythms in the world belong to one or other of two basic patterns—either the rapid tattoo of animal hooves or the measured beat of a human heart. The animal hoof pattern is easy to understand from the ritual and sympathetic magic of hunting cultures. Yet, interestingly, the heart beat rhythm is more widespread in the world—even in groups like the plains Indians who hunted the great herds of bison. Is this rhythm deeply imprinted on human consciousness from foetal life? [Liley, 1972, p. 104]

These are only questions, but they do point up the possible significance of the reactional biography. Can learning in the uterus as the earliest behavior acquisition have such far-reaching effects because of its priority? What is needed is more objective evidence of *the fact* of prenatal learning. Once more, Liley (1972) comes to our help with evidence of an inferential sort. First, he calls attention to the extreme measures that must be taken to get the fetus to lie still for some diagnostic or therapeutic procedure. The mother must be still for 15 to 20 minutes, to allow the fetus to be quiescent. Touching or listening to the sounds of the mother's abdomen must be avoided during this period. Compare these precautions with the activity generated by many pregnant women at night, when discomfort causes much restlessness. Then there are such conditions as leg cramps, heartburn, and a trip or two to the bathroom. With the family away, daytime may be a relatively more restful period. Liley seems to be saying that when children enter the world they are only maintaining the diurnal schedule imposed on them during their sojourn in the uterus. But, instead of attributing lawfulness to the behavior of their new offspring, the distressed parents see only perversity in their neonate's lack of appreciation of the fact that nighttime is a time for sleep (Liley, 1972, pp. 104–105). But Liley's example is only circumstantial evidence. We need more solid proof of uterine learning, a topic we discuss in the following section.

Conditioning of the Human Fetus in Utero

Outside of the maternal singing, murmuring, movements, heartbeat, gurgles, grunts, and groans, there is little else of a stimulating sort impinging on the fetus. There are no toys, buses, streetcars, and brothers and sisters to interact with—a really impoverished situation for behavior acquisition. That's why Spelt (1948) realized that he had to get through in some way to the fetus, to get a rise out of it, before he could demonstrate any learning. His procedure will provide us with an opportunity to discuss classical conditioning, a paradigm for one mode of behavior acquisition.[3]

Spelt's apparatus.   Spelt rigged up an oak clapper 5 inches wide, 22½ inches long, and 1 inch thick (much like a fraternity paddle). It was released so as to strike the face of a box sharply, thus producing a very loud noise. This was Spelt's unconditioned stimulus. Why is it called unconditioned? Because without any prior contacts, the loud noise evoked a definite movement response of the fetus.

How could Spelt be sure he was getting what he thought he was getting? By a special arrangement of three registering instruments, tambours, consisting of a membrane in contact with different points of the pregnant mother's abdomen. Each tambour was connected by a rubber tube to a recording stylus so that any fetal movement would be transmitted via the membrane and would be recorded by the stylus on a moving piece of paper. Tambours were positioned on the mother's abdomen so as to register movements of fetal head, arms, and legs. Also recorded were the mother's breathing, the mother's push-button signal of a *felt* fetal movement, the instant of unconditioned- and conditioned-stimulus presentation and a time line registering 5-second intervals. (See Figure 3-3 for experimental setup.)

Now we must talk about the conditioned (or conditioning) stimulus, which was provided by means of a door bell, the gong of which had been removed and the striker so adjusted as to strike perpendicularly to the surface of any part of the abdomen. Such an arrangement would transmit a vibration through to the fetus via the mother's abdominal tissues. A crucial point about the conditioned stimulus is that when it is first presented it must not elicit the response that the unconditioned stimulus calls forth. The vibratory stimulus, applied to the mother's abdomen, passed the test because there were no fetal movements in response to it.

Spelt's subjects and procedure.   Except for one pregnant and three nonpregnant control subjects, the 16 experimental subjects were all patients of an obstetric clinic of an urban hospital. All but two were past the seventh month of pregnancy. The purpose of the experiment was not divulged to them. In fact, they were simply informed that observations of fetal move-

---

[3] Classical conditioning is also called *Pavlovian* or *respondent* conditioning.

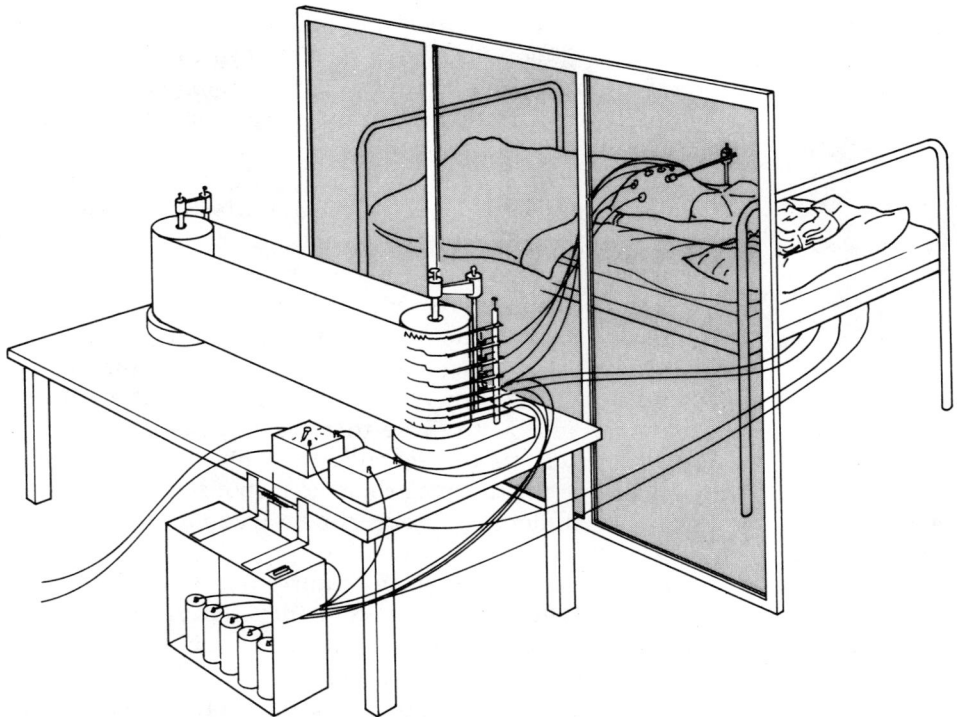

Figure 3-3 Sketch of apparatus arranged for Spelt's conditioning of the human fetus *in utero*. (From Spelt, 1948, Figure 1.)

ments would be conducted, providing only that they were willing. The only incentive for their participation was free delivery of their babies at term.

The procedure involved presentation of the vibratory stimulus for 5 seconds, terminated by the loud noise of the clapper. Because the mothers had been warned about the loud noise, they adapted to the situation and did not give a startle response, which would have been registered by the three tambours as a total movement of the mother.

Spelt's results.   One fetus gave evidence of a conditioned response to the vibratory stimulus alone by the eighth session (8 to 16 trials constituting one session). Subject 16 showed the first fetal response to the conditioned stimulus alone *without* the loud noise (unconditioned stimulus) after only 21 paired presentations. In the sixth session, seven conditioned responses occurred *in succession* after 59 reinforced presentations of the vibratory stimulus. The next morning, testing with the conditioned stimulus alone (that is, without any further reinforcement), four more conditioned responses appeared, thus indicating a certain degree of stability of the newly acquired fetal response. Similar results were obtained in other subjects, and Spelt was able to demonstrate both extinction and spontaneous recovery as well.

Spelt's control group.   The subjects of this group were tested for a control of the vibratory stimulus. These mothers were in the late eighth or ninth month of pregnancy. The specific point involved here was that, since the fetus was approaching full maturity, would it be sensitive enough to the vibratory stimulus to react to it alone? The answer was no. None of the vibratory stimuli alone operated to elicit a fetal response. Three nonpregnant subjects also served as controls when results for them showed that the two stimuli in various arrangements and combinations produced no records remotely similar to those that demonstrated fetal conditioning. Two pregnant subjects in the seventh month of their pregnancy showed no fetal conditioning, indicating that the response of the fetus to the loud noise did not occur under Spelt's experimental conditions before the eighth month.

Conclusion.   By use of a vibratory–tactile stimulus as a conditioned stimulus and a loud noise as an unconditioned stimulus, Spelt was able to establish a conditioned response in the human fetus while it was in the uterus during the last 2 months prior to birth. After as few as 15 to 20 paired presentations, it was possible to demonstrate the learned response to the point where one could expect a series of three or four successive responses to the vibratory stimulus alone. With some additional reinforcement, as many as 11 successive conditioned responses occurred. Experimental extinction, spontaneous recovery, and retention of the conditioned response over a 3-week interval show that a more stable response is only a function of the proper experimental conditions. These features and the fact that the fetal reactions that Spelt demonstrated share some of the properties of psychological events (historical, differential, integrative, variable, modifiable, and inhibitive) place them squarely in our domain. One final point—the fetuses that participated in Spelt's study serve to illustrate an important point about the reactional biography. That moment in their fetal development at which they *began* to respond to the vibratory stimulus alone signaled the start of their reactional biography, but only with respect to the vibratory stimulus alone. Likewise, the zero point was behind them at the stage at which they began to perform reactions manifesting properties of psychological events.

Intrauterine Biological Factors

Because biological factors are constant participants in psychological events, we should take account of the special ways in which they may influence the psychological development of the fetus and, later, the infant. At this point, we are mostly interested in negative biological factors that can affect the reactional biography.

According to Langman (1975, p. 109), "Until the 1940s it was assumed that congenital defects were caused mainly by hereditary factors." Then it was discovered that German measles early in the mother's pregnancy caused abnormalities in the embryo. Since then, a host of factors have been found in the environment of the embryo that can damage it and handicap it from the start. Among them, Langman (p. 108) lists infectious agents contracted from the mother, radiation, hormone imbalances, chromosomal abnormalities, diabetes of the pregnant mother, and a lengthy list of organ and systems defects. Fortunately, congenital malformations occur on a worldwide basis of only 3.3% of live births (p. 109).

Malnutrition of pregnant mother. This listing does not, by any means, exhaust the number of conditions that may handicap the fetus' future psychological development. Among others, Hurley in his provocative book, *Poverty and Mental Retardation: A Causal Relationship* (1969, p. 182), asserts that malnutrition of the pregnant mother "plays a role in prematurity and birth defects including mental retardation and . . . irremediable brain damage." Guthrie, Masangkay, and Guthrie (1976) examined mental development in a Philippine community where there was severe malnutrition. They found (p. 175) that the intelligence-test scores of children who had or were experiencing malnutrition showed a trend to obtain such low scores that there was "virtually no overlap in their scores with those of their more adequately nourished peers." (However, that does not mean that eating will raise the IQ.)

Effects of maternal smoking. According to *Smoking and Pregnancy* (no date, p. 5), "maternal smoking during pregnancy exerts a retarding influence on fetal growth, increased incidence of prematurity, and a significantly greater number of unsuccessful pregnancies due to stillbirth and neonatal death as compared to non-smoking mothers."

Chronic alcoholism in the pregnant mother. Jones, Smith, Ulleland, and Streissguth (1973) studied eight unrelated children from three different ethnic groups, but all born to chronic alcoholic mothers. They found similar craniofacial, limb, and heart and circulatory defects that they connected with prenatal growth and developmental delay. "The insult to growth rate has continued during early childhood" (p. 12) despite adequate nutrition in hospital or foster home.

Drug addiction of the pregnant mother. Phenobarbital and amphetamine are being taken by "an undetermined but substantial number of pregnant women" (Zemp and Middaugh, 1975, p. 316). Therefore, Zemp and

Middaugh (1975) decided to inject pregnant mice with d-amphetamine sulphate and check the outcome on their offspring. The open-field behavior at Day 75 was increased over that of a control group. Prenatal injections of phenobarbital resulted in decreased litter size, increased mortality and later behavior deficits. Applications from mice to humans should be guarded and suggestive.

We are on more solid ground in a study on humans by Zelson, Rubio, and Wasserman (1971). During a period of 10 years, they observed 384 infants born to heroin-addicted mothers. Signs of withdrawal were noted in 67.4% of the offspring and low birth weight in 49.4%. Fourteen infants (3.6%) died in the neonatal period, but incidence of congenital anomalies appeared to be no higher than in the general newborn population. Morphine and quinine were demonstrated in the urine of newborn infants within the first 24 hours of life.

In a study on the effects of Miltown and Librium on human embryonic and fetal development, Milkovich and Van den Berg (1974) observed a series of 19,044 live births as part of a longitudinal study of pregnancy and child health. The most relevant part of their findings concerned the rate of fetal abnormalities related to drug intake by the mother in early pregnancy. Rates of the anomalies after prescription and use of Meprobamate or Chlordiazepoxide during the first 42 days of pregnancy were higher, 12.1% and 11.4% respectively. The rate for children of mothers taking other drugs was 4.6% compared with 2.6% for children of no-drug mothers.

Effects of obstetrical medication on fetus and infant.   With the multiplication of drugs given during pregnancy, labor, and delivery, Bowes, Brackbill, Conway, and Steinschneider (1970, p. 4) point out that "now the fetus is potentially at greater risk from well-intentioned medicaments than from the vicissitudes of pregnancy and delivery." Their paper notes that, until very recently, drug effects have been studied from the standpoint of the adult. Bowes and his colleagues do point out that the sedatives and anesthetics given the mother at delivery do have a depressing effect on the infant's functioning. In summarizing their study, we read that, beside the fetal malformations caused by such drugs as Thalidomide, anesthetics and analgesics given before or at delivery may cause the newborn infant to be "so severely depressed at birth from the use of these drugs that he is unable to establish spontaneous respirations" (p. 36).

In a more recent study, Standley, Soule, Copans, and Duchowny (1974) confirm and extend these observations. They note that pain-relieving drugs disorganized the neonate's nursing and visual attention and adversely affected muscle tension and the orienting response. But their main interest was to note the effect on normal babies whose mothers received low spinal, local, and no anesthesia.

Results showed that the babies of women receiving drugs showed the following effects in tests administered to them at Day 3: "jerky movements in small arcs, startles and tremulous motions, and frequent state changes and crying were common in babies of mothers who received anesthesia" (Standley et al., 1974, p. 635). Yet, the most alert, least irritable, and—from the standpoint of motor development on the third day of their lives—the most mature behavior was shown by babies whose mothers received no medication (p. 635). Their conclusion is probably the best way of bringing this section to a close. "Our data raise questions about the assumption that routine usage of these anesthetic agents is inconsequential, even for the normal, healthy infant" (p. 635).

Psychological Aspects of Childbirth

Many of our accepted practices are not supported by scientific research and appear to be rooted more in hospital and medical tradition than in human physiology.[4]

[Jerold Lucey, M.D., in Haire, 1972, p. 3]

In childbirth, the mother has long occupied center stage. In a crisis in which survival of one or the other is at stake, the mother usually gets first consideration. But recently more attention has been given to the role of the tiny participant in the birth process.

Leboyer's Babies

Leboyer, a French obstetrician, has delivered 10,000 babies since 1953, but the last 1000 had a most unconventional delivery. The radical change in Leboyer's practice involved a shift of attention from the mother to the baby. Leboyer details his present delivery-room procedure in *Birth Without Violence* (1975), an international best-seller. Because his methods run contrary to well-established hospital procedures, one might guess that they have not yet been very widely adopted. The following brief account of the Leboyer method reveals why, and it also brings out some of the psychological aspects of the human events occurring in the delivery room.

Psychological aspects of delivery. As noted, the mother traditionally gets most of the attention from the attendants at her delivery. She is treated as if she were a patient, and she is assigned to a bed under what has often been

[4] And, one might add, than in psychology.

called a pathological attitude toward delivery. The mother may be so heavily drugged (and, incidentally, her child too) that neither can be very active in *facilitating* birth. As a consequence, forceps may have to be used in extracting the infant from the birth canal, with some possibility of the child incurring structural damage. Once the infant has exited, it is held upside down and slapped on the buttocks "to get breathing started." Placement on a metal scale comes next, and further processing. Throughout, the neonate is handled as *an object* in a noisy room under intense illumination.

"Outrageous!" says Leboyer. Here is how he operates. The floodlights are turned off so as not to blind the newcomer emerged from the mostly dark cavern. The brightest light the fetus could even have been subjected to during uterine life is indicated in the following sentence from Leboyer (1975, p. 17): "If a woman more than six months pregnant is naked in the sunlight, the infant within her sees it as a golden haze." No wonder the burning lights of the delivery room evoke such screaming and flailing of arms and legs. Therefore, Leboyer permits only a night light sufficient to attend the mother. But should an emergency arise, more illumination is instantly available.

How about sounds?   We are already familiar with the stroking and massaging of the fetus by the mother with every step she takes. And, when she sits, stands, lies, and turns, "the fetus swims about buoyantly" (especially in early pregnancy) within a uterus that maintains a constant temperature. Not so after birth in a room the temperature of which is adjusted to suit the attendants. All the gentle touches are gone. The infant is dangled head down and slapped in that position. Its weight must be known at once, and so there is an encounter with the hard, cold, metal tray of the scale. Leboyer considers the whole procedure just described "hell for the child" (1975, p. 19).

According to Leboyer, the continuity of the touch that the fetus experienced in the uterus must not be broken. So the whole birth process is watched over patiently, allowing it to advance naturally. When the baby's head emerges and then the arms, the physician slips a finger under each armpit and gently eases the baby out into the world. In the next instant, contact with the mother is reestablished by nestling the infant on its mother's belly.

There is no rush to cut the umbilical cord. The wait makes for an easier transition to respiration and provides the newborn with a double supply of oxygen. When respiration has taken over fully and the umbilical cord has stopped beating, then, as a now-useless-link with the mother, the umbilicus is ready for separation. On assuming responsibility for its own oxygen supply, the newborn "will have uttered no more than one cry. Or two. Or three" (1975, p. 52). Why? Because Leboyer's "birth without violence" has made crying unnecessary; it does not arouse crying.

Getting born continues.   Leboyer's program takes into account the infant's recent touching experiences in the uterus. The goal is to provide the infant with the same exquisitely gentle contact with the mother after birth as existed prior to birth. As the infant continues to nest on the mother's abdomen, flat on its stomach, the mother is encouraged to make her first acquaintance with her baby by touch. She fondles and caresses it as gently as the uterus did, not as it did in labor, but like the uterus of the early days, in slow, continuous motion.

One last step.   Following the pacifying massage by the mother and attendants, Leboyer reinstates one more uterine condition as a security factor in the infant's passage to independent status in the external world. As the child is led to abandon the soft, warm belly of its mother, a bath of warm water has been readied, maintained at a temperature of 98 or 99° F. The child is placed in it (see Figure 3-4). The situation is very like a return to the watery womb. All tensions dissolve. Movement is reinstated. Hands open and close. The eyes open. By contrast with newborn infants who howl and scream and wear ugly masks, Leboyer's babies display beatific smiles even within 24 hours of birth (as shown in Figure 3-5), an unheard-of phenomenon among babies delivered in the traditional way.

In another book, *Loving Hands* (1976), Leboyer describes the traditional art of baby massage that has been passed on, from mother to daughter for countless generations, in India. The practice fits in with, and complements, his birth-without-violence procedures. If we once more recall the dramatic movement, massage, and close touch that the fetus experienced in the uterus for 9 months, we can easily empathize with the infant's tomblike situation after birth as Leboyer describes it in *Loving Hands* (1976, p. 12)

> Here is the child in the cradle.
> All alone.
> Not a sound. Not a whisper.
> And worst of all . . . there is no movement.
> Everything is dead. A horrible dead feeling everywhere.
> A horrible loneliness.

"What we are doing here is softening the pain of an almost total upheaval by carrying the past forward into the present. We are giving the child company on its journey. We are soothing by sending the echo of the familiar and loving uterine waves along its back" (Leboyer, 1975, p. 62). Leboyer is saying that it is best to provide for the infant the same secure psychological base enjoyed in the uterus for integrating the unpredictable, new experiences it will meet in the external world. For the same reason, Leboyer recommends that the child be returned to the water following the massage,

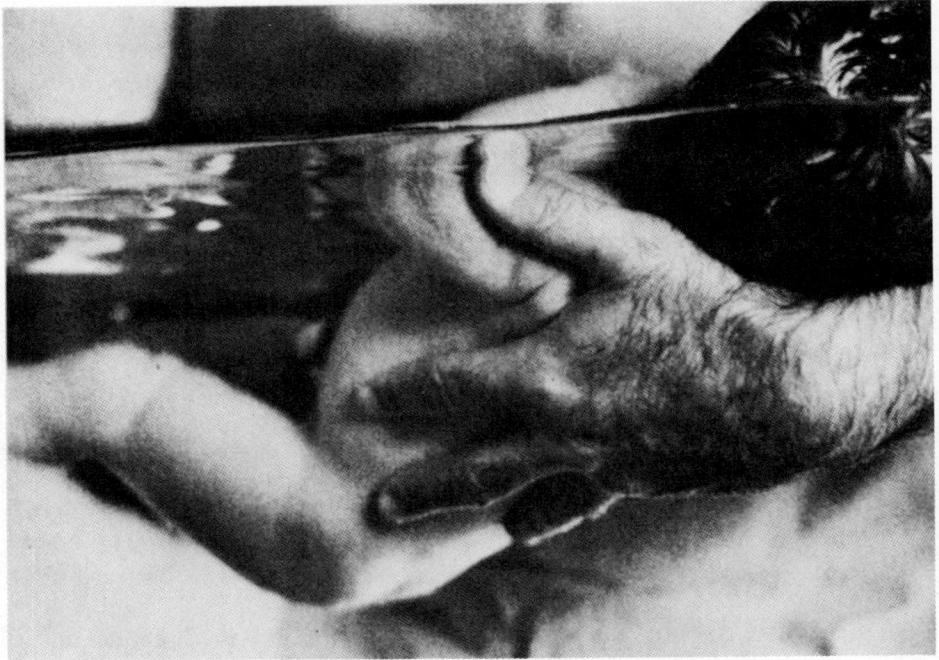

Figure 3-4 After the newborn has nested on the mother's abdomen and the child and mother have made their acquaintance, the infant is *not* placed on the hard, cold surface of a scale. Instead, it is placed or "replaced" in water, in a bath at a temperature of 98° or 99° F. (From *Birth Without Violence*, by Frederick Leboyer. Copyright © 1975 by Alfred A. Knopf, Inc. Reprinted by permission of the publisher.)

not for a bath so much as to let the child float once more as it used to. Note the connection to the statements made about baby swimmers in the preceding chapter.

A follow-up of Leboyer's babies. Leboyer has never made any extravagant claims for the superiority of his procedure over the conventional methods. He thinks that a humane and painless birth for child as well as mother is benefit enough. But one cannot help speculating about more lasting effects of birth without violence. And, in fact, a follow-up study has been reported by Trotter (1977). Researchers assigned 120 women randomly to Leboyer-type delivery rooms at a hospital in a middle-class neighborhood. Leboyer babies, consisting of three groups of 40 each, were aged 1, 2, and 3 years respectively at the time of the study. But it should be made clear that all had entered the world under a Leboyer type of delivery. Their psychomotor

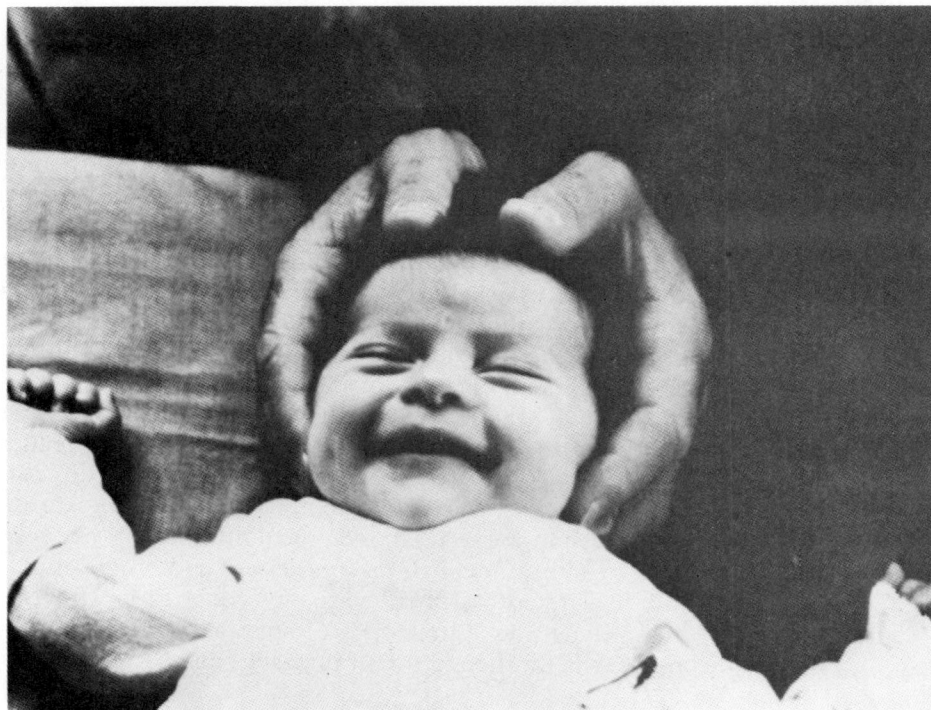

Figure 3-5 Most people would guess the age of the child in this photo at about 6 months, yet this baby is not yet 24 hours old. The secret? Birth without violence. (From *Birth Without Violence*, by Frederick Leboyer. Copyright © 1975 by Alfred A. Knopf, Inc. Reprinted by permission of the publisher.)

development yielded an average score of 106 on a scale of 129, on which 100 is average. These results indicate that their physical development was somewhat advanced over that of non-Leboyer babies. They were also more resourceful in the use of both hands.

> These children also began walking at an earlier age (13 months on the average, compared with the usual 14 or 15 months). They have displayed less than the normal amount of difficulty in toilet training and self-feeding and seem to be protected from manifestations of colic and shortness of breath sometimes seen during the first months of life. [Trotter, 1977, p. 59]

There were fringe benefits as well. The mother of Leboyer babies felt that they had had a rich and rewarding experience as participants, and the fathers also took a greater interest in their children. Apparently, the bonding between parents and children was strengthened by engaging all the concerned actors in the drama early on.

Reciprocal Interaction Following Birth

The rich psychological drama that occurs between the mother and her newborn has been captured by Klaus and Kennel in their fascinating book, *Maternal-Infant Bonding* (1976). The rapidity of what they call *bonding* (quick buildup of a close interrelationship), can be explained with the aid of Figure 3-6. The situation demands minute analysis of all the factors and all the processes going on simultaneously. In the center of Figure 3-6, one sees a mother feeding her child during the first hour of its life. However, the still scene at best can portray only what was happening at the instant the photo was snapped; all the dynamic action is omitted. What we should have is a frame-by-frame analysis of a motion-picture recording. But the arrows in the diagram must substitute. Some arrows are in the direction from mother to infant and others from infant to mother. They indicate all the variables that are involved in the series of reciprocal interactions between mother and child occurring simultaneously in a variety of combinations. Here follows a brief, piecemeal inventory of the variables constituting the interactions, most of which Klaus and Kennel (1976) support with research findings. We first consider the mother-to-infant interactions.

1. *Touch.* There is a rapid buildup of touch interactions, with most mothers at first timidly touching the baby's hands and toes until they gradually establish contact with the body and soon are massaging the entire body of the child.
2. *Eye-to-eye contact.* Many studies support the notion of the importance of the eye in bonding mother and child. Stimulus qualities of the eyes—such as the shininess of the globe, the mobility of the eyes despite their fixity in space, and the distinct pupil—iris—cornea aspects—give them a powerful attentional advantage over other bodily features (p. 70).
3. *High-pitched voice of the mother.* Klaus and Kennel cite research showing that mothers talk to their babies in a high-pitched voice by comparison with the voice pitch to which they will immediately change when speaking to a physician or nurse. According to investigators, this voice quality gives an advantage to the voices of mothers over fathers (p. 73).
4. *Entrainment.* When people speak or listen to others speak, such process may be accompanied by synchronous *movements* such as head nodding, tongue clucking, and touching. This is what Klaus and Kennel call *entrainment.* They support the concept with research citation.

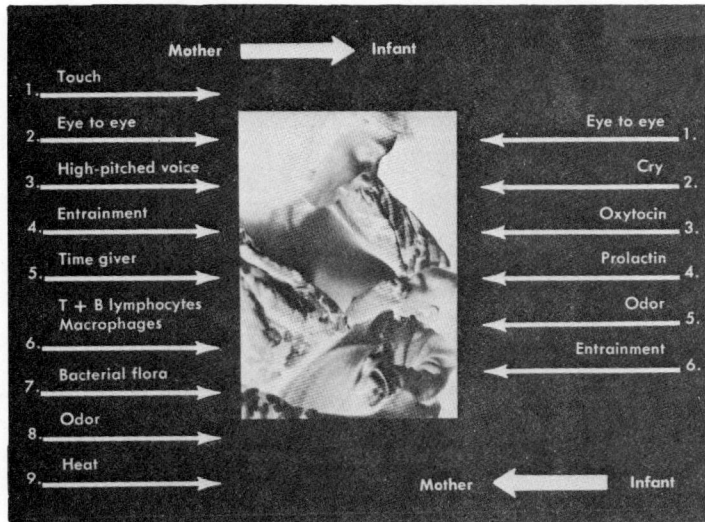

Figure 3-6 Mother-to-infant and infant-to-mother interactions that can occur simultaneously in the first days of life. (From Klaus and Kennell, *Maternal-Infant Bonding*, St. Louis: Mosby, 1976, p. 67.)

5. *Time giver.* We have already seen how an infant may become adjusted even *in utero* to the mother's schedule or lack thereof. After birth, the infant will also gradually become attuned to the mother's own sleep cycle, feeding schedules, and so on.

6. *T and B lymphocytes, macrophages.* The baby is bequeathed immediate immunity to diseases through the maternal milk, which contains T and B lymphocytes and macrophages, which all provide protection against enteric pathogens. These are biological in nature and, therefore, of no special psychological interest.

7. *Bacterial nasal flora.* Exchange of bacterial nasal flora is another biological interaction that confers immunity to the infant against such organisms as *Staphylococcus.*

8. *Odor.* According to research, "by the fifth day of life, breast feeding infants can discriminate their mother's own breastpad from the breastpads of other mothers with significant reliability" (p. 76).

9. *Heat.* Traditionally, the mother's body has been the reliable source of body heat, research indicates that when babies are *wrapped* and placed against the mother (in place of naked body contact) they show a slight temperature drop. This condition is of diminishing importance today.

Now, we very briefly consider the infant-to-mother interactions (the full account in Klaus and Kennel's *Maternal-Infant Bonding*, 1976, is highly recommended).

1. *Eye-to-eye contact.*   Klaus and Kennel emphasize the powerful effect that the infant's eye contact has on the mother. By contrast, they cite research showing the difficulties that mothers of blind newborns have in establishing closeness with their babies (Klaus and Kennel, 1976, p. 77), and they show how eye contact of each (mother and child) reinforces the other (as when eye contact elicits a smile or touch on the part of the other).
2. *Cry.*   Crying is another potent stimulus that gets prompt response from the mother, not only in terms of movement to reach the baby but in inducing "nursing readiness" (p. 78).
3. *Oxytocin.*   When the mother breast-feeds her baby right after birth, the child's nursing or even licking her breasts releases hormones that reduce uterine contractions and bleeding (p. 78).
4. *Prolactin.*   Research suggests strongly that the infant's licking, sucking, or even touching the maternal breast increases prolactin, which induces milk production, which induces nursing, and so on.
5. *Odor.*   According to Klaus and Kennel, reports of many mothers suggest that each baby has a characteristic odor (p. 79), which may reinforce the mother's behavior toward her infant.
6. *Entrainment.*   Klaus and Kennel also stated that, in order for parental attachment to occur, the infant must provide some "feedback" to the parent. The factor that operates here is a movement on the part of the infant synchronous with some action of the parent: speech, touch, or whatever. A shortened statement of the principle involved here is stated as "You cannot fall in love with a dishrag" (p. 79).

What we have achieved so far is a fragmentation into little bits and pieces of what is actually a totality, a dynamic process, a series of interactions. If we try to reorder the pieces of the jigsaw puzzle, we get close to the picture intended by Klaus and Kennel. The partners in the reciprocal interaction just noted may be simultaneously involved with each other on a number of sensory levels simultaneously even though we analyzed them sequentially and separately (see Figure 3-7).

Another point that needs to be stressed is that mother and infant reinforce each other's behavior; that is, the response of each has an effect on the other. When the infant is picked up, it becomes quiet, opens its eyes, and follows the mother with its eyes. The mother likewise looks into the eyes of the infant, and so on.

Looking at the process in the opposite direction, when the mother touches the infant's cheek, he is likely to turn his head, bringing him into contact with

Figure 3-7 "Mother and Child," by Mary Cassatt, circa 1900. Note how well the artist has captured the rich visual and tactile interactions between mother and child. (Courtesy of the Art Institute of Chicago.)

her nipple, on which he will suck. His sucking in turn is pleasurable to both of them. [Is this simultaneous reinforcement?]. Actually, this is a necessarily over-simplified description of these interactions. These behaviors do not occur in a chainlike sequence but rather each behavior triggers several others. Thus the effects of an interaction are more like that of a stone dropped into a pool, causing a multitude of ever increasing rings to appear, rather than like a chain where each link leads to only one other. [Klaus and Kennel, 1976, p. 68]

What we have accomplished in reassembling the pieces that we started with in our analysis is a reaffirmation of the *event*. What we actually acknowledge is the intimate interaction of mother and child on a number of sensory levels (smell, touch, movement, and eye contact, for example). But the paramount principle that ties the flow of events together and seems to make sense of them is *reinforcement*. The infant's cry elicits the mother's touching and holding of the child, reinforcing its action, while contact with the infant's body reinforces the mother's action of cuddling it, and so on. As Klaus and Kennel put it in nonreinforcement terms, "Their behaviors complement each other and serve to lock the pair together" (p. 67). For us, we might say that the action of each member of the pair is a source of reinforcement for the action of the other member.

What Can We Learn from Prematures?

As appealing as birth without violence may be, it would be well to have some reaction to it from other investigators. Fortunately, such is available from an American investigator, Ruth Rice, who specializes in premature babies. Writing in the *APA Monitor* (1975), she reveals a philosophy of childbirth similar to that of Leboyer. Rice shows a sensitivity to the "emotional" needs of the newborn, pointing out that failure to do so can cause "colic, hyperactivity, feeding difficulties and sleeping problems" (p. 8). She stresses the increased morbidity for premature children. Like Leboyer, Rice notes the continued activity of the fetus and its perpetual intrauterine bombardment by auditory, touch, and kinesthetic stimulation as a function of the intimate contact with the mother. When the premature is suddenly evicted from the exciting womb to the cold, sterile tomb of an incubator, all the previous rich stimulation comes to a grinding halt.

What are the consequences of the premature's confinement to the incubator? Rice believes that the premature obtains much less total stimulation during its entire developmental period than does the full-term baby. The result is an interference in biological development and in the mother-infant attachment relationship. In fact, Rice speculates that the higher proportion of prematures among abused children may derive from the prolonged separation of mother and infant. She says "All newborns need their mother's close intimacy and frequent touch but the premature infant, cheated of the normal nine months of stimulation in the uterus, needs these things the most" (Rice, 1975, p. 8).

Rice's question.   Rice's observations and reflections prompted the formulation of the following question. Would it be possible to facilitate neurological development and maturation in the premature infant? Because touch is ahead of the other senses, Rice developed a tactile–kinesthetic treatment program. As indexes of developmental progress, she took nine primitive reflexes that *disappear* in full-term infants by the age of 4 months.

Rice's procedure.   Rice placed 30 prematurely born infants randomly into experimental and control groups. Treatment consisted of stroking and massaging the infant's entire body. Such stimulation, taught to the mothers of the experimental group of babies, was administered for 15 minutes daily for 30 days, beginning with the day the infant came home from the hospital. Control mothers were given only the usual instructions on infant care. In order to make sure that sufficient nutrition was available to all the subjects, a 4-month supply of formula was given for each child.

Rice's results.   Developmental progress of the 30 subjects was evaluated by a pediatrician, a psychologist, and a pediatric nurse who had no knowledge of which subject was experimental and which control. Briefly, in assessing the disappearance of the primitive reflexes, the experimental group was far different. Six of the nine reflexes pinpointed for study were absent in the experimental group, and a significant difference in weight gain in its favor. Psychological functioning as measured by the Bayley Scales of Infant Development also showed a statistically significant difference in favor of the experimental group.

Rice's conclusion.   In conclusion, Rice (1975, p. 9) notes that

> In short, the infants who were systematically stroked and rocked by their mothers for 30 days after arriving home from the hospital made significant gains in weight, neurological development, and in mental functioning.[5] In addition, it is suggested that they surpassed the rate of growth of normal, fullterm infants by virtue of age adjustment. A baby who was eight weeks premature at birth, and who was 16 weeks at examination date, would have an adjusted age of eight weeks total age. Thus, this infant would have made a 24-week gain in 16 weeks. In other words, at four months, chronological age, not only would this infant have "caught up" with a fullterm infant, but would have accelerated another eight weeks in developmental functioning. This was also evidenced in weight gain. The average weight gain for a fullterm infant is double his birth weight by four months. All the experimental infants more than doubled their birth weight in four months. One infant, who was 32 weeks gestational age and three pounds at birth, weighed over 15 pounds at four months of age—a gain of five times her birth weight.

---

[5] This is Rice's inference, not mine.

The Cultural Warping of Childbirth

How bound we are by custom is startlingly revealed in Haire's (1972) critical analysis of childbirth, especially as it is managed in the United States. Here are some salient objections she raises against current practice:

1. Requiring all normal women to give birth in the hospital with much "obstetrical tampering" (p. 16)
2. Induced labor when not called for
3. Separating the mother from familial support during labor and birth
4. Confining the normal laboring woman to bed
5. Shaving the birth area
6. Dependence on drugs for pain relief
7. Chemical stimulation of labor
8. Moving the normal mother to a delivery room for birth
9. Requiring the mother to lie flat on her back with knees drawn up and spread far apart by "stirrups," making spontaneous birth more difficult or impossible
10. Routine use of forceps for delivery

Haire (1972) has 20 more complaints against traditional methods associated with childbirth. She points out that obstetrical techniques give primary consideration to the attending physician and nurses, sometimes even handicapping mother or child. Haire supports her arguments with 102 references from the medical literature and presents data from countries where more natural methods are used with more favorable consequences to mother and newborn. Both Leboyer's method and Rice's experimental study need to be evaluated within the wider context of childbirth management as represented in Haire's exposé.

The Foundation Stage of the Reactional Biography

The foregoing sections on maturation, on the fetus' activities within the uterus with its opportunities for interacting with the myriad surrounding conditions, and on childbirth of the full-term as well as the premature infant, have given us a glimmer of what is to come. We have already witnessed the conditionability of the human fetus in the uterus, and we have "caught" the fetus sucking its thumb or toes as early as 25 weeks from conception. In other words, we have watched psychological action emerge from the ceaseless life activity of the fetus.

Our purpose now is to try to get to the bottom of things, to try to determine how the interbehavioral history starts. This brings us to the foundation stage of the reactional biography, that developmental phase during which we *begin to observe* interactions that are essentially psychological, namely, historical, differential, integrative, variable, delayable, modifiable, inhibitive. It is the stage in which the organism is launched on its reactional biography, of which we have seen only the meager portion. The uterus provided only limited possibilities for behavior acquisition, but once the newborn is ejected into the "big, buzzing, booming confusion" of the outside world things really begin to happen.

The Raw Materials for Psychological
Interactions

Reflexes. A convenient example of one source of psychological development is Spelt's conditioning of the human fetus *in utero*. With the loud noise produced by the paddle against the box, Spelt evoked a startle reflex in the fetus. For simplicity's sake, we may say that without any prior history, between fetus and loud noise, the startle reflex occurs. Not so with the vibratory stimulus. The first meeting between it and the fetus apparently produces no consequences. But, as the two stimuli are paired in presentation, at some point in the sequence the vibratory stimulus comes to function *as if* it were the loud noise. If we consider the response to the loud noise as a physiological reflex, then the eventual or final reaction to the vibratory stimulus is a psychological or conditioned response. And now we have a paradigm for one source of raw materials for the interactional history, namely, the reflexes.

Our example of a reflex happens to be one that involves the total organism. One is not startled in an arm or a leg; the action takes place all over. However, other reflexes are more restricted or local, such as the pupillary reflex. If we shine a light into the infant's eye, the pupil contracts. Remove the light, and the pupil dilates to normal. What we have here is a structure-function operation. An organismic structure is so built that it can function only in one way to a stimulus that will set it off. Now, if you tell the infant that a big bear has entered the room, the pupil does not change in size. But if you convince the infant's mother of the same piece of news, we may be quite certain that the size of her pupils will change. Two points are important here:

1. The infant's pupillary reaction to light stimulation qualifies as a physiological reflex, the mother's reaction to news of a bear as a psychological interaction with its implicit history involving language, stories of bears, and so on.
2. Unlike the all-over startle response, the pupillary reflex involves predominantly the eyes but we had better keep the rest of the organism around, too.

Although we have in previous chapters differentiated between physiology and psychology, our present discussion offers another opportunity to elaborate the point and to learn more about one source of "psychological reflex." The table of reflexes in *Stedman's Medical Dictionary* (Taylor, 1957, pp. 1206–1211) lists approximately 175 reflexes, a fact that makes the organism seem like a repository of reflexes. As varied as they are, reflexes nevertheless have certain common characteristics. They are more or less permanent and simple reactions that constitute gross adaptations to the environment. If you are choking, the gag relfex may succeed in disgorging the menacing object in your throat and thus save your life. Pepper, tear gas, or other irritant in the nose or eyes elicits sneezing or tears to rid the organism of the threatening substance. Thus, the gross response to the environment is an adaptation, not an adjustment.

Psychological responses. Besides these crude, built-in, unlearned reactions called *reflexes*, the organism must adjust to multitudinous, ever changing and more subtle conditions than pepper, tear gas, or a tap on the patellar (knee) tendon. These are acquired during the organism's own individual development. Let's take a simple example. A dog is in the conditioning laboratory. Every time the animal is administered a shock to the foot, we observe a withdrawal reflex; the response is unlearned, automatic, simple, and constitutes a gross adjustment to the environment. Suppose we flash a red light before the same dog; we get no "response" or a neutral response. Now, let us present red light and shock, red light and shock, for 50 trials. If we have hooked up the apparatus so that a lift of the dog's foot will *prevent* the shock by opening the switch, something else begins to happen. As we keep presenting, first the red light and then the shock, the foot comes up ever more quickly during the successive trials, until it successfully *prevents* the shock. Now, this is a finer adjustment to the situation than simply moving the foot and taking the shock as before. Here's another superior feature of the acquired or conditioned response in our dog: If we cut out the shock entirely, the reaction is gradually weakened until, eventually, it disappears or, as we say, is extinguished. The dog has stopped lifting its foot. Wouldn't it be "silly" for the dog to keep withdrawing a paw in perpetuity from a shock that was not being administered any longer? This response is also a fine and specific adjustment. One more point must not be overlooked: If we apply our criteria of psychological events to the present situation, we can, at least, discern the historical, differential, and modifiable features. This is the distinction between the reflexes that the physiologist studies and what *appear like* the same responses that are of such great interest to the psychologist. If we make the mistake of focusing attention only on the responses of the organism, confusion will certainly follow, but as long as we take into consideration how, and to what, the organism's reactions are hooked up we will be able to view them as two different kinds of events.

Physiological Reflexes Versus Psychological Responses

Now that we have a criterion for separating physiological from psychological events, let us test it out with some samples. Take trembling as our first example. The way to elicit this reflex is to put the organism in the deep freeze until we get a visible tremor. What a far cry from a student who complains that every time he must give a talk before his speech class, he is certain that his fellow students know that his legs are shaking because they can see his pants quiver. We may be sure that the student's trembling was not a "built-in" response demonstrable at birth. It had to be acquired during his interactional history.

At birth, urination and defecation are physiological reflexes that no one needs to learn how to do. "Toilet training" is essentially a method of transforming physiological reflexes into conditioned responses. At this point, we should recall the hangups that college students had about urination in the study referred to earlier. A cough as the result of a sore throat is one thing, but a cough produced as a way of hedging or delaying a response to an embarrassing question is a totally different event. We could go on through a long list of similar illustrations but that would be belaboring a point. The point simply concerns the relationship between the response and the condition or stimulus function that is connected with the response. If the condition operates from birth prior to any opportunity for learning, it belongs to the physiologist. However, if the eliciting variable comes to operate in that manner only *after* a series of events or *after* a history involving the organism and the eliciting variable, then we have an occurrence in which the psychologist has a justifiable interest. Now that we have differentiated between physiological and psychological events, we are ready to explore the principles of conditioning.

The Principles of Conditioning

Classical conditioning. Classical conditioning had its beginning shortly after the turn of the century in the physiological laboratory of Ivan Pavlov in St. Petersburg, (now Leningrad, USSR). Pavlov was interested in the secretion of stomach and salivary glands. On one occasion, in his early work on salivary secretion with dogs, he observed that a dog drooled not only when meat powder was introduced into the dog's mouth but even when the dog heard his caretaker walking in the corridor. Pavlov called the latter a "psychic secretion" and proceeded to make his laboratory sound-proof, odor-proof, illumination-proof, and vibration-proof, so as to control every possible barrier that might affect his experiments. He also isolated the dog subject in a special conditioning chamber with one-way windows. He then proceeded with experiments that yielded the principles of conditioning as we know them today.

The conditioning process.   We are already somewhat familiar with several basic terms such as *unconditioned stimulus* and *unconditioned response.* To use Pavlov's example, the meat powder is the unconditioned stimulus, and the dog's drooling is the unconditioned response. They are called *unconditioned* because no previous history or other special sets of conditions is required.

Now suppose we are in Pavlov's laboratory and we want to do some conditioning. We may want to use a ticking metronome, a flash of light, or a bell. Let us select the ticking metronome. Our first procedure must be to test the metronome to check that it does not already elicit some response. We do this and find that our canine subject barely notices it, so we say that the metronome elicits a neutral response. We may diagram our two situations as follows.

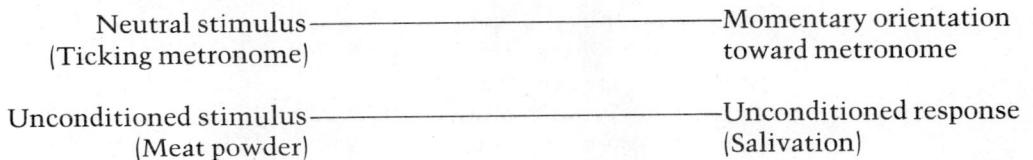

Neutral stimulus————————————————Momentary orientation
(Ticking metronome)   toward metronome

Unconditioned stimulus—————————————Unconditioned response
(Meat powder)   (Salivation)

We are now ready to proceed with conditioning. We do so by presenting the ticking metronome set at an arbitrary 100 beats per minute, followed a half second later by meat powder in mouth. We continue presenting the *paired* stimuli at varied intevals for, let us say, 20 to 50 trials. Now let us test the efficacy of the metronome. We set the metronome to ticking but withhold the meat in the mouth. The dog drools anyhow, just to the metronome alone. We have established a conditioned response. The formerly neutral stimulus is neutral no more. In fact, the metronome acts *as if* it were meat powder. What we have done is to change the metronome's stimulus function to approximate that of the meat powder. The traditional diagram pictures the conditioning process as follows:

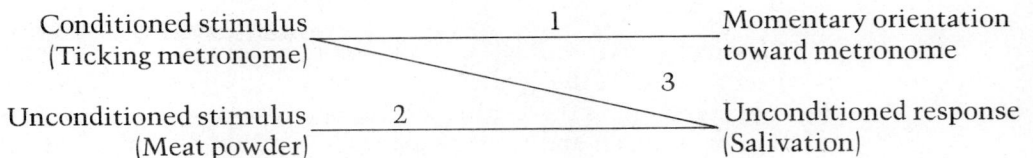

Conditioned stimulus ————————1———————— Momentary orientation
(Ticking metronome)   toward metronome
                                                                              3
Unconditioned stimulus ———2———————————— Unconditioned response
(Meat powder)   (Salivation)

Some psychologists talk about the process in terms of *stimulus substitution* because a new stimulus (the ticking metronome) has been substituted for the meat-powder stimulus that was originally connected with the salivating response. But, because the meat powder still functions as it used to, it may be more fitting to say the conditioning procedure has succeeded in extending the stimulus function of the meat powder to the metronome as well. In my opinion, it is more an *extension* of stimulus function rather than a *substitution* for it. The principle of generalization that will come up for consideration later tends to support such a connection. A final point about the outcome of conditioning as just discussed, from an interbehavioral viewpoint: we may say that the stimulus function of the metronome is equivalent to the action of meat powder, because both stimulus objects are connected with the same response.

Reinforcement.   If we ask, in the case of conditioning just discussed, how conditioning occurred, the answer is clear-cut: the chief factor is the role of the meat powder. Without it, conditioning would never have occurred. Psychologists speak of its role as reinforcement. It is the unconditioned stimulus that strengthens or reinforces the reaction to the metronome once established. The conditioned response does not need to be reinforced in every trial. In fact, once in every five trials is adequate to keep the conditioned response occurring with high frequency.

Generalization.   In our experiment, we set the metronome at 100 beats a minute. After we have achieved a successful conditioned response, suppose we reset the metronome at 120 and start it ticking. We get a conditioned response to it even though we had not used that rate during our conditioning. Then let us set it at 80 and try it; we get a conditioned response (CR). Let us be bolder and try again at settings of 60 and 140, in turn; we still get a CR, but not as much salivary secretion at any of the settings as at the 100 used originally. We have demonstrated *stimulus generalization of a CR.* This term means that the CR occurs not only to the conditioned stimulus but also to other, similar stimuli, even though they were not used in the initial conditioning experiment. We also have before us a generalization gradient, which is a gradual decrease in the strength of the CR with decreasing similarity of the stimuli used in testing for generalization by comparison with the original conditioned stimulus (CS). We should note in passing that what we observe here reveals a certain orderliness, lawfulness, or pattern.

Extinction.   Because we discussed extinction in the previous chapter, we need only state at this point that if we stop reinforcing the CR with the unconditioned stimulus (UCS) after successful conditioning, eventually the salivary secretion will cease entirely. When this happens, we say that the CR has become extinguished. For example, it is fortunate that extinction has eliminated our crying; otherwise we would all be walking around crying at the drop of a hat.

Spontaneous recovery.   The term *spontaneous recovery* is also not a stranger to us but let us have a brief restatement in terms of our experimental model. Following the extinction series just referred to, suppose we let a day or two pass after the salivary response has extinguished. Now let us try the metronome set at 100; we find that we get a fairly strong CR. This is spontaneous recovery, which we have discussed earlier. To give an everyday example, you are in an exam and have gone completely blank for an answer to a given question. You walk out of the exam, and now, unfortunately, it "comes back" to you in its full strength.

Differentiation.   In a sense, differentiation or discrimination is the opposite of generalization; it is the presence of specificity. But, if we may go back to our generalization gradient of CR to a whole range of metronome ticking rates, let us set up a method for demonstrating differentiation. We shall use the 100 setting on the metronome and a 60 setting also. Now let us consistently reinforce the 100 beats per minute and never reinforce the 60 beats per minute. The eventual result will be a strong CR to the 100-beat rate and no response to the 60-beat rate. This is differentiation or discrimination. By selectively reinforcing the response to one stimulus and not to the other, we have restricted generalization and achieved specificity in its place. Such results demonstrate the fineness of psychological adjustment possibilities that are not apparent in the physiological type of adaptation. The sharpness of discrimination in animals of different species has been studied in this fashion. And, in the everyday world, if a child has had a cat described as "a four-legged animal with pointed ears," it must still learn to react differentially to cats, horses, and rabbits. Continued generalization would plunge it into linguistic problems.

Inhibition.   Let us return to our paradigm conditioning experiment at the stage at which we have a well-established CR. We have been consistently getting a very dependable salivary response as we are demonstrating the laboratory to a visitor. We set off our ticking metronome, but just at that moment a fly buzzes past the dog's eyes and nothing happens. We have just witnessed an instance of inhibition, which we define as the interfering effect of an extraneous factor on the CR so as to prevent its operation. In the everyday world, some of the hangups that people have in their elimination, sexual, and affectional reactions may be subject to the conditioning principle of inhibition.

Higher-order conditioning.   Our model conditioning experiment will again serve our purpose. We use the metronome CS, which is connected with a strong CR, but now we want to know if we can use the metronome the way we used the meat powder. In other words, can we, with the metronome ticking at 100, reinforce a previously conditioned response to an arbitrarily selected new conditioned stimulus such as a light? We try it, after 200 trials, let us say, we have conditioned the dog to secrete saliva to the light by means of reinforcement with the metronome (but *not* meat powder). This is called *second-order conditioning,* and our original reinforcement with meat powder was first-order conditioning. Pavlov failed to obtain third-order conditioning with dogs, but with human behavior the interrelationships between stimuli and stimuli, and responses and responses, and stimuli and responses or, better, between and among behavioral events, are so utterly complex as to almost discourage an analysis of their interconnection.

Experimental neurosis.   There is one other type of experiment that Pavlov carried out that we must consider, because it shows how behavior can be controlled or manipulated to the point of breakdown. Briefly, Pavlov started with an experiment involving differentiation essentially. He started out with two stimuli: a circle and an ellipse. When he showed the dog the circle, he rewarded it with food, but when he presented the ellipse the dog got nothing. Of course, Pavlov was wise enough to randomize the presentation of the two stimuli, so that on different trials, the figures would appear sometimes on the right and sometimes on the left. This was done to prevent a sequence habit.

When Pavlov had a well-established salivary CR going, he started to present stimuli that made a differential response increasingly more difficult. He did this by drawing the ellipse more and more like a circle. When he reached the point where the ellipse had diameters in a proportion of four to five, the dog's behavior showed a general breakdown. Failure to be able to make a differential response resulted in barking, snarling, growling, aggression toward the experimenter, defecation, urination, and blood-pressure increases, as well as pulse rate, raucous breathing, and sexual responses occurring indiscriminately. Pavlov called this breakdown "experimental neurosis." But there was no way of checking on the state of the dog's nervous system, and no one did. It is much simpler to explain the situation as a *behavioral* breakdown. Consider the fact that we had previously established two distinct responses correlated with two distinct stimulus functions. By narrowing the difference between them, we reach a point at which the discriminatory response breaks down. In place of the two differential responses, we now see an explosive, all-out response. Under the "impossible" circumstances, this was the type of "adjustment" available to the organism.

The Significance of Classical (or Pavlovian) Conditioning

We have come around to conditioning as a topic in a roundabout way within a chapter concerned with behavior origins. The reason is that the two are inextricably interconnected. Where we find behavior emerging, we also find conditioning as the means by which those emerging behaviors get organized. That does not mean that conditioning operates *only* during the early stages of the interbehavioral history. Not at all. It will be doing its work throughout the individual's life span. But, because it does make its appearance in the foundation stage of the reactional biography, it seemed appropriate to discuss it at this point.

Now, first of all, the principles that we have examined show us how reactions that are biological functions of structures change into psychological interactions through a certain history. For example, in the early history of classical conditioning, Pavlov (1927) reports a relevant instance. In Pavlov's laboratory, Krylov (a colleague of Pavlov) was injecting dogs with morphine five or six times a day. The consequences were the usual nausea, secretion of saliva, vomiting, and sleep. So far, we have an unconditioned stimulus (morphine) eliciting an unconditioned response (vomiting, and so on). But, after the experiment got under way, the mere sight of the experimenter opening the syringe box was enough to call out all these marked reactions. Even in those dogs in which sight of the syringe box did not function as a conditioned stimulus, mere injection with saline solution worked effectively.

Applications of conditioning principles.   Further instances can be found in the treatment of behavior problems; for example, alcoholism. A substance such as Antabuse causes nausea and vomiting when taken with alcohol—a simple illustration of unconditioned stimulus—unconditioned response. The idea is to form a conditioned response to the sight and smell of alcohol. In one European institution, I witnessed such a treatment. A glass of vodka mixed with the nauseous liquid was placed on a table before the patient, who was instructed to drink it. The poor patient dreaded consuming the mixture, but finally, with much retching, succeeded in getting it down (momentarily); afterward, there was the inevitable vomiting and nausea. The hope of the physician was that he had established a conditioned response so that the mere sight and/or smell of vodka would do the job of the nauseating mixture. Some may, in passing, question the validity of such a "cure," but it could serve as a step in a further and more basic treatment of that patient's problems.

Enuresis and foresight.   Another application of conditioning principles has been made to enuresis (bed-wetting) in children. According to some investigators, enuresis occurs because children are insensitive to bladder tensions that stimulate other children to walk to the bathroom during the night and micturate. The problem is to get the bed-wetter to respond in a similar way. The procedure applies conditioning principles to the situation. A bell is attached to a special wired pad placed in the bed, under the child. The first drops of urine close the circuit and ring a bell, at which signal the child has been instructed to get up, go to the bathroom, and micturate. Eventually the bladder tensions do the job of the bell, so that the child responds to them instead of waiting for the bell. The conditioned-response paradigm should be apparent in this setup, with the bell acting as unconditioned stimulus for the unconditioned response (awakening and going to the bathroom to urinate). Conditioning has done its work successfully when the child's bladder tension elicits the sequence of waking, going to the bathroom, and so on.

Again it is questionable if the conditioned-response method is always justified in treating enuresis, particularly in the context of deep emotional problems. But at least we have established that the principles of conditioning permit prediction and control or, in Toulmin's (1961) words, foresight.

How about understanding? Classical conditioning research is important not only because it permitted prediction and control of behavior. As the principles of conditioning were discovered, psychologists were able to make much greater headway in making sense of behavior. They were able to discern the underlying rhyme and reason, the orderliness or patterning.

If we inquire further into that rhyme and reason, we are led into the realization that the principles of conditioning reveal how reactions are connected with their specific stimuli, unconditioned stimulus with unconditioned response, and conditioned stimulus with a neutral response. Then, as we follow the behavioral sequence, we note that the conditioned stimulus becomes related to what was an unconditioned response but now becomes a conditioned response as a function of the little bit of history that connected them all. So it is with the other principles. For example, higher-order conditioning reveals, as an addition to the preceding statement, that once a conditioned response has been established one can transform other neutral stimuli into conditioned stimuli. In other words, one can build still more conditioned responses out of once-established conditioned responses, or behavior on behavior. And, if we reexamine experimental neurosis with the same kind of analysis, we find that an organism is involved in two clear-cut, distinct behaviors such as Response X to the circle and Response Y to the ellipse. Now, as we narrow the difference between the two stimuli, we make the differential responses more difficult to perform until a certain point is reached that makes neither response specifically appropriate, and we get the familiar "breakdown." In relational terms, when too much similarity but not identity between the two conditioned stimuli is introduced, one also changes the relationship between the corresponding reactions.

What the type of analysis resorted to reveals is relations. The important point about the relations is that they are all *observable*. We have not dealt with any hypothetical or inferential entities as causes, such as a conceptual nervous sytem. Although we should note that when Pavlov (1927) made his astute laboratory observations, he was convinced that he was dealing with brain processes, as revealed by the title of his treatise: *Conditioned Reflexes: An Investigation of the Physiological Activity of the Cerebral Cortex.* He *never observed* cerebral activity but what he did observe he tried to explain in terms of hypothetical brain activity.

In my opinion, the principles of conditioning, stated in terms of observable conditions and behavioral relationships, as we have analyzed them, constitute the most solidly established area of psychology. They do not require statistical treatment to perceive them and they do not require any exceptions to the rule. Best of all, conditioning principles teach us how behavioral events flow along the way they do and how they are interconnected with each other or how they are related to one another; as Woodger (1929, p. 192) points out, "It seems hardly possible to speak of independent events because every event is related to every other event by the relation of 'extension'." The principles of conditioning spell out what some of those relationships are.

Random Movements as Raw Materials for Psychological Interactions

If reflexes were the only building blocks for behavior, both behavior and psychology would be much more simple. Fortunately, we find another rich source for behavior development in the random movements of the living organism. Imagine the kind of calamity in which parents are told that their new baby is stillborn. To be stillborn is to be lifeless, inert, utterly inactive. To be born alive is to be active, for whatever else life means, it means "spontaneous" movement, wriggling, squirming, turning, kicking, and so on. Life is action; even in plant life movement is not absent in any absolute way.

The Seeming Inexhaustibility of Random Movements

I have devised a simple scheme for observing and recording the apparently endless variety of movements in a "biologically normal" newborn. ("Biological normality" may be defined by such a standard as the Apgar test.[6]) Let us fix very weak lights to forehead, hands, elbows, knees, and toes of the child. Next let us rig up a motion-picture camera above the subject, turn out the room illumination, and watch and record. If our subject is lethargic or asleep, we can prompt some activity by sprinkling cool water over the body or pinching the foot. Now, watch for action; for the time being at least, the infant acts like a perpetual-motion machine. It reacts all over, with everything it has. Its head twists and turns up and down and sideways, and crying issues forth from the mouth. Arms and hands flail in every direction, and legs pump the air and kick back and forth and sideways. The interesting thing is that none of this activity is set off by any strong stimulus—cold, heat, loud noise, sudden displacement in space (falling), injury, and so on.

All these stimuli are reacted to in the same way. There seems to be a total lack of specificity, the hallmark of psychological events. There is the same lack of specification on the part of the behaving organism's action.

---

[6]In the Apgar test, within one minute of birth the infant is rated on a scale of 0–2 on (1) skin color (blue, 0; pink, 2), (2) respiratory effort, (3) muscle tone, (4) heart rate, and (5) reflex irritability. Virginia Apgar developed this test for biological fitness of the neonate.

Every response is an all-out, massive, apparently uncoordinated series of movements of the total organism. The important point is that such movements should be understood in terms of biological stimulus—response activity at the biological level, in which the total organism is put into action by any adequate stimulus. The organism acts this way simply by virtue of its being alive and presumably without learning playing any part whatsoever.

The advantages of the amorphous nature of random movements.   The amorphousness of random movements confers uncountable psychological benefits on the organism. Their unorganized state permits all the more latitude in the way that future interactions may organize them. Consider the psychological possibilities of the arm and hand movements alone. Imagine the infant in its crib with a large plastic ring suspended within reach. When we first introduce ring and child, there is no psychological response. But, through successive interactions, progressively more complex visual discriminations occur. Soon the dangling object begins to elicit random kicking, arm waving, head nodding, and vocalization. Gradually, through shaping, excessive movements drop out as they are not reinforced and the reactions become more and more precise until the infant can actually grasp the ring. Even kicking and vocalization drop out. By the fourth month of this aspect of the infant's career, we have seen emerge a clean cut, definite psychological response. In subsequent interactions, the baby will transfer the ring from one hand to another, bring it to the mouth, inspect it and repeatedly drop it to the floor, to the annoyance of Mama. What we have seen in the developmental theater that we have been observing is the gradual evolution or shaping of a response out of shapeless, mass-organismic action. The whole process deserves the metaphor of the sculptor shaping a statue out of a "shapeless" block of marble. In a similar way, we have witnessed the shaping of a response in a series of situations in which all the relevant variables were observable. Again, we feel no need to resort to inferences about hypothetical brain processes or invisible mental happenings.

Do babies learn to cry?   According to Rosenzweig (1954), babies *do* learn to cry. But, one wants to interject, "But don't babies cry at birth when they are slapped on the buttocks?" The (paraphrased) answer is "Yes, and that kind of crying is unlearned but that is reflex crying, a reflex akin to the knee jerk." According to Rosenzweig, what happens during the child's interactional history is that, in times of distress, such as hunger, cold, or pain, *prior to* crying, the infant reacts by putting out its tongue, or licks its lips when hungry, trembles or sneezes when cold, squirms when hurt. But parents do not attend to the child when these signals occur. They start running only when the child cries, thus inevitably and unwittingly reinforcing the crying response, which becomes a generalized distress call in times of trouble. If parents do not want to have cry-babies, Rosenzweig advises that they reinforce the precrying signals that the infant "emits." Rosenzweig suggests that "babies cry largely because they are taught to do so" (p. 81).

Other evidence.   Occasionally cases come to light of children who have been reared in extreme social isolation, the so-called cupboard children or attic children. Davis (1954) reports the case of Anna, who was reared in an attic room of a farmhouse for five years with a minimum of attention. She was taken to a country home, nourished, and otherwise cared for. According to Davis' report, "She was believed to be deaf and possibly blind. . . . She neither smiled nor *cried* in our presence" (Davis, 1954, pp. 555–556, emphasis added). Davis' observations of Anna support the notion that crying as a reflex suffers extinction in the absence of a conditioning process. Even smiling, as well as seeing and hearing, seem to call for a conditioning process.

From crying to speaking.   The ultimate in studies of crying was carried out by Karelitz, Karelitz, and Rosenfeld (1965). These investigators recorded and analyzed 1300 tapes of the crying of babies. Their longitudinal study of crying shows a definite pattern. The first cries are sharp and intense and last as long as an exhalation, followed by a rapid inhalation. At 1 month, coughlike sounds start off a crying spell. At 3 months, a plaintive quality and inflectional variations are introduced. At 9 months, pitch variations and an "ah-ha" quality appear. Vowel-like sounds insinuate themselves into the crying patterning, and at 18 months recognizable words such as "Mama!" or "I wanna go bye-bye!" are interwoven into the pattern of crying. From the cry reflex to sentence-long language takes 18 months.[7] After that, crying and speaking have more or less separate careers, but their common origin has been definitely uncovered by the Karelitzes and their coworkers.

On learning Chinese.   We have not said much about such vocal expressions as the endless coos, gurgles, babble, and chatter of infancy that appear between crying spells. They, too, play a role in the infant's development of language. We realize the great potential in this respect when we consider the following statement from Mussen (1963, p. 24): "Children of all nations and cultures make the same sounds, and in the same order. English and American infants pronounce French nasals and the French guttural 'r' as well as German vowel sounds." One could add "Swahili, Polish, and Hindi sounds, and so on." Mussen seems to be saying that *any* infant on this planet has the biological vocal raw materials for speaking any (not necessarily *just one*) of the more than 3000 languages spoken on this planet. Today millions of babies are learning Chinese; they happen to live in China. In the interest of international amity, perhaps American babies should be learning Chinese and become bilingual.

---

[7] There is no implication that maturation has brought this about; rather, a reactional biography is behind it.

Operant Conditioning

In analyzing the embarrassing wealth of random movements as raw materials for psychological interactions, I did not point out differences between them and the reflexes, a job that we must tackle now. Because the reflexes involve discrete organismic *structures* that can be activated by adequate stimuli, that property separates them from random movements. Pepper in the nose produces sneezing, onions yield tearing, a tap on the patellar tendon elicits a knee jerk. As noted earlier, the infant seems to be in perpetual motion "for no apparent reason." There is no way to demarcate stimulus–response units in observing random movements. Some people explain random movements by saying that the organism "emits" behavior. To me, this sounds too self-actional. I prefer the concept of "spontaneous" movement as an essential property of a living thing, particularly a member of the animal kingdom. To be alive is to move. Here, in my opinion, is another area where we have reached "rock bottom." There is no need and no use to inquire as to who or what is being "emitted." The animal is alive, and life manifests itself in movement. This movement is "rock bottom."

Training pigeons to play Ping-Pong.   Suppose we want to train pigeons to play a loose kind of Ping-Pong game commensurate with their limited biological possibilities (no arms, no hands–only beak). We know from past experiences that pigeons have had busy careers of pecking at most anything (their chief occupation). We can start their game in the setup shown in Figure 3–8. Our two subjects are Gary and Ron. To start things going, we place the Ping-Pong ball before Gary, who immediately pecks it on its way toward Ron at the opposite end of the table. Ron does not "catch on" to the game immediately, so we coach him in the same way as we did Gary. Placing the ball before him a few times is enough; the game is on. For pecking the ball, we reward them with a pellet of food, every peck at first, then intermittently, ensuring a fast game. When they have become expert, we can make the game more competitive by rewarding each player only when he succeeds in pecking the ball *past his opponent.* In time, the experiment has succeeded in bringing under control an arbitrarily selected reaction of each pigeon that it performed at a proper time and that was immediately reinforced. (The demonstration described was *not* hypothetical but was actually carried out at Wichita State University under the supervision of my colleague, Gary Greenberg.)

Operant conditioning distinguished from classical conditioning.   In classical conditioning, the stimulus is followed by a reinforcement as shown by the diagram on p. 114 that we used to illustrate it. In operant conditioning, the reinforcement follows the response. Not until the Ping-Pong playing pigeons pecked at the ball did they obtain a pellet of food. The diagram used to illustrate operant conditioning looks like this:

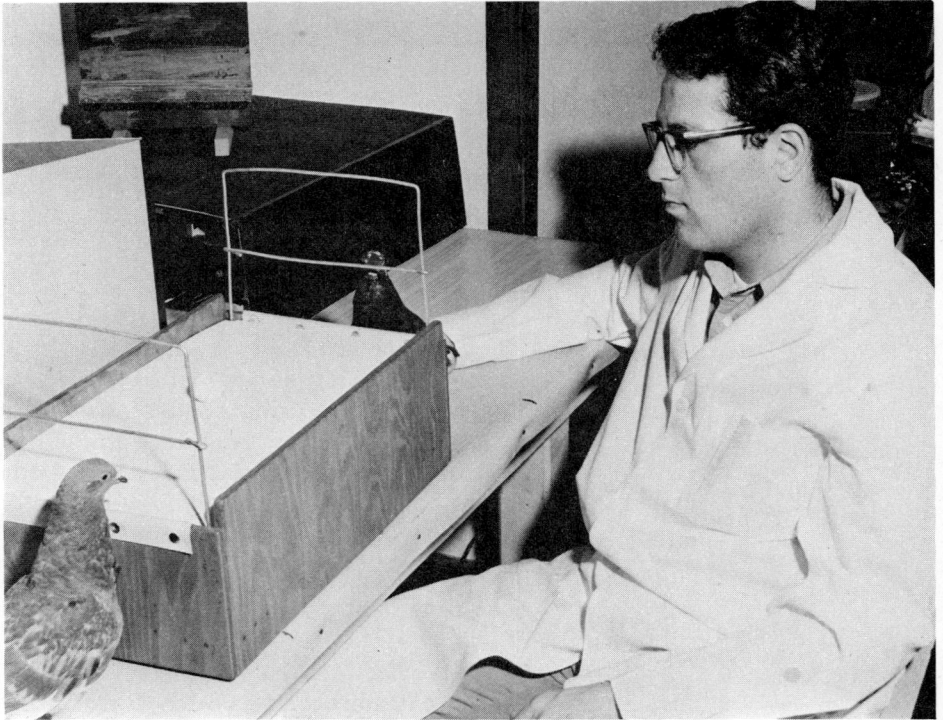

Figure 3-8   Pigeons being "coached" to play Ping-Pong by shaping, or the method of successive approximations. At first, crude approximations are reinforced and then, gradually, closer approximations, until the desired end is achieved. (Courtesy of Gary Greenberg.)

$$R \longrightarrow S$$

A response leads to or is followed by a reinforced stimulus. Another way to state the case is that the occurrence of the stimulus (S) is dependent or contingent upon the occurrence of the response (R). The response produces an effect on the environment. That is why operant conditioning is also called *instrumental conditioning.* The response is instrumental in changing something. It produces a reward or is instrumental in avoiding an electric shock. Pushing the light switch (R) illuminates the room (S). That is how operant behavior gets its name; operant behavior "operates" on the environment.

Reinforcement.   If our Ping-Pong players pecked at the ball and nothing happened, their pecking responses would soon be extinguished and the game wouldn't even get started. But because they are hungry pigeons, their pecking increases in frequency. We say, then, that the food strengthens the response of pecking or that it reinforces pecking. To take that fact into account, we modify our diagram as follows:

$$R \longrightarrow S^R$$

The superscript R stands for "reinforcing" (*not* to be confused with "response"). The reinforcing effect of a stimulus is indicated by the increasing frequency of the response that produced that stimulus. The food, then, is a reinforcer, a positive reinforcer. To prove it, all we have to do is withhold reinforcement long enough; eventually we get extinction, just as we did in classical conditioning.

Negative reinforcement. In addition to positive reinforcement, it is possible to increase the frequency of an operant response by using aversive stimuli such as electric shock. Escape conditioning will help to explain negative reinforcement. If a rat is placed in a Skinner box (see Figure 3–9), it can be administered a shock through the metal cage floor. But pressing the bar in the cage will succeed in terminating the unpleasant shock. In other words, by doing something, the rat escapes from the shock. The rate of the escape response increases; the reinforcement in this case is the *removal of the shock,* not *the* shock by itself. Putting pillows over our ears to avoid loud noises and turning off bright, hot, television-studio lights to escape being hot and sweaty also illustrate negative reinforcement. The essential difference between positive and negative reinforcement is this: In the former, the response is strengthened through the *presentation* of a stim-

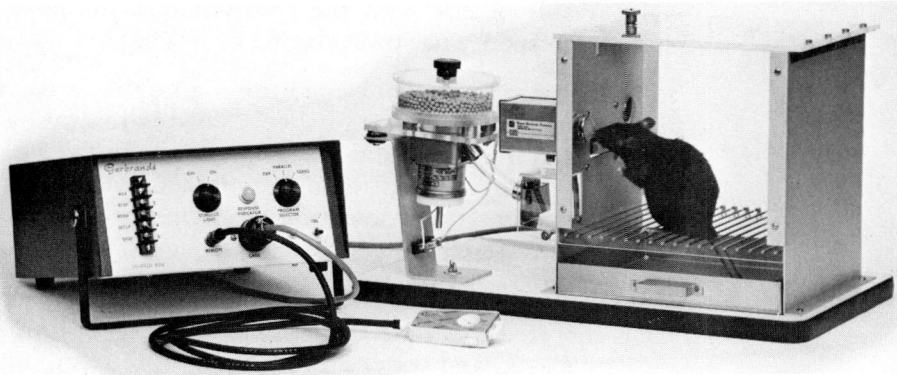

Figure 3-9 A Skinner box. Whenever the rat presses a bar, a feeding mechanism automatically delivers a pellet of food into the food tray just below the bar. Every time the bar is depressed, it also activates a recording device (outside the box) that makes a blip on a continually moving piece of paper, permitting a record of the frequency of response. (Courtesy of B. F. Skinner.)

ulus (food, in the case of the Ping-Pong playing pigeons). In negative reinforcement, the bar-pressing response of the rat in the preceding example is
strengthened by *removing* the unpleasant shock.

Punishment.   We have seen that both positive and negative reinforcers
have something in common in that they both increase the frequency or
strengthen a response. In one case, *presentation* of food increases the frequency of bar-pressing responses; in the other case, *withdrawing* electric
shock also increases the frequency of bar-pressing responses. How does punishment fit into this schema? In operant terms, punishment is defined as
"withdrawing a positive reinforcer or presenting a negative" (Skinner, 1953,
p. 185). Taking candy away from or spanking a child fits Skinner's definition
of punishment. So does imprisonment, because it denies the prisoner the
freedom of movement and privileges that the rest of us enjoy. Withholding
love and affection, as when the mother says, "If you don't behave, I won't
love you," constitutes the threat of *withdrawing* a positive reinforcer. Heap-
ing criticism, blame, disapproval, or nagging amounts to *presentation* of an
aversive stimulus (just the opposite of a negative reinforcer). Both the withholding of a positive reinforcer and the presentation of a negative reinforcer
are used to produce the same effect; that is, suppressing or decreasing the
frequency of a response.

Further comparison between classical and operant conditioning.   We have
mentioned some differences between classical and operant conditioning
at points where they were relevant. Now we finish the job. In operant
conditioning, stress is on the response as it is instrumental in achieving
some result or effect on the environment. In classical conditioning, the
subject's response has no such effect.

Reinforcement.   Operant conditioning implies a reward such as presentation of food or avoidance of shock. Food is rewarding if Ping-Pong playing
increases in frequency and precision of response as a consequence of obtaining it. In classical conditioning, reinforcement follows the CS (metronome)
and strengthens the interaction of eliciting the salivary reflex. In operant
conditioning, reinforcement is a consequence of the response.

Primary and secondary reinforcement.   Unconditioned responses as we
have analyzed them are the best illustrations of primary reinforcers. Food,
electric shock, and water possess their reinforcing function from the start.
But approval, gifts, threats, blame, awards, honor rolls, badges, and such
come to have their respective stimulus functions only after a certain history
or a process somewhat like Pavlov's higher-order conditioning.

Shaping and chaining.   One of the principal advantages of operant conditioning is its power for bringing under control complex patterns of behaviors
by contrast with the "local" or reflex behaviors that classical conditioning

governs so well. Suppose that, as a classroom demonstration, we want to train a pigeon to carry out some arbitrary act. On the table, at the front of the class, is a feed box with a manual switch that, when pressed, delivers a pellet of food in the food tray. Our pigeon for the day, Blondie, has already been trained to go to the food box as soon as she *hears* the switch close (secondary or conditioned reinforcement). I ask the students what response they want to condition. Someone suggests putting a book at one end of the table and requiring Blondie to walk about it clockwise. All agree, so we release Blondie, who fortunately does not engage in a sit-down strike. If she did, all would be lost. Instead, she moves about in different directions. We do nothing until she takes a step or two in the direction of the book on the table. As soon as she does, we close the switch, and Blondie is at the feed box in an instant. Now, instead of "starting from scratch" with her movements, Blondie's early "random movements" drop out, and she is oriented more and more only in the direction that produced results (that is, reinforced reactions with presentation of food). In a short time, Blondie continually heads for the book after picking up her reward at the feed box.

Now, the problem is to get Blondie to circle the book clockwise. But there really is no problem because the plan is simply a continuation of our previous procedure. If Blondie makes a move in a counterclockwise direction, she is not reinforced, but the slightest move in a clockwise direction is instantly reinforced with food, which Blondie collects. She then goes back in the vicinity of the book. It is tempting to anthropomorphize and say that Blondie acts as if she tried to find out what we want her to do so she could do it and collect her reward. But we will resist that temptation and simply say that we are reinforcing successive approximations of reactions that will eventually constitute a clear-cut pattern. We reach our goal of having Blondie circle the book in a clockwise direction in the same step-by-step fashion that we used before.

After our quick success with that response, some student suggests that we stand a blackboard eraser at the other end of the table and have Blondie knock it over. We accept the assignment and reward every slightest move in the "right direction." In only a few minutes, Blondie is on her way and in front of the eraser. The final step is easy for her because pecking is a "preformed unit" elicited by almost any object. It fits easily into her total repertoire.

Now, we require that Blondie execute *both acts* one after the other, which she does easily. The completion of her book-circling act cues her to start her next act, which appears as one continuous, integrated act.[8] Skinner has named this procedure *chaining*. It seems to be "a functionally coherent unit of behavior; but it is constructed by a continual process of differential reinforcement from undifferentiated behavior, just as the sculptor shapes his figure from a lump of clay" (Skinner, 1953, pp. 92–93).

[8] In the interest of brevity, certain technical details are omitted.

This demonstration is particularly effective in making the following points: behavior is observable; is a function of certain, specifiable variables; and is lawful, manipulable, controllable, and predictable. You can see it take shape before your very eyes; in fact, you yourself can actually and literaly *shape it* before your very eyes.

Discriminative stimuli. Because of its close connection with interbehavioral analysis, we should include a brief discussion of Skinner's (1953, p. 107) concept of discriminative stimuli. We may take the example Skinner uses of reinforcing neck stretching in a pigeon when a light is on in the experimental chamber and not reinforced or extinguished when the light is off. After some time, neck stretching occurs only when the light is on (p. 107). But even though this looks like a Pavlovian CR, Skinner (p. 108) explains it otherwise: "a *stimulus* (the light) is the occasion upon which a *response* (stretching the neck) is followed by *reinforcement* (with food)." This is what Skinner means by the term *discrimination*. The light *as well as* the reinforcer affect the behavioral outcome. As Skinner puts it, "Most operant behavior . . . acquires important connections with the surrounding world" (p. 107). To borrow Skinner's further examples, a smiling person is likely to be the occasion of an approved social approach, the opposite with a frowning one. But essentially what we have here is Kantor's (1933, p. 34) interactional setting factors. Both theoreticians recognize that there is more to behavior analysis and description than simple stimulus and response. They acknowledge that the conditions under which behavior occurs also play a role in the outcome of an event.

"Walking" in the Newborn

Babies normally begin to walk alone between 12 and 14 months. According to commonsense notions, this is proper and "natural," and attempts to start the infant walking earlier might be deleterious. Zelazo, Zelazo, and Kolb, (1972b) felt that there was no scientific evidence to support such a belief and so they went about trying to check it out. In a preliminary study with only one subject, this is what they found out (Zelazo, Zelazo, and Kolb, 1972b, p. 1060):

> Our initial pilot baby, who received active exercise of the walking reflex and opportunities for motor activity beyond the first 8 weeks, walked alone at 7½ months of age. He is now 6 years old and in excellent physical and intellectual condition. He has always showed good coordination—maneuvering a marble with a hocky stick at 14 months and riding a two-wheel bicycle with training wheels at 3½ years of age, for example. He combined as many as three words at 11 months and learned to read and write at 4 years of age. His thorough medical examinations have confirmed his sound physical and intellectual development.

Zelazo and his colleagues describe other cases of parents who, entirely on their own, provided opportunities for their newborn babies to stand and walk shortly after birth. One mother reported that her three sturdy babies walked without support at 7, 9, and 11 months respectively. The mother said that the children were quite independent and intelligent and now in their twenties and in good health (Zelazo, 1972b, p. 1060).

The cases just described did not seem to demonstrate any harmful consequences of early walking. In fact, in a follow-up, motor performance of these children seemed to be above average, as did other behaviors. But Zelazo and his colleagues did not think that early walking brought all these benefits on. Because there were so many uncontrolled variables, one cannot be certain of a casual relationship between the two sets of factors.

Zelazo's experiment.   After reflecting on the paucity of data on the effects of early walking, Zelazo, Zelazo, and Kolb (1972a) decided to settle the matter by conducting an experiment. As subjects, they used 24 white, 1-week-old male infants from middle-class and upper-middle-class families. Two local physicians helped in obtaining the infants. Part of their question was "Will stimulation of the stepping and placing reflexes during the first eight weeks of life facilitate walking and will it lead to an earlier onset of walking alone?" Stepping and walking as reflexes are easily elicited. Stepping or walking occur even in the newborn when it is held under its arms and its feet touch a flat surface; coordinated "walking" movements are evoked, as shown in Figure 3-10. The placing reflex is elicited when the infant, held in a similar way, lifts its legs and places the feet on the table on stimulation of the dorsal part of the feet. These two reflexes have all the appearance of unconditioned reflexes because they operate without any apparent previous conditioning.

The experimental groups.   Controlling for birth order and socioeconomic status of the parents, Zelazo and associates set up four different groups, six babies in each. The first was the experimental group, the other three, controls; their treatment was arranged as follows.

1. *The active-exercise group.*   During four 3-minute sessions every day from the beginning of the second week through the end of the eighth week, the six infants of this group received active exercise. Supported under the arms, these babies were handled so as to permit them to make foot contact with a table or other flat surface. As they made walking steps, they were permitted to move forward as in true walking. This procedure encouraged their taking right and left steps alternatively.
2. *The passive-exercise group.*   This group received a daily, 12-minute session of passive exercise and social stimulation minus the encour-

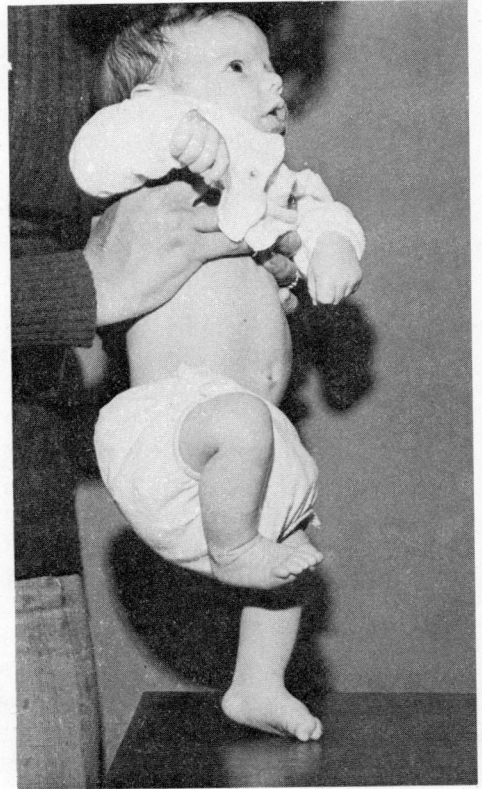

Figure 3-10 Six-week-old infant, Alexander Taylor, displaying the stepping response after several weeks of "active exercise." (Courtesy of Philip R. Zelazo.)

agement of walking and placing reflexes. Gentle exercise of arms and legs by means of pumping them with the infant on its back was the distinctive treatment of this group.
3. *The no-exercise group.* This group simply participated in the weekly test sessions of the other groups but received no training.
4. *Test-effect control group.* As a control for the possible facilitating, cumulative effect of the weekly testing, this group was tested only once, at the end of the 8-week period.

The results. Although all the babies began the experiment at approximately the same point, Figure 3-11 shows the active-exercise group far superior to the other three groups after 8 weeks of practice in walking. The before and after results for them show an increase from an average of eight steps per minute at the start to 30 per minute by the eighth week of life.

The passive-exercise group started out with an average of 7.8 steps per minute and ended up with an average of three. The no-exercise group performed comparably, starting with an average of 5.4 steps at the beginning

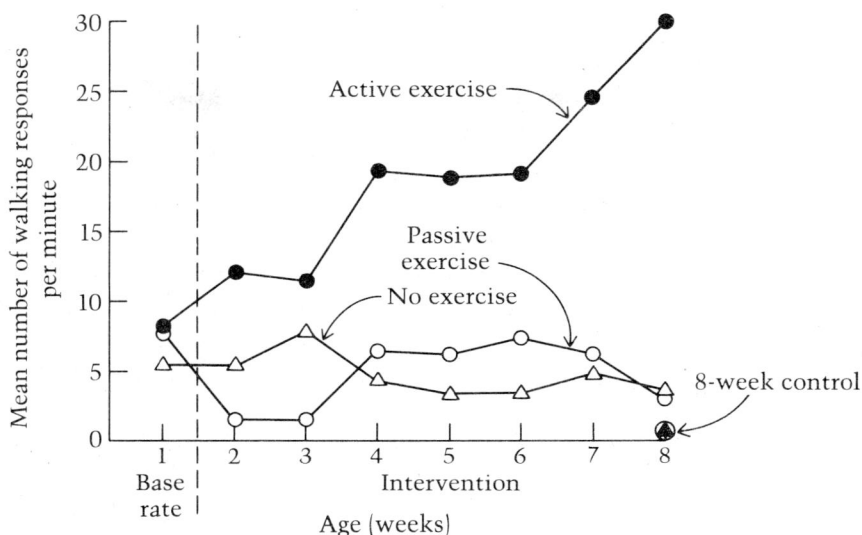

Figure 3-11 Mean number of walking responses for the experimental group (active exercise) and the control groups (passive exercise and no exercise). (From P. R. Zelazo, N. A. Zelazo, and S. Kolb, "'Walking' in the newborn," *Science*, 1972, *176*, 314–315. Copyright 1972 by the American Association for the Advancement of Science.)

and finishing with three as a mean. The 8-week control group showed the poorest performance of all with an average of less than one step per minute at the eighth week.

Conclusions on newborn walking. Zelazo and his colleagues (Zelazo, Zelazo, and Kolb, 1972a, p. 314) concluded that

> Brief daily exercise of walking and placing reflexes in the newborn leads to a high rate of responding by eight weeks and to an earlier onset of walking alone. There appears to be a critical period during which the walking response can be transformed intact from a reflexive to an instrumental action.

Reflex or instrumental learning? Stepping and walking reflexes are universally considered to be reflexes. And it is beyond dispute that learning did occur in the active-exercise group. The question is how. Analysis of the walking in the active-exercise group would seem to indicate only unconditioned stimulus (contact of infant's foot with table)—unconditioned response (lifting and stepping reflex). However, in Pavlovian conditioning this does not of itself produce increased learning. As Zelazo, Zelazo, and Kolb

(1972a, p. 315) point out, "There is normally no increase in salivation with repeated presentations of meat powder in the dog's mouth, nor does the pupil constrict more and more with each flash of light." In a similar fashion, the walking reflex, *as a reflex* elicited when the infant's foot contacted a flat surface, should remain constant. But, since there was undoubtedly learning, Zelazo and colleagues believe that the walking responses of their active-exercise group came under instrumental or operant control. They interpret the increase in walking responses by the rewarding *consequences* of walking. Each step was *reinforced* by *the upright position of the infant, movement forward through space* and *changing visual stimulation* that *followed* each step. These consequences of the walking responses reinforced the infant just as presence of food in the food tray reinforced the pigeon's bar-pressing response.

When Rice studied the importance of maternal contact on the infant's development, she stated that certain primitive reflexes disappear by about 4 months. At the time Zelazo, Zelazo, and Kolb (1972a) did their study, they were of the opinion that the stepping and placing reflexes would fade by the second month, making walking more difficult after that time. But, instead of sticking with that belief, they tested it experimentally. They worked with three groups of babies, 2, 6, and 10 weeks old, administering daily active exercise to the babies of each group. "active exercise produced gradual but consistent increases in walking steps in all three groups" (Zelazo, 1976, p. 94). The results also seemed to show that the stepping reflex does not disappear and that actually "no critical period exists" for learning to walk (p. 96).

As to Zelazo's purpose in conducting research in newborn walking, the following statement speaks for itself: "It is not our desire to encourage all parents to walk their newborns, but to encourage more research on newborn walking" (Zelazo, Zelazo, and Kolb, 1972b, p. 1060).

The Significance of Operant or Instrumental Conditioning

In our discussion of classical conditioning, we considered the significance of that process in furthering our understanding of behavior origins. We also noted that many of the principles of classical conditioning apply to operant conditioning as well. And both are so inextricably interwoven with the emergence of behavior in the foundation stage of the interbehavioral history that neither topic can be considered apart from the other.

Operant conditioning, just as classical conditioning, reveals how behavioral events may emerge from a biological matrix, how they are related to one another and to the surrounding conditions in ways that permit the formulation of principles that yield foresight and understanding or control and prediction. The same statements applicable to classical conditioning hold for operant conditioning. Together they offer both the psychological theoretician as well as the practitioner valuable ways to understand behavior and modify behavior problems. But, of the two, operant conditioning should be given first place for the following reasons. Classical conditioning derived from the study of reflexes, the functioning, as we saw, of the more-or-less circumscribed portions of the organism (nose sneezing, eyes tearing, throat gagging). And classical conditioning is beautifully suited for handling such interactions, both theoretically and in an applied way, the latter as illustrated in a method of treating alcoholism. But when we consider the tremendous breadth of data that operant conditioning encompasses (everything that has been called *"voluntary"*), then it must be given priority over classical conditioning. To support this claim, we need only be reminded of the tremendous wealth provided by the infant's random movements. These countless, unshaped biotic activities are only "waiting for" surrounding conditions to be related to. This is where operant conditioning helps in understanding behavioral events. No longer can infantile behavior be looked on as emanating from within in accordance with a program laid down by genes, brain, or by maturation. Such a view is rendered obsolete by a framework that can relate the infant's behavior to the persons and objects and happenings in its environment as causal. With such an orientation as operant conditioning provides, behavioral events become observable, lawful, dependable, and orderly, and they offer foresight and understanding.

We can gain an additional insight into the value of operant or instrumental conditioning from a slightly different perspective. The traditional outlook in terms of voluntary and involuntary may help us out. Although contemporary psychologists are wary about the use of the terms, roughly we may use the word *involuntary* to refer to reflexes and the word *voluntary* to everything else you do.

> When you pick up a pencil, or when you merely ask someone to hand it to you; when you signal the bus-driver, or climb on the bus; when you make a telephone call; when you hum a tune, or glance at your watch, or work on a problem in mathematics—in these and in thousands of other everyday acts, you illustrate operant behavior. [Keller, 1954, p. 2]

I am suggesting that all these samples of so-called voluntary behavior, and thousands of others even more subtle, originate from the myriad, random movements present in the living, human organism at birth. I am also suggesting that they are shaped and perpetuated through reinforcement, the basic principle.

An illustration.   I watch with fascination an 11-year-old girl, Susan, playing a piano with the excellence expected of college piano majors. I recall that, at the start of her pianistic career 5 years ago, she was laboriously picking out the separate keys (responses) to the separate notes (stimuli). Now, through countless "preformed units" retained from many other pieces that she has played, she performs in ways describable in terms of learning by operant conditioning. For example, she fragments her Chopin nocturne into a thousand pieces. The notes are, in Skinnerian terms, the discriminative stimuli, which lead to key-pressing responses. Here's where self-monitoring and reinforcement come into the picture. The young pianist monitors her playing in a way very similar to the way in which she monitors herself while she carries a bowl of soup filled to the brim as she walks to the dining-room table. Any spills on her part are duly noted. So with her practicing the new Chopin nocturne. A wrong tone is instantly "punishing" with a wince on her part (self-reaction) and, maybe, a comment from her mother as well. Thus, wrong key presses tend to be "suppressed," while the correct ones are reinforcing and become shaped as the most frequently occurring ones.

Chaining is also involved in the terribly complicated series of events which we know as "playing a Chopin nocturne." I would suggest the following construct. In the beginning, the instant that our young pianist strikes a given note, she is brought into visual contact with the next note, and so on. Eventually, the notes will not be necessary when each response "cues off" the next response and the entire chain is performed smoothly and efficiently through shaping and constant reinforcement. In the present instance, reinforcement can be translated as *practice*. "Keeping in practice" means "getting reinforced for the correct responses." How? Through self-auditioning, as well as through approval by family, friends, teacher, and by prizes in competitions. After the recital, if the piece is not practiced, reinforcement has no opportunity to do its work, which opens the door to extinction. Months later, I ask my young pianist friend to play that beautiful Chopin nocturne. She replies "Oh, I've forgotten that one." Such a construct as I have here proposed "makes sense" of what we might metaphorically call the birth and death of a Chopin nocturne in the piano repertoire of an 11-year-old pianist.[9]

Ecological Interactions

Following Kantor's (1933) lead, I am including the ecological class of interactions under the foundation stage of the reactional biography because of its apparent validity. As noted earlier the term *ecology* is borrowed from biology: it refers to the study of the interrelationship between living organisms and their environments in a biological sense. The chameleon's change of color with change of background and other instances of protective coloration, the lungs of air-breathing animals, and the gills of fishes are all adaptations to the life circumstances of those organisms.

[9] Perhaps we should say that the piece is only "rusty" and that a few practice sessions would bring the nocturne up to par.

Kantor (1933, pp. 87–91) also uses the term *ecological* in a psychological sense, to refer to interbehaviors manifesting some of the characteristic properties of psychological events such as historical, differential, integrative, variable, modifiable, and inhibitive. The particular reactions that are identified by the term *ecological* are "elementary forms of differential reactions to things based primarily upon the character of those objects" (Kantor, 1933, p. 87).

Ecological Acts as Discoveries

According to Kantor, ecological reactions are "acts of discovery" (p. 87). The child finds out about objects in its surroundings. Daddy's razor blades can cut one's hands; syrup is sweet like candy and is sticky, the piano can be counted on to stay put when one grabs hold of it to restore balance, but not the tablecloth. The window pane is transparent but one cannot put one's finger through it as one can through air or water. And water can be warm, hot, or cold. If one falls down the stairs, one gets hurt. Fire burns. Balloons burst and pop and go away. Soap in the eyes stings. And, if Daddy swings one round and round, it makes one dizzy, and so does the merry-go-round and the carousel at the park. Sirens are terribly loud and scary. And of the variety of foods that Mama puts in one's mouth, certain ones taste good but others are awful and one spits them out.

In an experiment by Kellogg and Kellogg (1933), an ape and a child were reared together for 9 months, and a comparison was made of their behavior during that period. One of the tests that was carried out during that interval was the observation of the two subjects' *first* response to ice in the mouth (p. 105). They did react differently to the novel stimulus, but the incident is important to use because it fits Kantor's conception of ecological reactions as "acts of discovery." For the first time in their lives, the ape and the child each learned what it was like to experience ice in the mouth. But essentially, what all of the foregoing means is that, in the foundation stage, the organism is involved in the earliest and most fundamental discriminatory reactions, as a foundation for further behavioral acquisitions. All together, reflexes, random movements, and ecological interactions constitute the raw materials for behavioral beginnings. In this first stage of the reactional biography, we see the organism launched on a psychological career.

Chapter Summary

Regarding the origins of behavior development, the concept of maturation is best applicable biologically rather than behaviorally. There are possibilities for behavior origin in the fetal environment of sounds and movement opportunities. Spelt's (1967) experiment supports the conditionability of the organism at this stage.

A consideration of biological factors as they condition the psychological development of the fetus leads to the psychological aspects surrounding the birth of full-term babies as well as that of the premature. The cultural warping of childbirth affects this process.

In the reflexes and random movements of the organism, behavior originates shaped by classical and operant conditioning principles. While the principles of conditioning are very pertinent in the earliest stage of behavior development, they operate throughout the life of the organism as well.

4 The Basic Stage of the Reactional Biography

The basic reactions are among the most fundamental of the individual's psychological equipment. Upon them as a basis are developed the great mass of psychological responses which constitute the individual's behavior patterns. Unless the person becomes wholly reformed, we have here the substructure of his future character and intelligence.

[Kantor and Smith, 1975, p. 112]

This quotation from Kantor and Smith helps us define basic interbehaviors. We can more clearly conceptualize them by comparing and contrasting them with interactions developed in the preceding foundation stage. There, we simply noted the emergence of psychological action from biological activities such as reflexes and random movements. That phase of the reactional biography is a transition from the biological functioning of the living organism to a level of adjustment characterized by the historical, differential, integrative, variable, modifiable, delayable, and inhibitive properties of psychological events. There, too, we observed an intimate connection between psychological events and the anatomical and physiological characteristics of the organism.

In the basic stage, biological factors are not so prominent, although they are always participating factors. Speech is a useful example. In the foundation stage, the "organs of speech" are essential for producing the infant cry, the gurgles, cooing, and so on, but such verbalizations may not develop, as with the "attic" or "cupboard" children. In other words, they can be extinguished. However, the continued presence and functioning of speech organs in the basic stage do not determine whether a given child will speak at all or whether it will speak in English, French, or Swahili. The anatomical conditions are necessary but not sufficient conditions. What will determine the particular language(s) that the infant will speak will be the particular language-speaking group(s) in which the child grows up. Thus, social factors appear much more prominently here than they did in the foundation stage.

Let us pursue this example further. It has been said (with tongue in cheek) that in the polyglot nation of Israel one can hear more languages spoken than exist on the face of the earth. But there is pressure on everyone to learn Hebrew, the official language. When established immigrants master the language, they speak it with an accent that instantly reveals the country of their origin. One may speak Hebrew with a recognizable Russian accent, another with a French accent, and others with Polish, German, Czech, or Algerian accents. Their "mother tongue" comes through; the country in which the immigrant learned his or her "native language" proclaims itself. Thus, the basic stage sets its mark not only on an individual's mother tongue but also on one's second- or third-language acquisition.[1]

Let us take as another example the random kicking of legs and flailing of arms of the foundation stage. In the basic stage, both become integrated —the swinging motion of the arms and the stepping movements of the legs—into the individual's basic walking, which will last throughout the individual's life span (barring any interfering anatomical or physiological accidents). But that is not all, for out of these basic walking interbehaviors can be elaborated any or all of the following: running, skipping, hopping, jumping, swimming, skating, skiing, dancing, acrobatics, and mountain climbing. Once acquired, basic behaviors are like money in the bank, to spend as one likes or, more properly, as one's caretakers like.

Bijou (1976, p. 1) has devoted an entire book to the basic stage, which he defines as the period "from the time a child begins to talk to the time he enters kindergarten or first grade." Despite my admiration for his work, I would not define the basic stage in chronological units but in terms of the origin of *specific behaviors* that endure, such as walking and talking. Beyond this minor criticism, Bijou's book must be considered a landmark in the area of literature on child development. He deals exclusively with interactions, not with self-actional entities; he says, for example, "There are no genes that can be directly traced to abilities, knowledge, and problem-solving skills" (p. 89); "An ability is viewed here not as a capacity or 'a possession'

---

[1] The question at this point is "Could one possibly escape from the apparent determinism here? Or, if one practiced strenuously to speak Hebrew like a native and achieved it, would *that also* illustrate determinism?"

but rather as the probability of occurrence of an operant in an operant class" (p. 52). Bijou traces out the development of exploratory behavior, curiosity and play, cognitive behavior (including intelligence and competence), and the roots of moral behavior. All are viewed naturalistically as events involving child and stimulus objects in a functional analysis in which setting factors and interactional history also play a role.

As a closing *introductory* commentary on the basic stage, we offer the following quotation from Bijou (1976, p. 1): "Longitudinal studies show that personality patterns are fairly stable by the age of five, and, barring drastic changes in the child brought about by previous illness, accident, or radical changes in his external environment, persist along the lines observed at this time."[2]

Students of abnormal psychology, the psychoanalysts in particular, search for the origin of adult behavior problems in the early or basic stage of the individual's interbehavioral history. In the following sections, we examine a variety of sources, not necessarily limited to the literature on "psychopathology," to determine how well the data support our conception of the basic stage. Our first case is traditionally classified as an obsessive-compulsive reaction, conventionally considered as one of the "neuroses" or "psychoneuroses." It is especially appropriate because it involves such a young child.

A Baffling Case of Trichotillomania (Compulsive Hair Pulling)

A 2½-year-old baby girl was referred for psychiatric study because of a precocious loss of scalp hair, a condition that had persisted for a year. After an organic basis for the condition was ruled out, the psychiatrist (Phillip Seitz) went to the home of the child and her mother for the purpose of making naturalistic observations.

As Seitz observed the child sucking milk from a nursing bottle, he saw an unusual sight. As the child cuddled herself in the arms of the mother and sucked at the nipple of the bottle, she searched for what few hairs were left on her fast-balding head. When she found some, she pulled them out. This condition of compulsive hair pulling has been labeled *trichotillomania*. After the child pulled the hairs out, she carried them to her upper lip, where she rolled them between her lip and nose. She continued this activity as long as she nursed but stopped promptly as soon as she had finished. The mother reported that the trichotillomania occurred at no other time, only when the baby was nursing from the bottle.

---

[2] Until we arrive at the chapter on personality, I am using this term to mean the sum total of a given individual's acquired reactions.

At this point, Seitz (1950) began a search for the antecedents of the child's disturbing behavior. As a result of his inquiry, the following reactional-biography factors of the child's development came to light. Briefly, the mother described the uneventful birth of the child at term and her desire to nurse her baby at her breast. All went well until the mother panicked and discontinued nursing during the third week because she felt she lacked an adequate supply of milk to properly nourish the child. The baby was switched to nursing from a bottle and was weaned when she was a year old. At this time, the mother put the baby on solid foods and had her drink fluids from a cup.

Weaning proceeded satisfactorily until a severe toilet-training program was instituted, when the child was 18 months old. Scoldings and spankings became the order of the day in the formerly peaceful home. The mother then recalled that during the turmoil of their toilet-training program the child refused solid foods, insisted on having her milk from a nursing bottle, and began to pull out her hair and tickle her nose with it while nursing. During that period, the child was negativistic in other ways, which made her quite unmanageable.

About this time, Seitz (1950) entertained the hypothesis that, perhaps, during the tense, unhappy days of enforced toilet training, the child unwittingly duplicated the earlier, happier days when she nursed at her mother's breast (regressive behavior). The nose tickling suggested that such a condition may have actually existed. From here, the next step was to examine the mother's breasts. Sure enough, examination showed a ring of long, coarse hairs surrounding each nipple of the mother's breasts.

Being a pragmatist, Seitz (1950) put his hypothesis to the test by constructing a nipple with a circle of coarse human hairs around its base. The apparatus worked. The child accepted the arrangement. As she slowly turned the bottle around while nursing, the hairs attached to the bottle brushed against her upper lip and nose. The nose tickling apparently substituted satisfactorily for the mother's breast during the earliest 2-weeks' nursing period. In terms of stimulus function, the "hirsute" nursing bottle and the mother's hairy breast served equivalent stimulus functions. The fact that hair pulling did not occur during the child's nursing at the redesigned bottle supports that construct.

The significance of this case lies in its relation to the basic stage under consideration here. Apparently, a response was so well established during the first 2 weeks of a child's life that even though it was *apparently* extinguished it made its reappearance at 18 months as an adjustment to a stressful situation.

Seitz (1950, p. 188) concludes his report with some *basic* questions. "To what other neurotic traits and psychosomatic reactions may an individual be predisposed in later life by specific cutaneous conditioning of this type? Psychocutaneous disorders of the nose? Nose picking? Hay fever or allergic rhinitis?"

The Locomotive God: A Phobia That Originated in the Basic Stage

William Ellery Leonard was a distinguished professor of literature at the University of Wisconsin. Among his achievements was a translation, in verse, of *On the Nature of Things*, a philosophical poem by the Roman Lucretius (55 B.C.). Despite an illustrious academic career, he lived a life filled with countless fears that hemmed him in within a most circumscribed life space. When his anxieties mounted, at times, he dared not go farther than five blocks from his home. The theme that ran through his multiple anxieties was a terrifying fear of trains (siderophobia) and, later, of other situations.

Phobias Defined

By their definition, phobias are irrational fears of what appears to be a harmless or neutral stimulus object—a fear of elevators or enclosed spaces, high places, dirt or contamination, and so on. Leonard admitted to himself and others that his fear of trains was irrational. However, when he tried to modify his phobia by boarding a train, the terror that he experienced at that moment was real. It forced him to leap from the train at risk of life rather than suffer the panicky feeling that seized him when he was aboard the train. A lifetime of such phobic situations as this are described in Leonard's (1927) book, *The Locomotive God*.

In this book, Leonard tells how he tried to make sense of an apparently nonsensical phobia. He tried to get help from an analyst and others, but finally decided to do it himself. His procedure was to lie down and achieve a woozy condition that he called "twilight sleep," during which he would recall incidents in his past life. Here are some highlights of his reminiscences. A number of episodes occurred while he was a university student in Germany. On one occasion, he was riding a bicycle in the country. When he heard a church bell ringing, he was propelled into a state of turmoil. Another time, also in Germany, he bought a railroad ticket to visit a college friend at his home, but when the train pulled into the station Leonard was paralyzed by panic and canceled his trip on the pretext of illness.

Other recalled experiences took Leonard into his childhood. He remembered how, when other boys ran after parades, he would run away from them. Loud, sudden noises, whatever their origin, aggravated his "nervousness." His mother even got him a toy drum so that, by beating it himself, he could master that fear. Mostly, it was trains that distressed him. They dominated his life so completely that he knew the train schedule completely. When it was time for him to leave a friend's home, he made sure he would not be caught under a trestle with a train thundering overhead. He knew there was "nothing to be afraid of," but, nevertheless, each fright experience had a core of panic and pandemonium. The following recollection of a slightly different sort, but related to the siderophobia in feeling tone, is in Leonard's own words (1927, p. 27):

> When I was alone in the house, aged six, with my sister one morning, a whimsical cow stuck its head into the window of the downstairs back bedroom and lowed at me. She might, of course, have startled any child *qua* cow. I knew cows; I had seen this very cow tethered in the field between our house and the next. She did not startle me *qua* cow. But the feel of uproar and menace was overwhelming.

The Basic Incident

Leonard's reveries, extending over thousands of hours, finally recovered a vivid memory of a terrible fright from a train that came at him too suddenly, too loudly, and too close on a day when he was slightly over 2 years old. He recalled how on the afternoon of that day he, along with his mother, the maid, and the family doctor had gone to the station to meet his father, who was due to arrive on the five o'clock train. He had never seen a train close up and therefore begged his mother to let him walk down the platform alone. She gave her permission but cautioned him not to get too close.

In the next scene, the monstrous, clanging, hissing locomotive was on him, flashing "a fiercely shaking Face of infinite menace, more hideous and hostile than Gorgonshield, or the squat demon in a Chinese temple, with gaping jaws, flanked by bulging jowls, to swallow me down, to eat me alive—and the Thing is God" (Leonard, 1927, p. 12). In that instant, he was convinced that God had come roaring down from heaven to kill him as punishment for disobeying his mother in going too close to the tracks. As the locomotive swept by little Will, it discharged steam from under the piston box into his anus (pain in that spot wakened him from sleep over many years). In his panic, his sole thought was to find security in his mother's arms. Screaming, at last he found her. Years later, with hallucinatory clarity, he relived grabbing the knees of his giantess mother, who was three times his size. She succeeded in comforting and quieting the boy. She even had him touch the cow-catcher on the locomotive to convince him that there was no face, that it was not alive, and that it was not God but only a locomotive. The next Christmas, his father put a wooden train on the tree for Will, and Will was delighted with it "but the excitement almost made him sick" (p. 26). The parents explained that and the little boy's fear of all kinds of noises—cars, church bells, hand organs, and bands as an indication of a constitutional "nervousness."

Leonard wondered how it could be that, as wise and perceptive as his parents were, they missed the precipitating incident of his phobia.[3] But, then, we want to ask what assurance do we have that Leonard had not

---

[3] Note the term *precipitating*, which indicates that there were other background factors, such as talk of a vengeful God.

simply invented the Locomotive God incident out of fantasy? In reading the account of Leonard's phobia, one comes away with a respect for the scientific attitude that he showed toward the memories that he recaptured of his past life. He was extremely cautious in accepting them at face value and did everything he could to verify that they were bonafide. For example, he might write the city clerk of a boyhood hometown for blueprints of a building or map of a city section. Or he would write the police department in another city to confirm the name and badge number of a policeman that he recalled as "Pat" with Badge Number 2. He was thoroughly objective in checking out the data that he stumbled across in his self-analysis. And, finally, the origin of his tragic phobia was also confirmed for him when he discovered a diary that his mother had kept for him. In it, he found the following item under date of June 4, 1878, part of it even in his baby talk (Leonard, 1927, p. 16):

> I went to the depot to meet my papa for the *first* time. I had never been so near to a Locomotive, or "locomoti" as I call it. I was so frightened when it came rushing along past us that I screamed and mama had to hold me in her arms. My papa did not come home from Westfield on that train and so we had to come away without him, but I have been to the depot and seen a "locomoti and the pattenger cars" and I have been talking a great deal about it ever since.

Leonard asks and answers the question, "Can ten minutes' time control fifty years? It can. . . . That afternoon changed my whole life" (Leonard, 1927, pp. 16–17). The following quotation from Leonard's book (p. 17) adds eloquent testimony to the enduring nature of basic reactions that concern us in the present chapter.

> Children's diseases—measles, scarlet fever, infantile paralysis—how parents dread them, for, even if the little lives are saved, they may be maimed, in eyes, ears, or legs, for life. And nursemaids must not drop or bump them—for a scar is a life-long misfortune. We must guard their morals and manners too —training them not to tell lies or to spit or to do nasty things in the clothes-closet. But a scare, with a few shrieks and tears, is soon a neighborhood joke. Yet what was this scare of mine? Sex, self-respect, self-confidence, friendliness to the world, the will to roam and the will to know, wholesome promise, were abruptly disintegrated in the explosion of complete collapse before the attack of alien and incomprehensible power, to be replaced by terror, guilt, shame, and the cringing need of shelter. In a nervous system a little more than two years out of the womb, I was born again that day.

Significance of the Locomotive God

Much of the basic behavior that we acquire is so neutral or "blah" that we can lose sight of it. But Leonard's phobia as described in *The Locomotive God* is so dramatic and attention compelling that we cannot miss it as a valuable paradigm. The fear of trains that emerged when Leonard was a little over two years of age was acquired so thoroughly that it survived during his entire life span. In fact, through a generalization process, it spread into sex, marital, social, travel, occupational, and many other life situations. How much more *basic* could an interaction be?

Touch: Encore

During the foundation stage, we observed the ubiquity and significance of the fetus' contact with the maternal uterus.[4] And, later, Leboyer taught us of the effect of continuing contact in the neonate and in the postnatal development of the infant. Now, touch again comes into our discussion, but from a different perspective.

Touch from a Developmental Standpoint

Viewed developmentally, the earliest rich touch interactions between mother and infant eventually tend to thin out. Bosanquet (1970) points out that, as the baby becomes more active, the mother's attitude changes from one of pleasure and encouragement to prohibitions against touching. " 'Don't touch' must be one of the most common injunctions a baby receives from its mother when it starts crawling about" (Bosanquet, 1970, p. 53). A bit later, sexual connotations creep into the child's exploration of its mother's body and, even more so, of its own genital region, both forbidden territories in our culture. Bosanquet surmises that many adults have an unsatisfied longing to touch and be touched and suggests that, because of "hangups," the keeping of pets serves as a substitute form of satisfaction of such needs. After all, petting and fondling of pets is freely sanctioned. Spouses often demonstrate much affection toward a pet but none at all toward each other.

Touch Viewed Culturally

In Japan, people do not touch one another publicly. At a railroad station bidding each other goodbye, they will not embrace nor even touch each other on the shoulder. It is as if everybody had a touch-me-not phobia. Instead of touching, they bow incessantly to each other, over and over again, at a distance that will grant each enough space to execute the characteristic deep bow without collision. In Western culture, we also have a perfunctory ritual, the handshake—in the United States, pretty much restricted to male–male interaction.

---

[4] These points are enhanced by Gottlieb's (1976) finding that the cutaneous or skin senses are the first to develop in a number of mammalian and avian (bird) species. Thus, touch has a headstart on the later-appearing auditory and visual senses.

Actual cross-cultural studies of touch are rare. However, Jourard (1966) carried out naturalistic observations to determine under what conditions people permit touching by another, the meaning ascribed to touching, and where people will permit being touched. He observed individuals in pairs at coffee shops in San Juan, Puerto Rico, in Paris, and in London. He kept a tally of the number of times each person touched the other. The score for San Juan was 180, for Paris 100, and for London 0. But all of these data are sociological in perspective. It would be more profitable for us to be in possession of more intimate, psychological (individual) data. Such are available to us in the following exploratory study by Marc Hollender.

The Need or Wish to Be Held

Decrying the dearth of studies on the need to be touched, held, or cuddled, Marc Hollender (1970), a psychiatrist at Vanderbilt University School of Medicine at Nashville, Tennessee, carried out an investigation of his own.[5]

The subjects.   The subjects were 27 paid volunteers and 27 psychiatric patients, all women, ranging in age from 18 to 59 years. All had completed high school and were, or had been, married. Because the two groups of women showed no differences in body-contact experiences, Hollender treated the two groups as one. In fact, Hollender found that the two groups did not differ psychologically in terms of the nature of their problems but only in the manner in which they coped with their problems.

The procedure.   Hollender saw each woman for two or three 1-hour interviews. Interviews were tape-recorded.[6] There was no attempt to disguise questions about being held or cuddled other than to treat them as one aspect of a detailed life history.

The findings.   Hollender (1970, p. 446) found that the need or wish to be held or cuddled could be placed on a continuum ranging from "indifferent" at one end to "intense" at the other end. For a few women, the need was so strong that it resembled an "addiction" and determined a way of life (as we shall see later). Most women expressed a "marked" or "moderate" interest, a few were indifferent, and another "small group" reacted with aversion to body contact. These last are the people who act as if they were stung when someone touches them. Why? Well, before we go on with the rest of the

---

[5] My use of the term *need* is *not* to be identified with some presumably inherent or instinctive, self-actional entity. Please read it to mean the same as an acquired response.

[6] Should the reader raise objection to the interview method, let me point out that our "break-through" to knowledge about human sexual behavior was achieved through Kinsey's scientifically rigorous interviews. One cannot do much else in exploring an unknown territory.

findings, let us dispose of this puzzling question. The following quotation from Bosanquet (1970, p. 52) is suggested as a possible explanation. "Touching inhibitions are introduced at various stages in development. Initially in infancy, longings for tactile [touch] contact which are not met and satisfied become repudiated as a defense against the pain of longing. This leads to an aversion to touching later on. So do early traumatic experiences of touching."

In a mentalistic framework, the defense mechanism illustrated here is what Freud (in Brill, 1946, p. 584) called "reaction formation," or the development in the conscious sphere of the opposite of what is demanding expression in the repressed sphere of the Unconscious. Stated otherwise, in a nonmentalistic framework, the individual can be thought of as saying, "What I can't control (my deep longing to be cuddled), I repudiate. It isn't important to me." A kind of denial or even disgust at the mere thought of such a thing, or a sort of "sour grapes" mechanism. In any case, the defense can be traced, in a positive way, to the need to be touched or cuddled in the individual's reactional biography and disgust is one way of handling the problem.

Dissociation of touch from sexual intercourse.   The common notion is that touch inevitably leads to and is intimately connected with sexual intercourse. According to Hollender, this is not so. Some of his interviewees said that they would much prefer *being held* to participating in a sexual experience. Others confessed that, in order to be held and cuddled, they would do anything. They would barter or trade sex for being held, the more imperative need for them. Does this situation imply that touch (or the need to be held or cuddled) has priority over sexual behavior because the former had a prior or more "basic" start over the latter? That seems to be the implication. Later on, it may or may not be integrated with sexual interactions.

Some of Hollender's subjects confessed that they would freely grant a man sexual favors as the price for getting their needs for cuddling met. One stated that all she wanted was to be held, to have someone put his arms around her and to be allowed to relax. And, if she went to bed with a man, he would reciprocate by holding her for a little while.

> When asked what she would do if her sexual partner did not hold her, she responded, "I would say 'the hell with him.'. . . I figure I have to settle for something I don't want to get what I do want, so they should do the same." [Hollender, 1970, p. 451]

Several women admitted to being sexually provocative or to engaging in premarital sexual activity or to involvement in extramarital intercourse as *the price for being held as an end in itself.* Some women cried and acted like little girls to gain their husband's attention and the eventual cuddling.

Others achieved their goal by pouting accompanied by crying or by pouting alone. Are not these *basic* interbehaviors?

The importance of being held is indicated in women's reactions to frustrations of body-contact needs. Feelings of loneliness, rejection, hurt pride or vanity, a let-down feeling, and tension were reported. When being held was unavailable, a woman might turn to her children and *hold them* instead. A blanket held tightly over the shoulder, or a heavy, fuzzy sweater would do the job for others. Rocking, holding an inanimate object, eating, or smoking served to console others.

The childish nature of the wish to be held.   Some women denied the childish nature of the wish to be held.[7] According to Hollender (1970, p. 449), "Many camouflage their childlike wishes from themselves as well as others with the veil of 'adult' sexuality." A few blamed themselves as being dependent, insecure, lacking control, or immature. One woman considered her wish to be so childish that she kept it secret so as not to be laughed at (p. 450). Others openly admitted the childish origin of their need for cuddling. One woman even pinpointed the start of her intense need as originating in childhood. As a little girl, she shared a bedroom with her sister. Every night, when they went to bed, there would be a fight as to whether or not her sister would cuddle her because she could not go to sleep unless she was cuddled. When she happened to be sick, there were no fights because at those times her mother would sleep with her and her mother always cuddled. (There is a hint here as to when and in connection with whom cuddling or being held really got started.)

The wish to be held as basic behavior.   Because individuals are in such intimate contact with their own past histories, they occasionally experience "flashes of insight" into their own behavior. The following quotations from three of Hollender's subjects, particularly the first one, are eloquent expressions of such intuitions. Her interpretation ties together all that we have learned from Liley, Leboyer, Rice, and others. In a sense, we were held and cuddled in, and by, the uterus *before* we were caressed in our mother's arms. Did it start there for some and later for others? Whatever the answer, we can be sure that the behaviors under scrutiny meet the definition of basic interbehaviors because of (1) their demanding nature and (2) their persistence even into the later years.

[Subject 1:] Why does a child want to be held when it cries? It is held and it doesn't cry anymore. . . . The closeness, I think, with the newborn is necessary because the newborn has been inside of you for nine months and suddenly

[7] As students of psychology, we must not understand the term *childish* in a derogatory sense. We should translate it as *basic.*

comes into the world and has to lie on cold sheets all by itself, alone, far away from everything it is used to . . . and maybe . . . something like that just stays with you.

[Subject 2:] Preverbal children will crawl and stumble for a while and they will come to their mother to be held and then wander off, like their battery has been recharged. Adults do this too.

[Subject 3:] It is very important for me to be held. . . . It is one of my biggest problems. . . . Especially when I am upset and feel all alone, I have to be held and told that everything will be all right—just like a baby, I have to be held. It's just a longing that I've always had. [Hollender, 1970, p. 449]

How about men? One cannot help speculating how men fare in the wish or need to be held by comparison with women. Hollender speculated along these lines and found himself involved in another study, this time of men (Hollender and Mercer, 1976). Because our culture considers it "unmanly" for a man to cry or want to be held, Hollender hypothesized that men would find it easier to admit and to discuss their wish to hold rather than their wish to be held. Another factor that would tend to support that hypothesis is that American mothers hold and cuddle girl babies more than they do boy babies (Hollender and Mercer, 1976, p. 51). Without going into Hollender's procedure, comparison of 30 men and 45 women, he did not find support for his postulate (p. 51). In fact, for men he found no significant difference in the means between the wish to be held and the wish to hold. The chief difference between men and women was that there was a trend in favor of women being held over holding, but the difference was not statistically significant. Hollender concluded that men do wish to be held, but less intensely than women. Perhaps culture does not reinforce these particular basic interbehaviors equally for men and women. But there is little doubt that the wish to be held is basic.

The Hite Report

Because of its wide appeal as a best-seller and because of its congruence with Hollender's findings, *The Hite Report* (Hite, 1976) deserves a brief account, particularly the section on touch. The report itself is based on a nationwide questionnaire study of a *selected sample* of American female sexuality. The total number of women who answered questions on all aspects of their sexual activity was 3019 (Hite, 1976, p. xx). But it is the chapter on the relationship of touch to sexuality that concerns us here.

The bulk of Hite's book is constituted of direct quotations from answers to questions posed in the questionnaire. The final chapter, "Touching Is Sex Too," dealing with physical closeness, asks what, among other changes, would women like to see in physical relations. The answer, clear and sharp, is "One of the most basic changes involves valuing touching and closeness just for their own sakes—rather than only as a prelude to intercourse or orgasm" (p. 384). Here follow some relevant quotes from individual responses:

1. Closeness with another person is more important to me than orgasm. . . . If I had to *choose* between the two, I'd choose touching" (p. 385).
2. "General body touching is to me more important than orgasms" (p. 386).
3. "I am a snuggler and a toucher" (p. 387).
4. "Sex itself is not terribly important to me, but physical contact in the form of touching, hugs, embraces, caresses, etc., is most important" (p. 387).
5. "I really enjoy it [touching], but I find that some men do not understand this and so become aroused and want to have sex. Yet I just wanted closeness and affection. So at times, in order to get this, I have ended up having sex, which is not what I started off wanting" (p. 389).

All this echoes Hollender's report. But, for us, the greatest significance of these quotations lies in their relationship to the basic stage of the interbehavioral history, the main business of the present chapter. One cannot, by any stretch of the imagination, believe that the wishes or needs referred to came into existence only last week. They appear to be quite basic, which, for us, means *acquired early* and *persisting*.

Child-Abusing Parents

Child abuse has lately reached epidemic proportions, with the most severe cases occurring in children under three years of age.

[Blumberg, 1974, p. 21]

Most people look on child abuse as a heinous crime. According to Blumberg (1974, p. 22), 60,000 detected cases occurred in the United States in 1972. If one could somehow include undetected cases and lesser degrees of the battered child, the number would surely be enormous. How shall we understand such monstrous behavior on the part of parents who (according to popular theory) are alleged to harbor an "instinct" for loving and nurturing the offspring that they themselves created? The study of child-abusing parents from a psychological angle is only in its initial stages, but let us examine some of the literature in this area for whatever illumination it may throw on a serious social problem.

A Typical Story

Miriam Muravchik (1972), a social worker, tells the story of one family, a story that begins with Lilly, a 10-year-old, neglected, unloved child. Her mother had come to New York, jobless, poor, and illiterate, with only one child. Falling prey to the predators of her slum community, she soon acquired five more children. At one time, she lived with an older, alcoholic man who drank up part of her welfare check. Eventually, a court order led to the removal of Lilly and two of her brothers from the mother's custody and to their institutionalization.

The next scene took place 7 years later, when Lilly appeared before Muravchik accused of child abuse. At the age of 14, she had left her alien home, very much rejected, and had taken up with Carlos, himself a neglected, abandoned child. They had set up housekeeping. Strife soon entered the household. Lilly could not cook, they were in deep financial difficulty, and they were rejected and isolated by both their families. Increasing tension resulted in their screaming and striking each other, and pretty soon their children became the scapegoats. The end result was a battered child (the youngest) with "hematoma [a swelling containing blood] of the right side of the skull, ecchymosis [black and blue area] of the right side of the face, contusions, and fracture of two ribs" (Muravchik, 1972, p. 29). Here, we see two generations of a family each responding in an "unloving" way to their offspring. What is the explanation?

Because poverty was common to both families, one is tempted to seize on socioeconomic deprivation as a likely cause of child abuse. But if it is true, as Paulson and Blake (1969) point out, that the majority of socioeconomically deprived parents do not batter their children, while some upper-middle-class parents do "clobber" theirs, then one must look elsewhere for antecedent conditions. Certainly, Paulson and Blake caution against picking out education, occupation, health, social, or economic stresses as sufficient causes of child abuse.

Psychological Characteristics of Abusive Parents

In a penetrating review of the literature on the child-abusing parent, Spinetta and Rigler (1972) summarized 88 different articles. Their interest was in the psychological aspect of the problem, not the medical, legal, social, or economic phases of it. First they point out the lack of "well-designed studies of personality characteristics of abusing parents" (p. 296). In their review, they assembled the opinions of concerned professional people as to the psychological attributes of abusive parents, to derive the broadest generalizations that might lead to hypothesis testing. Here are some of the findings that they report.

1. A group of 39 men and women imprisoned for cruelty to their children had hostile and rejecting parents.
2. Of 10 mothers who had murdered their children, *all* grew up in an emotional icebox, with rejecting parents with whom identification was impossible.
3. One of the best-controlled studies showed among other findings, "a probable history of emotional deprivation in the [abusive] mother's own upbringing" (p. 298).
4. Sixteen studies are grouped together as offering "further support for the hypothesis that the abusing parent was once an abused or neglected child" (p. 298).

The following quotation puts forward the broadest generalization that Spinetta and Rigler (1972, p. 298) were able to derive from their examination of professionals' opinions about the psychological attributes of child-abusing parents.

One basic factor in the etiology of child abuse draws unanimity: Abusing parents were themselves abused or neglected, physically or emotionally, as children. Steele and Pollock (1968) have shown a history of parents having been raised in the same style that they have recreated in the pattern of rearing their own children. As infants and children, all of the parents in the groups were deprived both of basic mothering and of the deep sense of being cared for and cared about from the beginning of their lives.

Child Abuse as Basic Behavior

We must not overlook two points that need to be made about the findings just reported.

The first point concerns the applicability of the construct of the reactional biography to the abusive parent. The implication seems to be that, if a given individual is to become an abusive parent, then that individual must be put into the hands of abusive parents from the earliest days of the reactional biography.

The second point concerns basic interactions. The implication of the findings seems to be that if a child is neglected or battered, that child is a likely candidate for an adult status as a child-abusing or neglecting parent. Stated otherwise, early behaviors involving anger, frustration, hatred, rage, fury, and brutality become so basic that they are readily available in adulthood for perpetrating on others. In the words of the title and theme of a paper by Richard Galdston, "Violence Begins at Home" (1971). Conversely, "To be tender, loving, and caring, human beings must be tenderly loved and cared for in their earliest years, from the moment they are born" (Montagu, 1971, p. 121).

The Roots of Competence (or Incompetence)

Because of his special interest in the earliest years of the child's psychological history, it is appropriate at this point to review some of the findings and theory of Burton White and his coworkers at Harvard University, as reported in "Competence and Experience" (White, Kaban, Shapiro, and Attanucci, 1977). In 20 years of research in early childhood, White and his colleagues found that, across the various socioeconomic and ethnic groups in the United States, divergence in educability and early competence showed up at 2 years of age. At this phase of development, it became possible to pick out those children who would be competent in school from those who would not be. However, it was not possible to do so at 6 months because behavior development at such an early period is so modest as to prevent differentiation. Between 6 months and 2 years of age, because of the child's greater possibility for language development and expanded world (via crawling), differences in behavioral opportunities can accumulate and, by two years, show great divergence in the behavior acquisitions of different children.

> Along with such variation, there occurs a gradual crystallization within each child [note this self-actional construct] in regard to structures involved in language learning, curiosity, problem-solving skills, and social skill and attachment development. By 24 months of age, reasonably reliable indicators of future trends in these and other fundamental areas are usually present. Furthermore, recent evidence from experiments in remedial education suggest that these trends are difficult to modify significantly from 24 months on. [White et al., 1977, p. 120]

Subjects and Procedure

Without going into specific details, what White and his colleagues did was to go into the homes of 39 children in order to make naturalistic observations of their normal, everyday activities. They tape-recorded their comments and coded their data.

Highlights of White's Findings

Their most unexpected and most frequent finding in the 12- to 33-month age range was *staring* at one object or scene for at least three seconds; in other words, by this procedure the child is gaining "information" and also learning to attend. This is a form of behavior that will later stand the child in good stead in the schoolroom.

While the 12- to 15-month-olds spent far more time in interactions with physical objects, by 33 months of age social tasks doubled. Other social tasks included efforts to please, to cooperate, to gain approval, to gain attention, to direct, to compete, to converse, and to maintain social contact. Nonsocial tasks included the following activities: to gain auditory (and the previously mentioned visual) information, to find something to do, to procure an object, to explore, and to construct a product.

The main goal of White's longitudinal study was to identify those behaviors that contributed to the development of competence in children. They selected children over a wide range of socioeconomic levels on the assumption that they would be studying some children who were developing well and others not so well. Since groups of 1-year-olds resemble each other behaviorally, White was most interested in experiences between 1 and 2 years of age that produced that divergence.

Criteria of Competence Development

Children who were most competent at 3 years of age showed certain developmental trends that began to separate them from the less competent even as early as 12 to 15 months of age. The outstanding criterion was almost a doubling of social experiences of children who were most competent at 3 years of age. Specifically, seeking attention (usually the mother's) and attempts to please someone else (also, usually the mother) were the outstanding social criteria of competence. To a lesser degree, seeking assistance was also involved.

Children who were developing well spent almost twice as much time in "steady staring: at objects, people, scenes, at various and sundry items in their worlds" (p. 133). Note that steady staring is not the same as looking at things randomly and desultorily without really "taking them in." Another outstanding index of competence development was the amount of live language directed to the child. The children who were most competent at 3 years of age had almost four times more language directed at them between 12 and 15 months than children who were less competent. The former also overheard about four times more language than the latter. On this point, White and his colleagues (1977, p. 134) comment "Here, we believe, we have one of the key clues as to how to rear children well." Children who were developing well spent much more time in task-oriented behavior; the others had much more empty time on their hands. But it is not any particular task that separates the two groups, only "a pattern of tasks" (p. 137). "Restoring order" turned out to be another measure found more commonly in well-developing children. This category included such acts as picking up a piece of paper and putting it in the wastebasket or arranging something that is not quite right, like a misplaced book on a table or an ashtray too far over the edge of a coffee table.

Competence in Relation to Basic Behavior

Many other significant data in White's research are interesting in themselves, but my point in referring to his work has been to use some of his findings as a test of the construct of basic behavior. Our fundamental question is "Are there antecedent events in the early psychological histories that explain the later development of competence or lack of its development?" The answer from White and his colleagues' observations appears to be affirmative. White is now projecting an "experimental confirmation" of his findings. Thus, there is hope of someday specifying more precisely than we can today the basic ingredients of a full development of potential for every child. This requires a perspective that will appreciate the full significance of the basic stage of the reactional biography. We may learn to view a successful college career, for example, as beginning, not with high school or even in the first grade, but in the early months in the home. In my opinion, the prerequisites for college (sustained attention, cooperation, task orientation, discipline, and, above all, language) are either laid down or missed in the basic stage. From a simple lack of opportunity, a child can just as easily learn not to attend to stimulus objects as the opposite, and such behavior can become as basic and enduring as its opposite. And so the roots of competence or incompetence appear to lie in the basic stage of the reactional biography.

Genie: A Modern-Day "Wild Child"

In November 1970, there came to light the case of a 13½-year-old girl, Genie, who had spent practically her entire past life in what amounted to solitary confinement. Before we inventory her psychological status at the time she entered society, we shall go into Genie's background as reported by Susan Curtiss (1977).

When Genie's mother married, she said that her life ended. Her tyrannical husband kept her under virtual imprisonment or house arrest. He repeatedly threatened to kill her and rubbed in the lesson with frequent beatings. When she became pregnant with her first baby, he beat her and almost succeeded in killing her by strangulation. The first child, a girl, died from pneumonia and overexposure in the garage where the father ordered her to be kept because the baby's crying irritated him. There were two more children, one of whom died from choking on his own mucus at 2 days of age. The third child, a boy, presented developmental problems and, at the age of 3, was given to the paternal grandmother to be reared. Eventually, he was returned to his parents in much better condition.

Genie was born 3 years later, as unwanted as the other children. Not much is known about her life during the first year and a half. At 14 months, acutely ill, she was taken to a pediatrician, who thought that the feverish and unresponsive child might be retarded. That diagnosis was all the excuse the father needed to isolate and abuse Genie from that point on.

About that time, the father's mother died, so they moved into her home. Embittered by the death of his mother, Genie's father now cut off all contacts with the rest of the world. The whole family was to feel this isolation but "for Genie, it was the beginning of her extreme abuse, neglect and isolation" (Curtiss, 1977, p. 5). For a short time, Genie was "privileged" to spend some time in a play pen in the backyard or on the back steps.

> In the house Genie was confined to a small bedroom, harnessed to an infant's potty seat. Genie's father sewed the harness himself; unclad except for the harness, Genie was left to sit on that chair. Unable to move anything except her fingers and hands, feet and toes, Genie was left to sit, tied up, hour after hour, often into the night, day after day, month after month, year after year. At night, when Genie was not forgotten, she was removed from her harness only to be placed into another restraining garment—a sleeping bag which her father had fashioned to hold Genie's arms stationary (allegedly to prevent her from taking it off). In effect, it was a straight jacket [straitjacket]. Therein constrained, Genie was put into an infant's crib with wire mesh sides and a wire mesh cover overhead. Caged by night, harnessed by day, Genie was left to somehow endure the hours and years of her life. [Curtiss, 1977, p. 5]

We may be sure Genie got precious little stimulation during her years of confinement. Genie was confined in a small bedroom, situated next to an unoccupied bedroom and a bathroom.[8] Bathroom noises were about the extent of her auditory stimulation. There was no radio or television to be heard, and conversations (if any) had to be low in volume on account of the father's sensitivity to noise. The only exceptions were the father's swearing or growling to frighten Genie into silence on the rare occasion when she tried to get attention by making a noise with her body or an object. The enraged father would then enter the room and bare his teeth to Genie and would bark like a dog. If she repeated the offense, he would beat her. Besides those inhuman sounds, Genie may have heard occasional traffic noises through the windows, which were always kept open a few inches. Because her room was in the back of the house, away from the street, there was very little chance for Genie's hearing much more.

Before her progressive blindness set in, Genie's mother tried to give Genie a bit of attention, but as she grew worse Genie's brother attended to Genie's few wants. Coached by his father to growl and bark, but not to speak to Genie, the brother gave no language experience to Genie.

For "play" materials, Genie had two plastic raincoats to touch, an occasional empty cottage-cheese container, empty thread spools, and the like. In the entire room, the only furniture was the potty seat and crib unless one includes the bare floor and bare walls and a bare ceiling light bulb. The only other visual possibilities were a patch of sky and the side of a house next

---

[8] We learn later (Curtiss, 1977, p. 9) that her visual field was restricted to a depth of about 10 feet for almost her entire past life and she was nearsighted to that distance although a causal connection has not been established.

door from two windows open a few inches at the top. These are some of the conditions under which Genie built up her basic reactions.

Things came to a head when Genie was 13½ years old. Genie's mother, blind and afraid to call her own mother (under threat of death from her husband) finally rebelled. Now she threatened to leave unless her husband called her parents, which he did. That day Genie's mother fled with Genie. The police took custody of the girl and brought charges against the parents. On the day the case came to trial, Genie's father committed suicide. Genie, much malnourished, was taken to the hospital for treatment and observation.

Genie's Psychological Status at
13½ Years of Age

Here follow some of Curtiss' (1977) observations on her introduction to Genie. She found that, similar to other "wild children," Genie was indifferent to heat and cold, probably as a function of her rearing without clothing.[9] Since Genie had not been given solid food, she did not know how to chew and had a great deal of trouble swallowing. Her immobile condition over the years prevented her from standing upright. In fact, she was unable to extend her arms or legs, and running, jumping, hopping, or climbing were out of the question. Her walking was difficult and crude, executed with a swaying movement. Her only vocalization was a whimper. She weighed 59 pounds, and her height was a mere 54 inches. She was absolutely not toilet trained and would not swallow her saliva.

Genie's language facility. Genie had no language behavior. According to Curtiss (1977, p. 11), "Genie was faced with learning her first language when she was 13 years, 7 months of age." Outside of her whimper, she was totally unvocal. Her crying was sobless, and her most violent tantrums were also silent. In moments of frustration, she would explode, "flailing about, scratching, spitting, blowing her nose, and frantically rubbing her face and hair with her own mucous, all the time trying to gouge or otherwise inflict pain on herself—all in silence" (p. 10). We are also told (Curtiss, 1977, p. 10) that except for a few words, Genie never spoke. The hospital staff was able to communicate with her, yet they all admitted that such communication was mediated by pointing and other gestures.

Genie's intelligence-test performance. On admission to the hospital, Genie was administered two intelligence tests. On the Vineland Social Maturity Scale, she earned a score that gave her a mental age of 1.05 years. Her mental age on the Preschool Attainment Record was 13 months. Four

[9] This implies that during their reactional biographies people *learn* to react discriminatively to temperature differences.

months later, she achieved an MA (mental age) of 4.9 years on the Leiter International Performance Scale. With the wide scatter on these tests, she was believed to be somewhere at the 2-year level. There were some encouraging factors in Genie's meager behavior repertoire: her maintenance of good eye contact and the fact that she was active, interested, and curious.

Progress report. Curtiss has worked prodigiously with Genie and deserves special honor for her efforts. What are the results to date? Well, according to Curtiss (1977, p. 204), "Genie has language". But when we study samples of Genie's speech after 3 or 4 years of Curtiss' dedicated work, we are forced to admit that Genie's linguistic achievements cannot match, by any means, the sheer effort exerted by Curtiss. Here are some of Genie's speech samples.

1. 10/6/73 (past 16 years of age): "Where is may I have ten penny?" (p. 164).
2. 6/15/74 (at about 17 years of age): "Where is stop spitting?" (p. 164).
3. 4/24/74 (at approximately 17 years of age): "Talk Mama to buy Mixmaster"—translated by Curtiss to mean, "I should tell Mama to buy me a Mixmaster" (p. 183).

There are many other fascinating details about Genie's past and present reactional biography and irresistible speculations about how it will turn out. Predictions about the final outcome are difficult to make. Much depends on the heroic efforts that Curtiss continues to put forth in her laudable attempt to enrich a heretofore poverty-stricken reactional biography. But, surely, part of the end result will be determined also by how yielding or unyielding Genie's basic behavior will be—the nonhuman behavior that she showed on her entrance into society, behavior that she had practiced "vehemently" for 13½ years.

Basic Behavior in a Lighter Vein

Dear Abby:

Awhile back a grown man wrote in saying he liked to chew on rubber objects as it relaxed him. Then someone caught him chewing on a rubber duck and he was embarrassed. Well, tell him not to be ashamed as my husband is the best in the world and he has a similar peculiarity.

When our daughter was a baby, I found her pacifier in our bed. I thought it had dropped out of her mouth while she was in our bed, but later I found the pacifier in the drawer of our nightstand table and I couldn't for the life of me figure out how it got there.

Then one morning I woke up early and saw my husband sound asleep with the pacifier in his mouth! We had a good laugh over it and that evening when I fixed the baby's bottle I jokingly asked him if he wanted a bottle, too. He said yes, so I fixed him one.

He loved it, so I kept fixing him a bottle right along with the baby's. I took the baby off the bottle when she was 14 months old, but my husband still has one every night and he is 37. Please don't use our name as my husband is well-known here. He works on the Space Program. Thank you.

Happy Wife [Van Buren, 1970, p. 6b]

As a guess, where would you place the origin of the behavior displayed by this 37-year-old man? Would you speculate that his act of sucking on a nipple was of recent origin? The right answer can come only from a thorough investigation of his reactional biography. However, assuming that the act began in infancy or early childhood, its persistence into mid-life (at least) would label it as basic behavior. In any case, I would suggest that his response is governed by the principle that present events are a function of antecedent events.

Observational Learning, Social Learning or Modeling

The following domestic situation is a common one:

Mother stealthily entered the kitchen and walked over to the pantry. She opened the pantry door and reached for a can of coffee. She lifted the plastic lid and took out four gum drops. As he watched his mother from a partially opened door, a smile crept across Junior's face. In the past, he had searched high and low for the candy, but without success. As soon as his mother left the room, he ran over to the pantry and got a mouthful of candy for himself. [Karen, 1974, p. 242]

The time between Junior's observation of his mother's sneaky act and his securing of the candy was quite short, but even if his mother had stayed in the kitchen painting for several hours, the same event could have occurred despite the time lapse, whenever the coast was clear. This brings us to an important difference between observational learning, on the one hand, and operant and classical conditioning, on the other.[10] The latter require some surrounding condition to reinforce a particular reaction, directly and immediately. But, according to Bandura (1974, p. 860), whose name has been identified with observational learning or modeling, "Had humans been ruled solely by instant consequences [such as in operant conditioning], they would have long ago become museum species among the extinct species."

[10] Observational learning is also sometimes referred to as *imitation, identification, copying, vicarious learning, social facilitation,* and *role playing.* The construct of imitation is not acceptable to all psychologists. Skinner (1953, pp. 119–120) treats these data as operant conditioning subject to reinforcement the same as other operant responses.

Note the term *solely* in Bandura's statement. He does not deny the importance of operant and classical conditioning. Much of our behavior is the result of direct and immediate consequences but that is not the whole story when it comes to human behavior in particular. People are more than "mechanical pawns of environmental forces" (p. 859). Bandura also questions the automaticity with which operant reinforcers do their work. People *reflect* on the consequences of their action and note which behaviors are appropriate under which behavior settings. By evaluating consequences of their acts, they provide themselves with a guide for future action. They can *anticipate* favorable or unfavorable results of their action and act in accordance with those anticipations.

Learning Vicariously

But there is more to observational learning than that. People (outside of prison) do not live in solitary confinement. They live in a social world, and they note what reactions of those around them are rewarded, punished, or ignored. They learn "at the expense of others" without having to undergo the observed experiences themselves. According to Bandura, this way that people have of evaluating the behavioral consequences of the action of others introduces another variable into the way reinforcement works. People weigh the consequences to themselves for behaving the way somebody else did with certain consequences. Had Junior's mother become violently ill or dropped dead from eating the four gumdrops, his reaction to the gum drops at the first available opportunity would have been different from what it was. He would have "profited from" her experience. Children in the classroom observing another child spanked for destroying a plant do not have to destroy a plant themselves and get spanked in order to desist from engaging in such vandalism. The vicarious experience is sufficient.

How to Peel a Banana

Suppose we bring a child into the laboratory, place a banana before it, leave at once, and watch their interaction by means of a one-way window. Assuming that the child has never seen a banana before, the banana may or may not ever get peeled. But suppose the same child has, on just one occasion, watched a parent perform that operation. The interaction is radically different. The point is then that one can learn how to peel a banana vicariously, simply by watching how someone else does it.

Here are two more illustrations that show how subtly observational learning does its work. Three-year-old Nicki and I are going up on an escalator, side by side. I casually and spontaneously place my right foot on the step above. Instantly, Nicki puts her right foot on the step above, and I realize that I have just served as a model for her. In another case, 4-year-old Kristen has attended her first funeral. She observes many people shedding tears. Kristen sheds tears. She has just learned how to "act" at funerals. These examples of children learning in a social situation illustrate Bandura's (1969, p. 118) statement that "virtually all learning phenomena resulting from direct experiences can occur on a vicarious basis through observation of the persons' behavior and its consequences for them." We should note that some learnings may involve both conditioning and modeling. The violin or piano teacher or the skiing or swimming instructor may model how something is to be done, then shape the behavior of the student as the latter imitates the instructor.

Does Television Teach Violence?

Consider the following (paraphrased) incidents reported by Liebert, Neale, and Davidson (1973).

A Washington, D.C., judge told about a case of burglary committed by kids who entered a building by forcing a skylight. When he questioned them, they told him that they got the idea from a TV program.

Four young boys who needed a human skull for their club's furnishings broke into a Jersey City mausoleum, pried open a coffin, and helped themselves to one.

A 16-year-old boy was arrested entering the cellar of a home. He was wearing gloves, a trick he said he had learned from TV to avoid leaving fingerprints.

In Brooklyn, a policeman's son, only six years old, requested real bullets from his father because his "little sister doesn't die for real when I shoot her like they do when Hopalong Cassidy kills 'em."

In Los Angeles, a housemaid caught a 7-year-old sprinkling ground glass into the family's lamb stew. With malice toward none, he was only experimenting to determine whether he could get the same results as he saw the scheme yield in a television program.

Do these examples prove conclusively that watching television programs showing violence and criminal behavior inevitably leads children into violence and crime? Obviously not, because we could find many children who had watched the same programs and who are still law-abiding citizens. And we do not know what other factors were involved in the delinquencies or attempts at delinquency reported earlier.

Bandura's Classic Study

Why not settle the question experimentally? This query takes us back to an experimental investigation by Bandura (1963), a study that is now almost a classic. Bandura attempted to determine whether children would imitate aggression after exposure to aggressive adult models. He used three groups of children. Group I watched an adult engaged in verbal and physical aggression against a large, inflated, plastic Bobo doll. Group II subjects were exposed to the same model, who now acted in a mild, subdued manner toward the doll. Group III had no model to imitate. There was another condition that prevailed in the two groups that watched a model. Half of the subjects in each group watched a model of the same sex and the other half a model of the opposite sex. This condition was meant to test for effect of the sex of model on imitation of aggression.

To compare models in real life, as he used them in the studies just referred to, with film-mediated models as seen on television, Bandura used the same aggressive models in a film version, which he showed a group of child subjects in the form of a movie. Another group was shown the same aggressive scene but in a cartoon form, in which the female aggressive model was costumed as a cat. This television cartoon version was projected onto a screen in a television console as a television cartoon program.

After the children had viewed their respective versions of the modeling situations, they and the control group were mildly frustrated and tested for the amount of imitated or nonimitated aggression they manifested. According to Bandura (1963, p. 208),

> The results of these experiments leave little doubt that exposure to aggressive models heightens children's aggressive responses to subsequent frustration. As shown in [Figure 4-1], children who observed the aggressive models exhibited approximately twice as much aggression as did subjects in the nonaggressive model group or the control group. In addition, children who witnessed the subdued nonaggressive model displayed the inhibited behavior characteristic of their model and expressed significantly less aggression than the control children.[11]

Sex of model. Bandura's use of both male and female models yielded an interesting finding. He learned that the male aggressive model stimulated more aggression than the female aggressive model. Apparently, reacting with widely prevalent sex stereotyping, children thought the female aggressive model was out of character. But both boys and girls considered appropriate and approved the aggression displayed by the male model.

How precisely did the children imitate? The aggressive models that the children watched were instrumental not only in releasing their aggression but also in shaping it precisely. Children who observed aggressive models performed a "great number of precisely imitative aggressive acts" (Bandura,

---

[11] Note that Bandura's statement is in statistical form and thus constitutes a generalized description of *a group* and not a specific description of the behavior of individual children. (See Figure 4-1.)

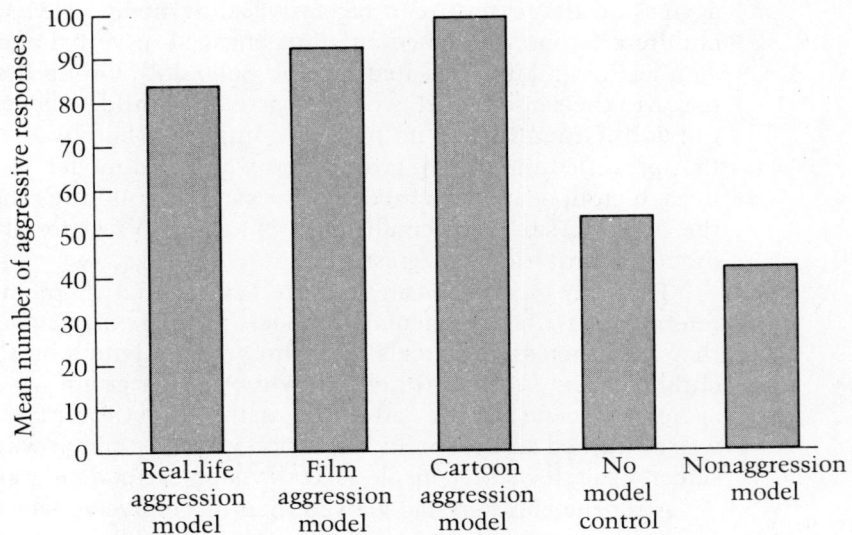

Figure 4-1 Mean number of aggressive responses performed by children in each of five groups. (From Bandura (1963), p. 209. Courtesy of Albert Bandura.)

1963, p. 209) by comparison with the nonaggressive model group or the control group. Their "carbon-copy" responses are illustrated in Figure 4-2. The top row of pictures shows the female model in aggressive action. The middle row shows a boy and the bottom row a girl, both of whom had watched the film version of modeling. The similarity is indeed striking.

Consequences of the model's behavior. Does it make any difference in imitation whether the model is rewarded or punished for the behavior modeled? In brief, Bandura found that children who saw a model, Rocky, rewarded for his aggressive behavior readily imitated his verbal and physical aggression. On the other hand, children who watched Rocky punished for the same action showed as little imitative aggression as a control group that had not been exposed to either model.

In still another experiment, Bandura (1969, p. 128) provided three different conditions for his child observers. The three films showed, respectively, (1) severe punishment of the aggressive model, (2) generous reward of same, and (3) no consequences for the aggression. These findings were consistent; that is, children who observed the punished model showed fewer imitative responses than the children in the model-rewarded and the no-consequence groups. But these differences were eliminated in the next experiment in which three groups observed the model rewarded, the model-punished, or the no-consequences condition. Now in order to promote performance of the

Figure 4-2 Imitative aggressive responses. The top frame shows a female "model" engaged in four different aggressive activities. The lower frames show a boy and a girl reproducing the modeled behavior with shocking accuracy. (From Bandura, Ross, and Ross, Imitation of film-mediated aggressive models, *Journal of Abnormal and Social Psychology*, 1963, 66 (1), 8. Copyright 1963 by the American Psychological Association. Reprinted by permission.)

model's behavior, the children were rewarded when they reproduced the behavior of the model that each group had been exposed to. Thus, regardless of which model the children had observed, the introduction of positive incentives eliminated the performance differences noted in the previous experiment. Regardless of condition (model-rewarded, model-punished, or no-consequences), the children in the three groups reacted in pretty much the same way when they were encouraged to imitate the model. Even the sex differential observed in previous studies did not show up, for girls were about as aggressive as boys when both were rewarded for imitating an aggressive model. Does this mean that, regardless of training, "every man [and woman] has his [her] price?"

Can Children Learn Socially Desirable Behavior from Television?

In an extensive review summarizing an 85-item reference list, Liebert and Poulos (1975) also discuss their own work. While most research on the effects of television have centered on the possible transmission of aggression, some workers have also looked for possible beneficial effects. One immediately thinks of *Sesame Street, Mister Rogers,* and *The Electric Company.* Following their own theory and research, Liebert and Poulos (1975) made an attempt to see if they could teach prosocial behavior via television. They decided to use 30-second spots (the usual length of commercials) to teach cooperative behavior through imitation. They had each spot represent an interpersonal situation that had a possibility for ending in aggression and/or violence or in cooperation and a satisfactory solution for the two parties concerned.

"The Swing."   The 30-second spot opens with a boy and a girl about 8 to 10 years of age, both running toward a swing from opposite sides of a playground. A struggle ensues, each contender claiming property rights, but before they engage in battle, one of the pair suggests that they each take turns and that the other child go first. The last segments of the half-minute drama show each child, in turn, enjoying the swing while being pushed by the other. It all ends happily.

Testing the effect of "The Swing."   Liebert and Poulos (1975) obtained boys and girls from the second and fourth grades of a public school. Some of the subjects viewed "The Swing" twice in a row; others saw one of two commercials directed to children. They then played a game in which they could earn points. When the game was over, the players could turn in their points for a prize, the quality of which was determined by the number of points. The higher the point score, the better the prize. The structure of the game was such that cooperation would expedite both children in earning points. Now, they had to choose between cooperating to their mutual advantage or to go it alone to make certain of their individual outcome. The choice was analogous to the conflict and its resolution as depicted in "The Swing," which these subjects had observed and which the commercial-viewing subjects had not seen.

The results.   Here is the outcome as reported by Liebert and Poulos (1975, p. 91):

> The mean number of seconds of cooperation and competition was calculated for children who saw "The Swing" and for those who saw the commercials. "The Swing" group cooperated for an *average* of 151 seconds and competed for an average of 146 seconds; youngsters who had viewed commercials cooperated for 89 seconds and competed for 207 seconds on the *average.* Watching "The Swing" clearly made cooperation a more likely outcome.

The answer to the question.   In a review of the many studies carried out during the past decade since Bandura's pioneering investigation, Liebert, Neale, and Davidson (1973, p. 157) are still asking the question "Does extensive viewing of violence by our youth contribute significantly to the prevalance of violence in our society?" Here is their answer:

While some quibble, violence continues to become a way of life. On the basis of evaluation of many lines of converging evidence, involving more than 50 studies which have included more than 10,000 normal children and adolescents from every conceivable background, the weight of the evidence is clear: The demonstrated teaching and instigating effects of aggressive television fare upon youth are of sufficient importance to warrant immediate remedial action.

Not all researchers agree with Liebert, Neale, and Davidson's assessment of the effects of television viewing on children. Chaos and confusion seem to rule the interpretation of the masses of data accumulated in pursuit of a solution of the problem. But, if we recall that psychology is the study of the individual, this situation should not surprise us. Any single variable in a child's life, such as viewing violent television programs, is likely to have different stimulus functions. Besides, that condition is only one factor within a multiplicity of other reactional-biography factors. Small wonder that there is no clear-cut pattern when any of those factors are averaged out. Finally, although we do not have a definitive answer to the question of how accurately children model antisocial or prosocial behavior that they see on television, we may be quite certain that they are acquiring basic reactions through observational learning of the children and grownups in their surroundings.

Chapter Summary

Early and frequently occurring interactions become established because of their priority. Two examples of basic interbehaviors were given, a case of compulsive hair pulling and a case of phobia. Touch plays an important role in human behavior, from its origin as basic behavior in the infantile and fetal stage to its operation in the adult.

Abusive parents were themselves abused or neglected in their own basic stage. White's naturalistic observations of how babies acquire competence (or incompetence) as basic behavior were measured against a contrasting view that children come into the world already competent or incompetent. In attempting to answer the question "How basic are basic interbehaviors?" we investigated the behavioral acquisition of a 13½-year-old "wild child." And we asked the question "How much basic behavior do children acquire simply by imitating other people's behavior and its consequences?"

Our entire focus here has been on the enduring nature of the individual's earliest behavioral acquisitions. We can only guess that the reason for this interactional stability is that being first gives them an advantage. Perhaps they do not meet the competition or interference that later interbehaviors meet, for present events are a function of antecedent events.

5 The Societal Phase of the Reactional Biography

Man is custom made, tailored according to the pattern prevailing in each culture.

[Ashley Montagu, 1956, p. 14]

In the two preceding chapters, to make sense of behavior we adopted a developmental or longitudinal approach with the help of the concept of the reactional biography. Implicit in that concept is the notion that behavior development is continuous, which still prevails in our present consideration of societal behaviors. We shall now be studying interactions that flow in an uninterrupted succession with behaviors that originated in the basic stage, which were, in turn, continuous with foundation-stage behaviors.

Let us recapitulate before proceeding with our analysis of societal interactions. In the foundation or transitional stage, we saw behaviors just beginning to emerge out of their biological matrix. In the basic stage, we observed the establishment of psychological interactions that tended to become fixed and stable, and that came to constitute the frequently occurring or enduring activities of the individual. Now, we have arrived at the mature or societal phase of the reactional biography to learn what we can from this vantage point.

In our analysis, we shall follow Kantor (1924, chapt. 7) who, over a half century ago, ascertained four distinct types of societal behaviors: suprabasic, contingential, cultural, and idiosyncratic. Before proceeding with their analysis, I must stress one point. I have purposely avoided the term *societal stage* of the reactional biography in favor of the term *phase* because the former strongly implies a more *definite point* than the latter. The term *societal phase* calls attention to the behaviors an individual performs on attaining adult status in relation with others, domestically, occupationally, and so on. Some of these behaviors originate in earlier phases of the reactional biography. Without stressing when societal interactions were acquired or how they are performed, we note that *by the time* a person enters on an advanced social role we find performance of the following four types of societal behaviors.

Suprabasic Interactions

The prefix *supra-*, meaning "beyond" or "above," clearly reveals its relation to the term *basic.* One might easily guess that suprabasic interactions are an unbroken progression of basic interactions. Actually, we meet here with elaborations and extensions of basic reactions that were built up in simpler forms in earlier phases of the reactional biography.

If we were to study people in various occupations or professions such as carpentry, masonry, dentistry, and surgery, it would be possible to trace such behaviors to earlier and simpler (basic) forms in uninterrupted continuity. Going in the other direction, we could start with the child's basic manual responses that give way to simple piano or violin playing or finger painting to eventual elaboration into virtuoso, concert performances or portrait painting as suprabasic reactions.

Vocabulary

The gurgles and goos of the foundation stage become gradually shaped into the child's words, phrases, and sentences of, first, baby talk and, later, more mature expressions in the basic stage. But suprabasic speech can involve a multisyllabic and far more complicated spoken and written vocabulary. High school is expected to lead to an expansion of one's basic stock of words and college even more so. Both facilitate the acquisition of suprabasic linguistic behavior. In the preceding chapter, Genie lacked suprabasic language behavior because she had missed out on the requisite basic behavior.

Secondary-Language Acquisition

Learning a second language (for example, Spanish) in high school or college provides another illustration of suprabasic behavior. Obviously, if the individual concerned had never before been in contact with Spanish, then foundation and basic behaviors in Spanish are out of the question. They are non-existent. The individual concerned must learn by studying vocabulary lists that literally translate from the known *basic* (English) into the to-be-learned Spanish lists; for example, *table* is *la mesa*. The process is not, typically, the same as learning one's "mother tongue" directly from infancy on.

Deceptive Cognates

We may approach suprabasic behavior by way of deceptive cognates. First we must define the term *cognate*. A cognate is a word in one language that has, in common with a word in another language, the same original word or root but with some phonetic differences. For example, the German word *Vater* and the English word *father* are cognates. But *deceptive cognates* can complicate the picture. These are words in two languages that, despite the fact that they have a superficial resemblance, nevertheless have radically different meanings because they do not share the same root word. If you and I have a nodding acquaintance with Spanish and see the word *ropa* somewhere, we may translate *ropa* to mean *rope*. We would be wrong, because *ropa* means clothing. Similarly, if we stumblingly expressed our embarrassment to someone with the Spanish word *embarasado* (a close resemblance), we would actually have stated that we were *pregnant*, because that is what *embarasado* really means in Spanish. Similarly, if we heard someone talking about being *constipado*, Spanish-speaking people would know that the speaker had a cold, not an intestinal obstruction. And if soap were missing in one's hotel room in Spain, one should not ask room service to send up some *sopa*, because a bowl of soup would be sent. These words are deceptive cognates, not cognates. Thus, one's culturalization may cause trouble if one engages in a direct translation from one culture to another on the basis of a superficial resemblance of words.

During a stay in Poland, I found that many of the young people were well read in English literature but their pronunciation was in terms of their very phonetic Polish language. Thus, the English word *sweater* was rendered *sweeter*; the English word *hotel*, accented on the second syllable, as *hótel*; and the English word *beautiful*, which we pronounce as three syllables, was uttered as if it had five syllables, thus: *be-a-u-ti-ful*. What the young Polish students were doing was reacting in an unfamiliar situation with behaviors that they had acquired in the past in like situations. Kantor (1924, p. 193) points out the limitations of suprabasic behaviors in that they are limited in scope, permitting the individual to react only analogously to new objects and situations. This means that the individual responds in *new* situations (requiring finer, for example, pronunciation adjustments) in terms of earlier-acquired pronunciations of different, Polish pronunciations, which are not as suitable in the new situation.

Contingential Interactions

In addition to routine activities that we perform in our day-to-day living, we are confronted with situations for which we have no ready response. Emergencies arise in everyone's life. A motorist was driving on a California freeway when she discovered that her accelerator pedal was stuck. She stepped on the brakes but that only slowed the car down. And after a mile the brakes burned out, and the heat that was generated set fire to the tires. The woman later explained that her only recourse was to jump out of her car, at a cost of cuts and bruises and a total loss of her crashed car.

That driver was involved in a contingential situation. A contingency is an unforeseen or unpredictable event.[1] Let us assume that the woman had never before been in such a situation. Her behavior that developed under the stress of the particular situation emerged as a function of previously acquired specific action; namely, depressing the brake, which she had done in other situations. But that did not solve the emergency, so, as she saw it, the only thing left for her to do was to jump out of her car, roaring along at 60 miles an hour! That was contingential behavior. Never before had she performed that particular response. It arose on the spur of the moment, situationally. Of course, that woman felt like a fool when the police asked her, "Why didn't you right away simply turn the ignition key off and bring your car to a stop?" In everyday terms, we say, "That never occurred to her."

In our terms, we say that particular set of previously acquired interactions did not occur, apparently because other interactions had priority in her individual history. Others, with different reactional biographies, would have behaved otherwise. Therefore, contingential or emergency reactions are not specific to the individual's past behavioral history. But that dependency on past behavior acquisition is only a *general* dependency, because the individual has no suitable, specific behavioral equipment to bring to bear in the emergency. That does not mean that the adjustment will be absolutely novel or different but the total situation defines the response as extraordinary indeed. Furthermore, the unique set of factors in a contingential situation are hardly likely to reoccur. Nor is the frenzied driver of our illustration likely to respond the way she did if she were confronted with another similar emergency. Therefore, contingential responses are occasional or temporary behavioral performances, not permanent behavior acquisitions. Some of them may be even once-in-a-lifetime activities. As an additional point, let us note that even where people are equipped through training with prepared reactions, as are firemen in fighting fires, no two fires are alike. A grass fire, a barn, a skyscraper, a gasoline-storage tank, will each evoke a mixture of

---

[1] The word *contingency* is used in the everyday sense. The same term also has a specialized meaning in operant conditioning.

routine actions as well as some degree or other of contingential behavior, simply because no two contingential situations are identical.

Emergencies as Contingential Interactions

Because emergencies occur in everyday life situations, that is where we find our illustrations. When bank tellers are handed a note demanding money under threat, they usually do as they are told. But the press reports the case of a bank teller who, confronted by a robber, *pretended* to faint and crashed to the floor. The robber, unnerved by all the commotion, left the note and money behind and ran out the door. That bank teller's pretended faint, never before rehearsed, fits our definition of contingential action; so does the robber's.

Would it be wiser to select as your surgeon a recent young graduate of the best medical school in the country or a reputable surgeon who had performed several thousand such operations as you require? Assuming that a surgeon is likely to be confronted with highly unusual conditions during the operation, the latter would seem to be indicated. Why? Because, out of the vast repertoire of his surgical reactions in the past, if he should find himself in a rare circumstance, even one he had not experienced before, he would have a better chance of developing, then and there, an appropriate measure by comparison with the young graduate without any previous experience. One can think of contingential action as recombinations or rearrangements of preformed, reactional components that take a particular configuration as a function of the complex, specific, emergency *situation.*

Wit and Repartee as Contingential Action

The following examples show that wit and repartee qualify as contingential interactions. A young man, home from college, tries for some time to convey an important piece of information to his father. Finally, he blurts out, "Dad, I'm in love with a girl." The father replies, "Son, you couldn't have made a better choice." Note that there is nothing original in the father's statement. The factor that gives it freshness, "spontaneity," and humor is that such a remark might be expected and unfunny if the son had said, "Dad, I've decided to marry Joan and not Jane." It is the specific situation that makes the difference.

A Freudian Joke

The "schadchen" (Jewish marriage broker) had assured the suitor that the father of the girl was no longer living. After the engagement had been announced, the news leaked out that the father was still living and serving a sentence in prison. The suitor reproached the agent for deceiving him. "Well," said the latter, "what did I tell you. Do you call that living?" [Brill, 1905/1938, p. 662]

What makes Freud's joke contingential is certainly *not* originality but the marriage broker's attempt to get out of his difficulty by resorting to punning. He tried to extricate himself by turning the word *living* to mean not the opposite of death but as a term to down-play the prison existence of the girl's father: "Is that living?" The novelty of the broker's response *in the particular situation* makes it contingential, not the quality of the response.

Graffiti and Contingential Action

Our final illustration of wit and repartee comes from a collection of graffiti or wall writings gathered from a variety of contemporary and historical sources by Reisner (1971). Repartee, in its ordinary spoken form, is fleeting, passing quickly into and out of existence. Graffiti, as written repartee, are preserved and become available for analysis. Especially when there are cumulative contributions by different individuals at different times, they facilitate analysis comparable to a frame-by-frame study of a motion-picture recording.

Here is a specimen from Reisner's (1971, p. 115) book.

A now far-famed homosexual graffito alleged

MY MOTHER MADE ME A HOMOSEXUAL.

[And a witty cynic added]

IF I SENT HER THE WOOL, WOULD SHE MAKE ME ONE, TOO?

The following, collected from toilet walls in New York City, are from an earlier edition of Reisner's (1967) *Graffiti: Selected Scrawls from Bathroom Walls* (1967, pp. 16, 39, and 39, respectively):

DO NOT WRITE ON WALLS!

(Underneath)

YOU WANT WE SHOULD TYPE MAYBE?

GOD WAS HERE.

(Underneath)

I SURE WAS
—GOD

THE LORD GIVETH AND THE LORD TAKETH AWAY,
THE LORD IS AN INDIAN GIVER.

Summing up contingential interactions, note again that there is no great originality in the separate items, taken item by item. Their adroitness and cleverness is bestowed on them by the specific situation in which they occur. That is why we say that contingential action is situationally generated out of what might be called previously acquired or "preformed" acts, but the specific behavior that occurs was not acquired in the past *in the exact form* in which it occurs in the contingential situation, and only *looks* "brand new."

The Cultural or Social Psychological Response

As students of psychology, we must remind ourselves from time to time that our focus is always on the behavior of the individual. But the titles of the present chapter and of this section imply some sort of relationship with society or the group of which every individual is a member.[2] That relationship has been formulated differently by different scholars. For example, Judson Mills (1969) has brought together a number of experimental studies concerned with interpersonal relations, such as hostility and attitudes toward others, beliefs about people, and group pressure and conformity. Such approaches contribute interesting data but they tend to swamp out the individual's interactions, which are our prime object of study.

Shared Reactions

With our continued attention on the individual in our study of shared reactions, our job is to try to isolate a distinctive psychological occurrence from other human events occurring in nature. There are two criteria that we can use in carving out such a datum. On the side of the organism, we can watch for behaviors that a given individual performs in common with other members of a particular group. For example, we may be stationed near a church where we observe some men (not all) raise their hats reverently as they walk past the church door. We may be certain that those that do are engaging in cultural or social psychological behavior. Their shared reactions are also called *conventional* or *uniformity responses*, and we will have more to say about them.

Common Stimulus Functions

Now, if we shift our attention from the responding organism to the stimulus object, we come on our second criterion. What we note here is whether or not the stimulus object operates or functions in the same way for sets of people. If it does, then we have isolated a cultural or conventional stimulus

---

[2] Even Genie was growled at and fed.

function. The church in the preceding example functioned similarly for members of a particular religious group and, therefore, qualifies as a cultural, conventional, or social psychological stimulus function.

It is important to point out that the two criteria that helped us to isolate the social psychological datum are being discussed separately for emphasis only. Depending on the interest of the moment, we may stress either the action of the organism or the action of the stimulus object. But, regardless, we must not lose sight of our basic datum: that is, the integrated, unified organism–stimulus object interaction or, better, field event. With that stricture before us, in the following sections we sometimes emphasize the cultural institutions that are found among various human groups or the shared reactions of diverse cultural groups. But first we need to know something about the manner in which social psychology or cultural interactions come about.

Origin of Cultural Interactions

War orphans provide a convenient illustration of the origin of cultural interactions. Vietnamese and Korean babies have been scattered throughout a number of countries of the world. If we restrict ourselves to those in the United States, let us note what different kinds of individuals, psychologically speaking, those children will become as adults by contrast with what they would be had they remained in their native country. Customs, language, occupation or profession, religion, dress, ethics, morals, diet, attitudes—all can match similar behaviors performed by individuals who were born and reared in the United States. Thus, simply by living as a member of a group and being reinforced in certain ways, one comes to act, in many ways, like other members of that group. How subtly and thoroughly one becomes socialized has been sensed by Užgiris (1977).

Užgiris (1977, p. 105) points out that a classification of our interactions with people versus interactions with objects is erroneous. Why? Because people are also a class of objects with certain stimulus functions, and objects are an integral part of responding to people. For example, some of the earliest reactions between children are integrated with some object such as a toy desired and fought for by both. "More importantly, either through example or specific demonstration, persons lead the child to engage in certain kinds of interactions with objects, adding to the child's network of meanings attached to those objects, *so that the child gains the sociocultural view of even the physical world*" (Užgiris, 1977, p. 105, emphasis added). Apparently, what Užgiris is saying is that it is impossible for us to experience physical objects in some raw, pure form, because we impose human meanings or cultural-stimulus functions. Objects are either "good" or "bad," "nice," "dirty," "nasty," or "fun," and Užgiris adds the British view that "the infant is engaging in communication with others from the moment of birth" (p. 105). If that is so, then it seems that we are being shaped into the cultural beings that we eventually become from the moment we enter the world, a thoroughly social world, in the delivery room.

How to Make a Chinese Out of an American Child

The effectiveness with which culturalization does its work is demonstrated in the following case from Kluckhohn (1960). It concerns a young white American who, from infancy, had been culturalized in a radically different manner from that of most American children. When he visited New York, he was "a stranger in his own land." Kluckhohn's statement follows (1960, pp. 21–22):

> Some years ago I met in New York City a young man who did not speak a word of English and was obviously bewildered by American ways. By "blood" he was as American as you or I, for his parents had gone from Indiana to China as missionaries. Orphaned in infancy, he was reared by a Chinese family in a remote village. All who met him found him more Chinese than American. The facts of his blue eyes and light hair were less impressive than a Chinese style of gait, Chinese arm and hand movements, Chinese facial expression, and Chinese modes of thought. The biological heritage was American, but the cultural training had been Chinese. He returned to China.

Psychologically speaking, the young man was Chinese through and through, in his language, dress, diet, religious and political beliefs, customs, manners, and so on. Apparently, yellow skin and "slant eyes" are not prerequisites for becoming Chinese in a psychological sense. Dwelling among Chinese from infancy on will do the job.

Now, let us survey the seemingly endless variety of ways to behave among various human groups.

On the Alleged Homogenization of Our Planet

It is a pretty safe proposition that, *in some ways*, our shrinking world is becoming homogenized. For example, denim has encircled the globe, and unisex denim jeans are fashionable even in noncapitalist countries, where they fetch a fancy price on the lively black market. The man's white shirt (alone, without coat) is almost a uniform in Israel, to be seen even in Parliament. In Japan, too, the white shirt has become a widely accepted symbol of the business and professional man. Japanese commuter trains, particularly in the summer, present an impressive display of white-shirted men, a scene ripe for incorporation into a television commercial for some superwhitening detergent. If further examples are needed, the Golden Arches of McDonald's are by now a familiar sight in the Ginza district of Tokyo (see Figure 5-1). And Pepsi Cola has recently intruded itself into the communist economic system of the USSR. We should not be too surprised, one day, to behold the

Figure 5-1 A cultural "import." McDonald's golden arches in the Ginza district of Tokyo. McDonald's hamburgers have "caught on" in Japan, and more than 125 restaurants have been built throughout the country. This means that Japanese children can be culturalized to crave hamburgers and french fries the way American children have been. (Courtesy of McDonald's System, Inc.).

Pepsi logo at some oasis in the Sahara Desert. But the spread of specific cultural ways of behaving from country to country must not tempt us to conclude that we are becoming one cultural world. The examples before us are spotty and infrequent. The difference in reactions between national and other ethnic groups exceeds the similarities by far. If this were not so, the Chinese and the Soviets would see eye-to-eye with each other and with the Western world. The fact that both countries espouse communism does not override other more powerful cultural factors that unite the people of each country. Similarly, if this were not so, the Arabs and the Israelis would be living side by side in perpetual peace.

For an illustration of the force of traditional cultural ways, we revert to Japan. About a hundred years ago, the emperor of Japan started the radical custom of wearing Western dress, to spur imitation of the West. That custom persisted down to the present. But, now that the Japanese feel that they have caught up with the Occident, some groups are complaining because the emperor is never seen wearing a kimono. The issue is even being raised in the Japanese parliament: a member is quoted as saying, "This is a good time to reevaluate the good things in our own tradition" ("Emperor Pressured to Wear Kimono," 1978, p. 8a). The kimono is a broad-sashed, wide-sleeved robe that has been worn by both sexes as an outer garment for hundreds of years.

There are many other institutions that Japanese share and that distinguish them. Among others, there are art forms of flower arrangement and tea ceremony, haiku (a form of poetry), their gods, their food, music, their Kabuki theater, their geishas, and, above all, their language. I now propose to concentrate on such shared reactions, in a whirlwind tour from one country to another, to compare distinctive ways of behaving in different cultures. But, first, a procedural matter. When I say, "Japanese do so and so," you, the reader, must *not* understand that statement to mean that 100% of Japanese do so and so. I would ask you to kindly qualify such statements to mean, "more Japanese than not" or "a significant number of Japanese." The actual count is not important to us; the salient point is that *sets of people* are acting thus and thus.

Human Diet

The favorite American meat is probably steak, which most Americans assume would be equally appetizing to any human on the face of the earth. This is simply not so. Europeans generally prefer the less chewy roasts and fried cutlets. And a Chinese or Japanese cook would be aghast at a huge slab of sirloin steak on a plate, would probably consider it an obscenity, and might comment that the cook was too lazy to prepare it properly. For the Asian, proper preparation of meat requires that it be sliced thin and mingled intimately with the vegetables.

Insects as food.   In an article entitled "Insects in the Diet," Marston Bates (1959) points out the abhorrence North Americans display for the consumption of insects, except possibly in sophisticated cocktail circles, which may tolerate such exotic delights as chocolate-covered ants, maguey worms from Mexico, silkworm pupae from Japan, and fried grasshoppers, available in the gourmet sections of the supermarket. Yet elsewhere, according to Bates (1959, p. 46) wherever grasshoppers are in sufficient supply to permit collection, they form a part of the diet of the inhabitants of the region:

> They are especially important in many parts of Africa. The explorers of that continent have described a variety of ways in which grasshoppers may be toasted, fried, or boiled. Ground, dried, and salted, they may be kept for months, making a food reserve. Grasshoppers were also an important element in the diet for those tribes of North American Indians that lived in regions where swarming species occurred.

Bates points out only one exception to the American repugnance to insects—one of their by-products, honey, "a very intimate product at that, for the bees have to carry the nectar home in their crops to regurgitate it into the honeycomb" (p. 44). Fortunately, most Americans do not know that.

Dogs as food?   Writing in *Science*, Miller (1974, p. 394) suggests a possible solution of the recent canine population explosion: "Too many dogs are uncontrolled, unwanted and unowned. . . . Why not consider excess dogs a significant nutritional resource that deserves our attention?" Certainly not in our country, simply because the very thought would be repulsive to many Americans.

But, the fact is that dog meat [or horse meat or, for that matter, any flesh] has sustained humans in history. Miller (1974, p. 394) informs us that

> . . . in many cultures, dogs have been a traditional component of man's diet. In much of Oceania, dogs have been preferred over pork. Early British visitors to Hawaii and Tahiti described Polynesian methods of dressing and cooking dogs and compared the product favorably with English lamb.[3]
>
> Undoubtedly some will raise objections because, in Western culture, dogs have been sanctified as pets. Such objections are without merit. In the first place . . . stray and unknown dogs (which are not pets) are a major part of the dog problem. Second, many animals (chickens, ducks, rabbits, calves) fill dual roles as pets and as food. In my experience, such pets have been every bit as delicious as their relatives with whom I have had no personal relationship. Third, could anyone bestow a higher honor on a pet than to make it part of oneself?

The sacred cow of India.   Famine has been a recurrent theme throughout India's history. Capricious rains, lack of irrigation, and dependence on primitive farming conditions work against providing an exploding population with an adequate food supply. An American or European finds it difficult to reconcile the widespread malnutrition and starvation with the common scene of cows ambling freely about, even in the most heavily congested chief cities of India (see Figure 5-2). One runs into cows while crossing the street or walking along on the sidewalks. Cows block traffic, drop excrement anywhere, and compete with humans for scraps of garbage.

When a stray cow appears in the center of a busy city on any other continent, it is promptly hauled away. But in India it is considered sacred in the Hindu religion, the religion of the majority. Devout Hindus treat the cow as an object of veneration with a status far and beyond the Hindu principle of *Ahimsa*, which unifies all living things. Hindus depend on the cow as a beast of burden, and they accept the cow's gift of life-sustaining milk and cheese, and use its dung for fuel (see Figure 5-3). However, they would never slaughter it or eat its flesh; such an act would not only be abhorrent, but even sacrilegious. According to Williamson and Payne (1959, p. 137): "The Hindu would rather starve to death than eat his cow." She is *Go Motha* (cow mother). As a result of their rearing, the whole cluster of attitudes, practices, and feelings connected with the "holy-cow complex"

---

[3] In *Redbook* Magazine (1966, p. 32), anthropologist Margaret Mead writes that "the Aztecs bred dogs for food."

Figure 5-2   Typical street scene in India's capital of New Delhi.
Roaming cattle tie up traffic and require pedestrians to watch
their step, but no one gets upset over this common situation.
(National Observer photograph by John F. Bridge.)

appears natural, normal, and eternal to religious Hindus. And, because of
their rearing, Americans are likely to look on the Hindu's ways as bizarre,
irrational, and ludicrous.[4]

There are anywhere between 85 and 250 million cows in India (Griffiths, 1967, p. 483). As a capitalist stimulated by the profit motive, an American may make a quick calculation of how many billions of hamburgers
are hoofing it all over India in pursuit of potential (and famished) Hindu customers.

Superficially at least, the Hindu's response to cows appears to Western
eyes to be an inflexible, irrational, traditional institutionalization of a state
of perpetual hunger or starvation in the presence of food. Yet preservation of
the cows may once have saved Indians *from* starvation by assuring a continuous supply of dairy products.

Before the mid-19th century, the tomato was widely regarded as a
curiosity and not as an edible object. Many people rejected it as food, not
because of scientific tests but because they were *told* that it was poisonous.
Of course, its sociopsychological status has been reversed since then; we

---

[4] Vijayalakshmi Shastri, a Hindu, asked a difficult question about George Washington's troops.
While on a tour of Valley Forge, she was told that they starved during the severe winter of
1777–1778. She wanted to know, "Why didn't they eat their horses? That would have
nourished them as it does people in various countries today." What would *you* have said?

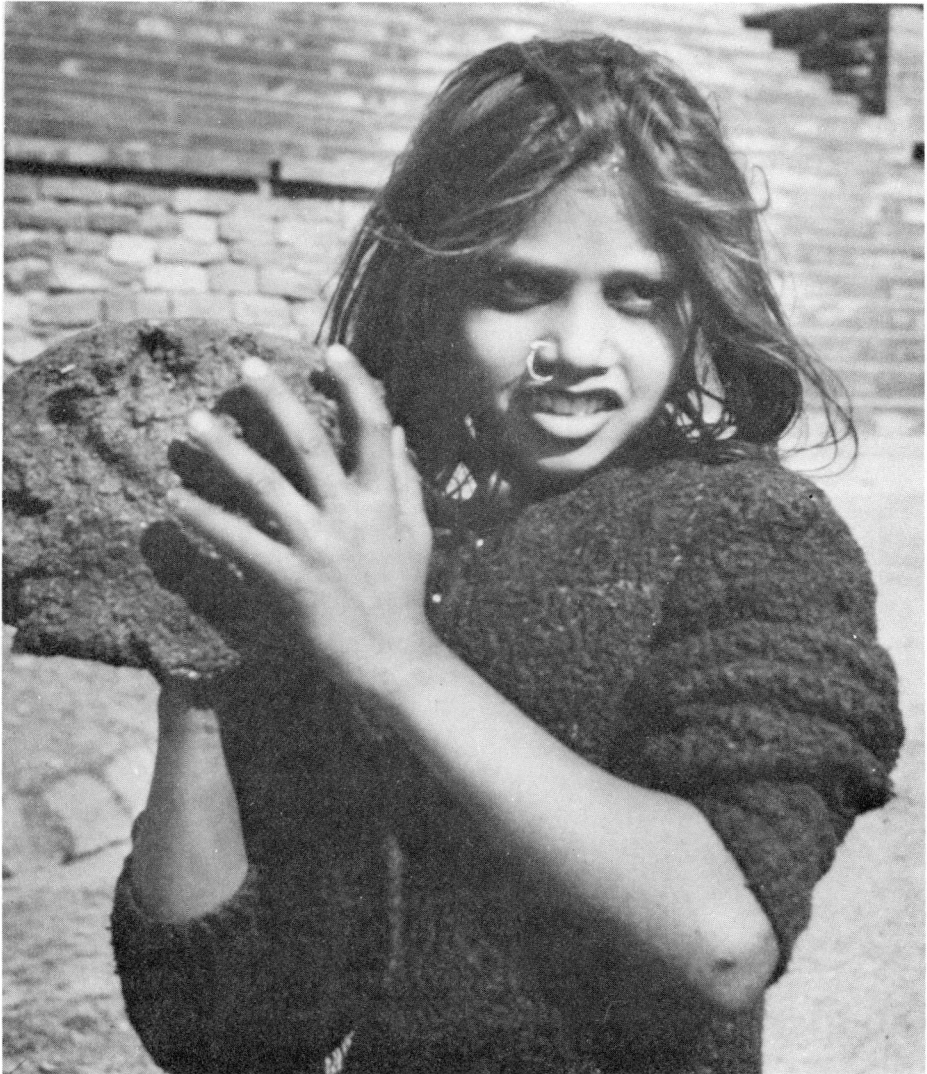

Figure 5-3 An Indian girl shapes fresh cow dung bare-handed. Her activity, which would be revolting to a child in our culture, adds to her family's income: the cakes are sold as fuel. (From Izard, 1977, p. 9.)

now know it to be an excellent source of vitamins A and C. The tomato's earlier status offers a less dramatic example of unreasonable social behavior in contrast to the Hindu veneration of cows, with its apparently far more drastic results.

One person's meat is another person's poison.   Anthropologist Jean Briggs made a 17-month field study of the Utker, a small, isolated group of Eskimos, who live at the mouth of the Back River, northwest of Canada's Hudson Bay and north of the Arctic Circle. She was "adopted as a daughter" into an Eskimo family and lived intimately with the family in their summer tent and winter igloo. In describing the erratic food supply, Briggs (1970, p. 164) says that "on some days there is nothing to eat except rotting whitefish from the dog food caches, not bad for a change but still a less desirable food than the boiled heads of salmon trout and char that usually provide the evening meal in summer and early winter." What would the Eskimo reaction be to White civilization's stinking Liederkranz cheese and moldy Roquefort cheese? At a later point, Briggs (1970, p. 229) writes, "It was hard to accustom myself to a diet of raw fish, eaten skin, scales and all. I never did succeed in mastering the skin, but at first I tried valiantly, though the scales stuck in my throat and the slime made me retch."[5] But the 3-year-old girl in the Eskimo family was "courted with specially hoarded delicacies: fish eyes and skin, bannock, jam and spoonfuls of dry milk" (p. 110). Apparently, among Eskimo children, fish skin and fish eyes are comparable to American children "licking the bowl clean" after Mama mixes a cake or candy. Surely, these dietary illustrations should suggest strongly that any food might elicit "smacking one's lips" among members of one cultural group and retching among members of another cultural group. These illustrations may also glut our curiosity about the variability of human diet, as we proceed to *methods* of feeding babies.

Fashion Cycles in Breast Feeding[6]

According to Jelliffe and Jelliffe (1975, p. 57), "The widespread use of infant formulas based on cow's milk in the Western world is a development of only the last 50 to 70 years, made possible by revolutions in dairy farming and food technology." Up until quite recently, then, the unquestionable source of nourishment for the human infant was human milk. If, for some reason, a mother was unable to breast-feed her baby, a wet-nurse had to be hired to suckle it.

What happened to cause such a radical change that succeeded in substituting the baby bottle for the human breast in infant feeding? According to Nicholas Wade (1974, p. 45), it was a radical shift in moral attitude. He writes, "In the United States, the breast has been gradually transmogrified

[5] Of course, as my colleague Grant Kenyon points out, even within American culture, some individuals have been culturalized to "adore" and others to "abhor" caviar and oysters on the half shell.

[6] This section is based on an article by Nicholas Wade, "Bottle-Feeding: Adverse Effects of a Western Technology," *Science*, 1974, *184*, 45–48.

from its nutritional role into a cosmetic and sexual symbol so potent that an American woman may no longer nurse her baby in public." But, as a boy, I can recall instances of women (in such situations as at railroad stations or while visiting at homes of friends) unashamedly baring the breast to their baby at feeding time, in the presence of mixed company. Now, as Wade points out, there is a grass-roots movement aimed at a return to breast-feeding babies. But the minority of women who have resumed the practice do so in the ladies' restroom, as inconspicuously as possible, or schedule their comings and goings by feeding their babies at home.[7]

Fashion cycles often show strange, erratic patterns. It is hard to predict the eventual outcome of the return-to-the-breast movement in the United States but we do know the effect that the practice of bottle feeding is having on the rest of the world. "Ironically, just when American mothers are putting babies back to the nipple, women in underdeveloped countries are imitating in droves the Western fad for the bottle" (Wade, 1974, p. 45). And with disastrous consequences!

The economic cost of bottle feeding.   In the succession of international conferences on the world's food problems, little or no consideration is given to human milk. Because human milk is "neither grown nor purchased" (Jelliffe and Jelliffe, 1975, p. 557), it is not usually recognized as food when food is being discussed. And, as Wade reminds us, human milk is hygienic and cheap, while cow's milk is neither. In underdeveloped countries, a worker who follows the trend, imported from the West, of bottle feeding his baby, must sacrifice anywhere from 20 to 50% of his day's wages to buy cow's milk to put in the baby bottle. According to Wade, in Kenya alone, the annual loss in breast milk amounts to $11.5 million, equivalent to about one-fifth of Kenya's annual foreign aid. "In Chile, where the proportion of children being breast-fed at 13 months fell from 95 to 5 percent during the last decade, the annual loss of human milk is equivalent to that produced by 32,000 cows" (Wade, 1974, p. 45). For the developing world as a whole, that figure may rise to a billion or more dollars.

Hygienic considerations.   Aside from purely monetary considerations, bottle feeding of babies in underdeveloped countries causes grave health and medical damage to the babies concerned. Human milk has perfect nutritional and antiinfective value for the child, beside being hygienic. No sterilization of human milk is required. But, in third-world countries where illiteracy abounds, mothers are likely to have trouble following instructions in preparing the baby's formula. As a result, they may overdilute the formula

---

[7] This incident provides a powerful lesson on the force of cultural attitudes that shifted from acknowledging the female breast's true mammalian function to endowing the same structure with erotic connotations.

or contaminate it with unclean water, thus creating health problems for their babies. According to Wade (1974, p. 45), illnesses such as diarrhea are more common among bottle-fed babies, and their mortality rate is much higher than for exclusively breast-fed babies. Malnutrition and its consequences are appearing earlier and with greater frequency among the former. And Wade states that medical costs are "usually ten times greater for bottle-fed babies than for breast-fed" (p. 45).

If breast feeding has such clear-cut advantages over bottle feeding, why would women who are already living from hand to mouth adopt such a punishing practice? They do not do it because they must go to work, because (Wade tells us) in Latin America only one out of four women of childbearing age holds a job. It is simply a matter of their mirroring the example of a small, Westernized elite in Latin-American towns. As Wade puts it (1974, p. 46), "The bottle has become a status symbol. Breast feeding is considered a vulgar peasant custom, to be abandoned as part of the process of urbanization." Other culturalizing factors are advertising campaigns by the baby-food industry, which have been accused of encouraging "commerciogenic malnutrition" (p. 46). Indifferent pediatricians have also been criticized for sitting by in silence.

Implications of the importation of bottle feeding.   The chief significance of Wade's study concerns culturalization or the adoption of ways of behaving of individuals in one culture by individuals of another culture or cultures. According to Wade (1974, p. 48), "the stigma of breast-feeding began to spread from the United States and Europe to third world countries following World War II." A factor that facilitated such a spread was the distribution of large quantities of dried skim milk under the Food for Peace program. The program was intended to prevent starvation, but its side effect was to aid and abet the practice of bottle feeding. One important point about the socio-psychological response must not be overlooked. Its adoption by members of a group is not the result of rationally thinking things through and deciding that a given practice of a certain group is worthy of adoption because it will confer certain benefits *if* adopted. In fact, it is adopted *despite the fact* that it may be *detrimental* to the group, just as bottle feeding of babies was unhygienic, medically unwise, and financially burdensome. Why, then, was it embraced? Simply because it was a "status symbol." Bottle feeding of babies was more highly regarded than the "vulgar, peasant custom" of breast feeding. That was "reason" enough for its adoption.

Americans Abroad

Americans go abroad in ever-increasing numbers. Among the countries of Europe, England is a favorite because it is considered to be our "Mother country." Our legal system is patterned after the English, we are both democracies, sharing the same values and customs, and we speak the same language, don't we?

But what "culture shock" unsophisticated Americans experience from the moment they set foot on English soil. Even crossing the street becomes hazardous. One's customary (American) "reflexes" are all wrong because the flow of traffic is "all wrong." In the American system, when we begin to cross the street, we automatically turn our gaze to the left, and as we approach the middle of the street, we check for approaching vehicles in the opposite direction. Such behavior in an English street amounts to gross irresponsibility and is almost guaranteed to get you killed, as it almost did me.

Manner of eating.   Dietary differences aside, there is trouble enough inherent in the way in which the English and Americans manage their common table tools—knife, fork, and spoon. In the busy tourist season, the English go to see Americans eat and vice versa. The Americans nudge each other as they observe the English spreading their food on the *bottom* of the fork with a knife; the fork is held upside down, gripped by the left hand, and it stays there for the duration, while the knife *stays* in the right hand. In other words, the English are as are Europeans generally, *left-handed eaters.* Americans, on the other hand, insist on conveying food to the mouth with the right hand. But, because they cut their meat or fish also with the right hand, they involve themselves in a considerable amount of acrobatics. For example, with fork in the left hand, they take up their knife and proceed to detach a small portion of flesh. But they cannot seem to convey the morsel on the fork to their mouth with the left hand. No, they must first put down their knife on the plate, transferring the fork to the right hand, which in turn transports the fragment to the mouth. Thus, Americans are *right-handed eaters.*

Another difference in the way in which Americans and English feed themselves shows up by observing the food specimens that appear on successive forkfuls as they eat. Each English fork is certain to contain a proper portion of, let us say, meat, potatoes, and peas, all molded together on the bottom of the fork, with the knife used like a bricklayer's trowel. The American, with his customary acrobatics, will end up with each food *in turn* on the fork, one at a time—for example, one fork of meat, the next one of potatoes, and then the peas by themselves, by contrast with the English blend.

The English language.   So far, we have gotten into considerable trouble, and we have only crossed a London street and eaten at an English restaurant. Now, we are out on the town. At Piccadilly Circus, we ask a friendly bobby (not cop) for the subway. He points to an opening to a descending stairway and we set off, go along a passage, up an ascending stairway and find ourselves on the other side of the square at Piccadilly Circus. With the help of another bobby, the matter is straightened out. Our mistake. We should have asked for the underground, not the subway, because a subway is only an underground passage for the English, and our "subways" are the English underground. One could go on and on with numerous instances of perplexing misunderstandings and confusion between people who are supposed to be speaking the English language. I offer a condensed version of such a dictionary.

AMERICAN	ENGLISH
apartment	flat
baby carriage	perambulator or pram
bill (money)	banknote, or note
box car	goods wagon
candy	sweets
chain store	multiple-shop
cookie	biscuit
daylight-saving time	summer time
dishpan	washing-up bowl
elevator	lift
gasoline	petrol
guy	bloke
hood (of a car)	bonnet
letter box	pillar box
livingroom	sitting room
molasses	black treacle
monkey wrench	screw spanner
oatmeal (cooked)	porridge
package	parcel
roast	joint
Sensational!	Smashing!
silverware	plate
spool of cotton	reel
sugar bowl	sugar basin
TV	telly
thumbtack	drawing pin
undershirt	vest
water heater	geyser

Even a brief comparison of the translation of word pairs in this American–English dictionary, plus a bit of imagination, are sufficient to envision countless situations that might give rise to embarrassment, bewilderment, frustration, or even anger on the part of visiting Americans. Children reared

under the two different cultural systems become two immediately recognizable different "end products." Asked, "What kind of a time did you have at
the party?" one says, "Sensational!" and the other one says, "Smashing!"

Culturalization

*Strange to say, babies born to us need not grow up to be what
we think of as human; their humanity seems to be
transmitted to them after birth.*

[Shotter, 1974, p. 215]

The cases of Genie and of the cupboard or attic children, reported earlier,
support Shotter's statement that we are not born (psychologically) human.
Our humanity is "thrust on us." We must now give some consideration to
the process that humanizes, domesticates, or socializes us.

The intimate details of culturalization would draw us into child
psychology, which is a specialized study (for example, see *The Integration of
a Child into a Social World*, Richards, 1974). Our purpose will be served by
a brief and general treatment. By *culturalization*, we refer to the succession
of psychological events, involving individuals, that shape them into people like those under whose auspices they acquire their behavior. As Shotter (1974, p. 215) puts it, "People are made by other people, and they attempt
to make them in their own image." We have seen what might have been an
American boy become a Chinese, complete in all respects. We also saw it in
the variability of human diet, in the cyclical changes in breast-feeding in the
same or different social groups, and in our comparison of American and
English manner of eating and speaking.

Institutions. We must say more about culturalization than a statement
that a person becomes like the various groups of individuals with whom he
or she lives. In every group, there are objects, persons, or situations that are
already endowed with stimulus functions that elicit, via learning, identical
responses from members of the group into which the individual is born. Our
previous example of a church eliciting hat-tipping responses is an apt illustration of an institution.[8] A person such as a president of the United States, a
king, a bishop or a mayor is, by our definition, an institution in relation to
the individuals that share common reactions toward them. Such reactions
could be a posture such as a bow or a form of address ("Mr. President"). An
institutionalized stimulus object can possess any number of stimulus functions; examples are such events as Christmas Day, the Sabbath, the priest,
rabbi, church, synagogue, or temple.

---

[8] The specialized usage of the term *institution* must not be confused with the family or school,
which are sociological, not social psychological institutions.

Where culturalization occurs.   One immediately thinks of the home as the earliest and most important culturalizing medium. The child learns to share not only behaviors common to the family only, but also the behavior of those groups which the family members are associated with, such as the community colloquial group, religious organization, and political party. Peer groups, with their slang, musical tastes, drug or drinking customs, sexual, ethical, political attitudes, come along later as additional socializing influences. And, of course, the school, church, and organizations such as Scouts, Brownies, Campfire Girls, fraternities, and sororities are also culturalizing loci. Nor should we overlook the radio and television, newspapers, comics and books. This list of possible auspices of behavior is only suggestive. The best criterion of culturalization is that process by which at least two people perform an identical or uniform response. Twins who spend much time alone together often develop a "language" that only they understand. This is an example of culturalization, and the twins constitute a social psychological or cultural group because they (alone) share certain names for certain objects that (presumably) no one else shares. And, by our definition, the objects that they have endowed with the mutually shared stimulus functions are institutions. And when Hitler elicited the Nazi salute and the verbal response "Heil Hitler," he too functioned as an institution for crowds of possibly 10,000 supporters.

Characteristics of Cultural Responses

In describing the following properties of cultural responses, we should preface them with a sentence such as "not every cultural response but, among them all, many will show the adjectives we ascribe to them now."

Cultural reactions are artificial.   Cultural reactions need not be based on hygienic, economic, medical, or any rational considerations as we have already noted. Dress need have no necessary relation toward protecting one against warmth, cold, or immodesty. Further examples are using cosmetics and ornamentation; filing teeth; perforating ears, noses, or cheeks; scarring the skin, or tanning it (as under sun lamps); foot binding; wearing corsets, and deforming heads of babies by binding rings. On the island of Madagascar off the southeast coast of Africa, the natives (called Malagasies) breed a Brahma-type cow with huge, spreading horns and a fat hump on its neck. If you were to make a count of the number of such cattle, you would find more cows than people, with the cows numbering about 8 million. Immediately, one thinks, "Ah, these cattle are being raised for economic profit." But that is not so. Those cows are not exported, and they are not eaten or milked. Nor do they have any religious significance, as do the sacred cows of India. Well, of what earthly good are they? They are a status symbol, because the more cows a Malagasy owns, the greater the prestige. Should you comment on the foolishness and artificiality of such a custom to a Malagasy citizen, you are likely to be asked (glancing at your huge diamond rings), "Of what earthly use are your diamonds?"

Cultural reactions are arbitrary.   Should you ask, "Why do Christians celebrate their holy day on Sunday, the Jews on Saturday, and Moslems on Friday?" the only answer is, "Well, that's the way we've always done it." George Bernard Shaw, who tried (but failed) to reform the arbitrariness of English spelling, pointed out the possible consequences of following what looked like dependable rules. Suppose, as a foreigner, you did not know how to spell *fish* in English, but you were familiar with the English words *enough, women,* and *nation.* From an analysis of the relevant phonemes of those three words, you might conclude that *fish* should be spelled *ghoti,* but you would be wrong. And how would you go about explaining to a non-English-speaking person the pronunciation of *cough, weigh,* and *thorough?* My guess is that he or she would consider our pronunciation quite arbitrary.

Cultural reactions are formal.   Many social psychological responses are rigorously prescribed. If you want to address a letter to your congressman, senator, or governor, you should look in your dictionary under "Forms of Address." At the dinner table, one must use the *proper* utensil for various dishes. At a banquet, I overheard an 8-year-old ask his mother, following the salad course, "Mama, did I use the right fork?" Any utensil or even his fingers would have conveyed the salad to his mouth, but he had been too thoroughly culturalized to engage in such barbaric action. Formality is illustrated in religious rituals such as weddings, funerals, and baptisms and in ceremonies such as graduation exercises and parades. The formal aspect of cultural reactions is prominent where groups engage in uniform or shared reactions that must be performed in a rigorous, prescribed, or obligatory fashion. Etiquette and grammar are prime examples.

Cultural reactions are distributive.   Cultural reactions are found in certain regions of the world and not in others. Hewes, an anthropologist, has made a study of "World Distributions of Certain Postural Habits" (1955). From a biophysical point of view, says Hewes (p. 231), "the number of body positions capable of being maintained steadily is probably on the order of one thousand." But of the many possible combinations of trunk and limb positions, cultures in different areas fixate certain ones, and these become the mode. For example, a one-legged resting stance occurs in the tall-grass region of the Sudan and in a few other scattered regions of the world. The deep squat, "with the soles of the feet flat and the buttocks either actually resting on the ground or floor, or only an inch or two above it, has a very wide distribution except for European and Europe-derived cultures" (p. 238). I have seen elderly people in Turkey, India, and other Asian countries assume such a stance—while waiting for a bus, for example—and maintain it for periods of 20 minutes or longer without creaking bones or groans when they stood erect (see Figure 5-4). The posture is equivalent to our sitting in a chair to relax or rest. "In the culture of the contemporary United States, the deep squatting posture is reliably reported among males in the backward mountain communities in the southern Appalachians and the Ozarks" (p. 238). The more than 3,000 languages of the world, dress and native costumes, religions, political beliefs, diet, and customs would also show the scattered distribution of cultural reactions. (Note the stylishly dressed woman from Singapore in Figure 5-5.)

Cultural reactions are diffusive.   Cultural reactions spread from individual to individual and from one region to another. Our illustration of breast-feeding qualifies in this respect. The custom spread from one woman to another among the "Westernized elite" in third-world countries and from them to women in the "lower classes." New slang terms, fashions, and fads show the same dispersion.

Figure 5-4   Elderly villager in the interior of Turkey shown resting in deep squat while fingering prayer beads. Both cultural behaviors may go together, but only in certain regions of this planet.

Figure 5-5 A stylishly dressed woman of Singapore about a decade ago. Today, she may be appearing in denim jeans.

Cultural reactions are powerful.   Cultural reactions may show such fierce loyalty to group institutions that the cost of maintaining them may be martyrdom or suffering. Christian martyrs, conscientious objectors, "underground" operators, terrorists, and those prejudiced against other national, racial, or religious groups are instances of how dominating cultural reactions can be.

Cultural reactions are imposed on us.   At birth, not one of us had any choice as to what language we would speak, what religious or political beliefs we would hold, and so on. Quite unwittingly, we "adopted" via learning the ways of our family, school, church, and so on and became the kind of persons we are now. Simply by exposure to such ways of acting as surrounded us, we became culturalized. "People partake of culture the way they do of oxygen—carelessly, continuously and unconsciously." (Anonymous). (Figure 5-6 illustrates a religious form of culturalization.)

Implications of Cultural Reactions

The preceding sections presented a kaleidoscopic view of shared reactions of different, scattered human groups. We observed that the uniform reactions

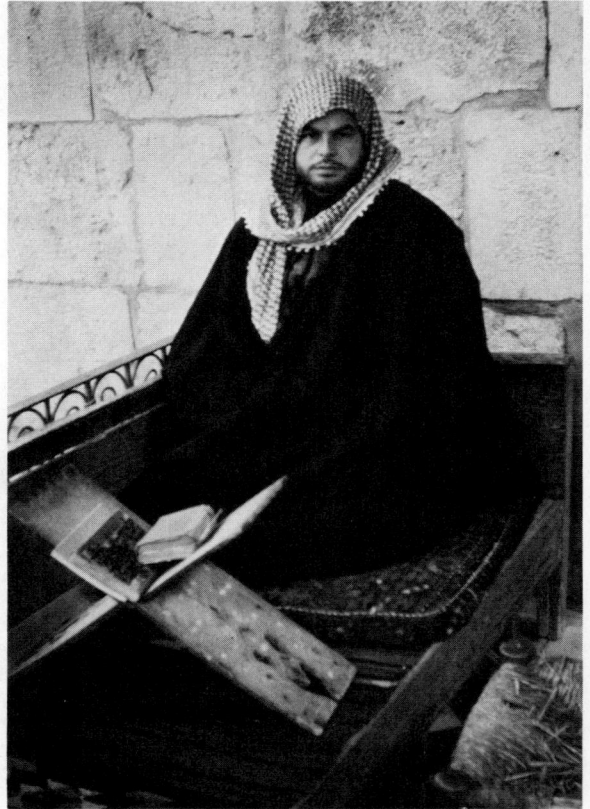

Figure 5-6 A serious theological student of the Koran, Istanbul, Turkey. Note the headdress, robe, and sitting posture in cross-legged, "tailor" or "Turk" fashion, a cultural characteristic found only in certain geographical areas.

of one group might be totally unacceptable to some other collectivity of individuals. People over the world just do not see, taste, or believe the same way about objects, persons, practices, and situations in their surroundings. The difference lies in the way those objects, persons, practices, and situations are institutionalized via learning. (For another illustration, see Figure 5-7.) Clearly realizing the relativity of the institution's stimulus function provides the basis for the following two insights.

1. A comprehension of what culturalization is and how it works should give us greater understanding and appreciation of our own culturalization, a fuller awareness (via self-reaction) of what kind of individuals we are psychologically. Although as an infant and child I partook of my culture the way I partook of oxygen, "carelessly, continuously, and unconsciously," I need not be so naive now, for I can, in a sense, step aside and observe myself.

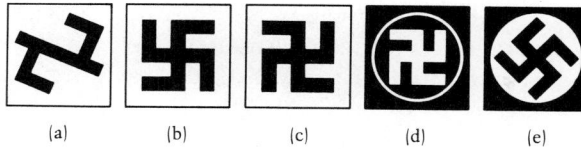

(a)   (b)   (c)   (d)   (e)

Figure 5-7 The swastika—a case of possible spread from culture to culture. (a) Aleph, the first letter of the Hebrew alphabet. (b) A "good luck" sign used by the Navajos for centuries and now abandoned. (c) *Swastika*, an American magazine dealing in psychic healing and psychic experiences. (d) Sign of a Japanese house of prostitution. (e) The Nazi swastika, official symbol of the Nazi party, adopted as the official insignia of the German government under Hitler. (From Krout, 1942, p. 518.)

One of the best books written about Americans is Geoffrey Gorer's *The American People* (1948). Gorer was a foreigner, a Britisher, who traveled extensively over the United States. Perhaps the very fact that he was a foreigner permitted him to see us more clearly than we ourselves could, because he was freer of "the astigmatism which we all invariably have for our own society and its values" (p. 14). One can often understand one's own culture better from the stance of a visit to a *different* culture. It has been said that, if fish were scientists, the last thing they would discover would be water. Because social scientists are first of all products of their own culture and only much later become social scientists, detecting the influence of their own cultural milieu is as difficult for them as discovery of water by the fish. But we must try.

2. A thorough understanding and appreciation of culturalization also help expose its tremendous power in shaping people. Earlier, we saw that an offspring of a Vietnamese couple can become an American, and an American child can become a "100% Chinese." Moreover, if one starts culturalizing a child early enough, that child can enjoy eating fish eyes, and fish skin and scales, or it can be taught to vomit at the same fare. We would retch if we knew we were eating dog meat, while other humans, otherwise culturalized, might find that flesh as tasty as lamb. And what women feel and do about breast-feeding (pro or con) depends on what women they model feel and do. One shudders to think what can be achieved by leaders who exploit the evil in all of us. But control can be beneficial as well as detrimental. Both demonstrate the tremendous potential of culture.

As a way of tying up the loose ends of our piecemeal views of cultural reactions, and as a way to show their potential, we now shift to the story of the last "wild" Native American in North America, who within his last five years, also became a "civilized" American. We shall see how two vastly different forms of culturalization worked on one individual.

Ishi in Two Worlds: A Biography of the Last Wild Indian in North America[9]

Ishi's story starts in the early morning of August 29, 1911, in the corral of a slaughterhouse near Oroville, California. Barking dogs had wakened the sleeping butchers, who soon found a crouching Native American, terribly frightened and near the point of exhaustion. They called the sheriff, who hauled the man off to jail for his own protection as much as anything else. Communication was impossible, for the prisoner knew not one word of English. However, the man was emaciated from starvation, his hair was burned off close to his head, and he was naked except for an old piece of canvas that served him for a poncho. Native Americans, Mexicans, and Spaniards from the surrounding country tried to talk with him, but his speech was as incomprehensible to all as if he had come from another planet (see Figure 5-8).

Kroeber's Intervention

At this point in the drama, two prominent figures appeared on the scene: the eminent anthropologist, Alfred Kroeber, and his colleague, T. T. Waterman, a linguist. Both men eased Ishi's entrance into a world radically different from the one he had inhabited for over half a century. Kroeber got government permission to assume responsibility for the wild Indian and moved him to the anthropology museum of the University of California in San Francisco. Fortunately, Phoebe Hearst, an heiress, had provided living quarters for the museum caretakers. Consequently, Ishi found a perfect, sheltered home in his sudden ejection from the Stone Age into the Iron Age. Ishi lived for 4 years and 7 months in his new world, participating in the new culture to the fullest until his death at about age 54 (in 1916, of tuberculosis).

If Ishi's language was so impenetrable, how could anyone learn about his past? Waterman's knowledge of California Native American languages finally broke the code. He recognized Ishi's language as Yahi, a variant of the Yana tribe's tongue, spoken by the Native Americans around Mt. Lassen. Waterman and Ishi became fast friends. Each coached the other in his own native language. Theodora Kroeber eventually pieced together all that could be known of Ishi's life (1) from what he was able to recall of it, (2) from what he said on a camping trip in his own home territory about 40 miles north of

---

[9] This is the title of a book by Theodora Kroeber (1961).

Figure 5-8   Ishi, making a harpoon for spearing salmon. (From Kroeber, *Ishi in two worlds: A biography of the last wild Indian in North America.* University of California Press, 1961. Lowie Museum of Anthropology, University of California, Berkeley.)

San Francisco, and (3) from facts and rumors passed on by residents of Mt. Lassen. Alfred Kroeber made his contribution by developing a very close relationship with Ishi over the remaining span of Ishi's life.

The Last Wild Indian

During the middle of the 19th century, California was inundated with hundreds of thousands of immigrants from the East. As a result, the Native Americans were pushed farther and farther into the less desirable wilderness and mountainous areas. This is exactly what happened to Ishi's tribe of 200–300 Yahis near Mt. Lassen. Disease, exposure, and shock of displacement, as well as massacre by White settlers decimated his people until only five were left; two men, two women, and a child. From here on, concealment was their only recourse. Eventually, after his mother died, Ishi was the sole surviving Yahi. He singed his hair as a sign of mourning her death, and then walked aimlessly south for 40 miles, ending up exhausted at the slaughterhouse.

Ishi's Past

As a Yahi, Ishi was a member of a tribe that spent most of the year in the great outdoors, requiring the lightest of shelters. During most seasons, the Yahis wore no clothes at all. Women wore a round basket hat, and a breech-cloth for men served the requirements of modesty. A buckskin skirt and a wildcat or rabbit cloak thrown over the shoulder sufficed in cold weather for both men and women. Baskets of intricate design were used for storing and for cooking. Hot stones were dropped into water held in baskets, for cooking. Pottery and wood containers were not used.

The Yahis' staple food was acorn flour made into mush or bread. Salmon, deer meat, and nuts extended the basic diet. For delicacies, they roasted grasshoppers, certain grubs, and worms. They were hunters, fishermen, and gatherers of wild grains, seeds, fruits, and roots. Their digging sticks suggested the derogatory name early White settlers gave them—Diggers. "Ethnologists are agreed that they pursued a way of life the most totally aboriginal and primitive of any on the continent, at least after the coming of the white man to America" (Kroeber, 1961, p. 100).

Ishi's Entrance into the Wilds of Civilization

When Ishi first set eyes on the huge metropolis of San Francisco he could not believe that there were so many people on earth. Policemen, firemen, trolley cars, the crowds in the street, and the shops were, for him, "out of this world." He adopted White man's clothing at once but long resisted shoes. Invited to Waterman's, his first dinner at a White family's table, he imitated the hostess perfectly, using knife, fork, spoon, and napkin in unison with her. Soon he was given a job as assistant janitor at the museum, learning to endorse his check with the signature *Ishi*. With $25 a month as salary, he was able to keep himself in necessities. He soon learned to ride the trolleys and to shop for his personal needs. When he went on a shopping spree, he would return with "bread, jelly, honey, tea—and later, coffee—sugar, canned salmon or fresh, salt pork, beef to boil or stew, sardines, dry cheese, potatoes, beans, dried and fresh and canned fruit, and a choice of fresh vegetables" (Kroeber, 1961, p. 163). He also liked candy, ice cream, and ice cream sodas. He did not like whiskey but considered beer a medicine, to be taken only by the spoonful.

As to personal habits, Ishi had no apparent sexual life, being very reticent with White women with whom he came in contact. Continuing his tribal custom, he bathed daily. He also meticulously plucked out any beard hairs daily, washed his long hair frequently, and brushed and combed it daily. He could have won the Good Housekeeping Seal of Approval for the neatness of his living quarters. Whenever he worked in the museum, he spread a tarpaulin or newspaper to catch any mess and cleaned up everything on completing his job. All his clothes and personal belongings were arranged neatly on shelves or wrapped in paper and stored in drawers.

Ishi in Two Worlds

It is not correct to leave the impression that Ishi became completely culturalized into, and by, White culture. A unique situation, a coincidence that reads like fiction, made it possible for him to continue some of his Yahi behaviors. The museum already had many Native American artifacts, such as spears, bows and arrows, and stone tools of all sorts. Soon Ishi occupied his time at the museum by adding to its collection. Soon he was attracting audiences of as many as a thousand observers (Kroeber, 1961, p. 179) who watched Ishi fashioning tools or weapons or making fire with his simple fire drill. Supplies had to be brought for Ishi from the country. The museum was well repaid, not only with his "manufacture" of display materials but also with his demonstration before the public of a highly skilled Indian craftsman at work. Some of his behavior matched the behavior of "Stone Age" people the world over. In other ways, such as enjoying a movie, in bargaining for an item at the food market, in using the miraculous matches, in his use and appreciation of flush toilets, electric lights, automobiles, and stoves, he shared the behavior of San Franciscans. Ishi lived in both worlds. (See Figure 5-9 for the "Americanized" Ishi.)

Theodora Kroeber's comment calls attention to the full significance of Ishi's life in two worlds:

> He [Ishi] was . . . a living affirmation of the credo of the anthropologists that modern man—*homo sapiens*—whether contemporary American Indian or Athenian Greek of Phidias' time, is quite simply and wholly human in his biology, in his capacity to learn new skills and new ways as a changed environment exposes him to them, in his power of abstract thought, and in his moral and ethical discriminations. [Kroeber, 1961, p. 230]

Idiosyncratic Interactions

We are now ready to discuss the last type of societal behaviors, idiosyncratic interactions, which we set off as being different, and apart from, cultural responses.[10] But how can we reconcile such a segregation with the following statement by Montagu (1956, p. 42): "The evidence indicates quite clearly that everything that human beings ever do *as human beings* they have had to learn from other human beings." Montagu's statement encompasses *all* of

---

[10] *Idiosyncratic* is the adjective form of the more familiar term *idiosyncrasy,* which means "a characteristic distinguishing an individual" or "an eccentricity."

Figure 5-9 Ishi shown after he entered "the wilds of civilization." On the left is Sam Batwi, his early interpreter; in the center, A. L. Kroeber, the anthropologist. (From Kroeber, *Ishi in two worlds: A biography of the last wild Indian in North America.* University of California Press, 1961. Lowie Museum of Anthropology, University of California, Berkeley.)

an individual's behavior repertoire and appears to contradict the possibility of any other kind of activity than cultural, but I think the apparent contradiction can be reconciled.

Let us take Beethoven's composition of his *Seventh Symphony* as a starting point. The component reactions out of which idiosyncratic responses evolve are culturally derived. Some of the themes of Beethoven's symphony have been related to familiar folk songs. Obviously, too, Beethoven was instructed to read music and to combine notes in accordance with the instruction prevalent in his culture, and we know that he studied with Haydn. Undoubtedly, without such culturalization, there could never have been a *Seventh Symphony.* But no one *instructed* Beethoven *how* to write that particular composition. It resulted only from his individual, *solitary* interactions with his notes, paper, pen, musical instruments, his reactional biography. We have already noted how he agonized, scratched, and rewrote passages countless times. Beethoven's composing was in a class apart from his wholesale adoption of his linguistic behavior. The words of his German vocabulary (*Brot, Milch, Wasser*—"bread," "milk," "water") he acquired just by hearing his family members speak in the presence of the named objects.

Thus, what stands out in idiosyncratic behavior is not *shared contact* with institutions but *private* contact with stimulus objects or institutions. The acts that concern us under the present category are original, innovative, and creative. It has been said that the classic composers, writers, and artists are "dead radicals." As innovators, they failed to fit conventional tastes, but in time they themselves became conventional. When they were first played in Berlin, Tchaikovsky's symphonies were considered barbaric noise. Today, they are quite conventional. And it is a matter of historical record that Beethoven's "radical" notions so offended his teacher, Haydn, that all further lessons were discontinued.

The term *idiosyncratic* applies not only to each work of art, composition, and so on, but also to the artist's style, or a distinctive, overall characterization of a creative person's works. It does not take much musical sophistication to recognize a previously unheard work by Bach, Schumann, or Beethoven, and we talk about Hemingway's or Joyce's writing style. The last is an excellent example of an idiosyncratic mode. In *Ulysses* (1934), Joyce attempted an experiment in which he set down not only what people did on a particular day as they went about their work but *all* their thoughts, and he did it without any expurgation or censorship. One passage in *Ulysses* continues without a sentence break for 38 pages. This is an idiosyncratic way to write a novel.

Every individual acquires some peculiar, highly individualistic reactions. For example, one person may eat only one kind of food at a meal—only potatoes or only cabbage, but not mixed. Another puts ketchup on practically every food. People also develop fears, attitudes, and beliefs as individual, private responses. When many of these are unshared, the individual is characterized as an "oddball." It is questionable whether the Peeping Tom, the "flasher," or the child molester become so through culturalization. Because the acquisition of sexual behavior is largely unshared, the situation provides a ready opportunity for the buildup of idiosyncratic behaviors. Much solitary thinking without correction or modification provided by contact with others may easily lead to delusional or fantasy thinking, which involves psychopathology.

The American humorist Josh Billings (a pseudonym for Henry Shaw) said, "It is better to know nothing than to know what ain't so" (Shaw, 1919, p. 53). Certainly, powerful cultural "knowledge," beliefs, and attitudes can prevent individuals from getting a different slant or making a discovery that departs from traditionally accepted ways of doing or thinking about things. The following quotation shows how accepted ways may block discoveries or other, perhaps better, ways of thinking in a number of fields of human endeavor.

Resistance by scientists to discovery involves devotion to accepted (traditional) substantive concepts, methodological preconceptions (antitheoretical or inability to place the novel into the favorite model), religious ideas, professional standing of an authority who spoofs the novelty, theoretical preconceptions (schools), or professional specialization. Such historical evidence led the English geneticist C. D. Darlington to state that it is no accident that "bacteria were first seen under the microscope by a draper, that stratigraphy was first understood by a canal engineer, that oxygen was first isolated by a Unitarian minister, that the theory of infection was first established by a chemist, the theory of heredity by a monastic school teacher, and the theory of evolution by a man who was unfitted to be a university instructor in either botany or zoology." [Wohlsetter, 1964, p. 12]

Chapter Summary

The societal phase of the reactional biography, the final phase, wraps up the developmental picture of behavior acquisition. The individual performs four types of interactions by the time of attainment of the adult stage, although those behaviors (suprabasic, contingential, cultural, and idiosyncratic) may have originated earlier.

Suprabasic interactions are continuous with the earlier basic reactions of childhood and are simply extensions and elaborations of the earlier behaviors. Extended vocabularies, or secondary-language acquisition, professional skills, and virtuoso performances are examples of suprabasic interactions.

Contingential interactions are behaviors that emerge in unpredictable or emergency situations under the stress of the particular conditions. Wit and repartee are examples. Setting factors or situation, not originality of response, contribute to wit and humor.

The class of cultural or shared reactions is set apart by a common stimulus function or institution and by common, identical, or shared reactions on the part of the individuals composing a given group. Culturalization is the process by which individuals come to share reactions with others, originating in the family and capable of, for example, creating an American out of a Vietnamese infant or a Chinese out of an American child. There is extreme variability among different human groups in preferred diet, in customs such as breast feeding, in manner of eating and speaking. Then, we moved on to a more thorough analysis of how culturalization works, what cultural reactions are, and what their significance is. A brief biography of Ishi, the last "wild" Native American in North America, shows the tremendous potential that culturalization exerts in shaping people to its mold; Ishi learned to function in two vastly different cultural systems.

Idiosyncratic interactions, the last societal behavior to gain our attention, are *unshared*, unique, original, and creative acts of individuals. The manner by which they are acquired is totally different from that of shared interactions in that they involve private, individual contact with stimulus objects, even though their component reactions are acquired under cultural auspices. Innovators (artists, composers, writers, inventors, and fashion designers) are idiosyncratic; their followers are cultural organisms. The construct of idiosyncratic action can also be applied to odd or "psychotic" behavior and powerful cultural patterns can prevent the development of idiosyncratic action even when it might lead to progress.

6 Personality

But man is the only animal, if you will understand the locution, that ceases to be an animal in the most significant respect when he becomes a person, and to be a person it is necessary that one live in the world of persons and personal entities, and personal organization, and so on, which we ordinarily call the social order or the world of culture. And insofar as a person is separated from the world of culture, he begins to deteriorate in his attributes as a person.

[Sullivan, 1950, p. 331]

The term *personality* is a noun, and a noun is usually defined as the name of a person, place, or thing. It might be reasoned that, because personality is not a person or place, it must be a thing—a semantic error that has induced clouds of misconception. Popular psychology has conceived of personality as a fuzzy something-or-other, a mystical, inner entity that somehow effuses "charm," "magnetism," "perversity," or "charisma." *Webster's Seventh New Collegiate Dictionary* defines charisma in a theological sense as "a power bestowed upon a Christian by the Holy Spirit for the good of the church." A nontheological definition of charisma is "a personal magic of leadership arousing special popular loyalty or enthusiasm for a statesman or military commander." Certain political leaders are said to possess charisma, while certain others are said to lack it. "It" is believed to be an entity or quality "you can't put your finger on."[1] All such purported explanations of personality are stated in terms of evanescent entities behind, or apart from, actual reactions of people. Far from facilitating the understanding of personality, they actually succeed in obscuring it.

A more positive explanation of personality, but still unacceptable, is phrased in terms of one's social stimulus value for other people or how one affects others. The trouble with such an explanation is that a given person, X, would have as many personalities as there were different responses of individuals in interaction with X. Conversely, a hermit living alone on a desert island and having no social stimulus value would by this criterion have no personality, which reduces to an absurdity.

Personality Defined

Our specification of psychology has been in terms of interactions between organism and stimulus object; that is our basic datum. We are also committed to a study of the individual. Therefore, our definition of personality must not violate that commitment. Accordingly, I suggest that we view personality as the totality of the individual's interactions with the relevant stimulus objects—everything that the person does and can do. This would cover the individual's tastings, touchings, smellings, seeings, hearings, desirings, lovings, hatings, fearings, thinkings, knowings, skills, anxieties, despairs, aspirations, and so on.

Personality Must Be Dated

As soon as personality is defined as the total series of a given individual's interactions with the relevant stimulus objects, one immediately thinks, "But people change from infancy, to childhood, adolescence, middle age, and senility. Surely personality cannot be a permanent and abiding characteristic of an individual." True. The ancient Greek philosopher Heraclitus asserted that "You cannot step twice into the same river." This holds for personality as it does for all else. Everything is in a state of flux; so is personality.

An inventory of one's personality would stop only with the death of the individual. If we were following a student around from one class to another, let us say, that student would continually be adding certain behaviors to his or her total repertory and deleting others. Personality is a dynamic, ongoing concern, so we can only speak of Jane Doe's personality *as of a certain date*. Jane Doe's personality before and after an automobile accident that wipes

[1] Irvine Shiffer has attempted to bring this whole topic down to earth in his book *Charisma* (1973).

out her parents and three siblings can show drastic changes. Are you talking about her personality as an enthusiastic scholar before the accident or after it, when "she is not herself," having become a withdrawn person with no interest whatsoever in her studies? Religious conversion or the ethical and moral shifts of the soldier (prior to induction, during the war, and following discharge and return to peaceful pursuits) also show the need for a durational dimension in the study of personality. From a social, legal, or biological standpoint, Jane Doe can be treated as "the same Jane Doe" over long stretches of time, but the same does not hold in personality study, for Jane Doe's personality as of her eighth birthday is not identical with her personality as of her 21st birthday, which is not identical with her personality as of her 72nd birthday. By now, the need for specifying the particular period in which personality is being assessed should be obvious. After all, what can *you* say in a letter of recommendation about an employee or friend whom you have not seen or contacted for 10 or 15 years? Later in this chapter, we examine some apparently radical shifts in personality.

Personality as an Interactional System

An investigation of any personality will show that the behavior equipment of that individual is not helter-skelter or hodge-podge. For example, the individual does not begin a sentence in English, shift to Mandarin Chinese (which that person *never* heard before), weep and cry in turn, and turn a cartwheel before finishing that sentence. But if that person did engage in such unusual behavior, I believe we would be able to "crack the case" with serious study. Contrary to this kind of imagined "craziness," each person's behaviors show a certain organization, coherence, or order. They fall into some sort of pattern or system, some of which are stable and enduring. Both students and professors behave in certain expected ways in the classroom, in the tavern, on the golf course, or in Sunday school.

What about So-Called Behavior Disorganization?

But do not the "insane" carry out "crazy" actions? I believe that when we come to the topic of "personality disorders" in the next chapter, we shall find that they, too, are not chaotic—they make sense. For example, the ravings of the "maniac" can be understood in terms of past behavior. They are in the language that was acquired, and refer to things that were experienced, in the reactional biography. Even the so-called insanities permit classification (systematization), so that personality interactions may be classed under such categories as schizophrenic, paranoiac, hysteric, and obsessive-compulsive and may be dealt with accordingly. Thus, even so-called behavior disorganization can be expected to show organization.

The Organism as Host

To refine and extend my definition of personality and to provide an additional insight into the concept of personality, I now offer some thoughts from a provocative article, "The Organism as Host" by Donald Baer (1976). It is only fair to say that my presentation of his essay is both selective and colored perhaps by my own theoretical position. I should also point out that Baer uses a metaphor that stresses an objective conception of personality in terms of the component reactions—nothing above or beyond that.

Baer starts by pointing out that, in writing up a lab report on learning, a student may comment that "the organism was reinforced" (p. 87). Actually, "organisms are not reinforced; responses are" (p. 87). Whenever we say that organisms learn, the procedures that eventuate in learning do so by reinforcing one response instead of another or by reinforcing a particular response in one stimulus setting instead of another (discrimination). Thus, one does something not to the organism but to its responses, and it is not the organism that changes but the responses of that organism that show change.

Baer goes on to show that even an organismic variable (such as hunger or thirst) can be stated in terms of a stimulus operation; that is, as an absent stimulus instead of "a deprived organism" (p. 88). In my terms, the farther away we move from a focus on the organism, the more interactional or interbehavioral we may become. Baer shows that even the self-actional "instincts" can be formulated "in terms of eliciting stimuli and elicited responses, then, once again we have a statement, not about the primal organism, but only about some of its responses and their controlling stimuli" (p. 89).

Next, Baer talks about responses as the basic data with which he deals. He says,

> The responses are the basic entities of this account. They lead lives of their own, dictated by their separate interactions with the surrounding environment, and by their interactions with one another, because, to a considerable extent, they are the surrounding environment of one another. However, they lead their own lives as guests of the organism; the organism is their host." (Baer, 1976, p. 89)

"The first and perhaps most obvious implication is that organisms do not truly have traits. They have guests; but the guests can come and go as individuals" (Baer, 1976, p. 89). As separate entities, the individual behaviors will "come and go" in accordance with the rules of conditioning governing each. Should the environment treat a number of responses alike, they might coalesce and become a group or class. If they covaried together, they would reflect predictability. But they could also have a different fate through a differential reinforcement and depart or be incorporated into a different class. "Thus, traits are artifacts of the environment: To the extent that the environment has been simple and uniform, an organism may contain a number of very large response classes, and thereby appear to be characterized by traits" (p. 90).[2] But if the organism is situated in a complex behavioral setting, the resulting responses may be highly specific and varied and numerous, making prediction more difficult with probable charges of an inconsistent personality.

"However," quips Baer (1976, p. 90), "those others who view the organism essentially as host will not complain: Why blame the host for the varied lives pursued by the guests?"

Implications of Baer's metaphor.   Baer's metaphor of the organism as host and responses as guests, from my standpoint, properly assigns the organism *as* organism a very incidental role. Stress is placed on the separate destiny of the specific reactions organized in relation to the organism and governed not by the organism, but by "the environment." It requires only one additional step to a full interbehavioral conception of *interactions* involving, on the one hand, stimulus objects and, on the other hand, organismic activities. But the organism and stimulus object are only the loci between which psychological events occur. Baer's metaphor chiefly helps to supplant the organism as the locus of an imaginary theater, from within which the self-actional drama has been alleged to have proceeded.

Every Personality Is Unique

Baer called our attention to the need for dealing *specifically* with the reactions collectively referred to as *personality*. When one considers the number of the reactions we are dealing with and the differential destinies of their "comings and goings," it is not difficult to understand how each personality is unique. From the very beginning, each organism is a separate and distinct biological entity. Thus, my personality becomes organized with me as a locus and your personality with you as a locus. And, because we cannot occupy the same space at the same time, our interactions are differentially reinforced with different outcomes. This is the way I understand the fact that each personality is unique.

Uniqueness is not peculiar to psychology. It prevails in every field. For example, in astronomy, no two solar systems are alike, and no two planets in our own solar system are identical with each other. And no two oak trees match each other in every respect. When I pass people in the street, my amazement never ceases over the fact that I have not yet observed duplicate

---

[2] The term *contain* should not be understood self-actionally but in terms of Baer's metaphor of organism as host.

faces.[3] "Albert Jay Nock called this the greatest of miracles, the continued production of millions of human beings 'guaranteed no two alike!' " (Goode, 1972, p. 3).

Roger Williams, a biochemist, has written a book, *Biochemical Individuality* (1963) that effectively demonstrates not only the uniqueness of the organism but that of the organs and systems as well. According to Williams, stomachs, for example, vary tremendously in size and shape in a range that is considered normal: "Some stomachs hold six or eight times as much as others" (p. 22). The emptying time of stomachs and still other features also show marked variability. (See Figure 6-1.)

The uniqueness of personality, then, need not disturb us any more than the unique data of any other scientist. Actually, if we took the trouble to inventory the personality interactions of different individuals, we would find that the difference between them can be accounted for by the fact that a highly developed personality has a far greater number of interactions than a "deprived" or "mentally retarded" person. Another way in which two people can achieve their uniqueness is in the kinds of component reactions each acquires. One person excels in mechanical skills, another in arts or crafts. Thus, the uniqueness of personality is not evanescent but can be pinned down to the number, varieties, and ways of performing all of the constituent reactions organized into a personality system. Above all else, the reactional biography provides a unique set of conditions during which individuals acquire their constituent personality interactions.

Loneliness

We wander through life in a semidarkness where none of us can distinguish exactly the features of his neighbors; only from time to time through some experience we have with our companion or through some remark he passes, he stands for a moment close to us as though illuminated by a flash of lightning.

Albert Schweitzer

Thomas Wolfe, in *You Can't Go Home Again*, characterized loneliness as "the central and inevitable experience of every man." The psychological literature on loneliness is practically nonexistent, but poets and writers have recognized it. But Skinner is an exception. The following quotation from *Science and Human Behavior* (Skinner, 1953, p. 165) packs a powerful-

[3] Are twins an exception or do we *perceive* them as identical in the same way as it is said that to Asians all Westerners look alike?

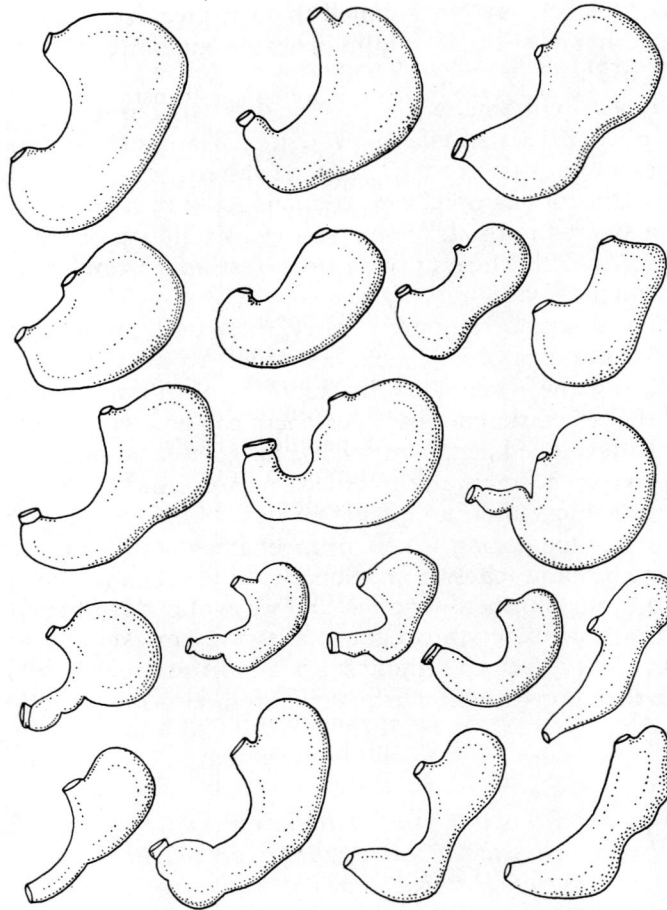

Figure 6-1 Note the marked variation in the size and shape of human stomachs. The uniqueness characteristic of personality also operates in the biological realm, as shown by comparisons of stomachs, livers, nerve distributions, or finger prints. Does the same hold for the data of astronomy? (From Anson, 1950, p. 287.)

ly creditable description of the data of loneliness and a satisfying interpretation as well:

> The condition which the layman calls loneliness, for example, appears to be a mild form of frustration due to the interruption of an established sequence of responses which have been positively reinforced by the social environment. The

lonely man has no one to talk to. No matter where he turns, powerful behavior has no chance to be effective. Loneliness which is due to the absence of a single person who has supplied reinforcement in the form of affection may be especially profound, as the lovesick individual demonstrates. The loneliness of the amiable man who finds himself among strangers for a long time will be of a different character. A child lost in a large crowd suffers in still a different way: all the behavior which has been previously reinforced by the appearance of his mother or father now fails; he looks about but does not see them; he calls and cries, but they do not answer.

The Lonely Crowd. David Riesman in *The Lonely Crowd* (Riesman, Glazer, and Denney, 1953, p. 23), sees loneliness as an affliction of contemporary society, particularly people who are "other-directed." A society of high growth potential encourages adherence to tradition and conformity. The result is tradition-directed people. A society of transitional population growth encourages early acquisition in the lives of its members, of an internalized set of goals, thus developing inner-directed people. A society of incipient population decline encourages the development of "a social character whose conformity is insured by [the] tendency to be sensitized to the expectations and preferences of others. These I shall term *other-directed* people and the society in which they live [is] *dependent on other-direction*" (Riesman, Glazer, and Denney, 1953, p. 8). My own understanding is that when the days of easy success are over (and population growth is about to decline) there is greater dependency on others for success. All of these ideas, however, are hypotheses, not hard facts.

One way to understand the "other-directed" type of character prevalent in our society of incipient population decline is to contrast it with the "inner-directed" type of character. The latter, early in life, developed what Riesman and his associates, in self-actional terms, called "an internalized set of goals" (p. 23). Riesman (personal communication, 1978) points out that the "internalized goals have been adopted from parents and other authoritative adults. 'Inner-directed' and 'other-directed' alike conform, as all human beings must do unless they are autistic, but to different audiences. The 'inner-directed' person appears more independent because the audience has been internalized and is not visible." By contrast with the "other-directed," the "inner-directed" feel that they have control of their lives, are strong, self-reliant, independent, hard-working, ambitious, and stable. It is as if the "inner-directed" had a psychological gyroscope to keep them on course.

The "other-directed" people are characterized as being shallower, friendlier, and more dependent on approval from their peers. Because their contemporaries provide the source of direction for their lives, they are very sensitive to signals from their contemporaries, either directly or indirectly, through friends and the mass media. Their goals shift with changing signals sent out by others.

Now, Riesman and his associates point out that "while all people want and need to be liked by some of the people some of the time, it is only the modern 'other-directed' types who make this their chief source of direction and chief area of sensitivity" (Riesman, Glazer, and Denney, 1953, p. 38). By contrast, the "inner-directed" remain stable even when social approval is not available.

Another way in which the two types differ is in the handling of their children. The "inner-directed" parents would show their children how they might have fallen short of their own (their children's own) standards and that they must surpass those standards. "Other-directed" parents would operate in a wider, socialized framework. They would be more permissive and might be anxious about their offspring, not for failing to come up to their own standards but for not being popular or for not conforming to their peer-group standards. Such standards are reinforced through pressures from the peer group, the school, mass media, and popular culture. Let one sixth-grader "con" her mother into buying her a pair of boots, and any other sixth-grader has leverage against her other-directed mother's resistance toward the purchase of same.

Now, how does loneliness enter the picture? Other-directed people "stress the dangers of aloneness and the virtues of group-mindedness" (Riesman, Glazer, and Denney, 1953, p. 183). Beware of success, for success may only succeed in ostracizing one from the group; one must not depart too far from the group norm for it may bring loneliness. But does the "other-directed" person achieve adjustment in clinging to the group? Not according to Riesman. Such a person becomes "anomic," which Riesman would like to define as "maladjusted" except for the negative connotations of that term. But, by clinging to his group, the "other-directed" person may achieve a kind of bland adjustment that can yield only boredom and restlessness because it ignores the individual's own idiosyncratic interests and wishes. Apathy follows the conflict between group pressures and personal aspirations and leads to anomie, proving that conformity has not brought meaning or success to anomic individuals.

Anomie is a condition of alienation from self and others in one's society, a sense of normlessness resulting from too great a sensitivity to conflicting signals from others. Anomics are contrasted with adjusted and autonomous people. The adjusted and autonomous, whether inner-directed or other-directed, fit into their society. The anomics are social "misfits." They are unable to conform or feel comfortable about not conforming. They are too sensitive to other people; they try too hard. They become apathetic, resembling—but to a lesser degree—patients in mental institutions. There is a vacuum in their lives; they are alienated from themselves and others, because they do not know what the norms are and are frustrated. According to

Riesman, Glazer, and Denney (1953), the way out of the risk of anomie and the flabby character of superficial "adjustment"is greater autonomy or independence.

Riesman's handling of loneliness is oblique and sociological rather than direct and psychological; but, in view of the scarcity of materials, it is better than nothing. Anyhow, we move on to a consideration of another worker's viewpoint, who points out one source of the problem.

Frieda Fromm-Reichmann.   In a paper entitled *Loneliness,* Frieda Fromm-Reichmann (1959, p. 1) puts her finger on the main difficulty in the study of loneliness: the term has served as a catch-all to include such diverse data as "loneliness, self-imposed aloneness, compulsory solitude and real loneliness" (p. 1). She concerns herself with severe loneliness, which "seems to be a painful, frightening experience that people will do practically everything to avoid" (p. 1). Fromm-Reichmann would probably consider the "lonely crowd's" loneliness a mild form of that which she is considering, distressing as the crowd's loneliness may be.

Fromm-Reichmann traces the origin of severe loneliness to the human "need" for intimacy that goes back to the infant's contact with the mother and tenderness from her. During weaning and later stages of separation from the mother, substitutions (such as fantasy) may not keep pace with the reduced intimacy, thus preparing the way for isolation and loneliness. Fromm-Reichmann believes that this kind of loneliness comes close to matching panic in intensity (p. 5). Quoting Ludwig Binswanger, Fromm-Reichmann points out that people "are terrified of the 'naked horror' of real loneliness" and that they are "more frightened of being lonely than of being hungry" (p. 7).

Fromm-Reichmann's own view of loneliness appears to be reflected in the following statement (1959, p. 8):

> Many psychiatrists now believe that the lack of real attention and acceptance by the significant adults of his infancy and early childhood hits him especially hard because of his innate specific potentialities for sensitive responsiveness to love and intimacy. This situation forms the cradle of his later loneliness and simultaneous yearning for, yet fear of, interpersonal closeness.

The existentialist theory of loneliness.   Existentialists from Kierkegaard (1938) to Sartre (1948) and Heidegger (1935) talk about the horrors of not being and entreat the lonely individual "thrown into existence to face bravely his fundamentally lonely, unique, and finite existence; to face death, the awareness of which is so often covered with layers of repression and denial" (Weigert, 1970, p. 70). Because people have become a mediocrity in mass society, the existentialists appeal to individuals to rise to the authenticity and uniqueness of their being in the world, to choose to become themselves and to accept responsibility for their own decisions even if such decisions should have bad consequences. Only in this way can mankind transcend its meaninglessness, powerlessness, and uniqueness (Weigert, pp. 70–71).

Pronko on loneliness.   Having thought much about loneliness, I feel compelled to add my speculations to the foregoing. The topic is especially relevant at this point because my hunch relates to the uniqueness of personality. I am tempted to think that loneliness may be connected with that uniqueness. The only way my hypothesis could be tested would be to rear two people who would be identical to the last response. In effect, they would be what we might call "psychological twins." Could we achieve such an impossible feat, all we would have to do is to check and see if our "psychological twins" experienced loneliness. Because such an achievement is utterly unattainable, it can never be tested; nevertheless, the possible relationship between personality uniqueness and loneliness keeps on nagging me. I continue to recall Rainer Maria Rilke's (De Forest, 1951, p. 61) phrase: "even between the *closest* human beings infinite distances continue to exist."

To some degree or other, each person revolves in his or her own peculiar orbit. Whatever degree of compatibility may exist between any two spouses, lovers, or friends may be an expression of the amount of overlap in their respective orbits. Alienation, with its resulting loneliness, may itself be the result of separate and distinct orbits, as caricatured so well in the following quotation from Rollo May's *Love and Will* (1969, p. 22):

> Ionesco has a scene in his play, *The Bald Soprano,* in which a man and woman happen to meet and engage in polite, if mannered, conversation. As they talk they discover that they both came down to New York on the 10 o'clock train that morning from New Haven, and, surprisingly, the address of both is the same building on Fifth Avenue. Lo and behold, they also both live in the same apartment and both have a daughter 7 years old. They finally discover to their astonishment that they are man and wife.

The Organization of Personality

We have already noted that an individual's personality shows a certain degree of order, coherence, system, or organization and stability.[4] The question before us now is "How shall we understand those personality attributes? Why is there any stability or orderliness among the too-numerous-to-count stimulus–response units that comprise personality?" That question is answered by an examination of the conditions surrounding the development of personality interactions during the individual's reactional biography.

If we pay particular attention to the conditions under which personality development takes place, we find a considerable degree of stability of such

---

[4] See Mahan (1968) for a thorough discussion of stability and change in personality.

conditions. Even the atmospheric envelope cooperates in maintaining a constant supply of oxygen for respiration. But radical changes in personality might result from radical (insufficient) amounts of oxygen in the air or from sudden and extreme temperature changes. Even gravitational changes disrupt walking, jumping, dancing, and so on—witness the readjustment astronauts required in walking on the moon. These conditions and other factors are easily overlooked and taken for granted, but they are there.

Other things being constant, one also finds relative stability in political conditions and therefore relative stability in the personality of citizens. We can illustrate this with a hypothetical case of a benevolent, peace-loving professor in Germany. Over long periods of time, his personality shows a sameness and repetitiveness.[5] Then, Hitler takes over, there is an upheaval in political, social, economic, religious, and legal conditions, and we see dramatic changes in the professor's behavior. His personality shows opposite kinds of reactions to those he previously showed. He becomes an "underground worker," carries a gun and is prepared to shoot to kill, dynamites defense plants, wears filthy clothes, goes days without end unbathed, and adopts vulgar speech. At war's end, he resumes his earlier behavior, which manifests the former day-to-day similarity and repetitiveness. This example reminds us that the study of personality is the study of psychological events, interactions, or interbehaviors. We cannot study a person's reactions apart from the conditions under which they occur. So, if we have stable conditions, we have a stable personality; when setting factors are chaotic, personality is chaotic.

The "sameness" we have referred to can be seen only over a period of time. If we observe the flow of events involving a certain individual, we note that certain events *recur*. Every successive event is *not* utterly different from every event that ever preceded it. In fact, certain events are "repeated."[6] That is one kind of pattern to be observed in personality analysis. If we pursue the matter further, we find that the "repetition" or "sameness" of the events constituting personality is determined by their setting factors. This is an appropriate time to hark back to Barker (1968) who, as we noted in Chapter 1, found that he could predict more about behavior from a knowledge of behavior settings (soda fountain, gymnasium, classroom) than he

---

[5] In his perennially popular play, *Our Town*, Thornton Wilder effectively depicts this repetitiveness and similarity of personalities not only of the same individuals over time but even of two generations of individuals dealing with similar situations in similar ways.

[6] The English biologist Woodger's warning is pertinent here:

> *Strictly speaking*, an event cannot be repeated because a given event is unique . . . and can never be again. . . . What happens when we are said to "repeat a process" [or event] is that we put certain things in certain relations and another event happens which may to a close degree of approximation exhibit the same mode of characterization in its serial changes as did the former ones. [Woodger, 1929, p. 186, emphasis added]

could from a catalogue of particular individual's "motives," "drives" or "experience." Apparently, then, the kind of "stability" of personality that we have been discussing is a function of stability or, to use a more appropriate term, "repetitiveness" of setting factors and, of course, the reinforcements of their correlated responses.

Multiple or Split Personality

Stability is one kind of pattern that an analysis of personality yields. If we persist in an attempt to make still more sense of personality, we can discriminate another pattern in the flow of events, a pattern that at first does not look like a pattern at all. When we make an across-the-board comparison of an individual's behaviors, we also find that personality reactions are sometimes at odds with one another. The same person can react in opposite ways within a short space of time. Imagine the German professor just returned home to a loving family after just sabotaging a railroad bridge and killing several men. What contradictory reactions within a short space of time! Here's another example: I knock at the front door of a friend's house. Through the glass in the door, in plain sight, the mother, in obvious rage, is beating her child. The mother's face is contorted with anger at her child. She soon answers my knock, opens the door, and is instantaneously transformed into a smiling, gracious hostess. What a turnabout in such short order!

Similarly, in Maxwell Anderson's play *Anne of the Thousand Days*, Anne Boleyn, the second wife of Henry VIII, is first shown passionately in love with the king, whom she soon comes to hate with equal passion. From passionate lovers to hated enemies long before a thousand days? George Bernard Shaw commented, "When we want to read of the deeds that are done for love, whither do we turn? To the murder column."

These are exactly the kinds of contradictory or polarized responses within the same personality system that we are now examining. At least superficially, it seems that there is no rhyme or reason to such inconsistency. But what right have we to expect personality interactions to be homogeneous? Homogeneity will not work as a metaphor, for to homogenize is to make a mixture uniform throughout. The fat globules in homogenized milk are broken up into fine particles that remain evenly dispersed throughout the liquid. The metaphor of homogenization is simply inappropriate if we expect to find personality responses to be consistent or harmonious with one another. Instead, we discover a pattern of variegated responses, sometimes inconsistent and incompatible with one another or even antagonistic to each other. Yet I think we can make sense of the apparent hodge-podge. But let Balzac set the stage for us in his devastatingly frank description of himself (O'Brien, 1966, p. 27, emphasis added):

> In my five feet three inches I contain every possible inconsistency and contrast, and those who find me vain, extravagant, obstinate, frivolous, illogical,

fatuous, negligent, idle, unpurposeful, unreflective, inconstant, talkative, tact-less, crude, unpolished, crotchety, and of uneven temper are no less right than those who would say that I am economical, modest, courageous, tenacious, energetic, neglected, hard-working, constant, reserved, full of finesse, polite, and always cheerful. The man who calls me a poltroon will be no more wrong than the man who says I am extremely brave. In short, learned or ignorant, talented or inept, I am astonished by nothing more than myself. *I conclude that I am simply an instrument played upon by circumstance.*

Balzac's last statement is almost prophetic of recent views of personality. In decrying psychology's failure to predict personality, Bakker (1975, p. 165) attributes the default to a too-close focus on the organism and attempts to get at "essentials" and "inner traits" instead of looking at social contexts. Here's the way he views the problem:

> Man's behavior is not primarily determined by unchangeable personality traits or other essential characteristics; on the contrary, his behavior is extreme-ly changeable as a function of the situation in which he finds himself. Change the situation and the person's behavior will change. If one wants to predict his behavior it is more important to know the situation than the person. [Bakker, 1975, p. 165]

People behave differently in different situations. A humorous anecdote concerns Mrs. Smith's son. A policeman knocks on her door and brings her bad news. He tells her that her son, Jimmy, had just held up a bank and shot a teller and a security officer, run outside, and shot another police officer. Then he ran into an apartment building and raped a woman before he was finally apprehended. Mrs. Smith commented, "I'm surprised. Why, he never acts that way around the house!"

Bakker provides other sober illustrations of the need for specifying the setting factors of personality interactions. He discusses the Storm Troopers (the SS) who, during Hitler's regime in Germany,

> . . . engaged in what is undoubtedly the most cruel and destructive behavior ob-servable among human beings. One would postulate, therefore, that they had personality traits of, for instance, a sadistic type which predisposed them to this kind of work. However, those who have studied the concentration camps and their guards have observed that the SS men consisted of normal individuals. [Bakker, 1975, p. 165]

Quoting another writer, Bakker continues, "The SS man looked upon him-self as normal, and when he had finished his job he went home quietly, kissed his wife and children, played with his dog, called on his friends, etc." (p. 165).

Bakker also tells about the war experiences of Professor Kremer, chairman of the histology department at the University of Muenster. He joined the SS and was ordered to replace the physician at the concentration camp at Auschwitz, where he kept a diary. The entries for September 2 and 5 reflect the shock that he felt as revealed by such entries as "the most horrible of horrors" (Bakker, 1975, p. 166). But by October 17, he was recording taking out of presumably living concentration-camp victims "fresh material of liver, spleen, and pancreas after injection of pilocarpin" (p. 166). Subsequent entries are routine, expressing "tranquility and a primary interest in food and scientific experiments on the prisoners. In just a few short weeks Dr. Kremer changed from a horrified observer to a calm participant" (p. 166). The following comment from Bakker (1975) is most insightful. "One is easily inclined to jump to the conclusion that monstrous men created the abhorrent situation, while in fact it appears that the situation created monstrous men" (p. 166).

Another fact that argues against an inherently pathological view of those participating in atrocities perpetrated in the concentration camps is the magnitude of that participation. Workers in the horror camps were not some small, special group of "crazies." They were recruited from the general population. The extent of their involvement is revealed by Alexander Donat (1967) in an article in which he reviews *Simon Wiesenthal's Memoirs* (Wiesenthal dedicated his life to searching out Nazi persecutors of Jews). "After the war, Nazis were readmitted to all walks of life. The state offices, the judiciary, the police force, industry and army, legal and medical professions were flooded by ex-Nazis, unrepentant but forgiven" (Donat, 1967, p. 33). In 1951, three SS generals established an organization of former armed SS men. They became the spokesmen for 400,000 SS veterans who collect pensions, retain all civil rights, and constitute one of the largest voters' groups in Germany. No wonder the historian Golo Mann, Thomas Mann's son, asserts, "If we are to be exact about the guilt . . . one half of our nation would have to sit as judges of the other half. So let's get used to the idea that the street car conductor, or, for that matter, the postman, or milkman, or bank teller may have been a child murderer, or the lovely saleslady or waitress a former concentration camp overseer" (Donat, 1967, p. 33).

Some Multiple Personalities

Eldridge Cleaver.   A one-time Black revolutionary leader and one of the founders of the Black Panther Party, Eldridge Cleaver fled the country when he faced trial on charges of attempted murder in connection with a shootout in 1968 between police in Oakland, California, and members of the Black Panther Party. At that time, he declared, "The only good pig [policeman] is a dead pig."

In his book, *Soul on Ice,* Cleaver (1968) describes his 9-year imprisonment for his drug dealing (p. 17) and rape (p. 26). For 8 years, as a fugitive, he traveled on false passports in various communist countries, such as Cuba, Algeria, North Korea, China, and North Vietnam. In 1973, he and his family entered and lived in Paris, illegally. At last, through the efforts of Giscard d'Estaing (then Minister of Finance and Economy), he was able to establish legal residence in France, where he could have lived with his family for the rest of his days (Cleaver, 1978, p. 206). But a religious experience, which he describes in *Soul on Fire,* converted him (Cleaver, 1978). He states that he is now a Christian with a heart full of goodwill, and if it is God's will that he be imprisoned, so be it. He chose to return to the United States in November 1975, where, after 9 months' imprisonment, he is out on bail, studying and preaching the gospel. Here is an extreme personality change—or a sensible way to end his exile.

This case, like others to be touched on later, raises an important question. How can one evaluate the genuineness of such radical personality transformations as Cleaver has manifested? Admittedly, it is difficult, but the problem is usually raised only when people change from "bad character" to "good character." Would we be suspicious of Cleaver's "motives" if he had suddenly changed from a career in the Christian ministry to one of crime? About his earlier spree in delinquency, we are not likely to ask "was he a sincere rapist and drug dealer or was that faked?"

Charles Colson.   Charles Colson was Richard Nixon's chief confidant and counselor. In his book *Born Again* (1976, p. 14), Colson writes, "For three long years, I had committed everything I had, every ounce of energy to Richard Nixon's cause. Nothing else had mattered. We had no time together as a family, no social life, no vacations." During the 1972 presidential campaign, Colson was widely quoted to have said, "I would walk over my grandmother to reelect Richard Nixon." Colson was charged in the Watergate coverup and in the burglary of Daniel Ellsberg's psychiatrist's office. But since then he declares that he has been "born again" and has dedicated his life to Jesus Christ. In short, he has manifested a radical shift of allegiances.

Will the real Mr. Nixon stand up?   The two foregoing brief biographical sketches showed radical changes that took place over a considerable period of time. But a lengthy time interval is not essential to expose contradictory reactions, as shown in the following quotation from Jeffrey Hart describing Richard Nixon as he appears in private and the way he comes on in public.

> There exists a huge gap between the private and the public man. With a small group of people he knows, Nixon is direct, realistic, humorous, and often startlingly candid. He swears. He uses vivid imagery. He is frequently scatalogical.

In public an amazing transformation occurs. An oppressive respectability settles over the fellow. He becomes almost prim. He walks without swinging his arms. His speeches are full of stale protestations of virtue. He seems to think that everyone expects the President—as distinguished from Dick Nixon—to be some sort of civics book, a Sunday school paragon.[7]

Obviously, such a transformation as Hart describes could occur in a very short time period—for example, during a Cabinet meeting and immediately after. Whether such dramatic changes occur over a long or short period of time is not important. The important thing about them is their bipolarity or oppositeness, a feature with which we must now come to grips.

Subsystems in Personality Organization

> There was a little girl
> Who had a little curl
> Right in the middle of her forehead
> And when she was good,
> She was very, very good
> And when she was bad, she was horrid.

Could a nursery rhyme be offered seriously in attempting to make sense of the diametrically opposite clusters of responses that we observed in the cases directly above? As a reminder, we observed contrary responses in the German professor, the woman beating her child, Anne Boleyn, the guards in the concentration camps, and, finally in the cases of the three political figures, Cleaver, Colson, and Nixon.

The nursery rhyme does furnish a clue to the solution of the coexistence of contradictory responses in the same individual. Let's consider the little girl with the little curl. Everything is going her way; she is happy, having fun; suddenly a cousin snatches her new doll. There is an instantaneous personality switch; she grabs the doll, bites her cousin's hand, and sends her sprawling to the floor. Her mother remonstrates, but the little girl only sasses her mother and slaps at her. This sequence of events is one chain reaction of a coherent set of responses, followed by another chain reaction of another coherent set of responses. And they operate lawfully in relation to their organizing stimuli as evolved during the little girl's reactional biography.

Place yourself in the following situation. A young woman comes to you and initiates talk about her boyfriend. Although in love with him, she is distressed by a puzzling change in his personality, *on occasion.* Usually kind, gentle, and considerate of her, when he has had too much to drink, he

[7] From a newspaper column by Jeffrey Hart. © King Features Syndicate, Inc. Reproduced by permission.

becomes cruel, abusive in his language toward her, and vulgar. She then asks you, "Which is the real Tommy?" You might answer, "One Tommy is not more real than the other. Both are real. Whichever Tommy prevails depends on the attending circumstances." However, the "good Tommy" and the "bad Tommy" both follow a definite psychological rule; namely, that behavior is a function of stimulating conditions, setting factors, and antecedent events.

A work by Slater (1970) may help us understand Tommy's compartmentalized reactions. Slater believes that the contradictory responses commonly observed in people reveal a conflict, one side of which is strongly stressed while the other, also quite strong, is partially but not completely suppressed.[8] We deny the suppressed side but it is still there. Slater uses a metaphor to explain such split-personality shifts (his metaphor is in self-actional terms, but it can be fitted into an interactional framework):

> An individual who "converts" from one orientation to its exact opposite appears to himself and others to have made a gross change, but actually it involves only a very small shift in the balance of a focal and persistent conflict. Just as only one percent of the voting population is needed to reverse the results of an American election, so only one percent of an individual's internal "constituencies" need shift in order to transform him from voluptuary to ascetic, from policeman to criminal, from Communist to anticommunist, or whatever. The opposite sides are as evenly matched as before, and the apparent change merely represents the desperate efforts made by the internal "majority" to consolidate its shaky position of dominance. The individual must expend just as much energy shouting down the new "minority" as he did the old; some of the most dedicated witch hunters of the 1950's for example, were ex-Communists [Slater, 1970, p. 4].

As noted earlier, Slater's construct of multiple personality in terms of hypothetical "internal constituents" or "internal majorities" and "minorities" is self-actional, which is criticism enough. Baer's (1976) metaphor of "the organism as host" is equally applicable here. The kind of "conversion" that Slater mentions ("from voluptuary to ascetic, policeman to criminal, from Communist to anticommunist or whatever") can be handled in terms of Baer's concept. Assume that for the "voluptuary turned ascetic," we have a macho group of vulgar, pleasure-seeking, brawling conventioneers. They depart, to the satisfaction of the host, and are succeeded by a strict, evangelistic religious group. The former noise and chaos contrast with the present peace and quiet prevailing among the new guests.

Now, it is also possible to formulate a construct in terms of events or interactions that cohere in certain ways that may be considered as lawful subsystems of the larger system referred to as *personality*. For example,

[8] This conflict can be handled interactionally as a competition of reaction systems.

pleasant, loving, affectionate interactions stick together, just as angry, hateful, yelling, and screaming interactions do. But each subsystem obeys a "law and order" of its own in terms of a similarity of its respective stimulus functions. It is we, the onlookers, who make so much of the alternations or "conversions" from one extreme to the other. After all, the options are limited, so some situations do require a "two-valued orientation." But "birds of a feather flock together," and so do some interactions. Coherence of particles or other entities is no stranger to science, and the organization of personality into subsystems requires no special principles.

One final point: in this chapter we have not considered behavior that, traditionally, goes by the name of "abnormal psychology" or "psychopathology." *Everyone* has "contradictory" sets of reactions. I believe that such opposite blocks of interactions simply reflect contradictory sets of conditions during their acquisition and reinforcement. Furthermore, the same principles that we have here considered as applicable to "normal" personality also apply to our understanding of "abnormal" personality. No new principles are necessary.

The following case history illustrates some of the points we have been considering.

James Morris to Jan Morris: A Case of Transsexualism

James Morris (1974) was no run-of-the-mill man. At the age of 17, he volunteered for the army, after which he enrolled at Oxford. From there he went into journalism and became a successful foreign correspondent. For a full decade, he had a grandstand view of the world's great events, serving in turn the Arab News Agency in Cairo, the *Times* of London, and the *Manchester Guardian*. As foreign correspondent of the *Times*, Morris accompanied the first successful ascent of Mt. Everest with a British expeditionary team. He was also an observer at the war in Palestine. As a world traveler and adventurer, he was in vigorous physical condition; he had to be. In mid-life and at the height of his career, known on both sides of the Atlantic, Morris seemed headed toward still greater success whether in newspapers, television, politics, or diplomacy. Yet he turned away from it all and returned home to England to write books and to travel on his own. As an indication of his worth as a writer, he won the Heinemann Award for Literature in England and the Polk Memorial Award for Journalism in the United States. He is author of a dozen or more books.

With such great achievements in hand and great promise of more to come, why would James Morris so totally reject further prizes just within his grasp? Morris answers that question as follows: "I wanted none of it. It was repugnant to me. I thought of public success itself, I suppose, as part of maleness, and I deliberately turned my back on it, as I set my face against manhood" (Morris, 1974, p. 93). Now the secret is out: Morris loathed his manhood. Ever since childhood, he had longed and, literally, prayed God to make him a girl. On this point, he explains (p. 26), "It all seemed plain enough to me. I was born with the wrong body, being feminine by gender but male by sex, and I could achieve completeness only when one was adjusted to the other. I have thought about it for four decades since then."[9]

One must read Morris' *Conundrum* (1974) in its entirety to understand his obsession. The following snatches from his account may help in understanding his yearning for womanhood, not merely for a change of genital apparatus. Nor did he consider himself a transvestite, for he did not get any sexual pleasure from wearing the clothes of the opposite sex (p. 48). Some thought he might be a "repressed homosexual," but he rejected that notion. All he wanted was a match of his sex with his gender; if he could achieve that, it would "make a whole" of him (p. 49). In the fourth decade of his life, he decided to do something about it. Since to himself he had always been a woman, he was getting rid of the falsity. "With Elizabeth's [his wife's] loving help I abandoned the attempt to live on as a male, and took the first steps towards a physical change of sex" (p. 102). The alternatives were suicide or a ruinous melancholy and despair.

Morris now put his long-incubated plan of action into operation. He would *start* altering his body. Under a physician's care, he took synthetic female hormones, and, by the time he had swallowed 12,000 pills in 8 years (p. 105), his bodily contours were gradually taking on a more female form. With his long hair and a contralto voice, it took only a bit of makeup and a bracelet or two to establish James as a female. Morris found out that "people see in you what they expect to see" (p. 118). In certain settings, he was known as a man and people accepted him as a man; in others, they saw a woman. At his male traveler's club, he was greeted as a male. But he was also a member of another club a short distance away where he was known only since he had begun "passing" as a woman. When he went from one club to the other, changing roles, James comments, " 'Cheerio, sir,' the porter would say at one club, and 'Hello, madam,' the porter would greet me at the other" (p. 120). In time, James adopted the female mode of dress completely and went on trips with his wife, both of them greeted at motels as "girls."

The last situation called for important changes. It was obvious that the Morrises could not continue to be "man and wife," so in the interest of legal propriety, they were divorced and became, to the world, "sisters-in-law." But their personal and family relationships continued to be close and affectionate as before. James initiated action with the government for a change of identity and soon became, legally and officially, Jan Morris in all government records even down to a driver's license.

[9] The term *gender* refers to the behaviors that indicate to others or to oneself to what degree one is male or female (also referred to as *gender role*).

Jan was now ready for the last phase of his transformation. This required surgery, which was done in Casablanca, Morocco. The operation involved removal of penis and testicles and the creation of a vagina out of the erotically sensitive tissues, thus making orgasm possible. The complete changeover required a two-stage operation—the second stage in an English nursing home. On recovering from surgery, because Jan was no longer producing male sex hormones, she filled out in cheeks, hips, and bosom and could not have passed for a man if she had wanted to (p. 152). She sat, walked, and gestured like a woman, and the more she was treated like a woman by others, the more womanly she became (p. 149). Jan and Elizabeth Morris live together in close friendship, even though they are divorced. For Jan, the story ends happily because she (he?) got what he (she?) always wanted—his (her?) womanhood.

Implications of Jan Morris' Case History

The most glaring feature of James Morris' personality problem was its basic nature. It began early—somewhere in childhood, according to Morris (1974) —and persisted until the fourth decade of his life, at which point it had to be attended to, or there would have been only suicide or anxiety and frustration as alternatives. One wonders what powerful reinforcers did their work with such thorough efficiency! (In that respect, this case is similar to the case of siderophobia recorded by Leonard, as considered in Chapter 2.)

Another point that should not be overlooked in this admittedly extreme case is the potential for personality development. We may assume that, under certain antecedent conditions and certain kinds of reinforcement, an anatomical male can become so unhappy with a male gender role that, after being a male for four decades, he decides to become a woman not only psychologically but even anatomically. Personality is rich, complex, and many-faceted.

Pseudopersonality

Actors are the only honest hypocrites

William Hazlitt

According to original Greek meaning, the word *hypocrite* (as defined by *Webster's International Dictionary*, second edition), refers to "one who plays a part on the stage, a dissembler, a feigner." The actor admittedly takes on or assumes the personality characteristics of Julius Caesar, Napoleon, or President Truman—whomever he may be portraying. The audience also shares in that dissembling or pretense and shows its appreciation to the degree to which the actors match the assumed personalities of the characters they are "playing."

Movies, and television soap operas, comedies, cartoons, and sports, sex, and violence dramas occupy a great deal of the American family's leisure hours. Even the commercials, which take up a good fraction of viewing time, have actors who do not necessarily have headaches, nausea, bad breath, or loose teeth, but only act *as if* they did. Yet, despite the plethora of data, what we might call "the psychology of acting" is quite skimpy.

One concept that I found useful was formulated some time ago by Kantor in Volume 1 of his *Principles of Psychology* (1924). He introduced the construct of pseudopersonality, which he defined as reactions that are distinct from the more-or-less stable or permanent personality interbehaviors. Pseudopersonality includes reactions that "are more or less artificial; they may be acquired because the individual wants to create a particular sort of impression upon other people or because he wishes to disguise his more fundamental and permanent personality" (Kantor, 1924, p. 85).

If "actors are the only honest hypocrites," then it follows that some people are dishonest hypocrites. For example, imagine a man who never had any medical training, yet acts like an obstetrician and gets away with it for a long time because he carries off his act successfully until someone checks up on his qualifications. He is dishonest because, although he knew he was acting, his patients did not know that. He was an "impersonator" because he borrowed certain (delivery room) personality reactions of the bona fide obstetrician. His act would have been perfectly legal if he had performed it on the stage before an audience. In that case, he might have been applauded instead of imprisoned.

Recently, a pertinent item in the press (*Wichita Eagle & Beacon*, March 5, 1978) reported the four-year-long masquerade of Henri Michel Poirier as a consultant in the emergency ward of a hospital in Toulouse, France. He was the official physician for the national tennis team of France and won acclaim for a thesis on dreaming that he had published. He was arrested while driving a stolen car and was charged with practicing medicine without a license. His training? All the medicine he could learn in his jail cell while serving a 4-year term for burglary.

In the theater, so-called impersonators are perennially present. One marvels at the precision with which they can match the walk, gestures, facial grimaces, and even speech of public officials, actors, and others. To the degree to which they achieve those excellences, we might say they "are" the person whom they are impersonating. How far such impersonation could go, given enough opportunity and time, no one can say. Obvious limitations of both have yielded only limited degrees of impersonation. Apparently, personality interactions must be objective and concrete if they can be appropriated fairly easily. It seems as though one might "steal" at least some portion of an individual's personality more easily rather than that same person's property or money.

A cartoon shows a mother helping get her teenage daughter ready for a date. When the girl has finished dressing, she turns to her mother and says, "I hope he doesn't want to go to a movie. I don't know him well enough to wear my glasses." She is impersonating a girl who does not wear glasses. Similarly, the Japanese have an eloquent rule of conduct that "away from home, one need feel no shame." And someone has defined courtship as a time after which a man and a woman begin to act like themselves. Apparently, everyone at some time or other wears a mask (except ingenuous children or the severely mentally retarded.)[10] For example, suppose you and I have a close relationship and I make some blunt, brusque remark for which I immediately express regret. I say, "I did hurt your feelings, didn't I?" You deny it, but not too convincingly, and you and I both know that you are hurt. You (unsuccessfully) act like a person who is not hurt. That is pseudo-personality.

The hero of the Shakespeare play *Hamlet*, in anger and jealousy over his mother's hasty marrige to his uncle (the suspected murderer of his father), chides her and advises her to "assume a virtue if you have it not." The idea behind the suggestion is that if she continues to practice a pseudopersonality response (chastity) long enough, it will become "second nature" or a permanent part of her personality.

There are other varieties of pseudopersonality, such as affectations. An affectation is defined as an act of taking on or displaying an attitude or mode of behavior not natural or not genuine. If I *assume* an Oxford English accent to impress someone, I am "affected." Regarding young people who act in imitation of an admired film hero, heroine, or teacher, someone has said understandingly, "Don't laugh at their affectations; they are only trying on one face after another to find their own."

The trouble with the term *pseudopersonality* is its connotation of spuriousness or falsity of the behavior so labeled. But even a thoroughly cowardly person can occasionally perform a brave act. And a miser may, on rare occasions, act magnanimously. Both aberrations are, nevertheless, cases of pseudopersonality because they are fleeting and transient "guests of the organism."

There are still other kinds of pseudopersonality interactions. For example, suppose you reside in England for a few months. You make friends, who say goodbye by saying, "Cheerio." You respond in kind, but somewhat artificially. However, after a while the salutation begins to feel natural, and you

---

[10]It would be an interesting exercise to trace out the meaning of masks, which are found worldwide in a variety of cultures. Our own use of masks to impersonate even nonhuman creatures in Halloween rituals belongs in this spectrum, as do the masks worn over the eyes during masked balls.

use it frequently. Yet when you leave England you never again think of saying, "Cheerio." Thus, some pseudopersonality components are transient and fleeting. Further examples could be illustrated with drugs or smoking. Some try such things once or twice and never again, while others become addicted on a more or less permanent basis.

Personality and Character

The terms *personality* and *character* suggest two different referents, one for each term, thus forcing us to make a semantic analysis. We have already defined personality as the totality of interactions involving a given individual and the interrelated stimulus objects. Such a definition would suggest that, because the term *personality* is all-inclusive, then *character* cannot refer to anything over and above and beyond personality. Because the term *personality* is all-inclusive, psychologically speaking, then the term *character* can only refer to an *aspect* of personality. The following analysis may clarify the relationship between the two terms.

Character in Everyday Usage

The term *character* is often used in a judgmental way. Ask Person A about C and you get a favorable report, but B gives you an unfavorable one. In this case, you may learn more about A and B than you do about C. You may find that A is tolerant of other people and B is overly critical. So we end up studying A and C instead of B.

Peter sees Paul in terms of his own personality. When we later discuss projection as a defense mechanism, we shall see how readily people attribute their own insecurities, anxieties, fears, and wishes to others. Therefore, because Peter's reports about Paul are not reliable, we now attempt a psychological specification of character.

Character from a Psychological Standpoint

If we want to learn about Paul's character, we must focus on Paul's action, because we have been defining psychology as the study of the individual's behavior in relation to stimulus objects. As we go about our job, we observe Paul at a cafeteria. For lunch, he selects roast beef, spinach, and mashed potatoes. On his way back to work, he stops at a department store and shoplifts a bow tie, which he pockets undetected by the store's security guard. He returns to work late and states that he had a flat tire on his way back from lunch, when he actually did not have a flat. Thus, we know that he lied. We make one more observation about Paul that is relevant to our purpose. We see him take a small motor belonging to the plant, put it in his overcoat pocket, and walk out with it when the whistle blows.

Now, we have some concrete behaviors of Paul's to sort out. If we start with his lunch, we find that his selection from the menu is not subject to any social or legal standards. No one cares whether he had selected fish, spaghetti, and string beans. And society is indifferent to Paul's choice of bow ties over four-in-hand ties. But his *stealing* a bow tie is unacceptable to the store management and to administrators of justice who must execute the law legislated by representatives of the people (society). Then, too, Paul's stealing his company's motor conflicts with another standard, as does his lying about his tardiness. Thus, we arrive at a definition of character; namely, *character* is a blanket term that includes personality reactions that are approved or disapproved in a particular society in certain situations. Thus, when we talk about character, we are talking about concrete, specific behaviors. Rules and regulations disapprove shooting people with guns except in wartime, when the more enemy soldiers one kills, the more approval one gets. Killing out of season labels one as a bad character and a criminal. Killing in season may make one a hero and a good character.

In one year, a rich Moslem fathered four children. How can this be, when most fathers cannot achieve more than one legitimate child a year? The answer is that, as a Moslem, he is in a religious and legal sense allowed to have four wives. Each wife gave birth to a child within the space of a year. Does that make him a bad character? That depends. Certainly not in his own Moslem country, which allows every Moslem up to four wives. He certainly would be in our country, which allows only one wife at a time (*serial polygamy*).

We are concerned with character, then, only when behavior is judged from the standpoint of some code or social norm and is labeled as right or wrong. In other words, when we have inventoried an individual's personality, certain behaviors are approved or disapproved according to prevailing standards (legal, ethical, moral, or religious) in that society. Those behaviors can be classed as honesty, generosity, cooperation, and so on and constitute that person's character. Now, if we simply want to comprehend an individual's personality without regard to group standards, then we have personality. Character is an *aspect* of personality. My purpose in this brief exercise has been, more than anything else, to avoid possible semantic confusion of two terms closely related in everyday usage which *seem* to point to two different phenomena where there is only one—namely, personality.

Catalogue of Personality Interactions

Our survey of personality up to this point has revealed the richness, complexity, and diversity of a given individual's interactions that we label with the comprehensive term *personality*. The total number of personality interactions is nearly astronomical. We can manage such masses of data by adopting the same procedure that other scientists have found useful in the same situation; that is, classification. The physicist, chemist, botanist, zoologist, and astronomer have not yet completed their respective jobs of ordering their last datum into groups or categories according to established criteria. They may never finish that job, but they nevertheless have a procedure for classifying their data so that they can study interrelationships. We shall try out a system for classifying personality interactions that Kantor and Smith (1975) have proposed. The following categories are suggestive, rather than fixed, as are the chemist's categories, and are not mutually exclusive or exhaustive.

Abilities

In the category of abilities are performances such as bricklaying, surgery, dancing, carpentry, painting, cooking, sculpting, baking, and mechanical abilities of all sorts.

Skills

People may consider themselves typists or mechanically able, but typing tests and various mechanical abilities tests select those who are excellent from those with ordinary or poor performance. Thus, a certain agreed-on score on such tests could be used to separate skills from abilities.

Capacities and Aptitudes

After an individual learns how to solve a number of mechanical puzzles, future puzzles are easier to solve. The locksmith's past experience with locks and the "safecracker's" with breaking into safes pave the way for performing process responses (see Chapter 1). Similarly, if one has learned to type on a manual typewriter, one can also type on an electric machine. The same applies to driving a car or to surgical or dental work.

Talents

When capacities and aptitudes reach a certain high degree of excellence, the individual is said to be *talented*. The expert can "sight-read" a piece of music that the novice must hammer out bit by bit. The term *talent* is semantically contaminated with self-actional notions; for example, that some individuals have been endowed with "God-given talents." Others limit application of the term to musical and artistic excellence. But Kantor and Smith (1975, p. 140) would extend the term to expertise in performing process responses in "salesmanship, in conversation, in watchmaking, in apparatus making, as well as in the arts." And they explain virtuoso performance, as they do all talents, as reactional-biography developments.

Tastes

Some people like classical music; others cannot stand it but prefer popular music; still others care only for "rock"; and so on. The "jocks" may scorn all the foregoing because all they want are sports programs. Another person is angry when the latest episode in a favorite continuous "soap opera" is interrupted by a presidential address. Personalities differ in likes and dislikes.

Habits

Habit interactions are the most dependable of the individual's personality responses. Suppose you describe someone's saying or doing something to your group or friends without identifying the person. Someone is very likely to remark, "Only X would have said (or done) that." Habits, therefore, characterize or identify the individual because they stand out "like a sore thumb." This is why detectives study a burglar's "m.o." (mode of operation) to identify that burglar by habitual procedures. In more ordinary ways, people have coffee- or tea-drinking habits (sometimes culturalized); smoking, gum-chewing, drug, and swearing habits; or habits of neatness, cleanliness, or orderliness. These responses are tightly knit with their corresponding stimulus objects because they have been powerfully reinforced in the past.

How easily and "automatically" even complex habitual personality interactions can come to be performed with precision is illustrated by an example from William James (1918). He tells of a juggler who "early practiced the art of juggling with balls in the air" and achieved such expertise that, while keeping four balls in the air, he could read without hesitation from a book placed before him. The same juggler, even after an interval of 30 years with scarcely once touching the balls, could "still manage to read while keeping *three* balls up" (p. 117). The power that William James attributed to habit is revealed, as is his elegant literary style, in the following quotation from his *Principles of Psychology* (James, 1918, p. 121).

Habit is thus the enormous flywheel of society, its most precious conservative agent. It alone is what keeps us all within the bounds of ordinance, and saves the children of fortune from the envious uprisings of the poor. It alone prevents the hardest and most repulsive walks of life from being deserted by those brought up to tread therein. It keeps the fisherman and the deck-hand at sea through the winter; it holds the miner in his darkness, and nails the countryman to his log-cabin and his lonely farm through all the months of snow; it protects us from invasion by the natives of the desert and the frozen zone. It dooms us all to fight out the battle of life upon the lines of our nurture or our early choice and to make the best of a pursuit that disagrees, because there is no other for which we are fitted, and it is too late to begin again.

Attitudes have sometimes been considered to be "predispositions" to act, but if we are accustomed to dealing only in terms of interactions between the organism's responses and their correlated stimulus objects, this definition implies that there is something else above and beyond the responses, a self-actional entity, and that is unacceptable. A definition suggested by the American psychologist Cameron may help. Cameron (1947, p. 54) distinguishes between "the attitude and the responses as constituents of a unitary reaction." He defines an attitude as "the relatively widespread, diffuse aspect of a reaction which functions as a behavioral background, preparing for, supporting, and prolonging certain responses and not others. In contrast to this, a response is the more specific, localized aspect of a reaction which emerges from, and is supported by, the more sustained attitude" (Cameron, 1947, pp. 54–55).

With a slight revision, it is possible to make Cameron's construct useful to our purpose. One can, then, conceptualize an attitude as a subtle, continuing orientation or overall interaction that, as Cameron says, "prepares for, supports, and prolongs" certain responses selectively. In metaphorical terms, particular responses can be considered as operating similarly to the way we saw setting factors working in our analysis of psychological interactions (Chapter 1). In relation to his metaphor of the organism as host, Baer (1976, p. 92) suggests a concept of "inter-guest interaction." He says, "It seems inevitable that . . . responses may interact to determine whether other responses will increase or decrease" (p. 92). It is also possible to consider a closely related conception—competition of reaction systems. It appears, then, that an individual's interactions interact with each other affecting the eventual outcome.

For example, a suspicious attitude acts selectively to "aid and abet" corresponding reactions as long as that attitude continues. A friendly attitude begets specific friendly responses. If we know X's racial, religious, and national prejudices (attitudes), we know roughly what X will do when sitting at a cafeteria table with a member of a given group, when shaking hands, and so on. Knowing that a person's attitude toward pain is supersensitive or stoical prepares the dentist for dealing with that patient. People's attitudes toward the women's liberation movement, the Equal Rights Amendment, abortion, the ecology, the energy crisis, gay rights, war, fluoridation, and the Panama Canal are examples of attitudes as personality components. All these attitudes condition the specific interactions subsumed under them.

Kantor and Smith (1975) offer still other personality categories. However, our aim is not to achieve a final and complete classification of personality components but only to suggest how the job might be attacked *if* we were ambitious enough to undertake it. Even more importantly, our present analysis was intended to show that law and order prevail under apparent complexity and diversity.

Biological Factors in Personality Development

In Chapter 1, we gave thorough consideration to the relationship between biological conditions and psychological development. Here, we briefly note how anatomical and physiological factors participate in the individual's behavioral repertoire, or personality.

Permissive Biological Factors

If the human species had failed to evolve hands, then obviously "patty-cake" games and applauding would not exist. But, of course, most humans are born with hands. The question is "What is the proper role of the hands in applauding?" First, let's take the case of the rare unfortunates who are born without hands. Certainly, they cannot be expected to applaud an operatic performance (which they may, nevertheless, thoroughly enjoy anyhow). But Genie was born with hands, and yet at 17 years of age was not applauding anything. Apparently, then, being born with hands does not of itself guarantee applauding behavior. A reactional biography is also essential. Hands simply permit or make it possible to acquire the behavior if the opportunity to learn to applaud is also made possible. Thus, a simplistic formula for applauding would be *Applauding = Hands + Reactional biography*. One could write similar formulas involving vocal chords, ears, eyes, and so on as participants in personality development.

More Positive Biological Factors

Because biological organisms and their behavior are intimately connected, biological conditions may provide a rich source of stimulation for such behaviors as pride or shame of (1) one's figure or (2) size or (3) disfigurements. Exactly how these factors operate has been demonstrated clearly in a classic work by Barker, Wright, Meyerson, and Gonick (1953). Barker and his colleagues (1953, p. 28) first remind us that there are certain cultural expectations of what adults may do as compared with children. Obviously adults have an advantage over youngsters with their restricted, limited opportunities.

Barker and his colleagues present an ideal case for our purpose: two pairs of girls, each pair of which consisted of a biologically mature and a biologically immature girl. We shall consider only one pair, Child S and Child M, shown in Figure 6-2. S is 13 years, 11 months, and 20 days old; and M is 13 years, 11 months, and 21 days old. They differ in age by no more than 24 hours. Each pair of girls was not only the same chronological age and mental age but was in the same grade in school and from the same socioeconomic background. M had experienced menstruation, but S had not. An inspection of Figure 6-2 shows that M is much more feminine in appearance, while S "looks like a child." But what is far more dramatic is the judgment about the *psychological* maturity of the two girls by parents, teachers, and other significant adults who knew the girls. Naturally, the people judging the girls were

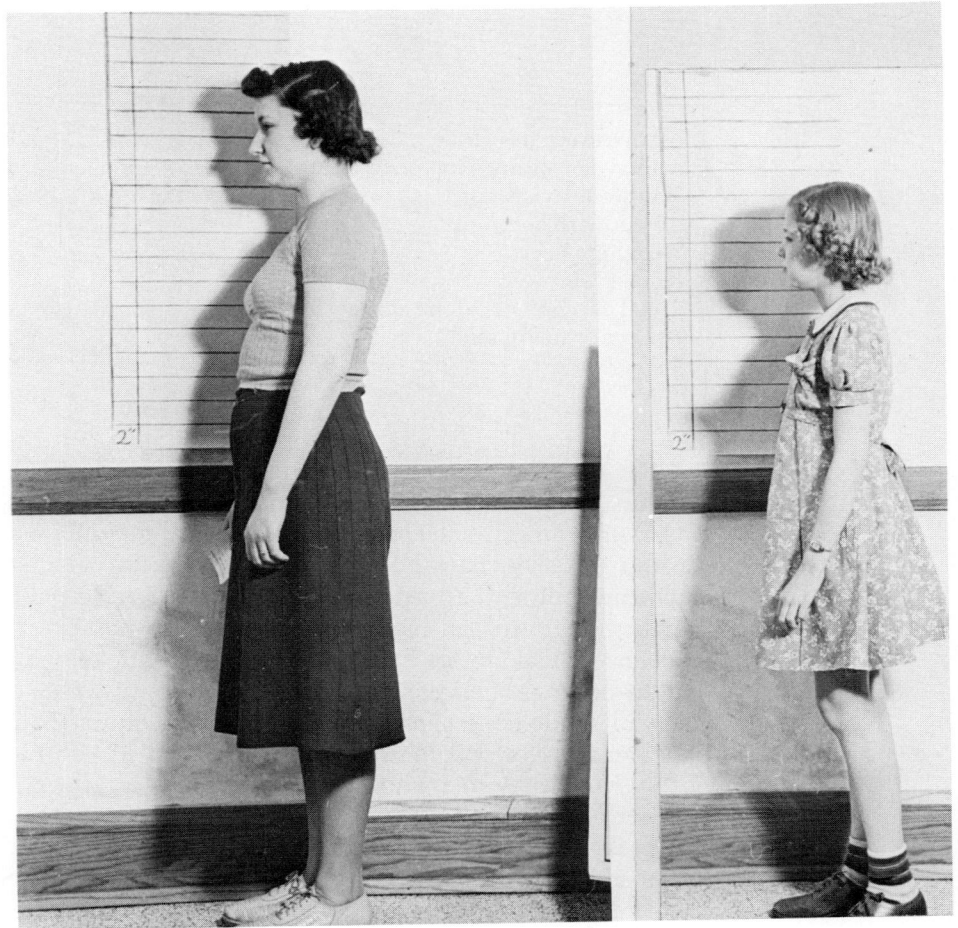

Figure 6-2 Two girls, M (left) and S (right). M is 13 years, 11 months, and 21 days old. S is 13 years, 11 months, and 20 days old. Their different biological status affects their respective personality development. (From Barker, Wright, Myerson, and Gonick, 1953, p. 32. Photo courtesy of Dr. Barker.)

never told the purpose of the study. In fact, they thought it was an inquiry into parents' and teachers' standards of discipline.

A comparison of judgments.   The four judges of each girl were asked to consider which of a list of activities they thought proper for each girl to engage in. Here are some comparisons.

	NUMBER OF JUDGES AGREEING	
	CHILD M	CHILD S
Go to the movies alone	4	2
Attend dances unchaperoned	2	1
Stay alone overnight	2	1
Go out with boys	2	0
Wear high heels	3	0
Pluck eyebrows	4	0
Social engagement alone at night	4	0
Use rouge and lipstick	4	1

The overall findings are summed up in the following statement by Barker and his colleagues (1953, p. 30): "The physically more mature girl of each pair is judged to be behaviorally mature enough for adult-like activities more frequently than the physically less mature girl." We would miss an important point in all this discussion if we overlooked the detailed way in which the differential biological maturation works in the case of M and S. The anatomical factors by themselves do not make one girl more womanly and the other girl childish. It is the social-stimulus value that each girl has for the adults who control their lives that really counts. Think of the boundless opportunities for personality development for M, who is allowed to go out with boys, denied to S who does not have that privilege. Self-reactions enter the picture, too, for M, who is allowed to wear high-heeled shoes and pluck her eyebrows, comes to think of herself as a young woman with certain rights and privileges formerly denied her. In this respect, S continues to play her role as a "second-class citizen." In short, as concerns personality development, biological factors play an *indirect* role. They do not themselves produce or cause the organism to behave in certain ways. They do serve as stimuli to which others (such as parents and teachers of M and S) react in ways that either facilitate or inhibit acquisition of personality interactions by providing or withholding opportunities for such.

Negative Biological Factors

In addition to permitting or facilitating certain personality acquisitions and serving as social stimuli to others, biological factors can also operate in a negative way. We have only touched on this point in our discussion. If an infant at birth is lacking essential organs such as brain or heart, it cannot live and is thereby denied a rich and varied personality development. A spastic child with a scarred brain cannot develop into a finely coordinated ballet dancer or tightrope walker. The scarred brain operates as a negative factor. It prevents certain personality acquisition. However, I know of a severely spastic young man with an IQ of 150 (whatever that may mean as an index of intellectual development).

The case of Helen Keller is instructive in the role that biological conditions serve as negative factors. Her loss of hearing and seeing eliminated the possible acquisition of a number of personality interactions. For example, she could never hope to paint nature on a canvas. But we should note that, even when so many biological factors worked against her, threatening her even with institutionalization, she nevertheless rose to great heights as a writer, a poet, an administrator of a world organization in behalf of the blind, and, in a sense, as a public speaker.

As one more illustration, let us take the case of Johnny, whose parents suspect he is falling behind in his development. A medical inquiry establishes that Johnny lacks a thyroid gland, a biological structure essential for normal biological functioning. Without it, Johnny is apathetic and indifferent to people and things in his surroundings. The parents say, "He's just a vegetable."

The medical diagnosis calls for regular injection of thyroxin. Soon, we notice a significant change in Johnny's behavior. He is more alert and energetic. He begins to move and turn and to notice people and things and to acquire reactions to the toys, kittens, bottles, and other things in his surroundings. Suppose thyroxin is not available. The child again sinks into indifference, lethargy, or even stupor. If Johnny did not receive thyroxin for years, eventually he would be declared "severely retarded" and institutionalized. But if thyroxin injections are continued over the years, Johnny can rate as normal or even superior on an intelligence test.

How shall we fit such negative biochemical facts into a personality framework? Shall we say that the thyroxin injection *produced* a higher IQ in Johnny or that it maintained the organism in a "normal" biological condition that *made possible* interactions between Johnny and the stimulus objects in his surroundings. In other words, thyroxin is a *necessary*, and not a *causal*, condition of personality development. Negative biological conditions would have prevented Beethoven from acquiring *any* musical behaviors if he had been born deaf. But the mere fact that at birth his hearing was intact did not of itself guarantee musical virtuosity. A reactional biography was also essential. And, as we noted earlier, Beethoven's deafness in middle age did not interfere with his finest compositions.

Freud's Theory of Personality

Now, by contrast with the theory of personality just considered, we are going to explore a competing theory, one developed by Sigmund Freud (1856–1939) in his system, psychoanalysis. One reason we are doing this is because of this system's wide influence. La Piere (1959) has attempted to show how the implications of Freudian theory have pervaded child rearing, the school, the handling of crime, welfare, and other aspects of modern life. In his book, *Freud on Broadway* (1955), Sievers convincingly traces out the impact of Freud's theories on the American theater. Significant dramatists such as Eugene O'Neill, Elmer Rice, Thornton Wilder, Lillian Hellman, Arthur Miller, and Tennessee Williams have dealt with such themes as the Oedipus complex, guilt, repression, homosexuality, dreams, and fantasies. The motion-picture theater has also fallen under the spell of Freud's system. Finally, psychoanalysis has had an effect on academic psychology, even though some theoretical points, such as defense dynamisms, have been revised or reformulated in other terms. While acknowledging the mentalistic or dualistic nature of psychoanalytic theory, nevertheless, if we are to achieve any understanding of it, we must enter into the spirit of the game and become, temporarily at least, dualists, or the devil's advocates.

From the outset, we should be clear that psychoanalysis is both a theory and a form of treatment of human problems. Our interest is in the former. We want to know how Freud conceptualizes human personality.[11]

Psychoanalysis as a Dualistic System

The most basic point about Freud's systematic view (Freud, 1933) is its dualistic (body–mind) foundation. However, Freud is not concerned with how body affects mind or vice versa, but with what goes on in the mind.

Conscious, Preconscious, Unconscious

The conscious.   As far as Freud is concerned, the mind is divided into three compartments—the conscious, preconscious, and the unconscious. The conscious is least significant. It is conscious mind that notes what time it is,

---

[11] As sources, Freud's *Basic Writings of Sigmund Freud* (Freud, 1938) and his *New Introductory Lectures on Psychoanalysis* (Freud, 1933) are recommended in addition to those mentioned in the text.

that we feel hungry or sleepy, and that the birds are singing. It maintains contact with the outer world and gets us through the day's business, but it is not important.

The preconscious.   Can you remember how you celebrated your birthday three years ago? Perhaps not right away, but if given enough time maybe you can "drag it up." Should you do so, Freud would say that that particular memory was lodged in your preconscious, a "half-way house" between the conscious and the unconscious. The preconscious, then, contains that which at the moment is unconscious but that can be brought into consciousness with some effort.

The unconscious.   However, the largest and most significant portion of the mental apparatus is the unconscious. Figure 6-3 represents the "iceberg theory of mind," which has become associated with psychoanalysis. Most of an iceberg is under water. In the same way, the unconscious constitutes the largest part of the mental apparatus. It is deep, mysterious, and hidden from view. The visible portions of the iceberg represent the much less significant preconscious and conscious. The metaphor suits Freud because, according to him, most of human behavior is motivated by unconscious factors. Why do people fall in love with the people that they do fall in love with? They do not know, because their past experiences that determine such things have been

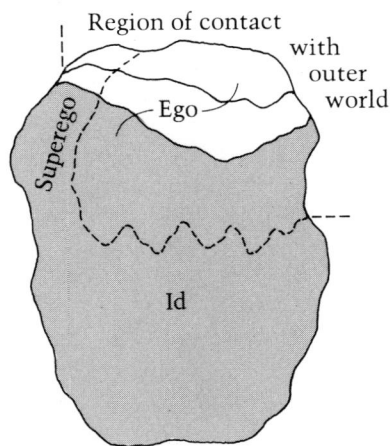

Figure 6-3   The psychoanalytic or "iceberg" theory of personality. The white part at the top, like the part of an iceberg above water, represents the conscious aspect of mind. The intermediate gray part just below is the preconscious, and all else belongs to the vast unconscious. Note also the interrelationships between these three compartments and the id, ego, and superego.

buried in the unconscious, and although these experiences are hidden, they nevertheless still cause people to make certain choices.

According to Groddeck (1950), a disciple of Freud's, it is not right to say that we "live our lives," because our lives are really lived by the unconscious and by motives that manipulate us like puppets on a string. Freud pushes the self-actional view to the extreme when he pictures the mind as a stage on which invisible psychic forces such as the conscious contend with the unconscious, determining what the individual will ultimately do.

Id, Ego, and Superego

The id.   In addition to the conscious, preconscious, and unconscious, but with different boundaries, there are the id, ego, and superego. In the deepest layers of the mind lurks the id, the untamed, animal seat of urges and impulses. The id is the locus of the instincts that know no prohibition, no law, no morality, no denial, no contradiction—only immediate expression of biological impulses. The id lives according to the pleasure principle.

The ego.   Around the core of the id, a new development gradually takes shape. Faced with delays and frustration of id impulses, the ego emerges as an agency that learns to adapt to the realities of existence and so, eventually, to live according to the reality principle. Obviously, the two principles are going to be in opposition from time to time.

The superego.   At first, the parents provide the earliest curb on the untamed passions. But, just as the ego develops out of the id, so does the superego develop out of the ego. It is as if one part of the ego stood apart and could observe and criticize the other part. Eventually the superego takes over the "parental function" of prohibition, blame, and the upholding of moral principles. In a psychoanalytic sense, people "carry their parents around with them" to curb id impulses. Conscience, then, becomes one of the superego functions; the other function is to hold up ideals for the ego to attain; failure to do so causes anxiety.

With the hypothetical entities that Freud has proposed, the stage is set for war. Freud uses striking metaphors to illustrate the imaginary, internal forces and their interrelationships. A horse and rider (Freud, 1933, pp. 108–109) represents the relationship between the id and the ego. The horse symbolizes the wild, unbridled id. The ego, living according to the reality principle and knowing the right road to take, is the rider. Sometimes the rider is successful in directing the horse where it should go, but sometimes the horse takes the rider where it chooses to go. But the ego gets it from still another side, from the superego. As Freud (1933, p. 108) puts it, "The poor Ego has a still harder time of it; it has to serve three harsh masters, and has to do its best to reconcile the claims and demands of all three." When any entity gains power over the others, and with variations provided along the conscious—unconscious dimension, things can get pretty rough in this so-called mind.

Infantile Sexuality

Freud's pronouncement that the sexual function is present from birth horrified the world. But he did not mean that it was there from the start in the adult form. Sexuality in the infant, according to Freud, is diffuse, expressing itself simply in the filling and emptying of such body cavities as mouth, stomach, bladder, and rectum and through touching, rocking, petting, seeing, and so on. Also certain erogenous zones channel the expression of infantile sexuality. The first beachhead of the sexual instincts is the oral zone, which is so closely connected with nourishment and survival. The anal zone becomes established early and assumes a sexual (pleasurable) function. The genital zone is activated when the instincts express themselves via the genital structures. Freud does not consider any zone as dominating the others. In fact, he considers the infant to be "polymorphously perverse," a term meant to denote the richness and variety of expressions of infantile sexuality. All the later (adult) perversions, such as voyeurism, exhibitionism, sadism, and masochism, are present from the start and become only exaggerated and uncontrolled in the adult "pervert."

Autoerotic, Narcissistic, and Object-Choice Stages

The erogenous zones indicate bodily regions at which the sexual instincts are expressed in more or less concentrated form, but the skin (all over) is also an erogenous area, as manifested in touching, patting, massaging, petting, and cradling. At this early stage of functioning, the organism is said to be *autoerotic.* Pleasure is derived from the mere activity of the organs concerned. But later developments usher in a narcissistic stage. The direction of the instinctual impulses now is reflexive, which means that they are directed toward oneself. In psychoanalytic terms, the ego takes itself as an object, causing people to act as if they were in love with themselves. Freud questions whether anyone ever gets *completely* over one's narcissistic fixation. Nevertheless, most people go on to the next, still more mature developmental phase, the object-choice stage in which, not oneself, but another person, becomes the goal of instinctual impulses. And this brings us to the Oedipus complex, a construct of central importance in psychoanalysis.

The Oedipus Complex

The Oedipus complex proceeds naturally out of the narcissistic stage. The first objects in the external world are those that cater to the child's narcissism, to its comfort and bodily pleasures, so that the instincts come to be directed toward the caretaker. The first object choice can determine later, adult object "choices."

The first caretaker of almost everyone is the mother. A fixation of the instincts on the mother results in the most important of all complexes, the Oedipus complex. According to Freud, the boy's sexual wishes are directed toward the mother as object choice, while jealous and hostile impulses are aimed toward the father as rival. One sometimes hears children say that they will someday marry their opposite-sex parent; Freud would probably say that such children are expressing the Oedipus complex in that "incestuous" relationship and that the eternal triangle has started to shape "the family romance."

The Oedipus complex in the boy.   To proceed with an analysis of how the Oedipus complex develops in the boy, we must consider the castration complex, another momentous Freudian concept. The castration complex arises from what Freud considers a preoccupation of children; namely, the problem of the difference between the sexes. This is the way Freud thinks that the problem is solved: both the boy and girl soon note that girls lack an organ that boys possess. In their speculations, they come out with different answers. The boy reasons that at one time the female also possessed such an organ but that she was deprived of it on account of her incestuous wishes. Fearing a similar tragedy, he resolves to give up his wish to possess his mother and to get rid of his rival, the father. Thus, the castration complex smashes to pieces the Oedipus complex, and the boy then starts looking around for "a girl just like the girl that married dear old Dad," a mother substitute.

The Oedipus complex in the girl.   According to Freud, there is an interesting inversion of the two main complexes in the girl. Her castration complex comes first and, in fact, ushers in her Oedipus complex. In her speculation about her lack of a phallus, the girl reasons that she too, at one time, had such a prized organ but now lacks it because her mother deprived her of it. Therefore, she rejects her mother as an object choice and turns toward her father as an object choice, eventually going on to a father substitute who will give her a boy who will symbolize and compensate her for the missing organ. But Freud thinks that the woman will suffer, to some degree, from "penis envy" and will seek restitution in joining women's liberation movements, supporting equal-rights amendments, and so on.

Dynamics and Dynamisms

What we have been discussing up to this point might be considered an anatomy of the mind. Now we are ready to delve into what we might compare to a physiology of the mind; that is, how the various components function in relation to each other or, as it is sometimes put, the dynamics.[12] The chief agent of all the alleged goings-on in the mental apparatus is the unconscious ego. All the warring elements are harmonized, neutralized, resolved, or somehow transformed by the unconscious ego. Its failure to bring the warring parties to terms means anxiety, neurosis, or psychosis or, if all works well, absence of tension and disharmony. The variety of dynamisms or mechanisms are all functions of the unconscious ego. We now consider some of the most important of them, because they are offered as throwing light on personality. As Healy, Bronner, and Bowers (1930, p. 196) argue, "All defense dynamisms are to be found in a moderate degree at work in the normal individual."

1. *Repression.* When the unconscious ego banishes a potentially painful impulse from consciousness, that is repression. However, when a person intentionally and knowingly tries to forget an unpleasant experience, that is suppression, not repression. Repression must go on unconsciously, not consciously. Its defensive purpose should be evident: it protects the conscious ego from the id's shocking disclosures by "keeping a lid on them."

2. *Sublimation.* Assume that a crude sexual urge is seeking expression, but the unconscious ego is on the job and will not permit it. The energy representing that impulse may still be allowed expression if it can be expended in more socially approved ways in the form of affection, filial devotion, and social involvement as in teaching, social welfare, or missionary work, or the "brotherhood of man." There is also a strong implication that physical exercise can sublimate sexual desire. (Or is that only a distraction technique?) At any rate, this defense mechanism ensures that all that energy is expended in tiny dribbles in an asexual manner.

3. *Displacement.* If the psychic energy that Freud assumes to exist is repressed, it can still find another outlet and obtain satisfactory expression thereby. The expression, "She got him on the rebound," illustrates a shift in object choice from one person to another. Kicking the cat is another. You stumble from your own awkwardness, and the cat is handy, so you kick it in anger. Or perhaps Papa comes home from the office after being thoroughly bawled out by his boss. His wife and child are convenient targets for the resentment that he failed to express toward his boss. Psychoanalysis would treat Leonard's siderophobia (Chapter 1) as a displacement, the notion being that his conflict did not really involve trains but that the unconscious picked on them as a dodge to throw the unconscious off the track where the real conflict might be found. Compulsions and obsessions are also viewed as illustrating the defense dynamisms of displacement.

---

[12] For a nonpsychoanalytic interpretation of dynamics and dynamisms, *see* Skinner (1953, especially pp. 288–294 and 372–379).

4. *Symbolization.*   If certain id urges are linked up with ideas that would outrage the superego, those ideas can still get expressed if they are, so to speak, disguised or symbolized in less blatant ways. There must be a comparison of sorts between the symbol and the thing symbolized. For example, as in fairytales, so in dreams parents are symbolized as king and queen, brothers and sisters as little animals or vermin, birth as falling into or climbing out of water, death by setting out on a journey or traveling by train. The sexual life, probably because it is so repressed, has a rich assemblage of symbols to represent it. Sticks, umbrellas, poles, trees, knives, daggers, swords, and firearms symbolize the male sex organ. Pits, hollows, caves, jars, bottles, boxes, chests, cupboards, stoves, rooms, churches, and chapels are female sexual symbols.

5. *Projection.*   When an external danger threatens the organism, fight or flight is possible. But when there is an "internal" danger, such as a powerful id urge threatening the peace and security therein, the only alternative is to *externalize* that danger. If it is "out there," it seems easier to deal with. So the individual who is tempted to extreme sexual or aggressive impulse can "disown" that urge and claim that it is really being forced on him or her by the devil or by evil voices beamed over radio waves. The murderer may claim that "The Lord made me do it. It wasn't my idea." According to a disciple of Freud's, Theodor Reik (1949, p. 85), it is better not to get involved in lovers' quarrels, for "Lovers ask themselves . . . whether the fault is really theirs and regularly answer, no, the blame is with the other person. Sometimes it is better not to ask yourself this question, for then you will not hear lies about yourself."

6. *Rationalization.*   Rationalization is probably the most common of the defense dynamisms. According to Freud, we are *supposed to be* rational creatures, but most of our behavior is really motivated by unconscious, irrational impulses, so the unconscious ego manipulates and revises them to appear rational. We act in certain ways and *then* find reasons to back them up. In a sense, the unconscious ego is defending the id by pretending that the id is conforming to reality instead of pushing its own demands. We explain our slips of the tongue, the pen, and so on as "accidents" or "chance" happenings, but the Freudians, with their belief in strict determinism, are likely to suspect rationalization.

7. *Idealization.*   Idealization is most clearly visible when individuals fall in love. In this manifestation of it, people endow the beloved with attributes of excellence and beauty that others simply cannot see. Idealization amounts to an unconscious overestimation and endowment of "spiritual qualities" in the object choice. The actual situation is that the "spiritual attributes" have been "loaned" to the beloved because of sensual attraction, not that the sexual allure is the result of "the spiritual merits." A popular song of a

by-gone era asked (rhetorically), "Do I love you because you're beautiful or are you beautiful because I love you?" Theodor Reik would say it is the latter, as revealed in the following statement from his book, *Of Love and Lust* (1949, p. 43): "The love object is a phantom to a great extent, a peg on which we hang all the illusions of ourselves which we longed to fulfill. The living person is, so to speak, only the material from which we create a fantastic figure, just as a sculptor shapes a statue out of stone."

The psychoanalytic term *idealization* bears some relationship to our everyday use of the term as when we *idealize, idolize,* or attribute a halo to someone. The difference is that as a defense dynamism, in psychoanalytic usage, idealization is said to bear a relationship to certain id impulses. Idealization should not be confused with sublimation, in which the sexual aim is deflected and expressed in highly attenuated or nonsexual ways. Idealization eats its cake and has it too, simply by pretending that the sexual attraction is something other than what is really is.

8. *Introjection.* Mothers are sometimes heard to exclaim to their babies, "Oh, I love you so much I could gobble you up!" Here, we have an excellent illustration of the defense dynamism of introjection or incorporation. To incorporate means to take in and combine or blend so as to form one body. At first, the child is omnipotent because it *is* the universe, but later the world of objects and other persons becomes differentiated and separate. But the child can regain some of that omnipotence by psychologically assimilating what is not the self through incorporation, after the physiological prototype of the swallowing reflex. The schizophrenic is said to fail to differentiate between reality and fantasy because, through incorporation or introjection, the two have become so blended that they are one for that person. Therefore, we say that the schizophrenic has lost contact with reality.

9. *Identification.* When the little boy says, "Someday I'm going to marry Mom and buy her lots of nice things," the psychoanalyst would see the dynamism of identification working there. He or she would mean that the son unconsciously molds himself after the father. The boy "plays the role" of his father or wants to *be* him. In a similar way, the little girl plays mother and treats her dolls after the model furnished by her mother in her handling of real, live children. In addition to shaping their adult role, the psychoanalyst believes that identification may help in resolving the Oedipus complex by enabling the child to act *as if* he or she were the mate of the opposite-sex parent. Identification also operates while we watch soap operas, plays, or read mystery stories during which we can identify with the hero, heroine, or the Boston strangler and, thereby, perhaps, sublimate our erotic or murderous id urges.

10. *Conversion.* Repression does not always work effectively, in which case the affective (emotional) energy of what is repressed is directed into the

bodily sphere. For example, a soldier may be terrified at the prospect of going into battle, but he does not dare to acknowledge it for fear of being declared a coward. So, unwittingly, he may develop a paralysis of the leg, which the unconscious ego worked out as a successful defense dynamism. Now he does not have to go to battle, and he will not be considered a coward. What a nice solution! This hypothetical case is an illustration of hysteria, or expression of repressed instinctual impulses by means of physical manifestations.

11. *Reaction Formation.* Reaction formation or reversal formation is a coverup of instinctual impulses in the id by the development of the direct opposite in the conscious ego. Thus, aggression can express itself as an excessive sympathy, hatred as love or love as hatred, touching as disgust (see Hollender's 1970 study on touch), and anal interests as orderliness, miserliness, and stubbornness.

Freud considers reaction formation as hypocritical, because one feeling masquerades as its opposite. For example, a mother may react to an unplanned-for child with Hollywood gushiness and sweetness, really a disguise for her feelings of resentment toward the unwanted child. But if the defense works by hiding the mother's true feelings from herself, then the defense dynamism protects the mother from guilt feelings.

One of Freud's American advocates, A. A. Brill (1946), offers some interesting speculations on how smell operates in humans as a reaction formation. Taking an evolutionary viewpoint, he points out how feces and urine have been important in species territoriality and sexuality. Even detection of criminals is achieved with the aid of bloodhounds by means of dogs' superior smell. With a romantic freedom, Brill (p. 187) speculates that humans have substituted vision for an earlier epoch's domination of smell. "We say, 'How beautiful she is!' In the olden days, it was, 'How beautiful she smells!'—as one can still observe in dogs when they meet" (p. 187). He goes on to say,

> Repression of the sense of smell is responsible for many changes in the behavior of civilized man. But the interest in odors has not been given up. Millions are spent annually on perfumes and odoriferous powders and pomades which are supposedly used to disguise our dislike for human odors. Yet all these artificial perfumes come from the same source as the human odor. The most expensive perfume is made from the sexual glands of the civet cat, musk ox, and of certain deer, obtained when these animals are in rut. A drop of such secretion can make gallons of perfume. The other ingredients of perfume are from blossoms of the sexual glands of plants. These unconsciously serve the same purpose as the original ones—namely, to attract the sexes. [Brill, 1946, p. 188]

Poor humans, the very thing that they tried to cover up or get away from, they end up anointing themselves with!

12. *Unconscious fantasy.*   Freud believes that some fantasizing takes place entirely in the unconscious, where it is free from the restraints of reality. As proof, he suggests that solutions to scientific and other problems may occur during sleep. But psychoanalysis also considers conscious fantasizing or daydreaming an important "defense" by providing gratification of impulses that would be denied motor discharge. The origin of daydreaming is traced to childish play with objects that are woven into the fantasy involved in play. In daydreaming dependence on real objects is abandoned. Children are quite open in their make-believe fantasying, but adults make a great secret of their daydreams and are reluctant to share them with others. But adult daydreams "pay off" anyhow in relieving some of the id pressures. The schizophrenic's "autistic thinking" is a defense against the harsh realities of life and a compensation for them.

13. *Dream work.*   The term *dream work* refers to a combination of defense dynamisms that shape the impulses motivating the dream into their final form as reported by the dreamer. The dream as reported in its often absurd form is called the "manifest content." But the true, hidden, or latent content must be analyzed out by noting which dynamisms were involved in disguising the forbidden latent content into the acceptable manifest. The following dream, analyzed by Alexander (1948), may help in understanding dream work.

A German businessman reported a dream in which he was taking a walk with a high-ranking officer of the Russian army and gradually realized that it was the czar. Suddenly a stranger with a sword attacked the czar, with the obvious intention of wanting to kill him. The patient wanted to intervene and save the czar's life but failed to do so. The czar was killed (Alexander, 1948, pp. 161–162).

Asked to associate to the different parts of the dream, the patient reported that the czar is called "little father" in Russian. He also recalled a recent armistice situation when, as a German soldier, he with his comrades faced Russian soldiers in their trenches. On one occasion, he violated the armistice agreement by firing at a Russian soldier, "which appeared to him 'strange' because in normal life, 'he wouldn't kill a fly' " (Alexander, 1948, p. 162).

When asked to associate with the word "stranger," he hesitated. Nothing came to his mind, and he stated with annoyance that he did not know who the stranger was. He was then told that the stranger probably meant the strange part of his own personality which had committed murder. It was pointed out to him that he used the word "strange" when he described how unlike his naturally kind character it was to shoot at the Russians. The patient protested energetically and said, "How could it be myself when in the dream I try to save the Tsar?" It was then explained to him that he was the author of the dream and if he had wanted to, he could have saved the Tsar. Intellectually the point became clear, and he later produced memories in which hostile feelings toward his father were recalled. [Alexander, 1948, p. 162]

Several dynamisms enter the picture here.

a. *Projection.*   Note the patient's disowning of his aggressive impulses by dumping them onto the "stranger."

b. *Symbolism.*   At first, the patient was walking with a Russian officer, apparently an inadequate substitute for his own father, so the dream work produced the czar or "little father."

c. *Reaction formation.*   This defense transformed the hostile impulses already projected on the stranger to solicitousness and protectiveness on the basis of the formula *Hate = love.* But hostility won out in the end because the czar was killed. And, as Alexander pointed out to the patient, he (the patient) was the author of this scenario. If he had really intended to save the czar's life, why didn't he "write the plot" accordingly?

One more point. The patient's Oedipus complex is quite transparent in the dream the patient reported to Alexander.

The defense dynamisms or mechanisms, as they are sometimes called, have been set forth here in a psychoanalytic framework; they are considered important in understanding personality. The defense dynamisms are the various ways in which the primitive, unsocialized id desires and wishes are manipulated by the unconscious ego to avoid tension, frustration, or pain by keeping the various mental systems in harmony with each other.

It seems hardly necessary to point out that psychoanalytic theory relies on a thoroughly self-actional viewpoint, with all the criticisms pertaining thereto. However, it is also important to note that whatever *data* the psychoanalyst deals with can also be translated into other theoretical frameworks, a task that would require another book.

Chapter Summary

The approach in this chapter was a synthetic one, in which the person is seen whole. Personality is an integrated interactional system, the totality of a given individual's interbehaviors. Personality must be dated, is organized even in "disorganization," and is unique. Multiple or split personality involves organization into subsystems, while pseudopersonality involves behavior unlike the usual self. The diversity and magnitude of personality interbehaviors can be organized into classes. Biological factors also play a role in personality development. Freud's theory of personality stresses the defense dynamisms as explanations of personality dynamics. Behavior development is extremely flexible and has great latent potential. It is even possible, psychologically speaking, to "make a woman" out of an individual who had previously been, for 40 years, "a man."

Lastly, both continuity (or stability) and change in the constituent personality responses are important. Some responses endure for decades, while others come and go. In the case of the constituent responses of personality, their stability or change will be determined by the stability or change of their controlling stimuli.

7 "Abnormal Personality," "Psychopathology," "Mental Illness," or "Problems in Living"?

Some occurrences which appear astounding when only partially understood, become simple and natural phenomena when one gets complete information.

[Goddard, 1927, p. vii]

In the days when house calls were the order of the day, a physician was returning from the country where he had seen a patient.

> It was long past midnight when an acquaintance going in the opposite direction saw the doctor in the middle of the country road on his hands and knees, feeling around in the dirt. He stopped his machine and called to him to know what he was doing. The reply came back promptly in all seriousness, "hunting for goldfish." The acquaintance was horrified as the thought went through his head, "My God, the doctor has gone crazy." Who would not have had some such thought upon finding a man in the darkness, hunting for goldfish in the dust of a lonely country road? But the doctor was not crazy; he was behaving with complete intelligence. The other facts that belong to this story are: the doctor's patient had given him a bowl of goldfish which he had placed in his car. Driving in the dark the car had hit an unseen bump the shock of which had broken the bowl, spilling part of the water and with it the fish. One he had picked up in the bottom of the car, but two seemed to have been thrown out into the road and he hoped to find them. [Goddard, 1927, pp. vii–viii]

If the physician's acquaintance had driven off at the moment he learned that his medical friend was hunting in the road for goldfish, he would have been puzzled by the unusual event he had just witnessed, ascribed it to "craziness," and dismissed the incident.

"Panchrestons"

A woman confined to a state psychiatric institution walks up and down the corridor of her ward and, highly agitated, keeps repeating the phrase, "I do, I do." Some refer to her as "a nut" or "a crazy." As long as such disdainful views prevail, unusual acts are simply labeled as "crazy" without further consideration, a procedure still extant today, particularly in popular psychology. Some people think that, if they give a particular event a name, they have thereby explained it. Hardin (1957) has called such a name a *panchreston*, a term he defines as an "explain-all," a word that is intended to explain everything and therefore explains nothing. To say that a person is "off her rocker" or "nutty as a fruitcake" may make one feel smug but adds *not* one iota of understanding. To call someone "crazy" amounts to saying, "I don't understand your behavior. It is 'out of this world.' " And with that attitude, we close the case, obstructing further study and understanding.

Instead of applying the panchreston *crazy* to the woman's repetitious "I do" in our example, let us expand our inquiry to see if we can relate her present behavior to prior events. If we take enough patience to study her case history (reactional biography), we learn that, just hours before her eagerly anticipated church wedding, her husband-to-be was killed in a traffic accident. Doesn't her apparently unusual behavior make sense now? It looks as though her constantly repeated phrase "I do" is part of a rehearsal of the anticipated wedding ceremony. Both our procedure up to this point and the multiplicity of terms in the title of this chapter suggest that there are more ways of construing such events than we have examined so far. Let us look at the approaches toward such events that have been adopted in different places and different times.

The Medical Model

Today, the most prevalent way of understanding personality problems is by way of the medical model, although this has not always been true. One can imagine that if our case of the woman repeating "I do" were being discussed at a cocktail party, someone would suggest that the woman is "sick." Any unusual behavior of an individual is likely to be so labeled. We hear talk about "sick humor," "sick economies," and a "sick society."

In an article, "Psychiatrists Use Dangerous Words," American psychiatrist Karl Menninger (1964) pointed out the danger of applying labels to people's behavior. For example, calling a person "psychotic" or "schizophrenic," implying that the term refers to a "disease," can wreck a career. Menninger believes there are only behavior patterns that can be worked with, not some incurable disease state with the customary institutionalization and pessimistic outcome. It is interesting to note that, although Menninger rejects the old, static, fatalistic concept of mental disease, he nevertheless clings to the metaphor of mental illness. He says that if people are demoralized, frightened, confused, worried, or depressed, those are ways of behaving. Nevertheless, he considers their complaints as "symptoms" of an illness, a "mental illness," which, as a physician, it is his obligation to "treat" and to "cure."

Now we move on to the view of a psychiatrist who considers the concept of mental illness itself a myth.

The Myth of Mental Illness

When psychiatrist Thomas Szasz published his book, *The Myth of Mental Illness* (1961), he dropped an intellectual bombshell that aroused argument, attack, and counterattack in the psychiatric literature. Now, when Szasz says that mental illness is a myth, we need to understand that he is not *denying* the behavioral facts that are *labeled as* mental illness. He acknowledges that people do suffer from anxiety, fears, worries, distress, frustration, depression, confusion, and so on. He only objects to applying the inappropriate metaphor of "illness" to such happenings.

Szasz is of the opinion that the mental-illness metaphor is derived from the disease, syphilis of the brain. Certainly, such a biological condition may be related to behavioral changes too (as we noted in Chapter 1); but, medically speaking, we are dealing with a brain disease. But some reductionists believe that "mental illness" is also of this type and that some day some neurological or chemical condition will be found to explain all the neuroses and psychoses. Szasz is opposed to such a view, insisting instead that people also have difficulties that are *problems in living.*

A comparison between neurological defects and behaviors labeled as "mental illness" is in order. If a patient complains about double vision, we make an anatomical and physiological inquiry, find a lesion in the optic pathway, and feel satisfied with the finding as an explanation. Now, if we return to our case of the patient who kept incessantly repeating the phrase "I do," we cannot (and need not) explain her behavior by a defect or disease of the nervous system. A dimension involving that woman's reactional biography is sufficient. Furthermore, says Szasz, just as bodily diseases and defects are related to anatomical and physiological conditions, so are the actions of people labeled as mental illness inextricably interwoven with social and, especially, ethical considerations.

The question of norms also arises in a comparison of bodily versus mental illness. If we take bodily illness, the norm is the structural and functional effectiveness of the organism stated in anatomical and physiological terms. The norm, departure from which defines mental illness, is not so easily stated, but one thing is clear—that norm must be stated in social, ethical, and legal terms. For example, by maintaining that only a person suffering from mental illness would commit murder illustrates use of a legal concept as a norm of mental health. If one grants that, then it is apparent that medical measures such as diagnosis, prognosis, and cure are inappropriate. Murderers, child molesters, and wife abusers are not "sick" the way diabetics, arthritics, and asthmatics are. The latter are identified by anatomical and physiological criteria and the former by social, ethical, and legal standards. Child abusers and exhibitionists simply happen to behave in ways that society strongly condemns. To take another illustration that shows the shiftiness of social norms: homosexuality in ancient Greece was not disapproved. In our own culture, it used to be very taboo and definitely illegal, but today the social and legal norm is, at least, ambivalent.

> To recapitulate: In contemporary social usage, the finding of mental illness is made by observing a deviance in behavior from certain psychosocial, ethical, or legal norms. The judgment may be made, as in medicine, by the patient, the physician (psychiatrist), or others. Remedial action, finally, tends to be sought in a therapeutic—or covertly medical—framework. This creates a situation in which it is claimed that psychosocial, ethical, and legal deviations can be corrected by medical action. *Since medical interventions are designed to remedy only medical problems, it is logically absurd to expect that they will help solve problems whose very existence has been defined and established on non-medical grounds.* [Szasz, 1970, p. 17, emphasis added]

"Mental Illness" as a Metaphor

The term *mental illness* forces an analogy of human conduct with biological disease and defect. One assumes the existence of mental illness and then uses it to explain someone's not getting along with someone else. So one "treats" the mental illness in the hope of "curing" it, thus making it possible for that person to get along. Szasz sees this as a futile exercise—one of fighting battles on false fronts. We should be tackling ethical, personal, and social conflict. The mental-illness metaphor, for example, encourages "treating stomach acid and chronic fatigue instead of facing up to a marital conflict" (Szasz, 1970, p. 23). When we drop the metaphor of mental illness, then we see clearly that what confronts us are problems in living. We are not involved in anatomy, physiology, physics, and chemistry. Rather, we find ourselves in the area of human relationships, not in medicine with its proper role in treating broken bones, tumors, inflammations, and infections.

On Classification

One possible starting point for a classification of the data ordinarily included under the category of "abnormal personality" or "psychopathology" appears to be with existing classificatory schemas. We start with the widely accepted *Diagnostic and Statistical Manual of Mental Disorders*, adopted by the American Psychiatric Association (American Psychiatric Association, 1952, 1968).

Analysis of the diagnostic manual reveals a serious logical error. It resorts to a dual foundation for ordering psychiatric data: (1) a biological basis and (2) a psychological one. The results produced by application of two different criteria may be made clear by the following example. Suppose we have the task of sorting out all the mixed "races" of people on earth. Suppose we first separate them on the basis of height. After we have finished sorting according to height, we start to segregate them on the basis of color. Our two categories of people will include a mixture of red, brown, yellow, and white ones and tall, medium, and short ones. In place of order, we have confusion. Our trouble comes from applying both criteria. Had we sorted according to only one criterion, we would have had only one continuum or gradient; if according to height, then very tall at one end, stepwise, to very short at the other, or, if by color, then black would be at one end and, by small gradations, white at the other.

The dual system of classification used in the *Diagnostic and Statistical Manual* (or DSM) is similarly plagued. One large class is designated as "disorders caused by or associated with impairment of brain tissue function" (pp. 2–4). The criterion here is anatomical and physiological, including such factors as infection, tumors, and injuries. Then all of a sudden we come on a totally different class designated as "disorders of psychogenic origin or without clearly defined physical cause or structural change in the brain" (pp. 5–8). And, here, we find the more familiar schizophrenia, paranoia, anxiety, phobia, and obsessions-compulsions or—"problems in living" (to be discussed later), not anatomical–physiological considerations.

We must not overlook the inconsistency in this classification schema. We start out applying anatomical or medical criteria, and suddenly, in midstream, we change horses and criteria and now apply psychological standards. A classification using a single criterion would yield a consistency in results. With the system we are analyzing here, we find that behaviors with related brain injuries may be matched with the behaviors when there are no brain injuries. We may be sure that *the behaviors* that occur in connection with intoxication, brain infection, or lead poisoning will not be radically different from those categorized under disorders of psychological origin without tissue involvement.

Daniel Goleman, a clinical psychologist and associate editor of *Psychology Today*, has written an article entitled "Who's Mentally Ill?" (Goleman, 1978). Essentially, the article keenly analyzes the newest version of the *Diagnostic and Statistical Manual of Mental Disorders—III*, in preparation since 1973 but not yet adopted. According to Goleman, the proposed classification is being intensely debated over such items as the omission of "hysteria" and "neurosis" from the new classificatory scheme and the fact that the latest version is "ten times as long as *DSM-II*" (p. 34). It is important to compare this presumably scientifically based classification with something like the chemist's periodic table of elements. The latter is never debated or revised from convention to convention of assembled chemists. It is fixed and dependable. Consider the fact that some psychiatrists are "displeased the draft omits some favorite new diagnosis—for instance, a veterans' group successfully lobbied for a syndrome they wanted to call 'Post-Vietnam-Combat Disorder.' Feminist women forced a change in a category called 'Sexual Sadism' which they argued would excuse rapists from responsibility for their acts" (p. 34). The following points need to be underscored: (1) the vagueness of the entire classification; (2) the omission of classes that had been included and used over decades; (3) the introduction of *new* classes such as the "Post-Vietnam-Combat Disorder" (may not some future war or other social catastrophe require the introduction of still another "new" disorder?); (4) perhaps, the most important question at this juncture is "How do the proposed changes fit into a medical model?" For example, how do "new mental illnesses" come into being, and why are former illnesses abolished? Goleman educes many other fine points, but these will suffice for our purpose.

A Suggested Orientation Toward Classification

We must constantly remind ourselves that our discipline, psychology, is the study of the behavior of the individual. We should also note that, certainly up to this point in our analysis, we have found no behavior that is supernatural or "out of this world." There is no need to change that approach in our study of "abnormal psychology" or "psychopathology." Whatever data come within our purview will be assumed to be continuous with other common, familiar behaviors.

Another problem arises from psychiatry's attempt to classify *people* rather than behaviors. Psychiatry and sometimes psychology have shown a preference for assigning only one name per customer; for example, A is labeled paranoiac, B manic-depressive, and C schizophrenic. But even psychiatry has been forced to admit use of two categories, as in a diagnosis of *schizophrenia, paranoid type.* I would like to suggest that matters are even more complicated than that. As Kline and Gerard (1953, p. 201) have pointed out, "The 'psychiatry' of an individual is an end product of processes which themselves are not essentially 'psychiatric'."

The Minnesota Multiphasic Personality Inventory (MMPI) is a paper-and-pencil personality questionnaire. If we were to take that test, we would find that each of us "normals" would acquire a certain score on each of the following scales: hypochondriasis, depression, hysteria, psychopathic deviation, masculinity–femininity, paranoia, psychasthenia, schizophrenia, and hypomania. How can that be if we are "normal"? Or are "the people on the outside looking in" different from the "patients" *to a degree* and not *in kind?* That is why noninstitutionalized people do not score zero all across the board. Everybody earns a score, some higher than others.

I have pointed out some problems resident in the traditional classification. Yet we have a certain obligation to become acquainted with current terminology and corresponding behaviors. Elsewhere (Pronko, 1963), I have suggested the following plan of action. In everyday life situations, at work, at play, in their homes and elsewhere, people act in an almost infinite number of ways. Many actions are commendable or neutral in the eyes of the other citizens, but certain actions are judged "insane," "crazy," "psychopathic," "pathological," or as evidencing "mental illness" and as requiring restraint, incarceration, or institutionalization of the person involved. It is obvious, then, that it is not the act itself that labels a person with the common terms listed earlier, but the existence and application of a certain value judgment of the social group in which the act was committed. The situation is a far cry from the organic conditions of staphylococcal infection or pulmonary tuberculosis. The latter proclaims itself as a certain organ or tissue condition, identifiable by means of routine laboratory techniques. The former are *ways of acting*, of saying, thinking, and imagining that are disapproved depending specifically on who commits the act, who judges it, the social status of the former, the latter, and so on.

As students of psychopathology, let us take the behaviors that are labeled as *psychotic.* Because the way they are judged socially does not add one bit to our knowledge of the behavior of the individual concerned at the time he performed the act in question, we cannot use such a criterion for distinguishing those behaviors psychologically from nonpsychotic behaviors. Perhaps Allport's (1937, p. 52) phrase that "character is personality evaluated and personality is character devaluated" will help to make the point that when we strip away the social convention that stamps certain behavior as psychotic, there is no psychological essence that permits us to distinguish psychotic from nonpsychotic behavior. Nevertheless, let us take such behaviors as simple exaggerations or accentuations of behaviors performed by nonpsychotics and, without involving ourselves in a futile psychotic-versus-nonpsychotic controversy, place them in a common matrix. Let us recall Kline and Gerard's (1953, p. 201) previously quoted statement, "The 'psychiatry' of an individual is an end product of processes which themselves are not essentially 'psychiatric.' " If this is true, then our study should repay us by revealing behavioral trends in all alike, the institutionalized and the noninstitutionalized. As a tentative approach, we shall adopt existing classes of behavior disorders, to be judged in terms of the progress we make in formulating and interpreting the behaviors with which we start.

A Tentative Adoption of the Traditional Classification

To guide our discussion, we will consider the following traditional classes and subclasses of the data of so-called mental illness.

NEUROSES (OR PSYCHONEUROSES)	PSYCHOSES
Anxiety reactions	Paranoia
Hypochondriasis	Schizophrenia
Hysteria	Manic-depressive
Obsessions-compulsions	

The Neuroses

Our first job is to try to define the neuroses (or psychoneuroses) and the psychoses. Both terms are, as Menninger (1964) reminded us, "dangerous," and both are "panchrestons." Despite those handicaps, we must treat them as sympathetically as possible. The "neuroses," then, are usually considered *minor* personality disorders, and the psychoses are considered *major*. In the same loose fashion, neurotics are not considered dangerous enough to warrant commitment to an institution, while psychotics are more likely to be committed. Delusions and/or hallucinations are supposed to be more characteristic of psychotics, not neurotics. But all these "criteria" are so imprecise that they are not by any means dependable. And now, being properly warned of the looseness of the framework within which we shall find our data, we proceed to a consideration of anxiety neurosis or anxiety reactions.

Anxiety Reactions

Ours is supposed to be an age of anxiety. Surely, down through the centuries, all the wars and pestilences that flesh is heir to have caused humans much stress and tension. Anxiety is a human response to threatened or unknown dangers. We can approach a definition of anxiety by contrasting anxiety with fear. Fear has a definite object or situation that the person can point to, such as flying in an airplane or the dentist's drill. The fear seems reasonable. But anxiety involves a diffuse apprehension as when a person declares, "I'm anxious and jittery, but I don't know why." The psychoanalyst would interpret that situation as "free-floating anxiety" and considers it a displacement from some repressed unconscious impulse.

On the response side of the anxiety picture, we find visceral and muscular tensions as aspects of the anxiety pattern. If we get down to details, we find that almost every nook and cranny of the organism that has a muscle may be incorporated into the anxiety picture. Some headaches may be the result of a hangover or from other kinds of intoxications. These are not anxiety reactions because they are explainable on a physiological basis. But for some people, their marital or business situation or life itself can "be a headache." Other people react to threat with high blood pressure or a stroke. Russek (1960) states that coronary disease was seven times more frequent in ambitious males with an intense, sustained aim to achieve success, by comparison with a control group. Russek also found that in a group of patients under 40 years of age, extended emotional stress connected with job responsibility preceded heart attack in 91% of cases versus 20% for controls.

There are other variations on the anxiety theme. Stomach ulcers, asthma and hay fever, arthritis, and even cancer have been scrutinized for possible psychological involvement, as have absence of menstruation, painful menstruation, pregnancy, and a number of sexual problems. Often such problems are misidentified as medical cases. The distinction between the medical or biological and the psychological response is always made on the following basis: did the reaction occur as a function of (1) a tissue-excitation response (such as pollen in the nose) or (2) a history of argument at the dinner table (for example)? Marks and Lader (1973) have pinpointed the most frequent anxiety reactions in terms of the biological reaction systems involved: headache, heart palpitation, breathlessness, faintness, dizziness, chest pain, easy fatiguability, sighing, and the complaint of apprehension. The overall picture is one of tension and stress, but this is the important point: the apparent hyperactivity of various organ systems is not a function of the individual's running around a race track or doing hard work. The heart may palpitate while the defendant sits still in a chair in the courtroom just before the jury announces its verdict.

Phobias.   Traditionally, phobias have not been classified under anxiety responses, and yet, on the response side, they resemble the reactions we have been discussing so far. It is the stimulus characteristics of phobias that create a certain awkwardness. In "free-floating anxiety," for example, the person is not sure what the anxiety-provoking thing is. As we noted in regard to Leonard's siderophobia, he knew that he was anxious about trains. His anxiety was out of all proportion to the potential danger of trains, however, so that others would consider his behavior irrational, a fact he readily admitted—but his problem persisted anyhow. Freud would say that the situation demanded a search for something that had been repressed in the unconscious. But Skinner would probably say that the situation demanded a search for a response that had been originally conditioned to an aversive stimulus but that was now conditioned to a neutral stimulus.

A catalogue of phobias.   The older textbooks on psychopathology included long lists of phobias dressed up in forbidding Greek words, with the suffix *-phobia* meaning fear and the prefix indicating the specific stimulus that was the source of the problem. The following partial list is offered as a transient distraction from our more serious discussion.

STIMULUS	PHOBIA	STIMULUS	PHOBIA
animals	zoophobia	heart disease	cardiophobia
bacteria	bacteriophobia	nakedness	gymnophobia
being alone	monophobia	open spaces	agoraphobia
being stared at	scopophobia	pain	algophobia
blushing	ereuthophobia	poisoning	toxicophobia
corpse	necrophobia	sea	thalassophobia
crowds	ochlophobia	sexual intercourse	coitophobia
death	thanatophobia	snakes	ophidiophobia
dirt	mysophobia	strangers	xenophobia
electricity	electrophobia	surgical operations	ergasiophobia
elevated places	acrophobia	touching or being	haphephobia
everything	panophobia	touched	
fire	pyrophobia	women	gynophobia
		worms	helminthophobia

This list of phobias, which used to provide instructors with a rich source of exam questions, shows

1. The absurdity of naming the stimulus objects of phobias in a foreign language
2. The possibility of creating endless lists of such terms
3. The apparent specificity of conditioning involved in the acquisition of the phobic response
4. The need for delving into the phobic's reactional biography in order to understand its origin

Hypochondriasis

Reduced to simplest terms, *hypochondriasis* may be defined as "overconcern with body." An exaggerated response to one's own organ functioning or general health status elaborates the definition. In terms of an interbehavioral analysis, hypochondriasis involves a self-reaction. The individual reacts to some specific or general feature of the biological makeup in certain ways. For example, a dictatorial father may rule his family with an iron hand under the threat of a heart attack if anyone crosses him. The mother whose children have left home ("the empty-nest syndrome") may turn her attention to herself and her bodily functioning and seek more attention for herself by making the rounds of medical practitioners. A child may escape an exam at school by having an upset stomach. Alfred Adler (1929) describes the case of a woman married for years to a difficult man; but when she had occasional headaches her husband was very nice to her.

There are still more situations that can elicit a hypochondriacal response. Our culture tolerates or even rewards illness or defect. If a man drinks and fails to support his family, we throw him in jail. But if he does not work because he claims he has "heart trouble" or arthritis, we take care of him through the county hospital or welfare system. With such a sympathetic attitude toward illness so prevalent in our culture, it is small wonder that people build up "adjustment by illness" or bodily complaint? Society reinforces such responses. Insurance companies have a difficult time in distinguishing between genuine back injuries and pain from whiplash and what has been labeled as "compensation neurosis." It is not hard to guess whether happy workers or disgruntled ones are likely to file suit for compensation following an on-the-job injury.

Still other situations can elicit a hypochondriacal response. For example, a placebo effect is the effect that is attributed to a pill, potion, or procedure because of the patient's belief in its effectiveness, not on the basis of its medicinal properties. A sugar pill is one type of placebo. We must not think, though, that the effect is "only imaginary." The response is a psychological response of the patient to the total treatment situation.

Some years ago, Beecher (1956) contrasted wound pains in civilian surgery patients and in wounded soldiers. He administered the same questionnaire to both groups and found that only 25% of wounded soldiers wanted drugs to relieve their pain compared to 80% of civilians who did desire pain-relieving drugs. Why the reversal in the two groups? According to Beecher (1956, p. 110), the wounds had different meanings for the individuals of the two groups. Although we are told that the pain sensation from the wounds of the two groups may be presumed to be equivalent, their *reaction* to the wounds was radically different. The wounded soldier had just escaped death on the battlefield and rejoiced at being alive—"his wound was a good thing" (p. 110). To the civilian, the wound was an unwanted, unexpected tragedy even when it was essential, as after an emergency surgery.

Therefore, pain occurred more frequently and with greater severity in the civilian group. Beecher's conclusion (1956, p. 110) is that "there is no simple, direct relationship between the wound *per se* and the pain experienced. The pain is in very large part determined by other factors and of great importance here is the significance of the wound."

The hypochondriacal response is the same regardless of whether it occurs (1) under placebo to one's dizziness, nausea, or other complaint or (2) to one's wounds under battle or hospital conditions, with or without drug, or with placebo. "Placebos, organically ineffective, can only affect reaction" (Beecher, 1956, p. 112). Placebos, just like drugs, have *some* effect on the response. But even drugs do not have an absolute effect. One drug user may have an out-of-this-world "high," another experiences a "bummer," and a third, nothing, after taking the same drug. This is another way of saying that hypochondriacal responses are like other responses. The "meaning" or stimulus function of one's biological makeup or illness, wound, or drug intake will be determined by the individual's past history, life circumstances, and such setting factors as presence of others and their interpersonal relationships.

Hysteria

A case of reactional dissociation.   The case of Kate Fox (Carter, 1937) concerns a well-developed adolescent over 13 years of age. The incident that brought her to the clinic occurred about 9 months previously while she was in school. Her left leg suddenly became paralyzed, numb and prickly. She was put to bed. Two weeks later, while on crutches, she acted as if she had St. Vitus Dance, a toxic disorder of the central nervous system causing involuntary movements or spasms. Several weeks later, she calmed down, but a lack of appetite caused her to lose weight, and she still relied on crutches.

Clinical studies showed that Kate could use her left leg while lying down. Furthermore her gait was so untypical of any biological condition that organic disease was ruled out. It was not St. Vitus Dance. So Kate was brought to the psychological clinic in a wheelchair. Her paralysis and lack of appetite were discussed with her, but she had no insight into the reason for their occurrence. Her counselor suggested tht such incidents as hers were often connected with "emotional crises." Kate finally broke down and tearfully narrated the following family drama.

Up until three years prior to her paralysis, Kate's home had been a happy one. Then, a love triangle intruded itself into the family situation when the mother fell in love with a roomer and eloped with him. The mother's return initiated a series of violent and abusive scenes, with many charges and countercharges and threats of divorce.

The rest of the story concerns Kate's reaction to those climactic events. She avoided thinking of the sordid happenings that had disrupted the once peaceful home. Brooding much and communicating little, she kept herself obsessively occupied both at home and at school. However, the strain of social intercourse made her reluctant to mix with the other children, especially at recess time. It is interesting to note that her first paralysis occurred just prior to one of the recess periods.

Kate's story had a happy ending. Her counselor encouraged her to talk about the bitter, past family incidents, to ventilate her feelings, and, after many retellings of the ugly family happenings, to accept them. She also came to see the relationship of her paralysis to the antecedent family tragedy.

Carter's account (1937, pp. 223–224) of Kate's hysterical response stresses its development as an aspect of her reactional biography. Prior to the family crisis, Kate's behavior equipment fitted her well for her domestic, school, and community life as shown by her excellent health, progress in school, and in her social adjustment.

> Then, into her developing reactional biography there intruded a parental triangle situation which was wholly foreign to and at violence with anything previously experienced. From this point on, this individual was precipitated into an environment in which the various objects, persons, and situations did not constitute a homogeneous unity. The result was that in the two years following she built up additional behavior equipment that did not hang together very well. Then, under the stress of a specific fear of social intercourse (the recess period) a part of her reactional equipment sejoined [split off], a specific reaction system (her left leg) became nonfunctional. Hence our descriptive term, *reactional dissociation*. [Carter, 1937, p. 224, emphasis added]

Cameron's (1947) phrase, *reactional inactivation*, is equally appropriate, and his definition of the term is equally acceptable. For Cameron, this term refers to "a persistent selective reaction-insensitivity, which involves a loss in activity related to need or anxiety, but lacks a background of organ or tissue pathology adequate to account for it" (p. 321).

The case of Kate Fox shows a dissociation or splitting off of her walking responses by means of her left leg in an interpersonal crisis.[1] Essentially, what we have here is the nonoperation of a previously acquired response or, to be more precise, a group of closely related responses. Note that when Kate was in bed she could use her left leg. And anatomical and physiological conditions were checked out and ruled out as possible factors in the paralysis.

Next, we look at cases of hysteria that show dissociation of larger clusters of personality reactions. Our extended discussion of personality

---

[1] The term *splitting*, even in its slang form, is appropriate here when we note that Kate's walking reactions by means of her left leg "split."

"switches" (Chapter 6) might just as well have been included here—we find nothing distinctively or essentially different in "abnormal personality" that we do not find in "normal personality" or vice versa. Recall the conflicting or directly opposite personality reactions in the German professor going underground, the Auschwitz concentration camp physician, the "conversion" of Charles Colson after Watergate, and the change of James Morris to Jan Morris. They, too, are cases of what we there labeled as *multiple* or *split personality*. Now, we should add the terms *double personality* and *alternating personality*. Some authors differentiate between the first two terms and the latter; we will not. We round out our discussion with a famous case of split or multiple personality written up in *The Three Faces of Eve*, a book by Thigpen and Cleckley (1957). The case attracted widespread attention when the popular press published its particulars and when a movie portrayal of Evelyn Lancaster's dramatic life was shown on the movie screens across the land.

The three faces of Eve.   The story began when Evelyn Lancaster came to her psychiatrists, Thigpen and Cleckley, complaining about headaches. Sitting in her chair, she presented the picture of a drab, colorless, uninteresting woman, a very plain dresser, quite inhibited, a little anxious, not at all lively, very reserved. She was formal, meek, humble, serious, even sad and immobile. She told the story of how she married Earl White and some of the trouble they had been having. She had a little girl, and she appeared to be a devoted mother, but she was unhappy that she made the agreement to send her daughter to her husband's church for religious training. She made this promise in good faith, but could not go through with it because she felt it unfair to the child; she was now convinced that the child should have an opportunity to determine her own religious beliefs. This was one source of conflict. She also had bad headaches, and sometimes—she was not sure— she thought she suffered from momentary "blackouts."

During one of her office visits, a very startling thing happened as this drab housewife sat in her chair opposite the psychiatrist. There was a sudden transformation in her behavior. Now, instead of this reserved, frozen-faced woman who just answered in short phrases, one saw a vivacious, uninhibited flirt. The grim little housewife with drooping shoulders was instantly metamorphosed into a spontaneous, impertinent, jocular, even flippant hoyden.

Thigpen and Cleckley were to witness many such personality conversions in their office, reconstructing a still greater number of far more radical and complicating episodes that involved both Eve White, the puritanical, grim housewife, and the saucy, suggestive coquette, Eve Black. The eventual appearance of Jane as an alternative to the antagonistic and opposite personalities gave some hope of synthesizing the split personality, for, superficially speaking, Jane was a kind of compromise between the other two.

Obsession–Compulsions

The older literature treated obsessions and compulsions as if they were two different entities. *Obsessions* were defined as persistent, uncontrollable *thoughts*, while the term *compulsion* was limited to *acts* that the victim was compelled to carry out "involuntarily." Perhaps the only difference between the two was that the preoccupations, or obsessions, were not followed by compulsive acts, while in the latter they were. Examples of obsessions include preoccupation with death, obsessive doubts, suicide, or violence towards others. The traditional compulsions include compulsive stealing (kleptomania), compulsive fire setting (pyromania), compulsive window peeping (voyeurism), compulsive display of the nude body or genitalia (exhibitionism), compulsive dressing in the clothes of the opposite sex (transvestism), compulsive infliction of pain on others associated with sexual pleasure (sadism), and compulsive "need" for infliction of pain on oneself associated with sexual pleasure (masochism).

Today, there appears to be little value in separating the gross *doings* of the organism from the subtle *thinkings*. Besides, when people suffer from a phobia such as a fear of contamination of dirt (mysophobia), it may cause mounting *anxiety*, which in turn elicits a hand-washing *compulsion* and a temporary relief from that anxiety. Because one type of response can spill over into another, we need not be obsessed with differentiating between obsessions and compulsions, but shall use the two terms interchangeably or in the hyphenated form. A still more acceptable term is *obsessive-compulsive reactions*.

A down-to-earth view of the obsessive-compulsive reaction. We have already acknowledged the repetitiveness of human behavior in our discussion of personality. In the present connection, we note the exaggeration of certain behaviors of everyday living. We do this particularly to prevent getting an "out-of-this-world" view of obsession-compulsions by observing the dedication, perseverance, and striving for perfection of creative people in a variety of fields. For example, Erikson (1958, p. 45) has said about George Bernard Shaw that his apprenticeship in writing for five years while he "starved" and got nothing published came "close to what clinicians call 'obsessive compensation' " (p. 45). And he quotes Shaw as saying, "I have risen by sheer gravitation, too industrious by acquired habit to stop working (I work as my father drank)" (Erikson, 1958, p. 45). Both were "obsessive-compulsives"—Shaw's father, an alcoholic; the son, a "workaholic." My point about the relatedness of the so-called abnormal or pathological forms of obsessive-compulsive reactions to other everyday expressions of such behavior is elaborated in the following quotation from Graham Greene.

Everyday expressions of obsessions–compulsions. Obsessive-compulsive behavior can be found in everyday interactions as well as in the interactions of institutionalized mental patients. According to Graham Greene,

Every creative writer worth our consideration, every writer who can be called in the wide eighteenth-century use of the term a poet, is a victim: a man given over to an obsession. Was it not the obsessive fear of treachery which dictated not only James's plots but also his elaborate conceits (behind the barbed network of his style he could feel really secure himself), and was it not another obsession, a terrible pity for human beings, which drove Hardy to write novels that are like desperate acts of rebellion in a lost cause? What obsession then do we find in Mr. de la Mare—one of the few living writers who can survive in this company? The obsession is perhaps most easily detected in the symbols an author uses, and it would not be far from the truth—odd as it may seem on the face of it—to say that the dominant symbol in Mr. de la Mare's short stories is the railway station or the railway journey (Greene, 1952, p. 79).

Graham Greene himself is obsessed with evil. Hemingway was driven by the thought of death, even embracing it himself before it was due him. Tennessee Williams is obsessed with sex, Steinbeck with a belief in primitive goodness, Faulkner, as Dostoevsky and Greene, with a heavy sense of evil, Scott Fitzgerald with wealth and glitter, Thomas Wolfe with life itself, and Sinclair Lewis with sham and hypocrisy. Every creative artist shows an *idée fixe*, a hallucinatory preoccupation with some aspect of life. The products of the poets', the writers', and the artists' obsessions have brought them honor and acclaim because they are on the socially useful side of life (cf. Mairet, 1929). When obsessions are on the socially useless side of life . . . they bring punishment or incarceration. Aeschylus, Homer, Plato, Aristotle, Wilde, Shakespeare, LaPlace, Descartes, Darwin, Bach, Beethoven, Debussy, Michelangelo, Leonardo da Vinci, Faraday, Newton, Marconi, Einstein, Ehrlich, Dickens, Tolstoy, Kreisler, Rubinstein, Caruso, Carnegie, Schweitzer and Edison—this is a skimpy list of creative workers whose magnificent obsessions brought boundless benefits to mankind. On the other hand, Hitler is a reminder of the deadly efficacy of an evil obsession. [Pronko, 1963, p. 253]

We now consider some deviations of the obsessive-compulsive category that are not as socially desirable or approved as those we have just examined.

Obesity in humans.   Reflections on eating suggest that obesity and its lawful precursor, overeating, are strictly human "inventions." It is very doubtful if animals, such as bears, birds, fish, snakes, lions, and wolves, under natural (nonhuman) conditions, ever "eat themselves to death." There are fat cows, pigs, and geese raised under artificial ("domesticated") conditions, which account for their abnormal shape and weight, but the human is the finest example of self-inflicted obesity. Such studies as have been done (Pronko, 1963, pp. 217–220) show that compulsive eating serves as a substitute satisfaction or compensation for lack of human companionship, or as an anxiety-reducing factor in stressful situations.

From fat humans to fat rats.   An experiment by Ullman (1951) revealed that compulsive eating can be produced in rats by manipulating certain conditions. Without going into details, *essentially* Ullman determined the percentage of pellets his rats ate under shock versus no-shock conditions. He divided each minute of each day's 20-minute sessions into twelve 5-second periods. His results indicated that during shock intervals the rats ate over twice as many pellets as they did during no-shock intervals. But the most significant portion of his study concerns what happened when he allowed his rats to eat to the point of satiation *before* he put them into the shock versus no-shock situation. Now, with hunger eliminated by letting the animals "stuff themselves" before they were put into the apparatus, they acted as if they were anywhere from seven to 14 times as hungry during the shock intervals as they were during any of the following no-shock intervals. Apparently, some other condition than hunger was working to produce such results. The rats ate ravenously (although satiated) only when they were being shocked. Their eating stopped when the shock was discontinued. Ullman suggests that the rats had learned to eat when they were hungry and that this adjustment carried over into the painful (shocking) situation even when they were not hungry. If so, then eating can go on not only in the absence of hunger but in a condition of satiation of the organism, at which time it serves some other function than hunger appeasement. The adjustive act available to the animal in the situation was eating. The increase in eating during shock is thought to occur because eating becomes a generalized tension-reducing response in the situation. This argument is buttressed by the fact that when shock was applied the animals ate even after having been satiated. This behavior is thought to be analogous to the kind of abnormal behavior in which the behavior is quantitatively rather than qualitatively "queer" behavior (p. 581). In other words, eating in Ullman's rats appears to serve a nonnutritive function because it occurs in painful situations similar to the distortion of the nutritive function of food in the obese human.

Sexual compulsions.   We should not be surprised to find distortions of human sexual behavior hemmed in as it is with ethical, moral, religious, and socioeconomic factors plus individual conditioning. Zoophilia, or sexual congress between a human and a member of another species, is one such strongly disapproved sexual deviation.

Zoophilia.   The following case from Menninger (1951) deserves to become a classic instance of zoophilia.

> For reasons of discretion I can report this case only in vague outline. This was a traveling salesman of thirty, unmarried, of good appearance, and extremely well regarded by his firm. He had business contacts in many parts of the country, and carried out his business activities quite satisfactorily. It was his wont at the conclusion of a day's work in a new town to eat his dinner alone in the hotel, read a book or go to a moving picture show until 10 or 11 o'clock at night, and then start out on a curious, furtive search for an approachable mare or cow. He had acquired an efficient technique for doing this: For example, he would repair to the suburban fringes of the city before darkness and mark certain

barns and corrals where such animals were kept. Then, under cover of darkness, he would return to these places armed with pieces of meat with which to deflect dogs and make his entrance into any barns or lots where the horses and cows were kept. He would then begin a process of petting and wooing the animal, so to speak, in almost precisely the way a normal man would make amorous advances to a woman. From long experience he had learned just how fast and how far he could proceed. His object was to have sexual congress with the animal, and this he claimed to be able to accomplish in most instances. The excitement of the search, the wooing, possibility of discovery, possibility of being kicked or otherwise hurt by the animal, the surreptitiousness of the entire business, all added to the pleasure. He had no interest in sexual relations with women or homosexual relations with men.

His excellent appearance, good manner, business efficiency, and generally "normal" demeanor made the contrast of his reputation and his secret sexual activities all the more striking. He evinced considerable curiosity as to why he should be so different from other people. He was in the main quite satisfied with his way of life and had no wish to change it. On subsequent visits to the same town he would renew his contacts with previously discovered animals precisely as if they were former human acquaintances. [Menninger, 1951, p. 67]

Fetishism.   Fetishism is defined as a sexual response to inanimate objects of the loved person or nongenital portions of the body. Articles of clothing such as gloves, handkerchief, stockings, underwear, aprons, or shoes may elicit powerful erotic responses, as can a foot, leg, breast, hand, ear, or even voice (as when someone refers to a "sexy voice"). The deflection of the sexual response is apparent in the nongenital range of stimulus objects to which the fetishist responds. In fetishism, the stimulating person is desired obliquely and peripherally but not genitally. It is natural to look for repression or suppression or other antecedent events in the reactional biography of the fetishist. The following quotation from Alexander (1966) covers homosexual behavior in addition to a "recipe" for conditioning fetishism in a cat:[2]

Homosexual behavior is an acquired taste, the result of one or several conditioning experiences to which the person was subjected in one form or another in an early phase of his life. . . . Conditioning can produce sexual deviation even in animals in which a deviation can be produced which could not possibly be inborn or exist in nature. Kinsey has shown that cats which were regularly masturbated with the aid of a yellow rubber glove, will become sexually excited at the sight and smell of yellow rubber gloves. Homosexuality is no more invariably inborn in man than sexual attachment to yellow rubber gloves in cats. It is in both cases a learned behavior, reinforced by the experience of sexual satisfaction. [Alexander, 1966, p. 202]

There is a clear implication here of the ready conditionability of the sexual reponse.

---

[2] The entire range of homosexuality is covered with scientific excellence in Tripp (1975).

Odds and ends of obsession–compulsions.   Surely no other human compulsive behaviors have the tenacity of drugs and alcohol. Our common use of the terms *social drinker* and *alcoholic* roughly distinguishes the noncompulsive from the compulsive drinker. In the lingo of the alcoholic, as far as the latter is concerned, "One drink is too many and a thousand aren't enough."

Gasoline and glue sniffing add to our list of addictions or compulsive behaviors. Transvestism also belongs here as does television addiction. Some people write bogus checks as addictively as others eat starch (see Pronko, 1963, p. 254) or smoke tobacco or marijuana. Theodore Reik (1959) has devoted a whole book, *The Compulsion to Confess,* to a compulsion found not only in the case of the criminal, but in innocent people and in myth, religion, in art, and in language. Were we to keep on adding to our list of obsession-compulsions, we would end up with a long and meaningless inventory of imperious habit reactions.

Obsession–compulsions as adjustments.   Cameron (1974, p. 315) sees certain powerful habit reactions as "an indirect method of solving conflicts, or substituting permissible satisfactions for taboo ones, of increasing reward from and acceptance by other persons and of avoiding punishment and deprivation." Then why aren't they effective adjustments? Because they offer only transient "tension reduction" and must be repeated. Nothing ever gets settled; people with such habits only succeed in "spinning their wheels."

The Psychoses

Having sampled the "minor personality problems" or "disorders" (the neuroses), we are ready to invade the field of the "major personality problems" or "disorders," the psychoses. As usual, we are once more confronted with a choice between a criterion based on deviation from a social norm or from the medical model we explored above. We now look further into the suitability of the social norm criterion of the psychoses.

As children of our culture, it is almost impossible for us to realize how readily we fall into expected ways of behaving in our daily transactions with family, neighbors, and colleagues. It is only departures from "correct" reactions that call attention to such "routine" behaviors in the home, school, factory, or business. Violations of social norms may label a person as ignorant, criminal, bad mannered, or sinful. Over and above these categories, there are violations of social norms that label the violator as "mentally ill." In other societies, that label could be associated with witchcraft, demonic possession, or divine inspiration. The following quotation reveals how subtly social norms operate in defining how we may "stray from the straight and narrow."

There are innumerable norms . . . over which consensus is so complete that the members of a group appear to take them for granted. A host of such norms surrounds even the simplest conversation: a person engaged in conversation is expected to face toward his partner, rather than directly away from him; if his gaze is toward the partner, he is expected to look toward his eyes, rather than, say, toward his forehead; to stand at a proper conversational distance, neither one inch away nor across the room and so on. A person who regularly violated these expectations probably would not be thought to be merely ill-bred, but as strange, bizarre, and frightening, because his behavior violates the assumptive world of the group, the world that is construed to be the only one that is natural, decent, and possible. [Scheff, 1968, p. 10]

According to Scheff, deviations from certain ethical, legal, and moral social norms are labeled as crime, perversion, professional or business malpractice, departure from "common decency," and so on. "After exhausting these categories, however, there is always a residue of the most diverse kinds of violations, for which the culture provides no explicit label" (Scheff, 1968, p. 10). They cannot be defined legally, morally, or ethically. Scheff suggests the term *"residual deviance"* (p. 10) for these assorted deviations, the possessors of which our society labels as mentally ill. Because the medical metaphor assumes that a disease originates and unfolds within the individual, and is therefore inappropriate, Scheff prefers the term *deviant behavior* as an alternative label.[3]

A Social-System Model of "Mental Disorder"

Scheff (1968) modestly proposes "a social system model of mental disorder," not as a finished system but only as a research framework. Toward that end, he states nine propositions as basic assumptions to guide research in this area. As an alternative to the medical model, we now briefly set down the component propositions of Scheff's theory.

Proposition 1. "Residual deviance arises from diverse sources" (Scheff, 1968, p. 10): organic causes, individual psychological peculiarities (see the discussion of idiosyncratic behavior in Chapter 7) and what we call the reactional biography, stress in civilian or in combat life, and deprivation of food, sleep, and sensory experience.

Proposition 2. When one considers the number of people who receive treatment for their "mental illness," the number who do not must be extremely high. According to Scheff, there is evidence that grossly deviant behavior occurs but is "unrecognized, ignored, or rationalized," as when the eccentric gives away his or her money, or sees visions under religious auspices, is a

[3] The term *deviant* is defined as deviating from some accepted norm, which should include the genius. But in common usage it almost always has a derogatory meaning as something undesirable or disapproved.

genius (such as Beethoven), or is a recluse who may freeze or starve to death in self-imposed solitary confinement. Scheff quotes surveys that reveal a high incidence of problems of living. The problems that people report in those surveys are like those that "the mentally ill" who can afford it seek treatment for.

Proposition 3. "Most residual deviancy is 'denied' and is transitory" (Scheff, 1968, p. 12). It is unrecognized or rationalized away or does not become crystalized. Examples are "battlefield neuroses," which "go away" if the soldier is kept with his unit but which may be "established" if he is sent to base hospital. Other examples of transient deviation are phases in child development during which children show temper tantrums, head banging, and fear of persons, animals, darkness, ghosts, and lightning and thunder. How, then, do transient deviants develop deviant "careers"? Chiefly, but not entirely, through the group's reaction to the behavior in question.

Proposition 4. Certain prevailing beliefs and practices account for, and support, the institution of "mental illness" or the conception that people are "crazy." Stereotyped notions of mental disorder are learned in early childhood. From scattered observations, Scheff (1968, p. 15) concludes that children learn a lot of notions about what it is to be "crazy," not so much from adults but from other children. These notions are couched in vague and mysterious terms.

Proposition 5. "The stereotypes of insanity are continually reaffirmed inadvertently among adults, in ordinary social interaction" (Scheff, 1968, p. 15). In the media and in social discourse, the childhood stereotypic acquisitions are reinforced through a news item, for example, that an apprehended rapist had been an inmate in a mental institution, but no mention is made of the fact that some rapists have never been institutionalized. "Actually, it has been demonstrated that the incidence of crimes of violence, or of any crime, is much lower among ex-mental patients than among the general population. Yet, this is not the picture presented to the public" (p. 16). Phrases used in conversation, such as "Are you crazy?" or "He's off his rocker" constantly reinforce childhood stereotypes about "mental illness."

Proposition 6. Once such conceptions of "mental illness" become entrenched, they are available as societal reactions to a given individual or by a given individual against oneself or society. When a deviant person is in a behavioral crisis, because of the "crazy" stereotype available in the culture, it becomes the guide for action both by others and by the deviant as well. Those around the deviant and the deviant also react uniformly in terms of the traditional stereotypes of insanity. Then, the deviant's behavior becomes crystalized in conformity with those expectations, "thus becoming similar to the behavior of other deviants classified as mentally ill, and stable over time" (Scheff, 1968, p. 17). Labeling the person, then, is an important factor in explaining the deviant's acceptance of a social role as a mentally ill person. The deviant's acceptance of the label may bring "benefits," such as more and kinder treatment by staff, visitation rights, and "campus privileges." These reinforce the sick role.

Proposition 7.   "Labeled deviants are punished when they attempt to return to conventional roles" (Scheff, 1968, p. 19). Job, marital, and social difficulties arise for the deviant who tries to conform, once labeled as a deviant. The system reinforces the assigned social role as deviant and punishes attempts at stepping out of that role.

Proposition 8.   When persons are publicly charged with deviance, they may, in their state of confusion, shame, and suggestibility, accept the role of insanity as the only alternative. Because the charged deviant also learned the stereotype about crazy people, a self-fulfilling prophecy ensues. That person is "hooked" and enters on a chronic career in "mental illness."

Proposition 9.   The preceding eight hypotheses lead to this final one: "Among residual deviants, labeling is the single most important cause of careers of residual deviance" (Scheff, 1968, p. 20). Whether labeling occurs or not depends, first, on the "visibility of the deviant behavior; second, the power of the deviant, and the social distance between the deviant and the agents of social control; and, finally, the tolerance level of the community, and the availability in the culture of the community of alternative, nondeviant roles" (p. 21).[4]

Paranoia

Traditionally, paranoia has been identified with disordered thinking. A now-obsolete term, *monomania*, called attention to the fact that the "monomaniac" was "crazy" along one particular line. For example, one retired man has developed a career in lecturing on UFOs, during which he insists he has communicated with creatures from Venus and other planets. He has even published a book in which he reproduced vocabularies of languages spoken on other planets. Otherwise, this man's behavior shows no apparent deviations. In cases where there is no deterioration or disorganization, the term *true paranoia* has been applied. If there is intellectual impairment, as in schizophrenia, then the term *paranoid schizophrenia* has been favored in the traditional framework.

Also, the term *delusion* is closely synonymous with paranoia. Cameron (1947, p. 390) defines delusions as "convictions based upon misinterpretations, unwarranted inferences or unjustified conclusions." Such a definition would include much of our everyday behavior, for how could we validate all

---

[4] As a possible juror, the reader might remember the unreliability of diagnostic labels in evaluating the testimony of "expert witnesses" in so-called sanity hearings.

of our premises for action? Communications do misfire. A wrong inference while driving in traffic can cause a serious accident. Unjustified conclusions about where or when to meet or how to get there are revealed when we have to say, "I thought you meant so and so." Fortunately, the bulk of our reactions that meet Cameron's definition do not violate social norms. The "UFO specialist" just mentioned may be derided, but he is tolerated. The following incident fits in with the down-to-earth view of "mental illness" that I have tried to develop here. It shows the ease with which a British intelligence officer fitted a given set of facts into a perfect, logical system. A number of other alert and competent officers were also involved in the case. Perhaps their very alertness and experience as intelligence officers were responsible for their joint, transient delusion.

An incident at Dieppe.   The story starts with the intelligence officer reading the evening newspaper. This man was among a handful of ranking officers who had advance knowledge of the Dieppe raid, a top secret military plan. Imagine his surprise when he spotted and analyzed an advertisement in the paper for Sylvan Flakes, the British equivalent of our Ivory Soap. The "ad" carried the headlines "Beach Coat from Dieppe" and showed a beautiful girl in a beach coat (see Figure 7-1).

The officer jumped into a cab and hurried to headquarters with the suspicion-arousing newspaper. On closer scrutiny, some even more striking features were noted. The word "coat" could easily be a code word for "Combined Operations Attack" which was the designation for the Dieppe raid. Furthermore, the girl was shown cutting the thorny stems of roses with hedge shears. The suspicious officers even counted the number of button holes on the girl's dress and derived the exact hour that had been specified for the start of the raid!

The case was taken to Scotland Yard, where it created some stir before it was finally realized that the items in the "ad" and the planned raid had certain common features through mere, remotest coincidence. The officers were eventually convinced that the advertisement was not intended to convey secret information to an enemy agent, who might count the buttons on the girl's dress and who would translate her use of garden shears into the British use of tanks against barbed wire, which was a part of the real plan.

The intelligence officer burdened with a military secret shared by a very few responsible people was conscientiously and sensitively responsive to any evidence of possible interception of the critical information and of its relay to the enemy. Under the circumstances he *found* the evidence, but, just as readily, abandoned his interpretation of the facts when another interpretation appeared more plausible. Had he persisted in his first approach to the facts, we would label him "psychotic," but when we focus on the intellectual operations involved, his action is essentially the same as when the psychotic experiences "sudden clarification" or evolves a "pseudo-community" (Cameron, 1947).

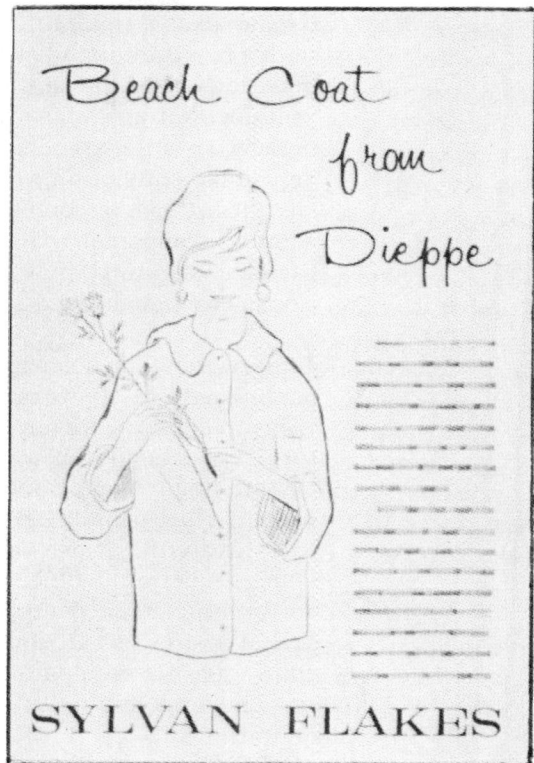

Figure 7-1 Pictorial representation of the Sylvan Flakes advertisement that prompted a highly inferential, paranoid military investigation concerning the Dieppe invasion.

Sudden clarification. The intelligence officer involved in the incident at Dieppe showed a certain flexibility when he shifted his perspective by abandoning his first interpretation of "the facts" in the ad. He was also able to surrender the "sudden clarification" that preceded that interpretation, by which Cameron (1947, p. 438) means the conviction that comes to one with great, logical force that the explanation for someone's behavior or the sizing up of a situation is correct.

Pseudocommunity. Cameron's construct of pseudocommunity may also throw light on the behaviors that we label as *paranoid*. People react selectively to persons and objects in their milieu. The "sensitiveness" of the artist to color and design, the reformer to signs of evil, the botanist to plant life illustrate how the world is organized differently for different people via the psychological history. Things pass unnoticed for one that arouse the other to interested activity. "When we say that the world has 'special meaning' for the lover, the scientist, the soldier, or the mystic, we are referring to the special ways of reacting each has developed in relation to surroundings that are common to them all" (Cameron, 1947, p. 425). Cameron sees the paranoiac as a rigid, inflexible person, who, from a lack of communication with a resultant inability to change perspectives, becomes locked into a rigid perspective which leads to a pseudocommunity. Cameron (1947) defines the pseudocommunity as "an organization of a patient's reactions to the observed or inferred behavior of actual and imagined persons, on the basis of delusional conviction, which makes the patient seem to himself a focus or a significant part of some concerted action, malignant or benign" (p. 438). It should be apparent that any action based on the attributed properties of a pseudocommunity may involve the individual in legal or other complications, which make him a social deviant.

Projection.   The defense mechanism of projection is closely identified with paranoia. Baer's (1976) metaphor of the organism as host may help clarify the way projection works in paranoia. We have noted the presence of contradictory response in the behavioral repertoire of the individual. If these are threatening to the person, they may be unwittingly "disowned" and attributed to other people. An uncontrollable sexual or aggressive impulse seems less threatening if one can believe that it comes from the devil or from evil voices. A certain woman claimed that men were following her on the street and making sexual overtures to her. Actually, she "disowned" her demanding sexual desires and attributed them to men in her surroundings. She attempted to solve her problem via projection.

The epidemic nature of paranoia is clearly illustrated in the following quotation:

> There is no harder scientific fact in the world than the fact that belief can be produced in practically unlimited quantity and intensity, without observation or reasoning, and even in defiance of both by the simple desire to believe founded on a strong interest in believing. Everybody recognizes this in the case of the amatory infatuation of the adolescents who see angels and heroes in obviously (to others) commonplace or even objectionable maidens and youths. But it holds good over the entire field of human activity. The hardest-headed materialist will become a consulter of table-rappers and slate-writers if he loses a child or a wife so beloved that the desire to revive and communicate with them becomes irresistible. [George Bernard Shaw (1906) 1930, p. 13]

Schizophrenia: Classic Treatment

Of all the psychoses, schizophrenia has traditionally comprised the most bizarre and incomprehensible set of behaviors. Before the term *schizophrenia* came into general use, the term *dementia praecox* was in vogue. The word *dementia* referred to the gradual deterioration or disorganization of behavior with the passage of years, and *praecox* to the precocious or early beginning of the "disease." It most frequently occurred in young people.

The term *schizophrenia* is frequently confused with split personality. But we have already discussed that problem as a neurosis under the category of hysteria. The split in schizophrenia refers to the break between the patient's thinking and feeling. The schizophrenic is said to show a blunting or flattening of affect, or complete apathy. Laughter may occur when crying is more appropriate, or vice versa. The split also refers to the detachment of feelings from "reality." In fact, the psychosis has been considered a flight from reality with a compensatory fantasy life. The schizophrenic is believed to adjust to problems of a harsh reality by autistic thinking. Self-centered autistic thinking or fantasy can transform the schizophrenic into a billionaire or the "ruler of Europe."

Traditionally, four major types of schizophrenia have been delineated: simple, hebephrenic, paranoid, and catatonic; but such delineation is found with a far greater frequency in textbooks than in real human beings.

Schizophrenia, simple form.   The drifters, ne'er-do-wells, frequent job changers, hoboes, prostitutes, "bar flies," racetrack touts, and drug peddlers are among those who have been considered as simple schizophrenics. Presumably, their shirking the ordinary responsibilities of daily office, shop, or household in favor of an "easier" way of life characterizes them as a group. A patient at one of our largest institutions, a former hobo, diagnosed as a simple schizophrenic, admitted to me that he had written crank letters to the president of the United States in order to secure a comfortable, easy country-club style of life. Only when these individuals violate a social norm are they labeled as simple schizophrenics; otherwise, they "do their thing" unnoticed and unmolested.

In a movement against forced institutionalization, Hansen and Emery (1978, p. 6) state that "the choice of a Broadway bench over drugs, hospitals and white suited 'parents' makes good sense to many 'lost souls' and 'shopping-bag ladies' just as it makes good sense to many of us." The "shopping-bag ladies" referred to are homeless women in metropolitan cities such as New York who survive by sorting through trash cans. They carry all their worldly possessions, and sometimes their bankbook too, in their shopping bags. They sleep in Grand Central Station, in subways, on park benches, or on doorsteps. If and when they get institutionalized, they must have a label, the most likely of which will be "schizophrenia, simple form." If they are not institutionalized, they are labeled only as "shopping-bag ladies."

Schizophrenia, hebephrenic form.   As a result of withdrawal from social contact, depersonalization occurs, which, in its most severe degree, is known as the *hebephrenic* form of schizophrenia. Again, from the traditional standpoint, regression is supposed to occur even to the child or infantile stage. Other behaviors conventionally associated with this form of schizophrenia are silliness, grimacing, laughing, gesturing or talking to oneself, and baby talk or incoherent speech. The patient may be so deteriorated that he or she may smear feces, may show bizarre delusions and hallucinations. Stereotyped words or phrases and the French phrase *salade des mots* (word salad) have also been identified with hebephrenia, as it has sometimes been called. A former schoolteacher wrote the following word salad letter, requesting me to deliver it to the judge in her county.

> Sirs: Kindly free from Hospitol Miss Margaret Rapp because of the following reasons:
>
> 1. Family neglect—Incompetent Health
> 2. Physician's Pride—Disobedience
> 3. Incompetent Hospitol Staff—Sacriligious impudence (Drink)
> 4. Incompetent Judge—Partiality—Teacher of negligence
> 5. Brilliant nurse
> 6. Incompetent Pay
> 7. Illness—(Optimism with surety for spiritualistic win)
> 8. Best Gift for Adaptation for service
> 9. Improvement
> 10. Destruction
> 11. Divorce
>
> Sincerely,
>
> Margaret Rapp

Withdrawal and a progressive loss of contact with others is bound to result in less effective linguistic communication.

Schizophrenia, paranoid form.   The traditional notion of the paranoid form of schizophrenia or paranoid dementia praecox has stressed the presence of delusions, but the delusions are far-fetched, remote, and bizarre. They are also supposed to show a loss of contact with "reality" by contrast with so-called true paranoia. Grandiose delusions may be present, which cartoonists burlesque as "Napoleons," "Generals," and so on. Persecutory delusions may involve harassment by the FBI or the Pope, according to the paranoid schizophrenic. Artistic creations of institutionalized patients, one of which is shown in Figure 7-2, have been of interest for many years.

The following letter to the president of a university reveals the *unrealistic* nature of a farmer's invention for separating eggs according to their sex and viability. A prominent item in the letter refers to the special relationship between the patient and "the source of all wisdom."

> Dear Sir
>
> I am a farmer, but the last six years I have been concentrating my thots on an ideal—to separate eggs—male and female and dead germs. also this discovery will denote sex in humans I have the wisdom, thru connection with the source of all wisdom. The ability to do this is all clear in my mind. but demonstration not finished. I wrote the O.S.C. [Ohio State College] sometime ago but

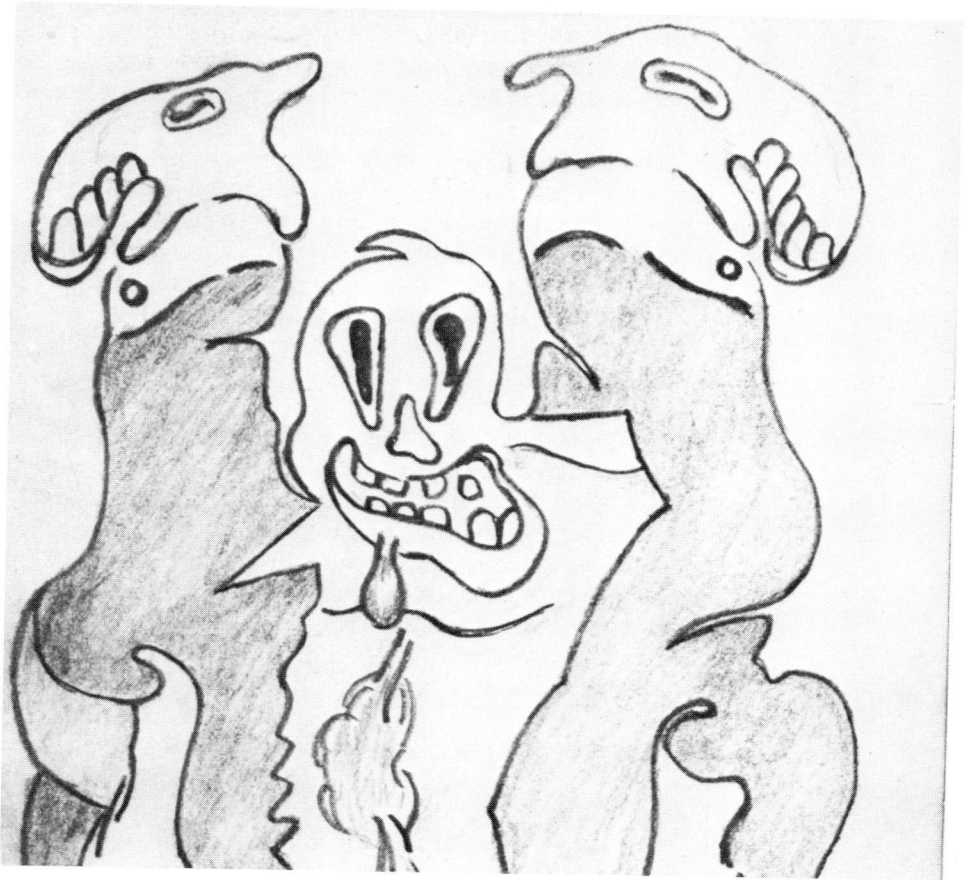

Figure 7-2 Artistic creation of an institutionalized patient. Is it "crazy" or highly imaginative? What would you think of it if you saw it as a character in "Sesame Street" or a Walt Disney cartoon?

they ignored my letter which I registered. History of course shows it is a rocky road. Therefore I expect to have to work hard to make it a reality. I left school in the North of England when I was 12 years old so you can understand this wisdom was not thought out in my brain desire plus concentration. But this I would like to know have you got X rays at your mental power house? If so would you be willing to let me come and use them a little and me to pay you later for the same? I am sure it will help your institution in many ways. I for one will do all I can So if you can be of any assistance to me kindly let me know

And oblige

Dick Kramer

Schizophrenia, catatonic form.   According to the traditional view, the catatonic form of schizophrenia, or *catatonia*, as it was formerly called, is distinguished from the other schizophrenias by "motor symptoms." Inactivity
is manifested in many spheres. For example, speech is greatly retarded,
sometimes progressing to the point of mutism. Patients may refuse to feed
themselves, so that tube feeding may be required. Some cases end in a
stupor, arousal from which may be very difficult. In a classic series of cases
studied by Hoch (1921), preoccupation with death or its simulation are said
to be prominent features of the catatonic form of schizophrenia. It is as if the
catatonic "acts dead" rather than commits suicide.

The Schizophrenias: A Variety of Theories

The biological school.   The hodge-podge of types of schizophrenias that we
have considered opens the door to a problem involving roughly half of our
mental-hospital population. A bewildering array of theories attempts to explain the schizophrenias. Some look on the problems as an organic disease
and have searched for its cause in the cells, tissues, and biochemical makeup
of the patient. Besides the brain and nervous sytem, the liver, kidneys,
glands, blood, vitamins, enzymes, urine, and other metabolic products have
been eagerly analyzed for *the cause,* which a century of research into the
tissues has failed to reveal.

The developmental school.   Opposed to the biological school of schizophrenia, with its stress on heredity and on constitutional and biochemical factors, is the developmental school, which views schizophrenia as a group of
learned reactions acquired during the individual's life history. A somewhat
older theory by Adolf Meyer (1957) held that schizophrenia was the end
result of habit deterioration, which reduced the individual's effectiveness in
dealing with concrete reality. A refinement of Meyer's biosocial viewpoint
by Cameron (1947, p. 451) considers "the schizophrenic disorders as disorganization and desocialization of the acquired behavior systems constituting
personality, and their replacement by behavior dominated or determined by
private fantasy, in the absence of organ or tissue pathology adequate to
account for the disorder."

The Freudian school.   For the Freudians, schizophrenia is a regressive
psychosis, the result of the individual's complete abandonment of object-
choice. In its place, love of other is transformed into love of self, and the
individual returns to the original infantile state of narcissism or autoeroti-
cism, with the libido now directed toward the self and toward bodily sensations (the libido is the hypothetical psychic energy at the disposal of the
mental apparatus).

Schizophrenia as a panchreston.   Our familiarity with the term *panchreston* will facilitate its application to schizophrenia as an "explain-all." Borrowing Hardin's (1957) term, Szasz (1957, p. 409) complains that class names such as schizophrenia may give the false impression that there 'exists' a homogeneous group of phenomena which are assignated by the word in question." In a recent work, Szasz (1976, p. 74) writes,

> Actually, insofar as the term "schizophrenia" designates some "problem" that an ostensible "patient" has, it refers usually to the fact that the "patient's" life is disordered—that it is, or the "patient" thinks it is, aimless and useless. If so, it can no more be "cured" by journeys than by drugs. Chaos, suffering, and turmoil can be remedied only by the subject putting his or her life in order. Whatever helps a person to achieve that goal will be "therapeutic."

And what gets the schizophrenic institutionalized is not a disease, to use a medical metaphor, but a way of behaving that offends or annoys somebody. Delusions and hallucinations "refer to behavior, not disease; to disapproved conduct, not histopathological change; hence they may loosely be called 'conditions,' but they are not, strictly speaking, medical conditions" (Szasz, 1976, p. 10). Szasz's view is a far cry from the more traditional view of schizophrenia as an imaginary pseudochemical disorder of the brain.

We have considered a number of discrepant theories of schizophrenia. They range from those that are self-actional to those that are harmonious with an ecological or interbehavioral type of construct. The choice is ours.

Manic-Depressive Psychosis

Fashions in labeling institutionalized people change, as do fashions in dress. What is called *manic-depressive psychosis* today was, 70 or 80 years ago, considered two separate psychoses, *mania* and *melancholia*. The term *mania* referred to violent, excessive motor activity and excitement ("overreacting"). By contrast, *melancholia* was characterized by severe depression and loss of interest in the world as revealed by inactivity, solitary behavior, and scarcely audible monosyllabic speech.

More recently, the two patterns have been united into circular insanity or the current hyphenated form *manic-depressive psychosis*. In explaining the behavior of the individual wearing the formidable label *manic-depressive*, heredity has been appealed to, particularly when this psychosis is found in more than one member of a family. In addition to heredity, the "constitution" of the individual has been suspect. Some people were believed to be tainted with a "predisposition" (whatever that is) toward manic-depressive psychosis, needing only a precipitating factor to bring it forth. Such theorists were confident that some anatomical derangement would be found somewhere in the manic-depressive cadaver's brain, if one cared to look. But greater profit may come to us from observing concrete behavioral events.

George Fox.   Let us start with the following portrait of a patient, labeled as a manic-depressive, a resident in one of our hospitals.

George Fox, a man of 47, formerly a typesetter, is, metaphorically speaking, "in high gear," an extremely energetic person but with much waste motion. First of all, he is extremely and loudly garrulous; with him a dialogue is next to impossible because of his monopoly of the conversation. In order to dominate the situation, George would, frequently with good humor, stand on a chair and raise his voice as he chattered of "ships and shoes and sealing wax, of cabbages and kings." Inventions, many of them sketched furiously on a growing pile of paper, plans, and plots come thick and fast and with *abrupt change of direction*, which is probably the outstanding feature of his behavior. An older psychiatry used the term, *"flight of ideas,"* to refer to this condition. There are no embarrassing silent periods in anyone's interaction with George. His abundant energy carries him headlong through a tireless and never-to-be predicted succession of acts. He is *in perpetual motion;* he is like a bee in that he buzzes constantly but never lights until exhausted. On one occasion, George kept up the mad pace of the sort indicated for several hours and then became so exhausted that he was forced to "recharge his batteries" with an hour's hard sleep. George's mad speed and abrupt changes in directionality may be detected even in the following short excerpt from an autobiography he was asked to write.

The Life and "Pedigree" of George Fox

Published by So Long & Co. N.Y. City—N.Y.	Edited by the "Big Chief" (himself) George Fox

Well on a Balmy and Clear Day in the month of December, to be Exact, Dec. 10, 1894, I selected for my dear old Mother, Mrs. Barbara Fox, whose maiden name was "Wilson" (that's all) a wee bit of Scotish methinks in her parents, probably born in Old Scotland, England,—perhaps thats where I Inherit my so styled "Pins" or "Buns"—some original—mostly "Antiques" but Dressed in Kilties or a new "Calico Wrapper" they sound new to some —its strange how "Illiterate" many of us are!

My father, not having an authenicated Data of my ancestry, I'll just say from memory, was born in the state of Virginia, where our Revered First in War, First in Peace, and First in the Hearts of his Countrymen and (the "First," but not *"Least"*) President of these Wealthy if not the Wealthiest (in *"Natural Resources"*) at least "Nation" on the "Face of the Globe" or in other words—The World—named "The United States of America"— America Right," "America Wrong"—"America Forever" or as said in the "Star Spangled Banner" May her Flag *Ever Wave* for the *Brave* and the *Free*, or United we *"Stand"* but Divided we *"Fall"* and as Rome *"Fell"* we trust God will Keep us by his *"Almightly Help"* from Ever Falling either by His Hands, "Earthquakes" "Floods," "Whirl Winds" "World Wars" or other *"Calamities"* or *"Catastrophies"* Since we are not writing the "End of the World" or The History of the United States, we might wisely return to our subject, the life of the writer George Fox.

Well, I was born, as I said, one of the most unpleasant things imaginable, especially for the mother of 1894, before "Twilight Series" and other *ISSUES* were published [and so on].

The second paragraph of George Fox's autobiography is particularly instructive in its rapid shift of attention. George happens to mention "the state of Virginia," which reminds him of the President who was "First in Peace," et cetera. From here on "Wealth" reminds him of "Natural Resources," the "globe," "the world," back to "the United States of America," the last word of which starts him off on another tangent to "America Right," "America Wrong," "America *Forever.*" Then a clang association elicits the phrase, "May her flag *Ever Wave,*" et cetera. Eventually, by a devious path, he returns to his life story, but in the other 49 pages shows the same madcap, headlong pace with its frequent change of direction. Note also the punning (*ISSUES,* connected with birth as well as publication) and the feigned jollity. [Pronko, 1963, pp. 368–369]

How shall we understand such frantic bursts of activity as George Fox manifests? Cameron (1947), among others, views manic-depressive reactions as continuous with the everyday behavior of people. Many individuals have fluctuations of mood and activity ranging from excitement to apathy or depression and reduced activity with poor or no productivity. Extreme degrees of both match what we observed in George Fox's case. Overexcitation can cause distraction and abrupt change in the direction of activity so that the resulting behavior appears incoherent and fragmented.

I propose that if schizophrenia can be interpreted as a *"flight from reality,"* then the manic response can be seen as a *"flight into reality."* However, the flight into reality is not directed, planned, or organized. It is a hit-and-miss attack in all directions at once, and it shows signs of panic and disintegration. In the most acute manic phase, the patient becomes incoherent, delirious, and exhausted. After the outburst of action, what is more natural than inactivity and depression? Does the manic patient dimly become aware of his or her failure to adjust to troubles during the manic explosion? We don't know. At any rate, he or she becomes depressed in a tense, agitated way. However, the patient then "recharges his or her batteries" and is once more ready for a wild onslaught on reality. But not all individuals alternate between a manic and a depressive phase. Those who do the labeling say that some patients have recurrent mania or recurrent melancholia. From an institutional standpoint, the manic is said to have a good chance for recovery (presumably because of his or her good contact with reality) in contrast with the schizophrenic, who has poor contact with reality. For that reason, the manic-depressive psychosis is considered an episodic disorder, with only one or several short periods of institutionalization being required. In between or after such episodes, the person may function well in the family and at his job as well as in society (pp. 300–301).

"Psychopathic Personality"

The American Psychiatric Association's *The Diagnostic and Statistical Manual* (1968) contains one large class that we must examine in order to round out our discussion of "abnormal psychology." The category labeled *Personality Disorders and Certain Other Non-Psychotic Mental Disorders* contains a long list of terms that have a familiar ring, such as *paranoid personality, schizoid personality, obsessive-compulsive personality,* and *hysterical personality.* They also appear here because these cases are supposed to be nonpsychotic and nonneurotic. Other subcategories that one finds here are drug dependencies, alcoholism, and such sexual deviations as fetishism, sadism, and masochism that we have already discussed as obsessive-compulsive reactions. But, it is the inadequate, passive-aggressive, asthenic or depressed, and antisocial subclasses of personality disorders that I wish to focus on now. Earlier editions of the *Diagnostic and Statistical Manual* had a wastebasket category, "psychopathic personality," covering a range of behaviors. Other terms that have been used are constitutional *psychopathic inferior, character disorders, moral imbecility, moral insanity,* and *sociopathy.* People so characterized have been said to be socially unadaptable, socially misfitted, impulsive, unstable, rootless, insincere, and unhappy.

Implications of Psychopathic Personality

The chief reason why we dwell on psychopathic personality is that it once more raises the question of Scheff's (1968) "social system model of mental disorder." The qualities of the psychopath or antisocial personality just listed are the opposite of those considered requisite to civilized communal living. They show in a glaring way, just as the neuroses and psychoses do less conspicuously, that neurotic, psychotic, or psychopathic behavior is "relative to the culture in which it flourishes and can be measured by no other rule than that of the prevailing ethic and morality" (Shoham, 1967, p. 23). As Shoham also points out, in a Brahmin society in India, where abstinence is absolutely mandatory, "getting high" on alcohol would constitute psychopathy. So would chastity among the prostitute priestesses of Astarte who were "consecrated to the distribution of erotic favors" (p. 23) among the worshippers of Astarte, the most important goddess of the Phoenicians, a goddess corresponding to Venus among the Romans.

Shoham (1967) makes another point that reveals the shiftiness of the social norms by which an individual is labeled a *psychopath* or *antisocial personality*. Take the aggressive psychopath as one example: the implication of the label is that the individual so diagnosed is way out of line. But, says Shoham, aggression is ubiquitous. One finds it in domestic, business, and tribal skirmishes, in national battles and world wars, in various forms of entertainment, sports (such as dueling, boxing, bullfighting, cockfighting), and so on. "The attitude toward aggression is laden with value judgment. We evaluate differently an aggressive business man and an aggressive robber, but *aggression per se* cannot be regarded as a diagnostic symptom" (Shoham, 1967, p. 39). It is simply too prevalent. The prevalance of aggression (as only one alleged attribute of the antisocial personality) makes it too difficult to limit it as a distinguishing characteristic of the individual so labeled. Also, if one attributes aggression (or lying or illegal activity) in a derogatory sense to the psychopath or in a neutral or commendable sense to a high government official caught up in Watergate, then the key to the differential treatment must lie in the social context of the action, in response of society to a given behavior. If that is so, then on what basis can we label one person as a psychopath or antisocial personality and pardon the other?

To wrap up our consideration of "psychopathology" in the present chapter, we must not overlook the danger of "name calling." Aside from the shiftiness of social norms, the following alarming statement from Szasz (1970) must give us pause: "I have discussed and documented elsewhere that *there is no behavior or person that a modern psychiatrist cannot possibly diagnose as abnormal or ill*" [p. 35, emphasis added]. As an example, he quotes guidelines that a psychiatrist offers for identifying types of behavior "symptomatic of deeper underlying disturbance." In academic problems, one should look for "underachievement, overachievement and erratic uneven performance" (p. 35). What else is there? According to Szasz, it is a "heads I win, tails you lose" proposition.

And this brings us to the most basic question of all. In bringing our discussion to a close, have we satisfactorily studied "sick" people in accordance with the "medical model" or have we been noting problems in living reflected in the flow of events as a function of antecedent events? We now turn to the interbehaviorist's response to that question.

The Interbehaviorist View of the So-Called Psychopathologies

As far as the interbehaviorist is concerned, the answer is clear. The behaviors labeled as neuroses and psychoses do not require any exotic set of explanations peculiar only to them. In fact, they can be easily subsumed under the same explanatory principles that apply to all the behaviors examined in the rest of this book.

In everyday life situations, at work, at play, in their homes, and elsewhere, people act in an almost infinite number of ways. Some actions are considered neutral in the eyes of others, and some are highly approved. However, certain others are considered "crazy," "insane," "pathological," "psychopathic," or as "evidence of mental illness." These may be thought to require "treatment," "incarceration," "restraint," or even "institutionalization." So it is not the act itself but its evaluation by a member or members of a particular society that determines the destiny of a particular response.

Nevertheless, when we study interbehaviors, labeled as abnormal or psychopathological, we see no exception to the reactional biography conception that all behaviors evolve during the person's individual psychological history. If those responses don't offend, irritate, or endanger others, the "host organism" is left alone. When reactions *do* annoy or disturb someone, the individual concerned is in trouble. There are other theoretical developments akin in some respects to the interbehaviorist's position. Let us consider them briefly.

Szasz

In his book *Ideology and Insanity*, Szasz (1970, p. 21) does not propose any radically new conception of the data labeled as "mental illness" or a new form of "treatment." His modest aim is to look afresh at the data designated by terms borrowed from medicine and to regard them as expressions of problems of living. Szasz's crude data are the individual's struggle for a "place in the sun," problems pertaining to the individual's conflict with others, with meaning, value, personal significance, and unhappiness. If and when these data are dismissed as illnesses and are studied in their own right, then Szasz (1970, p. 23) foresees that "human happiness, or well-being, is possible—not just for a select few, but on a scale hitherto unimaginable."

Sullivan

Harry Stack Sullivan, an assiduous student of schizophrenia, could not share the commonsense view that sees "a person" as existing in a kind of vacuum somewhat like a pawn on a chessboard. He always viewed the troubled individual who came to him in relation to the significant other people in that person's surroundings. Sullivan (1962, p. 258) defined psychiatry as dealing with "disordered living . . . not an impossible study of an *individual* suffering mental disorder; it is a study of disordered interpersonal relations nucleating more or less clearly in a particular person." Ten years of work with schizophrenics confirmed Sullivan (1962, p. 261) in the conviction "that *not* sick individuals but complex, peculiarly characterized *situations* were the subject-matter of research and therapy" (emphasis added). His "treatment" of schizophrenics involved their whole families. The significance of his comprehensive view is reflected in the title of a journal dedicated to the memory of Harry Stack Sullivan. The journal was named *Psychiatry: Journal for the Operational Statement of Interpersonal Relations.* As to the question of how interpersonal relations become disordered, we may be pretty certain that Sullivan would have accepted the reactional biography conception.

Laing

Ronald Laing is, perhaps, even a more controversial psychiatrist than either Szasz or Sullivan. His fundamental hypothesis is that society, not the individual, is "crazy." People are driven mad by mad, intolerable family conditions. In a book, *Sanity, Madness and the Family*, Laing and Esterson (1964, pp. viii–ix) state that when they considered the patients' reactions "without reference to family interactions, they may appear comparatively socially senseless, but . . . in their original family context, they are liable to make more sense."

In their study of over 200 families, Laing and Esterson were able to make sense of the patients' "queer" behavior "every time" (p. ix). The book reports 11 patients studied within the family context. The people with whom they worked carried such labels as "paranoid schizophrenics"—labels assigned to them by other psychiatrists.

How did they go about their study? Their near-transactional approach aimed at searching out "the relations between persons, and the characteristics of the family as a system composed of a multiplicity of persons (Laing and Esterson, 1964, p. 5). If necessary, Laing and Esterson went outside the family, but mostly they zeroed in on "the family as a total system, of each of its sub-systems, and of each of its members" (p. 10). Families might be studied for as long as three years. The complexity of their method is indicated in the following passage.

> Let us suppose that Jill has a father and mother and brother, who all live together. If one wishes to form a complete picture of her as a family person, let alone as a person outside the family, it will be necessary to see how she experiences and acts in all the following contexts:
>
> > Jill alone
> > Jill with mother
> > Jill with father
> > Jill with brother
> > Jill with mother and father
> > Jill with mother and brother
> > Jill with father and brother
> > Jill with mother, father, and brother.
>
> One sees that it is a fairly crude differentiation of the various positions that Jill has to adopt to characterize them as a daughter or sister. [Laing and Esterson, 1964, p. 6]

Conclusion

We have examined interbehavioral and several other non-self-actional approaches to events traditionally considered neurotic or psychotic. In my opinion, these newer approaches, by dealing with the data in a more comprehensive fashion, promise a better understanding than do the older viewpoints that focused on alleged actors (minds and brains) within the organism.

Chapter Summary

Traditionally, the data that are categorized as "abnormal personality" are handled according to the medical model. Szasz considers mental illness to be a myth; he does not deny the data subsumed under the label, mental illness, but demonstrates the inappropriateness of the metaphor of disease or illness when applied to human behavior. The traditional psychiatric classification can be criticized for its use of a dual criterion, a biological and a psychological one. The standard classification of "mental disorders" was tentatively adopted as a starting point for an analysis of the neuroses and the psychoses and subcategories of each. All were treated as continuous with everyday behaviors and not as strange, bizarre, out-of-this-world phenomena. In trying to make sense of the behaviors subsumed under the traditional categories, the construct of social deviance is useful. The artificiality and inutility of the "medical model" is revealed by applying social norms of what constitutes "crazy" behavior. Such norms are available and accepted by both the society and the deviant—our consideration of psychopathic personality, the operation of social norms in determining who shall be institutionalized and who shall be in charge of institutionalizing. When one realizes that "there is no behavior or person that a modern psychiatrist cannot possibly diagnose as abnormal or ill" (Szasz, 1970, p. 35), one must be grateful for being on the "outside" looking "in." The views of Szasz, Sullivan, and Laing offer several non-self-actional ways of looking at what are traditionally called neuroses or psychoses.

8 "Intelligence" and Intelligent Testing

Some of our most important beliefs about man and his development have changed or are in the process of changing.

[Hunt, 1964, p. 29]

Interbehavioral theory views psychological data as natural occurrences or events that obey the law "Present events are a function of antecedent events." The interbehaviorist insists on sticking to concrete facts. Accordingly, in the area of intelligence the raw data constitute, for example, children responding to questions on a test requiring bits of information, verbal definitions, and arithmetical calculations. All investigators start with such responses, but some assume something that the interbehaviorist cannot accept: an *unobservable* factor or entity, an innate capacity (intelligence). This inborn power, operating unseen, is thought to lie behind the child's responses to questions about information, language, or arithmetic. Because such a postulational procedure transforms the behaviors observed into manifestations of an in-dwelling, self-actional agent, the interbehaviorist rejects it.

The two views are irreconcilable because the interbehaviorist considers "intelligence" to be an unwarranted assumption derived, not from observation, but from tradition. According to the interbehaviorist, by dealing with actual behaviors of individuals (as in a test situation), one never observes any *inherent* power or genetically endowed general ability labeled *intelligence* that predisposes one individual to perform in a superior fashion to another individual and sets limits to the degree of development permitted a given individual. There are only differences in the performances (reactions) explainable on the basis of differences in the antecedent events in which the individuals being compared participated during their psychological histories.

Can we reconcile the two opposite views? Perhaps not. Our only hope lies in a patient examination of the broad historical record of theory and research. We begin with a semantic analysis of the term *intelligence.*

A Semantic Analysis of the Word

I have put quotation marks around the word "intelligence" in the title of this chapter to signal its imprecise meaning. The *Oxford Dictionary of English Etymology* (Onions, 1966) reveals that the terms *intelligence* and *intellect* have a common origin in the Latin word *intelligere,* meaning "to understand." The same source defines *intellect* as "knowing and reasoning faculties of the mind" (p. 479). If we consult Wolman's (1973) *Dictionary of Behavioral Science,* we learn that "in contemporary psychology it [intelligence] is generally defined as a hypothetical construct from which stem an individual's abilities to deal with abstractions, learning, and novel situations" (p. 197). Wolman also defines intelligence as "the ability to judge, comprehend, and reason" (p. 197) in a fashion similar to the ancient usage of the term. According to Wesman (1975, p. 142), despite centuries of study

> There appears to be no more general agreement as to the nature of intelligence or the most valid means of measuring intelligence than was the case 50 years ago. Concepts of intelligence and the definitions constructed to enunciate these concepts abound by the dozens if not indeed by the hundreds.

From the standpoint of semantics, the term *intelligence* as traditionally used points to a subsistential referent, not an existential one. Implanted in the genes from the start, intelligence is believed (by some psychologists) to refer to an imaginary "capacity" or "power" of some sort that will somehow limit or facilitate one's psychological history.

Alleged Characteristics of "Intelligence"

Today, the area of intelligence and intelligence testing is in a state of warfare. In drawing out the lines of battle, I believe we shall learn not only about intelligence and its testing but also about human nature in general from this perspective, and even about the manner in which psychologists do their work. For example, we shall find that the heredity–environment question insinuates itself into the arena of our present concern as it does in so many others, simply because this basic problem has not yet been settled. Some think it cannot be settled.

The Belief in Fixed Intelligence

In a book entitled *Intelligence and Experience*, Hunt (1961) reviews the history of the concept that intelligence is fixed and development is predetermined by the genes. Hunt narrates the bitter arguments as to what portion of intelligence is to be attributed to heredity and how much to experience. These debates proceed in lively fashion even today.

Historical and conceptual reasons.   According to Hunt, the belief in fixed intelligence had its roots in the Darwinian theory of natural selection. Francis Galton, Charles Darwin's brilliant cousin, influenced this conception of intelligence in his *Hereditary Genius* (Galton, 1869). Calling attention to the fact that the men (he did not consider women) of great distinction and reputation in Great Britain came from a relatively small cluster of families, Galton concluded that genius is inherited. Accordingly, he founded the eugenics movement, the aim of which was to breed for genius. Of course, Galton completely overlooked the favorable factors such as enriched environment, "pull," better education, and more opportunities provided by the leading English families of his time for their children.

Binet's radical approach.   In 1904, French psychologist Alfred Binet was appointed to a commission to study the problem of retardation among children in the public schools of Paris. Together with H. A. Simon, Binet devised a scale, many units of which were tasks or exercises that were in use in Parisian schools. Binet and Simon graded these tests in order of difficulty so that three-fourths of the children at each age level could pass them. Included in the tests were repetition of a series of digits, the execution of simple commands, knowledge of pictures, defining words, answering questions such as "Why do we have houses?" and attempts to evaluate comprehension, as in "What should you do when another child hits you?"

It is important to note that Binet did not believe that intelligence was fixed (Varon, 1936). In fact, after almost two decades of work on intelligence, he deplored the fact that

> Some recent philosophers appear to have given their moral support to the deplorable verdict that the intelligence of an individual is a fixed quantity.... We must protest and act against this brutal pessimism.... A child's mind is like a field for which an expert farmer has advised a change in the method of cultivating, with the result that in place of desert land, we now have a harvest. It is in

this particular sense, the one which is significant, that we say that the intelligence of children may be increased. One increases that which constitutes the intelligence of a school child, namely, the capacity to learn to improve with instruction. [Cited in Hunt, 1961, p. 13]

Goddard's influence.   Binet's optimistic outlook on the flexibility of intelligence took a turn for the worse when an American psychologist imported the Binet-Simon scale into America. This was Henry Goddard, who worked with mentally retarded children at the Vineland Training School in Vineland, New Jersey. He had translated Binet's scale into English in 1908 and used it in his studies. A fervent hereditarian, he could not work up much enthusiasm for educating his charges. Goddard influenced American psychology to conceive of intelligence as a fixed, genetic input prior to an organism's psychological development, a condition that permitted achievement only up to a level determined by the alleged amount of that genetic determinant.

Mercer and Brown (1973) point out that Binet's purpose in developing his intelligence tests was only to identify those children who could not do the work in regular schools and would have to be placed in special schools.

> Thus, the original purpose of "intelligence" testing was to predict which children would succeed academically. The ability to predict academic achievement through a test score has continued to be the primary criterion for testing the validity of "intelligence" measures. Perhaps the current dialogue about ethnic differences in "intelligence" would have never developed *if Binet had labeled his scales general measures of academic readiness rather than measures of "Intelligence." People tend to believe their own labels.* [Mercer and Brown, 1973, p. 58, emphasis added]

As noted before, a noun is defined as the name of a person, place, or thing. Once the noun *intelligence* was adopted, it was easy to go on and conceptualize it as an entity, and then as a stable, definite, or fixed entity. This procedure established the subsistential character of the term.

The Belief in Predetermined Development

"Faith in fixed intelligence has received a good deal of conceptual support from another belief which has been widely held in varying degrees. This is the belief in genetically predetermined development" (Hunt, 1961, p. 35). Older workers believed that evolution continued to do its work in the newborn individual of a species. The infant in its development realized its racial inheritance. The structures with which evolution had endowed the individual were innately determined to unfold by successive patterns of growth called *maturation.*

According to Hunt (1961, p. 36), other historical factors reinforced the conception of the genetic predetermination of behavior and intelligence.

According to the notion of preformation, the basic developmental anatomical as well as behavioral patterns exist at birth and simply unfold like the petals of a rosebud. According to primitive stages of this concept, the organism from the start contained, in miniature, all its structures—arms, legs, eyes, hair, and all. This view is self-actional. It has been partially supplanted by a later view known as *interactionism.* According to interactionism, the biological endowment of the organism interacts with environmental conditions that at each stage can produce irreversible changes in the direction of the organism's development. The same species of fruit flies can be divided, and variation of only the temperature during development can result in radical changes in wing size and shape. Interactionism, as a concept, did not completely displace the concept of predeterminism. The latter lingers on, and some psychologists still believe that walking in the human is simply due to maturation. According to them, walking does not have to be learned; it unfolds more or less automatically with the mere development of legs and other relevant structures. Washburn (1978, p. 411) offers a different explanation for walking in the human: "Through the process of natural selection, evolution produced a complex structural base which *makes human bipedal locomotion possible; yet the behavior has to be learned and it takes a child years to walk and run efficiently*" [emphasis added]. Could it be that the maturationists simply overlook the stream of thousands of interbehavioral events of infants learning to walk in interaction with the floor, chairs, and so forth in their surroundings? There are theoretical choices to be made at this point.

The Metaphor of the Genotype and Phenotype

When geneticists talk about plants or animals, they use such terms as *genotype* and *phenotype.* By *genotype* they refer to the constellation of "genes" that the organism receives from its parents. But *phenotype* refers to the visible characteristics of the organism, considered to be expressions of the interaction of the genotype and environmental conditions. To illustrate: if, in the first generation, red snapdragons are crossed with white ones, the result is all red snapdragons. But when any of these red offspring are cross-bred, their offspring (the third generation) show a ratio of three red snapdragons to one white one. Similar results have been obtained by crossing green peas with yellow ones and smooth peas with wrinkled ones. The results are said to follow Mendelian principles of heredity and are interpreted in terms of dominant and recessive genes (see Blum, 1978).

The appropriation of a biological metaphor by psychology.   In the example of Mendelian heredity, we talk about the shapes, sizes, and colors of flowers, vegetables, and fruit flies. These data belong to genetics, the branch of biology that deals with the similarities and differences of successive generations of organisms. But what have these things to do with Binet's children repeating a series of digits, defining words, or executing simple commands, *all in French*, of course? The only way the connection can be made is to impose the genotype and phenotype metaphor derived from the study of colors, shapes, and sizes of snapdragons to the psychological responses that we noted. Thus, the behavior that the organism performs has been transformed into the phenotype, from which one infers the genotype; that is, "the amount of intelligence" contained in the genes.[1] From Goddard on, some psychologists have wittingly or unwittingly adopted this metaphor. In fact, Hunt himself (Hunt, 1961, pp. 346, 361) writes about intelligence in terms of the genetic model of genotype and phenotype, even though he rejects the concepts of fixed intelligence and predetermined development.

Is it possible that Hunt and others have seen likenesses in two unlike things—namely, psychological activities and anatomical structures? Is this an instance of a misappropriation of a metaphor as a result of analogical reasoning? The following statement from Medawar and Medawar (1977, p. 38) seems to support that hypothesis:

> *Geneticism* is a word that has been coined to describe the enthusiastic mis-application of not fully understood genetic principles in situations to which they do not apply. I.Q. psychologists are among its most advanced practitioners, and it must be reported that some of their evidence on the relative contributions of nature and nurture to differences of intelligence—particularly in twins—has come under suspicion of having been "fiddled."

The following statement from Montagu (1956, pp. 42–43) reinforces the Medawars' stand:

> The fallacy is to assume that because the biological heredity of man is trans-mitted by mechanisms similar to those operative in other animals and in plants, the same mechanisms are responsible for fundamental human behavior. What is true in the biological context becomes a dangerous fallacy when it is applied to human material.

Apparently, investigators disagree on the appropriateness of taking a theory derived from a study of the anatomical and physiological characteristics of living things and imposing it on a radically different order of events, the behavioral. Constructs such as genotype and phenotype correctly refer to the visible color, size, and shape of living things because they were derived from a study of those things. But to apply them to the explanation of why some French children could name colors better than others or repeat a longer series of digits than others does not seem scientifically justified. Suppose a person were to become an expert in understanding engines, levers, fulcrums,

---

[1] According to this self-actional concept of heredity, the genes (just like the brain) are alleged to play a dual role, a biological one *and* a psychological one.

and other mechanical things. Would that person be warranted in imposing mechanical constructs on a study of living things, or should explanations of living things be derived from a study of living things?

Evidence About the Nature of Intelligence from Various Sources

There is an extensive literature on intelligence, ranging over experimental, theoretical, and applied reports. Goddard was not alone. Psychologists Cattell at Columbia University, Yerkes at Harvard, and Terman at Stanford had come under the spell of Galton's hereditary and eugenic notions about behavior. That influence affected both their observations and their interpretations.

Postulates of American Pioneers in the IQ Movement

What lasting effects resulted from the theoretical orientation of the American pioneers in the IQ movement? For example, in 1916 Terman revised the Binet-Simon scale of intelligence (now called the Stanford-Binet test) enlarging it from 54 tests to 90 and making other improvements. But Terman (and his colleagues) concluded that both his test and Binet's really tapped "native intelligence."

In his book, *The Science and Politics of IQ*, Kamin (1974) describes the common sociopolitical views of the early workers in the American mental-testing movement. They held "enthusiastic memberships in various eugenic societies and organizations" (p. 6). It is no surprise to read the following statement from *The Measurement of Intelligence* (Terman, 1916, pp. 6–7):

> In the near future intelligence tests will bring tens of thousands of these high-grade defectives under the surveillance and protection of society. This will ultimately result in curtailing the reproduction of feeble-mindedness and in the elimination of an enormous amount of crime, pauperism, and industrial inefficiency. It is hardly necessary to emphasize that the high-grade cases, of the type now so frequently overlooked, are precisely the ones whose guardianship it is most important for the state to assume.

Kamin (1974) makes a clearer and stronger case than I have of the infiltration of social, political, and economic assumptions into the mental testing of Goddard, Yerkes, and Terman. Here is the summation:

> The early history of testing in America fixed upon the Binet test an apparently indelible genetic interpretation. The hereditarian interpretation shared by Terman, Goddard and Yerkes did not arise as a consequence of the collection of

I.Q. data. Their involvement in the eugenics movement predated the collection of such data. [Kamin, 1974, p. 10]

Kamin also reminds us that, at the time they wrote, Terman and his colleagues did not have the support of quantitative genetics, because the science of genetics had not yet come into existence. Their assumptions took care of that lack:

> The scientific documentation offered by the mental testers that degeneracy and feeble-mindedness were heritable did not occur in a vacuum. Their views were responsive to social problems of the gravest moment. Their "findings" were politically partisan, and they had consequences. We can see clearly with hindsight how ludicrously beyond the bounds of science those views and "findings" extended. They fixed upon the succeeding generations of psychometricians, equipped with more sophisticated scientific tools, a clear predisposition toward a genetic interpretation of I.Q. data. That predisposition is still with us. [Kamin, 1974, p. 10]

This history has a lesson for us: Scientists do not operate in a vacuum. They are children of their culture, who often unwittingly absorb assumptions, opinions, and attitudes *prior to their entry on scientific work*, with serious consequences to their theoretical constructions. The following statement from MacLean (1970, p. 327) applies to the early 20th-century theories about intelligence: "It is . . . bewildering that the world order of science is able to live comfortably for years, and sometimes centuries, with beliefs that a new generation discovers to be false." Perhaps some future generation will discover the assumption of innate powers to be invalid.

Evidence from the Stanford-Binet Test Itself

As a witness to our further inquiry into the nature of intelligence, we call on testimony furnished by the Stanford-Binet test itself. The materials of the test are intrinsically appealing to children because they resemble toys that are familiar to them. Miniature spoons, dogs, and cats, and shoes, wooden blocks and beads, pictures, paper and pencil, and scissors attract and hold the child's interest. Here is a small sampling of the specific tasks required of the child.

The 2-year level.   At the 2-year level,[2] the subject is presented a three-hole form board with square, round, and triangular blocks to be placed in the proper recessed spaces. Other assignments include identifying parts of the body of a paper doll, building a four-block tower, and pointing out objects by name, such as *kitty*, *button*, and *engine*.

[2] The Stanford-Binet test *starts* at the 2-year level. Why not earlier, if intelligence is in the genes from the start (according to hereditarians)?

The 8-year level.   At the 8-year level, the experimenter reads a story and tests the subject's recall of it by asking specific questions about it. A *similarities and differences test* requires pointing out the ways in which a baseball and an orange, or a penny and a quarter, are *alike and different.*

The 12-year level.   The 12-year level requires such tasks as repeating five digits in reversed order and pointing out the absurdity of the following statement: "Bill Jones' feet are so big that he has to pull his trousers on over his head." Another task calls for writing in the one missing word necessary to complete a sentence such as: "_____ either of us could speak, we were at the bottom of the stairs."

Vocabulary.   The Stanford-Binet, like most other tests of general intelligence, is heavily loaded with tests of language facility. A vocabulary test runs through all age levels. Words such as *orange* and *envelope* appear at the lower end, but the list grows increasingly more difficult and ends with such exotic terms as *sudorific* and *parterre.*

Terman, the father of the Stanford-Binet, frequently acknowledged the importance of verbal fluency as a measure of intelligence. In fact, he (Terman, 1919b) suggested that, if time were a factor, the vocabulary test could well substitute for the *total* Stanford-Binet scale. In other references (Terman, 1916, 1919a), he stated that the vocabulary test has greater validity than any other single test item. In view of the crucial importance of language as a measure of intelligence, the following comment is in order. Suppose a child is reared in the backwoods of Appalachia. It seems appropriate to ask what power a gene would bestow on that child to define the word *orange* without any prior experience with the word or the fruit.

If the language is such an important basis for determining intelligence, does it offer a dependable base for deriving IQ; that is, can it be depended on to be stable over a period of time? The fact that neither the vocabulary test of the Stanford-Binet scale nor its method of scoring has changed since 1937 would imply a belief in its stability. Weaver and McPherson (1976) made a comparison of vocabulary scores on the Stanford-Binet vocabulary test given to two groups of children, one sample in 1942 and one in 1976. The first sample contained 1416 children and the second, 1727. They found "overall gains in vocabulary scores during the last 34 years. . . . For example, in 1942 a score of 8 words correct was typical of children who were 8 years, 6 months of age. Currently, this score is achieved by children who are 6 years, 5 months of age" (Weaver and McPherson, 1976, p. 520). There is a lesser gain at each higher level; but, even so, 34 years ago a raw vocabulary score of 15 was earned by children aged 12 years and 9 months. In their 1976 sample, that score was typical of children 11 years and 7 months of age. In other words, the increases were greatest at the younger ages, thinning out gradually with increasing age. Why the improvement? Weaver and McPherson

(1976, p. 521) answer that question by asking another: "Could these data possibly reflect a beneficial side effect of TV?" Their question is not as significant to our purpose as their findings, which imply that the venerated Stanford-Binet vocabulary test scale may not provide a solid bedrock basis for measuring the allegedly inherent intelligence. Perhaps a comparison such as Weaver and McPherson's should be carried out every 34 years.

In a survey of 70 tests of general intelligence, Mercer and Brown (1973, p. 67) found that 77% had subtests entitled Vocabulary, Language, or Verbal; 51% had sections labeled Arithmetic, Quantitative, or Numerical; and 53% had subtests entitled Reasoning, Logic, or Conceptual Thinking. They made a similar content analysis of another important intelligence test, namely the Wechsler Intelligence Scale for Children (WISC), and they came out with similar results, which they sum up in the following statement· "To rate as 'intelligent' in American society one must be highly verbal in English language, and adept at mathematical manipulation" (Mercer and Brown, 1973, p. 67). Is the highly verbal child one who has presumably inherited a high IQ or one who has simply learned more words? As usual, there are choices to be made.

Implications Arising from the Standardization of the Stanford-Binet Scale

In 1937, Terman and Merrill (1937) issued a revision of Terman's original scale, which had been a translation and modification of Binet's tests. He assembled a huge number of tests to provide more items, and more suitable items, that could be scored more objectively. He then tried these out on a sample of approximately 1000 students, for whom mental ages had been determined by Terman's original scale, and 500 preschoolers, for whom there were no prior records of test performance. After sifting out certain tests, Terman and Merrill rejected some and shifted others around so that there was an increase of children passing tests from one age to another. Thus, they had a series graded on the basis of increasing difficulty of test items. In the end, they had two tests, Form L and Form M, with 129 items each. Now, if a given child had to be retested, there were two forms to use in that situation.

Selection of subjects.   The next problem was to find a large, representative group of children from different regions of the country. Eventually, the standardization sample included 3184 subjects from communities in California, Nevada, New York, Colorado, Kansas, Virginia, Vermont, Texas, Minnesota, Indiana, and Kentucky. In selecting schools, Terman (1937, p. 12) states, "We chose average schools, and, as far as possible, recruited the preschool group from the siblings of school cases. *All subjects are American-born and belong to the white race.* There has been no elimination of any particular nationality groups" (emphasis added).

Selection of school cases.   Schools of *average social status* were selected in each community.

Derivation of the final scales.   After weeding out the unsatisfactory tests, Terman shifted the tests around so that the average mental age of each age group would be identical with that group's average chronological age (age in years). As an example, the performance of his 6-year-old group would *average out* to a mental age of 6 years. If we follow the formula for deriving an IQ, we divide mental age by the chronological age and get 6 divided by 6, which equals $1 \times 100 = 100$. Such matching of tests with chronological age was done at each age level so as to yield an average IQ of 100 at every age level.

Terman got what he asked for. He dealt with what American-born, White children of middle-class schools could do on a graded series of tests. There were no measures of any gene attributes. He dealt only with the average reactions of children at various age levels. It is not possible to over-stress the fact that Terman could only observe the concrete behaviors of those children. Now, what are we actually doing when we administer the Stanford-Binet to a child from a ghetto or "from across the tracks?" Are we not comparing the performance of each of those two children with the average performance of White, middle-class, American-born children? The alternative is to *believe* that we are comparing their "genotypes." As usual, we have a choice to make between the interbehavioral view, with its stress only on concrete performances as "intelligence," and the traditional view, with its claim of dealing with innate powers.

The Case of Jensen

In a Harvard Educational Review article provocatively entitled, "How Much Can We Boost IQ and Scholastic Achievement?" Jensen (1969), an educational psychologist from the University of California at Berkeley, answered, "Very little." Why? Jensen argued that compensatory education programs such as Head Start had not produced any lasting changes in IQ and that no amount of special education would ever bring Blacks up to the level of Whites. The furor aroused by Jensen's article brought many critical responses in the following issue of the Harvard journal. Kagan argued that one could hardly expect a *stable increase* in a short 8-week preschool program organized on a crash basis. In an article entitled, "Has Compensatory Education Failed? Has It Been Attempted?," Hunt (1969) claimed that such a program was too little, and too late.

But Jensen's criticism of the Head Start Program was only the opening barrage of his battle with the environmentalists. His next point concerns the inferior performance of Blacks on intelligence tests. Jensen (1969) states that, in the United States, Blacks *average* about 15 points or one standard deviation (S.D.) less on most standard intelligence tests by comparison with the *average* of the white population. Jensen also indicates that, in terms of scholastic achievement, "Negroes score about one standard deviation below the average for whites. . . . The one S.D. decrement in Negro performance is fairly constant throughout the period from grades one through 12" (pp. 81–82). The next point that Jensen makes concerns the largely genetic component of intelligence. His hypothesis is that intelligence is determined to the extent of 80% by heredity, only 20% by environment. He suggests that

> . . . genetic factors are strongly implicated in the average Negro–White intelligence differences. The preponderance of the evidence is, in my opinion, less consistent with a strictly environmental hypothesis than with a genetic hypothesis, which of course, does not exclude the influence of environment or its interaction with genetic factors. [Jensen, 1969, p. 82]

In support of his hereditarian argument, Jensen (1969, pp. 82–83) writes, "No one has yet produced any evidence based on a properly controlled study to show that representative samples of Negroes and white children can be equalized in intellectual ability through statistical control of environment and education." According to Jensen, the difference in IQs between Blacks and Whites argues for a differential educational program for children of the two races. Apparently, according to Jensen, one should not expect as much from Blacks because of their lower inherent IQ. Therefore, low-IQ children should be taught by rote or by association, and high-IQ children should be taught in terms of abstract and verbal concepts.

Jensen's supporters.   Jensen was not alone in his views. One staunch supporter was a Nobel Prize winner, William Shockley, a professor of engineering science at Stanford University. Shockley has won almost as much fame for his support of Jensen as for his coinvention of the transistor. Although Shockley has had no training in human genetics, anthropology, sociology, or psychology, according to Neary (1970) he is apparently convinced that "there is a difference in the wiring patterns of black and white minds."[3]

Jensen also won another advocate and popularizer of his viewpoint in Harvard professor Richard Herrnstein. Although not as certain about race differences in IQ as Jensen, Herrnstein does share Jensen's views that individual differences in IQ are largely inherited and that "the tendency to be unemployed may run in the genes of a family" (1973, p. 138). In fact, Herrnstein is of the opinion that the more successful we are in equating opportunities for the citizens of our country, the more will we allow genetic differences to manifest themselves. Eventually, we will have a caste system based largely on IQ, a condition already prophesied by the ghetto residents of our urban centers. As bearers of the lowest IQs, according to Herrnstein, they will produce future generations of the same, which will become a perpetual burden to society.

[3] Note the reductionist metaphor of wiring, which is congenial with an engineer's work and outlook.

Jensen's opponents. Because Jensen's thesis was loaded with social and political dynamite, it aroused more antagonism than support. Geneticists, sociologists, psychologists, and anthropologists arose to do battle. The Society for the Psychological Study of Social Issues criticized Jensen's articles, stating, "There is no direct evidence that supports the view that there is an innate difference between members of different racial groups" and suggested that "a more accurate understanding of the contribution of heredity to intelligence will be possible only when social conditions for all races are equal and when this situation has existed for several generations" (cited by Jensen, 1971, p. 24).

In 1969, the American Anthropological Association organized a symposium on "Differential Intelligence in Populations?" edited by Brace, Gamble, and Bond (1971) in a pamphlet, "Race and Intelligence." The following highlights are derived from its contents.

1. When we realize how utterly complex the culturalization of any individual is, "it has been a major challenge to psychologists to discover whether *any* aspects of human behavior are inherited" (Brace, Gamble, and Bond, 1971, p. 7).
2. If Jensen were really interested in an objective testing of the inherited component of differences in intelligence between Blacks and Whites, "he should have been devoting his efforts to setting up a scientifically acceptable test situation" (Brace, Gamble, and Bond, 1971, p. 8).
3. Jensen's estimates of heritability were based on studies of twins reared apart. He relied on *average* IQ scores and ignored the range, at the same time overlooking the similarity of environments of twins reared apart (Alland, 1971, p. 32).
4. While Jensen accepts *race* as a valid biological division, anthropologists consider the term an oversimplification, pointing out the diverse African origins of slaves imported into the United States. It is genetically improper to speak of an "average Negro American" (Alland, 1971, p. 34) or "average White American," for that matter.
5. "Black and white differences in intelligence appear to be primarily associated with differences in environmental advantages (Alland, 1971, p. 34).
6. In an article, "On Creeping Jensenism," anthropologists Brace and Livingstone (1971), quoting Hirsch, state that Jensen's studies deal with group averages and, therefore, "have nothing to do with *an* individual, nor are they based on the study of the development. The answers have been based on the test performance of a *population* of individuals at a given time" (Brace and Livingstone, 1971, p. 66).
7. If we define psychology as the *study of the individual,* then Jensen's work is sociological rather than psychological. Individuals as indi-

viduals are swamped out in his statistical characterizations of populations.

8. Brace and Livingstone (1971) point out that half of Jensen's article constitutes a review of quantitative genetics, which he admits is too complex for further consideration but which he believes supports his view. "It does not. Furthermore, we fail to see how, after pointing out that environment can change IQ by as much as 70 points, he [Jensen] can make the statement that 'in short it is doubtful that there is any significant environmental effect on IQ' " (Brace and Livingstone, 1971, pp. 66–67).

9. Jensen treats intelligence as if it were a single entity, such as eye color or green peas versus yellow peas. If we recall a child responding in varied ways to intelligence-test stimuli, we cannot accept Jensen's construct. The behaviors elicited on the Stanford-Binet require linguistic and mathematical skills, knowledge, picture recognition, and so on.

10. Considering the additional facts of the damaging consequences of poor nutrition, poverty, and low educational expenditure, Brace and Livingstone (1971, p. 69) write as follows: "We suggest that it is possible to explain all the measured differences among major groups of men primarily by environmental factors, while noting, on the other hand, that it is not possible to provide genetic explanations which are evolutionarily plausible for most of these differences."

Jensen's data.   So far, we have discussed only Jensen's conclusions and the implications of his study. But where did he obtain the data for his inquiry? Largely from the literature of the past 50 or 60 years. It is important to try to evaluate the validity of those data.

Jensen's theory about the inheritance of intelligence rests heavily on evidence drawn from identical twins reared apart. It occasionally happens that, when a single sperm fertilizes a single ovum, two organisms develop instead of only one. In that case, the pair are identical or monozygotic (MZ) twins. They are said to have identical genes (for their alleged "intelligences" as for anything else). They are always of the same sex and are strikingly similar in appearance. But sometimes two sperm at about the same time fertilize two different ova. The two different individuals that result from such a conception are fraternal or dizygotic (DZ) twins. Genetically, they do not resemble each other any more than if they were born at different times. In other words, genetically, they are no more alike than any two brothers or sisters or any brother and sister, and they, of course, may differ as to sex or appearance also.

Twin studies.   The suitability of monozygotic twins for genetic study is quite obvious. With their identical genes, the ideal experiment would put them under radically different conditions from birth on and, later, give them an intelligence test. If Jensen's genetic theory of intelligence holds true, such twins should manifest highly similar IQs despite radically different reactional biographies. Naturally, such an experiment would be immoral, so Jensen did the next best thing; he relied on the findings of "natural experiments" in which monozygotic twins were separated in early infancy and reared in different homes. Now, Jensen did not conduct such studies himself. He had to rely on comparison studies of identical twins reared apart that were carried out by others and reported in the literature (as already indicated). Here the work of the late Sir Cyril Burt, an English psychologist, comes under our purview as an important source for Jensen's conclusions.

Burt's twin studies. By 1955, Burt published a paper on 21 pairs of twins reared separately. The IQs of the separated twins were reported as correlated 0.771, an extremely high correlation. By 1958, he had accumulated "over 30 pairs" with the *same* correlation. A final report in 1966 on a total of 53 pairs (the largest ever) still showed the identical correlation of 0.771, a highly improbable statistical occurence. Burt also reported a near-perfect correlation of 0.944 through three successive different samples of IQ scores of identical twins reared together, also a statistical near-miracle. A perfect correlation would be expressed as 1.0, meaning that according to Burt's intelligence test, one twin earned *exactly the same IQ* as the other. A correlation of 0.944 comes "within a hair" of identity in scores, a figure that does not change over the years with the increasing sample.

Burt's prestige and power. Burt's prestigious studies on the IQs of separated twins overshadowed the work of others along the same lines. In fact, for his work he was knighted by King George VI and won the Thorndike award from the American Psychological Association. As an adviser to the government, he restructured the British educational system, which established a three-tiered school program, candidates for which were determined once and for all by their performance on an IQ test given at age 11. Of course, the guiding assumption of the program for many years was Burt's theory that intelligence is largely innate. Another source of power came to Burt from his editorship of the *British Journal of Statistical Psychology.* In that journal, he lambasted those who disagreed with him or criticized his work. And even after his death in 1971 at the age of 88, his colleagues suspected the authenticity of his data. So did Kamin.

Kamin's detective work. Since Jensen's sensational 1969 and other reports drew heavily on Burt's data, Kamin (1974) saw fit to make a thorough analysis of Burt's work. Here are some of his observations on Burt's overall procedural errors. First, data derived from the same study but published in different journals are often mutually contradictory. Second, seemingly impossible consistencies appear repeatedly in his publications. Third, procedures and methods are described in a very general or offhand manner. Various correlations with IQs are reported without naming the intelligence tests that were used. And, furthermore, with an ever-increasing sample size over the years, the correlations are astonishingly stable, even to the third decimal point. Fourth, zeroing in specifically on Burt's separated twin studies, Kamin (1974) indicates that Burt accumulated these cases over 45 years and reported them in 1966. Here are Kamin's charges against Burt's 1966 report:

> That paper indicates that all the twins had been separated before the age of six months, but it contains no information about the extent or duration of separation. There is no information about the sexes of the twin pairs, nor is their age at testing indicated. They were all, however, "children," and except in three cases "the tests were applied at school." Three very early cases had been dropped from the sample because of a relatively late age of separation. There were, "in the initial survey," some children outside London "originally tested by the local teacher or school doctor, but these have all been re-tested by Miss Conway." We are not told whether Miss Conway's test results corresponded to the teachers', nor whether discrepancies were averaged, or handled in some other way. [Kamin, 1974, p. 40]

This quotation is a tiny sample of the way Kamin hammers away at the slovenliness of Burt's work. His conclusion is that "the numbers left behind by Professor Burt are simply not worthy of our current scientific attention" (Kamin, 1974, p. 47).

More serious charges against Burt.   To be accused of carelessness and negligence in one's scientific work is bad enough. But far more damaging allegations have been brought against Burt, as the following quotation from Evans (1976, pp. 1–4) reveals:

> For 20 years, the most influential man of his era in the sphere of mental measurement deliberately, it now seems, faked the data in support of his theories about the relative importance of genetic as opposed to environmental factors in determining intelligence. He may even have invented fictitious collaborators to support his contention that 85 percent of an individual's performance in IQ tests was attributable to inherited characteristics. So Burt's alleged misdemeanors as a scientist clearly were serious and their effects far-reaching.
>
> The affair first came to the public's notice as a result of an article in London's *Sunday Times* by its medical correspondent Oliver Gillie. Gillie, who holds a doctorate in genetics, is an experienced researcher and writer. He had been commissioned to author a book—published at the same time as the newspaper article—and aimed at the intelligent lay reader on the whole area of heritability, during which he studied the nature versus nurture argument in relation to intelligence.
>
> In the course of this research Gillie uncovered evidence of Burt's manipulations from sources that, in fact, were already fairly well-known among the

psychological community here. The first of these was the book by Princeton psychologist Leon Kamin, *The Science and Politics of IQ* [1974], which had been available in Britain for about a year and a half but had not broken into the general public's awareness. In the book, Kamin demolished Burt's studies on twins, reared together and separately, by pointing out dozens of inaccuracies, inconsistencies and examples of statistical correlations staying constant against all laws of mathematical possibility. These twin studies, the mainstay of Burt's hereditarian platform, also showed evidence of Sir Cyril having taken data from one piece of work to slot into another because they would conveniently fit with his preferred genetic theories.

Some British researchers were also alert to some of these suspicious statistical shenanigans. Ann Clarke, a psychologist at Hull University, and her husband, Professor Alan Clarke, felt that Burt's figures were too often a perfect fit for the theories and set about reinforcing Kamin's case to the point where only one conclusion was possible. That the supremely competent and erudite Burt had, quite simply, cheated.

All this would have been bad enough. But Gillie went further. He set about trying to trace two people who could certainly have thrown light on these spuriously accurate calculations, a certain Margaret Howard and a J. Conway named as Burt's collaborators on papers in the *British Journal of Statistical Psychology* between 1952 and 1959. But here he came up against one huge problem. No one at University College London had any recollection or official record of either of the two women in question. Files were scanned and questions asked here and in the United States but Howard and Conway remained elusive. If they ever existed—and this is by no means an idle speculation—they have done a very good job of covering their tracks.

The case against Burt spread abroad. The popular media picked up the story and broadcast it far and wide. The *Times* (London) printed many eloquent letters pro and con. In the "News and Comment" section of *Science,* Nicholas Wade (1976) wrote a lengthy report entitled "IQ and Heredity: Suspicion of Fraud Beclouds Classic Experiment." In it, Wade quotes Jensen (to Jensen's great credit) as admitting that Burt's correlations were "useless for hypothesis testing" (p. 917). These were the very correlations that Jensen had used to buttress his own controversial hereditarian position.

Wade also raised doubt about the very existence of Burt's two collaborators, Margaret Howard and J. Conway who had coauthored some of his papers. The *Sunday Times* (London) failed to find such names listed in London University's records, and the two women were also unknown to many of Burt's colleagues. Furthermore, during Burt's editorship, there were numerous book reviews signed by his female collaborators in a style that some subscribers thought was very similar to Burt's distinctive style. And some went so far as to suspect Burt of writing the reviews himself under those two pseudonyms.[4]

---

[4] A fair appraisal of Burt's work and character is available in a biography by Hearnshaw (1979).

The story goes on and on, but we may as well stop at this point. There would be no purpose served in beating a dead horse. The moral of this scientific case history, if any, is that we should start our scientific work with raw data instead of secondary sources and that we should be alert to the witting or unwitting assumptions underlying our scientific work or the work of others.

But how about Jensen?   Did the exposé of an important source of Jensen's hereditarian stand finish him (Jensen) off? Not at all. Burt's papers were not Jensen's *only* source of data. For example, Jensen also relied on three other separated identical-twin studies. Under Kamin's criticial scrutiny, these also turned out to be full of error. The Shields study (1962) showed no effect of separation on genetically identical individuals. To take only one or two from a number of discrediting errors, Kamin found that Shields obtained different results in IQ difference of identical twins reared apart, depending on who tested them. Shields obtained an average score difference of only 8.5 for the 35 pairs of twins that he tested. But for the other five tested by other psychologists, the average difference score in intelligence was 22.4 (Kamin, 1974, p. 49)! Another point concerns the resemblance in rearing style of the separated twins. Shields' appendix "suggests that in *only ten* of the *40 cases* had members of a pair *never* attended the same school, nor been reared by *related families* (Kamin, 1974, p. 51, emphasis added). In a crude geographical sense, it is true that the twin pairs were "separated," but they were largely reared in common, as shown in the following quotation from Shields' study (quoted by Kamin, 1974, p. 50): "Bertram and Christopher were separated *at birth*. The paternal aunts decided to take one twin each and they have brought them up amicably, living next door to one another in the same Midlands colliery village. . . . They are constantly in and out of each other's houses." There are six other cases so described by Shields himself. At least, Shields offers rich (but condemning) details so obviously missing in Burt's reports.

Kamin also analyzes two other separated identical-twin studies, with equally damaging results, and reaches the following conclusion: "To the degree that the case for a genetic influence on IQ scores rests on the celebrated studies of separated twins, we can justifiably conclude that there is no reason to reject the hypothesis that IQ is simply not heritable" (Kamin, 1974, p. 67). Recent reanalysis of Burt's work appears to favor the interbehavioral view over the theory that intelligence is an innate capacity.

Is the IQ Constant?

Earlier in the present chapter, we made a semantic analysis of the hereditarian's belief in intelligence as a fixed, predetermined "entity." By adopting a biological metaphor, the hereditarian can easily conceive of intelligence in the same way as it is possible to think of a gene for a red or white rose and blue versus brown eyes. Now, from a strictly *logical* (not psychological) viewpoint, the hereditarian's argument for the fixity of intelligence would be strengthened if it could be shown that an individual's IQ is constant over a lifetime. This is the question that concerns us now. *Is* the IQ constant?

First let us examine a simple paradigm of a type that has been frequently offered in support of the notion that the IQ *is* constant. Figure 8-1, borrowed from Woodworth's (1940) textbook in general psychology, is offered by Woodworth as "proof" that the IQ does not change very much during an individual's life span. This diagram represents 25 children who achieved an IQ of 115 on an intelligence test administered to students enrolled in the Horace Mann and Lincoln schools of Teacher's College, Columbia University, New York, where Woodworth taught. To make things very clear, what Woodworth did was to pick out all the children who happened to earn that particular score. Then he decided to wait four years in order to find out if those 25 children would still earn an IQ of 115. A glance at the extreme right-hand side of Figure 8-1 shows that they *did not* all earn IQs of 115,

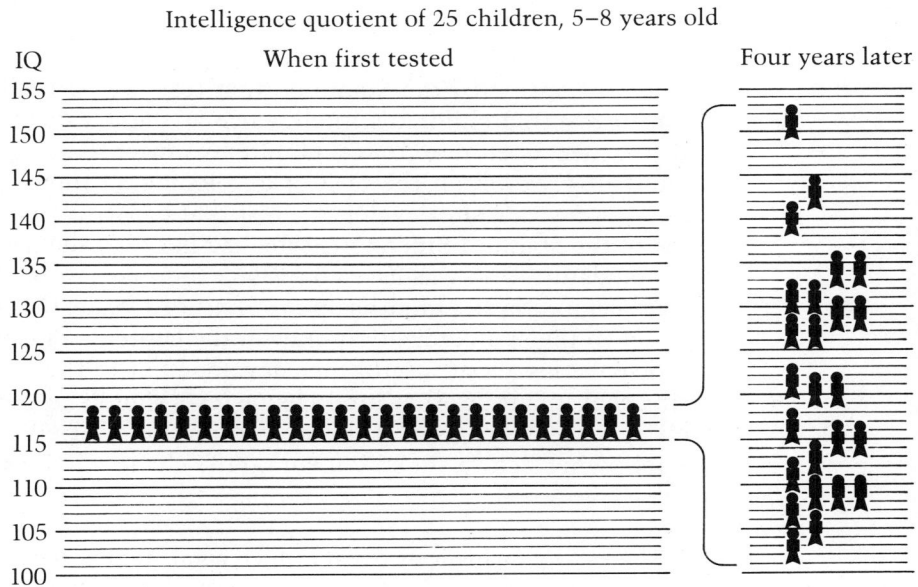

Figure 8-1 Data from the psychological records of the Horace Mann and Lincoln schools of Teachers College, Columbia University. Changes in IQ of 25 children whose IQ was 115 on first test. During four years in these stimulating schools, the IQ of some of these children went up, while the IQ of others went down. The changes were not large in comparison with the whole IQ range of 0–200. The average change was a gain of five points. (From Woodworth, 1940, p. 119.)

because one student is shown on the 149 level and another at the 101 level. If you count up from and down from 115, you will find that 15 students raised their IQs and 10 lost IQ points. But if you add up all the gains and subtract all the losses, you will find that the average change amounts to a gain of only five IQ points. And, since *any* individual can vary that much in any two successive testings, Woodworth argues that the IQ is relatively constant. Therefore, it *is* constant.

The heart of the problem lies in Woodworth's sociological approach. Actually, what Woodworth offers us is a comparison of *a population* at a certain time and that same population four years later. We should hardly need to be reminded that psychology is the study of *the individual*. If we drop a sociological approach for a psychological one, we focus on the scores of *individuals*. Now, we see a striking demonstration of change or *inconstancy*; for, we observe that one individual who had an IQ of 115 four years ago, now earns an IQ of 149, a gain of 34 points! Another child lost 15 points over the same period. The others range between those two points. The lesson in this exercise is that the same data can be used to prove contradictory claims. The IQ *is* constant; the IQ *is not* constant. Take your choice.

The IQ in Infancy

When we considered the Stanford-Binet test, we particularly noted that it began measuring children's intelligence at the advanced age of 2 years. In order to meet a felt need to test children younger than 2 years of age, Psyche Cattell (1947) took on the task of developing an infant intelligence scale. After 4 or 5 years, she developed a test that constituted an extension downward of the Stanford-Binet. Once she had her test, she had to standardize it. Her standardization was based on 1346 examinations made on 274 children at ages beginning at 3 months up to a limit of 3 years. Our interest, however, lies not in the standardization or even the contents of Cattell's tests but in her discoveries about intelligence development in the infant. After emphasizing that infant or other intelligence tests should be used with caution as well as with other observations or information, Cattell (1947, p. 60) makes the following significant statement on the changes in IQ scores that she and others have noted.

> There is a growing body of data which points to the conclusion that part of the I.Q. variations . . . and the crossing and recrossing of growth curves is *the result of changes in the tempo of development rather than the inadequacy of the tests.* An example is Case 198 [Figure 8-2]. This child had an obtained I.Q. of 73 at three months and one near 90 at both six and nine months. At one year and at each six-month interval thereafter up to the end of the third year she showed a comparatively steady gain. Between three and thirty-six months, eight examinations were made, and, with one exception, where there was a decrease of two I.Q. points, each test resulted in a higher I.Q. than the previous test. The mother, a

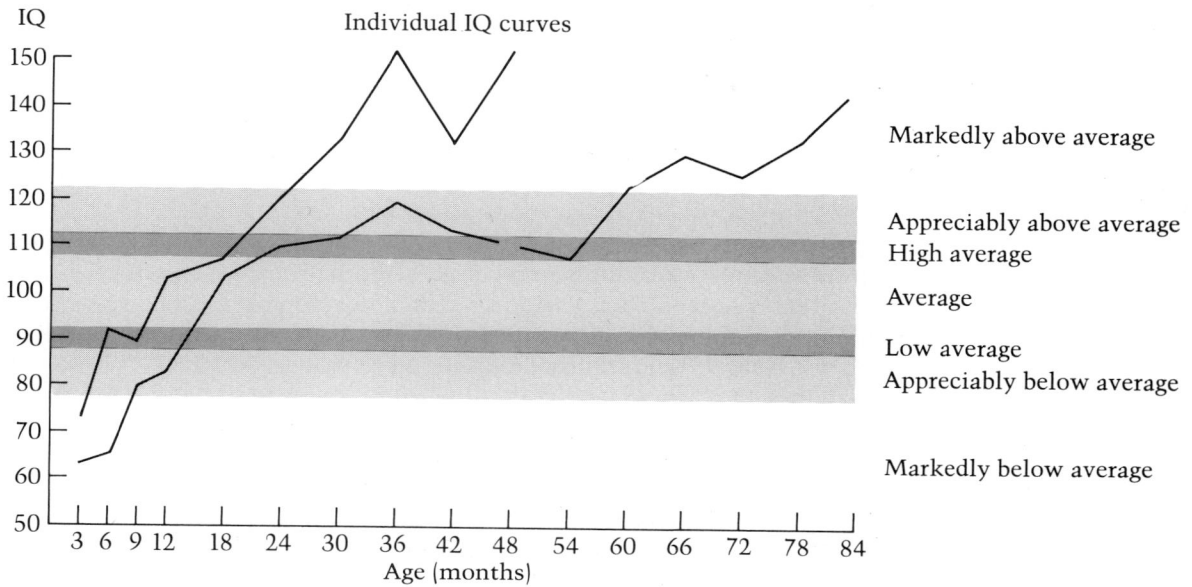

Figure 8-2 Individual IQ curves of two children whose development Cattell followed from the time they were 3 months of age. According to Cattell (1947, p. 62), the lack of constancy was *not* a matter of inadequate tests but a matter of the child's "development progressing at an increasingly rapid rate." (From Cattell, 1947, p. 61.)

patrol policeman's wife, selected the child's college at the time of her birth. At twelve months the pediatrician who examined the baby regretted that the mother was probably doomed to disappointment. The pediatrician's prediction was in line with mental test ratings obtained at that time, but at three years the child's I.Q. was 150 and at four years she informed the examiner that she was animate but her doll was inanimate. . . . Case 1H, also shown in [Figure 8-2], shows a somewhat similar rise in I.Q., though less regular and spread over a longer period. When but two or three tests are out of line the most probable cause may be an inadequate examination, but when seven successive tests show a consistent trend away from "constancy" this opinion cannot well be held. In these instances it appears more probable that the child's mental development was progressing at an increasingly rapid rate. [Cattell, 1947, pp. 60–61, emphasis added]

Cattell also found that IQ developmental curves declined after running along comparatively straight for a number of successive semiannual examinations. She suggests the operation of such factors as school entrance and illness. At any rate, we have seen what happens to intelligence development in infants. How is it with older age groups?

The Fels Research Institute Study of the IQ in
Children

> *Until recently, IQ was considered to be largely unchanging*
> *throughout life.*

[McCall, Applebaum, and Hogarty, 1973, p. 2]

Some research procedures use a cross-sectional method in which groups of individuals are studied at various stages of development. The hope is that a developmental picture of the behavior under study will emerge even though one tests *different* individuals at different ages. But the Fels Research Institute investigators preferred the longitudinal method, one in which *the same individual* is observed over a certain developmental period. In the longitudinal approach, a given individual is under scrutiny for the duration of the study, so one can be alert to significant factors related to any changes in behavior that may occur. In this respect, the longitudinal method is congruous with the concept of the reactional biography and its predilection for trying to make sense of the flow of psychological events.

Since 1929 the Fels Research Institute of Human Development at Yellow Springs, Ohio, has conducted a significant study of development in about 300 children. When the first generation of children grew up and married and had children, researchers then studied their offspring. They managed to administer the Stanford-Binet forms (among other tests) to their subjects at birthdays and half-birthdays between 2½ and 6 years and at birthdays from age 6 to 15 years.

Sontag, Baker, and Nelson (1955), who conducted the early studies, began to see a pattern in their data that was difficult to attribute to "chance." As they scanned the IQ curves derived from their data, they noted trends of decrease or increase in IQ that continued over several years. The picture for many children was not IQ stability or constancy; it was instability or change. Assuming that whatever changes occurred must be related to reactional biography conditions, they made an intensive study of the 35 children who had gained most and 35 who had lost most. This top and bottom group constituted one-half of the total group (140 children) in that particular study.

In searching for factors that might account for the changes in IQ, the Fels workers considered statistical errors, practice effects from successive testing, maturation patterns, anxiety, and "motivation." The last factor turned out to be the significant one.

Motivation and IQ change. Here is how Sontag and his colleagues saw "motivation" at work. A child is normally born into a sheltered, protective, loving atmosphere. Although the home offers comfort and support, it is also a threat to the child, as when a vulnerable child is temporarily deprived of love and attention directed toward siblings or on account of discipline and so on. In compensatory fashion, that child may derive substitute satisfaction from building up independence and reliance on self and from mastery of problems. In time, self-approval and group approval through competition sustain and comfort the child as substitutes of parental love. In the competitive schoolroom situation, such a child's IQ has a chance to rise.

But things may not go as smoothly as they have been pictured. Mothers may overprotect and infantilize the child, making it overdependent on maternal love and support. When this happens, the child's social maturation is inhibited. Such a child is less likely to develop resources for "independence, mastery of problems, and competition with peers" (Sontag, Baker, and Nelson, 1955). In the schoolroom, the same child may feel threatened and anxious in competition with others and may give up the fight and seek adjustment to the situation in other ways. The following two cases illustrate and support the Fels Research workers' theorizing.

Case M. J., the second child in a rural family, has little opportunity to play with other children except her sister, 8 years older. The mother is overprotective, and father and sister share in idolizing and pampering M. J. She is demanding of adult attention, indulges in almost no self-initiated play, and when with other children constantly turns to adults for reassurance. Her base Binet score is about 133. It drops until at 60 months, it is about 117. By 84 months it has recovered most of its loss and by 10 years is back to its base of 133.

Case E. R. shows a child whose score rose from a base of 118 at 3 years to 129 at 4 years. We attributed this to the fact that he was a slow maturer in motor development. Then, after no consistent change for 3 years, his scores began an ascent which carried them almost to 180. This boy, while not aggressive, is intensely competitive in school, gets great satisfaction from mastery of such subjects as mathematics and chemistry, and spends his free hours absorbed in a book. He depends relatively little on human relationships, either family or peers, for reassurance. [Sontag, Baker, and Nelson, 1955, pp. 561–562]

Intelligence and personality.   The earlier (1955) study spurred the Fels workers into further research on the nature of intelligence and possible personality correlates. This time Sontag, Baker, and Nelson (1958) included 200 subjects whose records were complete. They covered a span of over 20 years of the institute's history. In the Fels study, repeated measurements were made on the same subjects year after year.

The findings.   Individual curves drawn for 140 of the subjects are reproduced in the appendix of the original report (Sontag, Baker, and Nelson, 1955, pp. 58–80). Four of them are reproduced in Figure 8-3. What a diversity of patterns! Perhaps the most outstanding characteristic is the consistent and extensive change in many of the subjects. The greatest amount of increase in IQ score showed a gain of 73 IQ points from a raw score of 107 at

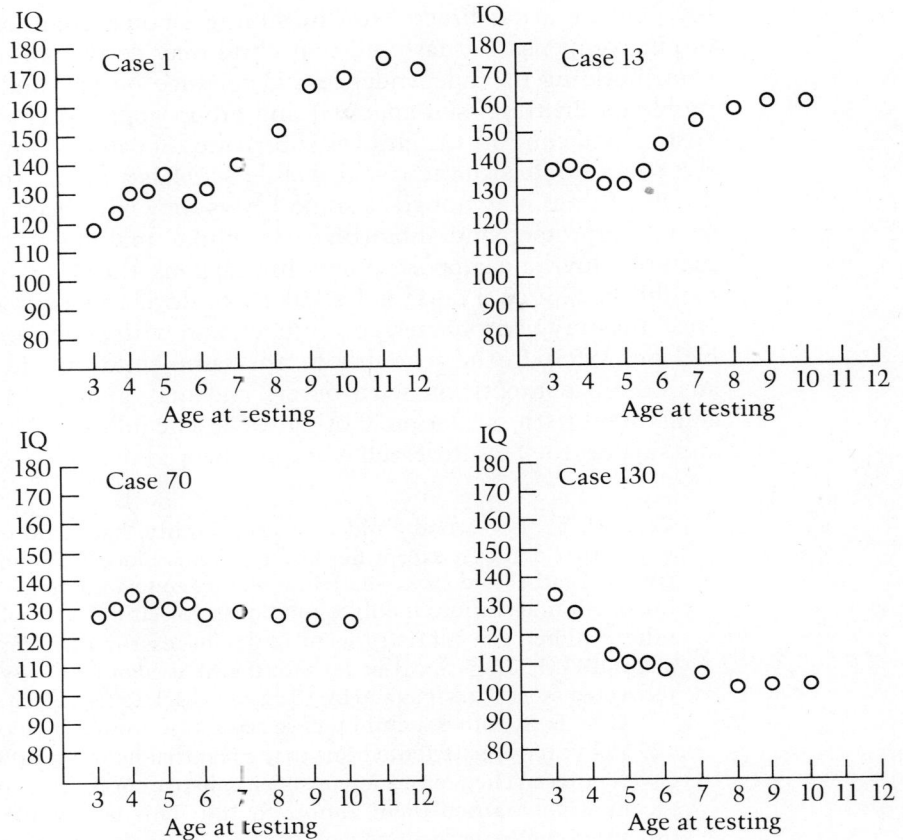

Figure 8-3 Four individual curves of intelligence development. Case 1 shows the greatest gain, one of 73 IQ points from a raw score of 107 at age 2½ to a score of 180 at age 10. Case 13 shows a decrement, then a gain. Case 70, a slight rise and a slight decline. Case 138 shows the greatest amount of loss, 40 points, from a raw score of 142 at age 3 to a raw score of 102 at age 8. (From Sontag, Baker, and Nelson, 1958, pp. 58, 60, 69, 80. Reproduced by permission of the Society for Research in Child Development.)

age 2½ to a score of 180 at age 10. The greatest decline in IQ score involved a loss of 40 points from a raw score of 142 at age 3 to a raw score of 102 at age 8 (p. 23). The changes were not necessarily linear, either. The same child's "curve" might be a V, showing first a decline, then an increment. The converse was also true. Some subjects showed little change. Many others showed prominent shifts in the shape of their curves at ages 5, 6, or 7, suggesting a relationship to the early school years. The irregularity of the patterns of change in IQ score caused by varying amounts of change at different age periods makes the classification of IQ change difficult. Clearly we cannot speak of individuals having a fixed increment of IQ change or a constant mental-growth rate, regardless of the age period during which these changes occur. Indeed, the highly idiosyncratic nature of the IQ changes found is an argument in itself for possible complex environmental causes of IQ change rather than simple hereditary factors (p. 23).

Implications concerning intelligence. Sontag, Baker, and Nelson (1958) consider that their findings concerning mental growth derived from longitudinal follow-up methods of study have "aided in dismissing the idea that the IQ is constant over any period during childhood" (p. 51). The individual cases argue against any "constant increment of IQ to be found in the majority of cases" (p. 51). Furthermore, they do not blame the tests as being unreliable, but go along with Bayley (1954), who "suspects that the failure of early tests in predicting a stable intellectual factor rests in the nature of intelligence itself" (Sontag, Baker, and Nelson, 1958, p. 30). Viewing the overall results, "it would appear that the extent of IQ change found during childhood has been previously underestimated" (pp. 53–54). Their conclusion is: "From the description of the nature and amount of change in IQ and from the analysis of possible artifacts in our data, we may conclude that real changes in relative mental ability do occur in childhood" (p. 54).

IQ and reactional-biography factors. Having found drastic changes in IQ over a span of years, Sontag and his coworkers (Sontag, Baker, and Nelson, 1958) began looking for related personality variables. To neglect such a procedure would be to act as if the changes were chaotic. Sontag and collaborators assumed no such thing. In general, they found that the children's personality adjustments were of value in predicting IQ score change and in understanding the nature of accelerated or decelerated mental-growth rate as related to personality factors. Emotional dependence on parents during the preschool years was definitely associated with loss in IQ scores. But children who, during the preschool years, developed behaviors characterized by such terms as *aggressive, self-initiation*, and *competitiveness* were laying a foundation for a subsequent accelerated development of intelligence. These behaviors then appeared to generalize to new learning situations.

The Fels workers found many other interesting relationships between intelligence development and personality variables. We close this brief report of their research with a statement of theirs that is rich with implications for an objective construct of intelligence. For them "intelligence" is not a thing apart, an entity within the person, a kind of "power behind the throne." They say, "We may regard intelligence as but one aspect of the total personality" (Sontag, Baker, and Nelson, 1958, p. 119).

In a monograph entitled "Developmental Changes in Mental Performance," McCall, Applebaum, and Hogarty (1973) report the results of a study that extended and elaborated the Sontag team research. In fact, they even used data from the Fels Research Institute "data bank." Before we examine their findings that are pertinent to our area of interest, we should note their review of previous investigations of IQ-score changes. The following is a partial but impressive list: the Harvard Growth Study, the Berkeley Guidance Study, the University of Colorado Child Research Council Study, the Chicago Study, the Brush Foundation Study, the Berkeley Growth Study, and the London Longitudinal Study

> . . . have all found nontrivial group and/or individual subject changes in IQ over age for the group as a whole, although there was often a small group of subjects who declined in IQ.[5] By contrast, a longitudinal study of black children from predominantly disadvantaged environments has shown a progressive decline in IQ between the ages of five and ten years. Similarly, children from rural mountain villages or other isolated or "disadvantaged" environments have also shown declines in IQ performance over age. [McCall, Applebaum, and Hogarty, 1973, p. 3]

What did McCall and his coworkers find? Their results are harmonious with previous findings. In their sample of "normal, home-reared, middle-class children" (p. 70) between the ages of 2½ and 17, they found an average change of 28.5 points. "One of every three children displayed a progressive change of more than 30 points, and one in seven shifted more than 40 points. Rare individuals may alter their performance as much as 74 points" (p. 70). One might easily foretell the following conclusion of the McCall, Applebaum, and Hogarty (1973) inquiry: "The failure to predict childhood IQ from infancy plus the present data on the extent of systematic IQ change during childhood argue against constancy" (p. 72). And here ends our exploration of infantile and childhood IQs—with poor support for the innate-capacity theory of intelligence. It follows from interbehavioral theory that the sequence of events involving a given individual need not be constant in any sense whatsoever.

The IQ in Adulthood

Forty or 50 years ago, psychologists believed that the IQ was at its highest in individuals in their twenties and that it declined gradually with advancing age. They reached such a conclusion from the type of data that they collected and analyzed. Their data were cross-sectional, that is, IQ scores obtained by studying, let us say, 5-, 10-, 20-, 30-, 40-, 50-, and 60-year-old subjects at a given time. Thus, such factors as superior educational opportu-

---

[5]Note that even in a study of whole populations IQ inconstancy manifests itself.

nities may have favored subjects in each antecedent age group. More recently longitudinal studies have been favored. What do they show? They uniformly show steady gains *with increasing age,* just the opposite of cross-sectional studies.

The Charles and James study.

While previous investigations chose either superior or retarded populations in longitudinal studies of IQ stability, Charles and James (1964) selected the "average person" group of individuals for their investigation. Their aim was "(a) to determine whether a mature population identified as 'average' in childhood could be located, (b) to retest a sample of this population, and (c) to determine what environmental factors might have influenced any changes of ability found" (Charles and James, 1964, p. 105).

From a departmental file listing test scores administered at an average age of 6 years and an average IQ of 100.2, 25 subjects in a Midwestern city were chosen who agreed to be retested. Roughly half of the subjects had been tested with the 1916 or 1937 revision of the Stanford-Binet test. The rest were administered the Kuhlman-Anderson or the Detroit Kindergarten tests. All were retested on the Otis Quick-Scoring Mental Ability Test.

Retesting.

To locate individuals after several decades in our mobile society was a difficult task, but 14 men and 11 women located in the same town agreed to cooperate in the project. All the men had completed high school. One woman had stopped her education at the eighth grade. Three men and five women had attended college without graduating. Four men and three women had graduated from college, and two men had taken some graduate work.

Occupations of the subjects' parents ranged broadly from unskilled labor to professional work, with business and professional categories most frequent. The occupations of the men themselves ranged all the way from unskilled labor to public school and college teaching. The most frequent women's occupations were in the sales and clerical areas, with a sprinkling of other fields.

Test results.

The average retest IQ score for the group of 25 subjects was 107.6, with a range extending from 90 to 132. As a check on possible IQ change, Charles and James (1964) found the difference between each subject's initial IQ and retest IQ. The difference between the two scores ranged from a loss of 8 IQ points to a gain of 29 IQ points! Because of our emphasis on the individual's behavior, the data, as displayed in Table 8-1, are worth inspecting. The data in the last column, showing the difference between the original and retest IQs were obviously arranged in rank order. The range of IQ scores from 90 to 132 extend from the lower end of the average level to the superior level.

Table 8-1   Subject Characteristics and Obtained IQ Scores

SUBJECT	SEX	ORIGINAL TEST AGE	RETEST AGE	ORIGINAL TEST	ORIGINAL IQ	RETEST IQ	DIFFERENCE
1	M	6	28	S–B[a]	101	93	− 8
2	F	13	42	K–A[b]	98	90	− 8
3	M	8	40	K–A	99	94	− 5
4	M	3	38	S–B	100	98	− 2
5	M	7	28	S–B	99	100	+ 1
6	F	8	26	K–A	98	100	+ 2
7	M	8	28	K–A	103	105	+ 2
8	F	5	36	D–K[e]	100	103	+ 3
9	F	6	28	S–B	99	103	+ 4
10	F	10	30	K–A	100	105	+ 5
11	F	6	41	K–A	104	109	+ 5
12	F	6	32	S–B	104	111	+ 7
13	M	6	29	S–B	100	108	+ 8
14	F	7	31	S–B	100	108	+ 8
15	F	6	28	S–B	96	104	+ 8
16	M	5	38	D–K	103	114	+ 9
17	F	5	34	D–K	100	112	+ 12
18	M	5	33	D–K	100	112	+ 12
19	M	6	28	S–B	100	113	+ 13
20	M	6	40	D–K	99	112	+ 13
21	F	6	41	S–B	100	113	+ 13
22	M	6	27	S–B	99	113	+ 14
23	M	6	33	D–K	100	116	+ 16
24	M	6	31	D–K	99	122	+ 23
25	M	7	40	K–A	103	132	+ 29

[a] S–B, Stanford-Binet.
[b] K–A, Kuhlmann-Anderson.
[c] D–K, Detroit-Kindergarten.
Source: Charles and James, 1964, p. 108.

Occupations also ranged from unskilled labor to professional. The ages of subjects at retest should also be noted. They range from an age of 26 years to 41 years. The time interval between test and retest ranges from a low of 18 years to a high of 35 years. The most significant experiences related to IQ-score change were what appeared to be persistence in attacking school study problems either on one's own or in seeking help from others. The small sample failed to yield any other outstanding biographical factors in explaining the observed changes.

The chief lesson to be derived from this study is packed into the following restrained statement quoted from near the close of Charles and James' report (1964, p. 110): "The great diversity of this population described as 'average' in childhood, suggests that caution should be exercised in making plans for the future of 'average' youngsters." "Average" youngsters can become "superior" adults.

Intelligence at Middle Age

It sounds too good to be true, but in 1969 Kangas and Bradway (1971) were able to round up 48 San Franciscans (24 men and 24 women) for whom periodic IQ scores were available going back 38 years! Such a rare occurrence started in 1931 as part of the standardization of the 1937 revision of the Stanford-Binet test in which the 48 participated. In 1931, their subjects, then 2 to 5½ years old, constituted the California sample of a nationwide standardization population for that revision. They were subsequently retested in 1941, 1956, and again in 1969 by Kangas and Bradway.

This is the way Kangas and Bradway obtained their subjects. In 1968, they wrote letters to 109 of the 111 subjects who had participated in the 1956 retest. They finally were able to administer the 1960 revision of the Stanford-Binet and the Wechsler Adult Intelligence Scale to the 48 subjects.

Was the sample representative?   Before discussing the results, an important question arises when we learn that the 48 participants in the 1969 retesting had been part of a group of 111 who had been tested in 1931, 1941, and 1956. How can we be sure that the 1969 group was a representative, rather than a biased, sample? One way to settle the issue is to compare the average IQs of the subjects in the 1931, 1941, and 1956 tests who participated in the 1969 tests with the average IQs of the *total group* of which they were a part in the 1931, 1941, and 1956 testings. Because Kangas and Bradway (1971) found that none of the differences between the sample of 48 and the total group were statistically significant, they concluded that their group of 48 subjects was a representative, not a biased, sample.

Constancy of the IQ.   The next significant question is: How stable were the IQs of the 48 subjects tested over a total span of 38 years, at successive intervals of 10, 15, and 13 years? Ideally, we should have results shown for each of the 48 individuals, but Kangas and Bradway (1971) provide data in terms of the group average IQ in each successive test. Those figures follow: 1931, 110.7; 1941, 113.3; 1956, 124.1; and 1969, 130.3. The correlation figures show a decreasing correlation between preschool IQ and later IQs as the 48 subjects grew older. That is another way of saying that the IQs of this group were not stable. We are not given the range of IQs in the successive testings, but the data were analyzed for the subjects whose ages in 1969 were between 39 and 44 years. When they examined the average IQs by yearly step intervals between 39 and 44, they found an "absence of any significant downward trend in IQ between those ages." In fact, Kangas and Bradway suggest that "there is growth even after the age of 34 years. The data do not indicate when growth ceases [but] "a strongly significant upward trend in IQ gain over the 38 years was found" (Kangas and Bradway, 1971, pp. 336–337).

Intelligence in the Declining Years

> *Clearly, "agedness" is not synonymous with advanced chronological age per se.*
>
> [Jarvik, Eisdorfer, and Blum, 1973, p. vi]

When we come to a consideration of the fate of the IQ in "the sunset years," the answer is very unclear. For example, in attempting to organize 600 summaries of studies on life-span development, John Horn (1970, p. 424) confessed that his hopes were "dashed on the rocks of contradiction and remoteness." There are other reasons than the statistical ones previously mentioned that tend to conceal, for example, the outstanding, still-productive 90-year-old.[6] Then, as Birren (1973) points out, cross-sectional studies ignore the dramatic changes in our culture over the years.

"While there is a high proportion of individuals over the age of 65 who are functionally illiterate, *there are not many illiterates of high school age*" (Birren, 1973, p. 153, emphasis added). In other words, in comparing populations at different age levels, there are more variables at work than simply age.

No one has stated this particular problem more clearly than Riegel (1976, p. 11). In censuring developmental psychologists of the past, he writes, "Without exception they failed to realize that people who differ in age also differ in their past histories and, therefore, in regard to the vast social changes that were brought about in education, welfare, health care, communication (newspaper, radio, television), transportation, etc." In comparing a cross section of 20-year-olds and 70-year-olds, say, in 1970, one must remember that the former were born in 1950 and the latter in 1900. Thus, they differ *also* in terms of the cultural and historical conditions under which each group developed their reactional biographies. The horse and buggy and the horseless carriage eras epitomize a whole class of vastly different cultural conditions for each generation. Imagine comparing 20-year-olds and 70-year-olds in 1920; one group was born in 1900 and the other in 1850. Such a perspective forces one to see more clearly the changing cultural dimension as a backdrop to individual psychological development.

The longitudinal approach comes in for its share of criticism, too. Even though developmental psychologists recognized the technical difficulties of

---

[6]This is an appropriate place to recall the case of the remarkable 100-year-old Charles Greeley Abbot discussed in Chapter 2.

evaluating the performance of individuals over a certain time span, "they failed to realize that as the individual changes so society changes" (Riegel, 1976, p. 11). For example, many times the physical and social environment may change faster and more dramatically than the changes that individuals may undergo. The horseless carriage made vast numbers of harness makers, blacksmiths, and wheelwrights obsolete. Droughts and industrially polluted lakes can eradicate farming and fishing careers mighty fast.

Static versus dynamic views.   Fundamentally, what Riegel (1976) is getting at relates to our discussion of static versus dynamic or process views of nature. Riegel is arguing on behalf of an approach that views (1) *the organism's interactions as changing* in (2) *a changing society.* Thus, there are two dimensions of change going on simultaneously, both sets of factors *interacting* with each other. It is possible to see the organism as a locus of a flow of behavioral events simultaneously occurring in a cultural-historical or social matrix. A fitting metaphor borrowed from astronomy suggests the rotation of the earth set within the orbit of Earth's revolution, within the solar system, set within the Milky Way, and so on. Developmental psychologists who held to the static view acted as if individuals themselves (as in the longitudinal approach) or groups of different aged individuals (as in the cross-sectional approach) were developing in a constant social environment if not in a social vacuum. "This viewpoint, too, is now being replaced among the students of a life-span developmental psychology that take both the development of the individual and that of the society into account" (Riegel, 1976, p. 246). The two-volume *The Developing Individual in a Changing World* (Riegel and Meacham, 1976) reflects the newer mode of thinking.

Are the tests fair to the aged?   In attempting to answer the question: "Does intelligence decline in old age?" there are still other problems than those we have considered. We shall touch on only one more: are the intelligence tests any fairer to the aged than they are to members of other cultures, minority groups, the illiterate, and so on? We have already observed that, because the Stanford-Binet as well as other tests were standardized on a middle-class, White population, they are fairest to those resembling that population. Similar arguments apply to tests given to the aging, tests that are more becoming to children and young adults.

With the realization that traditional tests are inappropriate for the aging, Demming and Pressey (1957) long ago devised a test that would be more closely related to the needs of older adults. Instead of paper cutouts and stringing beads, they had such items as depended on the "use of yellow pages of a telephone directory, on common legal terms, and on people to get to [sic] perform services needed in everyday life"; and they found higher scores on these tests for individuals who earned lower scores on traditional tests with their "kid-stuff" items (Demming and Pressey, 1957, pp. 144–148).

With a down-to-earth orientation, Riegel (1976) senses the artificiality of the sampling of the individual's actual behavioral repertoire by the traditional intelligence test. Does it really capture the rich, developmental status of an individual at a particular time?

> Does it, indeed, matter for an individual's daily success whether he or she cannot abstract some shared features from stimuli, solve some algebraic problems, trace a maze, or reassemble blocks? Granted that these performances and behaviors might be predictive of certain occupational and professional skills, they do not encompass the array of an individual's activities that occupy him or her and reflect lifelong experiences, feelings about one's past, and hopes for one's future. [Riegel, 1976, p. 6]

Experimental studies. We have just noted the unfairness of comparing groups of individuals who are one or more generations apart. Schaie and Labouvie-Vief (1974) shared this sensitivity and carried out a piece of work combining the longitudinal and cross-sectional approaches in an effort to get at the impact of sociocultural change on age differences in adult functioning of the type tested in intelligence tests, thus differentiating the effects of chronological age, on the one hand, and generation-related differences, on the other. Essentially, they followed the changes that occurred in groups originally tested in 1956 and 1963 and retested in 1970. Their subjects ranged in age from 21 to 84 years of age.

Schaie and Labouvie-Vief (1974, pp. 317–319) conclude that

> Traditional interpretations of intellectual decrement need to consider more carefully the confounding factor of cultural-historical change. . . . Concentrating on the generation-confound existing in conventional cross-sectional research, the data reported here lend minimal justification to the often stated stereotype of general behavioral deficit in late adulthood and maybe old age—a finding that, incidentally, is supported by recent longitudinal data suggesting that decrements may occur only in the years immediately preceding death.

Schaie and Labouvie-Vief, and Schaie in other writings with his colleagues, draw the following conclusions from his numerous studies: "Presumed *universal* decline in adult intelligence is at best a methodological artifact" (Schaie, 1974, p. 802). "There is a strong evidence that *much* of the difference in performance on intellectual abilities between young and old is not due to decline . . . but due to higher performance levels of successive generations. *Some* decrement . . . remains to be accounted for" (Schaie, 1974, p. 804). "*General* intellectual decline in old age is *largely* a myth" (Baltes and Schaie, 1974, p. 35). And "on at least *some* dimensions of intelligence . . . people of average health can expect to maintain or even increase their level of performance into old age" (Baltes and Schaie, 1974, p. 36).

These statements do not sound radical, but Horn and Donaldson (1976) have taken issue with Schaie's and his coworkers' conclusions. While admitting that some of the Schaie team's results "caution against the view that all of the abilities believed to be involved in intelligence necessarily decline or decline in the same way," they also state that "some abilities may decline little or not at all" (p. 715).

Perhaps, the problem pertaining to interpretation of results in related to dependence on statistics and the resultant neglect of the individual. Horn and Donaldson (1976, p. 715) seem to glimpse this when they write "There are results which caution against supposing that decline necessarily occurs *for all subjects* or necessarily sets in as early as might be supposed" (emphasis added). In a statement quoted earlier, Schaie (1974, p. 802) also discounted *universal* decline in old age. Can it be that the rare and outstanding individual's excellent functioning is obliterated in the process of statistical computation?

A look at the individual. In an evaluation of papers presented at a conference, Jarvik (1973) acknowledges a decline in performance on speeded tasks, a decline that begins between the ages of 18 and 40. But he reports that "the Iowa subjects who were entering the seventh decade at the time of their last testing had maintained their relative standing on mean total Alpha scores for 42 years" (p. 66). He further states that, if illness does not enter the picture,

> Cognitive stability is the rule and can be maintained into the ninth decade, as shown by one of our twins who was tested five times between the ages of 62 and 82 years. At age 82 this lady scored higher than she had at age 62 on Vocabulary, Similarities, and Digits Backward, and she equalled her earlier performance on Digits Forward. *Only on the speeded motor tasks were there prominent decrements.* [Jarvik, 1973, p. 67, emphasis added]

But, even in this area, Jarvik questions whether "psychomotor decline has to be accepted as inevitable. *Probably not,*" he states, *"because we know that there are wide individual differences"* (p. 67, emphasis added). Statistics have a way of dissolving individual differences.

Jarvik (1973, p. 66) also points out the influence of educational level on intelligence performance during later life. Education tends to set up intellectual habits that perpetuate themselves throughout life. But individuals who might stand out as the result of such differential life experiences are "homogenized" when they are presented as part of a group average.

In their study of the varied careers of specific individuals, Honzik and Macfarlane (1973, p. 46) "wonder at times if detailed biographies with emphasis [on] intra-individual coherence and change, are not the best way to contribute to valid knowledge in the field of human development." This is consonant with a definition of psychology as "the study of the individual."

Our discussion of group versus individual data is relevant to Skinner's (1953, p. 19) statement:

> A prediction of what the *average* individual will do is often of little or no value in dealing with a particular individual. The actuarial tables of life-insurance companies are of no value to a physician in predicting the death or survival of a particular patient. . . . A science of behavior which concerns only the behavior of groups is not likely to be of help in our understanding of the particular case.

Here again we are confronted with what may look like a choice, but which is not. The social matrix within which the individual develops must not be ignored or rejected, because it illuminates the individual's behavior, but neither must the individual's action disappear within the statistical manipulation of masses of data. Social and individual variables interact, so both must be taken into account.

One final point.   On the question of what happens to the IQ in the declining years, we get some help from Schaie's (1974) analysis of individual life patterns. "Such analyses show that at each age . . . level there are some individuals who (at least over a 14-year period of time) gain and others who lose, while many remain stable." Now, doesn't that statement have a familiar ring? It is as applicable to Psyche Cattell's study of infants, to the Fels Research Institute's findings with children, to the study of adults, and (we come full circle) to the aged. Thus, over the whole life span, there are some individuals who gain IQ and others who lose, while many remain stable. "Clearly, 'agedness' is not synonymous with advanced chronological age *per se*" (Jarvik, Eisdorfer, and Blum, 1973, p. vi).

Intervention Strategies

We have attacked the problem concerning the nature of intelligence from a number of perspectives. This time, let us try working at it from a different angle, that of intervention. To intervene means to introduce an extraneous condition into an ongoing situation in an attempt to modify that situation in some way. Suppose we learn that children in a certain ghetto show a decline in IQ score over the years. Why not try to do something about it to see if we can arrest that decline or even reverse it? One way to intervene would be to bring special teachers into the home to spur early development of the child. Such a plan would constitute an intervention strategy, and the results might throw light on the fixity or plasticity of intelligence.

Skeels' Study

Skeels' 30-year study (1966) did not start out as an intervention strategy; it just happened to become that by stages. The story goes back to the 1930s, when the prevailing notion was that intelligence was a fixed and abiding characteristic of the individual, determined by the genes. One could infer one's genotype from one's parents' occupational and educational achievements. Therefore, plans for adoption of a child were made on the basis of the parents' occupation, economic, and educational status. The theory was that that phenotype was the best prediction of the child's innate potentialities.

The subjects.   In the 1930s, 25 children (20 of them illegitimate) were sent by court order to an overcrowded and understaffed Iowa orphanage where Skeels was a psychologist. There was a fixed policy at this institution with two possibilities for children committed to it.

1. *The hospital.*   Children up to the age of 2 years were assigned to a hospital, a relatively new building. The hospital had a nursery for infants up to 6 months of age. This amounted to a dormitory equipped with cribs whose covered sides limited visual stimulation. Handling and care were minimal, consisting essentially in diaper changing and feeding via propped bottles.

Children beyond 6 months of age were assigned to crowded dormitories with anywhere from two to five larger cribs to a room. While there was a bit more freedom of movement in this area, human contacts were limited mostly to "feeding, dressing, and toilet details" (Skeels, 1966, p. 4).

2. *The cottages.*   Children aged 2 years or older were transferred to still-overcrowded dormitories in cottages. One matron, aided by three or four untrained girls, was in charge of 30 to 35 children of the same sex. In addition to taking complete care of the children, the matron maintained the cottage and mended her charges' clothes. Strict regimentation was the rule. There was some sort of schooling on the grounds with possibilities for transfer to the public junior high school. However, few of the "graduates" could carry on the work there. When the place became too crowded, children were sometimes transferred to another state institution for the mentally retarded. Skeels' story starts with his serendipitous follow-up of two frail, profoundly retarded little girls.

Early in Skeels' program, he came across two baby girls in the nursery. Abandoned by their mentally retarded mothers, these two frail, whiny waifs, emaciated, tearful, and with runny noses, spent their days rocking. Although they were, respectively, 13 and 16 months old, psychological tests placed them at 6 and 7 months developmentally. From additional observations of their behavior by the superintendent of nurses, and by the pediatrician, they were considered unsuitable for adoption; and so, with great confidence, they were recommended for transfer to an institution for the mentally retarded. The recommendation was carried out when the little girls were aged 15 and 18 months, respectively.

A surprise.   Six months after the two babies had been transferred, Skeels was touring the wards of an institution for the mentally retarded when his attention was caught by two little girls. They were alert, running about, interacting with adults much like any other "average" toddlers. Skeels hardly recognized them as the same two girls for whom he had predicted such an unfavorable outcome. He tested them again and could hardly believe that they were approaching normal psychological development for their age. However, he decided to leave them in the situation in which they had made such gains. Tests repeated a year later and again when the girls were 40 and 43 months old "gave unmistakable evidence of mental development well within the normal range for age" (Skeels, 1966, p. 6).

What's the explanation?   As Skeels pondered this heavy question, he felt that the real developmental spurt of his tiny charges was to be found in their changed life conditions in the institution for the mentally retarded.

> The two girls had been placed on one of the wards of older, brighter girls and women, ranging in age from 18 to 50 years and in mental age from 5 to 9 years, where they were the only children of preschool age, except for a few hopeless bed patients with gross physical defects. An older girl on the ward had "adopted" each of the two girls, and other older girls served as adoring aunts. Attendants and nurses also showed affection to the two, spending time with them, taking them along on their days off for automobile rides and shopping excursions, and purchasing toys, picture books, and play materials for them in great abundance. The setting seemed to be a homelike one, abundant in affection, rich in wholesome and interesting experiences, and geared to a preschool level of development. [Skeels, 1966, p. 6]

But Skeels realized that even though the now "normal" little girls were getting a lot of tender, loving care, their developmental needs could not continue to be met in the institution. So, in due time, they were placed in adoptive homes, presumably with a happy ending.

A daring experiment.   The impressive results with the two transferees from the hospital to the institution for the mentally retarded emboldened Skeels to send more "house guests" to the same institution. With some misgivings, the administration allowed Skeels to transfer 11 more children to the same institution. Thus, the experimental group consisted of 13 children, all under

3 years of age and all certified as "seriously retarded by tests and observation before transfer was considered" (Skeels, 1966, p. 8).

In a laboratory experiment, one must have a control group; but, since Skeels worked under naturalistic conditions, he could not, strictly speaking, arrange a control group. He did have what is called a "contrast group," which did not have the "advantages" that the transferees enjoyed. In other words, he *intervened* in the lives of 13 orphanage residents by taking them out of that condition, leaving the rest in the orphanage. Actually, what he did was to choose a contrast group from the records of tests given all the orphanage children periodically. At the time the transfer was made, the average age of the experimental group was 19.4 months. The range of IQs was from 35 to 89 with a mean of 64.3. Comparable data for the contrast group were 16.6 months for the mean chronological age; their mean IQ was 86.7, with the range varying from 81 to 103.

The results after two years.   Elsewhere (Pronko, 1973, p. 322) I have assessed the differential treatment of the two groups as follows.

Among the "house guests," every child showed a gain from 7 to 58 points. "Three children made gains of 45 points or more and all but two children gained more than 15 points ([Skeels, 1966,] p. 18)." Their average gain was 27.5 IQ points. The contrast group showed the direct opposite. With the exception of one child who showed a gain of 2 points from first to last, all subjects showed losses of from 9 to 45 points. Ten of the children lost 15 or more points over the course of the study. The average decline in IQ for the contrast group was 26.2 IQ points.

There was a follow-up study approximately 2½ years after the last test of the original study. Briefly, the experimental group still showed a mean increase of 31.6 points and the contrast group a mean loss of 20.6 points. Still more important, however, is the next follow-up study, which occurred 21 years later. It would seem absolutely impossible to locate all the original subjects, and yet the job was done with ingenuity and heroic effort.

What did Skeels find 21 years later?   Essentially, he found that the experimental and contrast groups had continued on their divergent paths through life. He learned that all 13 transferees were self-supporting; not one had to be cared for by public or private welfare. In the contrast group of 12 orphanage residents, 1 had died in an institution, 4 were still in institutions, and 7 were living in communities. One of those 7, still a ward of an institution for the mentally retarded, was discharged after his successful employment as a dishwasher in a nursing home. Another contrast group subject who remained in the orphanage until age 17 was returned to her mother; she was employed part time in a cafeteria, folding napkins around silverware. Two more patients were discharged and worked as dishwashers. Another man, free for a time as a farm worker, had to be returned to an institution. Still another became a "floater," plucking chickens and washing dishes in a hospital kitchen. The seventh, the successful one of his group, became a compositor and typesetter for a newspaper in a city of 300,000 (Skeels, 1966, p. 33).

The two groups were differentiated educationally, too. The median schooling of the experimental groups was at the 12th grade. Four members of this group had had one or more years of college work, and one had earned bachelor's degree and had done some graduate work. The median education of the contrast group was below the third grade!

Occupational levels also distinguished the two groups. The experimental-group subjects were all found to be self-supporting or married and functioning as housekeepers. They ranged from professional and business occupations to domestic service. Four members of the contrast group (36%) were institutionalized or unemployed. Those employed, with the exception of one case, were characterized as "hewers of wood and drawers of water" (Skeels, 1966, p. 54). In a comparison of maintenance cost to the state of Iowa, the two groups diverged radically. Thus the effect of Skeels' intervention strategy manifested itself eloquently in the manner in which it shaped the lives of the members of the experimental and contrast groups. Skeels' results do not suggest that intelligence is a constant, internal power.

An Experiment in the Prevention of Mental Retardation

If we analyze Skeels' report (1966) carefully, we note that what he did essentially was to intervene in the life circumstances of mentally retarded children in an effort to return them to "normality." He found the children already retarded and tried to rehabilitate them. His intervention strategy was a remedial one. But, as significant as his study turned out to be, one wants to ask, "Why wait until children are mentally retarded to do something about it? Wouldn't it be much more efficient to try to prevent behavioral retardation altogether, in the same way as preventive medicine aims to keep people from getting sick? This was the ambitious plan that Heber and Garber (1970) at the University of Wisconsin evolved, a plan that led to an exciting experiment that came to be known as the Wisconsin Project.

Background to the Wisconsin Project. The usual estimate of the prevalence of mental retardation in the United States is 3% of our population of over 220 million. That figure would include over 6 million people. But, according to Heber (1970), only 10 to 20% of that portion of the population has any demonstrable defect either in the structure or the function of the nervous system. Yet most of the research has been directed toward this minority of biologically defective individuals. How about the 80% or more of the mentally retarded without identifiable pathology of the central nervous system, found almost exclusively among the poor? It was this area of cultural and familial retardation that attracted Heber and Garber, a category that they felt had been too long neglected because of the widely prevalent view that it was genetic in origin and therefore nonpreventable.

What a survey revealed.   Heber and Garber (1970) decided to start with facts, so they made a survey in a typical urban slum in Milwaukee. The area that they selected for study had the city's lowest median family income and educational level and the highest unemployment rate and population density. Although containing only 3% of the population of Milwaukee, it contributed 33% of the total number of educable mentally retarded. They decided to limit themselves to Blacks only because, for follow-up purposes, Blacks might prove less mobile than other population groups.

Heber and Garber's next step involved the following considerations. They reasoned that most slum children learn school subjects normally, so mere residence in a slum cannot be the only factor responsible for retardation. Looking further, they discovered that not economic conditions *per se,* but maternal IQ predicted best the intelligence level of the child. They learned that, although mothers with IQs below 80 constituted only 45.4% of the total group of mothers, those mothers produced 78.2% of all children with IQs below 80! Another interesting datum turned up when Heber and Garber examined the IQ development of the same group of children longitudinally. In infancy, both the children of mothers with IQs below 80 and those of mothers who scored above 80 start out with equivalent IQs (about 95). But as Figure 8-4 reveals, they soon take divergent paths. For the offspring of mothers with IQs above 80 maintain a fairly steady IQ level, but those born to mothers with IQs below 80 show a progressive and fairly steep decline. By the age of 14 years, the latter have dipped into the sixties. The clear implication of these data point to the mother's role in the intelligence development of their children. Apparently mental retardation is not randomly distributed throughout the ghetto but results from the impoverished setting provided for her children by a retarded mother.

Project design.   From their survey data, Heber and Garber (1970) identified 40 mentally retarded mothers who tested below IQ 75. They assigned them randomly to either an experimental or control group. Beginning with the first week in the babies' lives, they intervened with a comprehensive program for the experimental group, the control group being left alone except for testing. Their purpose was to test the social-deprivation theory of mental retardation by trying to prevent it in the offspring of retarded mothers. Except for that intervention, those children were almost certain to follow the pattern of declining IQs that other such children had typically shown.

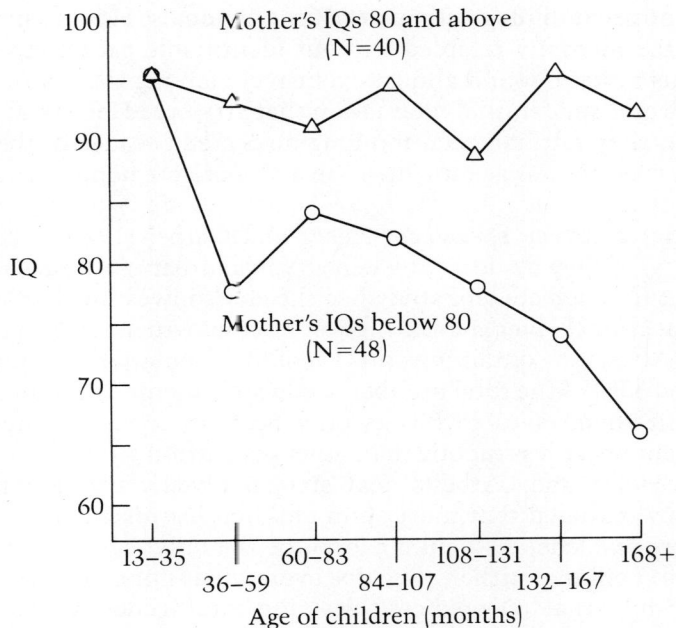

Figure 8-4 Age changes in average of IQ of 586 disadvantaged children whose mothers (*N* = 88) are mentally retarded. Note the differential results in the offspring of mothers with IQs of 80 and above in comparison with those whose mothers earn IQs below 80. The IQs of the former children are relatively constant. It is only the latter whose IQs deteriorate gradually into the sixties with increasing age. These results contradict the common notion that all slum-dwelling children show a decline in intelligence with age. Apparently only certain specifiable families make a disproportionate contribution to the ranks of the mentally retarded. Note also that on entrance into school only the lower IQ groups show a spurt in IQ before the decline resumes its progressive downward slope. (From Heber and Garber, 1970, p. 4.)

Heber and Garber's hypothesis. Here is Heber's (1976, p. 10) statement of his hypothesis.

> It was our contention that, should the experimental children reach school age and exhibit normal intelligence, we would know that it is indeed possible to prevent mental retardation from occurring at the present high frequency in this group. Should they exhibit a retarded level of functioning, at least we would know that their intensive exposure to learning experiences of the type we provided was not sufficient to displace their genetic or other biologic predispositions for intellectual functioning.

Treatment of the experimental group.   As soon as the experimental mother returned home from the hospital with her baby, a special teacher was assigned to build rapport with mother and child, secure their confidence, and work with the family. At 3 months of age, the infants were taken to an infant education center where specially trained teachers worked with the infants on a one-to-one basis. Each morning, the teachers picked up the baby in their charge and were bussed to the center. For approximately 8 hours a day, they engaged the baby in every phase of sensory and language stimulation that was believed to have relevance for developing intellectual skills. The intervention program was continued on a 5-day week, year-round basis, until the children entered public school. The goal was to foster the total development of the child by providing auditory, visual, motor, social, and emotional stimulation. Special teachers even provided lessons in science, art, and music.

Another aspect of the program was directed toward the rehabilitation of the mentally retarded mothers. This consisted of on-the-job occupational training and guidance in developing homemaking and child-care techniques. The idea was to change the mother's attitudes of hostility and suspicion toward social agencies as well as her self-reaction. It was hoped that improved employment possibilities, increased earnings, and self-confidence might improve the home situation. Remedial courses in reading, writing and arithmetic were also included.

The results.   Although both experimental and control groups were equivalent at the start, they soon began to diverge. For example, the experimental group showed a rapid increase in vocabulary after 19 months, a growth spurt that the control group did not show until 28 months. As for IQ development, at 42 months the experimental-group children earned an average of 33 IQ points higher than the controls, some of them scoring as high as 135!

From 24 months to 72 months, the experimental group has maintained better than a 20-point difference over the control group on the Cattell and Stanford-Binet, and at the mean age of 72 months the experimental group's mean IQ is 120.7, compared to the control group mean of 87.2—a difference of over 30 IQ points! These mean levels of IQ performance have been substantiated by an independent testing service using a "double-blind" procedure (in which both testers and testees were ignorant of the group to which the children belonged). Figure 8-5 shows a graphic representation of the mean IQ performance of the two groups.

Heber and Garber's (1970) intervention strategy ended three years ago when the children entered public school. That was as long as the experiment had been planned to continue. As to preparation for school, the experimental group was very well prepared to begin school work by contrast with the less fortunate control group. On practically every behavioral measure, the former were vastly superior, and on a number of measures there was little or no overlap in the performance of the two groups. Heber and Garber prevented

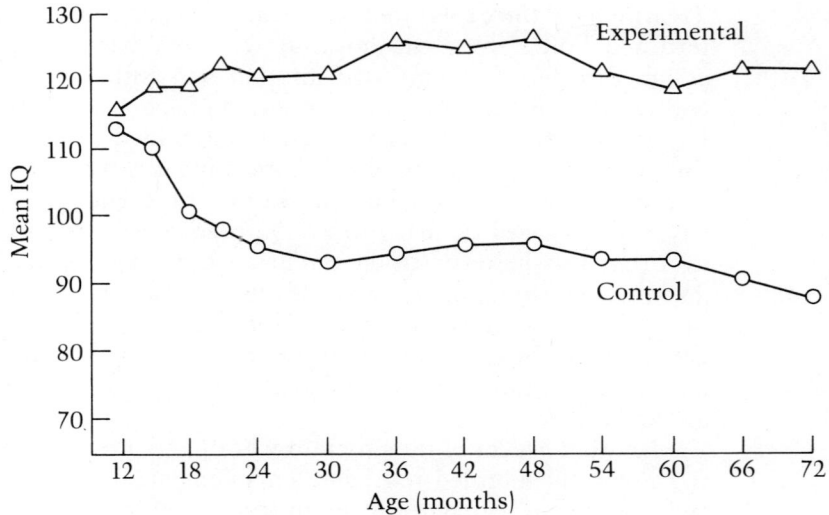

Figure 8-5 Mean IQ performance of the E (experimental) and C (control) groups from approximately the same position at the start of the study to their continued divergence from the 24th month on, with, at least, a 20-point spread. At the end, the two groups were 30 points apart. (From Heber, 1976, Fig. 5.)

mental retardation in children who would have gone the way of the control group except for the intervention. The experimenters radically changed the depressing environmental conditions in early development, thus preventing the relative decline in intelligence development that is apparent in the control group.

What has happened since the experiment ended 3 years ago? Heber and Garber only wanted to see if they could obtain an IQ difference between their two groups. They made no promises to maintain those differences throughout the life span of their subjects. But, if we consider the relative position of the two groups 3 years after the termination of the experiment, the effects of intervention are still there. According to Heber (1976, p. 24), "It is apparent that up to this point, at least the WISC differential, on the order of 20+ IQ points, has been maintained over a three-year follow-up to age nine." Figure 8-6 shows the mean IQ performance for the experimental and control groups over the entire 9-year period.

Will the differences hold? We do not know if the differences will hold. Was there constancy in the IQs of infants, children, adults, and the aged in the studies that we reviewed earlier? The IQ score changed with changing

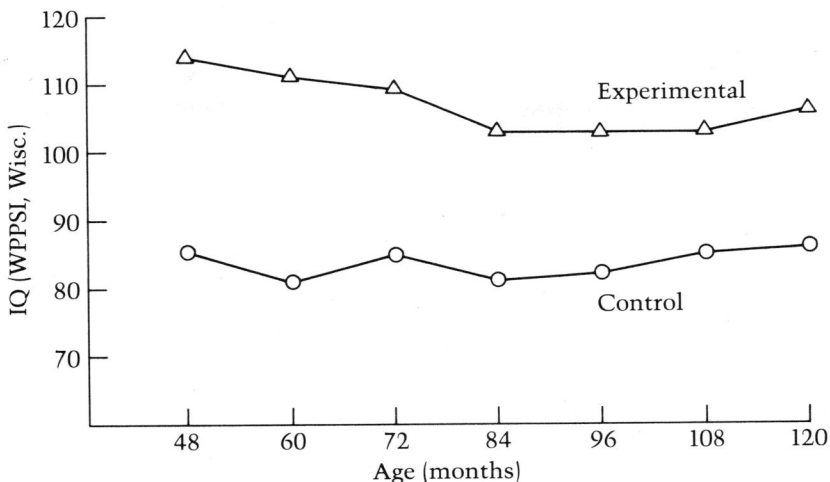

Figure 8-6 Mean IQ performance of the E (experimental) and C (control) groups over the extent of the Heber and Garber study, with emphasis on the *after effects* of the 6-year-long intervention. Following the termination of the 6-year intervention, and roughly 1, 2, and 3 years after school entry, the two groups are still 20 IQ points apart. (From Heber, 1976, Fig. 6.)

conditions. Given the radical change in the life circumstances of the experimental group (from a one-to-one basis to a wholesale classroom method of instruction), it is remarkable that there have not been some behavioral changes. Perhaps, they will come if behaviors acquired up to this point are not reinforced. Unplanned, uncontrolled interventions can also enter the picture. As Garber (1975, p. 301) puts it, "Why should we assume, considering all of our research into learning psychology, that there will be no extinction or learned interference of the behavior we worked so hard to develop but *somewhat foolishly think will sustain itself in a non-supportive environment* (emphasis added).

The IQ from a Sociological Perspective

Social factors that influence intelligence and intelligence testing have insinuated themselves into a number of topics in the present chapter. They were manifested in our content analysis of the Stanford-Binet test and in that scale's standardization on White children only. Both Jensen's and Burt's studies were found to be "loaded with social and political dynamite." Social factors were implicit in our consideration of the constancy of IQ in infancy, adult years, and old age, particularly as they affected generation differences. They were there also in the Skeels (1966) and Wisconsin intervention projects. All of this leads us naturally to an outright consideration of the relationship between intelligence and the social matrix in which it is embedded. The work we will use to explore this relationship is Jane Mercer's *Labeling the Mentally Retarded* (1973).

Who Are the Mentally Retarded?

As a sociologist, Mercer searched within the community for an answer to the question, "Who are the mentally retarded?" The city that she selected for her investigation was Riverside, California, a community with a population of 130,000, 8.5% of which was of Mexican-American heritage, and 4.7% Black (Mercer, 1973, p. 38). Her study involved 8 years of prodigious labor.

Mercer found certain ways of labeling the mentally retarded already in operation. According to Mercer (1973, pp. 2, 256), the helping professions—medicine, psychology, social work, and education—were operating from a clinical perspective. These workers saw mental retardation as a handicapping condition existing *in an individual,* as if "in a vacuum," without regard to the sociocultural milieu or to the manner in which that individual was viewed by others in that society. This pervasive and abstract view took two forms: (1) a pathological model and (2) a statistical model. The pathological model was derived from medicine, which defines *normal* as the absence of disease or of malfunctioning organs, while *abnormal* involves individual pathology characterized by "symptoms" irrespective of the retardate's social milieu.

The statistical model, used most often by psychologists and by formal organizations such as the public schools and law enforcement agencies, defines the extent of abnormality by the deviation of the individual's IQ score from the statistical mean, which is an IQ of 100. On the WISC scale, a standard deviation has been set at 15 points; on the Stanford-Binet, at 16. Therefore, a person is considered normal whose score is plus or minus one standard deviation from the mean of 100 or between IQ 85 to 115. A score between one and two standard deviations below the mean, with an IQ between 70 and 84, would be rated as "borderline." A score between two and three standard deviations, with an IQ between 55 and 69, would be rated as "mildly retarded." By the same calculation, the "moderately retarded" would be between three and four standard deviations below the mean, with an IQ between 40 and 54; the "severely retarded" with scores between 25–39, or between four and five standard deviations below the mean; and the "profoundly retarded" more than five standard deviations below the mean, with IQs below 25.

Mercer (1973) criticizes the clinical view because it regards mental retardation as a pathological attribute of an individual much as one either has, or does not have, measles. The clinician is also likely to look on mental retardation as a pattern of symptoms, which works best in such obviously biological conditions as Down's syndrome or mongolism. But where biological conditions are absent, one can easily assume that the hyperactive child, for example, is suffering from a "minimal brain dysfunction," which present techniques cannot detect as yet. Until such a time arrives, statistical criteria, or the IQ, must suffice, but the medical bias prevails. As evidence, Mercer (1973) points out that over half of the persons labeled as *mentally retarded* have no observable biological conditions that could be designated as causal. Yet during the 4-year period of her study, she found that "only 0.1% of the 2,013 etiological reports appearing . . . [during that time] studied this group of individuals (p. 11)." Biologically normal retardates are not sought after in studies of mental retardation. Because of the reductionistic bias, the study of biological defects is favored.

In her initial survey of the community of Riverside, Mercer (1973) concluded that the most prevalent model among practitioners in the field of mental retardation was the medical model, with its jargon of "etiology," "symptom," "diagnosis," "prognosis," "curable," "incurable," "remedial," and "irremedial." These terms were applied to all levels and all forms of mental retardation. Thus, if we ask "Who are the mentally retarded in Riverside?" the answer is "Individuals singled out and designated according to the metaphor provided by the medical model." According to that model, the trouble is localized within the individual.

Mercer's Social-System Perspective

As Mercer pursued her investigation, she found the medical model inadequate as a construct of mental retardation. Such a model might fit the range of cases found in a hospital for research purposes, but it was too narrow to fit the complexity and variety of data confronted in the larger community. Now, Mercer was not ready to discard the clinical view; she only thought it ought to be fitted into "a broader social system context" (1973, p. 21).

A social-system definition of a mental retardate views the individual as achieving a certain social status analogous to that of janitor, teacher, doctor, and so on. Mental retardation is a role associated with that status. According to the social-system perspective, there is no attribution of pathology to the individual as in the medical model. People who are retarded from a social-system perspective are "labeled retardates" as distinguished from "clinical retardates" who earn a low IQ or have a biological defect. A "labeled retardate" plays a role expected of people so labeled. As Mercer (1973, pp. 28–29) says,

> If a person does not occupy the status of mental retardate, is not playing the role of mental retardate in any social system, and is not regarded as mentally retarded by any of the significant others in his social world, then he is not

mentally retarded, irrespective of the level of his IQ, the adequacy of his adaptive behavior, or the extent of his organic impairment. From a social system perspective, a low score on an intelligence test is not a symptom of pathology but rather a behavioral characteristic, which is likely to increase the probability that a person will be assigned to the status of mental retardate in some social systems.

Locating the mentally retarded.   Mercer went to 241 organizations in Riverside who dealt with mental retardates. The following eight types of organizations were the sources of her subjects: public schools, law-enforcement agencies, private service groups, private organizations for the retarded, the California Department of Mental Hygiene, medical facilities, public-welfare and vocational-rehabilitation centers, and churches.

The survey provided Mercer with the names of 812 people labeled as mentally retarded by one or more of these organizations. Over half of the labeling was done by the public schools. In analyzing her data, Mercer found that the vast majority of her subjects were school-age children between 5 and 20 years of age. Only 7% were of preschool age, and only about 20% were above 20 years of age.

Why are the under-5 and over-25 groups so unrepresented? Mercer (1973) believes that, because schools have the primary responsibility for identifying the mentally retarded, most cases would be school-age children. The preschoolers, who may get labeled at some later time, prior to their schooling, fit into the family social system and are not identified as retarded by members of their social group. Only the most subnormal and biologically defective children are likely to be detected by some agency. By and large, then, the preschoolers are fairly safe from the labeling process.

On entrance into public school, when children assume the role of student, they are at risk of being labeled mentally retarded. Mercer (1973, p. 75) offers a vivid account of the pressure exerted on schoolchildren to acquire cognitive skills, intellectual achievement, and verbal facility—under strenuous conditions never before experienced. Furthermore, children are being constantly tested by standard tests and teachers' tests based on the statistical model of "normal," according to which somebody is destined to fail.

The "disappearing adults."   How about the underrepresented adults? If there was such an abundance of mentally retarded in school, what happened to them after they left school? Mercer (1973, p. 75) says,

> Here, again, the nature of societal demands appears to be a key factor. There is no single social institution comparable to the public school in which all adults must participate. The social groups in which they do participate are not constantly sorting and labeling persons, using the statistical definition of "normal," nor are they mainly concerned with cognitive and verbal abilities. Women may meet societal expectations as wives, mothers, and housekeepers even if their reading skills are rudimentary and their mathematical computations erratic.

Men may find work in occupations that require relatively little intellectual acumen. *They disappear into the general population* [emphasis added].

In other words, if the children who have acquired adaptive behavior can survive school, they may "have it made." After they leave school, they enter a different social system, take on different social roles (such as truck driver, factory worker, gardener, or domestic worker) and play those roles successfully. They may be "mentally retarded" in one social system but not in another, so we may talk sensibly about being "situationally retarded" (Mercer, 1973, p. 83). Even in a given child, to quote Mercer (1973, p. 89), "We now have what may be called a 6-hour retarded child—retarded from 9:00 to 3:00 five days a week."

The implication is that, in a discussion of intelligence as in other behaviors, we must speak of *specific* (not global) events. We should *not* say that *individuals* are mentally retarded. In a psychological sense, we should say that A behaves in a mentally retarded manner in a psychometric situation but also in a superior fashion as a member of a baseball team. And, if after leaving school, A is never required to take an intelligence test, he is never again labeled as mentally retarded. The dreaded label may be very transient. However, the person who is inadequate in *every* social system is *totally retarded.*

What misfired?   How does an intelligence test purporting to evaluate an individual psychologically fail so in predicting that individual's future behavior? The trouble, according to Mercer (1973), lay in the one-dimensional criterion that the schools used—the IQ score. But, Mercer tells us, the American Association on Mental Deficiency insists on a *two-dimensional criterion* for identifying the mentally retarded. One must not only state the individual's IQ score but also assess that person's adaptive behavior, even though the latter depends on a subjective evaluation.

Adaptive behavior is defined in terms of (1) the individual's participation in an increasing number of social systems (such as home, neighborhood, community, and play groups) and (2) in playing an increasing number and complexity of social roles comparable to others of that person's sex and age group. Adaptive behavior was not taken into account in the school's identification of the mentally retarded. The single dimension of IQ 75 to 79 or lower was used, and it failed because it did not take into account other behavioral dimensions available to an individual in situations outside the school.

The quasi-retarded.   Mercer (1973) made a special study of individuals who failed the intelligence test but passed the adaptive behavior test; these she labeled the *quasi-retarded.* In a follow-up study, when she compared the quasi-retarded with the comprehensively retarded (those who failed both the intelligence and adaptive behavior test), this is what she learned:

We found that eighty percent of the quasi-retarded adults had graduated from high school; they all read books, magazines, and newspapers; all had held jobs; sixty-five percent had white collar positions. All of them were able to work without supervision, participated in sports, traveled alone, went to the store by themselves and participated in informal visiting with co-workers, friends, and neighbors. In other words, *their social role performance tended to be indistinguishable from that of other adults.* [Mercer, 1972, p. 45, emphasis added]

An example of adaptive behavior. The specificity with which behavior must be considered is illustrated in the following case of adaptive behavior. In a staff meeting, a psychiatrist, E. E. Southard (1938), of a bygone era, was examining a boy who was rated low on intelligence tests but was nevertheless said to be a valuable clerk in a grocery store. The conversation between the patient and Southard went somewhat as follows (Southard, 1938, pp. 223–224):

> *S.:* You are a clerk in a grocery store and meat market?
> *P.:* Yes.
> *S.:* Are you a good clerk? (smiling as if it were a joke)
> *P.:* I guess so, pretty good.
> *S.:* Can you make change?
> *P.:* Sure.
> *S.:* If I bought something that cost 12 cents and gave you a quarter, how much change would I get back?
> *P.:* I don't know
> *S.:* You don't know?
> *P.:* No sir.
> *S.:* But I thought you could make change?
> *P.:* I can.
> *S.:* How can you make change if you don't know how much it is going to be?
> *P.:* Well, you see, it is like this. You said it cost 12 cents and you give me a quarter. Well, I give you a penny, that makes 13, and another penny makes 14, and another one makes 15 and then a dime makes 25 and that's your change.
> *S.:* Oh! Then how much would that come to?
> *P.:* I don't know but it will be right.
> *S.:* Now suppose a customer buys beefsteak, would you know how much to charge him?
> *P.:* Sure.
> *S.:* Well, suppose I buy three pounds of beefsteak at 29 cents a pound, how much would that cost?
> *P.:* I can't tell you here, but if the steak was on the scale, I could read it off. You just follow along till you get the place that says 29 and then read what the scale says.

That boy was a valuable clerk in that particular situation. He could make change correctly even if he could not add.

Socioeconomic level and IQ.   We must touch lightly on one more area of interest that Mercer uncovered. She found a positive relationship between socioeconomic level and IQ. Because Mexican-American and Black families were concentrated in the lower socioeconomic classes, they were overrepresented in the lower IQs (Mercer, 1973, p. 167) although the same relationship held for the low socioeconomic Whites. From two samples that she tested totaling 698 Chicanos, 386 Blacks and 1132 Whites, Mercer (1972) found "a strong and significant relationship between the cultural and economic factors of the respondent's background and his score on his IQ test" (p. 95). Both Chicanos and Blacks with higher IQs tend to match the socioeconomic characteristics of the average Anglo-American family. Their mothers were interested in educating their children beyond high school, their parents were married and owned their own home, the fathers had white-collar jobs and were educated, and so forth. When Mercer controlled for the cultural and economic backgrounds of the children, "there were no differences in intelligence between the Anglos and the Blacks, or between the Anglos and the Chicanos" (p. 96). Mercer's conclusion is that the IQ test measures largely how much exposure a child has had to Anglo culture. The more "Anglocized" children are, the higher their IQ (p. 95).

The Idiot Savant

The term *idiot savant* combines the familiar word *idiot* and *savant*, meaning "a person with detailed knowledge in some specialized field," "a wise person or sage." In psychology, *idiot savant* refers to a person who is mentally retarded with a low score on an intelligence scale but with a highly developed ability, such as playing by ear, having perfect pitch, or doing mathematical or calendar calculations. For example, an idiot savant might tell you right off, without access to a calendar, what day of the week your birthday fell on. The skill is a very concrete one and not displayed over all the centuries of the calendar but is limited to the block of years that have been memorized. The skills performed by idiot savants are very narrow, not creative, and usually useless. The following case may be an exception.

*A Case Report on the Artistic Talent of an
Autistic Idiot Savant*

Morishima and Brown (1977) report the case of a Japanese animal and insect artist, Shyoichiro Yamamura, with an IQ ranging between 48 and 53 on the Japanese version of the Stanford-Binet. He could understand language but could not speak and did not say the word "Mother" until he was 14 years old. He was unable to get along in school but did develop an interest in butterflies and other insects and would leave the classroom to chase after them when he saw them fly past the window. When he caught them, he would return to the classroom and observe them for hours. In addition, he developed a strong interest in drawing insects and animals. At the age of 11, Yamamura was sent to a special-education class where his teacher provided encouragement and every necessary facility for the further development of his interest.

When Yamamura was 19, he was sent to another educator, Tsutsumi, who had been working with retarded children in his home. Tsutsumi recognized Yamamura's artistic ability but questioned the value of teaching special skills to people who could not look after their own needs. So Tsutsumi taught him what amounted to adaptive behavior, even survival training, following which the young man showed development in "motor coordination, initiative in self-help skills, socialization, thinking processes, dietary habits and threshold for hot and cold weather" (Morishima and Brown, 1977, p. 35). On top of that, he provided Yamamura with intellectual stimulation in the form of picture books of insects. He also taught his protegé to raise and observe larvae through various stages, to observe and study insects minutely, and to do finger drawing. As a result, the young artist made rapid progress in developing "finger drawing skill rapidly from simple, flat pictures to dynamic pictures in six years. Ultimately his finger drawings became more precise and involved the use of all of his fingers including the finger nails" (Morishima and Brown, 1977, p. 35). Figure 8-7 is a sample of Yamamura's finger drawing.

In interpreting Yamamura's accomplishments, Morishima and Brown (1977, p. 35) suggest an idiosyncratic development of a cumulative sort promoted by powerful concentration and long hours of observation and practice. The process itself is the same as that manifested in the virtuoso's performance. If Einstein spent most of his waking hours thinking about physics while Isaac Stern spent comparable hours in practicing his concert pieces on the violin, then Einstein could not be a very good violinist or Isaac Stern a very good physicist. It seems that excellence in one area must be bought at the cost of "mental retardation" in some other area(s). That is why a psychologist may be a bad chemist or astronomer and a chemist or astronomer a bad psychologist.

Precociousness

Precociousness is defined as "premature or exceptionally early development." In that sense, it is the opposite of mental retardation or delayed development. From an interbehavioral viewpoint, precociousness is simply accelerated development. If we look at the whole spectrum of performance in any human area, some individuals perform very poorly, some in a mediocre fashion, and others superbly. Another aspect of that performance is that not all humans attain a certain level of performance at the same age. But why should they? The calendar as such is not the proper dimension for

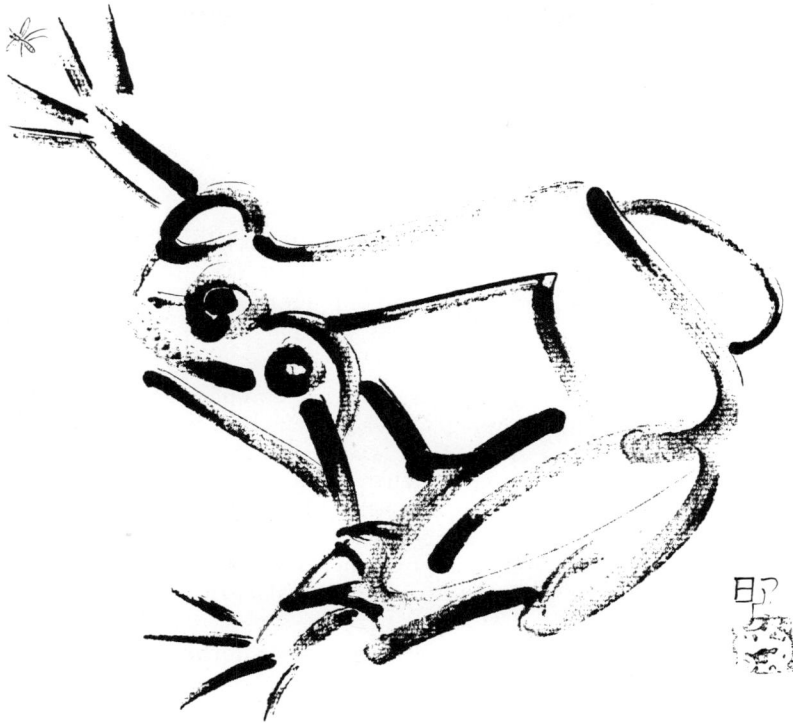

Figure 8-7   Finger drawing produced by a young, autistic artist, Shyoichiro Yamamura, an idiot savant. Compare the excellence of this drawing with Yamamura's IQ, which in successive tests ranged between IQ 48 and 53. (From Morishima and Brown, 1977, p. 34. Reproduced by permission of American Association of Mental Deficiency.)

explaining behavior. Donald Baer (1970) has proposed "an age-irrelevant concept of development." His thesis can be demonstrated with an experiment that he discusses. In that experiment, 7-year-olds could discriminate left from right; 4-year-olds could not. The experimenter could have waited 3 years when the customary environment would have processed that discrimination. But the experimenter intervened and gave the 4-year-olds some reaching responses to reinforce right and left discriminations. Within a half hour, through proper sequencing, that experimenter achieved a specified developmental outcome that "nature" ordinarily requires 3 years to achieve. At this point, Baer (1970, p. 240) comments, "What I want to emphasize is that by the end of the study, the four-year-olds had *developed*. They were not older than at the beginning, but their . . . learning behavior had become functionally like that of seven-year-olds." Baer's statement captures the essence of precociousness. But even intelligence tests take into account not only age but degree of development in relation to age as in the formula

$$IQ = \frac{\text{Mental age}}{\text{Chronological age}} \times 100$$

A radical accelerant. Julian Stanley (1975) has been studying precocity in mathematically and scientifically precocious youth under a 5-year grant from the Spencer Foundation. Here is a thumbnail sketch of one of his "radical accelerants":

> David was thirteen when he had completed the seventh grade of a junior high school in Baltimore. College entrance exams, Physics and Mathematics achievement tests, showed that David was intellectually equipped to do good work at the university level. When David's mother learned that her son's score on the physics and math tests exceeded those of most freshmen at Johns Hopkins University, she remarked that it was no wonder that he knew physics better than most university freshmen since he "had been studying physics on his own since he was three years old." [Stanley, 1975, p. 38]

The question was raised as to whether David could dispense with the courses he could get in the ninth through twelfth grades and still do satisfactory work at Johns Hopkins University. So the following fall he was enrolled as a freshman there. He took honors calculus and sophomore general physics and chemistry; but, because chemistry lab involved long periods, he changed to a computer-science course. He ranked fourth in the large computer class and earned an "A" in physics and a high "B" in honors calculus. His grade-point average for his freshman 13-hour program was 3.69, with 4.00 representing straight "A."

To make a long story short, David was graduated with a bachelor's degree at a little over 17½ years with a 3.4 cumulative grade-point average. "By age 17⅚ he had completed the Master of Science degree, specializing in computer science" (Stanley, 1975, p. 39). David has been very happy at Johns Hopkins and shudders when he thinks he might have been "turned off" had he been retarded in his career. David has put in more than a year's work toward his doctorate, has passed all his written comprehensive exams and two of his four oral exams. As of this writing, he plans to finish his doctorate by the time he is 19 or 20 and to teach computer science at a university.

Stanley describes many other such precocious youngsters, including some 10-year-olds who "had no difficulty with college algebra and trigonometry" (1975, p. 43). Some characterize such accomplishments as "amazing" and explain them self-actionally as "gifted." The precocious are considered as the elite, or, better, as the elect, who at birth were somehow dispensed an extra amount of "intelligence" making their accomplishment possible. But the real reason as to why we do not have many more such "radical accelerants" may lie with the traditional programming of our schools. At any rate, Stanley believes that "it seems uncomfortably probable" that many high-school graduates have been "turned off" from "having been educated at a snail's pace for too many years" (p. 43). But our main point might be stated in terms of the reactional-biography construct. First of all, the calendar is not a proper measuring instrument in evaluating psychological development. To take a hypothetical case, let us assume equivalent accomplishments during the reactional biographies of A and B. Yet A could accomplish in 5 years what took B 10 years to achieve. Surely, Mozart, in his sort span of 35 years, accomplished more than other musicians in 70 years. Or, as Baer (1970, p. 244) puts it, "Age has no relevance to development; sequence, or *program* has."

Toward an Interbehavioral Definition of Intelligence

> *[The term] "intelligent" is a word around which fantasies lurk: the belief, for instance, that intelligence is the very essence of the man, and that, somehow, somewhere inside the head, it exists in measurable amounts.*
>
> [Hudson, 1971, p. 1]

The preceding quotation embodies a prevalent self-actional view concerning intelligence. According to it, each person starts life with a resident faculty, a purely imaginary entity that sets limits to the individual's development. If an individual develops to a great extent, it is argued that that individual must have possessed a great deal of intelligence. On the other hand, a skimpy development is said to signify a skimpy IQ. The circular reasoning involved here should be readily apparent.

Robert Williams, a Black psychologist, nearly became a victim of such circular reasoning. He reports (Williams, 1974) that at 15 years his IQ was 82. Accordingly, his counselor advised him to take up bricklaying because he was good with his hands. Instead, he went to college, graduating with honors from Philander Smith College. From there, he went to Wayne State University in Detroit, where he got his masters and subsequently earned his doctoral degree from Washington University at St. Louis. Had Williams become a bricklayer, his counselor could have said, "I told you so. Williams just didn't have 'it'." Under the circumstances, the only thing he could say is, "Well, we made a mistake in pegging his IQ at 82 back there because Williams' accomplishments *prove* that he *must* have had a high IQ." No further comment is needed.

Wesman's Proposal

As a point of departure, toward an alternative construct for intelligence, let us consider Wesman's view. Wesman (1968) is of the opinion that our confusion about the nature of intelligence results from our ignoring two propositions which, he believes, should be obvious:

1. Intelligence is an attribute, not an entity. Here's where a semantic analysis is called for. Because *intelligence* is a noun, it is immediately converted into an entity or a substance. *Intelligence* has become reified or "thing-ified."

2. Intelligence is "a summation of learning experiences" (Wesman, 1968, p. 267). If one analyzes the specific content of any intelligence test (as we have earlier), one can find *no* response that the individual has *not* acquired. Each response has to be learned, and each behavioral acquisition changes the individual's status toward further behavioral acquisitions. Here we come back to our flow of behavioral events in which every individual participates. The behavioral events centering around some individuals are cumulatively rich, complex, and varied, or lead to excellence, while those involving others are scanty or impoverished. "Precocity" and "mental retardation" are rough assessments of the behavioral events in which given individuals are involved.

Another factor enters the picture as a replacement for the purely imaginary entity, the resident faculty (intelligence), in the person's genes. Since behavior is a function of surrounding conditions, those conditions must be given their proper place in interpreting the data of intelligence. Stimulus objects and setting factors must also be considered if one accepts the interbehavioral view of behavior. Lindsley's (1964) view that there are no retarded children, only retarded environments, helps to make the point, though overstressing it. But it does take the accent off the self-actional entity allegedly residing in the organism. Bijou (1966, p. 3) aligns himself with an interactional view when he states that "retarded behavior is a function of observable social, physical, and biological conditions, all with the status of independent behaviors." And Thurman (1976), writing in a paper entitled "Environmental Maintenance of Retarded Behavior: A Behavioral Perspective," suggests that retarded behavior is maintained by certain events in the life circumstances of individuals. He shows how reinforcement, avoidance behavior, and contingency schedules maintain certain behaviors. As an illustration, he offers a situation in which an 18-month-old child gets what it wants by crying and pointing. If the parents continue that practice for a year or two, they are maintaining that child in a state of retarded speech. Further examples are readily available in the studies of Skeels, Heber and Garber, and Mercer as well as in our consideration of the idiot savant and of precocity. And could anyone argue against the devastating consequences of the horrendous conditions during Genie's reactional biography (see Chapter 4)?

In an attempt at understanding "intelligence," mental retardation, precocity, or "average performance" from an interbehavioral viewpoint, no new principles are called for. All of these terms can be viewed as referring only to variable rates of individual behavior development by comparison with some arbitrary standard. Without such a standard, there are only "many different patterns of behavior each individual can show under varying circumstances" (Bakker, 1975, p. 167). An analogy with astronomy may help to make the point. Ask an astronomer how long a year is, and he or she will answer that it is 365½ days *on Earth*. That is how long it takes our planet to make one revolution around the sun. But a year on Venus is only 225 Earth days; on Mars, 687 Earth days; and on Pluto, 248 Earth years. But if one does not indulge in such comparisons with reference to Earth, then there are only "many different patterns of behavior each individual can show under varying circumstances" (Bakker, 1975, p. 167). To return to earthly psychological considerations, we make similar comparisons and transformations when we say that A is precocious, B is "average," and C is retarded. But, certainly when we view the data referred to with the term *intelligence* in a naturalistic fashion, we can only observe different developmental patterns involving different individuals. We can never observe any "essences" or hypothetical agents *behind* behaviors, *influencing* behaviors.

Then, despite the demonstrated changeability of human interactions, as indicated by changing IQs, why is the notion of IQ fixity and constancy so prevalent and persistent? Bakker (1975) feels that one reason for the perpetuation of the "unchangeability myth" is the dominant Western view based on the hypothesis that seeks for an "essence" in humans. This view prevents one from perceiving the kinds of changes, sometimes dramatic ones, we have examined. Another factor that sustains the constancy myth is a greater sensitivity toward perceiving that *many people do stay the same* simply because their life circumstances are stable.

Applications.   As a final commentary on the self-actional versus an interbehavioral construct of "intelligence," we should note, in passing, the possible applications of each theory. The self-actional theory, wedded to the concept of a "fixed intelligence" and a "genetically predetermined development" (Hunt, 1961, p. 35) is a pessimistic view, which, as we have seen, may condemn individuals to an impoverished psychological existence. Recall the case of Williams, (1974).

By contrast, an interbehavioral view, working with no internal principles, offers hope of modifying behavioral events by working with observable variables; that is, the constituents of those events. When, working from an interbehavioral viewpoint, we learn how to properly sequence behavioral events that can lead to ever-higher IQ scores, we shall be entering a psychological age.[7] By today's standards, precocious individuals may be much more common in the future than they are today, and they should arrive at that level less accidentally than they do today.

Chapter Summary

The term *intelligence* is based on an implicit belief in a genetically determined development ("geneticism"). The metaphors of "genotype" and "phenotype" were imported into the psychology of intelligence from the branch of biology known as *genetics*. We, then, considered evidence about the nature of intelligence (1) as developed by early American psychologists, (2) as demonstrated by the contents of the Stanford-Binet, and (3) as shown in the standardization of the Stanford-Binet, and (4) from an in-depth treatment of Jensen's work.

Regarding the constancy of IQ, both longitudinal and cross-sectional studies in infancy, childhood, adulthood, and old age show that "at each age . . . level there are some individuals who gain and others who lose, while many remain stable" (Schaie, 1974, p. 804).

Intervention strategies, described in Skeels' study and Heber and Garber's Milwaukee project, suggest that prevention of mental retardation is possible. Mercer's sociological research shows the need for extreme specificity in talking about a given individual's "intelligence" or "retardation," because they are situationally defined. The IQ is a superficial way to comprehend the richness and variety of human personality. The possiblity of overdevelopment in one area with low development in another is manifested in the idiot savant, while precocity shows the irrelevance of the age concept in understanding human development. Finally, an interbehavioral construct makes sense of the capsule data subsumed under the term *intelligence* and is proposed as a more useful way of conceptualizing intelligence than the traditional self-actional theory.

---

[7] Levinson (1971) has made a start in this direction. By training children in the verbalization of word definitions and simple concepts (none of which appeared on the Stanford-Binet), she increased their IQ by comparison with control groups.

9 Attending and Perceiving

Millions of items of the outward order are present to my senses which never properly enter into my experience. Why? Because they have no interest *for me.*

[James, 1918, p. 402]

Even a brief reflection on human behavior should reveal that not all reactions are alike. For example, memorizing a poem is not the same as grieving for a loved one. And playing a piano piece, arguing, dreaming, loving, praying, creating a painting, or recalling a childhood scene differ from each other. Now, if we agree that interactions differ one from another, then we might profit from ordering them into different classes to take a closer look at each.

An illustration from physiology may make the point clearer. If we were careless physiologists, we might be tempted to lump all the variety of biological functions into one undifferentiated lot. But scientific physiology has discriminated the following different kinds of physiological action: nervous-system coordination, feeding, digestion, excretion, respiration, circulation, reproduction, and secretion. By concentrated study of each specific kind of life function, physiologists have achieved a fuller, detailed knowledge of physiology.

If we can order our data into various categories, we can enjoy similar benefits from a concentrated study of each class in turn. Psychologists have classified their data, but the resulting categories have been no more fixed than the categories of other sciences. If we were to examine William James' (1918) *Principles of Psychology,* we would find such chapter headings as "Will," "Association," and "Conception." But contemporary psychologists no longer find those categories useful. However, the following categories still appear in today's textbooks: attending, perceiving, thinking, feeling and emoting, and remembering. The verb forms *attending* and *perceiving* are favored throughout this chapter because of their compatibility with an inter-behavioral view. The nouns *attention* and *perception* will occur only when stylistic variety requires but will be generally avoided because of their semantic connotations. In the following chapters, we shall examine these different classes of psychological interactions with the hope of achieving greater illumination of our subject matter from such a perspective.

Analysis of Attentional Reaction Systems

A little boy of two was sitting on a curb playing with a toy. When the toy rolled into the street, the boy ran out to get it and was killed by a passing car. The driver was not charged with the little boy's death. If we try to reconstruct the event, this is probably what happened. The little boy was so fascinated with his departing toy that his whole attention was directed toward it and not at all to the approaching car. Had we been in his situation, as a result of our training, we would have looked up and down the street before stepping into it, preventing the tragedy that befell him. The situation points up the importance of attention.

To achieve a greater understanding of attention, we need the concept of the behavior segment. In Chapter 1, we indicated that a complex response elicited at least three successive reaction systems. The first phase of a response involves shifting the direction of one's activity toward a given stimulus. For example, if I am to see the robin outside of my window, I must stop doing what I'm doing and turn my head in the direction of the window and what lies outside. If we can (analytically) "freeze" that phase of my response, we have analytically "frozen" my attentional reaction system. If we have a motion-picture recording of my action and play it slowly, we have a still better understanding of attention as the initial phase of every complex response in a behavior segment. This aspect of behavior paves the way for the next reaction system. In my case, it is discriminating or recognizing the robin. This is perception. Attention and perception merge into one another so closely that they can be treated separately only conceptually. Our problem is comparable to that of a physiologist trying to separate inspiration from expiration during the respiratory cycle. For special study, one must emphasize one and ignore the other. During our analysis of attention, I propose to ignore perception. When we consider perception, we will de-emphasize attention, but with the full realization that they always go hand in hand.

Skinner's Contribution

For Skinner (1953, p. 123), "attention is a controlling *relation*—the relation between a response and a discriminative stimulus. When someone is paying attention he is under special control of a stimulus." He offers a simple experiment as an illustration. A pigeon is reinforced with food when it pecks a key, but the reinforcement is given only when a small light above the key flickers. After a few such trials, the pigeon begins to watch for the light to flicker. In other words, the light "holds its attention." The pigeon's behavior is controlled by the light simply because it was reinforced in the past for looking at it. Traditionally, attention has been thought of as a *set* or *readiness to respond*. Certainly, Skinner's pigeon is oriented in the direction of the flickering light, ready to respond. This is what Skinner means when he defines attention as being "under special control of a stimulus." We might say that the pigeon in the situation described is "all eyes."

Now, to return to the example of my looking out of the window to see a robin. Just before I looked out of the window, I *heard* the robin's song. Because, in the past, the auditory discriminative stimulus was reinforced by the *sight* of a robin, that song was now related to, or, as Skinner would say, it "controlled" my head turning.

Skinner points out that a steady orientation of the eyes is not the only way in which attention manifests itself. He refers to the behavior of a lookout in the dark or in a heavy fog. That lookout's orientation may be toward the whole visual field or to successive portions of it. But, whichever it is, the lookout's present attending behavior occurs as a function of reinforcement in the past like a successful avoidance of a collision with another ship.

Kantor's Contribution

Kantor goes beyond Skinner in showing how attentional phases of interactions operate and what their effect is on subsequent phases of interaction. According to Kantor (1933) and Kantor and Smith (1975), attending reactions are preparatory and auxiliary. The term *preparatory* refers to the fact that the attending phase starts and prepares the ground for the occurrence of that particular response rather than a response to some other stimulus object. Having attended facilitates the perceptual phase. When (in everyday terms) we fail to see or hear something or someone, it is because attending failed to prepare the way for discriminating and subsequent reaction systems. Without it, stimulus functions are not actualized or realized.

According to Kantor and Smith (1975), attending reactions are also auxiliary. They pave the way for the adjustments that follow but are not "adjustmental" *per se*. That is, their facilitation of subsequent reaction systems are not, in themselves, adaptational acts. They are not like playing a chord on the piano after having attended to and discriminated the notes. They function in a subsidiary capacity by leading the way to the final adjustment of each behavior segment. They are more observable when the organism has to make a marked change of posture, but they also operate in subtle ways when bodily orientation is not involved. In any case, we may be sure that they are true behavioral occurrences.

Selectivity or Specificity of Attending
Interactions

For a long time, psychologists have characterized attention as being "selective." By that, they meant that we do not react indiscriminately to all of the mass of stimulation in our surroundings. Not all stimuli have equal value. Certain stimulus objects capture our attention, while certain others escape our notice altogether. This advantage of certain stimuli over others is what psychologists have meant when they refer to the "selectivity of attention."

In my opinion, the term *specificity* is superior to "selectivity" because of the latter's connotation that someone or something is doing the selecting. Specificity is a more neutral term, one that simply denotes the differential operation of a particular stimulus object by comparison with others.

How Shall We Understand the Specificity of
Attending Interactions?

The reactional biography.   How is it that, when the orthopedic surgeon walks down the street, he or she cannot help noticing the slightest limp, deformity, or crippling? The physician's past reactional biography has reinforced attention to that particular class of stimulus objects. Similarly, purses capture the attention of the purse snatcher; obese individuals, the weight watcher; drunkards, the reformer; building design, the architect; and color and form, the artist. From a self-actional standpoint, such people have been especially "sensitized" to a certain narrow range of stimulus objects through reinforcement. As a result, they live in what we might call "special worlds," in which certain stimulus objects have an edge in eliciting responses from such individuals over certain other stimulus objects. The specificity of each person's reactional biography partially explains the specificity of attentional reaction systems. But other variables are involved, and we consider them next.

Factors That Affect Attending

Since behavioral events involved a multiplicity of factors, a number of variables operate to influence attentional interactions. Some of these conditions are localized in the characteristics of the stimulus object.

Movement

Other things being equal, an object that moves has an advantage over a stationary one. An immobile lecturer rooted to the spot behind his or her lectern can gain instant and continued attention from the audience by walking back and forth before it. Here's another example. I am attending to my tomato plants when, all of a sudden, I notice one of those fat, squashy, green, horned worms. It was there *before* I spotted it, but it did not get a rise out of me until it raised its ugly head. Movement caused its actualization as a stimulus object for me. Beacons and railroad-crossing signals use lights as attention-getting devices, but when they add movement, they achieve greater effectiveness.

Change

When a boiler factory shuts down during the lunch hour, one can "hear the silence." Apparently, attention is not determined as a simple function of increase in energy impinging on the organism. Cessation of energy is an adequate condition to gain a person's attention. Similarly, when we are sitting in the living room, no one calls attention to the pendulum clock as it ticks away. But let it stop, and someone is bound to announce, "The clock has stopped!" As a final illustration, let us take a theater audience before the curtain goes up. No one pays attention to the illumination until the house lights are gradually dimmed.

Intensity

Other things being equal, more intense sounds command attentional priority over less intense ones. Despite the din of roaring auto engines, squeaking brakes, and honking horns, the ambulance or fire-truck siren holds a supreme position over the chaos of other noises because of its penetrating intensity.

Repetition

Other things being equal, the repetitive stimulus object is likely to get our attention over those that occur singly. The repeating alarm clock fits this condition. The notion is that separate and distinct blasts of the bell will be more effective in arousing the sleeper to attention than a continuous ring. Advertisers use a similar device in getting their message across, based on the idea of "repetition with variation" because repetition alone would lead to boredom.

Relative Size of Objects

A dwarf or a 7-foot person at the head of a parade may be equally effective in gaining the attention of parade watchers. Both individuals depart from expectation because of their relative size difference. The billboards and other signs in the Times Square district of New York compete savagely for the attention of passersby. As a consequence, advertisers erect on top of tall buildings giant boxes of detergents that spew forth bubbles. Others show a man who advertises a certain brand of cigarettes by puffing out smoke rings. The advertisers rely not only on size but several other factors such as the following.

Novelty

The bubbles issuing from the detergent box and the smoke rings in the illustrations demonstrate the application of novelty as well as repetition, movement, and relative size of objects. Use of animated cartoons in the Times Square area also illustrates the application of novelty, as does the use of comic books to sell a company's product or services.

Color

Because color has such an attractive value, it has been widely used not only in advertising but in merchandising as well. Many of the examples referred to earlier also belong here. In fact, if we consider only the packaging of products in the supermarkets, we can observe the use of a *combination* of many of the factors listed, including color. Each package must scream, "Take me," in competition with the same product under a different brand name. Primarily, the battle involves gaining the potential consumer's attention in the hope that attention will be followed by perception and by the customer's buying Product X.

These attentional factors are not exhaustive, but they point out features of stimulus objects that influence the direction of the responding organism's attention. But they are not the only determining factors, because, as noted, the interbehavioral history or the whole flow of events is interrelated. Because events are a function of antecedent events, attentional phases of events follow the same rule. It should be no surprise, then, that setting factors may also determine what stimulus objects have an edge in gaining our attention.

Setting Factors

I am sitting at the window reading while I wait for a friend who is to drive by to take me to a meeting. I have read in this same spot many times before without any distraction. This time, I am at the mercy of every car that goes past my window. My attentional reactions are really under the control of those passing automobiles. The setting factors of awaiting my friend do this to me.

A mother with an ill child in an adjoining room is so attentive that she responds to a dog barking in the distance by asking, "Was that the baby?" Or let us say we are walking through a city for a few hours. We started *after* breakfast, so at first we could not give the name or location of restaurants that we had passed along the way. But as lunchtime approaches we spot restaurants blocks away. Now, under conditions of food deprivation, they stand out like a sore thumb.

Attending Isn't Always "Psychological"

For us, attending reaction systems have referred to the initial phases of behavioral events that elicit either a shift in activity from one stimulus object to another or from one aspect of a stimulus object to another aspect of the same stimulus object. These shifts in activity (which, as noted, merge into perceptual reaction systems) are high-speed reactions that start off every behavior segment. The speed with which they occur, apart from their subtlety, make them difficult to study. But if we hold before us the notion of *psychological attention* as the brief, initial shift in activity that starts off every behavior segment, we will not confuse it with other behaviors that we turn to now.

Attentional Posture

Having been given the command "AT-TEN-SHUN!" the soldiers execute the order by standing erect, heels together, arms extended straight at side, and looking straight ahead. The military call this "standing at attention." The action displayed in this situation is quite different from psychological attention.

Suppose we inject a comic aspect to the situation we have before us. One soldier is preoccupied with the sight of his beloved in the grandstand and fails to execute the command. Why? Because his attention was under the control of another stimulus. As a consequence, he failed to shift his orientation away from the girl to his commanding officer's "AT'TEN-" in preparation for his perception of "-SHUN!" and execution of the final position. In other words, the soldier "missed the boat" because the attentional reaction system that brought his colleagues to carry out the officer's command failed to "get to him," and so the entire behavior segment never came off.

Now let's concentrate on the behavior of those soldiers who behaved in a militarily correct fashion. What are they doing? As they continue to stand at attention, they are simply maintaining the prescribed *posture*. Their stance does not prevent them from engaging in numerous, successive behavior segments such as looking and hearing things in their surroundings. Each of those behavior segments is, of course, introduced by an attentional reaction system. Shifting to a schoolroom situation, a student whose bodily orientation is directed toward the teacher may, nevertheless, be "miles away." Thus, attentional posture is not to be identified with fleeting psychological attention.

Inattention

The schoolroom suggests another situation, one in which the teacher complains that "Johnny isn't paying attention." What goes on here? If we examine Johnny's behavior, we find him strongly under the control of Mary's pigtail resting on his desk. He *is* paying attention but not in the direction required by the teacher. It is not a case of failure of attention but of misdirected attention, for Johnny could never have dipped Mary's pigtail into the fingerpaints on his desk if an attentional reaction system had not ushered in his perception of the pigtail and his subsequent manipulation of it. And so, inattention is not the absence of attention but attention elsewhere. Perhaps what we call "absent-mindedness" is simply a matter of not attending to one's *main* business.

Sustained Attention

We observe a student reading in the library. Nothing seems to distract her, she concentrates so thoroughly and persistently. When we compare her behavior with our model of an attentional reaction system as the introductory phase of every behavior segment, we find that she performs thousands of them in succession in her continuous *preoccupation* with her task. Her reading involves one behavior segment after another, each one initiated by an appropriate attentional phase that gets her from one fixation point to another in a line of reading matter and from one line to the next. In other words, her concentration shows not a single phase of one behavior segment but a whole series of them. This is sustained attention. Driving an automobile in heavy traffic also calls for sustained attention or concentration.

A Classic Experiment

A classic experiment was performed by Morgan (1916) that taught us the possible cost of sustaining attention under distracting conditions. Morgan wanted to find out what techniques people used in circumventing potential distracters. He required the subjects in his experiment to perform a task closely resembling typewriting with an instrument that had 10 numbered keys. The keys in the apparatus were constructed so as to measure the amount of pressure that the subjects exerted on them. A pneumograph set up around the subjects' chests furnished a breathing record.

The procedure involved exposing an alphabet letter in front of the subjects, which they were to "translate" into a number according to a code. As fast as they could, they struck the key that had that number on it. When the key was struck, another letter was exposed, and so on. For a certain interval (base period), Morgan allowed his subjects to work under quiet conditions. Then bells, buzzers, and loud phonograph records bombarded the subjects from all parts of the room. These noises were continued for 10 minutes, after which a 10-minute quiet work period was introduced.

Among the results, Morgan (1916) observed that when the noises were first introduced, there was a slowdown in work output. The noises functioned as distracters, apparently forcing the shift from the assigned task to the noises and back again. However, within a few minutes, the subjects regained their former speed and even improved beyond that point. The noises failed to distract, but Morgan found that the improvement was bought at the expense of greater energy expenditure on the part of the subjects. Under noisy work conditions, the subjects struck the keys with greater force. The breathing records also showed that the subjects tried to prevent distraction by talking to themselves, a technique that also required extra effort.

Another interesting result was found after the noises ceased. The quiet condition also caused a momentary slump in the work output, once more indicating that a *change* from a noisy to a quiet state can also function as a distraction. As an overall observation, Morgan found that, because his experimental subjects had had little preliminary training in the assigned task, they showed progressive improvement throughout the experiment. Had the experiment been continued long enough, Morgan's subjects might have adjusted completely to the noisy setting factors. When people gradually cease to respond to a continuous or repeated stimulus, psychologists refer to such a behavioral condition as *negative adaptation*. A traditional illustration tells about a man who applied a vibrating tuning fork to a spider's web. The alert spider came out of hiding, expecting a fly trapped in his web. Finding nothing, he returned to his corner. The man repeated the procedure and got another rise out of the spider. However, with continued repetition, the spider eventually failed to come out. Was this *negative adaption* or *extinction* the result of nonreinforcement?

Attentional Alternation

Continued inspection of Figure 9-1 is meant to illustrate attentional alternation. As you look at the figure, you may see a chair.[1] If you continue to look at it, you may say, "Now, I see a chair *upside down.*" If you persist in fixating it, you declare that the chair is right side up once more. But, a moment later, you are ready to swear that now it is upside down again. And so it goes on and on, right side up and upside down, and so forth. The situation illustrates the power of genuine psychological attention. Once attention has actualized a certain stimulus function, it seems as though its

[1] This discriminative act belongs under the category of perception, but we are ignoring that here and concentrating only on the attentional phases of interaction.

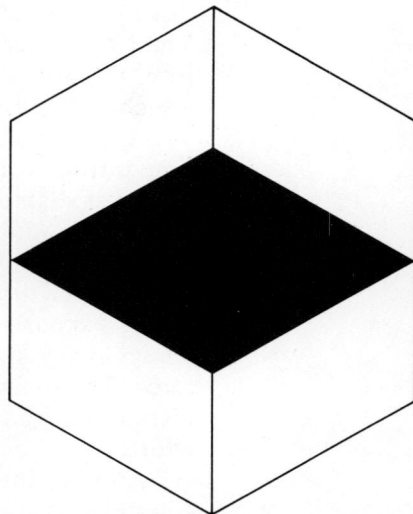

Figure 9-1   As you look at this figure, you may see "a chair." As you continue to look, you may see "a chair upside down." From then on, attentional alternation will result in a shift from one to the other, back and forth.

simplicity is soon exhausted (such as a chair right side up), so a shift actualizes a chair upside down. Because there are only the two possible stimulus functions, one can only alternate from one to the other in what may be ever decreasing intervals.[2]

In an experiment designed to study reversible perspective, Flamm and Bergum (1977) found that their subjects averaged 14.66 and 7.77 reversals per 1½-minute tests for the Necker Cube and Rubin figure respectively (for which see Figures 9-2 and 9-3).

We have discussed attention from a number of different aspects and have noted some of the conditions that influence it. Now, we are ready to explore perception, the next succeeding reaction system of every act unit.

Analysis of Perceiving

There is more to seeing than meets the eyeball.

[Hanson, 1958, p. 7]

"Do you see that sunset?" "Smell that honeysuckle!" "Feel the smoothness of this velvet." "How do you like the sound of that Mendelssohn piano concerto?" "I love this chocolate cake!" Such prosaic remarks are the com-

---

[2]A third possible stimulus function may be experienced by turning the figure 90 degrees, which may permit seeing the black area as a diamond.

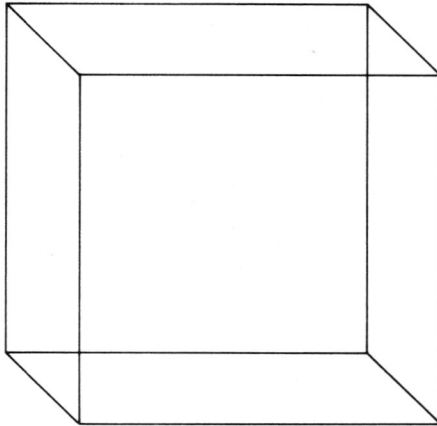

Figure 9-2 The Necker Cube, drawn as if it were transparent. It can be perceived as if one were viewing it from above or below.

Figure 9-3 Rubin's figure. The same geometrical form offers possibilities for two different discriminations, as a goblet or as two people, in silhouette, staring at each other.

mon currency of our daily life together. They reflect the various ways we have of contacting the world "in which we live, move, and have our being." They are accepted without question and raise no complicated philosophical questions about "reality" or the relationship of our perceivings to "reality." The entire "business" of the world, in all its human interrelations, is carried out as the result of our seeings, hearings, smellings, tastings, touchings, and so on. These events, which we shall group together under the term *perceiving*, are to be considered as earthly occurrences, all of them as natural as rain, sunshine, and wind, and all to be accepted at face value.

Perhaps, the best way to introduce the topic of perception is via the blotch in Figure 9-4. Let us assume that you have never before seen this figure. (If you have seen it before, then you must recollect your first look at it, at which time it *was* a meaningless blotch.) There it is directly in front of you. As you keep looking at it, let your attention shift to different aspects of it.

Typically what happens to most people is that they report seeing only a meaningless blob for some minutes. Finally, one hears a surprised "Oh" or "Ah," and they report seeing a cow, clear and sharp. At that very moment, we may say that a perceptual interaction came into existence. Although it is beside the point as to how long it lasts, for some people the interaction is enduring. Once established, you turn the figure upside down or on either of its ends, and it still remains *cow*.

Figure 9-4 If you do not see a cow instantly, keep trying. Patience will repay you with an interesting experience. Out of the left side of the blotch, there eventually emerges the head of a cow staring straight at you, her muzzle toward the bottom and the dome of her head at the top. The right side of her head is in deep shadow. Her left side has some black spots on an otherwise white flank.

What have we learned so far? First, that perception is not inherent in the stimulus object nor is guaranteed by it. One has to work at the job by continuing to participate in the interaction. And, one's reactional biography is brought to bear in the situation. All of one's past experiences with photographs of cows, paintings of them, or the actual cow itself count in actualizing the cow out of the puzzling blotch.

Another point that we must notice about the cow, once established, is its stability. Once you have seen the cow for some time, I challenge you to *not* see the cow. You cannot abolish it or will it out of existence. It will continue to stare right back at you regardless of how hard you try to negate your perception of it. I have not looked at it for as much as a year at a time, but it never fails to confront me with its placid, cowlike look on the next occasion. Stated otherwise, the pattern in Figure 9-4 is recognized as cow. And that verb, *recognize,* leads to a consideration of the role of recognition.

The term *recognition* derives from the Latin word *cognoscere,* meaning "to become acquainted with" or "to know." The prefix *re-* means "again" or "anew"; therefore, "to know again after having known before." To *re-cognize* a thing is to know it *again* after having made its acquaintance on a previous occasion. To state the matter otherwise, once the original meaningless blob takes on the stimulus function of *cow,* we cannot possibly return to our earlier state of "innocence," to our pre-"cow" naiveté. We just have to see the figure now again as we did then. We recognize it as *cow.* Our past perception of it as cow is having its effect now because, as we learned before, present events are a function of antecedent events. Therefore, our present cognition is a *re-cognition.*

Now we are ready to move on to Kantor's (1933, p. 153) characterization of perception as "semi-implicit." He means that we do not react to any stimulus object as if for the first time in our life. We respond to it in terms defined, in part, as we reacted to it on a past occasion. Since all events are historically connected, so is our recognition of the cow a function of an earlier discrimination of that blob as cow. Stating the matter in still another fashion, we may say that your present perception of the blob as cow cannot be understood if we treat it as if it were disconnected from your prior perception of it. The present perceptual interaction is indissolubly joined with the earlier one. Therefore, the two must be held together in our analysis. Arnheim (1971) has grasped the binding connection between present and past perceptions in the following statement, which could have been improved with the omission of the last four words ("and surviving in memory") referring to a superfluous, fictional, and self-actional construct: "Perception cannot be confined to what the eyes record of the outer world. *A perceptual act is never isolated; it is only the most recent phase of a stream of innumerable similar acts, performed in the past* and surviving in memory" (Arnheim, 1971, p. 80, emphasis added). Arnheim's view is a mixture of a self-actional and interactional orientation, but the italic passage is valid.

An Alternative View

The interpretation of perception that we have considered is not the only way to understand perception. A self-actional view (for example, see Morris, 1973, p. 287) holds that our sense organs are being constantly bombarded with information from "the outside world."[3] But this information is received

---

[3] The self-actional term "outside world" presupposes "an inner world" in which perceptions are said to really occur. As indicated much earlier, this "inner world" has a pseudolocation somewhere in the head.

in vastly different form. The eyes are said to receive light waves; the ears, sound waves; the skin, temperature and pressure. But there is no "meaning" in those sense data. They must be transmitted to the brain as neural impulses, still without meaning. According to the self-actional view, the brain receives these messages; it must sort them out, identify them, and interpret what they mean. The process of creating meaningful patterns out of the jumbled sensory impressions is known as perception" (Morris, 1973, p. 287).

The Two Views Compared

The two interpretations of perception are radically different. Essentially, an interbehavioral view finds the explanation of perception in the factors that participate in the perceptual event—that is, the organism, stimulus object, setting factors, and so on—and in the relationship of that event with a prior event or events. The self-actional view converts the stimulus object into the theoretical entities of physics—that is, light waves and sound waves. Their conversion into neural impulses carry "messages" to the brain, which eventually decodes them, *creating* the perception. The difference between the two theories boils down to this. In the interbehavioral theory, the factors that can be isolated in the event carry the theoretical burden.

Here is Skinner's (1953, p. 276) criticism of the traditional construct:

> When the physical organism is in contact with reality, the experienced copy is called a "sensation," "sense datum," or "percept." . . . Sensations, images and their congeries are characteristically regarded as psychic or mental events, occurring in a special world of consciousness, where, although they occupy no space, they can nevertheless often be seen.

Skinner seems to be saying that a self-actional theory translates a natural event into a fictional, supernatural occurrence. Furthermore, we can boldly assert that there is no scientific support for such alleged goings-on in the brain as the self-actional theory alleges. As usual, we must make a choice between them. But there is little choice because the hypothetical brain events of the self-actional theory can say no more. Therefore, let us tentatively try an interbehavioral form of construct in an attempt to throw further light on perception. Here, again, we follow the lead of Kantor and Smith (1975).

A Further Illumination of Perceptual Interactions

Because perception is so closely bound up with attention, it should not be much of a surprise that the two have certain characteristics in common.

Going back to the behavior segment as a unit, we fitted the attentional reaction system into it as the initial phase of that unit. The perceptual reaction system follows. But it, too, like its predecessor, is preparatory because it paves the way for the adjustmental phase of the behavior segment, the final reaction system. It is auxiliary also because it *facilitates* an adaptation to the stimulus object but does not, in itself, constitute an adjustment.

However, the role of perception must not be minimized. It does serve an important additional function, once attention has done its job, and that is to orient the organism in relation to the stimulus object. Suppose someone thrusts an object at you in a big hurry without giving you sufficient time to make out what it was. The consequence may be a valuable vase smashed to pieces on the floor. There was no time for you to stop what you were doing and to shift to the new stimulus, and then there was no opportunity for you to appreciate that a vase was being handed to you. Therefore, the final reaction system of reaching for the vase and holding on to it was prevented. This illustration should point up the manner in which perception orients the organism toward the stimulus object.

"Human error" is often responsible for two elevated, subway, or surface trains colliding with each other. In one instance, two surface trains on a straight track ran into each other from opposite sides. Five trainmen lost their lives. The trouble was due to the fact that no one was looking out of the window of either locomotive. In our terms, had a typical attentional and perceptual reaction taken place on the part of *one* locomotive engineer, the final reaction system of pulling the brake would have had a chance to occur, preventing a serious wreck.

Some of our commonly held modern views of perception have a long tradition. Morris' (1973) explanation goes back at least as far as Helmholtz, whose work dates around the latter half of the 19th century. According to Helmholtz (1866/1925), the elements of a sensation get combined as the result of an unconscious inference. An object is inferred to be there before us as would need to be there to produce just such a pattern of sensory impressions as we are experiencing. So goes the theory.

Allport (1955) finds such a fictional process troublesome. He does not go along with Morris' (1973) explanation in which the brain sorts out the sensory impressions that it receives, identifies them, and interprets them or draws inferences about them. The reason why Allport finds such a concept difficult is that

> There is no one to make an inference. Can a neuron or a group of synapses in the brain make an inference? . . . no "inferring agent" is to be found; so why complicate matters by setting one up? But the activity called inferring seems to require an "inferrer." To say that an inference is not made by anybody, but just goes on like the weather is to do some violence to the language. [Allport, 1955, p. 83]

Hanson (1958) can help us out further on the question of the brain's hypothesizing or drawing inferences.

Hanson's Contribution

To develop a proper exposition of Hanson's (1958) view of perception, we need the help of Figure 9-2, the Necker Cube. As we look at it, some will see a box from below; others will declare that it is a cube seen from above. If we agree to draw what we see, we all end up drawing a figure that matches the shape shown in Figure 9-2. The fundamental question is, "Do we all see the same thing? If so, then how are we to account for the fact that some saw a box from above, some a box from below (or even an ice cube, a wire frame for a kite, or an aquarium)?" Since we started with the "identical" stimulus objects, since our eyes registered in virtually the same fashion, and since we all drew the same configuration, how shall we explain the differences in the perceptual reports?

At this point, we must be careful not to be seduced by the facile explanation of the "inferrer" or "interpreter" allegedly residing in the brain. Hanson tackles the problem of the "middleman" directly when he asks if we are doing two things when we see *anything*. Are we first seeing a thing and then interpreting it? Adhering to the principle of parsimony, Hanson chooses the simpler interpretation declaring that "seeing does not designate two diaphanous components, one optical, the other interpretive. Figure 9-2 is simply seen now as a box from below, now as a cube from above, *one does not soak up an optical pattern and then clamp an interpretation on it.*" (Hanson, 1958, p. 9, emphasis added).

If you still insist on seeing the figure as a box from below first and then as a cube from above, interpreting the configuration of lines differently on each of the two occasions, Hanson would say that this is equivalent to saying we just see something different. It does not mean that we see the same thing and then interpret it differently. When I say that "I see a box from below," I do *not* refer to a different interpretation. In other words, Hanson seems to be saying that such interpretations are improper, they are forced on the data, they hinder instead of helping understanding, and they are fictitious.

Pursuing Hanson's novel orientation further, let us move on to Figure 9-3, the famous goblet–faces drawing. Here again, virtually the "same" stimulus object, sense data, retinal and brain conditions obtain for two different individuals, A and B. Their drawings are indistinguishable, yet A sees a goblet and B sees two men staring at each other. Looking at A's drawing of his goblet, B declares, "That's exactly what I saw, two men staring at each other." The problem is how to get B, for example, to see the goblet. When B's attention finally causes the goblet to be actualized, what has really changed?

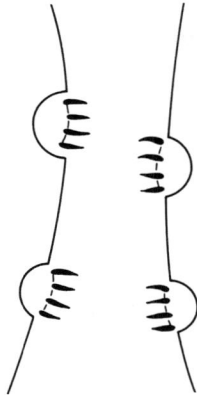

Figure 9-5 What do you perceive? Nonsense? Could it be a bear climbing up the other side of a tree? (From Hanson, *Patterns of discovery*, 1958, p. 12. Reproduced by permission of Cambridge University Press.)

"Nothing optical or sensational is modified. Yet one sees different things. The organization of what one sees changes" (Hanson, 1958, p. 12).

A greater appreciation of "organization" as used by Hanson may be had by inspecting Figure 9-5. The data are the same for all who view it: an assemblage of lines and arcs, reproducible in pretty much the same fashion by all. Yet it may be a nonsensical thing for you until I linguistically tip the scales in a different direction by telling you that it represents a bear climbing up the other side of a tree. At the moment that you see a bear, the component parts of the figure undergo a striking and sudden transformation. As Hanson (1958, p. 13) puts it, "You might even say with Wittgenstein, 'It has not changed, and yet I see it differently.' " This seeing the "same" thing differently is what Hanson means by organization. Figure 9-6 illustrates two possible organizations from *the same geometrical pattern*. One can see either long-horned antelopes or birds with open bills.

Figure 9-6 Antelopes or open-billed birds? Which? Or both? Can *one* geometrical pattern provide an opportunity for *two* psychological interactions? (From Hanson, *Patterns of discovery*, 1958, p. 14. Reproduced by permission of Cambridge University Press.)

In explaining the two possible discriminations of Figure 9-6, Hanson is adamant in rejecting the extraneous gimmick of "interpretation" or "inferring" as an *additive* to the seeing. Says Hanson, in regard to the reversible staircase, another ambiguous figure that can easily be imagined,

> To interpret is to think, to do something . . . The different ways in which these figures are seen are not due to different thoughts lying behind the visual reactions. What could 'spontaneous' mean if these reactions are not spontaneous? When the staircase 'goes into reverse' it does so spontaneously. One does not think of anything special: *one does not think at all. Nor does one interpret. One just sees*, now a staircase from above, now a staircase as from below. [Hanson, 1958, p. 11, emphasis added]

Try testing Hanson's construct on the three phrases in Figure 9-7 by reading them aloud. Even if you've had only a smattering of French (or none),

**PAS DE LIEU RHONE QUE NOUS.
SEAUX JE ROLE MAIN.**

**CAESAR ADSUM JAM FORTE;
BRUTUS ADERAT.**

Figure 9-7   Two phrases to be read as "French" and the third as "Latin," read by a Britisher. If the problem is solved, it will illustrate Hanson's construct of organization and spontaneity.

read the first two phrases *as* French. The only suggestion you need is that the letter *x* in *seaux* is silent. Read the third "Latin" phrase as the British might, who drop the initial *h* in a word when it precedes a vowel. If you succeeded, did you note the spontaneity and the radical shift in "organization"?

**DO NOT READ
THIS SIGN**

Figure 9-8   Did you *first* read this sign and *then* interpret it, or did you *only* read it? Were you able to obey what it directed you to do? Why not?

When you read the message in Figure 9-8, did you find yourself sensing something *and, then,* interpreting it, or was the "interpreting" instantaneous with the seeing of it? Is it possible that you did *nothing but* see the message? And, finally, were you able to obey the sign?

Evaluation of Hanson's contribution.   This completes our review of Hanson's approach to perception. We applaud his fresh insights in a troublesome area of psychology. Perhaps the only criticism to be leveled against his work is that it does not go far enough. But his penetrating analysis can be fitted into an interbehavioral framework for a still clearer interpretation.

Here is a sample of how we may apply an interbehavioral theory to Figure 9-6, "Antelopes or Open-Billed Birds?" Assume that we see one and then the other. How shall we understand that? We should first note that the figure is ambiguously drawn. Otherwise, it could not participate in two psychologically potential events. As such, it is involved in two separate and distinct interactions. If we stress the whole event, we do not feel the need of an "inferrer" or "interpreter." As a stimulus object, the figure serves two very different stimulus functions correlated with two very different response functions; namely, the organism's discrimination of antelopes and open-billed birds. It is a coincidence that a certain geometrical pattern has been involved in two different psychological events. We should not fault Hanson, for he has made his contribution by showing that there is more to seeing than meets the eye.

I have suggested that the stimulus object plays a role in perceptual interactions. If you want to elicit two different visual interactions in relation to the geometrically same stimulus object, you must draw it so as to provide two possibilities. Not *any* design will be seen ambiguously.

Using a famous ambiguous figure entitled "My Wife and My Mother-in-Law," Gerald Fisher (1968) hoped to work in a third aspect, a man's face. The result is the drawing shown in Figure 9-9, entitled "Mother, Father, and Daughter." His purpose was to add another item to the available repertoire of ambiguous spatial patterns for experimental purposes. But could he be sure just how his new figure worked? So he put it to the test. He showed the line sketch of Figure 9-9 to 179 subjects drawn at random from the customers patronizing a large restaurant in the English city of Newcastle upon Tyne, presumably a representative cross section of the general population. As Fisher handed them the figure, he asked them to tell him what they saw in the drawing. After they identified one aspect, he asked again if they saw anything else, and, a third time, too, if they gave a second response. His results showed that 177 participants perceived the daughter, 170 saw the father, and 106, the mother. Two respondents failed to "spot" the daughter aspect, nine failed to observe the father, and 73 were unable to identify the mother. Fisher concluded that the three-in-one drawing that he designed should be altered so that each aspect has an *equal* chance to be perceived. The mother aspect is out of balance. Anyhow, Fisher's study shows that the

Figure 9-9   Mother, father, and daughter are all three in the drawing. Can you find them? (From Fisher, *The American Journal of Psychology*, 1968, p. 275. © University of Illinois Press, Publisher.)

characteristics of the stimulus object do play a part in the outcome of perception.

The foregoing discussion of the role of the stimulus object in perception has led us naturally to a consideration of the Gestalt school of psychology, which is next on our agenda.

Gestalt Views on Perception

If you have been stopped at a railroad crossing by two flashing red light signals that go on and off alternately, you may have observed the phi phenomenon of apparent motion. Under the right conditions, even though the two lights are stationary and spaced apart, they are perceived as a single stimulus moving through the space between them. It is as if the red light were swinging *continuously* like a pendulum between the two loci.

The phi phenomenon (in its usual abbreviated form) is what started the Gestalt movement about 1910 in Germany. It was Wertheimer who studied this striking perceptual response in a simplified form in the laboratory. On the basis of his investigation, Wertheimer argued that there was no way to reduce that perception to a jumble of sensory elements that were then interpreted by the brain. The response could not be explained the way actual movement had been explained, that is, as the "sensation" (in self-actional terms) produced by a *continuous* movement of an object through space. The phi phenomenon was *immediately* given, and the "laws" governing its appearance could be stated in terms of the distance between the stimuli, their intensity, and the temporal relations between them. This kind of explanation weakened the theory of the "interpreter" within the brain, although the Gestalters did not entirely give up the nervous system in their theoretical development. However, we shall omit their psychophysiology and dwell on their more objective discoveries about the workings of stimulus objects.

Wertheimer's findings were only the start of a revolution waged against the prevailing atomistic psychology's attempt to reduce all psychology to certain basic component *elements*. Although Gestalt investigations were extended to thinking, memory, and recall, we shall here bring out only their main contributions to the area of perception. These may be considered rules of perceptual organization.

Gestalt.   The English word *gestalt* (plural, *gestalten)* comes from the German word *Gestalt. Webster's New Collegiate Dictionary* defines *gestalt* as "a structure, configuration or pattern of physical, biological, or psychological phenomena so integrated as to constitute a functional unit with properties not derivable from its parts in summation." We will expand and elaborate that definition by numerous examples.

Returning to our illustration of the phi phenomenon of apparent motion, that response has a certain *form, pattern, configuration, or structure.* That is the basic, irreducible datum. It has a *whole* character or organization that cannot be explained by adding the two separate and distinct (in time and space) flashing light stimuli. The same holds true for all perceptions. "The whole is different than the sum of its parts."

Transposability of gestalten.   That wholeness, form, or organization can even survive transposability as when a melody remains the same when it is transposed into a different key even though not a single note is the same as it was in the original arrangement. The transposability and endurance of form or organization are manifested when the lights go out. Through touch, we recognize our way in the dark throughout our homes even though we had never done so (tactually) before.

Figure and ground.   In observing the ever-changing scene, the perceptual field tends to be segregated so that certain aspects of it are organized as field, certain others as ground (or background). On such occasions, the figure is perceived as having a definite shape; it is more distinct and nearer than the ground. The drawing in Figure 9–3 (or any other, for that matter) can be used to illustrate figure and ground. When we perceive two men staring at each other, that portion of the drawing is figure, and all the rest is ground. But when we perceive the vase, it becomes figure and the rest, ground. When Jack is waiting for Jill and "spots" her in the crowd, Jill becomes figure for Jack and all else becomes an amorphous ground devoid of any interest whatsoever.

Similarity. In a complex of various elements, those elements that resemble each other tend to be organized together. The arrangement of X's and O's here favors perceiving them as alternating *vertical* rows of X's and *vertical* rows of O's over a horizontal arrangement as XOXOXO.

```
X  O  X  O  X  O
X  O  X  O  X  O
X  O  X  O  X  O
X  O  X  O  X  O
X  O  X  O  X  O
X  O  X  O  X  O
```

Proximity. Elements that are close together tend to be seen as belonging together over similar elements that are farther away. This arrangement of pairs of X's demonstrates proximity.

```
X  X      X  X      X  X      X  X
```

But by a special effort, we can overrule proximity as illustrated in the following adaptation:

```
X  |X      X| |X      X| |X      X|  X
```

We have also demonstrated the way that *enclosing* or *closure* (another organizational rule) operates (see next section). With the addition of the brackets, the wider space between the pairs of X's is better enclosed and the more distant X's appear to belong together.[4]

Closure. Any gap between elements of a continuing pattern will be perceived as closed—also sometimes referred to as "perceptual filling in." In the example shown here, the break in the circle does not prevent our perceiving it as a complete circle. There is a story connected with this particular rule. It concerns a Gestalt psychologist, Kurt Lewin, who was having dinner with some colleagues in a German beer garden. They were amazed at the performance of their waiter who could remember the details of their orders effectively as long as he served them, but after he gave them their bill, a simple question revealed that he could recall very little of what he had brought them. His behavior illustrates closure, meaning that once his task was completed he was also psychologically finished with it.

The incident suggested a study, which one of Lewin's students, Bluma Zeigarnik, carried out (Zeigarnik, 1927). She assigned a group of 32 subjects a

---

[4]A more extensive treatment of perception is available in Weintraub and Walker (1966).

series of simple tasks to perform. Among them were doing mental arithmetic and solving a riddle. Zeigarnik interrupted her subjects in the middle of one-half of the tasks and allowed them to complete the other half. Several hours later, when she asked them to recall the tasks that they had worked at, they could remember the interrupted tasks much better than the completed. The latter consituted "finished business" that illustrated closure. According to Lewin, the tension that presumably developed in the carrying out of a task that was interrupted did not result in closure. This lack of closure has been called the *Zeigarnik effect*.

Skinner (1953) has something to say about closure, particularly about seeing a circle with a small segment missing, as noted earlier. He would not favor "closure" as revealing an inherent power of a stimulus configuration prior to any response acquisition toward it. He favors an account in terms of an organism's previous history in contact with circular objects under all sorts of conditions. In other words, this would be a conditioned response, which some psychologists would categorize under generalization. But Skinner asks, if we consider a man whose daily job involves handling incompleted rings (such as piston rings), does "closure" compel him to see those piston rings as without a gap? (pp. 267–268). What do you think?

Continuity. Items that are marked by uninterrupted extension in space, time, or sequence are seen as belonging together. The sopranos belong together, as do the other voices. Try, if you can, to cross over back and forth from one voice to another at random, hearing each one separately, in turn.

Common fate. In the gestalt concept of common fate, elements that change or move in the same way tend to be perceived as belonging to each other. Two lines of chorus dancers, one of which kicks or moves to the right and the other to the left, illustrate this rule.

The Bent-Stick Problem

Have you ever stuck a branch from a tree into a stream or into the clear waters of a lake? If you have, then you must have noticed that the previously straight branch looks bent. If you have never made that observation, you can perform a miniexperiment by inserting a drinking straw into a glass of water. If you do so, you will note that the straw appears to bend at a sharp angle below the point at which it touches the water. This phenomenon of the bent stick has distressed philosophers and psychologists for a long time. In fact, even today, perception is said to be either *veridical* or *nonveridical*. *Webster's New Collegiate Dictionary* defines *veridical* as "truthful, genuine, and nonillusory," leaving *nonveridical* to mean "false or illusory." Another common term in psychology, *illusion*, has the connotation of deception or falseness. The ambiguous figures that we have studied in this chapter are also classified as illusions.

Allport's veridical and nonveridical perception.   Allport (1955) offers an extended discussion of veridical and nonveridical perception. For him, a veridical perception is one that corresponds to "objective reality." As an illustration, he uses two lines:

Do they look parallel? "Yes," you say, "they do." This is a direct experience of how the lines appear, "a phenomenological experience, observer-involved and private" (p. 23). But, Allport says, you have only given a report of how the lines "look," not how they "are" (p. 25).

Now, of course, says Allport, there's no way of finding out what the lines "really are, or would be apart from any possibility of human observation, [this would be] a meaningless question" (p. 25). But, he suggests the use of a more "objective" method in arriving at an answer to the second question. How about applying the straight edge of a card or a ruler to the lines and even measuring the distance between them at different points? This operation confirms that the two lines are straight and parallel. Therefore, according to Allport, your first perception in which the lines *appeared* to you to be parallel turned out to be a veridical perception.

Allport stresses the fact that use of one's hands and a ruler in checking the two lines makes for greater "objectivity." But are not hand movements themselves and ruler readings also subject to "private" perceptions even though another person is looking over your shoulder to check on you? This attack on the problem somehow (according to Allport) makes the whole operation "public" (p. 23). Allport never settles the question satisfactorily, probably because the framework he has chosen to work in is not satisfactory.

But we must pursue our attempt to solve the bent-stick problem even though we go about it in a roundabout fashion. This time, let us look into the nature of nonveridical perception. As our model, we shall turn to the same illusion that Allport uses. If you look at the pairs of long, horizontal lines toward the center of each diagram in Figure 9-10, the upper lines appear (metaphorically speaking) bow-legged and the lower ones, knock-kneed. According to Allport (1955), our phenomenological procedure tells us that the lines are not parallel. But, Allport argues, if you carry out a "physicalistic" check as to the facts regarding the lines" (p. 38) as you did earlier with a ruler, you will find that the lines are parallel. Therefore, according to Allport, your "phenomenological" perception of the lines as nonparallel is a nonveridical perception because it did not agree with the "physicalistic experience."

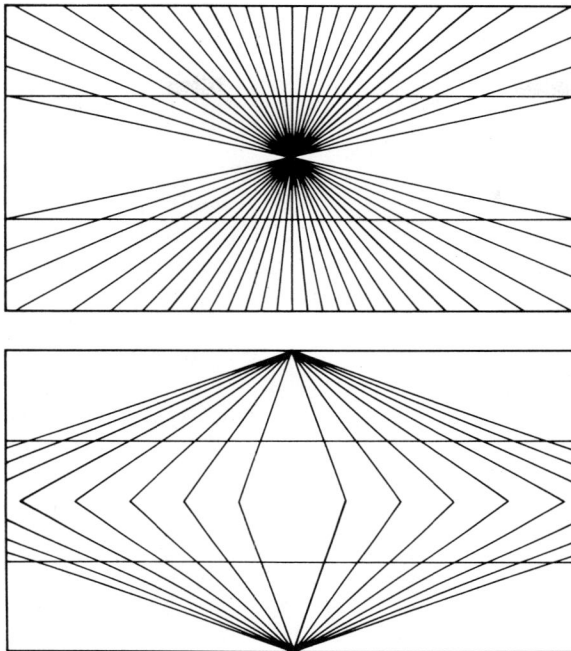

Figure 9-10 An illusion. The centrally located lines in the upper figure appear "bow-legged," those in the lower figure, "knock-kneed." Do the converging and diverging lines in the background have anything to do with it?

A test of Allport's two kinds of perceptions. If you turn Figure 9-10 sideways, bring it up to eye level, and sight down the pairs of lines, lo and behold, you perceive them as parallel. The test that we applied was what Allport has been calling a "phenomenological" procedure. No "physicalistic" operation with ruler was necessary to convert the first perception of nonparallel lines to a second perception in which they appeared parallel. The illusion is gone.

A suggestion toward a solution. Are two classes of perception necessary, as Allport suggests, or is there only one kind? Let's apply an interbehavioral analysis to the situation before us and see if it clears up the mystery. If we first consider the perceptual response in which the lines appeared bow-legged and knock-kneed, we must not overlook a critical factor, that is, the setting in which the parallel lines are embedded. In Chapter 1, we learned the importance of the setting factors among the several variables that have to be taken into account in analyzing behavioral events. This variable is crucial here. When we view the figure in the normal reading manner, the converging and diverging background of the lines is part of the whole. As a result, the parallel lines cannot be perceptually severed from the total pattern because the pattern is a factual gestalt. And yet Allport totally ignores the role of the setting factors for the parallel lines, acting very much as if the lines existed "in a vacuum."

Now, let us repeat the observation with the book turned sideways and sighted at eye level. Why do the lines look parallel now? In terms of my hypothesis, because we have made the setting factors (the converging and diverging lines) inoperative. They cannot do their work now as they did when we looked at the pattern squarely. Another way of ruling out the converging and diverging lines as "ground" (to apply Gestalt terminology) is to cut a piece of paper to fit exactly in between the two pairs of relevant lines. If you do so and look at the lines, you have eliminated the distorting effect of the setting factors and will, now, perceive the lines as parallel.

Note what we have achieved with this analysis. We have done our job entirely in terms of manipulating aspects of the stimulus object and/or setting factors. Nothing else is needed to explain one's perceiving the lines as parallel or nonparallel. The two perceptual interactions are indistinguishable from each other and naturalistic. Nor did we have to appeal to any internal "interpreter" or "inference."

And now the bent stick.   We are now ready to tackle the mystery of the bent stick. To refresh our memory, this is a stick partly in and partly out of the water and which seems to change direction under water. It no longer looks like a straight stick.

How shall we handle this case? To help us, we must call on the physicist. That scientist explains such a phenomenon with the concept of refraction. To the physicist, *refraction* means that light, like people, "behaves" differently in different media. Ordinarily, light travels in a straight path, but if it passes obliquely from one medium (such as air) to another (such as water), it is slowed down and is, therefore, deflected from a straight path. Actually, we can predict the degree of perceived bending by calculating the angle of refraction from the angle of incidence. In other words, we can predict the actual degree to which the stick appears to be bent. To dispel the mystery of the bent stick completely, we require only one more analytic tool, also discussed in Chapter 1, namely, the medium of contact. Certain variables facilitate, or make possible, the interaction between organism and stimulus object. These are commonly air, light, and so on.

In the case of the bent stick, we are interacting *simultaneously* with a stimulus object via two different media of contact, namely, air and water. But, since light does not behave in an identical fashion in both media, our perceptual interactions cannot be expected to be identical either. If we manipulate conditions by letting only *one* medium of contact operate (as by lifting the stick completely out of the water or by submerging the stick completely under water), then the stick no longer looks bent. The stick is perceived as straight either way. However, if we insist on interacting with it simultaneously under two different media of contact, then the result is the bent stick. But that does not mean that "appearances are deceiving" or that "our senses are not to be trusted," because the perceptual event known as "the bent stick"is as lawful and predictable as any other.

The lawfulness of illusions.   The foregoing argument raises the question about illusions or so-called "misperceptions." In my opinion, all perceptual reactions are lawful and orderly as long as we adhere to observables and deal with them. Then we can pinpoint such factors as the design of the stimulus object, the setting factors, or the media of contact as the variables that determine perceptual interactions. If you work with those factors, you change the perceptual interaction. Viewed in a naturalistic framework, all perceptions, including illusions, are subject to law and order, as is the rat who makes a "wrong turn" in a maze, or a subject in a learning experiment who makes an "error" in his or her response. Such an orientation also saves us from involvement in such pseudoquestions as Allport (1955, p. 24) raises as "how things look" versus "how things are," "objectivity" versus "subjectivity."

Factors That Affect Perceiving

Because of the intimate connection between attention and perception, the same variables that affect attention also operate in determining perception. We have already noted the role of setting factors and features of the stimulus object in both attending and perceiving interactions.

Linguistic Influence on Perceiving

In Chapter 1, we gave some consideration to the effect of language on our behavior. We saw how language shapes our reactions—the way we see things and the way we come to think of them.

The Carmichael, Hogan, and Walter experiment.   Carmichael, Hogan, and Walter (1932) decided to see if they could experimentally produce changes in the reproduction of visually perceived forms by the use of language. They prepared a set of 12 fairly ambiguous patterns. Two different sets of names were assigned to each of the patterns or figures, Word List I and Word List II. Figure 9-11 shows the figures which they used in the middle column and Word List I and Word List II in the adjoining columns.

In their procedure, Carmichael and his colleagues showed the same figures to all their subjects—two groups and a control group. But one group was given the names in List I when they viewed those figures, and the other

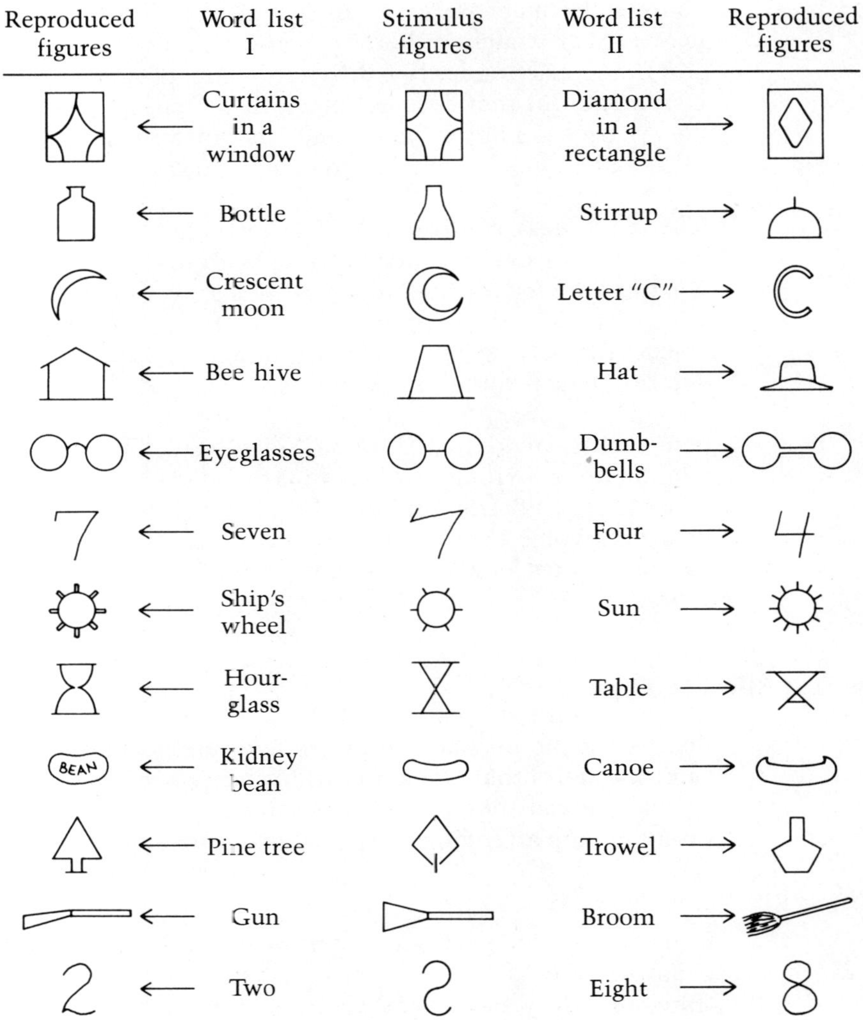

Reproduced figures	Word list I	Stimulus figures	Word list II	Reproduced figures
	←			→
	Curtains in a window		Diamond in a rectangle	
	← Bottle		Stirrup →	
	← Crescent moon		Letter "C" →	
	← Bee hive		Hat →	
	← Eyeglasses		Dumb-bells →	
	← Seven		Four →	
	← Ship's wheel		Sun →	
	← Hour-glass		Table →	
	← Kidney bean		Canoe →	
	← Pine tree		Trowel →	
	← Gun		Broom →	
	← Two		Eight →	

Figure 9-11 Stimulus figures used both in the Carnichael, Hogan, and Walter (1932) and the Herman, Lawless, and Marshall (1957) studies are shown in the middle column. Word lists presented to the two groups are entered in the adjacent columns and some of the corresponding figures drawn from memory in the two outermost columns. (From Carmichael, Hogan, and Walter, 1932.)

group was given the names in List II when they saw them. The control group viewed the figures without assignment of any names. The subjects were told that they would be shown a set of figures that they would be required to reproduce by drawing at the end of the series. The drawings were to be executed as accurately as possible and in any order.

The exposure apparatus was started, and before the appearance of each figure, the experimenter announced, "The next figure resembles [stating the assigned name of the figure in List I or II, as the case might be]." At the end of the series, if subjects were unable to draw a representation of each of the 12 figures, they were shown the entire series again, until a recognizable copy of every one of the figures was obtained. Forty-eight subjects viewed the figures under List I influence, and 38 under List II influence. Nine subjects viewed the series of figures without name attribution.

The figures in the first and last columns of Figure 9-11 are representative of the drawings that the subjects produced under the influence of the name attributed to each of the figures prior to exposure. It is apparent that those drawings bear a closer resemblance to the named object than they do to the object in common exposed to all the subjects.

The inescapable conclusion, according to Carmichael, Hogan, and Walter (1932, p. 85), is that "The present objective experimental results seem to show that in many cases the recall of a visually perceived form is altered by the fact that a particular word is said immediately before the visual presentation of the form."

The Herman, Lawless, and Marshall study.   Herman, Lawless, and Marshall (1957) did a follow-up on the Carmichael, Hogan, and Walter (1932) study with certain modifications. One important change concerned exposure of the stimulus figures. Whereas Carmichael, Hogan, and Walter allowed their subjects anywhere from three to eight exposures, Herman, Lawless, and Marshall decided on one exposure only with varying exposure times of 0.2 second, 1.0 second, and 5.0 seconds divided evenly among their groups.

Procedure.   They used the same figures and the same procedure but were more interested in determining the effect of set and exposure time on their subjects' reproductions of the figures exposed to them. And because Carmichael and his colleagues said very little about the control group's reproduction of figures named in Word List I and II *when these had not been given to them*, Herman and his colleagues were also interested in a checkup of this intriguing finding. Thus, their experiment boiled down to a test of the following two questions:

1. What will be the effect of omitting from the instructions to the subjects that they will later be asked to reproduce the figures that they will be shown?
2. What will be the effect of varying the time of exposure of the stimulus figures for 0.2 second, 1.0 second, and 5 seconds by contrast with Carmichael and his coworkers' use of a 1-second exposure?

Herman and his coworkers collected data on 407 subjects divided into 18 groups of 21 subjects each. Nine groups were divided so that they were given either Word List I, Word List II, or neither word list and either exposure times of 0.2 second, 1.0 second, or 5.0 seconds. These groups were told that they *would be* required to reproduce the figures at the end of the series. Another nine groups underwent the same procedure, with one exception: they were not told that they would be required at a later time to reproduce the figures shown to them.

Results.   In answer to their first question, Herman, Lawless, and Marshall conclude that *omitting* the instruction that the subjects will be asked to reproduce the stimulus figures works to increase the frequency of language-influenced reproductions, presumably because they did not, therefore, attend to, and perceive, features of the stimulus figures.

As to the effect of the variable exposure times, Herman, Lawless, and Marshall (1957) state that while there is some evidence that varying exposure time does have some effect on the frequency of language-influenced reproductions, particularly for the shorter exposures, the evidence is "not compelling" (p. 183).

Control subjects who were not given either Word List I or Word List II prior to exposure of the stimulus figures nevertheless reproduced the figures resembling objects in either Word List I or II, but with a *chance frequency* by comparison with subjects who actually heard the names in either Word List I or Word List II. As to how this happened with any frequency at all, the suggestion proposed by Herman and his coworkers is quite appealing. We note that, after all, the stimulus figures are, naturally, ambiguous. That is why they were drawn a certain way. As such, they have the same stimulus-function possibilities that either word list assigned to them has. But, since the experimenter did not name the stimulus figures for certain subjects, those subjects apparently did this for themselves. And, if this inference is valid, is it not in itself evidence of a sort of the powerful influence of language on perception?

Some evidence for the correctness of such a hunch is available in a finding by Herman, Lawless, and Marshall, who had an additional group of 29 subjects "free-associate" to each of the same stimulus figures that were shown to all the other subjects. Of course, neither word list was used with them. They were simply told to write down on a sheet of paper "the first word or phrase that came to mind" after each figure was exposed. These subjects were neither *told* in advance that they would be required to reproduce the figure stimuli, nor were they required to do so following their "free-association" task. When the experimenters checked on the frequency with which these subjects free-associated the names in Word List I or II, their data showed that a mean of 63% of the free associations were identical, or very similar, to the terms in those lists.

As to the most important finding of the Herman, Lawless, and Marshall (1957) study, the experimenters conclude that despite the differences between their own procedure and that of Carmichael, Hogan, and Walter, they, too, found that verbal labels given prior to visual presentation of stimulus figures did influence subjects' reproduction of those figures. With slightly different criteria than those used by Carmichael, Hogan, and Walter, Herman and his coexperimentalists found that 33% of the drawings resembled objects as they were labeled in Word Lists I and II, by comparison with 19% reported by their predecessors.

Implications of the Herman, Lawless, and Marshall study. Perhaps the most significant implication of the Herman, Lawless, and Marshall report (1957) is the futility of escaping the pervasive influence of language on the way we perceive things. If labeling of stimulus objects by others is unavailable, the past linguistic experiences of individuals can do the job for them. Contrariwise, beauty, pornography, and sin lie not only "in the eye of the beholder" but in the linguistic terms that others apply to them. Anyhow, Herman, Lawless, and Marshall's study points to two sources of linguistic influence on perception, those furnished by others and those provided by the individual's own available linguistic repertoire.

A confirmatory study. A study by Potter (1971) supports the preceding two studies and throws further light on how perception works, particularly the speed with which it apprehends meanings or actualizes stimulus functions. As background to her investigation, Potter (1971) points out that the average visual fixation lasts only ⅓ of a second, particularly in unfamiliar territory. It appears that perceptual interactions are constantly searching out what might be important to see or what one is likely to see, and confirming or refuting that expectation.

Potter wondered whether an observer could perceive an expected scene even when it is presented so briefly that it would not otherwise be remembered and, if so, what kind of advance cue would be required to permit such a rapid perception? Her procedure involved one practice session and eight test sessions in viewing 16 color pictures via motion-picture projection by two groups of 24 college students. The observers were told to look for a particular picture and, when they saw it, to press a lever that stopped the projector. One group saw the target picture before each sequence was shown. The other group was given only verbal descriptions of the pictures they were to look for ("for example, a boat, two men drinking beer, a child and butterfly"). Except for this difference, the procedure was otherwise identical for both groups. Subjects viewed the sequence of pictures at exposures ranging from approximately ⅛ of a second (125 milliseconds) to ⅓ of a second (333 milliseconds) per picture.

Results showed that errors for both groups were rare except at eight pictures per second. But to return to Potter's hypothesis, "one does not need to know exactly what a thing will look like to detect it in a ⅓-second glimpse" (Potter, 1971, p. 966). In fact, providing the name in advance of a stimulus object to be detected visually "permitted as accurate and almost as rapid selection as foreknowledge of exact appearance" (p. 965). Potter once again confirmed the efficacy of language on perception.

"Needs" or Setting Factors and Perceiving

The preceding experiments leave no doubt that language plays a role in the way we perceive things. In view of our findings about the greater sensitivity of behavioral events to surrounding variables over purely biological events (such as reflexes), we should not be surprised to find that what some have called "needs" of the organism also affect perception. The believer in UFOs perceives an unidentified flying object where others see a weather balloon or an unusual cloud effect. And a deeply religious person with a "need" to communicate with the Virgin Mary perceives her in the pattern of light and shade of a dimly lit church wall.

Hunger or food deprivation can affect perception. While some would treat such a condition self-actionally as a "need," it is also possible to handle the situation as a change in setting factors, localizable in an organismic condition. Several experiments have explored the possible influence of hunger on perception. In a preliminary experiment, Sanford (1936) found that when he presented children with (1) words to free-associate with and (2) ambiguous pictures to interpret before a regular meal, they gave more responses associated with food than they did shortly after a regular meal. So he performed another, more carefully designed experiment as a check on his earlier finding.

Sanford's question this time was "Will there be a greater effect on perception the longer a person is deprived of food?" Instead of working with subjects just before and just after a meal, he lengthened the food deprivation period to a 24-hour fast but also tested subjects at varying intervals since their last meal. Sanford used (1) a word-association test logically related to food and (2) interpretation of ambiguous pictures that could be connected with food and other stimuli that could tap food-related responses.

Sanford found no direct and simple relation between frequency of food-related responses and hours of food deprivation. When he compared results obtained from those who had fasted 24 hours with those tested at varying intervals between their breakfast and lunch or lunch and dinner, he found little difference in their scores. Increase in food response was almost as great toward the end of any abstinence period (between any two meals) as it was after a 24-hour fast. As Sanford (1937, p. 153) puts it, "Only slightly more food responses were obtained on the average after the fast than were obtained during the last hour of the normal eating cycle."

Reactional Biography and Perceiving

In our discussion of the specificity of attentional reaction systems, we inevitably were also involved in perception. The speedy attention and perception of anatomical deformities by the orthopedic surgeon serves as a reminder. It illustrates the specificity of perception, too, and for the same reason. What we attend to as well as what we perceive, out of the wealth of possible stimulation around us, is a function of our reactional biographies. As a personal example, I am sitting in a coffee shop, only dimly aware of the buzz of conversation about me until, instantaneously, the words, "child psychology," spring out at me out of the conversational blur of an adjacent group. My reactional biography must have had something to do with that event.

A geologist friend goes by a building and stops short in order to inspect, through a magnifying glass, columns of Indiana limestone in which he points out thousands of shellfish fossils. A colleague, who is an ornithologist, and I are walking across a campus. He discriminates many bird songs that simply pass me by. A carpenter friend walks into a newly built house and notes features of its construction, both proper and faulty, that others fail to see.

Perceptual constancy. Suppose we look at a circular mirror directly before us in the frontal plane where it is naturally seen as circular. Now, suppose we have someone tilt the mirror away from us. We still see it as circular. Let them tilt it still more, and we still perceive it as circular. From the standpoint of geometrical optics, or, to put it another way, if our eyes really acted like a camera, the circular mirror should appear to be elliptical, not circular. Because under varying conditions objects are still seen in the same way, psychologists have referred to such perceptions as object, shape, or form *constancy*. To continue with other illustrations, if we look down from a skyscraper, we say that the people down there "look like ants" and the automobiles "look like toys," but we nevertheless still perceive them as people and as automobiles. There is a "size constancy" in our perceptions regardless of the distance from which we view them. The same holds for color. I look at my fire-truck-red little stapler and it stays red in the brightest summer sunlight, in the shade of a tree, and in fairly dim light. It has a "redness" stability over a considerable range of conditions. This is an example of color constancy.

How shall we understand perceptual constancy? We certainly cannot understand it in terms of a strict determination by the features of the stimulus object. Self-actional theorists propose that perceptual constancies are "constructed by our own private, or inner, operations" (Allport, 1955, p. 42). As an alternative to such a self-actional construct, interbehavioral theory would naturally be stated in terms of the flow of events. We need to recall that a perceptual interaction is semi-implicit: no perceptual response is performed in severance of previous perceptual responses. They all hang together because of their historical interconnection. Would a person who had *never* seen an automobile fairly close up perceive automobiles from a skyscraper? If our construct about the effect of past perceivings on present perceivings is correct, then the answer to that question would be no. If all behavior is a function of a cumulative acquisition, why should perception be an exception? At any rate, if we adopt the view that present events are a function of antecedent events, we do not create the insoluble mystery (such as Allport is stuck with) of ascribing the business of converting "elliptical mirrors" into "circular" ones to an internal agent, a scientifically unverifiable construct. The answer to the question of how we perceive will come by studying the interrelationships of the flow of events. Potter's study, in particular, shows that visual perceptions may be about as intimately connected with prior linguistic action as with prior visual interactions and with about equivalent effectiveness.

Molyneux's question. William Molyneux was a Dublin lawyer and a learned member of the Irish Parliament. He was also a friend and correspondent of John Locke. On July 7, 1688, Molyneux wrote to Locke with the famous question as to whether a blind man who had recovered the use of his sight would recognize a cube and a globe presented before his eyes. Particularly, what Molyneux wondered about was whether the man's previous experience of touching the two objects would enable him to name the objects at first sight of them. Molyneux answered the question in the negative. Why? Here is Molyneux's explanation as reported by Morgan (1977, p. 6): "For, though he has obtained the experience of how a globe, how a cube affects his touch, yet he has not obtained the experience that what affects his touch so and so, must affect his sight so and so. Locke thoroughly agreed with the reply of 'this thinking gentleman.' " Since then, for almost 300 years, famous philosophers have engaged in endless pro and con argument on this question.

Senden (1960) has collected numerous cases of people with cataracts who had recovered their sight in later life. In general, Senden supports Molyneux's and Locke's argument. He states that "the process of learning to see in these cases is an enterprise fraught with innumerable difficulties, and the common idea that the patient must necessarily be delighted with the gifts of light and colour bequeathed to him by the operation, is wholly remote from the facts" (p. 20). Senden reports numerous cases of patients who, by touch, recognized such familiar objects as watches, knives, forks, spoons, and toys but could not recognize a single one of them visually even after considerable visual experience with them. He concludes that touch provides no bridge to a blind person newly sighted. Such a person must acquire visual space perception from scratch. The following case provides insight into the plight of such an individual.

Recovery of sight after 18 years of blindness.   Suppose a person had been born blind and were suddenly made to see. How and what would he or she perceive in view of a total lack of previous visual experience? The answer has never been clear-cut because the blind who recover their sight have had some degree of visual experience (no matter how vague) prior to restoration of their vision.

This is true in the case of George Campbell who, at the age of 18, had a surgical operation that permitted him to see somewhere nearly adequately for the first time in his life. How perceptual reactions became built up is told in Campbell's own words, although we leave to the reader the task of translating the everyday language into technical, scientifically acceptable terminology.

I entered a new world.

The room was full of objects completely new and strange to me. I did not recognize what anything was, or what it was for, as I had practically no visual experience. Most people do not realize how much of their "seeing" is actually brainwork, reasoning and past experience.[5] The doctor took me to a window and said, "George, do you see that hedge across the street?"

"No, sir."

I had no idea what it was among those strange forms.

"Where," I asked in confusion, "is the far curb of the street?"

This might help me. I had often crossed the street and knew it more or less by footstep touch. He explained carefully which one of those forms the curb was—and suddenly I understood. Yes, I could "see" it now! I was so thrilled I could hardly speak.

I could hardly take my glasses off to give my aching, new-born eyes a rest. I was fascinated by the details and colors of household objects such as ash trays, chairs, vases, carpets, and the friendly radio that I had known largely by touch.

I didn't know which color was which. Before my operation I could tell fireman's red if it was placed a few inches from my eyes, or perhaps bright blue, but any blends or gradations were beyond me. I asked Mother what the other color in the sky was. She explained the small white spots were clouds. After a day or two I went to a fruit store and asked what the color of each fruit was. I bought yellow bananas, green limes, red-and-yellow apples, lemons, oranges, and other fruits. I studied their subtle colors as I ate them. Why, there were thousands of shades of green alone!

My reactions to colors were different from the average person's. Dark green was like loyalty and tradition; light green was like touching a baby's skin. Light blue, to me, suggested something clean and fresh, like a cold drink on a hot summer day. Purple was like the cold, clammy feeling you get just before it

[5] To us, "brainwork, reasoning and past experience" can only be popular psychology's equivalent for reactional biography.

372 *Chapter 9*

rains. Pink was like eating delicious candy. Scarlet was like the burning sensation I had in my finger tips when I touched something hot.

That evening I went to a movie. I do not remember what the picture was, or its plot. All was confusion to me—there were so many things portrayed I did not recognize, and I could only look at the screen for a few seconds at a time. When I did look, I tried to learn what *caused* certain noises. Sounds that were not made by visible people or objects, such as an outer door shutting, added to my bewilderment. After a while, my eyes gave out. I had to leave.

When I walked out of the theater it was dark. I looked up. There were the stars! To my surprise, no one was looking at them except me. . . .

When I returned to high school, a few days later, I was in a predicament. An old friend would rush up to congratulate me. I would shake his hand, but until I heard his voice, I wasn't at all sure I knew him. During these first days I would often leave off conversation with boy friends in the halls to stare at pretty girls going by. *What* had I been missing?

At first I had faulty judgment of distance. When I'd reach for an ash tray, my hand would go beyond it. So I learned to measure distance by trial and error, like a baby. My glasses were focused at two distances, for reading and for far off seeing. I had to learn to use them effectively. As I said, most people do not realize how much of their "seeing" is actually brainwork, reasoning and past experience.

It was a job for me at first to go up and down stairs. But I had too much fun in my new world to bother about stumbling occasionally. [*This Week*, 1941]

"The things that we take for granted in our ordinary everyday life are as strange and unexplainable as anything one might find," (Sapir, 1926–1927, p. 892). Potter's (1971) experiment speaks to the speed, smoothness, and efficiency of perception. We take perception as much for granted as we do our respiration unless we are "out of breath" or have to "catch our breath." Since perception works so easily that its very efficiency works against our analysis of it, why not disrupt it in a controlled way so as to see what happens to it? One way to achieve that goal is to wear lenses that have the effect of inverting the visual space so that what was down is up and what was up is down.

Stratton's self-observations. Stratton (1896, 1897) set up experiments in which he wore an inverting lens system over his right eye and a blindfold over his left eye. In the first experiment, he wore the lenses for 21½ hours in the course of 3 days. In the second experiment, he wore them 67 hours during an 8-day period. When he was not wearing the lenses, he was carefully blindfolded.

In reporting his results, Stratton described an immediate disorientation of perceived objects lasting about 3 days but decreasing after that time. On the fourth day, while taking a walk outdoors and giving some thought to his body position, he states (1897, p. 354), "I had the distinct feeling that such a position was upside down." However, indoors, even by the second day, "there was no striking and obvious feeling that the scene was upside down" (p. 348).

At first, visual and motor reactions were very inaccurate. When Stratton located an object visually, his first movements were invariably in the wrong direction. At the table, the simplest acts of serving himself had to be cautiously studied and worked out. A glass of water that normally appeared in the upper right-hand portion of his place setting would appear to be in the lower left-hand position. Yet reaching there was ineffective. In settling himself into a chair, Stratton had to feel around carefully before he trusted himself to sit down. Even worse, the first day's frustrations resulted in mild nausea.

Subsequent days brought gradual improvement. Movements became less laborious and studied. By the third day, Stratton was beginning to feel more at home in his new experience. New visual and motor reactions were steadily built up until he no longer stumbled into things in trying to avoid them. He could reach to the proper place for the soap in washing himself and no longer *had* to feel for the proper location of the chairs in sitting. By the tenth day, the visual field no longer seemed upside down. The world seemed normal at last.

A surprise greeted Stratton when he removed the lenses and again saw things in his preexperimental manner. While things did not seem upside down, they did have a perplexing, bewildering appearance that lasted several hours. They just did not fit the order of things to which he had become accustomed during the experimental period. Even movements often turned out to be wrong. Going up steps was miscalculated by as much as a foot. Once, in going through the house, Stratton came to two doors side by side. He was on the verge of reaching for the wrong one when a difference in the metalwork of one called attention to his mistake, and he checked it. In the very effort to avoid things, he ran into them. His first day without lenses also brought on a spell of dizziness and nausea. Of course, in time there was a complete readjustment to the older way of doing and seeing things.

Ewert's laboratory study. In 1929, Harry P. Ewert, then a professor at Clark University, persuaded his friends, Norman L. Munn and Walter S. Hunter, to join him in an experiment. Two reversing lens systems held before the eyes by a headgear and mask were to be worn for 3 weeks. The purpose of the experiment was to observe in the laboratory what happened to movements that had to be learned with complete dependence on vision that had been disrupted (Ewert, 1930).

Results showed a great interference of various coordinated movements, but there was a rapid adjustment to the visual interference. At the end of 14 days of practice with lenses on, this interference was almost entirely overcome in some activities and almost overcome in others. The persistence of newly acquired behavior during the topsy-turvy period was not noted in any measurable form on removal of the lenses. In this respect, Ewert's results do not support those of Stratton. There appears to be a contradiction on this point. Furthermore, both experiments utilized lenses that magnified in addition to inverting the position of objects in space. A third point bears mention. An experiment that involves a radical change in seeing things must permit as long a period of time as possible in order to test for adaptation of perceptual reactions under these conditions.

The Snyder and Pronko study.   For these reasons, the experiment with Fred Snyder as subject (Snyder and Pronko, 1951) was carried out. The contradiction between Ewert's and Stratton's results needed to be checked. Do the new habits built up during the interval when the inverting lenses are worn persist or not? Since Snyder wore the inverting lenses for 30 days, much longer than the 195 hours and 56 minutes achieved in the Ewert experiment, the answer ought to be more clear-cut. We further improved the experiment by using lenses that do not magnify the visual field.

For a week prior to the day the inverting lenses were to be put on, Snyder was given a daily series of trials in various laboratory tasks. One of his jobs was to sort cards into nine different compartments. Another was the Minnesota Rate of Manipulation test. This requires that each of 64 checkerlike blocks of wood be lifted from a frame having holes into which the blocks fit, turned over, and replaced as quickly as possible. A third task involved the Purdue Pegboard. This test, which is used in some industries, requires lifting a small metal peg with one hand and a washer with another, assembling the two, and placing them in a row of holes in the board. A final job was to trace, via a mirror, a narrow star-shaped channel with a stylus. Every time the side is touched, an error is registered on an electric counter. Time was kept on all tasks. They proved to be satisfactory because of the graded difficulty in coordination they permitted. During his week's practice without lenses, Snyder's learning curves showed a leveling off for each of these tasks. In other words, the reaction involved was fairly stable and could be used as a base for comparing future performance with lenses on.

Then the day came to put the headgear on. The apparatus consisted of sheet aluminum bands running front-to-back and side-to-side over the head. Both of these were fastened to another band encircling the head much like the brim of a hat. The latter band had a goggles frame attached to it that served as a housing for the tubes containing the lenses. Sponge rubber was fitted around the goggles frame to exclude light and under the bands to cushion their pressure against the head. The headgear is shown in Figures 9-12 and 9-13.

Snyder's first sight of the world was a topsy-turvy scene in which up became down; down, up; right, left; and left, right. Things were not only upside down but reversed in a horizontal plane. (See Figure 9-14). Initial laboratory tests were almost impossible. Card sorting had to be given up. The

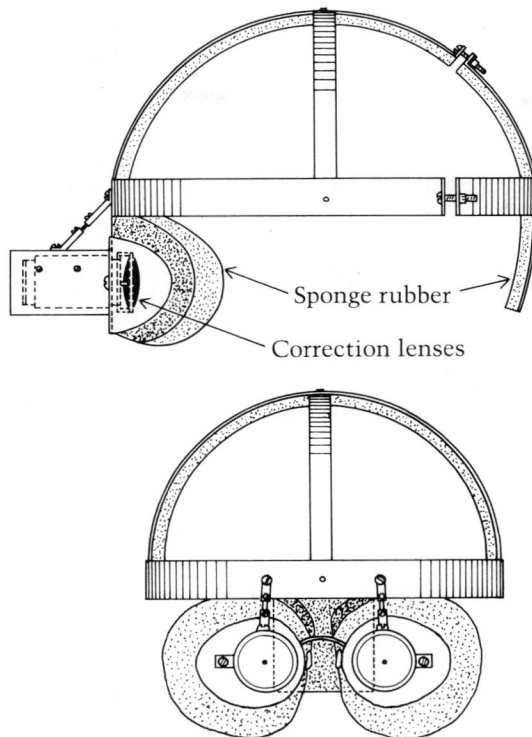

Sponge rubber

Correction lenses

Figure 9-12   Front and side view of headgear showing placement of lens system. (From Snyder and Pronko, 1952.)

Minnesota Rate of Manipulation test was fumbled. Occasionally, the subject reached for a fifth block that was not there. The Purdue Pegboard was quite hopeless and the Mirror Drawing almost futile. Snyder just could not get started. He insisted on going backward, which got him nowhere. During this task, he remarked, "Every move I make just gets me into trouble instead of on my way."

Outside the laboratory, things were no better. Snyder would climb into the back of a car, in reverse, attempting to sit against the back of the front seat. In walking on the campus walk, Snyder walked off it in the very effort to stay on it. The same occurred on the street. Since people on Snyder's left appeared to be on his right, he would shift to the left so as to avoid hitting them and thus collide with them. Steps and curbs gave trouble, too. Often he would step up too late and fall or else try to step up while still a foot or two away from the curb. Eating was painful to execute as well as to behold. Putting sugar into a glass of iced tea was accomplished by cautiously starting from the side nearest Snyder, bringing spoon and glass together, and

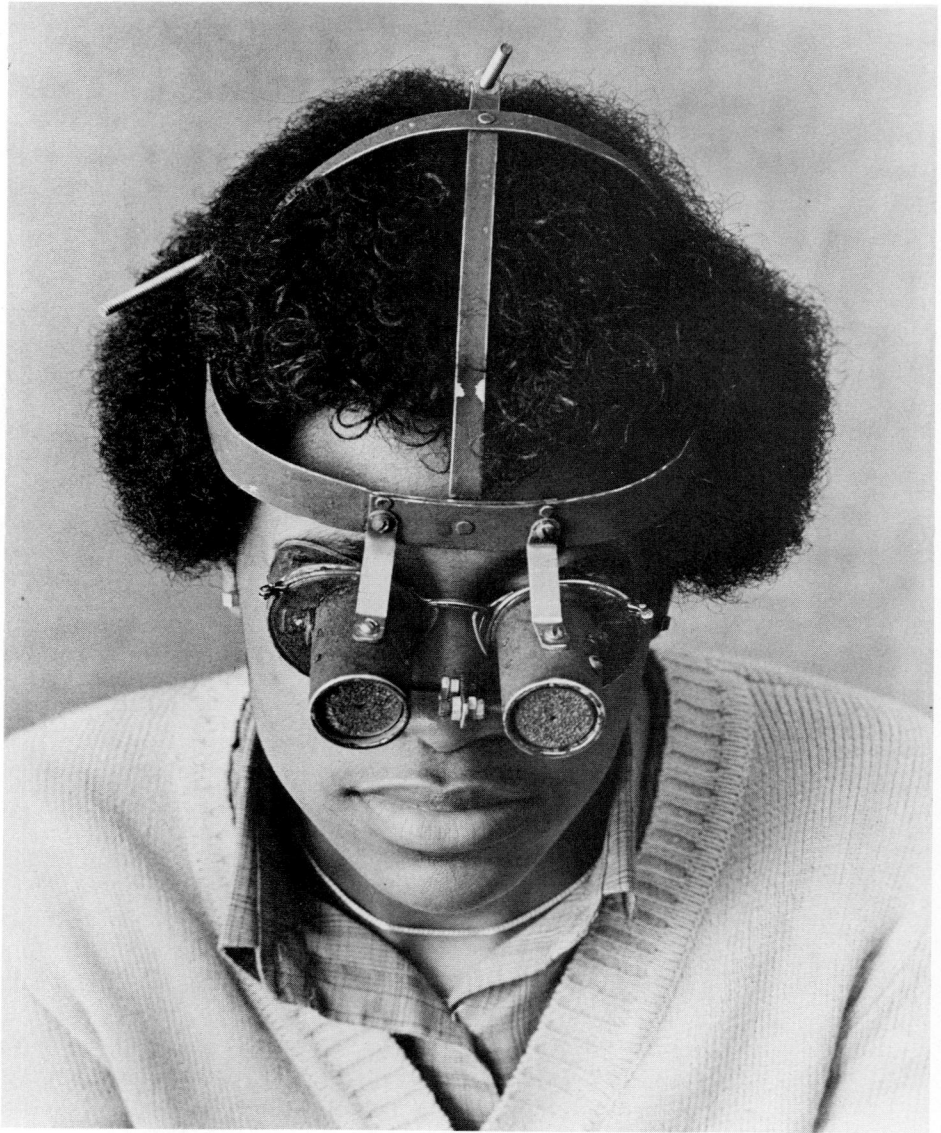

Figure 9-13   Front view of subject wearing inverting lenses. The small hole in the lens covering drastically restricts field of vision. (After Snyder and Pronko, 1952.)

pouring it in a direction away from him. Naturally, to Snyder, this looked as normal as the average person's putting sugar into tea by leaning the spoon from the farther side of the glass. Cutting a pie with a fork also had to be

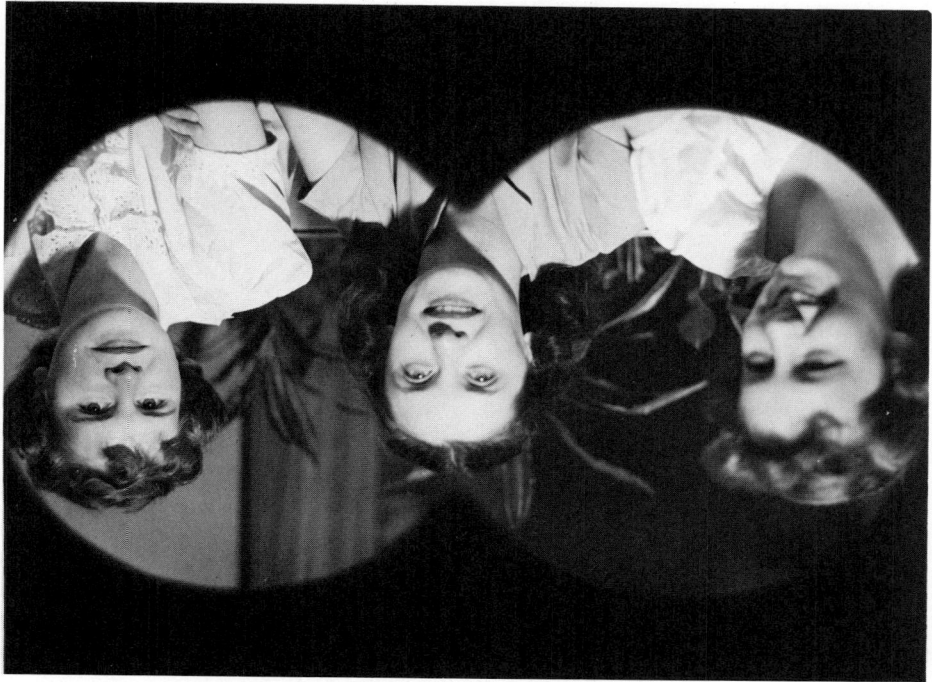

Figure 9-14   A view of Snyder's upside-down world through the upside-down lenses.

studiously worked out. Assume that the wedge of pie faces Snyder with the apex toward him. In attacking the pie, Snyder knew better. He realized that the apex appeared to be away from him but searched for it where the base seemed to be. Much trial and error was bound to bring some measure of success—although it should be stated that Snyder's first encounter with a lemon chiffon pie was a gastronomic catastrophe.

Putting the inverting lenses on Snyder produced a perceptual upheaval. The learning curves that had shown a continued drop in time and errors that leveled off showed a tremendous increase over both, but before the conclusion of the experiment, both curves continued to decline (to improve) until the point at which the lenses were removed. At this point, we had another rise in the time and error curve with early recovery and, again, continued improvement. Here is the significant implication. If you cover up the blips in the continuous learning curves that occur (1) at the point when the inverting lenses were put on and (2) when they were removed, you find a typical learning curve showing reduction in time and errors over the *entire experimental period!* This fact seems to show that perceptual adaptation is an ongoing affair that can overcome whatever conditions arise. Of course, the effect of once more removing the inverting lenses at the end of the experiment was not as long-lasting or as marked as putting them on turned out to be. But we must remember that Snyder had worn those topsy-turvy lenses only 30 days, after having *not* worn them for 25 years, so we should not expect marked changes in so short a time. What we need really, for comparison purposes, is for subjects to wear Snyder's inverting lenses for 25 years, then to *not* wear them for 30 days, and then wear them again. Do you think the results would be any different? Whatever your response, perceiving interactions, like other psychological interactions, shows the same modifiability, or change, over time. That's the main point of this particular discussion.

Social Factors in Perceiving

If you have ever looked down the roadbed of railroad tracks, you undoubtedly noticed that the rails seemed to converge instead of looking parallel. This is linear perspective, which the artist must apply to a painting with any depth in it. The kind of perception involved in sighting down railroad tracks is a three-dimensional (3-D) space. But with the experience that we have had in our culture with both 3-D space and with paintings and photos, which are only 2-D (or two-dimensional flat space), we can get a 3-D effect in photos and paintings, too.

The Ponzo illusion supports the notion that we can get a 3-D effect on a flat surface. If you look at Figure 9-15, representing a view of railroad tracks disappearing into the distance, noting particularly the two logs lying on the tracks, the one that appears to be farther away looks longer. Yet, if you measure them, you will note that they are the same size. Why is this? One explanation involves the misapplication of depth cues that have worked for us in three-dimensional space. They cannot be prevented from working in the two-dimensional Ponzo figure because all of our perceptions are of a piece. As Kilbride and Leibowitz (1977, pp. 409–410) explain it, "Since in our normal interaction with space we 'correct' for distant objects in the interest of size constancy, this same correction is misapplied in a two-dimensional presentation, thereby producing an illusory enlargement of the object located 'far away' near the point of convergence of the figure."

The next logical question is "Does everyone respond to the Ponzo illusion in the manner described?" No. For one thing, it develops with chronological age (and, presumably, experience). And "many cross-cultural studies have demonstrated that individuals from various cultural groups differ in their susceptibility to visual illusions" (Kilbride and Leibowitz, 1977, p. 408).

Kilbride, an anthropologist, and Leibowitz, a psychologist, joined forces in studying the Ponzo illusion in the Baganda. An earlier study by Leibowitz and Pick (1972) had shown that the Ponzo illusion is essentially nonexistent among the rural population of Baganda. In essence, the difference between those who perceived the Ponzo illusion and those who did not was given an

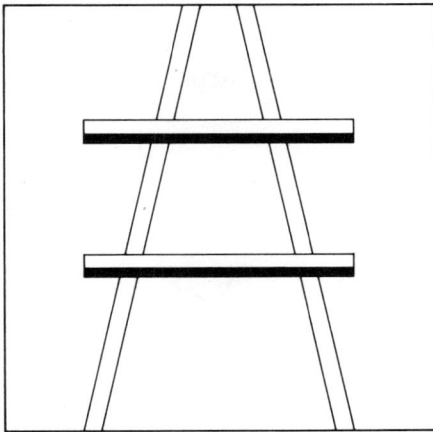

Figure 9-15 The Ponzo illusion, a three-dimensional effect on a flat surface. See text for explanation.

ecological explanation: Those who perceived the photos and other stimuli three-dimensionally resembled Uganda and Pennsylvania college students. Both perceived the Ponzo illusion. Not so with the rural Ugandan villagers, who found "essentially no illusion" (p. 416). Thus, exposure to reading materials, photographs, and representational art as social psychological variables plays a role in the kind of perception that Kilbride and Leibowitz worked with. Figure 9-16 illustrates the role of the reactional biography in what and how we perceive.

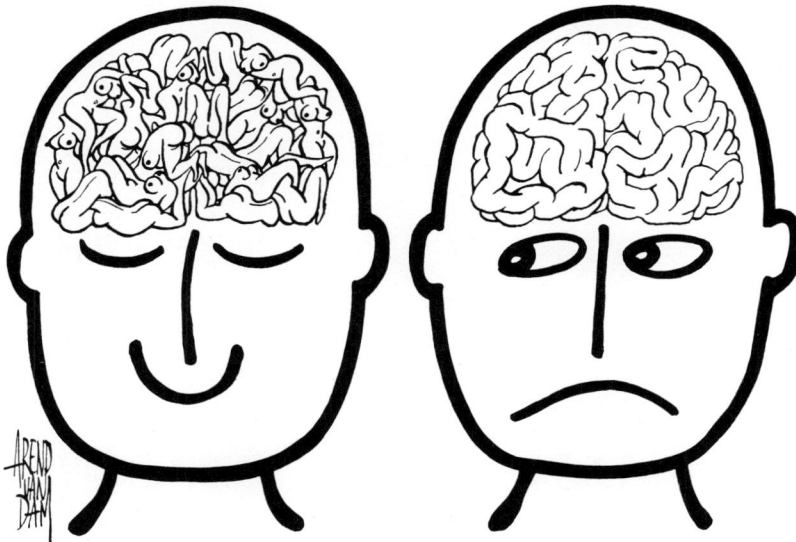

Figure 9-16 What do you perceive? Would a young child perceive what you perceive? (Arend Van Dam, artist.)

Chapter Summary

This chapter explored the two initial phases of every unit of behavior, attending and perceiving. Skinner defines attention as being "under the control of a stimulus" and Kantor's specification of it is preparatory and auxiliary. Extreme specificity is manifested in attention. Various factors affect attending, and there are many fine distinctions among inattention, attentional posture, sustained attention, distraction, and attentional alternation.

In analyzing perception, a self-actional and an interactional or interbehavioral view can be compared via Hanson's fresh and simple insights into the nature of perception. Gestalt views and rules about organization of aspects of stimulus objects provide valuable approaches to perception. The ancient bent-stick problem and illusions can be treated as "veridical" or "non-veridical" perceptions. Language, organismic "needs," the reactional biography, and social psychological conditions also affect perception.

10 Implicit Interactions: Thinking, Remembering, Forgetting, Recalling, and So On

No amount of looking inside the organism, or speculating about internal processes, is as relevant to the use of the term thinking *as are the history, current circumstances, and behavior of the person in question.* Thinking is purely and simply a behavioral concept, *and any other use of the term is either a corruption or the substitution of a different concept.*

[Bourne, Ekstrand, and Dominowski, 1971, p. 5]

As with other terms in psychology, the term *thinking* is also an importation from popular language. As such, its usage for us must be as sharply delineated as we can possibly make it. Certainly, we get no help from its conventional applications to such situations as the following.

1. I've lost my keys and I say to you, "I can't think when I had them last." What I actually mean is that I can't *recall* the occasion on which I used them the last time.
2. I ask you what you think of the Equal Rights Amendment and you say, "I'm for it." My question is a request for a statement of your "stance," "orientation," or "attitude" toward the Equal Rights Amendment.
3. "Do you think you'll go to Europe next summer?" This statement translates to "Do you anticipate going to Europe next summer?"

4. "Will you think to bring me the book you promised me?" This question does not ask you to sit down promptly and deliberate, cogitate, reason, or ponder. I am asking you to remember, to initiate an action that you will later complete by picking up that book and bringing it to me.

As seemingly diverse as these illustrations are, they nevertheless have something in common. They all involve a separation, in time and/or space, between the responding organism and the stimulus object involved. My attempts at responding to my keys now implicate me in recent *past* situations with those keys. When I inquire about your attitude toward the Equal Rights Amendment, the situation is different from one in which we stand before the Lincoln Memorial and I ask you what you "think" of it. There is no Equal Rights Amendment standing before us. Your anticipation of going to Europe is a psychological event that occurs *in advance* of your actually going. And your remembering to bring me that book connects your behavior *now* with your action on a *future* occasion and in a different place. Following in Kantor and Smith's footsteps, we shall call such interbehaviors *implicit*. For help in explicating the term *implicit*, let us refresh ourselves with the notion of perception as semiimplicit.

Perceiving as a Halfway House to Implicit Behavior

In our discussion of perception, we noted that no discriminatory interaction with a given stimulus object could be understood separate from interactions with prior related stimulus objects. To return to the cow illustration in Figure 9-2, your seeing it as a cow is not simply a cognition of it but a *re*-cognition. In a sense, what we have done by bringing you and Figure 9-2 together is to reinstate an interbehavior that was organized earlier. Here, incidentally, is an instance of prediction and control. By bringing together the variables that were involved in the earlier perceptual interbehavior, we can make it happen again. But what we need to stress in our present development is that the occurrence of the present perceptual interaction depends on a previous occurrence. It is really a recurrence or repetition of a prior event. Arnheim's (1971, p. 80) notion that a "perceptual act is never isolated; it is only the most recent phase of a stream of innumerable similar acts performed in the past" bears repetition because it helps to pinpoint the meaning of the term *semiimplicit*. With this term, we call attention to the fact that, although the cow is present before us, as we interact with it now, we nevertheless also react to it partially in terms of our past interactions with it. The words *implicit* and *implicate* derive from the same root Latin verb. *Webster's Unabridged Dictionary* defines *implicit* as "infolded, entangled, involved" and "not ostensible," and it defines *implicate* as "to involve deeply" or "to bring into intimate connection." Actually, we should think of a perceptual interaction as a large event comprising at least two related or connected perceptual events as the following diagram attempts to represent for our cow stimulus object. The present and prior perceptual events are "entangled" or "involved deeply" or are in "intimate connection." They belong together as a single unit.

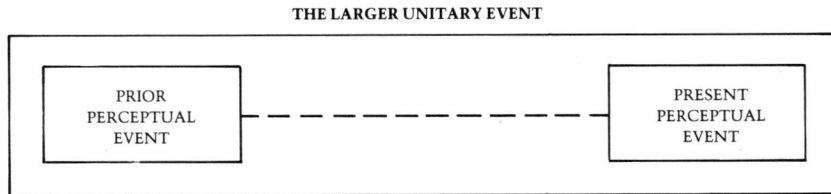

THE LARGER UNITARY EVENT

PRIOR PERCEPTUAL EVENT	– – – – – – – – –	PRESENT PERCEPTUAL EVENT

From Semiimplicit to Fully Implicit

We are now ready for the next step that will take us from semiimplicit to fully implicit interbehaviors. This time, with book closed, I ask you to "'think' about the cow you just saw in the book." If I question you in some detail about the cow, fence, and sky in the picture, you respond fairly satisfactorily, as we can verify by looking in the book. Now, here we have a fully implicit response because your response now is in total absence of the cow. You must get along without the illustration that was right under your nose during your perceiving act.

The situation described appears to violate our principle declared much earlier that there is never a response without a stimulus. Is this an exception? No, because if you reread my instructions to you, I *asked* you to "think about the cow you just saw in the book." This was the variable that connected your response with the (now) absent stimulus object, the cow picture. That variable we shall designate as the substitute stimulus (Kantor and Smith, 1975, pp. 198–199). It functioned to elicit your response. Something else might have had the same stimulus function, such as the word *cow* in a child's nursery book or even a glass of milk you might be drinking. In such instances, we may say that that stimulus object "pinch hits" for the absent stimulus object. In everyday terms, we call such stimulus functions "reminders." The following diagram contrasts a substitute stimulus function such as we have been considering here with a direct stimulus function that works to elicit reactions toward the eliciting stimulus object.

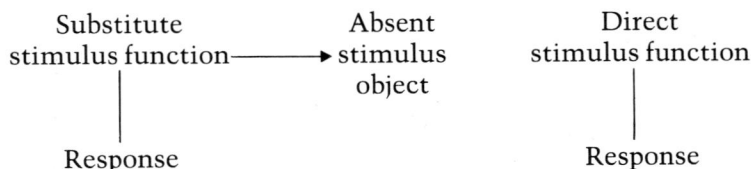

Substitute stimulus function———▶	Absent stimulus object	Direct stimulus function
Response		Response

So far, we have recognized the operation of stimulus functions residing in stimulus objects other than the stimulus object toward which a response is directed. But a stimulus object can elicit implicit interactions directed toward itself. For example, a little girl, looking at her well-worn doll, remarks how beautiful it was when she first gazed on it last Christmas. In this case, the doll (coincidentally) serves both a direct and a substitute stimulus function, the latter when the girl's response is directed toward the doll in a past situation (as when the doll was brand new). But a direct stimulus function is elicited when the little girl responds to the doll in the present by noting the doll's missing arm, cracked head, and so on. In passing, then, we simply mark that a stimulus object can function psychologically in such a way as to involve the responding organism with it in terms of a past relationship.

A further illustration of implicit interaction.   Let us proceed with more illustrations in an attempt to corroborate our interpretation of implicit action. A woman has just been widowed. She has just returned home from the funeral but is still "grief stricken." She weeps and will not be comforted. The striking feature about her behavior is that her dead husband is no longer there before her. The common saying (stated in mentalistic terms), "Out of sight, out of mind," does not hold in her case, for her reaction is to an absent stimulus object. How the interaction originated can be traced out from the series of preceding events. We may begin our account at the point when she gazed on her dead husband for the last time, just before they closed the casket. On this occasion, she gave full vent to her sense of bereavement. After the funeral, she returned home, but grief overwhelmed her even there. It is apparent that reactions to absent stimulus objects are not always subtle (inapparent). As for substitute stimuli in this case, we need look no further than the dead husband's watch, pipe, clothes, favorite chair, and so on, that were so *intimately* connected with him and that "pinch hit" so effectively for the dead husband in continuing to elicit the widow's grief reactions. In absence of the dead husband, the widow's sorrow can be as complete to the last detail (sobbing, moaning, crying, shedding tears) as when the corpse was before her. Thus, the action of the organism in the absence of a given stimulus object can be matched with a response to that stimulus object when it is actually present.

There is no such thing as pure thought.   It is a fact of nature that organisms do respond to absent stimulus objects. Such events are as undeniable as our comings and goings or as rain and snow. Several points follow from their full acceptance. Contrary to popular psychology's notion that thoughts just arise self-actionally—that they are uncaused—there is no such thing as "pure thought." "Thought" is always about somebody, something, or some situation. Therefore, the "somebody, something, or some situation" is as essential as the organism, for, without them, the "thinking" or implicit interaction cannot occur. There is no exception here to the scientific principle that all interactions are a joint function of at least two variables. If I can hum portions of the choral movement of Beethoven's *Ninth Symphony* for you now, that symphonic movement and I must have encountered each other in the past. As to how my implicit interaction with it came about at all, let us assume that you *asked* me if I knew it; that is, you provided the substitute stimulus function for that response.

Inapparent substitute stimulus functions. The incident directly above in which you ask me if I am familiar with the choral movement of Beethoven's *Ninth Symphony* reveals the operation of a substitute stimulus that is hard to miss. However, there are instances when the action of a substitute stimulus is of such a delicate sort that it can be detected with difficulty, if at all. The following incident illustrates the point.

I am walking on the outskirts of a certain town, when (as we say) "out of the blue" I catch myself humming the Scottish tune, "Loch Lomond," which has the lines "I'll take the high road and you'll take the low road." With faith in the kind of formulation I have presented for such interbehaviors, I begin to look for substitute stimuli in my surroundings. Taking note of my whereabouts, I observe that I had been walking in Maxwell Lane and at the moment had crossed into High Street when I recalled a phrase from another Scottish song, "Maxwelton's braes are bonnie." A moment later, I thought of the song "Loch Lomond." It satisfies me to interpret this event as the action of very subtly acting substitute stimuli. Had there been only a Maxwell Lane *or* a High Street, the event referred to might not have come about because of an inadequate stimulus function. Perhaps, the summation of both provided an effective substitute stimulus function. And, from an analytic standpoint, I might never have been able to isolate the substitute stimulus function if it had worked with only one of the two stimuli involved. In such a case, the operation of the substitute stimulus would have been inapparent. When the substitute stimulus function is not discernible, the layperson is likely to resort to self-actional interpretations in terms of hypothetical goings-on in the head.

Inapparent organismic action in implicit interbehaviors. We need to be occasionally reminded that implicit interactions always constitute field events in which organism, absent stimulus object, and substitute stimulus object are all interrelated. This point is particularly important as we now focus on the organism's action as an aspect of the total field. In some cases, as in the instance of the grieving widow, the organism's action is quite apparent. But, we need to realize that the organism's participation in implicit interactions can also be as subtle and difficult to detect as we have noted in the case of the substitute stimulus function. In such instances, the organism's action is both silent and invisible.

But are visibility and audibility the sole criteria for establishing scientific data? If this were true, the scope of the sciences would surely be greatly diminished. Physicists would ignore magnetism, cosmic radiation, and atomic particles. Chemists could not handle such data as catalytic action or even the ever-so-subtle gas, oxygen. Nor can the biologist actually see or hear nerves jump or move, but he or she nevertheless speaks of neural "action." Similarly, in psychology, we must subsume under the term *action* the organism's participation in implicit interaction that ranges from violent aggression at one end to passive revery at the other. Thus, the term *action* must be redefined to include, in all the sciences, action that may show a continuity ranging from gross or crude at one end to subtle at the other. We may expect to find various aspects of implicit interbehaviors at the subtle end of the continuum.

One's own behavior as a source of substitute stimulus function. Another subtlety enters the picture when it is impossible to pinpoint another object, person, or a situation performing a substitute stimulus function. For example, a student with self-actional theoretical leanings complains that he was lying in bed, alone in a pitch-dark room, and thought of something. How could that be? That student is overlooking an important point that we covered in discussing the self-reaction. We established there that people do respond to their own behavior. The singer monitoring his or her own rendition of a song and the actor his or her acting *while they are performing* are examples. But one's own behavior can also perform a substitute stimulus function. The singer can flatten a certain note and recall a similar accident that befell her in a recital in Chicago a year ago. Her flat note as a substitute stimulus functioned to elicit an implicit response to a past occasion. Her teacher could have served the same substitute stimulus function by asking her if she recalled the incident. But, that was not the case; it was her own behavior that called out her response. One's own substitute stimulus functions are easily overlooked because they operate so subtly and easily, probably because all our interactons are so inextricably interconnected with each other.

How Implicit Interactions Arise

Essentially, implicit interactions involve an attenuation, or a loosening up, of space and time variables. Because these aspects may give trouble in understanding implicit events, we must give them fuller consideration at this point. A study by Lipsitt and Kaye may provide us with a proper starting point for our venture. Lipsitt and Kaye (1964) were interested in finding out if they could condition a sucking response in 3- or 4-day-old infants. They used a tone as a conditioning stimulus and insertion of a nipple in the baby's mouth as an unconditioned stimulus. To make a long story short, they found that infants in the third or fourth day of life do learn, for they started sucking when they heard the tone. Translated into our present framework, what Lipsitt and Kaye are saying is that their babies did not have to wait until the nipple touched the interior of their mouth. The immediately preceding sound came to be an adequate "signal" for the oncoming nipple-in-mouth. Here, we begin to see the attenuation of space–time variables that is so characteristic of implicit psychological interactions.

Somewhat further along, the infant opens its mouth to an approaching spoonful of food delivered by Momma. This is more of the same thing, as is the game "Peek-a-boo" played by mother and child. Still later examples are furnished by intelligence tests that require the child to repeat digits that, although uttered once and are "gone with the wind," must be reproduced exactly as they were recited by the tester seconds ago. Or the tester reads a short story, on completion of which the child must either furnish a brief resumé of that story or answer questions about it in *retrospect*. In other words, the child must "hang onto" the story after being separated from it.

The Detachedness Permitted by Implicit Interactions

It is interesting to note that the developers of intelligence tests saw the attentuation of space–time variables that we have been discussing as an index of a child's psychological development. Full compliance with the aforementioned mentalistic adage, "Out of sight, out of mind," would surely reduce one to "idiocy." Suppose that all our interactions were restricted to the "here and now" of only those stimulus objects that happened to be "right under our noses." Surely, our behavior would not show the adaptiveness permitted by the spatiotemporal detachment characteristics of implicit interactions. They make it possible for us to "give heed to the morrow," to enjoy once more a past occasion, or to wear out our griefs in repeat performances following tragic incidents.

Different Kinds of Implicit Interactions

Our analysis thus far reveals a heterogeneous conglomeration of implicit interbehaviors. We have considered together (1) my attempts at recalling where I lost my keys, (2) an attitude toward the Equal Rights Amendment, (3) anticipation of a trip to Europe, (4) a remembering act, and (5) the widow's grieving over her husband's death. Despite their heterogeneity, they belong together because they involve interactions with an absent stimulus object via a substitute stimulus.

Now, following in the footsteps of Kantor and Smith (1975), we consider the different forms or configurations that implicit interactions assume. Our examination of them should teach us more about implicit behavior.

A brain is no more needed as the carrier through which thinking is conveyed than ether was needed to carry the light waves.

[Bentley, in Ratner, Altman, and Wheeler, 1964, p. 524]

Revived Interactions

Can you recall your most embarrassing moment? Imagine that you committed a serious breach of etiquette among a distinguished company. At such a moment, you can *reexperience* the loss of poise and the shame that you felt then; you may even actually blush at the recollection of the incident. That incident is past and gone, yet your response may be a close match to the original one. The present response, initiated by a substitute stimulus function, qualifies as a revived implicit interaction.

But it is Shakespeare's Lady Macbeth[1] that provides us with the best example of a revived interaction. Lady Macbeth goaded her husband to murder King Duncan so that Macbeth could succeed to the crown. She even collaborated in the act. Even if we knew nothing of the murder episode, we might reconstruct it from Lady Macbeth's revived implicit interaction during her somnambulism. A lady-in-waiting and a doctor witness Lady Macbeth's repeated "washing of her hands." Here are some excerpts from the famous sleepwalking scene:

> *Gentlewoman attending on Lady Macbeth:* It is an accustomed action with her, to seem thus washing her hands: I have known her to continue in this a quarter of an hour.
> *Lady Macbeth:* Yet here's a spot. . . .
> *Lady Macbeth:* Out, damned spot! out, I say! . . . Yet who would have thought the old man to have had so much blood in him?
> *Lady Macbeth:* What, will these hands ne'er be clean? . . . Here's the smell of the blood still: all the perfumes of Arabia will not sweeten this little hand. Oh, oh, oh!

Had Lady Macbeth been a practiced hit-woman (or hit-person), her sleep might not have been interrupted by her dramatic, repeated reenactment of the murder scene. Just incidentally, we may speculate that her sleep distur-

---

[1]Shakespeare's characters are so lifelike that I am analyzing Lady Macbeth's behavior as if she were a real, living person

bance is the result of "conflict and discord between warring aspects of her personality." Had she been as thoroughly innocent as Desdemona or completely and exclusively evil, the sleepwalking incident could hardly have come into being. But the chief lesson for us at this point lies in the details of her implicit action. Although her hands must have been washed clean immediately after the murder, she acts as if they were still bloodied. From her remarks, we may infer that, after the king's murder, she was appalled by the copious blood in which the king lay, by the unbearable smell of the blood, and by the horror of the whole sight. It is an interesting conclusion to Lady Macbeth's histrionic performance to note that the doctor and lady-in-waiting, sole observers of her performance, were convinced, thereby, of her complicity in the king's slaying. This is another way of saying that they understood her action as a *revived* implicit action.

Continuative Interactions

You and I have had a long and violent argument. You stalk angrily out of my office. The strange thing about your behavior is that your anger is not assuaged as soon as you are out of my sight. In fact, you may even grow angrier than before you departed. In any case, your behavior illustrates a continuative implicit interaction, starting out as a direct response with my contribution to our argument serving a direct stimulus function. However, at that point when I become an absent stimulus object, your behavior is classifiable as an implicit interaction of the continuative sort. The case of the grieving widow belongs here, for her grief began as she gazed for the last time on her dead husband, but it became implicit and continuative at the closing of the casket.

In the way of a more detailed explanation of continuative implicit interbehaviors, let us consider the case of a child who is spanked for a misdeed by an angry parent. The spanking starts off with a vociferous crying spell on the part of the child. Here is a direct response to a directly present stimulus function, the spanking. But the crying goes on and on, long after the spanking ceases. How are we to understand this? The answer is that we must look to the child's behavior to "keep the show going" in a chain-reaction sort of way. It is possible to see how the child's *boo* leads on to the next *hoo*, which leads to the next *boo*, and the next *hoo*, and so on. The behavior is, in a sense, "self-perpetuating," for we have observed that a person's own behavior can stimulate further behavior.

At this point, a charming (true) story can illustrate the point. A 4-year-old, spanked for an infringement of the adult code, "naturally" cried. After an interval, the mother advised, "Now, that's enough crying, Robbie, but if you want to cry some more, why don't you bring your little chair here by me and keep right on crying?" Robbie took his mother's suggestion and settled himself into his own chair, but the continuative implicit interaction had exhausted itself and his crying had come to a halt. So, Robbie said to his mother, "Well, help me get started." Fortunately, no continuative implicit response can go on forever, probably because psychological interactions are modifiable and other stimulus objects enter the picture.

Incipient Interactions

Webster's Seventh New Collegiate Dictionary defines the word *incipient* as "beginning to be" or "commencing." That definition is acceptable as a description of the type of implicit interaction presently before us. Let's assume that you met a man some time ago and you want to tell a friend about him. You are sure that the man's name began with the letter *J*, but that's as far as you get. Was it Johnson, Jackson, Jenkins? None seems right, so you give up. Later, the incipient response achieves "closure" when you are positive that the name was Jennings. A probable explanation for such "it's-on-the-tip-of-my-tongue" behavior is an inadequate substitute stimulus. Woodworth (1940, p. 350) suggests that one not persist in trying to complete the incipient response head on. He thinks it's better to "try-rest-try again." In my opinion, the lack of "closure" in the initial stages of recall points to an inadequacy of the substitute stimulus function. Letting the matter drop for a time permits another substitute stimulus object to function adequately so as to complete the response. Above all, we should not overlook the fact that the proper substitute stimulus function connects your behavior now with an absent stimulus object in the past (Mr. Jennings of our illustration). Here is another affirmation of the notion that behavior (as Skinner would put it) is "under the control of stimuli" or, with a more field type of orientation, behavior is a function of stimulus objects, media of contact, setting factors, and so on, rather than of hypothetical "internal" agents. As Bentley stated the matter in the quote at the beginning of this section (a statement that bears repeating), "A brain is no more needed as the carrier through which thinking [or implicit behavior] is conveyed than ether was needed to carry the light waves" (quoted in Ratner, Altman, and Wheeler, 1964, p. 524). If we can make sense of implicit behaviors by working with observable variables, we do not need imaginary, self-actional, internal agents.

Anticipatory Interactions

The dog cringes as its harsh master's stick is raised. The child cries as the hypodermic needle is being prepared. The patient in the dentist's chair winces before the drill contacts his or her tooth. People "jump the gun." These cases demonstrate that implicit interactions can look to the future as well as the past. The former are subsumed under anticipatory implicit interactions. However, before proceeding, we must not overlook the fact that the organisms in the preceding illustrations behave the way they do because they have had previous experience in the situations indicated. Otherwise, anticipatory implicit interactions do not occur. Thus, they have the same historical origin as all other behaviors.

Auto driving and anticipatory behavior. For many years, the National Safety Council has recommended that automobile drivers should practice defensive driving. This translates, I think, into anticipatory implicit interactions. One must try to out-guess the other drivers' intentions. Will they change lanes suddenly, cross the yellow line? Also, one must drive anticipatorily with respect to the road on the other side of the hill. Could there be a stalled car in your lane that your high speed would prevent your stopping in time to avoid an accident? The same applies to the invisible portion of the bend in the road that you are approaching. And shouldn't you be prepared, at least occasionally, for a tire blowout?

Anticipatory heart rate in rope climbing. Kozar (1964) reports frequent observations of heart rate increase immediately prior to sudden and violent exertion. Dogs that were studied experimentally showed an increase in heart rate that was too sudden to be explained by traditional mechanical or hormonal concepts. In dogs that had been exercised on a treadmill, marked increases in heart rate occurred "when the dog was lifted on to the treadmill, when the operator was reaching for the switch to start the treadmill, and at the sound of a loud noise" (Kozar, 1964, p. 311). These cardiac responses showed up in the very next cardiac cycle. But it is Kozar's experimental study of rope climbing in athletes that we turn to next for greater illumination of the details of anticipatory implicit interactions.

Kozar used telemetry, a recently introduced "wireless" technological development, for measuring heart rate at a distance. A miniature radio transmitter "broadcast" instantaneous heartbeats that were recorded at a distance for measurement and analysis.

Kozar (1964) obtained these telemetered heart records for ten gymnasts, in excellent physical condition, whom he studied prior to, during, and following, a severe, short-duration exercise—namely, climbing a 20-foot rope as fast as possible. Kozar told his subjects that they would be given a 2-minute warm-up session consisting of chinning and similar types of activities, after which they would hear a preparatory "ready" and then a "go" signal. He recorded their heart rate continuously from the point of the subjects' post warm-up.

Since we are here discussing anticipatory implicit interactions, our interest in Kozar's findings lies in the differences in heart rate in the period between the instant when they stopped their warm-up exercises and just prior to "Go." Table 10-1 shows the results for each subject from post warm-up to just prior to "Go" and percentage of total increase to that point.

Before we go on to a closer look at the results, one point must be emphatically stated, and that concerns the *heart-rate base* that Kozar (1964) used. His gymnasts were not in a state of complete rest and relaxation just before they climbed the rope. In fact, the base rate was obtained immediately following a 2-minute spurt of fairly vigorous exercise! So the gymnasts' hearts were already pounding fairly rapidly. Yet, they increased over and

Table 10-1   Heart-rate records of subjects in an experiment to measure anticipatory heart rate in rope climbing. Compare the figures in the "Post-warm-up" column with those in the column headed "Prior to 'go.' " The percentage of total anticipatory increase is shown in the last column.

SUBJECT NUMBER	POST-WARM-UP	PRIOR TO "GO"	PERCENT OF TOTAL ANTICIPATORY INCREASE
1	72	98	36.1
2	90	98	8.8
3	98	104	6.1
4	86	128	48.8
5	109	138	27.0
6	98	120	22.0
7	96	108	12.5
8	108	125	15.7
9	88	122	38.6
10	84	120	42.8

Source: After Kozar, 1964, p. 313. Reproduced by permission of *Ergonomics.*

above that rate at the mere anticipation of climbing the rope. The individual records can be compared in Columns 2 and 3 of Table 10-1 while the percentages of total anticipatory increases prior to "Go" appear in the last column. The range extends from 6.1% to 4.8%· For the entire group, the average anticipatory heartbeat increases come to 25%·

Kozar views the anticipatory behavior of his gymnasts as of possible adaptive value. On this point he writes as follows: "It may be beneficial to have the anticipatory increase of heart rate just prior to beginning the rope climb, or any other task of a short duration which requires an all-out effort" (Kozar, 1964, p. 314). Kozar seems to be saying that implicit anticipatory responses such as he worked with can add a margin of adaptation over and above that provided by adjustments of a physiological sort. In fact, he even recommends that coaches and physical-education teachers consider the application of his findings to the possible improvement of athletic performance. Aside from possible applications, the findings themselves are an instance of what I mentioned previously—that implicit interactions free the organism from reacting in the "here and now." Implicit responses not only connect us to the past in the ways indicated, but also make it possible for us to "jump the gun" in better shape than we would be without them. In either case, they have their origin in our reactional biographies.

Vestigial Interactions

Webster's Seventh New Collegiate Dictionary defines the noun *vestige* as "a fragment or remnant of what is past and gone." The term *vestigial* is the adjectival form of the root word. We can make use of that definition in our present treatment of implicit action, which has traditionally been identified with "images." If you fixate a strong light for some time and look elsewhere, you continue to see the light for some time. This has been called a "positive afterimage." But if you concentrate on a blue and green license plate for 20 or 30 seconds and then look at a gray wall, you will see a yellow and red license plate, the negative afterimage of the original visual object. A negative afterimage of a black and white figure will yield a white and black negative afterimage, the direct opposite of the original matter. In the case of colored objects or designs, the relationships are in terms of complementary colors of the original colors. Because experiences with positive and negative afterimages have little practical value, the layperson largely ignores them. But survival imagery, which we consider next, makes itself felt so strongly that it cannot be ignored.

Survival Interactions

Before we involve ourselves with survival interactions, we might profitably give brief consideration to the elusive concept of body image.

Body image.   You can look at your hand or toe or you can touch them. This is an obvious self-reaction (visual or tactual) of a perceptual sort. But, with closed eyes, you can also respond to your hand or toe without touching them, in which case you are performing an implicit interaction with your own "body part." It is reasonable to assume that during our reactional biographies we build up innumerable implicit self-reactions involving our geography, size, shape, distribution, and distance between parts, our relation to the horizontal and vertical. Even such extensions of oneself as crutches, prostheses, sword, gun, spurs, whiskers, and walking stick may be incorporated into one's body image or body schema. Gibson (1966) has suggested that touch should not be considered as being only a "proximity sense," as one requiring actual contact with the skin. In his opinion, "when a man touches something with a stick he feels it at the end of the stick, not in the hand" (pp. 100–101). In my opinion, the highly attenuated, indirect touch relationship here between organism and stimulus object borders on the implicit by comparison with skin contact with the same stimulus object.

As a test of Gibson's proposition, Vaught, Simpson, and Ryder (1968) did a study in which they required observers to perform, with the aid of a stick, a form discrimination of forms hidden from view. Of pertinent interest to us is the question whether their feeling of form discrimination was in the hand or at the end of the stick. The vast majority reported that they felt what they were probing "at the end of the stick and that sensation in the hand is of little consequence" (p. 848).[2] The important point for us is that a job ordinarily carried out by a hand in direct skin contact with an object can be assigned, so to speak, to the end of a stick (in Vaught, Simpson, and Ryder's case) 34 inches away from the hand. We see here the freeing or detachment of the implicit from spatial and temporal factors that we noted before.

Of more direct concern to us is the person's handling of self in certain situations. For example, surely, a woman who has worn a hat with a long feather in it must soon learn what passageways she can go through without damaging her feather. When she has achieved that feat, she has succeeded in incorporating that feather into her body image. Insofar as the feather operates in certain situations to determine her action, it is (in a psychological sense), an extension of herself. We are now ready to consider one type of survival implicit interaction, the so-called phantom limb and phantom sensations.

Phantom limb and phantom sensations. An anatomical loss of a leg, hand, arm, or breast does not necessarily mean what we might call a "psychological amputation." It is well established that amputees frequently report a persistent and strong feeling that the missing part is actually present as are various sensations localizable in it. Ever since 1871 when an American neurologist and novelist christened the phenomenon with the ghostly term "phantom limb," there have been about 400 reports on the subject. According to Kolb, Frank, and Watson (1952) of the Mayo Clinic, 98% of amputees in their study reported phantom limb, phantom breast, or phantom sensations. (Let us use the term "phantom phenomena" as a collective nomenclature.) They interpret the lower incidence reported in the literature as a reflection of the patients' reluctance to report such "bizarre" information about themselves or simply because no one bothered to inquire about them. Soon after their amputation, patients may "forget" that they are missing a leg, get out of bed, start to stand on their "feet," and fall flat on their faces. Some must convince themselves that they are really missing a leg by looking under the bed covers. A patient lying in bed with a mid-thigh amputation feels as if the leg is bent and that, in some unexplainable fashion, it passes through the solid mattress (without a sense of contact with it) and that it rests on the floor. Figure 10-1 represents the condition more concretely than any verbal description.

Douglas Price (1976a) of the Georgetown University School of Medicine has recently reviewed an extensive literature on phantom limb phenomena. He writes that "almost every individual who has lost a limb or part of one

---

[2] This is similar to the surgeon operating with rubber gloves on or industrial workers manipulating things with heavy asbestos gloves.

Figure 10-1 Artist's representation of a patient's phantom limb. The patient's phantom leg has the perplexing feeling of actually penetrating the solid mattress, with the foot resting on the floor. (Courtesy of Ciba Pharmaceutical Products, Inc.)

feels at one time or another that some portions of the missing part are still present" (p. 49). Included in the inventory of anatomical parts involved in phantom phenomena are the eye, ear, nose, facial tissue, tooth, larynx, breast, penis, and testicle.

Not only *presence* of the (missing) part is felt, but movement of the absent limb may also be experienced. For example, spontaneous reaching movements may be reported or a patient may attempt to catch a ball with the missing arm and hand and describe a corresponding sensation of movement. Touch sensations have also been noted. Writing about such cases, Price (1976a, p. 54) states that "a man felt in a phantom finger the former constriction of a wedding ring that had become so tight that it had to be removed some time before the amputation of his hand; and in another case, a man felt a corn on his phantom little toe, where there actually had been a corn."

Duration of phantom limb.   As to duration, Price informs us that phantom limb sensations may "survive" as long as 50 years. When we inquire about the dreams of amputees, Price states that "most amputees" dream of themselves as being intact and whole. After a year or two, some dream of themselves with the amputated part missing, but there are reports of some amputees "who have continued to dream of themselves with complete bodies for as long as thirty-two years" (Price, 1976a, p. 56). Working with 42 leprosy patients, Price (1977b) found phantom limb present in 38, or 90% of them. Six of the patients reported dreaming of themselves as being whole.

Of 24 amputees that he studied, Haber (1956) found that 12 of them could "will" movement in their phantom parts. These patients felt that they could bend their fingers. Some reported "pins and needles" sensations. Four patients continued to feel objects worn on the limb prior to amputation. One felt a watch around the phantom wrist and others felt rings on their phantom fingers. One said, "I feel a ring because it was bent and tight and so I feel it . . . on the ring next to the pinky" (Haber, 1956, p. 9).[3]

Postmastectomy breast phantoms.   In view of the recent increase in public awareness of, and greater interest in, cancer of the breast, phantom breast phenomena have come to deserve increasingly greater attention. Stimulated by the sparseness of relevant literature on breast phantom phenomena, Jarvis (1967) decided to do an exploratory study of breast sensations following amputation. He defined phantom breast sensation "as a feeling or sensation which seemed to come from the space the breast had previously filled as if the removed breast were still present" (Jarvis, 1967, p. 266).

Characteristics of phantom breast sensations.   Of the 104 patients whom Jarvis questioned, 95% reported experiencing one or more types of phantom sensations, 62% reported itching as the most frequent response, while pain occurred in 33%. "Tightness, tingling, fullness, burning, numbness, emptiness, and heaviness" (Jarvis, 1967, p. 267) occurred also but still less frequently. Since the breast does not compare in mobility to the legs, arms, or hands, it is necessarily *more or less restricted* to nonmobile phantom sensations.

An earlier study by Bressler, Cohen, and Magnussen (1956) corroborates Jarvis' findings. These workers interviewed a series of 25 patients in a follow-up study after removal of the breast. Of the 25 patients that they interviewed, 16 reported breast sensations, five of them painful ones.

Case 1.   A 45-year-old woman, seen 5 years after her operation, stated that she still felt as if the right breast were present. Sometimes she felt a mild burning or itching there.

Case 2.   A 34-year-old woman seen 3 days postoperatively complained of burning pain. She also reported that when she turned over on the operated

---

[3] Note the importance of the individual's psychological history in phantom phenomena. Do you think these individuals would have experienced survival interactions involving a wristwatch and a tight ring if they had not worn those objects prior to amputation?

side, she felt as if the breast were sliding down the side as it would have before surgery. (Here we find a *limited* mobility based on a presurgery experience of the same and, therefore, a survival of it.)

Case 4.　A 47-year-old woman, seen 3 days after a radical mastectomy with a partial surgical removal of the chest wall, stated she could not tell whether she had breasts or not until the dressing came off. "But if I should go on the feeling, I would think that both breasts were there" (Bressler, Cohen, and Magnussen, 1956, p. 182).

Making sense of phantom phenomena.　How shall we understand phantom phenomena? As usual, there are theoretical choices to be made. Probably the most popular theory involves a physiological framework. The centralists hold that, either through learning or natively, the brain somehow reactivates a given perceptual pattern in absence of the originating stimulus. The peripheral school hypothesizes that phantom sensations arise from nervous excitations in the stump or other excised area. For decades now, Kolb, a Mayo Clinic physician, has treated phantom pain, for example, as a biosocial phenomenon and has criticized physicians for dealing with pain in physiological terms. He cites the case of one patient who suffered pain in a phantom limb for over 30 years.

> During this period of time he had been exposed to 27 surgical and anesthetic procedures which had in turn severed peripheral, radicular, and spinal pathways purported as pain pathways subserving his painful leg. His final operation was a resection of the somatosensory cerebral cortex which again failed to modify his complaint. This patient's enduring painful symptom epitomizes the difficulty of reducing the problem of pain to simply physiological terms [Kolb, 1954, p. 118].

An alternative explanation.　In considering an alternative way of making sense of so-called phantom phenomena, as well as of body image, let us first set the facts straight. What are we dealing with? Neither images nor phantoms of any kind. All we can observe is people reacting to their own bodily portions and parts perceptually in myriad contacts, *in principle* no different than in their perceptual encounters with other stimulus objects in their surroundings. People also develop reactions to their bodily portions and parts of an implicit sort so that reactions that were built up involving a certain organ or part can survive an amputation. In such cases, survival implicit interactions, metaphorically speaking, have declared their independence of the anatomical portion involved *once they are established.* Consider the fact that "children up to about four years do not, as a rule, develop phantoms after limb amputations" (Jarvis, 1967, p. 271). Apparently, since flesh as flesh does not of itself produce behaviors that we label as phantom phenomena or (better still) survival implicit interactions, neither can it explain them. We need to consider the series of reactional-biography events during which individuals have acquired perceptual and, then, implicit interactions in relation to their bodily areas and parts. Once established, such responses continue for a time much as our other habitual, "automatic" responses in the form in which they were performed even after amputation of the organismic portion very essentially required in the acquisition of the response. We have reached another choice point in our attempt at understanding an important class of implicit interbehaviors.

Thinking

As mentioned at the beginning of this chapter, the term *thinking* has been used to refer to a variety of behaviors. It becomes our job at this point to try to isolate a distinctive form of psychological action. If a reminder is necessary, the term *action* comprises even the subtlest of behaviors in favor of mental states. As a first step in refining usage of the term *thinking*, we will separate it from daydreaming and fantasying. These activities have no purpose beyond titillating the participant. Berlyne, who has written a comprehensive book on thinking (Berlyne, 1965)—even though from a self-actional viewpoint—refers to daydreaming and free association as autistic thinking. His interest is in directed thinking, which he defines as "thinking whose function is to direct us to solutions of problems" (p. 19). Kantor and Smith (1975) distinguish between orientation and knowing on the one hand and thinking on the other. They include judging, evaluating and criticizing, deciding and choosing, and planning as prominent forms of thinking. They connect thinking with a need for taking some overt action not required in simply knowing something (p. 307). In this respect, their construct appears to be harmonious with Berlyne's notion of "directed thinking." Let us examine Kantor and Smith's "planning" as one type of serious thinking to see how it fits into our consideration of implicit action, after which we shall attack problem solving and reasoning.

Planning

Suppose you are an artist who decides to paint a landscape. You go at the job forthwith but are soon stopped because there is not enough space on the canvas and you lack the colors that you need in a painting that just grew as you went along. You didn't "THINK AHEA$_d$."

This time you start out with a fresh canvas, and you plan ahead. What do you do when you do that? You interact *implicitly* with the bare canvas, "visualizing" the detailed arrangement of the objects or persons or animals to be included *before* applying paint brush to canvas. This is planning. But note what else is included in our planning. You may use a pencil to sketch, in broad outlines, a trial arrangement of things on the canvas. And you check on the colors to determine if you have the necessary ones and if there is enough of each. And do you have the proper brushes, and so on? The latter operations are far from implicit, for they involve direct responses to directly present stimulus objects. But they are certainly an essential part of the planning procedure. Thus, planning, at least in the everyday example we have analyzed, involves both implicit and nonimplicit action. Planning the painting requires reacting to the canvas as it *would* look with the "projected" meadow, cows, farmhouse, sky, clouds, and so on, *prior to execution*. It also calls for nonimplicit action such as finding and examining brushes; preparing the easel, palette, and colors; and adjusting the illumination and temperature of the studio.

Problem Solving

The preceding situation, that part of it in which we found ourselves in a jam because we had not planned, can help to distinguish between planning and problem-solving behaviors. Because we had not started out by planning what we would paint on the bare canvas first, we thereby created a problem that called for a solution. We had to get out of the difficulty as best we could. The possibilities were to discard the ruined canvas and start with a fresh one, to paint out the most objectionable part and fit in the rest, and so on. Problem situations call out tension, perplexity, possibly frustration, hesitation, and uncertainty as to what to do next. But planning the painting in a second attempt was a "cool" operation, unhurried, unstrained, an implicit and nonimplicit combination of interactions.

Berlyne (1965, p. 281) reviews a number of theories about "problems and problematicity" proposed by various writers. Included among the properties attributed to problem situations are "stresses and strains," "gaps" in conditions that impel action so as to achieve "closure," variability of behavior, and unsuccessful attempts at reaching a goal and conflict (Berlyne, 1965, pp. 282–283). Berlyn collates these views and condenses them into a statement that problem situations reveal "a condition of high drive which is not promptly relieved" (p. 283). He sees a problem as implying a threat to the organism, a critical state causing conflict and disequilibrium.

Now let us move on to problem solving by apes.

Problem solving by chimpanzees.   Kohler, an early Gestalt psychologist, did some work with chimpanzees that is relevant to problem solving. He has reported this work in *The Mentality of Apes* (Kohler, 1927). Among his numerous observations on a number of chimpanzees, those on Sultan will serve our purposes best. Here is the situation: Sultan is, at the time, in a large cage. A prized banana lies on the ground outside the cage, but out of the chimp's reach. However, inside his cage lie two hollow bamboo rods. One is smaller than the other and can be fitted into either end of the larger one so as to make one long stick.

Sultan has a problem. He strives to reach the fruit, trying first one stick, then the other. Both are too short to touch the prized fruit. In his trial-and-error behaving, Sultan pushes one stick out as far as it will go. He then takes the second one and, with it, pushes the first one carefully along the ground until, at one point, it at least touches the fruit. But this does not solve his problem. The keeper intervenes at this point by retrieving the two sticks and putting them back into the cage.

To make a long story short, after an hour, Sultan gives up his pseudosolution of the problem. After a while, he picks up the sticks and plays carelessly with them. Accidentally, he holds the two sticks so that they are in a straight line. This time, he pushes the thinner stick into the opening of the double stick to pull the fruit to him. Kohler continues the account in the following passage from *The Mentality of Apes* (1927, pp. 127–128):

> Sultan is squatting at the bars, holding out one stick, and, at its end, a second bigger one, which is on the point of falling off. It does fall. Sultan pulls it to him and forthwith, with the greatest assurance, pushes the thinner one in again, so that it is firmly wedged, and fetches a fruit with the lengthened implement. But the bigger tube selected is a little too big, and so it slips from the end of the thinner one several times; each time Sultan rejoins the tubes immediately by holding the bigger one towards himself in the left and the thinner one in his right hand and a little backwards, and then sliding one into the other. The proceeding seems to please him immensely; he is very lively, pulls all the fruit, one after the other, towards the railings, without taking time to eat it, and when I disconnect the double-stick he puts it together again at once, and draws any distant objects whatever to the bars.
>
> The next day the test is repeated; Sultan begins with the proceeding which is in practice useless, but after he has pushed one of the tubes forward with the other for a few seconds, he again takes up both, quickly puts one into the other, and attains his objective with the double stick.

Thereafter, in such situations, according to Kohler, Sultan had no problem. He had acquired a ready-made response for use in such situations. But how about other chimps who did not have Sultan's reactional biography? Berlyne (1965, p. 281) says,

> A problem is often spoken of as something that exists in the outside world. It is presented to a subject on a piece of paper, or he discerns it in some part of nature. However, what will constitute a problem for one individual may not be a problem at all for another; despite identical external situations, a problem is more properly thought of as a condition of the organism.

As an alternative to "a condition of the organism," we have the choice of explaining this difference in terms of different interactional histories.

Jane Goodall's chimps.   The chimps in the Gombe Stream Reservation, where Jane Goodall has been conducting her research, find termites a delicacy. The baboons do, too, but they must wait until the termites attain their winged form and fly out to start other colonies. As a result, they can enjoy them during a short season only, because they have not solved the problem the way the chimps have.

Goodall (1964, pp. 1264–1265) describes a procedure used by the chimps in extracting the termites from within the termite nests. They first look for recently sealed openings on the surface of the mound. They pick the seal off with index finger and insert a tool that they brought with them into the opening. The tool may consist of a short stick, vine, or twig with the leaves stripped off. After the tool has been in the nest for some time, it is carefully and slowly withdrawn with termites clinging to it. The chimp picks off the delicacy with its lips. Planning (anticipatory implicit action) enters the picture, too. Goodall reports watching chimps pick up a grass stalk or twig and go marching off to a termite hill that was out of sight and about 100 feet distant. "One male carried a grass stalk [in his mouth] for half a mile, while he examined, one after the other, six termite hills, none of which was ready for working" (p. 443). Does this mean that the chimp can "think ahead"?

There is one other point that needs to be made with reference to Goodall's chimps. They did not show the conflict, trial-and-error behavior, false starts, pseudosolutions, and stresses manifested by Sultan. Why? Because they had learned how to behave in such situations through modeling. The reaction was a cultural trait "handed down" from one generation to another. Had Sultan lived in a chimp society that had evolved and transmitted a stick-using institution, he would have had no problem such as the one that confronted him. Problems can be avoided by individually or culturally acquired reactions.

Experimental study of problem solving. Birch and Rabinowitz (1951) arranged problems in the laboratory so as to enable them to isolate some of the variables affecting human problem solving. They contrived a problem previously used by another investigator (Maier, 1931). Two strings were hung from the ceiling. The problem assigned to participants in the experiment was to tie the strings together, but the strings were too far apart for a subject to reach one while holding the other. The solution lay in tying a weight to one string, starting it swinging, and catching it as it approached the other string. A relay and an electric switch lay on a nearby table.

Before the subjects entered this phase of the experiment, they participated in a preliminary phase in three groups. One group worked at a task in which they handled and used a switch like the one on the table to complete an electric circuit. Another group handled and used a relay like the one on the table to complete an electric circuit. A control group had no previous contact with either device.

Results.   Starting with the control group, 50% of this group used the relay as a weight to swing the string, and 50% used the switch for that purpose

But 100% of the experimental group that had had prior use of the relay in another type of situation ignored the relay on the table and used the switch as a weight. As for the group that had had prior use of the switch, 78% of them reached for the relay, while only 22% used the switch as a weight. Apparently, here as elsewhere, present events are a function of antecedent events. A more detailed interpretation of these results must wait until we have had an opportunity to examine some laboratory studies of human problem solving that deserve classic status. These were carried out by another Gestalt psychologist, Karl Duncker.

Duncker's investigations of problem solving in humans. Duncker (1945) assembled a variety of problem situations, some practical, some arithmetical, others geometrical, radiational, and so on. We shall need to analyze only the "box problem." The "box problem" requires the subject to arrange three small candles on a door in the laboratory, presumably for visual experiments. On a nearby table lie a profusion of things, including a few tacks and three unlike, small cardboard boxes (about the size of matchboxes) scattered over the table. The expected solution requires attaching each of the boxes, with a tack apiece, to the door where they are to serve as platforms for the candles.

Duncker introduced his subjects to different conditions prior to their problem-solving session. One group, which we might name the "without preutilization group," saw the three little boxes empty. The "after preutilization group" saw the three boxes as containers for candles in one, tacks in another, and matches in the third.

Instructions to all participants were the same. They were told that they were to carry out certain technical tasks, the solution of which could be executed with the help of objects on the table before them. They could use anything they wanted in any fashion whatsoever.

In addition to the objects essential for a solution to the problem were others utterly unsuited, such as paper, paper clips, tinfoil, string, pencils, pieces of wood, and ashtrays. The essential objects were never placed in a prominent place.

Results. Out of seven subjects in the "without preutilization group" who saw the matchboxes empty, all seven solved "the box problem." But of the seven who had seen the boxes as containers prior to their initiation of solving "the box problem" (the after-preutilization group), only three solved the problem, only 42.9% as compared with 100% of the other goup. Why the difference? According to Duncker (1945), the answer is "functional fixedness," by which he means that having seen the boxes as containers of various things hindered the members of that group from seeing them in any other context, for example, as objects that could be attached to a door with a tack, as platforms for candles. The members of the "without preutilization group" were freer, in that respect, because they were not hampered by any prior function of the same boxes when they viewed them in relation to the problem which they had to solve. Duncker (1945, p. 87) writes, "Under our experimental conditions, the object which is not fixed is almost twice as easily found as the object which is fixed." What is called for, Duncker thinks, is a recentering of attention from the basic difficulty created by the fixedness of function. The first function of any object determined by "after preutilization" becomes centered or dominant. Only the shifting of attention to the essential variables in relation to the basic difficulty in solving the problem can result in recentering.

Functional fixedness can operate in still another way. If an object is needed and sought for, it is not likely to be reacted to implicitly if it is *fixed;* that is, fastened to something or if it is a part of something. For example, suppose that we are dealing with Sultan after he has learned to use a stick as a tool. He is not as likely to react in this implicit way to a tree branch as he would to a detached tree branch leaning against a tree or lying on the ground. Duncker (1945, p. 85) says, "On the tree it is a 'branch,' a part of the visual figural unit 'tree,' and this part character—more generally, this 'fixedness' —is clearly responsible for the fact that to search for something like a stick, the branch on the tree is less 'within reach' than the branch on the ground." We may speculate that a branch on the tree as branch and an *almost identical* branch on the ground make an almost identical pattern on the retina of the eye and on the occipital lobe. Whence the difference in the behavioral response? Could it be that there is more to seeing than meets the eye? Goodall's chimps were not hindered by such object fixedness, because they had learned to tear off twigs or small branches from trees and to strip them of leaves for use as termite lures. Object fixedness, then, is only a function of presence or absence of a reactional biography in reaction to that object.

An alternative interbehavioral interpretation.   "Functional fixedness" and "recentering" can also be understood in terms of interactions. The term "functional fixedness" appears to say that, in the situation referred to as "after preutilization," the three little boxes on the table take on a definite stimulus function. They are seen as containers for small objects. In other words, they acquire what we may label as a "container stimulus function" for putting things into. In the new situation, they continue to function in the same way, interfering with a "platform stimulus function" or "something-to-attach-to-a-door-to-hold-a-candle stimulus function." This function operated more readily for the group for whom the little boxes had not already acquired a "container stimulus function." As for the "after-preutilization group" members who are blocked in solving the box problem, if they hope to solve it, one thing has to happen. Stimulus–response, setting, and other factors must attain a reorganization so that a different stimulus function (than the "box-as-a-container" one) has a chance to come into being. What we see here is an inhibition of one stimulus function by another. "Recentering" involves a shifting or change of stimulus functions preliminary to solution. Two very basic principles apparent throughout this analysis are that "behavior is under the control of stimuli" and that, in problem solving as in other situations, "present events are a function of antecedent events." How a little box was perceived in a previous situation will determine pretty much how it will be perceived in a new situation. Finally, problem solving requires more than perception; it demands implicit action toward stimulus objects with new or different psychological possibilities in dynamic, constantly changing problem situations.

Reasoning

Consider the following statements: (1) "All men are mortal"; (2) "Socrates is a man"; (3) "Therefore, Socrates is mortal." Here, in its clearest form, is an example of reasoning; that is, if the three preceding statements represent an individual's actual behavior, the conclusion in the last proposition is an inference drawn from the two preceding statements. According to Kantor (1977, p. 171), "The central core of reasoning is inferential action. Such action consists essentially of implicitly moving from one item of a system to one or more others. The conventional syllogism illustrates the process as it moves along from the premises to a conclusion." But reasoning does not require a formal structure to demonstrate inferential behavior, the essential property of reasoning. Homely examples will serve as well. The newspapers are piling up on our next-door neighbors' front porch. We infer that either (1) they are on vacation and forgot to suspend delivery or (2) something has happened to them. Mystery-story writers keep us in suspense by baiting us with one piece of circumstantial evidence after another. No sooner do we draw one inference than we must revise it because another inference from another bit of circumstantial evidence seems more plausible. For the police, "the smoking gun" is the strongest evidence for drawing inferences about who the victim's murderer was. When we compare reasoning with problem-solving behavior, it is true that reasoning may occur as an aspect of problem solving, although it need not. Besides, problem solving finds the individual in a quandary or dilemma. Reasoning may occur in a situation in which we notice a drop in temperature to below freezing, from which we infer that it might snow—only that and nothing more.

Fantasy and Dreaming

Dreaming permits each and every one of us to be quietly and safely insane every night of our lives.

[Dement, personal communication, 1978]

It is difficult to find a dependable distinction between fantasy and dreaming. Most writers see a continuum. For example, Vinacke (1974, p. 334) recognizes "more than one degree of fantasy." Thus, he views reverie as a freer form of fantasy than the daydream. The latter may have a beginning, a definite structure, and a theme that are lacking in the reverie, which is more like free association. But he considers both fantasy and dreaming as forms of autistic rather than the realistic forms of thinking that we observed in planning, problem solving, and reasoning. Autistic thinking is thinking that is engaged in for its own sake without any necessary relation to the rest of the individual's behavior.

Daydreaming. Although there is a scattered clinical literature on daydreaming, according to Vinacke (1974), daydreaming as a normal phenomenon, believed to be quite prevalent, has not received the attention it deserves. Singer and McCraven (1961) found that 96% of their subjects reported daydreaming daily, mostly when they were alone. Wagman (1967) learned that males reported daydreams that showed more assertive, sexual, heroic, and self-aggrandizing motives. In their daydreams, females were more passive, affiliative, self-centered, and more concerned with their physical attractiveness. Singer and McCraven (1961) also discovered a correlation between frequency of daydreaming and creativity.

Dreaming (night dreaming). Because Freud's (1900/1938) famous treatise, *The Interpretation of Dreams*, overshadows all other publications on dreaming, we might start with it as an introduction to our topic. According to Freud, a dream is a (disguised) wish fulfillment of a (repressed) wish. Presumably, if there were no repressions, there would be no dreams. And if there were no defense mechanisms operating in the unconscious ego, there would be no need for disguises. Direct expression of (largely) sexual impulses is prevented by a strict censor in the ego. Therefore, only *indirect* expression is permissible, and this must be achieved in a roundabout way, through the various dodges achieved via the defense mechanisms (also described in Chapter 7). The combination of defenses that translates the repressed and hidden impulses into the dream as reported by the dreamer is referred to as dream work. The analyst takes the dream as narrated by the dreamer but considers it only as the manifest content or *apparent* content and works backward to determine the latent (hidden or true) content of the dream. His analysis looks for such distorting mechanisms as displacement, projection, and symbolization, to arrive at the "real" meaning of the dream.

Among others, Hall (1953a, 1953) has disagreed with Freud's attribution of subtlety and complexity to dream work. He favors convenience of expression rather than devious disguise as an explanation for the data that are labeled as *symbolism*. The freer scope of night dreaming over daydreaming is undoubtedly due to differences in the dreamer's contact with reality. That is apparently the reason why some of our dreams fit the characterization attributed to them by Dement at the beginning of this section. As an interesting "experiment," try stating your dreams to your intimates as a statement of fact (as actual occurrences and not as dreams) and watch the raised eyebrows. If you do not recall your dreams, consider the following typical recurrent dreams of a "normal" female patient, reported by Epstein (1973, p. 53):

> [Dream 1] I was in the hospital. My teeth were coming out. It seems as though my tonsils were coming out. My teeth started coming out. As they were coming out, my tonsils started coming out and then my insides.
>
> [Dream 2] My mother was there with four men. They were looking at me, smirking. My mother gave me a sandwich. It was a hamburger. The hamburger had money in it. She wanted me to take the money to make me embarrassed. I ate the money sandwich and my teeth were coming out.
>
> [Dream 3] Someone was trying to push me out of the house, trying to kill me. They had their foot in my back. Somewhere along there my teeth came out.
>
> [Dream 4] He went to the bathroom. A woman from downstairs came up and saw me in bed waiting. I was embarrassed because she knew I was waiting and wanting to be raped.

The Experimental Study of Dreaming

> *There is not a muscle of the body which does not reveal thoughts and feeling.*
>
> [Story, 1949, p. 11]

The study of sleep and dreaming got under way only about 30 years ago with the discovery of two kinds of sleep. In his laboratory investigation of sleep at the University of Chicago, Kleitman observed that at certain times during the night his sleeping subjects' eyes showed very fast, jerky movements, apparent even to the naked eye. Later on, instrumentation was introduced to measure the brain waves via the EEG (electroencephalograph), eye movements with the aid of an electrooculograph, muscle activity by means of an electromyograph, respiratory rate with a pneumograph, cardiac, and still other physiological changes.

Dement joined the staff at about this time and named the periodic, quick shifting of the eyes "rapid eye movements" (REM). The name has stuck. The in-between periods were designated as NREM and pronounced as non-REM. Dement and Kleitman began waking up their subjects at different times during the sleep cycle to check on their subjects' dreams. They discovered that their subjects reported many more dreams during REM sleep (Dement and Kleitman, 1957).

As they continued their studies, they found other sharp differences between REM- and NREM-sleep. According to Dement (1974), NREM is a quiet and deep sleep in which snoring may occur; breathing is slow and regular, as is brain activity, and general bodily movement is absent.

REM sleep, on the other hand, is revealed by facial and finger twitches, snoring phases out, and breathing is irregular and even suspended momentarily. Dement (1974, p. 26) writes, "If we gently pull back the eyelids, the subject seems to be actually looking at something. Cerebral blood flow and brain temperature soar to new heights, but the large muscles of the body are completely paralyzed; arms, legs, and trunk cannot move. Throbbing penile erections occur in adult—and newborn—males."

REM sleep and dream recall.   What intrigued Dement most was a possible relationship between REM sleep and dreaming. Was dreaming restricted to the REM phase? So they began conducting more rigorous tests of their hypothesis, comparing REM with NREM periods. In 1957, Dement and Kleitman published the results of their findings. They had disturbed the sleep of their subjects 191 times during REM sleep and obtained impressive dream recall 152 times of 80% of the time. But when they wakened their subjects during the NREM phase, out of 160 times they got a report of dreaming 11 times or 6.9% of the time. The difference between the two conditions was not absolute.

Dement and Kleitman's earlier excitement over REM and NREM sleep as two distinct phenomena abated further with troubles stemming from a definition of dreams. They suspected that not everybody who participated in their study was defining the word *dream* in the same way. When they asked 500 undergraduate students to define the word, there were as many differences as similarities in their definitions. Eventually, they came to the conclusions that measuring REM time was not the same as measuring dream time and that the physiological differences between REM and NREM were more distinctive than the psychological aspects. And that is about the status quo today in the study of sleep.

At a recent international symposium held at Bardolino, Italy, reported by Lairy and Salzarulo (1975), Peter Hauri, an investigator of sleeping and dreaming at the Dartmouth Medical School, writes, "It appears that the relationship between physiological events and sleep mentation is much more complicated than earlier studies had led us to believe" (Hauri, 1975a, p. 279).

An interesting point that surfaced a number of times during the symposium concerns individual differences in dreaming. The symposium participants questioned whether there were people who never dream, or who do not report dreams spontaneously or who cannot recall them (Dement, 1975, p. 292). Hauri (1975, p. 308) is of the opinion that "these individual differences lie at the very heart of the problem." Here is another reminder of the concept that psychology is the study of the individual and that the individual's psychological history must be taken into account. Wholesale methods do not seem to yield significant results. As Hauri, (1975a, p. 279) summed up the work to date on sleep and dreaming, "We still lack a reliable physiological indicator of specific kinds of sleep mentation that would substantially improve predictions based on the REM/NREM dichotomy alone."

Nocturnal penile tumescence.   As early as 1940, Halverson (1940) described erections during sleep in male infants. Succeeding studies in adults, too, suggested a correspondence with REM, and because nocturnal penile tumescence was believed to provide a tool for the exploration of the Freudian (sexual) nature of dreams, it became an object of study in its own right. About 1965, there was an expansion of research in this area. In his doctoral dissertation, Karacan (1965, p. 89) found that "in young adult males a majority of nocturnal erections are related to REM sleep." Since then, Karacan has evolved more refined instrumentation for the study of nocturnal penile tumescence (hereafter referred to as NPT). He decided to determine how general the phenomenon was and to try to relate it to age.

Karacan, Williams, Thornby, and Salis (1975) chose as subjects 125 healthy boys and men between the ages of 3 and 79 years. They required their subjects to sleep in their laboratory for at least 3 consecutive nights, and a majority slept there for 7 or 8 consecutive nights. Data from the first night were never used. They classified an NPT episode as REM if at least one minute of it occurred during REM sleep and as a NREM episode if it occurred during NREM sleep.

As for results, we need not go into them in any depth because for us the mere occurrence of NPT is of interest. However, amount of tumescence which decreased over age range, averaged out to "1.5 hours per night, or 20 percent of sleep period time" (Karacan et al., 1975, p. 934). There was a close relationship between total tumescence time and total REM, except during the teen years, when NPT time exceeded REM time, independent of any increase in REM sleep time. The authors conclude (p. 935):

> These data provide clear evidence that NPT occurs consistently in healthy human males between the ages of 3 and 79. In fact, all of the 125 subjects whom we monitored for this study exhibited erections during sleep. There is evidence that an analogous phenomenon occurs in females and in some lower male animals.

Nightmares and night terrors.   The extreme in dream episodes are nightmares and night terrors. Nightmares involve fearful events that arouse great anxiety. Night terrors extend to the panic stage, arousing fight or flight associated with terror. Fisher, Kahn, Edwards, and Davis (1973), of the

Mount Sinai Medical Center, did a laboratory study of 11 subjects who suffered from extreme night terrors. They observed them for periods varying from four to 19 nights, for a total of 101 nights. Here is their description of the most severe dream incident: "The night terror in its full blown form is ushered in by a sudden loud piercing scream or series of screams of blood-curdling, animal-like intensity indicating uncontrolled panic" (Fisher et al., 1973, p. 81).

Ten of their 11 subjects frequently jumped out of bed and fled the house until they reestablished contact with their surroundings. During their sleep-walking stage, their participants reported carrying out complex activities and "several subjects have performed violent or destructive acts, such as striking a spouse, slashing a picture, or punching through a glass door before regaining contact. Several subjects have injured themselves before regaining contact" (pp. 81–82). Another aspect of the night terror involves physiological changes, such as radical increase in heart rate (doubling and even tripling the baseline rate), and equally dramatic changes in respiratory amplitude, eye movements, and in the electroencephalogram.[4]

Significance of night terrors.   We should not let this moving type of dream pass without milking its full meaning. In the grip of the night terror, the dreamer is quite obviously involved in intense activity. Yet the violent action is not in direct response to an attack on the dreamer! In fact, the stimulus object is absent and its function is mediated by a substitute stimulus. In this case of implicit action, we have a subtly operating substitute stimulus function connected with gross, extensive activity on the part of the organism. This should remind us that, from the standpoint of organismic response, implicit action is not restricted to the seemingly passive form of action apparent in daydreaming and reverie. We should expect all sorts of combinations, ranging from subtle to crude, both on the response as well as the stimulus side of implicit interactions.

Sensory Deprivation

Our linguistic habits permit us to pigeonhole phenomena into distinct categories when we should instead recognize a series of events having many common characteristics showing variation over a series of indefinite degrees. Daydreaming, night dreaming, nightmares, and night terrors are an example.

I am going to try to present a case for the argument that the kind of implicit activity we have been discussing under dreaming occurs in other

---

[4] One suspects the *possibility* of death from a cardiac crisis in people with structural defects of the heart.

situations, such as sensory deprivation. The term *sensory deprivation* refers to a condition of reduced stimulation far below the level to which the individual is accustomed. The facts of sensory deprivation organize themselves easily around three categories: (1) naturally occurring life situations, (2) observations from clinical medicine, and (3) experimental studies. We shall sample each area briefly.

Naturally occurring life situations.   In a comprehensive review of "fact and fancy in sensory deprivation studies," Wheaton (1959) has assembled a wealth of autobiographical and anecdotal material on the subject. He reports (p. 14) the case of Joshua Slocum, on a trip around the world in a solo voyage. Slocum hallucinated a bearded man who took over the navigation for him during a severe illness.

Another solo sailor, Bombard (Wheaton, 1959, p. 15), a medically trained man, reported how the extreme solitary situation threw him on his own psychological resources to keep his morale up. Explorers have similar problems. Wheaton (1959) describes Admiral Byrd's existence in a dark, non-dimensional world during his lonely vigil in Antarctica. He suffered extreme disorientation, particularly after waking. It became absolutely essential to exploit every possibility of his psychologically barren environment. For example, he tried strenuously to hear something, anything, in an environment where there was no sound.

Other examples of isolation reveal hallucinations in which nonexistent people are seen and heard—obviously implicit action. These seem to occur after a person has exhausted every possibility for sensory interaction in the condition of isolation. Wheaton's (1959, p. 19) case of Horvath is offered in support of my argument. For 20 days, Horvath was completely buried in a sleeping bag under drifting snow. His only sustenance was brandy, which he doled out to himself at the rate of a teaspoon a day. Even though he suffered from frostbite, he steadfastly believed that he would survive.

Horvath passed the time by busying himself with small tasks, magnifying each to extreme significance and reacting with concentration and interest. He kept in touch by fighting monotony and boredom through an occasional switching of tasks. Despite his extreme "busyness," Horvath did hallucinate sounds and sights of people and engaged in conversation with them. He experienced hallucination of death in the form of a person and even engaged in a battle with death for survival. Horvath won.

Cases from clinical medicine.   Cataract operations, which require enforced bandaging of the eyes, have revealed what has been labeled as "cataract psychosis" or "black-patch delirium." With recent improvements in surgical techniques and recovery programs, these conditions were more common formerly than they are today. In the recent past, Weisman and Hackett (1958) reported that 95% of patients who undergo eye operations with temporary loss of vision experience some form of delirium (confusion with possible accompaniment of hallucinations and delusions), while 65% show severe disturbance. This is especially likely when both eyes are bandaged.

Some investigators have labeled the conditions as "cataract delirium." However, it is not the cataract in itself that causes the problem, but the visual masking and resultant sensory deprivation. The term "black-patch delirium" is more appropriate because it calls attention to sensory isolation (visual) of the patient. That the condition is related to sensory deprivation is supported by the fact that the patient's delirium is worse at night. Why should this be so when under the eye bandages "it is night" 24 hours a day? Because at night, the decreased activity in the hospital adds auditory sensory deprivation on top of the visual. "Under these circumstances somewhat analogous to sensory deprivation, misinterpretations may become delusions and anxiety may become panic" (Weisman and Hackett, 1958, p. 1286).

Sensory deprivation in polio patients.   During an outbreak of poliomyelitis in the Boston area, Mendelson, Solomon, and Lindemann (1958) observed hallucinations in nonpsychotic patients. These severe reactions showed up sometime after their patients were being treated in the old-fashioned type of tank respirators. Many of them developed hallucinations, confusion, disorientation, and delusions. Let us look at the picture presented by one of their cases.

A 22-year-old married woman suffered paralysis of the neck, trunk, and legs. She maintained good contact with her surroundings until her fifth day in the respirator. She then began feeling disoriented as to person, place, and time. She had to be repeatedly told where she was and what her name was. Her "dreams" also began to take on a more vivid quality than her surroundings. As evening approached, which she dreaded, her "dreams" grew sharper, clearer, and more frequent than they had been during the day. The patient admitted experiencing auditory and visual hallucinations. She gave an impressive report of riding around the hospital in an automobile shaped like a tank respirator. (See Figure 10-2 for an artist's representation of her dream.) It seemed odd to her that she rode in the trunk compartment of the auto with her head sticking out of the rear of the car. She hallucinated certain nurses as companions during her excursions and kept asking when they would reach their destination. During her tenth respirator day, the patient's complaints cleared up and her dreams became more like dreams and reverie as she regained the use of her legs.

This patient's dream (hallucination?) fits the wish-fulfilling model of dreaming. It can be translated to mean, "I wish I were riding in an automobile instead of being flat on my back, paralyzed perhaps for the rest of my life, confined to the boring tank respirator. I would even settle for a ride in the car trunk with my head sticking out of the trunk in exchange for my present unbearable condition."

Figure 10-2 Artist's representation of a polio patient's hallucination during her confinement in a tank-type respirator. (Courtesy of Ciba Pharmaceutical Products, Inc.)

Experimental studies of sensory deprivation. The classic study in this area is the McGill University experiment conducted by Heron, Bexton, and Hebb (1953). They paid graduate students $20 a day for a required stay of 72 hours in their "isolation booth." The aim of the study was to observe what happened when their subjects were confined in a small room in which a fan and an air-conditioning unit were the only forms of sensory stimulation. The subjects reclined in a bed on a foam-rubber mattress. On their hands, they wore soft cotton gloves inside cardboard cuffs tied to the wrists and extending from below the elbow to beyond the fingertips. Both gloves and cuffs could be removed but only for eating or toileting. A foam-rubber pillow further reduced auditory stimulation by means of the ear phones it contained, which were connected to a microphone at an observer's post outside the subject's room. Translucent plastic goggles over the eyes transmitted a diffuse white light that prevented pattern vision.

The results of greatest interest to us concern the implicit behavior of the participants. Present conditions occupied them at first—their courses, and so on. Then followed past experiences and reminiscences about family and friends. Then some would take a highly detailed imaginary journey or count numbers into the thousands. Eventually, they drifted until, in 25 out of 29 cases, they reported hallucinatory activity. Confusion, apathy, boredom, restlessness, and emotional disturbance were also experienced, in some cases for several days following the experiment.

Remembering

Usage of the terms *remembering, forgetting, memorizing,* and *reminiscing* abounds in deep semantic confusion, due to their infiltration from popular usage into psychology. Where similar conditions have existed in other disciplines, progress came from a gradual refinement of the usage of everyday terms. It is worthwhile to clear up that confusion in our field by looking for concrete differences among the behavioral phenomena to which these four terms refer. Let us start with *remembering.*

In popular usage, the term *remembering* refers to the repetition of a previously learned act as when someone asks you, "Can you still remember 'Mary had a little lamb'?" and you recite it to prove that you "remember" it. Another meaning derives from a reference to any implicit action as when someone asks you, "Do you remember that storm last Sunday?" and you answer, "Yes, I remember." The two behaviors are quite different.

Remembering points toward the future.   It really does not matter what label we apply to a particular event. But there is a distinctive phenomenon that, by agreement, and because of prior usage, we may refer to as remembering.[5] Suppose you and I right *now* make an agreement to meet tomorrow morning at 10 o'clock in the student cafeteria for coffee and a discussion. If all goes well and I appear at the proper time and place, I have completed a remembering response. If I fail to do so, I am involved in *forgetting.* Thus, we may define forgetting as a remembering act that failed to achieve completion. And, if we prefer a bit of metaphor, we might consider forgetting as an aborted remembering act, just as a miscarriage is a failure to complete gestation. With forgetting out of the way, we are ready to continue our analysis of remembering, noting its specific characteristics.

Remembering involves an integrated time span.   If we stick to the facts, the most striking feature of remembering is the integrated time that binds it

---

[5] I am heavily indebted to Kantor and Smith's (1975) treatment of the area under discussion.

from its inception to its completion. From the moment I agreed to meet you until I appeared on the scene must be treated as a single analytic unit. You may argue that the clock is ticking off many hours in between the two points. That is merely a coincidence. After all, what does astronomical time have to do with the determination of plans for a business or medical career or retirement *years hence* into the future or reminiscences *going back* 50, 60, or more years? Behavioral space and time appear to be freer (or different?) than terrestrial space and clock time. This short deviation should give at least a hint of the as-yet unsolved problems concerning the evolution of the most advantageous behavioral space–time framework for psychological inquiry. But the factuality of the extended time interval in remembering as just described is beyond dispute. At any rate, under such a guiding assumption, we proceed now to an analysis of the integrated remembering act that we can dissect into the following three phases: (1) the initiation phase, (2) the delay or in-between period, and (3) the completion or final phase.

The initiation phase.   What happens when we initiate a remembering act? Suppose you call up your dentist's office for a semiannual appointment a month from now. You do not go to his or her office right now and sit there until the appointed time. That would be idiotic. Instead, if you have an appointment book, you jot it down there or even on the back of an envelope that you leave in plain sight somewhere. With that action, you have become involved in the organization of a response with the original stimulus and with the notation as a substitute stimulus. The latter is expected to do its job at the right time. Here we have a prominent and deliberate procedure in initiating a remembering act. There are, however, more casual ways of doing the same, as when you read about a shoe sale in the morning paper and decide then that at some later time in the day you will drop in at that shoe store.

The delay period.   The delay phase of the remembering act appears empty and lacking in activity as far as the remembering act goes. But that is only apparently so because there are many things going on. All of our psychological activity consists of an orderly flow of events that fits into each other and is organized in relation to each other. If the remembering act is crucial in our life, many of our ongoing reactions can serve as substitute stimuli. For lovers, "everything" reminds them of the beloved, which is another way of saying that the details of their life are tightly organized via a dominant theme, their love relationship. It seems reasonable to suppose that many of our remembering acts function without calling attention to themselves because of the smooth operation of any number of subtle substitute stimulus functions.

For contrast with the difficult-to-spot substitute stimulus functions in the hypothetical situation of the lovers, let us take a more obtrusive example. As an aid in helping you to remember to carry out a certain errand, you tie a string around your finger to initiate the act. Now, during the delay phase, the string is there continuously until you reach the place where the errand must be done and the string's job is finished. A still more blatant example is provided by a little boy who is sent to the grocery store. The mother says, "Now, here's a dollar. I want you to go to the corner grocery store and buy a loaf of bread and a quart of milk. Will you remember what you're to get?"

"Yes," the boy replies, "I'll remember." Now, what does the boy do? All the way to the store, he keeps reciting, "a loaf of bread and a quart of milk, a loaf of bread and a quart of milk," until he blurts it out to the grocer. Because of proper socialization, he may have whispered it to himself when he passed people, especially adults, in the street. Nevertheless, his action was continuous. Here, as if blown up large size, we see the uninterrupted operation of the substitute stimulus function during the delay period. In view of the subtlety and delicacy in the operation of psychological variables in other situations that we have noted along the way, it should not be difficult to envisage their work in remembering.

The delayed-reaction experiment. The detachment from the "here and now" that we have observed in psychological events, particularly in implicit behavior, is relevant to the much-studied delayed reaction in a number of species. The following experiment is typical. The animal (rat, for example) is placed in an apparatus in which one of several doorways leads to some reward (such as food). The correct doorway will vary from trial to trial, but it will always be the one with a light above it. The rat has learned this task well, for it consistently goes only to the lighted door. But now a delay interval is introduced by keeping the rat behind a clear plastic barrier. The rat is allowed to see the light go on and off but is prevented from entering the food compartment until after a certain interval. This interval can be increased from, say, 5 seconds to 45 seconds or longer.

The question is, "Will the rat still make the right choice or will its choice be random?" The answer depends on a number of factors. For example, the rat does better if it is allowed to maintain its stance in the direction of the door that had been illuminated. Turning the rat to face in the opposite direction spoils its delayed response. Thus, the posture of the rat plays a role in its delayed response similar to the little boy's recitation all the way to the grocery store. But the similarity must not be extended to imply that they are identical. In the first place, the rat's situation is contrived by the experimenter, whereas *you* initiated your dental appointment. Also, humans have to learn how to remember, as the little boy in our example and your appointment with the dentist demonstrate. Furthermore, your dentist's office isn't present before you in your initiation of the remembering act. The rat's doorway is. The rat's doorway is also the stimulus to which the consummatory act will be performed. The dentist's office in your consummatory phase is absent. You will respond to it *eventually* via substitute stimuli; the rat will not have to do so. And, finally, you have the advantage of language to organize your remembering responses, which the rat lacks but which the little boy is learning to utilize in remembering.

The consummatory phase.   In the case in which the string around your finger stimulates you to do the intended errand, the remembering act is concluded. The same in the case of the dental appointment. A glance at your note on the desk on the day and near the hour appointed and you are off to the dentist.

Remembering versus memorization.   Remembering and memorization are frequently confused. The term *memorization* refers to learning or behavior acquisition, as when you learn to recite a poem that you hope to recall at a later time. But your remembering to go to the dentist did not involve any behavior acquisition. Another difference lies in the uniqueness of the remembering act. Never again will you repeat your remembering to go to the dentist this next time. The following appointment will again be a once-in-a-lifetime, different affair. Each remembering act is a singular adjustment in each of its three phases to a specific event. This feature also distinguishes it from memorization. One could also conceivably learn or memorize something and never do anything with it beyond memorizing it.

Remembering joined with memorization.   Imagine students assiduously memorizing or "cramming" for an exam tomorrow. They are obviously involved in behavior acquisition. They must know the formulas, definitions, or dates (or multiplication tables, at lower levels). That is one thing. Now, after they have crammed to the point to which they are confident of knowing the material, they initiate a remembering act "projecting" it to tomorrow's exam. When they write down what they learned the night before, we see a combination of memorization and remembering. Their joint operation on such occasions should help in our distinguishing in them two different forms of psychological interactions.

Informational and performance memory.   One more point needs to be made. Earlier, we examined remembering acts that involved doing something, while in the previous paragraph we have been considering remembering acts involving informational responses. Instead of remembering a stunt to perform at a party, you may prefer to coin a witty phrase to spring on the group or memorize a joke or quip to deliver at an opportune time. Thus, not only "doings" but "knowings" may participate in remembering acts.

Remembering versus reminiscing.   Ralph Waldo Emerson once remarked, "Man postpones or remembers; he does not live in the present, but with reverted eye laments the past, or, heedless of the riches that surround him, stands on tiptoe to foresee the future. He cannot be happy and strong until he too lives with nature in the present, *above time."* (1969, p. 55; emphasis added.) We have already noted the frequent misidentification of reminiscing with remembering. There are events in which we recall pleasant or unpleasant (or neutral) happenings in the past. The *Comprehensive Dictionary of Psychological and Psychoanalytical Terms* (English and English, 1958, pp. 456–457) defines *reminiscence* variously as "the return unbidden and without associative cues of memories of past experience," and "relatively complete and unselective recall of past experience without specific purpose of guiding present behavior." We may settle for *recall of past events* as the essential property of reminiscence. In this respect, the time relationships in remembering and reminiscence are opposite, for remembering looks to the future, while recall turns to the past. If we take the present as a reference point, the following diagram represents the time relations between the two forms of behavior.

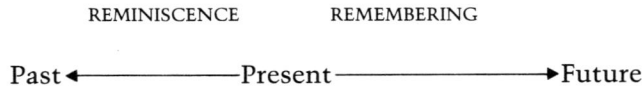

REMINISCENCE   REMEMBERING

Past ◀——————Present——————▶ Future

Cognitive Psychology

The term *cognition* has been traditionally defined to subsume any process by which we come to know objects. It includes perception, conceiving, imagining, judging, reasoning, problem solving, learning, thinking, and, often, speech. Many behaviorists shun such topics (except speech) because, traditionally, they have been identified with mentalism and dualism and because they are difficult to handle. They prefer to work with movements or utterances of organisms. But some psychologists have accumulated a formidable literature on what has come to be known as *cognitive psychology*.

Representative of the work in cognitive psychology is the experimentation carried out by Shepard and his colleagues at Stanford University. Shepard has also collaborated with Lynn Cooper (Cooper and Shepard, 1978) at the Center for Human Information Processing of the University of California at San Diego. Shepard has conducted a series of experiments aimed at determining how long it takes human subjects to react to visual objects (such as abstract, three-dimensional structures) rotated or otherwise transformed. Why? To measure the time it takes individuals to compare pairs of stimuli under different conditions in order to get at the "mental operations" behind their comparisons. Shepard seems to be saying that, "mentally," an operation takes place that is analogous to an actual physical operation. That is to say, when individuals are comparing two stimuli, one of which is upside down in relation to the other, they "mentally" turn one around to facilitate the judgment. Such a condition can be compared to one in which the two figures to be judged are both upright. The difference in time that the two operations take reflects the difference in the "mental operations." Other studies along this line are by Podgorny and Shepard (1978), Shepard (1978), and by Shepard and Podgorny (1978). Mainly, they are concerned with reactions to visual stimuli directly present versus those same stimuli out of sight, under different instructions.

Estes on Cognitive Psychology

A helpful insight into cognitive psychology is provided by Estes' (1978) introduction to the fifth volume of the *Handbook of Learning and Cognitive Processes: Human Information Processing.* The first three volumes deal with conditioning, behavior theory, learning and retention. The fourth is restricted to consideration of attention and memory. The fifth volume is limited to a single theoretical orientation, human information processing.

In his introduction, Estes (1978) points out the difficulties in handling such behavior as reading or problem solving. He writes, "We evidently need factual accounts of what the individual is doing between the initiation of the observed stimulus context and the ultimate observable responses indicating that the individual has obtained information or solved a problem" (p. 2). To solve the problem, cognitive psychology has reintroduced an old procedure, the use of reaction time, to measure the duration of, say, various stages in the solution of problems. The other important technique applied by cognitive psychologists comes from computer technology. The metaphor of the brain as a telephone switchboard has been upgraded in recent times to the brain as a computer.

Estes sees sharp limitations to analogizing the brain with a computer, because the two operate on different principles. Another important point that Estes (1978) makes refers to the "purely hypothetical" [imaginary] nature of the concepts developed to explain the internal brain processes analogized with the computer's storage, coding, retrieval, and so on. Estes raises other questions and problems with the metaphor of the brain as an information-processing system interacting with the problem solver and a task environment.

For another perspective on cognitive psychology, let us shift to Skinner's article, "Why I Am Not a Cognitive Psychologist" (Skinner, 1978).

Why Skinner Is Not a Cognitive Psychologist

Skinner's chief complaint is directed toward the cognitive psychologists' starting their investigations the same way that everybody does, "by studying the relations between the organism and evironment, but they seldom deal with them directly. Instead, they invent internal surrogates which become the subject matter of their science" (Skinner, 1978, p. 97). It is this *conver-*

sion of observable data into hypothetical internal processes that Skinner and other psychologists object to.

Skinner goes on to the notion that we carry around "copies" of the world in our heads. He rejects, as well, the construct that talks in terms of our "possessing" knowledge, which is "stored" (p. 106). He considers the question as to where "memories" are stored an unsuitable metaphor. He writes, "The observed facts are simple enough: I have acquired a repertoire of behavior, *parts of which* I display upon appropriate occasions. The metaphor of storage and retrieval goes beyond those facts" (p. 106). These are the main reasons why Skinner is not a cognitive psychologist, but his whole article is worth reading.

The powerful two-way metaphor so thoroughly entrenched in our thinking in a computer age is bound to reinforce the computer's alleged human attributes and the human's alleged computer attributes. At any rate, we have the choice here of interpreting such behavioral data as remembering, dreaming, and reminiscing in terms of hypothetical "storage " and "retrieval" in a brain or in terms of events that are a function of antecedent events.[6] For example, if I recall an incident that occurred yesterday, we may try to make sense of my recall either (1) by saying that yesterday's incident lay down "traces" in my brain that were reactivated today, or (2) by simply asserting that an event occurred today because a previous, related event occurred yesterday. Certainly, *in everyday terms*, I cannot recall something today that *did not* happen yesterday. The first theory is obviously self-actional, in which a portion of the organism (the brain) "carries the ball," theoretically speaking. The alternative theory deals in terms of fields consisting of interactions involving responses, stimulus objects, media of contact, setting factors, and the interrelationships of relevant interactions. The difference between a reductionistic and an interbehavioral interpretation of (let us say, in everyday terminology) a recall of a traffic accident last week may be stated as follows: for the reductionist, the link between the accident last week and my recall of it today is the "brain traces" (whatever *they* are) that were allegedly "laid down" at the time of the accident. No "linkage" is required in an interbehavioral account other than to indicate that the recall event is a function of the accident event. Event B occurred "because" Event A occurred previously. Instead of dealing with fictional entities ("brain traces" and such), an interbehavioral construct heeds the admonition to psychologists by Willard Day (1976, p. 608) in the following statement: "The profession greatly needs a lot more writing that consists of little more than careful description of what is actually observed by psychologists."

Despite its ancient vintage, the following quotation from John B. Watson's (1914, pp. 241–242) book, *Behavior: An Introduction to Comparative*

---

[6]McGaugh and Herz (1976, p. v) attempt to deal with "the neurological mechanisms that underlie our ability to learn, remember and forget."

Psychology, offers an alternative approach to cognitive psychology's way of handling the variety of implicit responses covered in this chapter:

> The term "retention" has been employed in a static sense . . . referring chiefly to the "persistence of modifications" in the nervous system. It seems possible to keep the term retention and make its meaning more definite. In behavior the term retention covers this phenomenon; viz., that an object to which an animal has learned to respond in a definite way will for a more or less definite period in which the given response has been prevented (*i.e.,* by not presenting the object) call forth in various degrees of perfection the old (or habitual) response. If the response is as definite at the end of the period of disuse as before we say that there has been no loss in retention or that retention was perfect. . . . So far as we know there is no longer any justification for assuming that a neural impulse, which is probably electrical, in any way modifies permanently the conductor over which it passes. While we are ignorant yet of what happens at the surfaces of separation of the conduction systems as regards permeability and the reverse, it seems quite unlikely that neuro-physiology will ever discover any structural modifications in the conductors themselves.

An Interbehavioral Interpretation of Implicit Interactions or "Thinking"

The illustrations of Buddha and Rodin's "The Thinker" in Figures 10-3 and 10-4 may serve to encapsulate or sum up our interpretation of implicit or "thinking" interbehaviors. Once more, we may either define implicit behavior as a self-actional generation of imaginary psychic "doings" within the organism's head, or we may define it as an organism's interbehavior with an absent stimulus object by means of a substitute stimulus. The interbehavioral view rejects the notion of pure thought. It assumes that "thinking" as an interaction involves "thinking" *about* some thing or somebody. The palpable brawniness of "The Thinker" reveals *action.* Because of Rodin's title and because nothing is before "The Thinker," we may assume that he is heavily involved in interaction with *absent* stimulus objects. If we knew much about his reactional biography and present circumstances, we might even guess what he was thinking *about.*

By contrast, the Buddha in the nth degree of relaxation and passivity, which is quite apparent, cannot be thinking at all. According to Buddhist doctrine, he has transcended contamination with the world. He is "out of this world." Also, in accordance with interbehavioral theory, if Buddha were thinking, he should show some sign of activity; as quoted before, "there is not a muscle of the body which does not reveal thoughts and feeling" (Story, 1949, p. 11).

Traditionally, the self-actional theory of thinking has prevailed. According to it, thinking is a hypothetical, wraithlike process alleged to occur in

Figure 10-3 Detachment from the world, living in it but being undefiled by its trivialities, and freedom from all desires and suffering are expressed in Buddha's state of Nirvana. Noninvolvement in the world—some would say, withdrawal from it —is the basic tenet of Buddhism. Contrast Buddha's passive posture here with that of Rodin's "The Thinker" in Figure 10-4. (Courtesy of Nelson Gallery—Atkins Museum, Kansas City, Missouri—Nelson Fund.)

the brain. As commonly conceived, it is the cause of itself. In interbehavioral terms, thinking is conceptualized as a field event, one in which an organism and absent stimulus object interact under very definite conditions. Also, the "thinking" or implicit event cannot be understood unless it is related to a relevant prior event. The two events *together* then make a meaningful behavioral chunk in line with our constant refrain: "present events are a function of antecedent events."

I believe that there are certain advantages to an interbehavioral view. For one thing, "thinking" or implicit activities are brought down to earth.

Figure 10-4   Rodin's "The Thinker." By contrast with the passive Buddha, "The Thinker" demonstrates the typical posture of a man heavily involved in thinking about *somebody* or *some thing*. The muscle tension reveals *action*. (Courtesy of E. F. Corwin.)

They are occurrences that can be "bounded" by the variables involved—organisms, absent stimulus objects, substitute stimulus objects, and so on. The factors involved can be analyzed and specified. An interbehavioral construct can also yield foresight and understanding, and it should permit application as well. For example, by providing ourselves with effective substitute stimuli (such as study notes), we should be able to "improve our memory." On this score alone, the self-actional brain theory of "thinking" leaves us bankrupt, for what can one do to one's brain to make it "think" effectively?

The following quotation from William Faulkner's (1950) *Requiem for A Nun* is a particularly appropriate annotation on both the chapter on perception and the chapter on "thinking" or implicit action. We enter the play at the moment when Mrs. Gowan, the former Temple Drake, in dissociating herself from her shady premarital career, exclaims, "Temple Drake is dead." Her uncle looks at her and answers, *"The past is never dead. It's not even past"* (p. 92). This is an eloquent way to say that "present events are a function of antecedent events!"

Chapter Summary

Interactions that involve perceiving are "a stream of innumerable, similar acts performed in the past." They are semiimplicit, which means that although the object is present in perceiving acts, it is responded to as a function of a prior response to that object. Fully implicit responses and "thinking" are interactions involving absent stimulus objects, interactions that were mediated by substitute stimuli that functioned in place of the absent stimulus object.

Contrary to the self-actional concept of "pure thought," "thinking" or implicit action always involves an absent stimulus object, and both the organism's participation or the participation of the substitute stimulus function can be subtle and inapparent. Implicit interactions reveal "detachedness" from a rigid space–time framework. Thinking is defined as implicit interactions directed toward the solution of problems; planning is one example.

Problem solving is behavior in a quandary or crisis. Reasoning is inferential behavior. Fantasy and dreaming are implicit interactions, with a wide variety of closely related behaviors observed in situations of sensory deprivation. Remembering is forward-looking, once-in-a-lifetime behavior, in contrast with reminiscing, which involves past time. Remembering is distinct from memorization. Reductionistic and interbehavioral constructs can be applied to a number of implicit forms of behavior.

11 Feeling Interactions, Emotional Interactions, and Motivation

I read books because they intrigue or excite me; I listen to music because it exhilarates me; I look at pictures because I find them beautiful; I associate with people I love or with whom I enjoy talking about everyday things with everyday words.

[Skinner, 1974, p. 244]

This quotation from Skinner introduces one kind of interaction that we shall consider in this chapter—feelings or affective responses. It is easy to identify with the common, everyday behaviors that Skinner describes.[1] But people also behave in more dramatic ways than their joys, sorrows, and despairs display. These are the emotions we shall consider next. Here, we examine interactions that are atypical, disruptive, and disrupted, illustrated by stuttering, fainting, startle, and so on. Although feelings and emotions are frequently bracketed together, I hope to show that they are poles apart. And, finally, we shall consider the question of motivation along with feelings and emotions because all three have been traditionally grouped together.

[1] Skinner (1974, p. 245) acknowledges feelings as "bodily states," but "there is an emphasis on the environmental conditions with which they are associated and an insistence that it is the conditions rather than the feelings which enable us to explain behavior."

Feeling Interactions

In the title for this chapter, I was sorely tempted to use the familiar and convenient terms *feelings* and *emotions*. But, as nouns, they are semantically dangerous, particularly because they suggest the notion of mental (or bodily) *states*. Such terms facilitate reification or "thingification" of feelings and emotions as static things that people "possess" inside them, a view inimical to the interbehavioral construct of interaction as a mutual activity occurring between organism and stimulus object under specific conditions. So I reduced the two terms to adjectives: *feeling* interactions and *emotional* interactions. The terms *motivation*, which has traditionally been associated with emotion, as well as *emotion* will receive separate treatment. For the present, it is sufficient to point out that, etymologically, the terms *emotion* and *motivation* derive from the same Latin root *movere*, "to move." Their ancient lineage and coexistence may help us to understand their relationship later, when we discuss motivation, or what allegedly "moves," "drives," or "motivates" us to act the way we do. But first we must tackle feelings, which we shall handle from an interbehavioral viewpoint after we define the kind of data that belongs in this category.

The Richness and Diversity of Feeling Interactions

Feeling "blue," depressed, joyful, anxious, angry, in love, jealous, lustful, or resentful are a few commonly observed or commonly experienced feelings. To appreciate more fully the tremendous number and variety of feeling interactions, one should glance down the column after column of Byron Barrington's (1963) catalog of "words descriptive of affective reactions." Here is a scanty sampling: *discouraged, mournful, sad, astonished, shocked, surprised, uncertain, frustrated, impatient, restless, affectionate, friendly, sympathetic, bitter, contemptuous, disgusted, vengeful, suspicious, grateful, annoyed, furious, bored, hopeful, awed, bashful, enthusiastic, apprehensive, panicky, lonely, patient, cynical, and hurt*. These are not precise scientific terms—they are everyday words that suggest the richness and variety of the crude data that come under our review as feeling interactions.

Affective Versus Effective Responses

We may make greater headway in our attempt to make sense of feeling interactions by trying out Kantor and Smith's (1975) distinction between affective and effective responses. We may sum up that distinction by focusing on the organismic side of the picture. When we observe people who are angry, jittery, discouraged, surprised, or bored, at the moment that they are behaving thus, we say that something or somebody "made them" act that way. For example, we say, "You make me angry." The consequence is to the person. Picture a person, Jane Doe, who is surprised by a group walking in to participate in a surprise birthday party for her. Jane stands there "dumb-founded," with gaping mouth doing nothing else; that is all that happens when one is surprised. But when you pick up a pen to write with, when you play a tune on a musical instrument, drive a car, hammer a nail, *you* are doing something *to something*. You are having an *effect* on something. Here, we have *effective* behavior, by comparison with *affective* behavior in the case of Jane's surprised reaction. We may say about Jane in everyday terms, "She was greatly moved or very much affected by the surprise party." That is affective behavior. Now, when Jane later takes a knife and cuts the cake, she is doing something to something. The direction of activity in the two cases is represented in Figure 11-1.

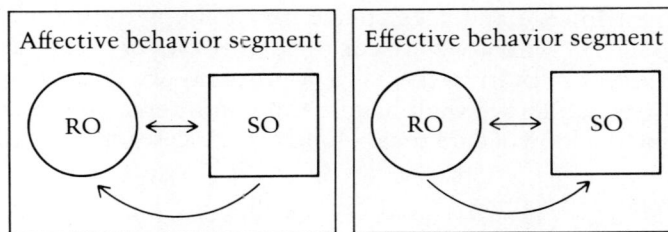

Figure 11-1   The direction of primary effect in affective and effective behavior segments. RO, reacting organism; SO, stimulus object. The "activity" in affective or feeling interactions is concentrated on the organism's side of the picture. In effective interactions, the effect is on the stimulus object as when the organism pushes or pulls an object, and so on. (From Kantor and Smith, 1975, p. 223.)

Analysis of Affective Responses

Some affective responses are quite apparent—for example, the responses of the grieving individual, weeping, nose blowing, moaning, and groaning; the fearful person, trembling and perspiring; and the angry one, breathing heavily and red in the face. Such people are obviously "doing something." In affective interactions, the action is primarily concentrated within the organism's biological systems. While these examples are easily open to inspection, other affective reactions are not. As we see later, some, like anxiety and tension, are so subtle that special techniques are required to detect them.

Affective Interactions Are Diffuse

Further inquiry into affective interactions reveals a prominent feature, namely, the widespread involvement of the organism in the response. Figure

11-2 helps to explain why. The illustration attempts to show the intimate connection among the visceral or internal organs situated in the abdomen. The autonomic nervous system interconnects the heart, lungs, stomach, gastrointestinal tract, bladder, colon, eyes, salivary and sweat glands, the digestive glands that secrete hydrochloric acid in the stomach, and so on.

The close interconnection of the various portions of the organism helps to explain the diffuseness of the responses we are now studying. Because the heart, liver, stomach, salivary glands, sweat glands, and so on are connected with each other, these organs participate in a sort of blanket response. In a

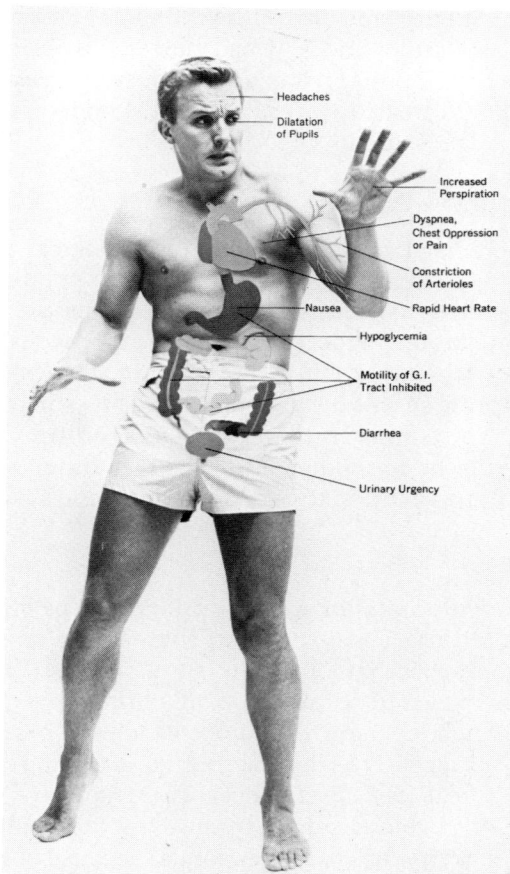

Headaches

Dilatation of Pupils

Increased Perspiration

Dyspnea, Chest Oppression or Pain

Constriction of Arterioles

Rapid Heart Rate

Nausea

Hypoglycemia

Motility of G. I. Tract Inhibited

Diarrhea

Urinary Urgency

Figure 11-2   Feeling, or affective, responses. A concrete illustration of the diffuseness of autonomically mediated affective or feeling responses. These are the well-known or common components seen in anxiety or "tension" reactions. Countless others are not illustrated here. (Courtesy of CIBA Pharmaceutical Products, Inc.)

sense, it is correct to say that the heart is connected with the surface arteries, with the tear glands, the sweat glands, spleen, stomach glands, and so on. The specific pattern of visceral action characteristic of a given individual can only be understood in terms of that person's own reactional biography. That's the only way we can understand why one person blushes, why another's stomach "flip-flops," and another's heart skips a beat.

Popular expressions show a genuine appreciation of the powerful organismic response to be seen in affective interactions. For example, we say that someone is "as white as a sheet," "as red as a beet," "speechless," (also "spitless"), "scared to death," "hot under the collar," "boiling" or "seething inside," "sweating it out," and "frozen to the spot." Or, that "makes me sick at my stomach" or "gripes me." "I had butterflies in my stomach." "My stomach turned a flip-flop." "That gave me goose pimples." "That made my hair stand on end." "It made my head spin." "My heart speeded up." "Now, don't get your blood pressure up."

Visceral Action as Psychological Response

It is important here as always to separate physiological from psychological events. We can do so by reference to the last two popular expressions just given. If someone's heart speeds up or the blood pressure shoots up because he or she is running around a racetrack, that occurrence is physiological. But if a thug holds you up with a gun while you are standing still waiting for a bus and your heart rate speeds up and your blood pressure rises, it is a psychological situation. To respond in the latter way requires a reactional biography acquired during the individual's life span. In other words, we "have to learn" to hate, fear, be affectionate, jealous, angry, and so on.

Affective Interactions Are Concrete

In the past, affective interactions were considered to be obscure, difficult-to-get-at psychic qualities. Today, we can view them as concrete as overt reactions. One approach that may help to achieve such an attitude is to speculate what the possibilities would be if a human were born as transparent as a jellyfish. Such a person would not be able to hide a single affective secret. Whatever provocative, threatening, or embarrassing stimulus was presented would reveal its consequences in the spleen's dramatic contraction and the shift of the blood supply to the skin. Stomach and heart action, accelerated heart activity, or arteries engorged because of increased pressure would reveal a correlation with whatever stimuli we would subject the person to. But, of course, people are opaque, and we cannot see through them. So we must use instrumental techniques such as the fluoroscope or "lie-detection" methods. With these aids we do no more than the physiologist does in inquiring into nerve action, heart activity, or bone conditions via oscilloscopes, galvanometers, or X-ray photography. They enable the physiologist to know what is going on. Because the human is not transparent, we need similar help in putting us in touch with events that differ somewhat from the effective responses.

The Simultaneous Performance of Affective and Effective Action

While we have differentiated between affective and effective action, it would be a serious mistake to think that organisms perform one or the other but never the two together. Two children are fighting in anger with each other. At the same time when they behave angrily (affectively) toward each other, they also grab one another, wrestle on the ground, pummel one another, and so on. The obvious point is that our example reveals both affective and effective action at the same time. Here are further examples: the surgeon in a crisis during an operation, the musician "feeling intensely" while manipulating the instrument, the mother feeding or rocking her baby. Almost all of our activities are carried out "accompanied by" a certain affective tone. We eat with gusto, we walk with enjoyment, play with enthusiasm, work with pleasure, frustration, or discouragement, and so on. All of our life activities are shot through with the great variety of affective responses mentioned earlier.

Carl Rogers' Critisicm of the Unfeeling Life

In an address at an annual meeting of the American Psychological Association, Carl Rogers (1973) touched on the point we have just reached, namely, the place of feelings in life, particularly in an academic setting. He argues that university life stresses thinking, reasoning, learning, and memorizing —that is, "the intellect." "It seems that we live on an either-or basis. We are aware of, and express, what we think; or we are aware of, and express, our emotional reactions. Almost never are the two sides of our life brought together" (p. 384). As a result we are dichotomized beings; we are not whole men and women. "Yet, in life, in therapy, in relationships with the opposite sex, in marriage, in parent–child relationships, in encounter groups, in university faculty meetings, we were forced to learn that feelings were an equally important part of living" (p. 384).

Student protests during the past decade or so support Rogers' notion that students more and more refuse to accept this dichotomization.

> Why are so many of our best students leaving universities? Because they find no place there for the whole person. Why are so many young people finding life perplexing and without meaning? Partly because they do not know that it is possible to live as a person of thought united with passion, of feeling suffused with intellect and curiosity. [Rogers, 1973, p. 384]

It is not necessary for us to resolve whether Carl Rogers is right or wrong. This quotation simply emphasizes the role that feelings play in day-to-day living.

Types of Affective Responses

Even the limited number of feeling interactions that we have inspected are difficult to classify. But Kantor and Smith (1975) offer the following suggestive schema for ordering feelings on the basis of (1) the kind of adjustment feeling responses require, (2) the kind of stimulus object involved, and (3) the intensity of response.

Passions. These feeling activities called *passions* are usually intense and specifically directed toward a particular stimulus object. We do not go around just loving, hating, or being jealous. When we love passionately, we love *someone*, or we hate *someone* "with a passion." Anger, jealousy, and revenging are further examples of passions.

Climactic feeling responses. A climactic affect has a development that rises to a climax ending in a release. Sudden disappointment, unexpected shock, overwhelming surprise, or sexual orgasm fit this category.

Affective sentiments. The patriotic sentiment provides an example of a powerful affective response, one that makes martyrs, for example, of volunteers for war. But religious feelings may work as effectively in the same way. Shame, pity for suffering creatures, modesty, charitableness, altruism, and feelings about hygienic conditions are additional examples. Some sentiments are culturally conditioned, for instance, sentiments toward children, the aged, and the dead. Some people around the Mediterranean region give unbridled expression of their grief at funerals of their loved ones even to the point of prostrating themselves on the casket or grave or kissing the corpse. Other cultures favor a more restrained expression of sentiment for the dead.

Moods. Children in a family may signal each other that now is not the time to ask Dad for permission to use the car because he is in a bad mood. If we inquire when his mood began, we learn that it started with an argument that he was involved in with his work supervisor. We can think of mood as a kind of "psychological hangover." Since the mood persists for some time after its origin, it apparently is not well organized or specifically directed toward a specific stimulus object. Metaphorically speaking, mood seems ready to attach itself to almost any stimulus object that comes along. Someone in a bad mood is ready to "pick another fight." When we want to request a favor of someone, we may ask (half jokingly), "Are you in a good mood this morning?" Pleasant moods that last for a considerable time period may have been initiated by a favorable report of a physical exam from the physician or by an unexpected check in the mail, although the individuals concerned may not be able to explain the origin of their happy mood.

Effect of "feeling good" on helping.

A study by Isen and Levin (1972) bears on the point of whether or not a mood may have an effect on other activities. More specifically, they wanted to determine whether "feeling good" would affect a person's subsequent helpfulness to others. They tried to "induce" a mood of "feeling good" by distributing cookies to a randomly selected group of subjects studying at individual carrels in the library. An equal number of students got nothing. The experimenter then solicited "help" from the subjects by asking them to participate as confederates in a psychology experiment. Half of the subjects were told that their participation in the experiment would help the experimental subjects, and the other half were told that what they were expected to do would distract and annoy the subjects. The experimenter, incidentally, had no way of knowing which students had received cookies.

Isen and Levin (1972, p. 386) state that

> The results of this experiment indicate that in terms of both number of subjects volunteering and amount of time volunteered, subjects who have unexpectedly received cookies help more, but distract less, than do those who have not received cookies. Thus, feeling good, induced naturalistically and in a way other than via report of success, seems to lead to increased helping, and to helping specifically, rather than to general activity.

Isen and Levin (1972) did another study to see whether "inducing" a mood of "feeling good" would affect *unsolicited help.* This time half their subjects found an unexpected dime in the coin-return slot of a pay telephone in an enclosed shopping mall. The subject was expected to help a young woman pick up papers that she had just dropped. Results showed that subjects who felt good by finding an unexpected dime were more helpful than control subjects in a situation in which "help" was not solicited. Their findings support the notion of mood as a continuing feeling response.

Methods of Studying Feeling Interactions

We have already noted the diffuseness of the organs that participate in affective interactions as a result of their intimate interconnection via the autonomic nervous system. And human anatomy is opaque. The only recourse left to us is to somehow tap the invisible, participating organs and systems within the organism. There is another important point here that must not be overlooked. Human arms and legs can become involved in gross operations such as in kicking, hurling, shoveling, or embracing the beloved. Their external attachment provides free scope to movements. But the heart, lungs, glands, stomach, eyes, and skin are anchored. Since they lack the freedom of movement granted to our appendages, they can only move in their fixed position. Therefore, their action is, of necessity, highly restricted. Thus, when John sees Jane, his heart can only beat more energetically or faster, the stomach glands can only increase or decrease hydrochloric acid production, a necessary ingredient of digestion, the tear glands can only secrete more or fewer tears, and so on.

Blood pressure.   When your physician wraps an inflatable cuff around your upper arm and blows it up, he is using a sphygmomanometer to check your blood pressure. Anyone who has studied blood pressure in the laboratory knows how difficult it is to get a "normal" reading. The physician, too, realizes that the patient's concern and even apprehension of the physical exam itself can affect blood pressure. Our interest in blood pressure comes in at the point at which it participates as an aspect of a person's total response in a "strained" marital, domestic, or business relationship. By contrast, the physiologist would be involved in blood pressure as a function of a condition of the blood vessels or some gland functioning or malfunctioning.

Blood volume.   When a person gets "white as a sheet" or "as red as a beet," there has been a considerable shift in the volume of blood in the upper part of the body. In the former case, the blood leaves the upper part of the body, and in the latter case there must have been a fairly rapid invasion of blood volume there. The spleen, a reservoir of blood in the abdominal region, is an important agent of such shifts in blood volume. The penile response we considered in the previous chapter may show spectacular changes in blood volume during acts of courting, and so on. Traditionally, blood-volume changes have been studied by means of the plethysmograph. This consists of a sleevelike apparatus filled with water that encloses a finger, hand, or foot. Increase or decrease in the volume of blood will be indicated by a rise or fall of the enclosed water level, which can be read in units of water pressure.

Heart rate.   The contractions of the heart can be conveniently felt at the wrist as a rhythmical throbbing of an artery produced by the increased volume of blood as a result of the heart action. Running in place can cause pulse increase or irregularity, which comes under the province of the physiologist. Our interests are served when the heart rate changes as a function of a heated argument or in the *anticipation of* climbing a rope.

Respiratory changes.   Under basal conditions, inspiration or breathing air in occupies a little less than half of the entire respiratory cycle (43%). But, in speech, inspiration takes only 16% of the cycle. We take a quick breath and let it out slowly during our speaking. In sudden fright, three-fourths of the cycle is spent in inspiration. In laughter, it is 23% (Young, 1973, p. 206).

Changes in the respiratory cycle are measured by the pneumograph, a flexible, air-filled tube that encircles the chest, adjusted to the comfort of the subject. A small tube extends from an opening around the larger chest tube and connects to a sensitive diaphragm. A stylus that rests on the diaphragm records the changes of rate, depth, and pattern of respiration on a recording paper.

The galvanic skin response.   The skin is quite an active organ in physiological as well as psychological ways. In fact, Montagu and Coles (1966, p. 261) consider the galvanic skin response (GSR) to be "the most sensitive physiological indicator of psychological events available to the psychologist."[2]

The GSR is obtained by applying a weak electrical current through the skin (too weak to be felt) and by measuring the resistance that the skin shows to the flow of current. The basic factor that affects skin resistance is the *activity* of the sweat glands, not the sweat as such. Temporary changes in the membranes of the sweat glands cause the fluctuations in skin resistance that can be read off on a meter. The use of the GSR in "lie detection" is based on the finding that neutral stimuli produce few or small decreases in skin resistance, while affective stimuli (pleasant or unpleasant) cause striking deflections of the meter indicator. Also novel, shocking, intense, or sudden stimuli produce larger changes than mild or familiar ones. It must have been a momentous discovery in the late 19th century, when researchers learned (see Neumann and Blanton, 1969) that the skin or "hide" of the organism, so apparently inert, played such an active, even sensitive, role in the psychological life of humans.

Lie detection as an art.   Lie detection as an art (it is not a science) is based on the premise that people with knowledge of a crime will try to conceal it in an effort to avoid punishment. If guilty, they may conceal their involvement by the proper facial expression and by lying. But their breathing, skin, and cardiovascular systems as components of psychological interactions "don't lie" when such people are questioned about the crucial aspects of the crime they are suspected of committing.

The concept underlying the use of the "lie detector" is based on a differential response to a list of words some of which are neutral and others of which have connection with the crime. The first lie detector relied on changes in breathing. Later, blood pressure (see Young, 1973, p. 216) and heart rate were added, and, finally, the galvanic skin response. While any one of the measures may be used alone, an operator feels more comfortable with a combination of measures. The four listed are considered basic, but today's "lie detectors" have added still other indexes such as finger and pulse volume and oxygen saturation measured by photoelectric sensors. As

---

[2] Other terms for this response are psychogalvanic response (PGR) and electrodermal response.

many as 20 indexes are used; hence the term *polygraph* (poly—means "many"). As to which measure is "best," Thackray and Orne (1968) complain about the lack of systematic laboratory research. Police and other users of "lie detectors" have reported a greater reliance on blood pressure and breathing measures and less so on the GSR. However, in line with the findings of other laboratory investigators, Thackray and Orne report that the GSR is most useful.

Does the polygraph work?   This is an important question in view of the widespread reliance on the polygraph. In addition to obtaining confessions and recovering losses in law enforcement, government has used it to test people already employed as well as job applicants. The hope is to obtain information on drug usage, homosexuality, medical conditions, or past criminal activity. "Business and government conduct an estimated 200,000 to 300,000 of these tests annually" (Abrams, 1973).

The urgent question is, then, "Does the 'lie detector' detect lying?" I believe that most psychologists would agree that the polygraph doesn't detect lying; at best, it "detects" the presence or absence of an affective or feeling response. Any person who feels guilty, embarrassed, ashamed, or frightened may provide "incriminating evidence." Suppose you or I were being subjected to a "lie-detection test" but that the *only* extent of our complicity in a crime was an intimate *knowledge* of the details of a crime. We might have obtained such by reading a police report or a newspaper account with no other involvement in the crime. Might we not incriminate ourselves by producing affective responses on the crucial words? Moreover, suppose the real criminal, who is a sociopath with no moral scruples, is also tested. Might not the machine declare such a person "innocent" because both crucial and neutral words elicited the same lack of affect? Such factors make lie detection an art and not a science. And, last but not least, might not all that formidable array of apparatus "work" by overwhelming the exhausted criminal into a confession? If so, what kind of a "lie detector" is that?

Muscle tension.   If one places electrodes over the muscles of the arms or legs and leads them by wire to an amplifier, one can pick up changes in the electrical activity of muscles under different conditions, even with the person lying still on a cot in a laboratory. Sustained contraction of certain muscles during anxiety can cause pain, such as tension headaches. Headache as the result of lead poisoning or alcoholic intoxication is a problem for the physiologist or physician, but when a person declares that "life is a headache," the psychologist sits up and takes notice. The apparatus for use in either case is called the *electromyograph.*

Headache as an expression of muscle tension.   In a biopsychological perspective, Bakal (1975) offers a thorough analysis of studies on headache. He first points out that headache is so common that it is difficult to find a person who has never had a headache (p. 370). Yet psychologists disown headache on the assumption that it has a physiological basis. Medical scientists reject it because they consider it to be complicated with psychological factors. Bakal's thesis is that both migraine and muscle-contraction headaches have psychological as well as physiological factors as underlying conditions.

Bakal suggests that migraine headache is connected with blood vessel tensions in the cranium and what he calls "autonomic nervous system instability" (p. 373). Another type of headache is thought to be the result of a chronic contraction of muscles about the face, scalp, neck, and shoulders. The latter is referred to as "muscle-contraction headache."

As for migraine sufferers, Henryk-Gutt and Rees (1973, p. 142) state that there is considerable clinical agreement that a migraine individual is a "tense, driving, obsessional perfectionist, with an inflexible personality, who maintains a store of bottled-up resentments which can neither be expressed nor resolved." Bakal (1975) pays lip service to "constitutional characteristics," (whatever they are), but he also points out that a minority of headache sufferers implicate the consumption of certain foods, alcohol, too much exercise, lack of sleep, and too much noise or light. Vacations, examinations, fear of failure, criticism, and too much responsibility have also been identified as precipitating factors. A high percentage of migraine patients blame their attacks on anxiety, personal problems, anger, or frustration. But the same kind of situation does not elicit the same response from all. So Bakal touches on a point agreeable to an interbehavioral viewpoint, namely, response specificity and idiosyncratic factors. It makes sense to study headaches within the framework of the individual's psychological history.

The pupillary response.   It is said that, in displaying wares before a potential buyer, the Chinese jade merchant watched the customer's eyes. Dilation of the pupils of the eye signaled excitement and interest, which told him how to proceed with the sale. Whether the story is true or not, it nevertheless fits in with recent laboratory findings. It is common knowledge that holding a flashlight before the eyes causes pupillary constriction and its removal, a dilation. That situation is obviously a physiological reflex. But when the pupil dilates in excitement, rage, fear, or pain, that is of psychological interest. The technique applied in either case is pupillometry.

The television pupillometer shown in Figures 11-3 and 11-4 uses a closed-circuit television system to observe the eye and to measure pupil diameter while showing it on the screen for continuous monitoring. Pupil diameter, in millimeters, is presented as a direct readout on a meter, but chart recording of pupillary action is also possible. The subject is positioned with the head comfortably supported by the chin rest and the forehead restraint bar. Because the field of vision is unobstructed, presentation of visual stimuli is facilitated. Such devices have been used as a unit of the "lie

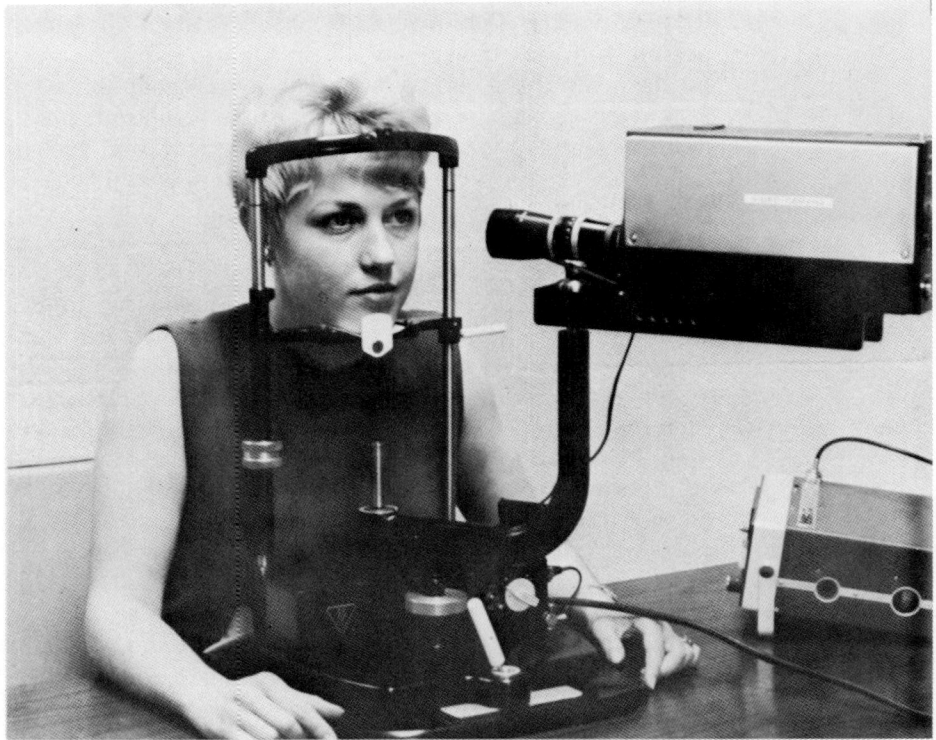

Figure 11-3 A pupillometer with subject positioned for response to presentation of auditory, visual, or other stimuli. The pupil is continuously monitored on a television screen, and the pupil diameter is shown directly on a panel meter. It can also be continuously recorded. See also Figure 11-4. (Courtesy of Whittaker Corporation.)

detector," as well as in consumer research, political and public opinion analysis, and drug-efficacy determination.

Studies in pupil size and affect. In 1965, Hess (1965) published a paper that created quite a stir. He tested four men and two women on a set of pictures, reasoning that pupil-size differences could not be explained in terms of brightness differences. Sure enough, the men showed greater pupillary dilation to female pinups and the women a greater increase to a male pinup and to a picture of a baby or one of a mother and baby. But when he showed them a stimulus such as a picture of sharks, the women's pupils narrowed, while the men's dilated (sharks were aversive stimuli for women, but not for men). Other findings forced Hess to conclude that unpleasant, uninteresting, or

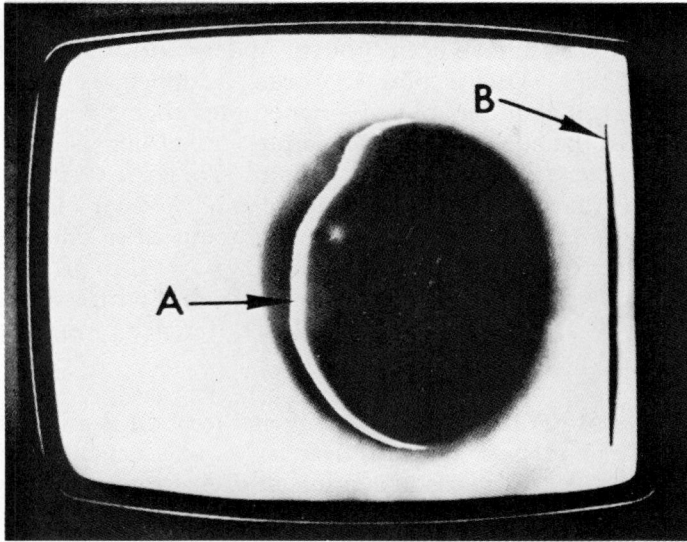

Figure 11-4 Pupillometer television monitoring screen displays an image of the subject's pupil diameter. The white crescent (a) aids focusing the image. The single black line (b) is equal in length to the height of the image, but a built-in recorder analyzes the data. (Courtesy of Whittaker Corporation.)

negative stimuli caused pupillary constriction and that positive, interesting, or pleasant stimuli had the opposite effect.

The trouble has been that a rapidly expanding literature in pupillometry does not support Hess' theory. In an extensive review article of the literature since 1960 on pupil size and affect, Janisse (1973) shows contradiction and confusion in the results obtained by a succession of investigators. After combing through more than 25 studies similar to that done by Hess, Janisse concludes that "Hess' conception of the bi-polarity of the pupil response to affect is not supported" (p. 320). Janisse also states that the important variable in pupillary-change studies is not whether an attitude toward a stimulus object is positive or negative but the intensity of the affect. "Stronger affect leads to greater dilation" (p. 322). Janisse also points out that the diversity of results may be partly due to the fact that what might be positive or negative to the experimenter may not be so to the subjects, a hint that statistical summing up of responses obliterates individual reactions. A reactional-biography approach may make more sense.

Biofeedback. Traditionally, a distinction was made between voluntary and involuntary responses. Striking a ball seems, on the face, different from heart rate, blood pressure, and brain waves. The latter seem to be beyond control, yet all have been brought under control via a technique known as *biofeedback*. This is how it works. A subject is connected with a continuously recording sphygmomanometer that gives an auditory or visual signal to the subject when blood pressure either rises or falls to a predetermined level. In this fashion, Shapiro, Turskey, Gershon, and Stern (1969) showed that human subjects could modify their blood pressure in either direction. Half of their subjects were required to raise their blood pressure and half, to lower it. A flashing light was used to provide feedback to male subjects who were rewarded after 20 flashes with a 3-second exposure of a picture of a nude woman. A marked difference in the final results emerged between the rise and fall groups.

Control of EEG activity.   As long as the brain is alive, it, like other living tissues, manifests electrical activity as one aspect of its life functioning. While its electrical action is miniscule, electronic amplification can make it visible. Recording is done by placing electrodes on the scalp or on the exposed brain directly. Under conditions of rest, the most common adult brain wave, alpha, occurs at the rate of 8 to 12 per second. In recent times, these waves have created great excitement because of their identification with Yogi and Zen monks' meditation.

It is true that humans can learn to differentiate between presence or absence of alpha waves, as Kamiya (1968) has demonstrated. He told his subjects whether they were right or wrong when asked to guess whether alpha waves were present or absent. Within seven 1-hour sessions, a majority of subjects achieved a significant proportion of correct responses. Following similar findings, some people went off the deep end in overestimating the results of the voluntary production of alpha. Buck (1976, p. 135) offers a restrained evaluation of alpha's possibilities in the following quotation:

> Many people have seized upon the relationship between alpha activity and meditation, on the one hand, and the apparent increases in alpha activity with feedback, on the other, as evidence that alpha feedback could facilitate the learning of meditation ("turn on the power of your mind" read one advertisement for an alpha feedback device), or at least providing a unique and pleasant high. These hopes have been disappointed by studies using control groups which do not receive feedback. Such groups have been found to produce alpha rhythms during rest that are as abundant as those of groups receiving feedback (Lynch and Paskewitz, 1971). Thus, although people can learn to increase and decrease alpha rhythms with biofeedback, they apparently cannot increase alpha past the level they would spontaneously have if resting. There is no evidence that alpha feedback can facilitate the learning of meditation.

Biofeedback has been applied to a number of organic problems such as cardiovascular disorders, headache, gastric disorders, epilepsy, and relaxation therapy, but, because experimental controls are hard to exercise in a treatment situation, the results so far must be viewed with caution. One note of hope comes from Basmajian (1972), who has applied biofeedback to the training of wind-instrument players who try to approximate the pattern of muscle potentials recorded from the lip- and cheek-muscle potentials of professional players. According to Buck (1976, p. 142), this application could lead to a new area of training in the development of human skills.

Selye's Stress Syndrome

Working in his laboratory at McGill University, Hans Selye (1956) was studying the effect of the injection of certain hormones on rats. He was surprised to find that they all got sick. Examining them in greater detail, he discovered that they showed similar symptoms, including stomach ulcers, enlarged adrenal glands, and shrunken thymus glands and lymph nodes. Suspecting impurities in the hormones he was using, he checked out his hunch and injected more rats with formalin, a solution of formaldehyde that acts as an irritant. He got the same results. Then he exposed rats to severe cold, drugs, and disease, conditions that subjected the organism to punishing strains on its adaptive capacity. He again found a similar pattern and named it the "stress syndrome," which he defined as a nonspecific bodily reaction common to all stress. There is more to the stress syndrome but, for our purposes, this brief explanation of it will suffice.

The topics in the present chapter seemed to call for, at least, a brief consideration of Selye's stress syndrome. As a reminder, we noted the role of the heart (as concerns its rate), blood pressure, blood volume, aspects of breathing, the galvanic skin response, muscle tension, and the pupillary response. They all show a readiness for participating in lively and abundant ways in stressful as well as nonstressful interactions (see Figure 11-5). As one example, tension headaches do not result from tension induced from painting the ceiling. That would be a physiological event. They come into our purview only because they were an aspect of interactions that were responses to stimulus situations eliciting anxiety, frustration, resentment, or anger. As transient responses, they may cause no problem. We know that a brief anger episode may show engorgement of the stomach mucosa, a resultant fragility, and increased gastric (hydrochloric acid) secretion (Wolf and Wolff, 1943; Wolff, 1953). But within minutes the gastric condition returns to normal. However, if a person continues for an indefinite period in a condition of apprehension, anxiety, fear, despair, frustration, or hopelessness, the stress syndrome can result in a bleeding ulcerated stomach. The following report, based on a publication, *Emotional Antecedents of Bleeding from Peptic Ulcer,* by Hollender, Soults, and Ringold (1971), illustrates the physiological consequences of a chronic affective (stress) reaction.

Bleeding from peptic ulcers as a stress reaction. Hollender, Soults, and Ringold (1971) came across two patients with peptic ulcers that they were

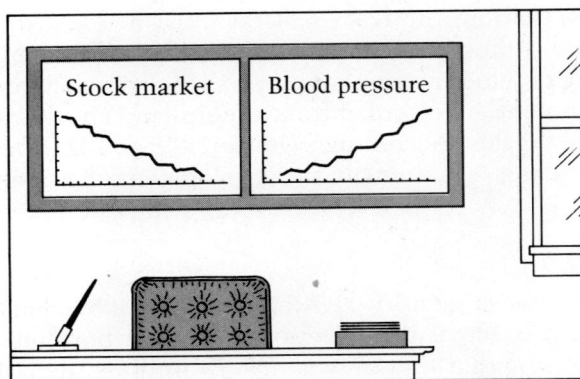

Figure 11-5 As the stock-market quotations continue to drop, note what happens to blood pressure.

studying for presentation to medical students.[3] Their attention was directed to the possible role of affective conditions as precipitating factors in the bleeding ulcers. As a result of other observations and from cases appearing in the literature, Hollender and his coworkers developed the following hypothesis: "A disturbing experience arousing intense feelings and creating a situation which seemed insoluble, might be a precipitating stress in producing hemorrhage from a peptic ulcer" (p. 199).

In interviewing a total of 15 patients, Hollender and his associates found seven instances in which bleeding followed an affective crisis and an additional one was equivocal (p. 199). One patient reported recurrent bleeding related to the following life conditions: when his wife left him with their children on account of his drinking, when he was almost run over by a train in the railroad yards, and when he was afraid his brother might have been killed in an airplane accident. Similar stressful conditions turned up in other interviews. Hollender and his coworkers state that the relationship between the crisis and the bleeding was so striking that "it seems unlikely that it is purely coincidental" (p. 199). Note that Hollender *obtained clear-cut evidence* of the presence of peptic ulcers in his patients (p. 203).

These cases were not isolated events. Hollender, Soults, and Ringold (1971) quote a study of 1000 men with duodenal ulcers, patients in an army hospital. There were 652 instances of bleeding (in 499 patients) and 124 instances of perforation. But other reports indicate that in the civilian population, bleeding occurs in less than 10% of patients. Could the radical difference between the two populations lie in the greater threat (stress) to soldiers in a military situation?

[3] The term *peptic* covers both gastric (or stomach) ulcers and those in the adjoining portion of the small intestine, the duodenum.

Stress and the sex ratio of offspring.   There is nothing beneficial about stress that causes peptic ulcers to bleed and perforate. But could a certain amount of stress be used in helping parents produce either boy or girl babies? At Iowa State University, Schuster and Schuster (1969a, 1969b, 1972) formulated a hypothesis that "the parent under less stress near the time of conception would reproduce its own sex in the offspring" (1969b, p. 335). The stress that the Schusters referred to was *mild* stress as shown by an ambitious, hard-working husband aiming for success. They assumed that a certain degree of continued mild stress in the man would inhibit the male sex gamete, favoring spermatozoa that produced girl babies. However, if the mother was a career woman, or socially or politically venturesome or socially aggressive, the resultant stress would provide a vaginal condition that would inhibit female-producing spermatozoa, thus producing mostly boy babies. If both parents were equally stressed, they would likely produce an equal number of boys and girls but maybe only one of each. Equal ratios of male and female progeny would be produced if neither parent was stressed.

The Schusters' thesis did not just come to them "out of the blue." An earlier publication by Snyder (1961) showed that pilots of fighter aircraft flying at lower elevations (at greater hazard to them) produced more girl babies, while pilots of bombers flying at higher and safer altitudes fathered more boy babies. Schuster and Schuster (1969b) also did a number of rat studies that supported their hypothesis that the parent under less stress close to conception tended to have offspring of the same sex.

They also checked out their hypothesis on a human population. They could not manipulate people by stressing them the way they did rats, so they selected people with certain personalities that already showed stress. Data from 94 parents in Los Angeles permitted the Schusters to produce a significant prediction of familial sex ratio from their subjects' anxiety scores.

The Schusters do not contradict the well-established finding that the male Y-chromosome from the sperm determines a male offspring. They say,

> However, our observations indicate that the female parent can influence whether a male-producing (XY) or female-producing (XX) sperm fertilizes the ovum. Our theory first postulates that the male parent under mild stress will produce predominantly female (XX) sperm; if not stressed, he produces both female and male sperm in about equal numbers. Our second postulate is that the female parent under mild stress has a vaginal environment favorable to the male (XY) sperm primarily; if not stressed, there is no differential penetrability effect. [Schuster and Schuster, 1969a]

Implications of the Schuster studies.   Apparently all stress is not bad, a notion that agrees with the most recent pronouncements of Selye, "the father of stress," who now talks about *eustress* ("good stress") (Cherry, 1978). In applying the idea of eustress to controlling the sex of one's offspring, here is some advice from the Schusters (1969a, p. 2):

If you are a man wishing for a son, it helps to pick a wife with a bit of a temper. If you are the one with a bit of a temper, try to find a way to relax for awhile. You don't need to play the best golf game, go to the farthest point on a vacation, mentally feud with people, earn a higher college degree than your brother, catch more fish than your neighbor, at least for a month or two! If this is not possible, plan conception after a major triumph. . . .

If you are one who is concerned about the underpopulation of the family rather than the overpopulation of the nation, perhaps the theory can be of some help to you. There seems to be a certain percentage of women who because of childhood conditioning or metabolic makeup find it extremely difficult to conceive and carry a female child, but who can conceive and carry a male child with very little trouble. But if the father can not solve or sidestep his anxieties, perhaps you both can play the game of deleting from your lives, actions and thought of proving yourselves, being right or doing your thing better than anyone else. Perhaps one of you will succeed and a son or a daughter will be conceived.[4]

The Schusters are not dogmatic about their theory or their findings and urge others to attempt to verify their results.

Emotional Interactions

With the terms *feelings* or *affective interactions*, we segregated a distinct form of behavior, behavior illustrated by passions, climactic feelings, affective sentiments, and moods. These reactions were characterized as very definite responses toward stimulus objects. In their patterning, they involved predominantly the visceral and glandular systems and the skin, and they reflected the direction of the primary consequence of feelings toward the organism. As such, affective interactions were contrasted with effective interactions in which the primary consequence was toward the stimulus object, the person turning, lifting, or carrying something. Now, if we can find a number of distinct phenomena, very different from feeling interactions, why waste the term *emotion*? Why not apply it to these events that, heretofore, have been treated indiscriminately along with feelings? In the following definition, then, borrowed from Kantor and Smith (1975), we shall delimit an explicit form of behavior, the emotional interaction.

Definition of the Term

In the emotional behavior segment, we find a very abnormal condition present. Whereas affective and all other responses show a follow-up of their attentional and perceptual phases with a final reaction system, emotional

---

[4] Wittels and Bornstein (1974) hypothesized that a female, when raped (presumably under extreme stress), would tend to produce boy babies. They found that, in ten cases of rape, nine of the ten resulting babies were male by comparison with the usual 50:50 ratio.

interactions stop short of the final phase. For that reason, they are abnormal or atypical. We may also think of them as aborted behavior segments, because they did not continue on to completion. Instead of the smoothness of operation of a normal behavior segment, the emotional behavior segment is disruptive, in that it causes at least a momentary gap in the flow of psychological events. The adjustmental feature so prominent in other events is lacking in this class of behaviors. With this as a working definition, let us move on to some concrete examples in which we hope to show the characteristic features of emotional-behavior segments.

Stuttering

Careful observation reveals occasional nonfluent speech in everybody. For example, Lay and Paivio (1969) gave a group of subjects three verbal tasks of increasing difficulty to perform while verbalizing. The number of filled pauses in relaxation to the total number of words spoken showed an increase with task difficulty. The most common filled pause was the indefinite article *a*, which was lengthened into the familiar and almost universal "ah" sound. Rate of word repetition also increased with word difficulty, as did false starts. Thus, there is evidence to show mild degrees of speech disruption in everyone's speech in tense situations.[5] We can see the breakup of speech more clearly in the so-called stutterer. In the stutterer's speech, we find repetition of sounds with alternating blocks and releases. Whereas speech organs in the nonstutterer function in an integrated way, in the stutterer they do not work in harmony. They seem to go their separate ways.

The following diagram represents an emotional behavior segment that starts out like any other. The man, a stutterer, wants to say, "There's the ball." We may assume that he has attended and perceived the ball prior to his vocal reference to it.

EMOTIONAL BEHAVIOR SEGMENT

Attention ---------------- Perception ---------------------- Incompletion of final ·
reaction system

"There's the   b-b-b-b-b-b-b," and so on.   Psychological gap

All goes well for a while until he comes to that dreaded sound *b*, which has always given him trouble. At this point, he gets "hung up" and keeps perseverating in a series of reflexlike spasms involving the jaw! For an interminable period, no matter that he puts ever more energy into the task, no other sound comes forth but *b*. The stutterer in this emotional behavior

---

[5] Bloodstein (1970) has proposed a continuity hypothesis that views speech disturbances, particularly in childhood, as of "almost universal occurrence" and avoids such terms as "stutterers" and "nonstutterers."

segment seems reduced to mere reflex functioning (as regards *this specific speech reaction*). There appears to be nothing psychological in his vocal action, any more than there would be if we were to keep tapping his patellar tendon to obtain a series of knee jerks. During his emotional block, he acts as if he were at the mercy of the tonic (continuous muscular contraction) and clonic (rapid muscular contraction *and* relaxation) spasms. If a new stimulus function happily intrudes into the stutterer's situation, he can complete his response and start another behavior segment. Because our example is so extreme, it shows the essential atypical features of an emotional behavior segment.

To most people, stuttering appears to be so abnormal and involuntary that they look on it as an exclusively biological event. Flanagan, Goldiamond, and Azrin (1958) speculated that, if stuttering were biologically determined, then it could not be modified with behavioral techniques. They decided to treat stuttering as operant behavior and see if they could bring it under control. In one experiment, Flanagan and his coworkers assigned three stutterers the task of reading aloud from printed copy. At each stutter, during a 30-minute session, the experimenters pressed a switch and obtained a base rate of stuttering. During the next 30 minutes, they delivered a blast of white noise to the subjects' ears via earphones on the occasion of every stutter. During the following 30-minute period, the quiet that prevailed during the first 30-minute interval was reinstated. The results? Stuttering was almost completely eliminated.

Because Flanagan, Goldiamond, and Azrin had been successful in converting high-rate stutterers into low-rate stutterers, they speculated about the possibilities of taking normally fluent speakers who are really "low-rate stutterers" and trying to change them into stutterers. This time during the recording session, they delivered a *continuous* low-level shock that was discontinued for a 10-second interval every time the subject reacted with a speech block. Obviously, if the subject could "stutter" every 10 seconds, the shock could be averted completely. The results were dramatic. Flanagan and associates had transformed a normally fluent subject into a stutterer.[6]

The facts that stuttering behavior can (1) be brought under experimental control and that it can (2) be "produced" demonstrate that we are dealing with psychological interactions that show modifiability, inhibition, and other identifying properties of behavioral events. The very conspicuous biological features during the "block" or "gap" phase of the behavior segment should not blind us to the psychological phases that precede it. In the case of stuttering, we should not overlook the fact that the reflex spasms are part of a psychological matrix. With stuttering to serve as a magnified emotional behavior segment, we now consider other varieties of a striking class of behaviors.

---

[6] This story has a happy ending, too; for Flanagan and his coworkers restored "the stutterer" to "non-stuttering" status through further conditioning.

Fainting as an Emotional Response

A nurse candidate has been assigned to observe her first surgical operation. She courageously watches the surgeon take scalpel in hand and cut through the abdominal tissues of the patient. So far, so good. She has attended and perceived, but when she sees the blood begin to collect in the incision, she collapses to the floor, from which point on she is "out of it." The attending nurses do their job, but she continues to lie prostrate on the floor. Obviously, there is nothing psychologically adjustmental about her limp-as-a-rag response. Here, we have another example of a disruptive, atypical interaction, another gap, during which the young woman has been reduced to mere physiological action. The heart keeps pumping, the lungs keep up their breathing function, but the continuity of her psychological interactions has been interrupted. Speak to her and she does not hear you. Offer her $1000 and you still get no response. But after some minutes she "comes to," looks around, and asks, "What happened?" Now the gap is closed, and she continues her psychological life where she left off. She was temporarily locked into an emotional-behavior segment from the moment she perceived the patient's blood until she saw, heard, talked, and behaved in other ways following the gap. Because her former interaction failed to go on to completion after she saw the blood, her action constitutes an aborted or truncated response—in other words, an emotional behavior segment. In an attempt to keep matters straight, we should note that fainting may be either a biological or a psychological affair. If you have been sitting a long time and the carotid reflex in your neck is not responsive enough to execute the proper blood-volume shift, you could feel dizzy or even faint. That would be a physiological event. But, if you read a telegram saying, "Your uncle left you a million dollars," and then fainted, your overwhelming response occurred in a psychological context.

The Startle Response

Our next exhibit is one that "comes and goes in less than one-half second" (Landis and Hunt, 1939, p. 27). If you are deep into an Alfred Hitchcock mystery story with the wind howling on a winter's night and all of a sudden the cat knocks over a pan onto the kitchen floor, you know what a startle response is. At a normal speaking rate, it takes 1 second to say *chimpanzee,* so your startle response is over before you get halfway through that phase. Obviously, we are involved with a high-speed phenomenon.

For a long time, the rapidity of the startle response discouraged its analysis. Then Landis and Hunt got a brilliant idea. Why not use high-speed motion-picture cameras in such a way that accurate timing of the stimulus and of the temporal sequence of happenings could be recorded? So they (Landis and Hunt, 1939) photographed the startle-response pattern with a superspeed camera running at about 1500 exposures per second. A timing unit made a photographic registration of time in one-thousandths of a second directly on the film (p. 27). With their clever procedure, Landis and Hunt did such a thorough analysis of the startle response that it has not required replication.

Once they had their startle response on film, they could run the film at slow speed or stop it at any particular frame. They found that the overall pattern could be described as a "shrinking" in which the eye blink was the first element of the pattern to appear. It took one-tenth of a second. Other aspects that followed were a head movement forward, change in facial expression, raising and drawing forward of the shoulders, movement upward of the upper arms, bending of the elbows, rotation of the lower arms, flexion of the fingers, forward movement of the trunk, contraction of the abdomen, and bending of the knees. All that action in less than a second!

The startle response as an emotional response.   How does the startle response fit in with the paradigm of emotional behavior? To begin with, total absorption in some other task and a lesser intensity of an auditory stimulus could be manipulated so as to fail to elicit the startle response. There must be precurrent attending and perceiving reaction systems and then the startle response. But would you consider the facial distortion, the shrinking, blinking, bending, and extending of the head and limbs an adjustmental act? No, this is the very opposite. During that less than one-half second, the organism is totally incapacitated for effective action. Thus, in terms of dealing with the stimulus object, the organism in the startle response is momentarily "out of it," manifesting a brief gap typical of the emotional behavior segment. Figure 11-6 illustrates how to exploit the startle reflex.

Is the startle response subject to modification? Landis and Hunt (1939, p. 54) succeeded in conditioning it by presenting a buzzer as a conditioned

Figure 11-6   Putting the startle response to work in producing exotic works of art.

stimulus and a revolver shot as an unconditioned stimulus. They also made an interesting observation on a group of experienced police officers during revolver practice on a police range. Under the conditions present, Landis and Hunt were only able to record head and eye responses. Despite their broad experience, these marksmen had not *completely* eliminated every phase of the startle response. "Convinced only by a demonstration of the film, they were quite surprised to find that they "made faces" when the revolver was fired, despite their years of training" (Landis and Hunt, 1939, p. 37). But most of the pattern had been brought under control. With rats, which do show the startle response, Moyer (1963) and Korn and Moyer (1966) have demonstrated habituation of the startle response and of heart rate to the sound of pistol shots; the habituation was shown over trials and over days.

Epilepsy as an Emotional Response

It is possible to arrange emotional interactions on a scale of intensity. At the low-intensity end, we might place the reaction of an individual during a near-collision. The gripping feeling in the gut region, with possible loss of control, can lead to embarrassing consequences. If you have ever seen a person in an epileptic seizure, surely you would agree that it should be placed toward the high-intensity end. It is the latter extreme, totally unrestrained activity, which we now examine.

Jacksonian epilepsy.   As a help in orienting us toward the role of biological factors, let us first consider the epileptic with a brain tumor—Jacksonian epilepsy. Such an epileptic shows convulsions confined to certain groups of muscles. How are we to understand this problem? I suggest that we consider the tumor as an invasion of foreign tissue with no other function except to interfere with "normal" biological functioning. As a growing lump, it is obviously a stimulus in its own right, metaphorically speaking, a "thorn in the flesh." If someone were to press hard on a person's brain through a hole in the skull, the consequences would be a convulsive seizure. The expanding tumor must have a comparable effect. I suggest that, because it is continuously present, that it has a disintegrative psychological effect—the person concerned is at a disadvantage as a participant in psychological interactions. In everyday terms, such a person has difficulty in maintaining personality integrity and unity. When the variables pile up against the person, the tumor has done its work and the result is a seizure. Is there any support for such a view? Yes. I believe that the high degree of success achieved with surgical removal of the tumor proves that extraction of the "thorn in the flesh" eliminates the seizures. I also believe that our analysis of this case gives due credit to the place of biological factors in psychological events. There is no doubt about their role as participating factors. But there is more to the etiology or "causation" of epilepsy than brain tumors.

Idiopathic or typical epilepsy.   The term *idiopathic* is usually defined as "arising spontaneously or from an obscure or unknown cause." Idiopathic epilepsy "occurs without any evident cause." The silent assumptions underlying those definitions are based on a self-actional, reductionistic framework. The thinking behind such views is that the only condition that can provoke an epileptic seizure must be anatomical, biochemical, or physiological. We shall consider other possible factors than those located in the biological makeup of the individual after we have obtained a clear picture of what a seizure looks like.

An epileptic seizure.   Let us start with a case of psychogenic (psychologically developed) seizure reported by Livingston (1956). A young man finds his previously healthy mother dead, whereupon he has an epileptic seizure. Reconstructing the scene, we are on sure ground in saying that he attended to, and perceived, the prostrate figure of his mother on the floor. We could find another person in a similar situation who would have followed up the perceptual act with a final reaction system of calling for an ambulance, and so on. But not this young man. In the place of that psychological adjustment, he "passes out of the picture" completely. From this point on, a psychologist has nothing to do for a time. The person in a seizure is reduced to mere physiological activity of a violent and chaotic sort. A kind of biological explosion occurs in which the organism appears to be under the control of a series of haphazard reflex reactions.

During this phase, epileptics fail to maintain posture. Unable to gravitate properly, they may fall to the ground, screaming. But the scream is not "voluntary"; it occurs only as a reflex spasm of the muscles of the lungs, diaphragm, and vocal chords. Epileptics may also reflexively bite their tongues unless precautions are taken against it. Many other muscles of the arms, legs, face, and eyes may twitch, so that epileptics look as though they were throwing themselves about. Drooling, urination, and sexual and defecation reflexes may assert themselves during this psychological gap. Yet the salivary gland, bladder, and rectal conditions are the same during the seizure as they were just before it occurred. Is it possible that the ordinary inhibitions operative during the epileptics' preseizure (psychological) period were no longer functional during the psychological gap? It appears that organisms are at the mercy of independently operating physiological reflexes as soon as they cease to participate in psychological events. This is the no-response phase of the seizure.

Such a picture of an epileptic seizure as an example of an emotional behavior segment is difficult to demonstrate experimentally. Therefore, we move on to a "field observation" of a typical seizure. The source of our picture of what an epileptic goes through is a literary one. However, it harmonizes with clinical descriptions because it was derived from self-observation. Since Dostoyevsky (1868/1925) was himself an epileptic, he describes, with clinical accuracy, the behavior of Myshkin, an epileptic and a character in Dostoyevsky's novel *The Idiot:*

> The staircase up which Myshkin ran from the gateway led to the corridors of the first and second floors, on which were the rooms of the hotel. As in all old houses, the staircase was of stone, dark and narrow, and it turned round a thick stone column. On the first half-landing there was a hollow like a niche in the column, not more than half a yard wide and nine inches deep. Yet there was room for a man to stand there. Dark as it was, Myshkin, on reaching the half-landing, at once discovered that a man was hiding in the niche. Myshkin suddenly wanted to pass by without looking to the right. He had taken one step already, but he could not resist turning around.
>
> Those two eyes, *the same two eyes,* met his own. The man hidden in the niche had already moved one step from it. For one second they stood facing one another and almost touching. Suddenly Myshkin seized him by the shoulders and turned him back towards the staircase, nearer to the light; he wanted to see his face more clearly.
>
> Rogozhin's eyes flashed and a smile of fury contorted his face. His right hand was raised and something gleamed in it; Myshkin did not think of check-ing it. He only remembered that he thought he cried out, "Parfyon, I don't believe it!" Then suddenly something seemed torn asunder before him; his soul was flooded with intense *inner* light. The moment lasted perhaps half a second, yet he clearly and consciously remembered the beginning, the first sound of the fearful scream which broke of itself from his breast and which he could not have checked by any effort. Then his consciousness was instantly extinguished and complete darkness followed.
>
> It was an epileptic fit, the first he had had for a long time. It is well known that epileptic fits come on quite suddenly. At the moment the face is horribly distorted, especially the eyes. The whole body and the features of the face work with convulsive jerks and contortions. A terrible, indescribable scream that is unlike anything else breaks from the sufferer. In that scream everything human seems obliterated and it is impossible or very difficult, for an observer to realise and admit that it is the man himself screaming. It seems indeed as though it were someone else screaming from within the man. That is how many people at least have described their impression. The sight of a man in an epileptic fit fills many people with positive and unbearable horror, in which there is a certain element of the uncanny. It must be supposed that some such feeling of sudden horror, together with the other terrible sensations of the moment, had suddenly paralysed Rogozhin and so saved Myshkin from the knife with which he would have stabbed him. Then before he had time to grasp that it was a fit, seeing that Myshkin had staggered away from him and fallen backwards downstairs, knock-ing his head violently against the stone step, Rogozhin flew headlong down-stairs, avoiding the prostrate figure, and, not knowing what he was doing, ran out of the hotel.
>
> Struggling in violent convulsions, the sick man slipped down the steps, of which there were about fifteen, to the bottom of the staircase. Very soon, not more than five minutes later, he was noticed and a crowd collected. A pool of blood by his head raised the doubt whether the sick man had hurt himself, or

whether there had been some crime. It was soon recognized, however, that it was a case of epilepsy; one of the people at the hotel recognized Myshkin as having arrived that morning. The difficulty was luckily solved by a fortunate circumstance. [Dostoevsky, 1868/1925, pp. 221–223]

We must not overlook the important details of Myshkin's preseizure behavior. Dostoyevsky carefully points out that Myshkin attended to, and perceived, his attacker. He even tried to see him more clearly, but instead of grabbing the knife out of Parfyon's hand and saving himself, he suddenly goes into a no-response phase and tumbles down the stairs in an epileptic seizure.

An inquiry into the nature of stimuli of the seizure response.   In the case of Myshkin, a life-threatening situation was the apparent precipitating factor in his seizure. What other stimuli do we find related to this particularly immoderate form of emotional response? The answer is "Quite a variety." For example, although "music hath charms to soothe a savage breast," it provokes others to an extravagant waste of uncoordinated action, as in musicogenic epilepsy. Daly and Barry (1957) have reviewed the literature on music-induced seizures including Critchley's 20 cases. If we inquire as to what kind of music had this unexpected effect, we find extreme variation from person to person. With some, it was any kind of music; with others, it was more specific. One patient experienced a seizure "only when he himself played the piano, another when he heard a brass wind instrument play bass notes" (p. 399). The popular song, "Green Eyes," always sent a third patient into a seizure. On one occasion, while eating in a restaurant, someone played "Green Eyes" on a jukebox, which brought on another seizure. Note the extreme specificity of stimulus-function operant even in such erratic, convulsive action as we are dealing with here. Unfortunately, the reactional-biography details are missing that would help us understand why "Green Eyes" had such a drastic effect on one man and so with the other cases.

As a test for ruling out epilepsy, Roman slave traders would rotate a potter's wheel before the eyes of slaves being considered for purchase. Recent research has shown that flickering light evokes seizures of every degree of severity. It is a short step from a flickering light to a flickering television screen. In 1966, Daube (1966) reported that in the previous 13 years there had been reports in the literature of approximately 100 patients who experienced seizures of all degrees of severity while watching television. Some patients had seizures only while watching television. Most of them went into convulsion while adjusting the set or sitting very close to it, especially in a dark room. Almost all were sensitive to light stimulation. And some patients had self-induced, visually precipitated seizures elicited by waving their hands with separated fingers before their eyes, others by jumping up and down in front of venetian blinds (Sherwood, 1962, p. 49).

"Reading epilepsy" has been reported by Bickford (1956) and his associates. Their patients were troubled with a clicking sensation in their jaws after prolonged reading. If they continued beyond that point, a major motor seizure would result. In all, about 25 cases of "reading epilepsy" have turned up in the literature. If we ask about the specificity of seizure-eliciting stimuli, we find it. According to Daube (1966), in many cases the reading material was highly specific "such as newsprint, Hebrew, or personal material. This material often had an emotional significance for the patient" (p. 528).[7]

We have previously noted musicogenic epilepsy, but there are other auditory stimuli that also produce seizures. Sudden loud noises have been effective, but so has cessation of noise (Daube, 1966, p. 529). Daube also reports "a significant component of startle" (p. 529) in some cases of auditory seizure (an intriguing comment in relation to my inclusion of startle as emotional behavior).

Other sensory-precipitated seizures reported by Daube (1966) occurred by rubbing or tapping certain parts of the body such as the right side or the thumb. We close with an instructive case among others in which a sudden movement of an extremity produced seizures. Out of a series of 15 cases, 5 patients could voluntarily induce the seizure. "Some of the convulsions could be precipitated by startle, or surprise, as well as by movement" (p. 531). Holding the leg could slow down or inhibit the convulsion. Daube (1966) describes the case of a 35-year-old man with fairly localized seizures of the right leg. He could initiate a seizure by movement of the leg. He was more likely to have a seizure when he was under stress. Eventually, a surgical operation on the brain revealed a scar on the cortex. Electrical stimulation in the region of the scar produced the typical seizure. Removal of the scar completely eliminated the seizure.

Our common two-valued semantic orientation makes it easy to think of epileptic seizures as due to either biological factors (such as tumors) *or* psychological ones. But the case just described shows the possible simultaneous complicity of biological *and* psychological variables: scar tissue pressing on nerves, thus facilitating the individual's disintegration, plus "stress," a shorthand way of acknowledging the presence of affective and/or emotional conditions.

The lesson of this case is that all the relevant factors must be searched out, biological and psychological. Yet we must realize that psychological factors such as fear, conflict, worry, alarm, frustration, anger, rage, grief, and resentment alone, without help from anatomical and physiological conditions, are capable of convulsing people. In fact, Daube (1966, p. 533) cites a number of physicians who conclude that "affective responses play a major part in the precipitation of convulsions." Above all else, we must not overlook the fact that the epileptic seizure fits our paradigm of the emotional

[7] These facts come close to the specific details that we require for a psychological (individual) study that would help make sense of otherwise strange cases.

behavior segment, with the usual attentional and perceptual reactions followed by a radical, no-response gap manifesting only a chaotic biological eruption in place of the usual adjustmental final-reaction system.

Sudden Death

> *My life* [Hunter said] *is at the mercy of any scoundrel who chooses to put me in a passion"*; it was indeed such an event which precipitated his sudden death.
>
> [Lown, 1977, p. 663, concerning John Hunter, 1728–1793, celebrated Scottish surgeon, anatomist, physiologist, and pathologist]

In the United States every year, about 450,000 people die when their hearts no longer contract as a unit. Their sudden death is the result of ventricular fibrillation (Lown and Verrier, 1976, p. 1165), a condition in which the individual muscle fibers contract separately in a totally uncoordinated way, preventing the heart from doing its job. And, yet, according to Lown and Verrier (1976, p. 1165), the fact that those who recover may live many years after the episode without structural damage to the heart suggests that such occurrences represent an electrical accident. But what could possibly evoke such a disorganization of heart action in which the heart is reduced to a nonrhythmic, quivering mass of muscle?

Lown and Verrier (1976) have experimentally produced irregularity of heartbeat in animals by means of electrical and drug stimulation. However, they criticize a too-narrow view of "the heart and vasculature . . . as a self-contained system" (p. 1169). They exposed dogs to two different situations, a cage in which the dogs were left undisturbed and a sling in which they received a shock at the end of each experimental period for three days. Comparison on Days 4 and 5 (without shock) showed that the dogs in the sling revealed extremely rapid heartbeat and extra heartbeats, a precursor of fibrillation. The authors conclude that "psychological stress can profoundly reduce the cardiac threshold for ventricular fibrillation" (p. 1169).

But how about humans? Obviously, one cannot subject them to experimental production of fibrillation. Fortunately, there is at least one incidence in a clinical setting of a violent attack of ventricular rapid action that was prevented from passing into ventricular fibrillation and death. The incident is reported in an article, "Paroxysmal Ventricular Tachycardia Due to Emotion: Possible Mechanism of Death From Fright," by Harvey and Levine (1952).

The patient, a 29-year-old woman, made multiple complaints about her heart such as shortness of breath, tensions, and palpitations. Laboratory investigation by fluoroscopic, X-ray, EKG, and other procedures showed no abnormalities of her heart whatsoever. Part of the medical work-up was an inquiry into the possible effect of amyl nitrite. The patient was a volunteer participant. She was connected with the phonocardiograph, a device for amplifying and recording the heart sounds. The instant the patient set eyes on the drug she was to take, the normal tracings and heart sounds were transformed into a machine-gun beat. According to Harvey and Levine (1952) a more severe fright might have caused a prolonged heart speedup leading to fibrillation and sudden death. "Scared to death" themselves when they heard the change in the phonocardiograph, the experimenters beat a rapid retreat with the drug and the patient's heartbeat returned to normal.

Outside of extremely limited laboratory or clinical evidence on sudden death, one is restricted to field observation of conditions in the life history of victims of sudden death. Lown, Verrier, and Rabinowitz (1977) report that "certain chronic emotional tension states have been associated with an increased prevalence of sudden death" (p. 900). Bereavement is one such factor. In one study of 4486 widowers, 55 years of age or older, within the first 6 months after loss of spouse, there was an increase in death rate that was 40% above the expected rate for married men of a matching age group.

In an inquiry into the antecedents of sudden death, Rahe (in Lown, Verrier, and Rabinowitz, 1977, p. 900) retrospectively interviewed the families of 226 victims of sudden coronary death in Finland. He found a pattern of significant life changes in the preceding 6 months. Divorce, grief, and disturbances and changes in work conditions were noted, factors that were lacking in the same time interval a year earlier. Twenty-six widows reported that anger and anxiety over work conditions and chronic depression preceded the sudden deaths of their husbands.

Greene, Goldstein, and Moss (1972) did a retrospective study of 26 patients who died suddenly in a population of 44,000 workers of the Eastman Kodak Company. Moss, who was largely responsible for conducting the study, studied the plant's medical records, those from the physicians, and interviewed the surviving next of kin, mostly wives. The data reveal that the majority (80%) of the victims had been depressed from a week up to several months prior to their decease (p. 729).

A case history.   One 55-year-old man, a long-time employee at the plant, a habitually disorganized man, during the summer months began getting things in order, both at home and at work. His wife suspected that he felt something was going to happen to him when he looked up his insurance policies and got his accounts and correspondence up to date, both at home and at work. The man was depressed over conflict with a son who had served a jail sentence for stealing. The couple was also ambitious to send another son to college with their savings, but he had turned them down. In fact, the boy was going to have to repeat another year of high school in the fall. On the day preceding his fatal heart attack at work, this man had learned that his son had again been caught stealing and was being held for petty larceny.

Other representative incidents preceding the sudden deaths of others were the departure of the last or only child for college or marriage, worry over the victim's own illness or that of others, and competitive games.

Greene, Goldstein, and Moss (1972) acknowledge the difficulty in gathering the necessary data in cases of sudden death. Perhaps, the best opportunity will accrue "from patients who die suddenly, but do not actually die, that is to say, patients who have potentially lethal arrhythmias (changes in the rhythm of the heartbeat either in rate or force) and are resuscitated" (p. 730).

Lown, Verrier, and Rabinowitz (1977, p. 900) frankly state that "direct evidence demonstrating a cause and effect relation between psychologic factors and sudden death will be difficult to establish with certainty." They feel a little more confident in the case of a 39-year-old patient who had on two occasions experienced fibrillation of the heart and also manifested premature heartbeats frequently. He had normal arteries and no indications of structural heart disease. During psychiatric visits, this man showed premature heartbeats, rapid pulse, cardiac arrest, and fibrillation during an REM sleep (dream) stage on the occasion of violent dreams. Meditation and drug treatment *decreased* the wild activity of his heart.

Cardiac irritability during sleep and dreaming.   Rosenblatt, Hartmann, and Zwilling (1973) have more to say on cardiac behavior during sleep and dreaming. They observed 10 patients with chronic cardiac problems in the sleep and dream laboratory of the Tufts University School of Medicine in Boston. They monitored their subjects during nighttime sleep in an air-conditioned room with continuous simultaneous recording of electroencephalogram (EEG), eye movements, and electrocardiogram (EKG). They tried to obtain data that would be representative of normal sleep. How? By locating the recording equipment in an adjoining room and having the subject sleep in a regular (not hospital) bed in a quiet, single room at a comfortable temperature. Eight of the subjects had proven heart damage; two had multiple premature contractions during waking EKG.

Since the object of their experiments was to try to relate electrocardiac changes with sleep stages, it is interesting to note the relatively consistent findings from subject to subject. The pattern of cardiac changes was similar for all 10 subjects despite the difference in cardiac histories of two of them. Although their subjects did not report any angina attacks during REM sleep, cardiac irregularities were observed in every case. Rosenblatt, Hartmann, and Zwilling (p. 133) conclude that the dream stage of sleep (or REM) "is a particularly vulnerable period for developing cardiac arrhythmias, especially by the mechanisms of rapid heart rate . . . and changes in blood pressure." While this experiment did not find any evidence of angina attacks, other investigators (such as Nowlin et al., 1965) have documented observations of multiple episodes of nocturnal angina-pectoris attacks during REM or dream sleep.[8]

In their comprehensive paper, "Psychological Aspects of Cardiac Arrhythmia," Lynch, Paskewitz, Gimbel, and Thomas (1977, p. 647) point out that "heart rate variability increases over 55 percent from non-REM to REM (dream) sleep, and blood pressure variability likewise increases by 50 percent." They speculate on the risk of sudden death during sleep and note another complicating factor that could work toward that end, concerning the relationship between heart action and respiration. During non-REM sleep, heartrate variability goes hand-in-hand with respiratory changes, but in REM sleep, they tend to go their separate ways. In that case, "such a dissociation could result in cardiac arrhythmias which might lead to sudden death during sleep" (p. 647).

If you are an alert student, my last footnote may have "gotten a rise out of you." You may realize that absent stimulus objects do not really have "power to catapult a heart into catastrophic reaction." Hearts cannot *really* react. Only *organisms* interact *with* (prominently), or *by means of*, their hearts. You might also have felt like accusing me of slipping into a reductionistic explanation. To make amends, I want to set the record straight after we have considered how sudden death could occur, to which topic we now proceed.

The illustrations that I choose come from homely incidents supplied by Hans Selye (1973). Here they are in paraphrase. You are walking along with a friend or spouse and are accosted by a far-gone drunk who verbally insults you but is too uncoordinated to do you any harm. You may ignore him completely, go on your way, and the episode is closed. You may, however, choose to fight, in which case dramatic changes occur throughout your organism. Adrenalin-type hormones pour into the bloodstream in profusion; the heart, lungs, and so on are alerted; heart rate and blood pressure rise beyond immediate demands as aspects of an "alarm reaction" (p. 694). The organism is in a "stress" situation, ready for "fight or flight." Selye (1973, p. 698) says, "If you happen to be a coronary candidate, the result may be a fatal brain hemorrhage or cardiac accident. In this case, who is the murderer? The drunk didn't even touch you. This is biologic suicide! Death is caused by choosing the wrong reaction."

An interbehavioral account. The self-actional concept of "choosing" which Selye brings in is questionable. Were you really involved in the deliberation and weighing of which side to take when confronted by the drunk, or is it more likely that whichever event occurred was a function of antece-

---

[8]We should not pass beyond this class of implicit interaction (dreaming) without noting the "power" of the *absent* stimulus objects (about which the dreamer is dreaming) in catapulting the heart into such catastrophic reaction.

dent events? If we may sum up certain past events that would permit us to label you as a "peacenik," the fighting event did not come off. On the other hand, if certain past events have shaped you in readiness to repay insult for insult, you stood your ground and fought it out. And if your vulnerable point (biologically speaking) was heart or cerebral artery, you succumbed to cardiac attack or cerebral hemorrhage in an emotional response.

The emotional response itself is only one variable of an event in which stimulus functions must be taken into account plus setting factors, and so on. But the job does not stop even there, for that particular event must be viewed in relation to the flow of events in which it is embedded. As to your possible death in the hypothetical situation under discussion, is it not simply a consequence or by-product of the drastic, all-out, catastrophic configuration that your response happened to evolve into, plus weak spots in your biological makeup?

And so forth.   There are still more examples of various kinds of emotional interactions. For example, there is so-called voodoo death (Mathis, 1964), made famous by the celebrated American physiologist, Walter B. Cannon (1942). Temper tantrums, breath holding (Lombroso and Pinchas, 1967), and convulsive disorders in children (Kemph et al., 1963), running amok (Westermeyer, 1972; Carr and Tan, 1976), and sudden infant death or "crib death" (Friedlander and Shaw, 1975) offer further samples for analysis as emotional interactions; but because they are only variations on a theme, we leave them for possible examination by the eager student.

Motivation

Psychologists today speak of instincts with lifted eyebrows,
but drives, whether we understand their nature or not, are still
in excellent repute.

[Young, 1936, p. 75]

Why do people stint and save, rescue others at risk to their own lives, become "workaholics," seek political power, strive for fame, gamble, commit murder or rape, or undergo rigorous religious discipline? According to some psychologists, because they are motivated to do so. More specifically, because they have drives, needs, wants, incentives, tendencies, impulses, appetites, dispositions, wishes, cravings, urges and purposes that make them carry out those acts.[9] Together, these "springs to action" constitute an area

---

[9] Freud's concept of a "death wish," residing in the individual, is one explanation for suicide (Freud, 1933, p. 147).

of psychology known as *motivation*, defined as the study of hypothetical processes that energize certain responses so that they are dominant over others. Thus these motives are said both to initiate the activity of the organism and determine its direction and strength.

Although many psychologists use the term *motivation* without defining the term, its clearest specification comes from a long-time student of this area, P. T. Young. According to Young (1936, p. 43), "In the strict sense of the term, a motive is that which arouses *movement*" (emphasis added). But movement requires release of energy, says Young, so we are immediately involved in biomechanics as when "hunger" "drives" a rat to activity in seeking food. The greater the amount of energy released, the greater the degree of drive. Studies of drive have been carried out largely on laboratory animals.

Primary and Secondary Drives or Motivation

According to Young (1936, p. 155), the secondary drives are "understandable organism; others, in the environment. Those within the organism are called "primary" or "unlearned" drives. These include hunger as well as food preferences, thirst, maternal behavior, sexual behavior (as worked out on rats, largely), general activity ("the urge for exercise after prolonged rest") (p. 131).[10] They depend on tissue or chemical condition of the organism. According to Young (1936, p. 155), the secondary drives are "understandable only by referring to the life history of the individual in relation to his social world" (p. 155). Thus, all drives that cannot be differentiated in physiological terms are, according to Young, secondary drives "until a specific organic basis can be clearly demonstrated" (p. 155). Among secondary (or learned) drives are curiosity, imitativeness, self-assertion, and self-abasement. Young suggests that organic motivating factors be called *motives* and that motivating factors in the environment be called *incentives*. "Thus desires, intentions, and goal sets are *motives*. Praise, reproof, punishment, money, food, mate, etc., are *incentives*" (p. 45).

Social and Nonsocial Incentives

According to Young (1936), incentives themselves can be classified as being either social or nonsocial. The mere presence of another person, or what that person says or does, constitutes a social incentive, but a volcano, a thunderstorm, or an avalanche are, obviously, nonsocial incentives. And, so, we come to a final definition of motivational psychology as formulated by Young (1936, p. 45) who proposes that:

[10] Judging from the millions of devotees of sportscasts, the "drive" for television watching has become dominant over "the urge for exercise after prolonged rest." The television-watching drive may be said to reach "double strength" when some people watch two sportscasts simultaneously.

Motivational psychology may be defined as the study of all conditions which arouse and regulate the behavior of organisms. The *arousal* or behavior necessarily implies a release of physical energy from the tissues. The *regulation* of behavior includes the control of activity through purposive determinations as well as the restriction of activity by organic structure.

In his more recent book, *Emotion in Man and Animal*, Young (1973) holds to essentially the same definition of motivation except to add that "there is not always a clean break between motivating and non-motivating conditions" (p. 62). In a summary statement, Young (1973, p. 88) says, "Motivation is the basic process of arousing, directing, and sustaining activity." The term *arousal* implies emotion with its liberation of physical energy within the tissues of an organism. That is why students of motivation have traditionally connected emotion with motivation.

The opening statement in Young's enduring reference work *Motivation of Behavior* is "All behavior is motivated." That universal statement apparently contradicts the preceding one about the lack of a clean break between motivating and nonmotivating conditions. It also contradicts his recent affirmative answer to the question "Are there psychological factors which do not motivate behavior?" (Young, 1973, p. 62). According to Young, among nonmotivating factors are the latent, inert habit organizations that we carry around with us and that are just there unless and until they are sprung into action.

Peters' Criticism of Motivation Theory

In the view of the conflicting statements, one tends to side with Peters' (1958, p. 153) statement, "Over and over again, in the field of motivation, it has been shown that there is conceptual confusion." Peters goes on to say that motivational psychologists who claim that all behavior is motivated are applying the term too broadly if by that statement they mean that we have a motive for everything we do (p. 152). He elaborates as follows:

> Drive theorists, for instance, use the term "drive" in such a way that a man can have a hunger drive, a drive to play poker rather than tennis, a drive to repeat acts in a compulsive manner, and even a desire to know. Now, surely this leads to confusion. For, apart from the fact that it is logically absurd to say that one could be driven to know anything, the use of the same term for all these very different types of action, is a case of unwarrantable assimilation in the interest of an over-all theory. [Peters, 1958, pp. 154–155]

Kantor's Cricitism

Kantor's (1942) indictment of traditional motivation theory applies to contemporary theorists. Here are some of his charges:

1. Instead of starting with observation of behavioral events, motivation theorists start with an assumption that organismic action requires internal "starters" or guides to action. This imposition of hypothetical agents confuses theory and data. They claim to be studying driving forces, not psychological events.

2. There is no clear-cut distinction between motivated and nonmotivated events, nor between internal or external motivators, or setting factors.

3. The verbal creation of drives or motives is a form of word magic that reifies or "thing-ifies" an imaginary biological condition into a self-actional, simplistic cause of organismic action. Giving a thing a name does not explain a fact. For example,

> *Question:* "Why does the rat engage in mating behavior?"
>
> *Answer:* "Because it has a mating drive."[11]
>
> *Question:* "How do you know?"
>
> *Answer:* "Because it engaged in mating behavior."

This is circular reasoning.

4. When an organism is interacting with a stimulus object under special conditions, the motivation theorists fixate on one aspect (such as a biological condition of the organism or pressure of a person) and force it to carry the total explanatory burden. As Dewey (1929, p. 194) said many years ago, "Events are explained as if one factor or another were the whole thing."

5. Motivational explanations are unhappy metaphors based on an outmoded physics. The notion that motivation is energy that makes the organism move is based on the old assumption that a psychological organism remains at rest unless some force sets it in motion, as in physical events.

6. It is difficult to see what possible connection physiological tensions, tissue needs, and physiological conditions such as hunger and thirst have with complex human behaviors such as creative activity, borrowing, lending, saving, divorcing, teaching, learning, hoping, going on hunger strikes, and abstaining from sexual intercourse.

Skinner on Drives

Skinner rejects drives just as he rejects all inner causes (Skinner, 1953, p. 29). He says,

---

[11] About 50 years ago, a "drive" was called an "instinct"—but fashions in science, as in clothes, change.

When we say that a man eats *because* he is hungry, smokes a great deal *because* he has the tobacco habit . . . we seem to be referring to causes. But on analysis these phrases prove to be merely redundant descriptions. A single set of facts is described by the two statements: "He eats" and "He is hungry." . . . The practice of explaining one statement in terms of the other is dangerous because it suggests that we have found the cause and therefore need search no further. Moreover, such terms as "hunger," "habit," and "intelligence" convert what are essentially the properties of a process or relation into what appear to be things. [Skinner, 1953, p. 31]

For Skinner, the important explanatory variables are not in the organism but in the environment. In the prediction and control of behavior, the behavior of the organism is the dependent variable. The independent variables are in the environment. "Relationships between the two—the 'cause and effect relationships' in behavior—are the laws of a science" (Skinner, 1953, p. 35). As far as Skinner is concerned, it is not possible to explain any system as long as you stay within the system. This is what the motivational theorists are guilty of doing. Eventually, one must get outside the system to the variables that act on it. Inner drives or needs are also useless for purposes of prediction and control because there is no way of getting at internal states. Instead of drives and needs, Skinner deals with deprivation and satiation in terms of their effect on behavior.

For comparative purposes, let us take Skinner's example of someone eating salty hors d'oeuvres. The motivation psychologist would say that the predinner snacks made the guest thirsty and the thirst "drove" that guest to drink. Skinner (1953, p. 104) dispenses with an imaginary thirst drive because "it is simpler, in both theory and practice, to restrict ourselves to the fact that hors d'oeuvres lead to drinking." If you want to drive people to drink, don't depend on an intervening hypothetical thirst drive—just feed them salty hors d'oeuvres.

Nissen (1953, pp. 308–309) appears to be even more vehemently opposed to drives, needs, and tissue conditions in his reference to the "very old and still prevalent superstition inherent in the word 'drive,' that the organism is driven and guided to certain external goals, such as money or murder, by a mysterious force or homunculus who sits somewhere inside, preferably in the heart or brain."[12]

In summing up this brief account of motivation, it is proper to say that some psychologists treat the data self-actionally and others interactionally or interbehaviorally. Here, as at other points, choices are available.

---

[12]Another excellent, critical treatment of motivation is given in Smith, *Motivation: What is it?* (no date).

Chapter Summary

This chapter covered three related topics: feeling interactions, emotional interactions, and motivation.

Feeling interactions are affective, in contrast to effective interactions. The visceral organs, glands, and skin interactions are prominent factors in affective responses. Simultaneous performance of affective and effective interactions is possible. Affective responses play an important role in everyday life. The passions, climactic feeling responses, sentiments, and moods are types of affective responses. There are several methods of studying such responses including those involved in so-called lie detection. Selye's stress syndrome is related to the possible involvement of affective interactions in illness and in the determination of the sex ratio of one's progeny.

Emotional interactions are atypical, aborted behavior segments without final-reaction systems. Stuttering, fainting, the startle response, epileptic seizures, and the possible occurrence of sudden death fit into the construct proposed for the emotional behavior segment and into Selye's concept of the stress syndrome.

Lastly, motivation is traditionally connected with emotion as the arousal or energizer of organismic action. Conventional motivation theory has been criticized by Peters, Kantor, and Skinner.

12 Language Interactions

People living at the seashore grow so accustomed to the murmur of the waves that they never hear it. By the same token, we scarcely ever hear the words which we utter.

[Ehrlich, 1965, p. 119]

We have already noted how easily we take for granted our attendings, perceivings, plannings, rememberings, and so on. The same applies to our language interactions. Our speaking and listening, writing, and reading are so pervasive, intimate, familiar, and "automatic" that we rarely catch ourselves in the act. Someone has said that we get ourselves into the middle of a sentence and trust Providence to get us out. Mark Twain's characterization of the human as the only animal that blushes and needs to may be true. But it is also a truism that humans talk (or listen) far more than they blush. It seems important, then, to pause and to hear the words we utter and, more important yet, *to reflect* on what goes on when we communicate. That is our goal in the present chapter.

The Multidisciplinary Nature of Language Study

The ubiquity of linguistic data has encouraged its investigation by a variety of disciplines. We now examine what aspects attract the attention of different specialists so as to delineate our own specific area of interest.

The Anthropology of Language

The anthropologist looks on language as a cultural product and a tool. A comparison of the structure of different languages is one job to be done here. For example, Holmes (1971, pp. 154–155) notes "that the Bantu and Bushman people of South Africa use lip and tongue noises, called 'clicks,' as we do consonants." And Farb (1974, p. 47) notes that "the Chukchi men of Siberia pronounce their word for 'people' *ramkichhin* and the women pronounce it *tsamkitstsin*. The pattern whereby women substitute *ts* for their men's *r* and *tsts* for their *chh* remains consistent in the pronunciation of all words that contain these sounds." That finding in itself may delight the anthropologist even if the Chukchi no longer existed. The pattern is there, and that is enough satisfactory datum for the anthropologist. Anthropologists take a more global view of things than do psychologists.

The Sociology of Language

The quickest and simplest example of the sociology of language is given in George Bernard Shaw's play *Pygmalion* or its recent musical version, *My Fair Lady*. Professor Higgins tries to make a "lady" out of a "guttersnipe," Liza. Even though they are both English, they have difficulty in communicating because they belong to very different social classes with radically different dialects. Sociology studies society, social institutions, and social or group relationships. Like anthropology, sociology takes group phenomena as its subject matter. A comparison of Black English with standard English would be a specific example.

The Philosophy of Language

What is the relationship of language structure and the structure of the world? Because philosophy is not limited to the rigorous methods of the scientific disciplines, it is freer to attack such grand problems or "the meaning of meaning."

The Physics of Language

Speech sounds *qua* sounds interest the physicist, who does not have to be concerned with meaning whatsoever because sounds can be analyzed by recording and analyzing them in terms of frequencies, stress, and so on. For example, by acoustic research Herman (1940) was able to pick out wave differentia between hoarse and nonhoarse speakers by means of an analysis of oscillographic records.

The Physiology of Language

A limited view of what might be called the "mechanics of speech" is afforded by a study of the biological participants in speaking and hearing

—the role of the lungs, diaphragm, vocal chords, tongue, and so on. When brain injuries interfere with speech, an assessment of the brain's participation is called for. Speech without a tongue or vocal chords is also of interest to the physiologist, as it is to the psychologist.

The Psychology of Language

The preceding differentiation of specialized interests of various disciplines shows that there is something for everybody in linguistic data. Our stress is neither on group nor on organ functioning but, as elsewhere, on the individual's behavior in linguistic situations. However, the field of psychology does not provide a united front in its interpretation of what happens when people speak to one another or listen to one another.

Theories of Language

We proceed now to an examination of different theories of language.

Body—Mind Theories

Mentalistic theories that work with the assumption of an invisible mind in a visible body consider language to be a means of conveying ideas, emotions, and desires from one mind to another. Figure 12-1 represents how the process is said to work. In the situation before us, assume that Jim is looking for his pipe. John knows where it is. The story goes that John has an idea of Jim's pipe in his mind and a desire to inform him as to its location. The idea and desire are somehow transformed into neural impulses to John's organs of speech. From John's mouth, sound waves are propagated to Jim's ears by a "purely physical process." From this point on, according to the traditional story, the procedure is an inverse order of the events that were said to have occurred in John. There is first a physiological transmission of the acoustic pattern (the sound waves) to the brain via neural impulses and, finally, a psychical production of the idea of the pipe. The whole series of transformations include the following chain of sequences: psychical–physiological–physical–physiological–psychical. The explanation is imaginary, with no way of getting at the presumed conversion of physiological to psychic events and vice versa.

Behavioristic Theories

With their strict avoidance of all things mental as beyond the pale of science, the classical behaviorists simply dropped all reference to alleged psychic happenings and described language in terms of the operation of anatomical and physiological mechanisms. The mentalists then objected to what they considered an impoverished account of the rich linguistic data. Notwithstanding their criticism, the behaviorists have continued to explain speaking as merely vocal organs, nerves, brain, mouth, lips, and so on, in action. The interbehaviorist objects to a reductionistic explanation of complex linguistic events in terms of only one aspect of those events. Certainly, anatomical and physiological factors play a part, but not a determinative or causal one. There is more to speaking and listening than organ functioning. Just as a single hint of other variables involved in communicative speech, how well would we do in a situation in which only Swahili, Chinese, or Roumanian were spoken?

Interbehavioral Theory

The interbehaviorist considers linguistic behavior as naturalistic as any other action. Therefore, from an interbehavioral viewpoint, there is one basic rule to follow in observing psychological language; that is, we must analyze each individual's behavior *separately* in line with our definition of psychology as the study of the individual. Accordingly, the diagram in Figure 12-1—because of its mentalism and because it analyzes two persons' behavior at once—is of no use to us as theory or construct. But let us assume an ordinary behavioral situation, one in which you and I are involved, and let us analyze it critically.

You and I are outdoors after a light rain shower. You decide it is a good time to pull weeds. Each weed calls out an attentional, perceptual, and final reaction system of yanking it out of the ground. There is nothing linguistic involved in your behavior. Because only one stimulus object occurs within each behavior segment, let us call that action "unistimulational, nonlinguistic behavior."

The speaker's (referor's) linguistic action.   At this point, I see a rainbow. Again, we have a unistimulational, nonlinguistic behavior unit. Now, wanting you to see it, I exclaim, "Look at the rainbow!" Within that behavior segment, I react, at the same time both to you *and* the rainbow. This is what the interbehaviorist (Kantor, 1977) calls "bistimulational referential language action." As the speaker, I am the referor because I refer you, or direct your attention to, the rainbow; therefore, I display referor language interbehavior (p. 71).

The hearer's (referee's) linguistic action.   Now, let us analyze *your* behavior so as to avoid the too-ready combining of the speaker's and hearer's action as illustrated in Figure 12-1. Even though the action of speaker and hearer occurs with great speed, we nevertheless (or, perhaps we should say, all the more reason that we) should take care in analyzing exactly what is occurring. Kantor would say that this is what is occurring on your part. Within the

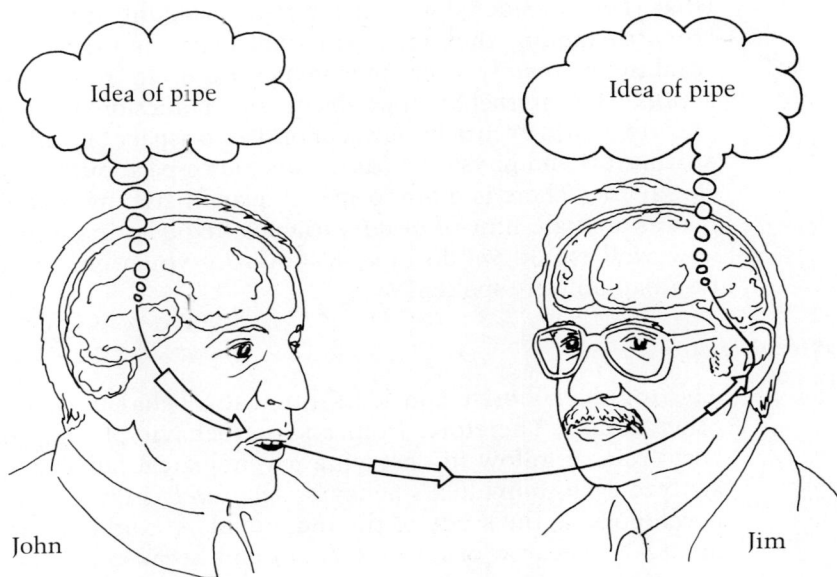

Figure 12-1 An account, in mentalistic terms, of a linguistic situation in which John tells Jim, "There's your pipe." The event is said to start with an idea of pipe in John's mind. Then neural impulses cause the organs of speech to utter the phrase. The physical impulses reach Jim's ears, where they are said to be transformed into neural impulses, which are in turn alleged to be translated into an idea of the pipe in Jim's mind.

behavior segment, within which you reacted to the rainbow, you *also* reacted to my exclamation, "Look at the rainbow!" In responding to both, you displayed bistimulational referential language. As such, you are identified as the referee because my action succeeded in referring you to the rainbow.

Suppose you are hard of hearing, or an airplane overhead prevents your hearing me clearly. You only know that I must have said something. In that case, the referee linguistic enterprise misfired, because you were *not* referred to the rainbow. So you ask, "What did you say?" This response of yours was a unistimulational behavior segment involving only my vocalization, nothing more. You might even elaborate by saying, "I know you must have said something, but I haven't the foggiest notion of what it was." Suppose now that instead of speaking in English, I repeat the phrase in Russian or Serbian, which you do not understand. This time the situation is unistimulational, because you are reacting only to my strange noises, which prompt you to ask again, "What did you say?"

Gesture as Psychological Language

> *There was speech in their dumbness, language in their very gesture.*
>
> [Shakespeare, *The Winter's Tale*, Act V, Scene ii]

Imagine another version of the rainbow situation. This time we are in a boiler factory in which the din very obviously obstructs any and all communication by conversational means. Does that stop me from performing referor linguistic action? No, for all that I need to do is to touch you on the shoulder and point to the sky through an opening in the factory. Have I done my linguistic job as referor? Yes, because I simultaneously responded to you *and* the rainbow. In other words, I was involved in a bistimulational linguistic event. Now, let's inspect your behavior. Did you simultaneously respond to my pointing gesture *and* the rainbow? Yes, you did; you succeeded in being referred to the rainbow by my action; or, stated otherwise, you responded to my action *and* the rainbow and thereby were involved in a bistimulational linguistic event.

If we are in a tight spot, for example, being held by terrorists or being interviewed as spies in a foreign country and assuming that our verbal communication is out of the question, we may still talk to one another with our eyes. For example, we can "point" to individuals or "point" directions by eye movements to the right-left or up-down. The many muscles of the head and ears hold possibilities, as do the legs. Incidentally, gestures should be recognized, too, for their potentiality as "punctuation marks" to express or accent shades of referential "meaning" in their accompaniment of vocal speech.

Gestures have their strongest claim to recognition as language when they function completely in lieu of speech. The sign language of the deaf (*not* including letter-for-letter signaling or spelling the words out) is a complete substitute for normal spoken language. Their manual language provides a rich system of bistimulational linguistic interaction. Trappist monks, obedient to their rule of silence, can nevertheless communicate with sign language.

Farb (1974) reports that one of the most widely disseminated systems of sign language flourished during the 19th century among the many Native American tribes throughout the great plains of North America. Their languages belonged to six different families, but even those who spoke languages within the same family could not understand each other. However, Farb informs us that

> All of these tribes, though, were in easy communication because of the elegant sign-language system they developed. . . . The early explorers of the Plains told

about Indian warriors who recounted their exploits—by the use of signs alone —at 'great length to members of other tribes incapable of understanding a word of the narrators' spoken language. As recently as several decades ago, a Shoshone Indian related to the anthropologist Robert Lowie his tribe's folk tale of a giant bird that snatched up and devoured people; *the myth was explained in all its detail by signs, without the utterance of a single word.* (Farb, 1974, pp. 208–209, emphasis added)

All of this communication was achieved in a language without true nouns, verbs, or adjectives. Incidentally, the Plains sign language for a *lie* was conveyed by the first two fingers of the right hand extended from the mouth and spread apart. The reference to "forked-tongue" is hard to miss.

Farb (1974) reveals another interesting linguistic discovery made among the Urubu, an isolated Native American tribe inhabiting a jungle in the Amazon Basin. Whereas, except for the deaf, sign language had always been developed between people who spoke different languages, the Urubu evolved a sign language for use exclusively among members of their own speech community. Their sign-language system apparently arose as a way of communicating with their disproportionately large number of deaf people. Whether because of disease or genetics, 1 out of about every 35 Urubu is deaf (Farb, 1974, p. 209). And yet, every member of the community learns the sign language as a coordinate or parallel language, *not* a "second language." It is as if, out of courtesy for the deaf, we all undertook to learn their sign language and were able to converse with them whenever the occasion arose.[1] Farb (1974, p. 210) says, "I have sat with four or five Urubu men and listened to one of them tell a story. But as soon as we were joined by a deaf person, the speaker immediately . . . [added] the sign language, apparently without omitting a thought."

With our analysis of conversational speech and gesture, we have delineated genuine psychological language. Both meet the criterion of referential language. When the speaker refers another person to some object (or person, and so on), referor language. When, simultaneous with the speaker's action, another person reacts to the speaker and the thing the speaker is referring to, we have referee language. The action of both the referor and referee are bistimulational.

The Symbolic Theory of Language

> *To call signs, characters, and symbols language is to speak metaphorically. They are no more genuine language than one's beloved is the apple of one's eye.*

> [Kantor, 1936, p. 19]

[1] American sign language is appearing with greater frequency on American television screens, as in severe weather warnings, religious services, and in some Presidential talks.

It is night, and you are driving in the mountains. Suddenly, in the glare of your headlights, you see a sign reading *DANGEROUS CURVE AHEAD.* This is not referential language, because *no one* is referring you to *something.* This is not a case of a speaker's (referor's) telling you about a sign. In this interaction, the sign stands alone. The situation is a symbolic interbehavior in which the sign operates as a unistimulational substitute stimulus object that elicits attending and perceiving reaction systems and a final implicit reaction system to the dangerous possibilities ahead. Nothing else.

You may object to my interpretation because the sign used words. But words are not the only symbols. Today, with so many people traveling in many "foreign countries" with unfamiliar languages, an international system of traffic "signs without words" is being developed and will soon be in worldwide usage. Pictures and symbolic signs are fast supplanting written messages for good reasons. First, they can be instantly perceived without having to be read. Secondly, they overcome language barriers, an important factor in view of fast-expanding international travel. These symbolic signs help foreigners traveling in the United States as well as Americans traveling abroad. Figure 12-2 shows a few signs in both old and new versions.

Webster's Seventh New Collegiate Dictionary defines the term *symbol* as "something that stands for or suggests something else by reason of relationship, association, convention, or accidental relationship." It is important to point out that there is a fixed, one-to-one relationship between the

Figure 12-2 The old and the new in traffic signs. Both are symbols—not psychological language. However, the old signs did use words. The new "signs without words" will work just as well. As they become familiar, the words will be phased out and the graphic design alone will do the job. (Note: in the actual sign, the ring and the diagonal are in red, the rest is in black.)

symbol and the thing symbolized. For example, imagine the chaos on the highway if the traffic symbols shown in Figure 12-2 "stood for or suggested" a *number of alternative driving possibilities.* It is the rigid relationship between the symbol and thing symbolized that makes the traffic sign so effective.

A significant consequence of this treatment of symbols is that symbols embrace a much larger class of objects than do words. The engagement ring symbolizes the mutual promise of a future marriage; the wedding band is a symbol of a mutual relationship of husband and wife. The Star of David symbolizes Judaism, and the cross is an emblem of the Christian religion. And some symbols may "stand for or suggest" more than one other thing. For example, a cross, " + ," may also symbolize "plus," as in the equation $2 + 2 = 4$.

A comparison of symbolic behavior and language behavior.   Now that we have some understanding of how symbols function, we are ready to take up the symbolic theory of language. According to this common theory, language is said to consist of signs or symbols that stand for ideas or things or both. If symbolic theorists overheard me say to you, "There's a rainbow," they would have immediately written down my words on paper and treated them as symbols. And, of course, they would be right, because the symbologists' transcribed words show a one-to-one relationship with my "verbo-vocal" action in addressing you. But the error lies in their equating that record on paper with my reacting to "the rainbow" and "you" in my speech adjustment. Transcripts of words used by the speaker must not be identified with the speaker's response to the listener and the thing spoken about.

Recall, too, that I needed only to point to the rainbow to get you to respond. Verbovocal action was not necessary. In that case, how was my act of pointing a symbol of a rainbow? Or does a rainbow demand a pointing action to it in a fixed relationship? Obviously not, or every time you saw a rainbow you would point or every time you saw someone pointing you would look for a rainbow.

If we venture further afield to other examples, how can we explain that some words have several referents? If words functioned as strictly as symbols do, what would you do with such words as *pool?* Would my utterance of the word *pool* refer you to a *pool of water,* a *numbers pool,* a *game of pool,* or to *pool one's resources.* If you should answer, "Well, that depends on the situation," I would note that *DANGEROUS CURVE AHEAD* is not a function of the particular situation or *context* in which it occurs. The sign has a one-to-one, fixed relationship with the road condition beyond the sign. Not so with *pool,* which can have four (or, perhaps, even more) referents because of the importance of the thing referred to in the actual speech situation. Or, to state it otherwise, *pool* does not act like a symbol in speech.

In actual situations, we know better what a word intends than what it *literally* says. For example, a sign in a restaurant reads, "If your steak is to rare, we'll cook it some more." On a strict symbolic basis, that sign should be meaningless because the sign maker used the preposition *to* as in "He gave the book *to* me." The sign maker should have used the adverb *too.* But the sign works *despite* its inaccurate symbolism. In fact, today, among some people, the distinction between the two is fast disappearing. The word *to* seems to do the work of both, and some people reading the sign referred to would not see any error. The same thing happens in speech situations. The thing referred to often dominates, overriding an unclear statement. Note how often misunderstandings occur—not because of a defective statement, but because the thing referred to does not stand out clearly enough. In frequent changes of topic during lively dialogue, the hearer may not know which "he" or "she" is being referred to in the speaker's statement. Yet the same individual may be referred to as James, "the louse," "the scoundrel," and so on. How different from the symbolic relationship indicated in the international traffic signs!

Another argument against the symbolic theory of psychological language is raised by Kantor (1936, p. 62) in the following passage:

Again, as everyone knows, in actual conversational speech much may be, and is, left unsaid. The hearer begins to speak, and to the point, before the speaker has finished his sentence. Are these missing members in any sense symbols? We hazard the suggestion that the symbolic conception here is based upon the notion that each word stands for something. If this is the case, the circumstance of good conversation with partial or truncated actions is a pitfall to the symbolic theory. This is true even if it be argued that in the case of unspoken speech the listener understood without being referred to something. For that situation plainly demonstrates that language adjustments need not be symbolic.

What would the proverbial visitor from Mars do with the following real-life situation if told to study it as symbolic behavior? X (husband) and Y (wife) are dining out. After their meal, X says to Y, "Do you have your purse?" Whereupon Y opens her purse and hands X three aspirin tablets. X thanks her and downs the aspirin tablets. The question is: how could the phrase, "Do you have your purse?" symbolize "Please give me three aspirin tablets"? But, if we know a bit of history about X and Y, we realize that Y has habitually carried aspirin in her purse for X's arthritis. So Y understood X's query to refer, not to the presence or absence of her purse, but to his after-dinner need for aspirin tablets. When the thing referred to is prominent, almost anything can work; for example, X might have obtained his aspirin tablets by an impolite extension of his arm with the hand held open. Where is the symbolism?

A final point. Some people talk to themselves. Others speak to someone as they carry out certain acts. A is building a fire in B's presence. As B looks on, A says, "First, we crumple up some paper" (and does so); "Then we put on some kindling" (and does that); and so on. There is no need for the symbologist to impose a symbolic interpretation on a situation when there is nothing for symbols to stand for or represent. What we have here is bistimulational referential action, superfluous as such action may seem.

A summing up. In this section on language considered as symbolic behavior, we first noted the rigid, one-to-one relationship between the symbol and thing symbolized, as exemplified in international traffic signs. In attempting to apply symbolism to language, we acknowledged a symbolic relationship between a person's transcribed speech (the words written down) and the things that the words stood for. But we saw no reason for identifying a record of the speaker's speech pattern with the bistimulational referential action of the speaker in the situation from which the record was derived. We also observed again that gestures that can be as eloquent as language refuse to be forced into the symbolic straitjacket. We also recognized that referential action on the part of the hearer can occur despite inaccurate symbolization, as it does also before the speaker even finishes "producing symbols." Finally, we saw an example, in X's and Y's behavior, of appropriate referee action in the face of the anything but symbolic linguistic patterning on the part of X. From the standpoint of a symbolic theory of language, strictly speaking, Y's behavior should be considered a complete breakdown of symbolism because of the lack of correspondence between X's utterance and Y's response. Yet, from a communicative standpoint, Y's behavior constitutes an appropriate and effective psychological reaction.[2]

Where Does Reading Fit In?

The lover and her beloved impatiently await each exchange of letters. Watch the lively series of facial expressions, which may range from delight through amusement to tears. The reader of such a letter is being referred to many common elements in their relationship.

To illustrate nonreferential reading, take the same reader of the letter, who now shifts to reading aloud a book in a foreign language after having *just* mastered the sound of each letter of that foreign alphabet. Obviously, the reader of that text is doing nothing more than" parroting." Is such action bistimulational or unistimulational? This last illustration leads us easily into a further consideration of events that at first seem to resemble bistimulational language but are not, on close examination.

Nonreferential Language

Verbal formulas. According to Kantor (1977), there is almost universal agreement among students of language that whatever sounds are produced

---

[2] Experimental studies from an interbehavioral standpoint have been conducted and are discussed in Kantor's *Psychological Linguistics* (1977).

by the tongue constitute language. He disagrees energetically with such a claim, pointing out that some of our forms of greeting are little more than verbal grunts of recognition or departure, such as "Hi," "How are ya?,"[3] or "See ya." The English "Cheerio" and "Ta Ta" are no more eloquent than the above. They are more or less socially prescribed forms for certain occasions, such as the manual salute in the military situation or the vocal address, "Your honor," in the courtroom situation.

Speech derivatives or products.   The conversations of the Watergate characters have been recorded on tape. They are products of real, referential utterances of the people involved. Certainly, they are *derived from* bona fide bistimulational referential action but must not be identified with the original, genuine bistimulational linguistic interactions. The recordings are comparable to a still-shot photo extracted from a dramatic moving-picture show or a theater production. They contain only a record of *what* was said and, perhaps, *how* it was said.

Language as Cultural Behavior

Culturalization, or the process by which a person is socialized or humanized, was considered in an overall way in Chapter 5. That process applies as well to the individual's manner of communicating with others. The person who is a thoroughgoing (100%) individualist in this regard simply does not communicate. We are forced to talk like other members of our group. And so we speak American English or British English, Eskimo, Portuguese, Croatian, and so on. Whatever society we are attached to, we will end up speaking its language; and, if we are fortunate enough to grow up in a social group with bilingual or multilingual people, we may acquire two or more languages. But such a characterization of language is too broad, for linguistic culturalization shows the same specificity as food tastes, dress, and religious beliefs and practices. Pronunciation, grammar, and politeness forms are a function of the particular locale in which the individual was reared.

As an illustration of regional pronunciation, we go to an erudite publication, *The American Language* by H. L. Mencken (1937). What do you make of the following sample of speech recorded in the Ozarks (for which Mencken gives no translation):

Lee Yancey allus was a right work-brickel feller, clever an' biddable as all git-out, but he ain't got nary smidgin' o' mother-wit, an' he ain't nothin' on'y a tie-wackin' sheer-crapper noways. I seed him an' his least chaps a-bustin' out middles down in ol' man Price's bottom t'other ev'nin', a whoopin' an' a-blaggardin'

---

[3] Some people may react to "How are ya?" as referential language and proceed to give an organ recital of pains and other malfunctions of the various parts of their anatomy.

an' a'spewin' ambeer all over each an' ever', whilst thet 'ar por susy hippoed woman o' hisn was a-pickin' boogers out'n her yeller tags, an' a-scunchin' cheenches on th' puncheon with a antiganglin' noodle-hook. [Mencken, 1937, p. 359]

Another interesting bit is to be found in Mencken's *The American Language* (1937). According to popular belief, dropping of the *r* before certain vowels in the South is believed to be due to the influence of Black slaves who reared White children. Mencken reports (pp. 361–362) that on April 15, 1842, Charles Dickens wrote to his wife, while visiting the United States, "All the women who have been bred in slave States speak more or less like Negroes, from having been constantly in their childhood with black nurses."

Mencken quotes several authorities who argue convincingly that the thing is really the other way around, that when the slaves were brought to America, "they learned the accent of their masters" (p. 362). Mencken quotes one authority to the effect that there was no pronunciation common among African slaves from various tribes that does not occur in "old-fashioned American speech" (p. 362). Had the slaves shared a common African childhood language, then one can see how they all might have learned to speak English with a common accent. Such was not the case, so Dickens' theory is not supported.

Even the ungrammatical *I is* for *I am*, attributed to the Black, has been tracked down in *Joseph Wright's English Dialect Dictionary* and found to be in common use in England as long ago as the 13th century (Mencken, 1937, p. 363). When the illiterate slaves came to the new country, they learned to speak the new language *as they heard it,* just as everybody else does.

The Role of Culturalization in Language Acquisition

We have already observed the power of culturalization in the societal stage of the reactional biography. An individual's language development also does not escape that incessant shaping during which adults correct the child with the admonition, "We don't say that, darling." Five-year-old Kristin rushes into the house with a complaint about her 12-year-old sister, who took some of her pine cones: "Susie *snook* three pine cones out of my basket!" Kristin will soon be saying *sneaked.* On another occasion, she stated that some "gooses" had chased her. Just as Kristin must learn to eat politely with knife, fork, and spoon and to say "Thank you" and "Please" in certain situations, so will members of her group impose a certain dialectal, stylistic, grammatical, and etiquette conformity on her utterances.

Idiosyncratic Linguistic Action

Even the few examples discussed under the section heading "Language as Cultural Behavior" attest to the richness and diversity of live, spoken language. No one becomes a talking robot. The linguistic situation is not so rigid as to demand absolute adherence to grammatical rules. Even "intellectuals" break the rules with such expressions as "I felt badly" or "He gave it to she and I." People speak as they speak and can be understood, even with expressions so offensive to the grammarian's ears as "I ain't got nobody." Speech is not bound by the grammarian's strictures or censures.

The resistance to an iron-clad linguistic conformity shows up in another way. There is nothing static about language as it is spoken. It is an ever-changing thing. New words come in, and old ones die out. There are even fashions in words that are considered vulgar or obscene. Some words are recycled the way dress styles are. In certain age groups, some four-letter words are coming into common usage that a decade ago were horribly shocking. If "Comin' Thro' the Rye" were sung the way Robert Burns (1965, pp. 39–40) published it, the Federal Communications Commission would not tolerate it. He certainly did not write, "Gin [if] a body *kiss* a body [person], need a body cry?" The reason why the other word did not offend the people of his time was that that particular four-letter word for intercourse was perfectly acceptable and, therefore, publishable. Times change. Today, everybody knows this word. It is among the earliest vocabulary acquisitions of the foreigner. Yet few use it in most "respectable" social situations. It could be, at some future time, that social changes set in motion today could make that particular four-letter word perfectly acceptable (as it was in Burns' time) as a synonym for "making love," the euphemism that is common currency today.

Slang.   Slang is the supreme example of the idiosyncratic linguistic response. A bit of reflection should reveal that a new slang term does not descend on the populace at one fell swoop. It spreads from person to person the way popular songs spread, but its origin is the most significant fact about it. A slang term must be created—brought into existence by someone. Its creator is an idiosyncrat because, out of the common stock of sounds of a given language, the idiosyncrat has coined a new term previously unknown and therefore unshared.

Despite the common occurrence of slang over the centuries, linguists have largely ignored the topic in their writings. The reason cannot be blamed on the ephemeral nature of slang because some slang words infiltrate common langage, become accepted, and survive for a long time. According to Mencken (1937, p. 557), the adjective *nice* was a slang word introduced in England about 1765. The purists frowned on its use, but it became accepted usage anyhow, and today no one questions "a *nice* day," "a *nice* wedding," or "a *nice* person." "So recently as 1929 the *Encyclopaedia Britannica* listed *bootlegger, speakeasy, dry, wet, crook, fake, fizzle, hike, hobo, poppycock, racketeer* and *O.K.* as American slang terms, but today most of them are in perfectly good usage" (Mencken, 1937, p. 565).

Slang is usually defined as a highly colloquial language sometimes considered undignified or as having a lower status than standard educated speech and containing either new words or old words given a new meaning, such as *square,* meaning "straight" or "conventional." Slang is noted for such attributes as novelty, freshness, ingenuity, amusement, brevity, and exaggeration. The following sample of recent slang from *The New Columbia Encyclopedia* (Harris and Levey, 1975, p. 2534) is offered for illustrative purposes: of madness—*bananas, bughouse, loony, screwy, nuts;* of women—*chick, quail, tomato, frail, skirt;* of drugs—*speed, bummer, tripping, downer, freakout;* of money—*lettuce, dough, bread, bucks;* of the command go—*scat, scram, split, scoot, vamoose.*

Idiosyncratic aspects of speech also manifest themselves in a certain degree of flexibility in what might be termed *style.* Certainly, one must speak in words of common coinage, but beyond the mere satisfaction of that requirement, there is room for individuality. Pitch, the rate at which words are uttered, intonation, intensity of feeling, and loudness illustrate the point. But, even beyond that, there are special features such as raising the eyebrows, momentarily sticking out the tongue, configurations of facial muscles, or even tics, some degree of lisp, rolling of r's, punctuating pauses, and accompanying manual gestures. All of these combine to confer a uniqueness of speech on every individual, a fact attested to by our identification of individual voices from tape recordings. These idiosyncratic features of speech are what the French naturalist Buffon must have been thinking of when (in male-chauvinist terms) he declared that "Style is the man." Imagine the very same speech delivered by both Billy and Jimmy Carter, and you'll get the point.

Language Acquisition

A thorough knowledge of psychological language is not possible without some understanding of how people come to be communicating organisms. But psychologists show no more agreement in this area than they do in many others. We now consider a number of theories about how humans come to use and respond to languages, beginning with a preliminary overall account of Skinner's view of language before we look into his explanation of human verbal behavior.

Skinner's View of Language as Verbal Behavior

In his *The Behavior of Organisms,* (1938, p. 442), Skinner hazards a guess as to the difference between human and animal behavior: "I may say that the only differences I expect to see revealed between the behavior of rat and man (aside from enormous differences of complexity) lie in the field of verbal behavior." Inevitably, Skinner was accused of reducing humans to talking rats, but what he really meant was that the same rigorous scientific method was to be applied to the study of verbal behavior as had proven successful in the study of rat behavior.

Skinner (1974, p. 88) reveals a semantic sensitivity in his avoidance of the term *language* because, as a noun, it suggests a "thing"—such as "capacity" or "ability" residing in the individual's mind. He prefers the term "verbal behavior" and considers it just as much behavior as pushing buttons, levers, playing ball, and so on.[4] In his book *About Behaviorism* (1974), Skinner uses the following illustration. The special feature of language is its effect on other people (pp. 88–89). For example, if, in their past experience, people have been reinforced by having a door open when they turned the door knob and pushed or pulled it open, they will do so in subsequent situations. But, if they have also been reinforced in the past by having the door opened by a listener on occasions when they said, "Please open the door," then that verbal response will be reinforced. There are admittedly differences between the two, but those differences don't require obscuring mentalistic explanations (p. 89). Skinner's theory is not self-actional. Like Kantor, Skinner has no need for internal "ideas" or "meanings" that get transmitted from the speaker's "mind" to that of the hearer. Skinner also rejects, as does Kantor, the conception of words as symbols. For Skinner, verbal behavior is under stimulus control. For Kantor, linguistic behavior is an adaptation to the thing referred to. Both view "meaning" naturalistically. For Kantor (1936, p. 122), "The technical description of a meaning reaction is any response which determines what a following reaction is to be." I say to you, "There's a water fountain," and you drink. The "meaning" of my remark is spelled out in your ensuing response—your drinking. For Skinner (1957, p. 91), the "meaning" of your verbal behavior lies in the "over-all function of the behavior. . . . A verbal response on the part of the speaker makes it possible for the listener to respond appropriately." This comes close to Kantor's linguistic response as an *adaptational act* toward the stimulus object to which the hearer is referred. The following definition, illustrated by means of a "primitive example," is offered by Skinner: "if one rat presses a lever to obtain food when hungry while another does so to obtain water when thirsty, the topographies of their behaviors may be indistinguishable, but they may be said to differ in meaning: to one rat, pressing the lever 'means' food; to the other, it 'means' water" (Skinner, 1974, p. 90). Both Kantor and Skinner give a new definition to an old term, one they both could do without.

---

[4] The interbehaviorist does not avoid the word *language* because, as Humpty-Dumpty says, "When I use a word it means just what I choose it to mean—neither more nor less" (Carroll, 1963, p. 79—originally published in 1872). So for us, *language* will mean behavior, neither more nor less.

Skinner finds no help in the formal and abstract analysis of words, phrases, and sentences issued by linguists. He rejects their assumption that words have inherent meanings and that humans have inherited an unconscious capacity for understanding grammar, a capacity said to allow them to use language with little training. Skinner does talk about an individual's "verbal repertoire," but with that term he does not refer to a storehouse of words in one's "memory" waiting to be matched with the speaker's or listener's "ideas." He means that certain verbal responses occur under certain identifiable conditions.

With an event type of orientation that Skinner espouses, there is no problem about where a word resides when it is not being spoken, any more than one wonders where the lightning is when it is not flashing. Events recur when the same constellation of factors come together. Such problems arise only in self-actional theories, in which a thing is forced to be the cause of itself. For Skinner, a given verbal event occurs when the same factors are present as obtained on a previous occurrence of that event. We should not be surprised to learn that, for Skinner, all verbal behavior is said to be acquired during the history of the organism, as is true of all other behavior. It follows, too, that, for Skinner, all behaviors are subject to the laws of operant conditioning, the details of which are presented in a comprehensive fashion by Kennedy (1975).

An Interbehavioral View of Language Behavior Development

Kantor and Smith (1975) recognize a vast literature in the linguistic development of children, but these works are largely a type of "word study." They concern themselves with developmental stages such as when children utter their first words, their first sentences, the ratio of nouns to adjectives, and so on. Because these are taken out of the context of the individual child's linguistic adjustmental act, they are not very useful in helping us understand referential behavior. Skinner (1957, p. 100) also complains that if the developmentalists and word-count investigators had not limited themselves to the surface features of children's language, "we should know more about how a child learns to speak." The conditions under which verbal behavior is acquired, what speech the child has heard, and under what circumstances, are the important variables for Skinner and for Kantor.

The interbehavioral view starts by rejecting maturation and all self-actional entities that are alleged to "generate" speech. Linguistic adjustments are said to be acquired in no way different from all other behaviors. Kantor and Smith (1975) acknowledge the participation of a variety of types of learning in the child's linguistic acquisition—classical conditioning, operant conditioning, imitation, or social learning.

Notions about the significance of the early, simple phases of the infant's prelinguistic activities differ from those stemming from an interbehavioral viewpoint. According to Lewis (1963, pp. 13–14),

> A child is born a speaker. . . . From birth he vocalizes and responds to sounds. . . . The child utters sounds and responds to the human voice, his mother responds to his sounds and speaks to him. If any of these four necessary conditions is impaired, the child's linguistic growth may suffer.

One wants to contradict Lewis in his claim that the "child is a born speaker." The sounds that the infant emits are a far cry from the speech that will develop out of those sounds. As important as the child's vocalizations are, as Mowrer (1952, p. 268) points out, "congenitally deaf children babble little, if any, and do not, without highly specialized training, learn to talk at all." Apparently there is more to talking than the mere possession of sound-producing equipment. Some of the other necessary conditions are revealed in the studies reviewed in the following sections.

Conditioning of vocalizations in the infant.   Rheingold, Gewirtz, and Ross (1959) decided to work with infants who were already at the "advanced stage" of babble, which evolves by about 3 months of age. After obtaining a baseline of vocalization for two days, the experimenters reinforced the infant's vocalizing during Days 3 and 4. The reinforcing stimulus consisted of three acts executed by the experimenter simultaneously—a broad smile, three "tsk" sounds, and a light touch on the infant's abdomen. Days 5 and 6 were nonreinforcing or extinction series. Under baseline conditions, the infants gave about 13 or 14 vocalizations per 3-minute period. The first day of reinforcement raised that figure to 18, an increase of 39%. The next day's conditioning increased vocalization to 25 or an additional increase of 34%. Thus, two sessions of 27 minutes each yielded an increase of 86% in the infants' vocalizings. Two days of extinction lowered the rate to 15, approximating the rate before the conditioning was begun. The conditioners concluded that the infants' vocalization can be brought under stimulus control.

The results suggest that mothers can increase not only their babies' prelinguistic sounds but also their going to or turning away from others, their crying, showing interest in strangers or fearing them, and so on. Perhaps more than that, Rheingold, Gewirtz, and Ross (1959) showed that the precursors of speech in the infant are a function of surrounding conditions as are all other behaviors. Stated otherwise, the development of the individual's linguistic adjustments follow the same principles that regulate every other type of psychological interaction.

Other confirmatory studies.   Weisberg (1963) used responding and nonresponding adults in a situation similar to the Rheingold, Gewirtz, and Ross

(1959) study and found that, once the child was accustomed to the experimental surroundings, a responding adult could increase its vocalization by contrast with the nonresponding adult. When the child was socially reinforced on vocalization, the rate increased markedly. However, social stimulation offered at other times produced as little effect as a nonsocial stimulus such as a chime.

With older children, 9 to 12 months of age, Dodd (1972) found that social and vocal reinforcement also increased the frequency and length of the child's vocalization but stopped short of imitation. Beyond this point, it is not difficult to see how eager parents will excitedly reinforce the child's "Dadada," shaping and refining it and other anticipated words to acceptable pronunciation. Vocabulary buildup grows rapidly. What else can the child do except to talk like others do in its surroundings? It may start with single word utterances such as "milk," which for the mother has a stimulus function equivalent to "I want milk." Progress beyond this point involves a hierarchy of behavior acquisition that builds up to phrases, sentences, idioms, and a chain of sentences. According to Kantor and Smith (1975, p. 333), "The child learns to do as others do in the craftsman situation when he uses a hammer instead of a chisel to drive a nail."

This sketchy account of a child's linguistic development has stressed verbovocal adjustment. For that reason, it might lead us to misidentify psychological language with word utterance. To guard against such error, I should point out a development that goes along hand in hand with oral speech. Concurrent with it, there is further development of gesture, which began long before the utterance of the first word. The outstretched arms lifted toward the giant adults spelled "Lift me up," long before the holophrastic word "Up!" appeared on the scene. And mothers everywhere recognize, clearly and sharply, the infant's extended hand with open palm as "Gimme." Also, long before the child started a career as speaker (referor), that child was performing adequately as hearer (referee). Or, as we used to say, the child has a "comprehension vocabulary" before attaining speech.

Words, Words, Words

The constant intrusion of words into our consideration of psychological language compels us to give due regard to a recent theory that has had a tremendous impact, not only on linguistics but also on the psychology of language. The theory has been elaborated by a world-famous linguist, Noam Chomsky.

Chomsky's theory.   Chomsky's theory is in direct opposition to theories of language acquisition that we have considered. According to the latter, the child acquires language from, and in, association with others in the same manner as all other reactions. Not so, says Chomsky, who puts language in a separate category, although he grudgingly admits the minor role of learning.

Chomsky (Allen and Van Buren, 1971) believes that language is the birthright of all normal children and that they come into the world with a blueprint for language, regardless of which language they will eventually speak. A built-in language-acquisition device (LAD) is said to receive speech input from others and to construct the grammar of that input language, which it then uses to "generate" sentences on its own. Chomsky is of the opinion that maturation largely accounts for speech development and gives little credit to the role that the reactional biography plays in language development.

Another pair of concepts that is important in Chomsky's theory is that of "deep structure" versus "surface structure." The surface structure of language is revealed in the speaker's utterance. It is the organization of the sentence into phrases, such as noun phrase and verb phrase. According to Chomsky, in the sentence, John kissed Mary (Allen and Van Buren, 1971, p. 59), *John* is a "noun phrase," *kissed* is a "verb phrase," and *Mary* is a "noun phrase." But this is only a superficial analysis. "The 'deep structure' of a sentence is the abstract, underlying form that determines the meaning of the sentence; it is present in the mind but not necessarily represented directly in the physical signal" (p. 2). It is the innate "deep structure" that generates the "surface structure." How does Chomsky know this? By inference from "surface structure."

Another fact that persuades Chomsky to assume that the individual is born with an unconscious knowledge of grammar is what Chomsky calls the "creativity of language" (Allen and Van Buren, 1971, p. 8). He is struck by the common observation that the speaker produces new sentences never before heard as such. A seemingly infinite variety of new sentences is uttered, and, furthermore, they are grammatically correct. Therefore, he concludes that they must be processed by the LAD, which, then, "generates" these never-before-heard, grammatically correct sentences.

All this convinces Chomsky that people are born with a "competence" that Chomsky defines as "what the speaker knows implicitly" (Allen and Van Buren, 1971, p. 7). "Competence," from a traditional viewpoint, is revealed in grammar. From Chomsky's viewpoint, competence implies a system of rules by which the "deep structure" of language is transformed into the "surface structure." According to Chomsky, people are born users of the underlying rules of grammar. How does Chomsky know this when he admits that "a person is not generally aware of the rules that govern sentence-interpretation in the language that he knows; nor, in fact, is there any reason to suppose that the rules can be brought to consciousness" (Allen and Van Buren, 1971, p. 7)? He infers it from the speaker's utterance or "what he does (his *performance*)" (p. 7). *Competence* is thus a purely inferential entity.

Critique of Chomsky's theory.   It does not take very much scientific sophistication to recognize Chomsky's constructs as purely fictitious, arbitrary, and self-actional. To endow maturation with power to "generate" speech is a (1) misuse of a valid biological concept and a (2) contradiction of what we do know about language acquisition by the child.[5] The inference of "deep structure" from "surface structure" and "competence" from "performance" reveals unwarranted, circular reasoning. There is no way to validate such purely imaginary constructs. As regards the "creativity" that Chomsky attributes to speech, and that so amazes him, we may endow the facts in the case with a special aura and a supernatural explanation, or we may handle them as naturalistically as we do other behaviors. The choice is ours.

If we examine the facts, we find that it takes a child four years to master the rudiments of a language (Farb, 1974, p. 249). Also, according to Farb, "the child continues to refine his speech until the age of ten, by which time he has internalized all the complicated rules of his native grammar" (p. 252). Ten years is a considerable portion of a normal life span.

On the point of creativity or novelty in our speech utterances (outside the clichés and social gestures such as "Hi"), Farb, who is quite sympathetic with Chomsky's view, notes the variables that lie at the basis of linguistic novelty or creativity.

> If English possessed a mere 1,000 nouns (such as *trees, children, horses*) and only 1,000 verbs *(grow, die, change)*, the number of possible two-word sentences therefore would be 1,000 × 1,000, or one million. Of course, most of these sentences will be meaningless to a speaker today—yet at one time people thought *atoms split* was a meaningless utterance. The nouns, however, might also serve as the objects of these same verbs in three-word sentences. So with the same meager repertory of 1,000 nouns and 1,000 verbs capable of taking an object, the number of possible three-word sentences increases to 1,000 × 1,000 × 1,000, or one billion. [Farb, 1974, p. 222]

With so many things in the world to be talked about, and so many verbal tags (approximately 500,000 in the English language) with which to refer to them, why should we expect much repetition in our utterances? The "creativeness" that Chomsky sees may merely mirror the unique adjustments that humans make in the flow of events in which they are involved. Also, the vastness of the linguistic facility (vocabulary) available to us permits us to "suit the action to the word, the word to the action."

One way to demystify the "creativeness" that Chomsky sees in language would be to find some other behavior that is comparable in richness and complexity but that does not mystify Chomsky. As he sees it, language is in a class apart from other behaviors (Chomsky, 1968, p. 11).

As a basis of comparison with linguistic speech, let us consider the manual movements that we perform in our everyday life. We are confronted

[5] In this connection, recall the case of Genie in Chapter 4. How much language maturation did she manifest in 13 years?

with an immediate disadvantage in not being able to fragment and "tag off" our continuous flow of movements the way we can our speaking behavior. We can *record* the latter and study the movements of the speech organs (for that is what they are) in the form of audible or written products through word analysis. Not having had a procedure for isolating components of manual movements, we have dealt with them in the gross and, thereby, overlook their richness and complexity. The painting of a lawn chair, the uprooting of a tree stump, the tying up of a tomato plant call for novel movements *never before* exercised in that same pattern of manual activities. These are unique performances also.

If these psychological interactions are too homely, let us move on to a more exalted level. Let us take the artist, the musical performer. As we noted in an earlier chapter, several years ago, Lili Kraus, a devotee of Mozart, played all 25 piano concertos of Mozart's in nine concerts in the United States. The mere thought of the combinations of notes (millions) that she executed is staggering. But, of course, the same would hold true for the composer. And, on a more earthy level, would we not find the same richness, complexity, and novelty, or, to use Chomsky's term, "creativeness," in surgery, dentistry, bricklaying, teaching, and so on? Variability and modifiability are the distinguishing attributes of behavior, so we should not be surprised to find them in speech as in other behaviors.[6]

Do the Infrahuman Animals Have Language, Too?

When circus dogs walk or dance on their hind legs, they resemble humans, but their evolutionary distance from humans limits them radically in their further imitation of *homo sapiens*. It is the nonhuman primates, the monkeys and chimpanzees, who hold adults as well as children spellbound with their antics. In the zoos, in circuses, and on television programs, they have entertained audiences with their acrobatics, bicycling, unicycling, boxing, smoking cigars, ice skating, roller skating, playing musical instruments in bands or orchestras and applauding themselves for their accomplishments. Even their "oil paintings" have (1) sold and (2) confounded art critics. Yet, in imitating human speech, despite their closer evolutionary kinship with humans, they have been surpassed by parrots and mynah birds.

Why the Contradiction?

Why are the nonhuman primates excellent mimics of such a range of human activities, excluding speech? The reason for their failure to talk to us certainly does not lie in a failure of human attempts to teach them. For the past

---

[6]Further evaluations of Chomsky's theory may be found in Riegel and Rosenwald (1975), Bowers (1969), MacCorquodale (1970) and Weigel (1977).

70 years, a number of experimentalists have made strenuous efforts in this direction with very scanty success.

Some have argued that the human organism's relatively larger brain capacity accounts for human speech. As tempting as such an argument is, Lenneberg (1968) reminds us that it is based on nothing more than intuition. He states that "the surgical removal of up to one-third of the cerebral mass early in childhood does not restrict the capacity for language acquisition" (p. 605). Lenneberg even doubts the traditionally assigned role of the left cerebral hemisphere in speech, pointing out that if this region is removed early enough in the life of an individual, "language may develop without impairment" (pp. 602–603).

The Continuity Theory of Evolution

Lenneberg is critical of anthropologists for assuming a continuity theory of evolution according to which evolutionary change proceeds at a constant rate. But gaps between closely related species show discontinuity; otherwise, we would observe a graded series of language behaviors up the evolutionary ladder toward *homo sapiens*. Because we do not observe a speech continuity, Lenneberg (1968, p. 611) concludes that the particular combination of speech-producing structures and their functions underwent a series of transformations during human evolution, transformations that were just right for speech production. However, this "assumption . . . must not be confused with the postulation of a 'gene for language' " (p. 611).

If Lenneberg's hypothesis is accepted, it would argue that because "all races have the same biological potential for the development of culture and the acquisition of language" (p. 608), then such evolutionary changes as he posited must have taken place prior to the dispersion of humans over the face of the earth. But how about the mynah birds' and parrots' superb echoic behavior? According to the discontinuity theory, we might say that that singular development was an evolutionary accident that led to a dead end (unless we acknowledge the amusement that the parroting of mynah birds and parrots provide humans).

The lack of proper anatomical structures for speech in the chimpanzee seems to have been substantiated by Lieberman, Klatt, and Wilson (1969). They analyzed the vocal tracts of the monkey and other nonhuman primates and compared them with that of the human. They discovered that the acoustical "vowel space" was different and that both apes and monkeys lack a pharynx like the human pharynx that is capable of much finer movement. "The inability of apes to mimic human speech is thus an inherent limitation of their vocal mechanisms" (Lieberman, Klatt, and Wilson, 1969, p. 1187).

However, we must not confuse the mimicking of speech with genuine bistimulational referential action. Our proper question should be "Can chimps function analogously to the way humans do when they tell someone something about so-and-so or when they are told something by someone about so-and-so?" And, since we have given gesture equal status with spoken language, why not circumvent the chimp's lack of verbovocal speech and try gesture as a communicative mode instead of speech? This is exactly what the Gardners decided to do.

Project Washoe

About 1966, psychologists R. Allen Gardner and Beatrice T. Gardner, of the University of Nevada at Reno, conceived of a plan that would overcome the speech-producing limitations of the chimp. They reasoned, "Why not provide a young chimpanzee with the opportunity to acquire the communicative language that an American deaf child has?" So they acquired a 10-month-old female chimp, Washoe, and proceeded to teach her the American Sign Language (ASL or Ameslan), a set of hand gestures in wide usage among the deaf of North America. Since chimpanzees have fairly mobile hands, sign language might have an advantage over oral speech.

The Gardners immersed Washoe in an environment of nothing but sign language. While they were in the presence of Washoe, they themselves, as well as Washoe's attendants, maintained the same rule of silence that the Trappist monks obeyed. Hand signals were used among the humans in communicating with each other whenever Washoe was present. Also, nonsigning humans (those not able to communicate in Ameslan) and all other chimpanzees were excluded from Washoe's living quarters (Gardner and Gardner, 1978). Note Washoe's signing "sweet" to Susan Nichols in Figure 12-3. Compare with Ameslan for "sweet" in Figure 12-4.

Washoe's home environment.   If one is going to compare the language development of a chimpanzee with that of a human child, the following reasoning should hold. One can hardly expect to use a caged chimp's language performance when the standard of comparison is a human child *in a home environment*. If one is to have a basis of comparison, then one must furnish similar conditions for both.

As Washoe's residence, the Gardners obtained a completely self-contained house trailer (8 × 24 feet) with provisions for her toilet, kitchen, and sleeping needs. A 500-square-foot backyard was made into a romping and play area. Her surroundings were kept as interesting to Washoe as possible. She was attended constantly by at least one human companion. Occasional visitors and excursions into the community made Washoe's life close to that of a middle-class American child. Her language teaching program was integrated with various aspects of her daily life, such as games, eating, and toileting. Her companions "talked" among themselves and with Washoe while keeping house, playing with her in her sandbox and during her eating, bathing, dressing, toothbrushing, and so on. The two-way use of

Figure 12-3 Two-way communication with an infant chimpanzee. Susan Nichols signs "What's this?" In reply, Washoe signs "Sweet." Compare with Figure 12-4. (Courtesy of Beatrice Gardner.)

Figure 12-4 American Sign Language for "sweet." Compare this with Washoe's rendition of the same sign in Figure 12-3. (From Watson, 1964, p. 7.)

"what's that?" approximated asking the names of objects by parents and child in the human family.

Methods used in speech training. As Washoe's first chief guardian, Roger Fouts (Fouts and Rigby, 1977) describes the techniques used in furthering Washoe's language acquisition. Shaping was used when Washoe made approximations to the correct Ameslan sign, but this procedure was not as effective as guidance. Guidance required physically molding the hands and arms in the proper position for the sign in the presence of the object. Washoe learned her sixth sign acquisition, *Tickle*, in this fashion (Gardner and Gardner, 1971).

More recently, Fouts has found molding to be an optimal training approach (Fouts, 1972). This method involved guiding Washoe's hands into the proper position and movement while she was engaged in the act. It might also require the experimenter's making the sign while encouraging Washoe to imitate it. But Washoe also learned signs by means of observational learning; that is simply from *casually* watching her companions' signings. This method was believed to be different from the deliberateness that was a part of Fouts' imitation in molding.

The results. Vocabulary acquisition came quickly; and when Washoe was between 18 and 24 months of age, she began using phrases at the same age that human babies begin to use two-word combinations.[7] In three years, she showed the use of 245 different combinations of three or more signs. She also indicated generalization of a sign from a specific object to a whole class of similar objects. For example, the sign *hurt* acquired in connection with bruises and scratches was later applied to stains, decals on the back of a hand, and the navel.

Washoe learned not only nouns, but verbs, pronouns, adjectives, and prepositions in proper combinations. After learning the sign for *open* for a certain door, she used it for car door, boxes, water faucets, capped soda bottles, and cupboard doors. To get Roger to unlock the refrigerator in her house trailer, she signed, *"Open key food."*

The following phrases illustrate Washoe's use of two- and three-sign combinations: *open drink, open hurry, you drink, please open, more food gimme, hug come hurry, you good Mrs. G., tickle me Susan, gimme please baby.*

The following interchanges among different people and Washoe testify to Washoe's complex interpersonal development. (Roger is Roger Fouts.)

---

[7] We should be reminded that Washoe was already about a year old when her linguistic reactional biography *started.*

Interchange A

Roger: What you want?
Washoe: Tickle.
Roger: Who tickle?
Washoe: Dr. Gardner.
Roger: Dr. Gardner not here.
Washoe: Roger tickle.

Interchange B (Washoe has wet the floor)

Washoe: Dirty dirty.
P [an attendant]: Bad Bad.
Washoe: Me sorry.

Washoe's idiosyncratic language response.   Another interesting observation (Gardner and Gardner, 1971) concerned Washoe's invention of the sign for *bib*. The Gardners had *decided* to use the sign for *napkin* or *wiper* to refer to *bib* also. On one occasion, before Washoe's learning of the sign for *bib* had been well consolidated, someone held up a bib and asked Washoe to name it. Beginning at the back of her neck where a bib is tied, she drew the outline of a bib on her chest with the index fingers of both hands, bringing them together at a point where a bib would naturally come. Later, when fluent signers of American Sign Language viewed films of Washoe's signing, they informed the Gardners that drawing an outline of a bib on the chest with both index fingers was the *standard* Ameslan sign for *bib*. Washoe's invention turned out to be more appropriate than that of her preceptors. In passing, we should note that human babies also coin words and sometimes induce the family to follow suit.

Project Washoe terminated when Washoe was 5 years old, at which time she had attained a vocabulary of 162 signs with no indication of a slowdown.

The Gardners broke ground with Washoe, who has "transferred" to the University of Oklahoma to work with Fouts. The Gardners are now proceeding with several chimpanzees in the same laboratory at the same time. Now that they feel that they have established two-way communication between humans and chimpanzee, they aim to determine the highest level of communication possible and to study communication among chimpanzees (Gardner and Gardner, 1978). Newborn subjects are being introduced to the group at intervals of 1 or 2 years so that at any given time there is an assortment of age groups and levels of development. Far more interesting and significant achievements are anticipated in their expanded program. For example, will chimps sign to each other and will chimp mothers who know the "lingo" teach their offspring sign language? Time will tell. Gardner (1980) has demonstrated that chimps can communicate with each other by means of sign language (see Figure 12-5).

Figure 12-5   Signing between subjects: chimpanzee Moja is holding a bottle of soda as her friend, Tatu, approaches and signs "Drink." (Courtesy of Beatrice T. Gardner.)

Work at the Institute for Primate Studies

At the termination of Project Washoe, Roger Fouts and Washoe shifted their respective functions to the Institute for Primate Studies of the University of Oklahoma. There, Fouts is studying 24 chimps and a number of monkeys at a primate colony. In addition to continued work with Washoe, Fouts is observing three chimps that are being raised in private homes as closely as possible to the way human children are reared. He is teaching sign language to all of them (Fouts, 1977).

Washoe at Oklahoma University.   Washoe, at her first sight of a chimp, called them "bugs." But, after overcoming her prejudice, she did sign to them. They, likewise, learned to sign, but in a more impoverished style (at that particular stage). Fouts reports one incident in which Bruno was eating raisins from the hand of a graduate student. Booee came up to Bruno and signed, "Tickle Booee." Bruno signed back, "Booee me food," which Fouts (1977) translates to mean (possibly) "Booee, I'm eating." At least, Bruno went on eating raisins.

Washoe's use of metaphor.   Washoe has shown continued progress in her sign-language development. As one instance, Fouts reports her attributing a new meaning to the term *dirty*. Originally, she used this term to signify soiled things or feces. Once she had a fight with a monkey. On her next encounter with that monkey, Roger asked her. "What that?" Her spontaneous reply was, "Dirty monkey." Following that experience, she used the sign for anyone who frustrated her wishes. On one occasion, she requested fruit from Roger. When Roger signed that he had none, she called him "Dirty Roger." This is clearly use of metaphor.

Sarah, the Chimp Who Reads and Writes

At the University of California, a psychologist, David Premack (1971; 1972), has taught a chimpanzee, Sarah, to read and write by means of a code of variously colored and shaped bits of plastic, each of which represents a word. These can be arranged on a magnetized board to form sentences. Sarah began her linguistic career in the way human babies do, by connecting a chip of a certain shape and color (a "word") with a certain object. She has mastered such relational concepts as "under," "name of," and "not name of."

Within a span of 6 years, Sarah has acquired a vocabulary of over 130 different plastic pieces. She often, but not always, makes the right choice when she is asked to judge stimuli as "same" or "different." Even grammar does not seem to be beyond her grasp, contrary to Chomsky's attribution of an unconscious knowledge of universal grammar to the human species alone. For example, when Sarah's experimenters spelled out, "Sarah, put the apple in the pail and the banana in the dish," she responded correctly. Note that she had to apply the verb *put* to both tasks and to relate apple to pail and not to dish, and so on—a rather complex operation in all.

Farb (1974), for one, doubts whether Sarah responds linguistically as humans know language. The fact that she performs correctly 75 to 80% of the time, and better with some experimenters than with others, suggests to Farb (1974, p. 232) that she has just learned a "bag of tricks." According to Farb, the fact that she does not "generate" sentences on her own but only responds to those that are presented to her further supports his hunch.

Lana, the Computerized Chimp

At Georgia State University, psychologists Rumbaugh, Gill, and Von Gloserfeld have been teaching Lana, a chimpanzee, an artificial language, christened "Yerkish," programmed into a computer. The built-in grammar demands rigorous adherence to the rules because nothing else will work. For example, the computer will accept and execute a request such as, "Please, machine, give milk," or "Please, machine, make music." If the computer buttons are pushed in the right sequence, the first request automatically activates a dispenser to give milk. The second one, if the input is correctly carried out, automatically provides music. However, if Lana should construct the sentence, *"Please* machine, *make* milk," the computer would reject that nonsensical request.

Rumbaugh's laboratory is so constructed that Lana is able to read her own sentence production on a projector above the keyboard. If she notes that she has made a mistake, she "erases" it by pushing a key, and she starts over again. She also recognizes mistakes that her experimenters make at their own keyboard when they want to communicate with her from another room.

Project Koko

In July 1972, Francine Patterson "adopted" a 1-year-old female gorilla named Koko. Ever since then, through modeling (imitation) and molding, she has been teaching American Sign Language to the young primate.

During the first year and a half, Patterson (1978b) reports that Koko's sign vocabulary grew at the rate of one sign a month. Because both Koko and Washoe had begun their sign language learning at about 1 year of age, comparisons were in order. Patterson learned that the progress of the chimp and the gorilla were equivalent. In 18 months, Koko had acquired 22 signs and Washoe, 21 (p. 77).

Sign-language "conversations" at the dinner table showed a comparable gain for each subject at the 29th month of the two projects. Washoe was reported to have used 50 signs during a 15- to 20-minute session at the evening meal. During a 1-hour dinner session, Patterson (1978b, p. 780) recorded a total of 251 signs for Koko. Their rate of production was similar. Subsequent progress showed Koko's expansion of vocabulary acquisition. In a recent report, Patterson (1978a, p. 453) writes, "I would estimate that Koko's current working vocabulary—signs she uses regularly and appropriately—stands at about 375."

Koko's IQ. Because of the close relationship between IQ and verbal facility, Patterson has felt that Koko is making great strides in intelligence, for she has spontaneously combined as many as 11 signs into meaningful and frequently novel statements. She also has a sense of past and future and is "clever" enough to know how to lie. As to actual scores on intelligence tests, despite an expected cultural bias toward humans, in February 1975, Koko's IQ on the Stanford-Binet scale was 84. Five months later, when she was 4, her IQ rose to 95, close to the average for human children. By January 1976, it slipped back to 85. Other tests gave comparable results. Figure 12-6 shows Koko responding correctly to the request, "Show me the dolly's hair."

Intraspecific communication. Once Patterson established that gorillas and humans could communicate with one another, she, like Fouts, wondered if

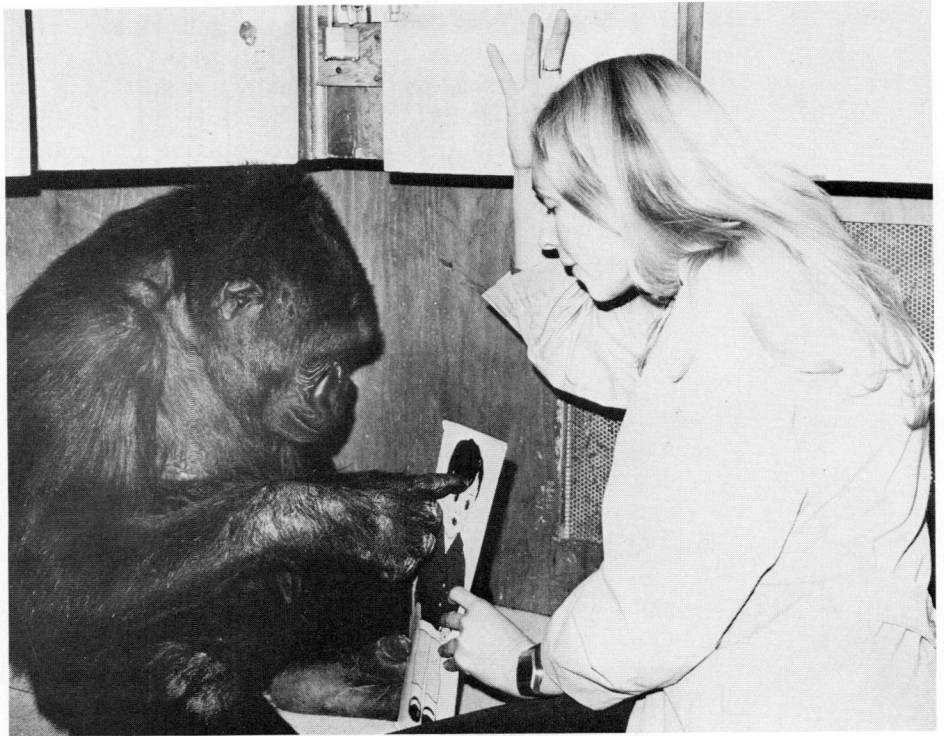

Figure 12-6   A preschool intelligence test adminstered by Penny Patterson gives Koko a chance to show her intelligence. Here Koko properly points to the doll's hair in answer to an item testing knowledge of body parts. (Francine Patterson and Ronald H. Cohn, Stanford University. Courtesy of National Geographic Society.)

gorillas could meaningfully sign to one another. So she acquired a younger, male companion, Michael, for Koko. Almost at once, the two were signing "come" to each other through the fence that separated them. Recently, Michael has learned to sign "chase." Both respond appropriately in inviting or executing the chase. Patterson (1978c, p. 3) reports that Michael is rapidly expanding his vocabulary from Koko's coaching rather than from that of his human caretakers.

From her observations of gorilla sign-language acquisition, Patterson (1978b) concludes that the gorilla and chimpanzee are equivalent in this respect and that both show a close parallel with language learning in human children. And, while admittedly nonhuman primates are slower in their acquisition of sign language, "this difference is one of degree and not of kind, however, and does not weaken the proposition that language is no longer the exclusive domain of man" (p. 95). However, what are needed are comparative studies of signing gorillas and chimps on the one hand and signing deaf children on the other.

A comparison of the methods.   In evaluating machine methods of teaching artificial language, Fouts (1977) argues that the exact recording of the experimental data provided by the use of machines is bought at the expense of excluding certain behaviors. Such methods as Premack and Rumbaugh use allow the chimpanzee to behave only in such ways as fit into the rigid experimental situation. "For example, the computer is not programmed to accept novel or innovative uses of the language" (Fouts, 1977, p. 1051), such as Fouts observed in the case of Washoe.

Gardner and Gardner (1978) add another point of criticism of the kind of condition that obtains in the Premack and Rumbaugh experiments. Their subjects were caged animals, and caged animals, just liked caged humans, develop pathological behavior with continued incarceration. Gardner and Gardner (1978, p. 12) quote Premack as saying that Sarah, after 7 years of cage confinement, "was too dangerous to handle. The difference, of course, is that at this time Sarah was being kept almost exclusively in solitary confinement in a 3 × 6 meter cage." Washoe's and her "siblings' " "home atmosphere" has not brought about any such radical personality changes. In fact, write the Gardners, "As Washoe becomes older, we found her more manageable and more easy to deal with" (Gardner and Gardner, 1971, p. 12).

But Is It Language?

Gardner and Gardner (1977, p. 59) suggest that instead of a categorical yes or no answer to the question "Can chimpanzees learn human language?" one should ask such quantitative questions as "How much human language, how soon, or how far can they go?" Can one really say at what point a human child has learned its language? Or, doesn't the baby's language, childish at first, *gradually* get elaborated into the form of the surrounding adults'? Why expect more from chimps?

But when the Gardners sum up a comparison of their chimpanzees' language learning with that of human babies, they find certain striking similarities; for example, immature or "baby talk" variations, generalization of application of sounds and words, a gradual increase in length of utterances, and in the use of order in early sentences.[8]

Limber's view.   In a recent article, "Language in Child and Chimp?" Limber (1977) questions whether the recent experiments just reviewed disprove the contention that language is an exclusively human invention. In his

---

[8] Many aspects of chimpanzee linguistic and other behaviors are covered in an engaging book, *Why Chimps Can Read*, written by Ann Premack (1976).

opinion, the results so far only demonstrate that chimpanzees can apply names to objects. While admitting that "naming plays an important, perhaps necessary role in human language" (p. 282), it is not sufficient evidence to prove that the organism is using human language. According to Limber, focusing on words distracts us from the role of the sentence with its structure of grammar, meaning, and creativity aspects. His definition of language permits him to write, "The ability of apes or even 2-year-olds to communicate and use simple names is not sufficient reason to attribute the use of human language to them" (p. 280).

Two points follow.   There are two points to be made here. First, unless we adopt an "all or none" definition of language, may we not say that the primates *share* the naming or symbolic function of language? If so, then, in this respect at least, the two species show a continuity rather than the gap previously claimed. Second, it is too early to demand a definitive answer to the question "Is language an exclusive attribute of *homo sapiens*?" Even Limber (1977), who appears to side with Chomsky's notion of an innate linguistic capacity in the human, looks with hope toward the coming work with conversational and problem-solving chimpanzees. He writes, "Such investigations may well advance our understanding of human psychology far more than any research heretofore involving infrahumans" (Limber, 1977, p. 294).

Chapter Summary

The psychology of language is distinct from other disciplines and can be considered via mentalistic, behavioristic, and interbehavioral theories of language. An interbehavioral orientation defines language as bistimulational referential behavior of an *individual*, whether speaker or hearer. Such a formulation subsumes gesture, recognizing it fully as an equivalent to speech. Symbols and symbolic behavior can be analyzed in relation to psychological language. A cultural perspective on language permits us to assess the social psychological and idiosyncratic influence on linguistic behavior. Skinnerians agree with interbehaviorists on how language is acquired and oppose Chomsky's hypothesis of a distinctly human, *innate* language faculty. Finally, we do not yet know if infrahuman animals also have language.

Epilogue

This book is the result of an attempt to develop an interbehavioral framework for understanding psychological data. While the approach here presented is identified with Kantor's interbehavioral psychology, kindred approaches, on a number of different fronts and from different perspectives, are emerging today. What distinguishes all of them is their common abandonment of theories that confine themselves to the skin and contents of the organism. I characterized these older procedures as self-actional. According to the dictionary, the term self-acting refers to "acting or capable of acting of or by itself." Many of the traditional theories interpret such facts as seeing, hearing, learning, remembering, and feeling self-actionally. As an example, although something other than the organism is involved in learning a poem, self-actional theorists interpret such facts in terms of imaginary brain or mind happenings. The internal principles that they apply cannot be scientifically verified because they are hypothetical or inferential ("brain traces"). Then, too, self-actional theories break down because the organism is forced to carry the explanatory burden by itself, even though it is only one of the variables in a complex psychological field. Finally, when we look for possible applications, we cannot do anything with such self-actional entities as "brain traces," "IQs," "drives," or "mental states."

The newer approaches differ from the traditional, self-actional ones in looking beyond the organism. For the former, behavior is a function of variables found in the surroundings of the organism. Another way of stating the same thing in a looser sense is to say that the responses of the organism are "under the control of the environment." For example, study the interbehaviors of people around you. Here's a boy in a shopping mall walking in a most peculiar fashion. This child takes long, stereotyped strides. Strange? Yes, if you restrict your observation self-actionally to *the boy* under study. But not, if you expand your field of observation beyond the action of the organism. If you do, you will note that the floor tiles are alternately white and brown. We now notice that the child steps on every other square, the brown ones. By broadening our field of observation beyond the organism, we make sense of the boy's behavior. We note a lawful relationship between the child's action and an environmental condition.

Here are other instances. A man seated at a table in a restaurant displays a grimace and "fans" his face with his hand. "Why?" Someone is smoking a pipe at an adjoining table. During a church service, worshippers kneel almost simultaneously. How come? The sound of a tinkling bell at the altar was the "occasion" for that response in unison.

These are only three samples of behaviors that make sense as soon as we connect them with their correlated other main variable in the event, the stimulus object. Here is where the lawful relationships must be sought. Thousands of such events are taking place around you. If you develop habits of looking beyond the organism to variables connected with the organism's action, you may need to give up imagining self-actional goings-on somewhere inside the organism. Or, at least, in addition to a self-actional approach, you will be able to view psychological data as larger than hypothetical intraorganismic occurrences—data that make a lot of sense viewed from the larger perspective.

But behavior is also a function of factors other than the organism's action and stimulus object. Still other conditions facilitate the confrontation between the organism and stimulus object. These are the media of contact, such as light, that make it possible for the two main participants to come into a functional relationship with one another. Setting factors must also be taken into account. How a boy and a basketball interact with each other depends on whether the two are in a gymnasium, in a classroom during an active class recitation, in church, and so on. Thus, we see the need for broadening our investigation still more to a situational, field, or event type of framework. As Barker demonstrated, how people behave depends on whether they are at the post office, Sunday school, tavern, or the Odd Fellows hall; therefore these additional factors must also be included. We do violence to the facts when we take in less investigative territory than the total event, situation, or field.

However, our job is still not finished. Let us return to the examples of the boy's peculiar walk in the mall, the man's reaction to the pipe smoke, and the worshippers' kneeling in unison at the sound of the tinkling bell. Even if we inventory the finest detail of those three events, we have not made much progress in understanding them until we start relating them to similar, prior events. Here the interbehavioral construct of the reactional biography or interactional history comes to our aid. When we apply the principle, "present events are a function of antecedent events," we have the answer to the question of why one particular boy walks on every brown square in the mall (while others do not). Only with this procedure can we account for the man's strong reaction to the smoke from the pipe and the church congregation's kneeling simultaneously. Our procedure yields foresight and understanding without resorting to hypothetical, internal "brain traces," "IQs," and such. All the variables that we need to deal with are observable. But can any system be perfect? Does it confer only benefits? One might well ask, "Doesn't interbehaviorism have any defects?" We explore that question next.

An Evaluation of a Field Approach of the Interbehavioral Sort[1]

It is a fair question to ask about the advantages and disadvantages of any systematic view. What scientific benefits does an interbehavioral framework offer and are there any drawbacks to its adoption? We frankly face this question at this point in our retrospective view.

The interbehaviorist finds a definite differentiation between the subject matter of psychology and that of biology. As a distinct subject matter, the interbehaviorist recognizes that the multiplicity of variables and unique factors that characterize psychological data cal for special procedures derived from its study and not from theoretical borrowings from biology, physics, and so on. While acknowledging the fact that psychology has much in common with the physical and biological sciences, interbehaviorists insist on developing their own models instead of copying the models of other sciences. For example, at one time Titchener adopted chemistry as a model, hoping to erect a science of "mental chemistry" in which he sought to show how mental elements could be fused into compounds that no longer resembled the original elements. Today, as another example, the computer (for some psychologists) serves as a model for brain functioning. The interbehaviorist rejects such imports from other sciences, preferring to discover any theoretical aids from the exclusive observation of behavioral data. This procedure serves as an acceptable limitation on the interbehaviorist but one that others might consider too confining.

---

[1] In this section, I received particular help from interchanges with my colleague, David Herman.

Interbehavioral psychology avoids the trap that derives from the two-valued orientation of matter (body) versus spirit (mind). Instead of imposing a supernatural metaphor on behaving organisms, interbehaviorism views them naturalistically, that is, of a piece with such events as gravitating objects, chemical interactions, and living things.

As a field view, interbehavioral psychology deals with behavior at its own level while recognizing that other disciplines provide relevant help in specifying the role of participating (such as biological, chemical, and physical) factors. As such, it rejects the prevailing reductionistic model of science, a procedure objectionable to those who favor reductionism.

An *apparent* disadvantage of interbehavioral theory is that it "looks" more complicated than self-actional theories in that it requires the accountability or specification of the relevant variables in the total event. Explanations in terms of more appealing hypothetical goings-on inside the organism are rejected, although opposing theorists consider such "explanations" easier or, at least, more acceptable.

Interbehavioral psychology has been criticized for not generating a distinctive research program (such as psychoneurology or animal experimentation). The rebuttal to that point is that interbehaviorism offers such a comprehensive approach that it can embrace the tremendous volume of existing data. Because data are neutral as far as theory is considered, they are available for all theories to try their hand at. As to the interbehavioral comprehensive reach, this feature gives it an advantage over what might be called "mini-systems" such as Gestalt and psychoanalysis, which prefer a more restricted set of data.

Although the interbehaviorist recognizes that the goal of psychology is the attainment of valid general principles, it emphasizes the individual and the applicability of general principles to the individual. The opposition might consider such an emphasis on the individual as a disadvantage, particularly to those investigators who favor quantitative methods that have been so successful in some other sciences. The interbehaviorist's retort to such a criticism is that much quantitative work in psychology deals with abstractive data in which individual behavior disappears in the group's average.

One test of the validity of a theory is the degree of foresight and understanding that it provides. On that score, you, the reader of this book, must be the judge. The basic question is "From the interbehavioral position adopted, how much lawfulness and orderliness have the 12 foregoing chapters reflected?" Another indirect test of the soundness of a theory is its successful applicability. If, for example, the principle of operant conditioning can be extended to the improvement of patients in an institution, to the solution of problems of schoolchildren, and so on, we have a confirmation of the validity of those principles. In the next section, we look further into the promise of field theories of an interbehavioral type.

Other Field Type Approaches

The most prevalent current view of "human nature" is a self-actional one. People are believed to become what they eventually become largely as the result of what they started with—a low "IQ" or a mediocre or a high one, "musical talent" (much, little, or none), neurotic or psychopathic "tendencies," sexual, criminal, or aggressive "drives" or "instincts," and so on. While self-actional theories grudgingly grant that an "environment" is necessary to bring the "talent" or "tendency" *out*, the dice are believed to be loaded for those who make it and against those who do not. The belief is a variation of the doctrine of predestination that has persisted in our culture for centuries.

But cultural beliefs are not eternal. They change along with other cultural institutions. During the Renaissance, the prevalent conception of "human nature" was radically different. As described by Skorpen (1965), the "Renaissance man" was proficient in many fields of endeavor.[2] The ideal of *l'uomo universale* (the all-around man) arose and spread over Europe. The Renaissance period produced such giants as Dante, Michelangelo, and Leonardo da Vinci, men who combined, within a single personality, the skills of artist, scientist, poet, philosopher, artisan, engineer, architect, and prophet. Inspired by the vision of unlimited human potentialities, these men and others of their period attained superb levels of achievement.

Have modern humans deteriorated? Skorpen (1965, p. 12) comments,

> When this dimension of the Renaissance ideal of the universal man is duly recognized, in the performance of men like Alberti and da Vinci, we may wonder if the human perfection which they instanced does not represent the peak of mankind's development in both theory and practice, such that, apart from improved techniques of scientific discovery and applied technology, little else of importance distinguishes modern man from his Renaissance ancestor. Indeed, we might wonder if modern man hasn't deteriorated in comparison.

As often happens, practice outstrips theory. In medical, educational, or psychological matters, people often do the proper thing through guess or accident. Certainly people of the Renaissance did not have the benefit of an objective psychological theory. They just stumbled onto a procedure that worked—that produced people of varied excellences. The Renaissance man happened to think of himself as an independent individual, free to rise to previously undreamed-of heights, and so he did. Our age, with its stress on inherent, self-actional "powers," or lack thereof, does not spur superb achievement.

[2] The Renaissance was blatantly and thoroughly a male chauvinist culture.

Newton believed in the concept of force concentrated in hard bits of matter. A parallel Newtonian view holds that a psychological "power" (IQ, creativity, drive, instinct, perversion, criminality, and so on) is encapsulated within people and that it drives them to excellence, mediocrity, or perdition. For example, the belief is still widespread that women are psychologically inferior to men. Nevertheless, where the prejudice has broken down and opportunities have been made available to women, it is common knowledge that they have become, and are becoming increasingly so, prime ministers of their countries (for example, Israel, Sri Lanka, and England), judges, legislators (as in the U.S. Senate and House of Representatives), members of the president's cabinet, executives in business and industry, members of boards of directors, physicians, scientists, lawyers, architects, engineers, coal miners, construction workers, locomotive engineers, jockeys, racing car drivers, commercial jet plane pilots, orchestra conductors, scientists, and officers in the army, navy, and air force. They are competing with men in criminal activity such as drug pushing, bank heists, robbery, and burglary. Several decades ago, women were considered unequal to men in these activities, which were considered strictly male. After all, there are very few occupational or professional activities that call for a specifically male or female genital structure. Today, women are catching up with men—even in the lung cancer rate from smoking cigarettes.

No one, today, would argue that racism has been eliminated from the face of the earth. Despite the fact that white people are an earthly minority, they are in the saddle, and many of them believe the yellow, red, brown, and black people (the majority) are inferior. Nevertheless, sporadically, there are rising in that majority (for example, in China and Africa) national leaders, physicians, surgeons, inventors, composers, poets, novelists, atomic scientists, musicians, singers, members of the United Nations, and so on. In the United States, Blacks are increasingly entering university as well as secondary and primary school teaching, and state and national legislatures, in addition to the well-established fields of entertainment and sports. Blacks are being appointed as cabinet-level officers, ambassadors, and United Nations representatives. They are developing into musicians, writers, poets, architects, physicians, scientists, and so on. One hundred years ago, such things were unheard of. And, yet, there is no scientific evidence that the genes or any other self-actional entities allegedly resident in Blacks have changed; only reactional biography opportunities have changed in that interval.

Let us now take a final hop, skip, and a jump through the preceding pages to highlight certain incidents:

- We observed that geniuses appear to be "made," not "born," for we noted the persistence, dedication, and hard labor correlated with excellence in creativity, with Beethoven serving as the supreme example.

- Preschool children have learned to use the touch method in typewriting and have been taught to read, write, and take dictation.
- Suzuki has taught 3- to 5-year-old children to play the violin with remarkable skill, such that some 5-year-olds can match or surpass college-aged violin students.
- A 3-year-old child manages not only to swim proficiently but also to pass a life-saving test. Today, toddlers in several countries are being "drown-proofed."
- A Black Papuan can rise from a primitive stone-age culture practicing cannibalism to an adulthood as a medical pathologist and political leader, spanning "ten thousand years in a life time."
- A mongoloid boy writes a diary that is published.
- A Black American family, two or three generations away from slavery, produces achievers, four of whom attain master's degrees and two, doctorates.
- We also observed the enduring nature of such basic behavioral examples as William E. Leonard's siderophobia, of the wish to be held, of child-abusing parents who were themselves abused, and of Genie, "a modern-day wild child."
- In the chapter on the societal stage of the reactional biography, we saw the indelible stamp that culture places on people in the example of an American-born boy who was psychologically transformed into a Chinese through and through because he was reared in China.

All of these behavior samples only hint at the tremendous possibilities for human development. Furthermore, they show that the achievements that we have noted have come about not *because* of a guiding theory of human behavior, but *despite* the traditional, pessimistic view of human nature that still holds sway over us. However, such data as we have examined are congruent with the event type of theories emerging today. Certainly, according to the hypothesis of the reactional biography or interbehavioral history, limitations to human development do not lie in some allegedly inherent quality ("IQ," "capacity," "talent," or "innate genius") that sets the limit of development at the psychological level. Present events are a function of antecedent events. Foresight and understanding come from studying the flow of events. The clear implication is that the only limits to the highest achievement of human potentialities lie in the number and quality of events in which organisms are enabled to participate.

This open-ended conception of human development sketched offers a breath-taking view of possibilities for the human species. Skinner, for one, has captured the full implications of technological applications of the science of human behavior even in its present, primitive stage. He writes, "There are wonderful possibilities—and all the more wonderful because traditional approaches have been so ineffective" (Skinner, 1971, p. 214). And as to the limits of those possibilities, he quotes Cabet in the following quotation:

> "The limits of perfection of the human species," said Etienne Cabet in *Voyage en Icarie*, "are as yet unknown." But of course there are no limits. The human species will never reach a final perfection before it is exterminated—"some say in fire, some in ice," and some in radiation. [Skinner, 1971, p. 208]

A kindred thought is expressed by John Dewey: "It [has] often happened that ideas strongly objected to when first presented take root and modify later views" (in a letter to Arthur Bentley, in Ratner, Altman, and Wheeler, 1964, p. 103). This offers an appropriate conclusion to our flight of fancy on what people can make of themselves.

References

Abrams, S. The polygraph in a psychiatric setting. *American journal of psychiatry,* 1973, *130,* 94–98.

Adler, A. *The practice and theory of individual psychology* (Rev. ed.). New York: Harcourt Brace Jovanovich, 1929.

Aebersold, P. C. Radioisotopes—new keys to knowledge. In *The Smithsonian report for 1953.* Washington, D.C.: 1954.

Alexander, F. *Fundamentals of psychoanalysis.* New York: Norton, 1948.

Alexander, L. Conditional reflexes as related to hypnosis and hypnotic techniques. *Conditional reflex,* 1966, *1,* 199–204.

Alland, A. Intelligence in black and white. In C. L. Brace, G. R. Gamble, and J. T. Bond (Eds.), *Race and intelligence: Anthropological studies* (No. 8). Washington, D.C.: American Anthropological Association, 1971.

Allen, J. P. B., and Van Buren, P. *Chomsky: Selected readings.* New York: Oxford University Press, 1971.

Allport, F. H. *Theories of perception and the concept of structure.* New York: Wiley, 1955.

Allport, G. W. *Personality: A psychological interpretation.* New York: Holt, 1937.

American Psychiatric Association, Committee on Nomenclature and Statistics. *Diagnostic and statistical manual of mental disorders I.* Washington, D.C.: American Psychiatric Association, 1952.

American Psychiatric Association, Committee on Nomenclature and Statistics. *Diagnostic and statistical manual of mental disorders II.* Washington, D.C.: American Psychiatric Association, 1968.

Anson, B. J. *An atlas of human anatomy.* Philadelphia: Saunders, 1950.

Arnheim, R. *Visual thinking.* Berkeley: University of California Press, 1971.

Baer, D. M. An age-irrelevant concept of development. *Merrill-Palmer quarterly of behavior and development,* 1970, *16,* 238–245.

Baer, D. M. The organism as host. *Human development*, 1976, *19*, 87–98.

Bakal, D. A. Headache: A biopsychological perspective. *Psychological bulletin*, 1975, *82*, 369–382.

Bakker, C. B. Why people don't change. *Psychotherapy: Theory, research and practice*, 1975, *12*, 164–172.

Baltes, P. B., and Schaie, K. W. The myth of the twilight years. *Psychology today*, 1974, *8*, 35–38, 40.

Bandura, A. The role of imitation in personality development. *Journal of nursery education*, 1963, *18*(3), 207–215.

Bandura, A. *Principles of behavior modification.* New York: Holt, Rinehart and Winston, 1969.

Bandura, A. Behavior theory and the models of man. *American psychologist*, 1974, *29*, 859–869.

Bandura, A., Ross, D., and Ross, S. A. Imitation of film-mediated aggressive models. *Journal of abnormal and social psychology*, 1963, *66*(1), 8.

Barker, R. G. *Ecological psychology.* Stanford, Calif.: Stanford University Press, 1968.

Barker, R. G., Wright, B. A., Meyerson, L., and Gonick, M. R. *Adjustment to physical handicap and illness: A survey of the social psychology of physique and disability* (Bulletin 55, revised). New York: Social Science Research Council, 1953.

Barrington, B. L. A list of words descriptive of affective reactions. *Journal of clinical psychology*, 1963, *19*, 259–262.

Basmajian, J. Electromyography comes of age. *Science*, 1972, *176*, 603–609.

Bates, M. Insects in the diet. *American scholar*, 1959, *29*(1), 43–52.

Bayley, N. Some increasing parent–child similarities during the growth of children. *Journal of educational psychology*, 1954, *45*, 1–21.

Beecher, H. K. The subjective response and reaction to sensation. *American journal of medicine*, 1956, *20*, 107–113.

Bentley, A. F. *Inquiry into inquiries.* Boston: Beacon Press, 1954.

Berlyne, D. E. *Structure and direction in thinking.* New York: Wiley, 1965.

Bernstein, L. *Leonard Bernstein on Beethoven: Symphony No. 5 in C Minor.* Columbia LP record, Omnibus Series, CL918.

Bickford, R., Whelan, J., Klass, D., and Corbin, K. Reading epilepsy. *Transactions of the American Neurological Association*, 1956, *81*, 100.

Bijou, S. W. A functional analysis of retarded development. In N. R. Ellis (Ed.), *International review of research in mental retardation*, Vol. 1. New York: Academic Press, 1966.

Bijou, S. *Child development: The basic stage of early childhood.* Englewood Cliffs, N.J.: Prentice-Hall, 1976.

Billings, J. (Henry W. Shaw). *The complete works of Josh Billings.* Chicago: Donahue, 1919.

Binet, A. *Les idées modernes sur les enfants.* Paris: Flamarion, 1913.

Birch, H. G., and Rabinowitz, H. S. The negative effect of previous experience on productive thinking. *Journal of experimental psychology*, 1951, *41*, 121–125.

Birren, J. E. A summary: Prospects and problems in research on the longitudinal development of man's intellectual capacities throughout life. In L. F. Jarvik, C. Eisdorfer. and J. E. Blum (Eds.), *Intellectual functioning in adults.* New York: Springer, 1973.

Bloodstein, O. Stuttering and normal nonfluency: A continuity hypothesis. *British journal of disorders of communication,* 1970, 5, 30–39.

Blum, J. M. *Pseudoscience and mental ability.* New York: Monthly Review Press, 1978.

Blumberg, M. L. Psychopathology of the abusing parent. *American journal of psychotherapy,* 1974, 28, 21–29.

Bosanquet, C. Getting in touch. *Journal of analytical psychology,* 1970, 15, 42–58.

Bourne, J. E., Ekstrand, B. R., and Dominowski, R. L. *The psychology of thinking.* Englewood Cliffs, N.J.: Prentice-Hall, 1971.

Bowers, F. The deep structure of abstract nouns. *Foundation of language,* 1969, 5, 520–523.

Bowes, W. A., Jr., Brackbill, Y., Conway, E., and Steinschneider, A. The effects of obstetrical medication on fetus and infant. *Monographs of the Society for Research in Child Development,* 1970, 35(4, Serial No. 137).

Brace, C. L. Introduction to Jensenism. In C. L. Brace, G. R. Gamble, and J. R. Bond (Eds.), *Race and intelligence. Anthropological studies (No. 8).* Washington, D.C.: American Anthropological Association, 1971.

Brace, C. L., Gamble, G. R., and Bond, J. R. (Eds.). *Race and intelligence. Anthropological studies (No. 8).* Washington, D.C.: American Anthropological Association, 1971.

Brace, C. L., and Livingstone, F. B. On creeping Jensenism. In C. L. Brace, G. R. Gamble, and J. R. Bond (Eds.), *Race and intelligence. Anthropological studies (No. 8).* Washington, D.C.: American Anthropological Association, 1971.

Bressler, B., Cohen, S. J., and Magnussen, F. The problem of phantom breast and phantom pain. *Journal of nervous and mental disease,* 1956, 123, 181–187.

Briggs, J. L. *Never in anger.* Cambridge, Mass.: Harvard University Press, 1970.

Brill, A. A. *Lectures on psychoanalytic psychiatry.* New York: Vintage Books, 1959. (Originally published 1946.)

Brook, D. *Masters of the keyboard.* London: King and Jarrett, 1947.

Brophy, B. *Mozart the dramatist.* New York: Harcourt Brace Jovanovich, 1964.

Brunswick, E. Scope and aspects of the cognitive problem. In H. Gruber, R. Jessor, and K. Hammond (Eds.), *Cognition: The Colorado symposium.* Cambridge, Mass.: Harvard University Press, 1957.

Buck, R. *Human motivation and emotion.* New York: Wiley, 1976.

Bugliosi, V., and Gentry, C. *Helter-skelter.* New York: Norton, 1974.

Burns, R. *The merry muses of Caledonia.* (G. Legman, Ed.). New Hyde Park, N.Y.: University Books, 1965. (Originally published circa 1800.)

Burt, C. The evidence for the concept of intelligence. *British journal of educational psychology,* 1955, 25, 167–168.

Cameron, N. *The psychology of behavior disorders.* Boston: Houghton Mifflin, 1947.

Campbell, G. I was born twice. *This Week,* 1941, 11, 6, 10.

Cannon, W. B. "Voodoo" death. *American anthropologist,* 1942, 44, 169–181.

Carmichael, L., Hogan, H. P., and Walter, A. A. An experimental study of the effect of language on the reproduction of visually perceived form. *Journal of experimental psychology,* 1932, 15, 73–86.

Carr, J. E., and Tan, E. K. In search of the true amok: Amok as viewed within the Malay culture. *American journal of psychiatry,* 1976, 133(11), 1295–1299.

Carroll, L. *Alice's adventures in wonderland & Through the looking glass.* New

York: Macmillan, 1963. (Originally published 1872.)

Carter, J. W., Jr. A case of reactional dissociation (hysterical paralysis). *American journal of orthopsychiatry*, 1937, *7*, 219–224.

Cattell, P. *The measurement of intelligence of infants and young children.* New York: Psychological Corporation, 1947.

Charles, D. C., and James, S. T. Stability of average intelligence. *Journal of genetic psychology*, 1964, *105*, 105–111.

Cherry L. On the real benefits of eustress. *Psychology today*, 1978, *11*, 60–63.

Chomsky, N. *Language and mind.* New York: Harcourt, Brace and World, 1968.

Chomsky, N. *Chomsky: Selected readings.* J. P. B. Allen and P. Van Buren (Eds.). New York: Oxford University Press, 1971.

Clarke, A. M., and Clarke, A. D. B. (Eds.). *Early experience: Myth and evidence.* New York: Free Press, 1976.

Cleaver, E. *Soul on ice.* New York: Dell, 1968.

Cleaver says he's full of good will. *Wichita Eagle*, August 30, 1976, p. 1b, col. 2.

Cleaver, E. *Soul on fire.* Waco, Texas: World Books, 1978.

Collier, B. 'Tis a hundred years. *Saturday review of the sciences*, 1973, *1*, 7; 12–13.

Colson, C. W. *Born again.* Old Tappan, N.J.: Chosen Books, 1976.

Cook, C. A. *Suzuki education in action.* New York: Exposition Press, 1970.

Cooper, L. A., and Shepard, R. N. Transformations on representations of objects in space. In C. E. Carterette and N. M. Freedman (Eds.), *Handbook of perception.* Vol. 8: *Space and object perception.* New York: Academic Press, 1978.

Corliss, R. The scarlet letters. *Bookletter*, 1976, *3*(3), 1–2.

Cowle, L. *Teaching your tot to swim.* New York: Vantage Press, 1970.

Craik, K. H. Environmental psychology. *Annual review of psychology*, 1973, *24*, 403–422.

Curtiss, S. *Genie: A modern-day "wild child."* New York: Academic Press, 1977.

Cushing, H. *The medical career and other papers.* Boston: Little, Brown, 1940.

Daly, D. D., and Barry, M. J., Jr. Musicogenic epilepsy. *Psychosomatic medicine*, 1957, *19*, 399–408.

Daube, J. R. Sensory precipitated seizures: A review. *Journal of nervous and mental disease*, 1966, *141*, 524–539.

Davis, K. Extreme social isolation of a child. *American journal of sociology*, 1940, *45*, 554–565.

Day, W. F. *Reconciliation of behaviorism and phenomenology.* In M. H. Marx, and F. E. Goodson, *Theories in contemporary psychology.* New York: Macmillan, 1976.

De Forest, I. The significance of countertransference in psychoanalytic therapy. *Psychoanalytic review*, 1951, *38*, 158–171.

Dement, W. C. *Some must watch while some must sleep.* San Francisco: Freeman, 1974.

Dement, W. C. Personal communication, 1978.

Dement, W. C. Report IV(B): Comments to Report IV. In G. C. Lairy, and P. Salzarulo (Eds.), *The experimental study of human sleep: Methodological problems.* New York: Elsevier Scientific Publishing Co., 1975, pp. 287–307.

Dement, W., and Kleitman, N. The relation of eye movements during sleep to dream activity: An objective method for the study of dreaming. *Journal of experimental psychology*, 1957, *53*, 339–346.

Dement, W., and Kleitman, N. The relation of eye movements during sleep to dream activity: An objective method for the study of dreaming. *Journal of psychology,* 1957, *53,* 339–346.

Dewey, J. *The quest for certainty.* New York: Minton, Batch & Co., 1929.

Dewey, J., and Bentley, A. F. *Knowing and the known.* Boston: Beacon Press, 1949.

Dodd, B. J. Effects of social and vocal stimulation on infant babbling. *Developmental psychology,* 1972, *7,* 80–83.

Donat, A. The hunters become the hunted. *Saturday review,* 1967, *50,* 32–33.

Dostoyevsky, F. *The idiot.* New York: Random House, 1925. (Originally published, 1868.)

Dunbar, E. Seven Dobbs against the odds. *Look,* 1969, *33*(24), 27–33.

Duncker, K. On problem solving. (Trans. L. S. Lees.) *Psychological monographs,* 1945, *58* (Whole No. 270), 1–113.

Ebbinghaus, H. *Memory: A contribution to experimental psychology.* (H. A. Ruger and C. E. Bussening, trans.). New York: Dover, 1964.

Ehrlich, V. *Russian formalism* (2nd ed.). New York: Humanities Press, 1965.

Einstein, A. *Essays in science.* New York: Philosophical Library, 1934.

Einstein, A. *Ideas and opinions.* New York: Bonanza Books, 1954.

Emperor pressured to wear kimono. *Wichita Eagle,* February 7, 1978, p. 8a, col. 1.

Emerson, R. W. *Essays* (2nd series). Columbus, Ohio: 1969. (Originally published 1841.)

English, H. B., and English, A. C. *A comprehensive dictionary of psychological and psychoanalytical terms.* New York: Longmans, Green, 1958.

Epstein, A. W. The typical dream: Case studies. *Journal of nervous and mental disease,* 1973, *156,* 47–56.

Erikson, E. H. *Young man Luther.* New York: Norton, 1958.

Estes, W. K. The information-processing approach to cognition: A confluence of metaphors and methods. In W.K. Estes (Ed.), *Handbook of learning and cognitive processes. Vol. 5: Human information processing.* Hillsdale, N.J.: Lawrence Erlbaum Associates, 1978.

Evans, P. The Burt affair . . . Sleuthing in science. *APA monitor,* 1976, *7,* 1, 4.

Ewert, P. H. A study of the effect of inverted retinal stimulation upon spatially coordinated behavior. *Genetic psychology monographs,* 1930, *7,* 177–363.

Farb, P. *Word play: What happens when people talk.* New York: Knopf, 1974.

Faulkner, W. *Requiem for a nun.* New York: Random House, 1950.

Fisher, C., Kahn, E., Edwards, A., and Davis, D. M. A psychophysiological study of nightmares and night terrors. I. Physiological aspects of the stage of night terror. *Journal of nervous and mental disease,* 1973, *157,* 75–98.

Fisher, G. H. "Mother, father, and daughter": A three-aspect ambiguous figure. *American journal of psychology,* 1968, *81,* 274–277.

Flamm, L. E., and Bergum, B. O. Reversible perspective figures and eye movements. *Perceptual and motor skills,* 1977, *44,* 1015–1019.

Flanagan, B., Goldiamond, I., and Azrin, N. H. Operant stuttering: The control of stuttering behavior through response-contingent consequences. *Journal of the experimental analysis of behavior,* 1958, *1,* 173–178.

Fouts, R. The use of guidance in teaching sign language to a chimpanzee. *Journal of comparative and physiological psychology,* 1972, *80,* 515–522.

Fouts, R. Talking with chimpanzees. In *Annual editions,* 1977–78. Guilford, Conn.: 1977.

Fouts, R. S., and Rigby, R. L. Man–chimpanzee communication. In T. E. Sebeok (Ed.),

How animals communicate. Bloomington: Indiana University Press, 1977.

Frederiksen, N. Toward a taxonomy of situations. *American Psychologist*, 1972, *27*, 114–123.

Freud, S. *Basic writings of Sigmund Freud* (A. A. Brill, Ed. and trans.). New York: Modern Library, 1938. (Originally published 1905.)

Freud, S. *New introductory lectures on psychoanalysis.* (W. J. H. Spratt, trans.). New York: Norton, 1933.

Freud, S. *The interpretation of dreams.* New York: Modern Library, 1938. (Originally published 1900.)

Freud, S. The standard edition of the complete psychological works of Sigmund Freud (J. Strachey, Ed. and trans.). Vol. 21: *The future of an illusion, civilization and its discontents, and other works.* London: Hogarth Press, 1961.

Friedlander, S., and Shaw, E. Psychogenic factors in sudden infant death: Some dynamic speculations. *Clinical social work journal*, 1975, *3*, 237–278.

Fromm-Reichmann, F. Loneliness. *Psychiatry*, 1959, *22*, 1–15.

Galdston, R. Violence begins at home. *Journal of the American Academy of Child Psychiatry*, 1971, *10*, 336–350.

Galton, F. *Hereditary genius: An inquiry into its laws and consequences.* London: Macmillan, 1869.

Gamalian, I. *Newsweek*, March 23, 1964, p. 64.

Garber, H. L. Intervention in infancy: A developmental approach. In M. Begab and S. Richardson (Eds.), *The mentally retarded and society.* Baltimore: University Park Press, 1975, 287–299.

Gardner, B. T. Personal communication, February 21, 1980,

Gardner, R. A., and Gardner, B. T. Teaching sign language to a chimpanzee. *Science*, 1971, *165*, 664–672.

Gardner, R. A., and Gardner, B. T. Comparative psychology and language acquisition. In K. Salzinger and F. Denmark (Eds.), *Psychology: The state of the art. Annals of the New York Academy of Sciences*, 1978, *309*, 33–76.

Gesell, A. *The embryology of behavior.* New York: Harper, 1945.

Gibson, J. J. *The senses considered as perceptual systems.* Boston: Houghton Mifflin, 1966.

Goddard, H. H. *Two souls in one body: A case of dual personality.* New York: Dodd, Mead, 1927.

Goleman, D. Who's mentally ill? *Psychology today*, 1978, *11*, 34–41.

Goodall, J. Tool-using and aimed throwing in a community of free-living chimpanzees. *Nature* (London), 1964, *201* (4926), 1264–1266.

Goode, D. M. Individuality and individualization. *Improving college and university teaching*, 1972, *20*, 3.

Gorer, G. *The American people: A study in national character.* New York: Norton, 1948.

Gottlieb, G. Conceptions of prenatal development: Behavioral embryology. *Psychological review*, 1976, *83*, 215–234.

Greene, G. *The lost childhood.* New York: Viking Press, 1952.

Greene, W. A., Goldstein, S., and Moss, A. J. Psychosocial aspects of sudden death: A preliminary report. *Archives of internal medicine*, 1972, *129*, 725–731.

Griffiths, B. The sacred cow. *Commonweal*, 1967, *85*, 483–484.

Groddeck, G. *The book of the it.* New York: Funk & Wagnalls, 1950.

Guthrie, G. M. Masangkay, Z., and Guthrie, H. A. Behavior, malnutrition, and mental development. *Journal of crosscultural psychology*, 1976, 7, 169–180.

Haber, W. B. Observations on phantom limb phenomena. *American Medical Association archives of neurology and psychiatry*, 1956, 75, 624–636.

Haire, D. *The cultural warping of childbirth*. Seattle: International Childbirth Education Association, 1972.

Hall, C. S. A cognitive theory of dream symbols. *Journal of general psychology*, 1953, 48, 169–186. (a)

Hall, C. S. *The meaning of dreams*. New York: Harper, 1953. (b)

Halverson, H. M. Genital and sphincter behavior of the male infant. *Journal of genetic psychology*, 1940, 56, 95–136.

Hansen, C., and Emery, R. D. *Behavior today*, 1978, 9, 6.

Hanson, N. R. *Patterns of discovery*. Cambridge, England: University Press, 1958.

Hardin, G. The threat of clarity. *American journal of psychiatry*, 1957, *114*, 392–396.

Harris, W. H., and Levey, J. S. (Eds.). *The new Columbia encyclopedia*. New York: Columbia University Press, 1975.

Harvey, W. P., and Levine, S. A. Paroxysmal ventricular tachycardia due to emotion. *JAMA*, 1952, *150*, 479–480.

Hauri, P. Categorization of sleep mental activity for psychophysiological studies. In G. C. Lairy and P. Salzarulo (Eds.), *The experimental study of human sleep: Methodological problems*. New York: Elsevier, 1975. (a)

Hauri, P. Discussion. In G. C. Lairy and P. Salzarulo (Eds.), *The experimental study of human sleep: Methodological problems*. New York: Elsevier, 1975. (b)

Healy, W., Bronner, A. F., and Bowers, A. M. *The structure and meaning of psychoanalysis*. New York: Knopf, 1930.

Hearnshaw, L. S. *Cyril Burt, psychologist*. Ithaca, N.Y.: Cornell University Press, 1979.

Heber, R. *Epidemiology of mental retardation*. Springfield, Ill.: Thomas, 1970.

Heber, F. R. Sociocultural mental retardation: A longitudinal study. Milwaukee: University of Wisconsin, 1976. (Mimeographed report.)

Heber, R., and Garber, H. An experiment in the prevention of cultural-familial mental retardation. Milwaukee: University of Wisconsin, 1970. (Mimeographed report.)

Heidegger, M. *Sein und zeit*. Halle: Neimeyer, 1935.

Henryk-Gutt, R., and Rees, W. L. Psychological aspects of migraine. *Journal of psychosomatic research*, 1973, *17*, 141–153.

Herman, D. T. *An harmonic analysis study of hoarse and non-hoarse voice quality*. Bloomington: Indiana University, 1940.

Herman, D. T., and Kenyon, G. Y. A contribution toward interbehavioral analysis: I. Some general concepts. *Psychological record*, 1956, 6, 33–38.

Herman, D. T., Lawless, R. H., and Marshall, R. W. Variables in the effect of language on the reproduction of visually perceived forms. *Perceptual and motor skills*, 1957, 7, 171–186.

Heron, W., Bexton, W. H., and Hebb, D. O. Cognitive effects of a decreased variation in the sensory environment. *American psychologist*, 1953, 8, 366.

Herrnstein, R. J. *I.Q. in the meritocracy*. Boston: Atlantic Monthly Press, 1973.

Hess, E. H. Attitude and pupil size. *Scientific American*, 1965, *212*, 46–54.

Hewes, G. W. World distribution of certain postural habits. *American anthropologist*, 1955, *57*(2), 231–244.

Hite, S. *The Hite report: A nationwide study on female sexuality.* New York: Macmillan, 1976.

Hoch, A. *Benign stupors.* New York: Macmillan, 1921.

Hollender, M. H. The need or wish to be held. *Archives of general psychiatry*, 1970, *22*, 445–453.

Hollender, M. H., and Mercer, A. J. Wish to be held and wish to hold in men and women. *Archives of general psychiatry*, 1976, *33*, 49–51.

Hollender, M. H., Soults, F. B., and Ringold, A. L. Emotional antecedents of bleeding from peptic ulcer. *Psychiatry in medicine*, 1971, *2*, 199–204.

Hollingsworth, B. Personal communication, no date.

Holmes, L. D. *Anthropology: An introduction* (2nd Ed.). New York: Ronald Press, 1971.

Honzik, M. P., and Macfarlane, J. W. Personality development and intellectual functioning from 21 months to 40 years. In L. F. Jarvik, C. Eisdorfer, and J. E. Blum (Eds.), *Intellectual functioning in adults.* New York: Springer, 1973.

Horn, J. L. Organization of data on life-span development of human abilities. In L. R. Goulet and P. B. Baltes (Eds.), *Life-span developmental psychology: Research and theory.* New York: Academic Press, 1970.

Horn, J. L., and Donaldson, G. On the myth of intellectual decline in adulthood. *American psychologist*, 1976, *10*, 701–719.

Hudson, L. Intelligence. *The Listener*, March 18, 1971. (Mimeographed.)

Hudson, L. *Human beings: The psychology of human experience.* New York: Doubleday, 1975.

Hunt, J. McV. *Intelligence and experience.* New York: Ronald Press, 1961.

Hunt, J. McV. The psychological basis for using pre-school enrichment as an antidote for cultural deprivation. *Merrill-Palmer quarterly of behavior and development*, 1964, *10*, 209.

Hunt, J. McV. Has compensatory education failed? Has it been attempted? In *Environment, heredity, and intelligence.* Harvard educational review reprint series, 1969, Vol. 39 (No. 2), 130–152.

Hunt, N. *The world of Nigel Hunt.* New York: Garrett, 1967.

Hurley, R. L. *Poverty and mental retardation: A causal relationship.* New York: Random House, 1969.

Isen, A. M., and Levin, P. F. Effect of feeling good on helping: Cookies and kindness. *Journal of personality and social psychology*, 1972, *21*(3), 384–388.

Izard, C. E. *Human emotions.* New York: Plenum Press, 1977.

Jackson, I. D. Personal communication, September 8, 1978.

James, W. *The principles of psychology* (Vol. 1). New York: Holt, 1918.

Janisse, M. P. Pupil size and affect: A critical review of the literature since 1960. *Canadian psychologist*, 1973, *14*, 311–329.

Jarvik, L. F. Discussion: Patterns of intellectual functioning in the later years. In L. F. Jarvik, C. Eisdorfer, and J. E. Blum (Eds.), *Intellectual functioning in adults.* New York: Springer, 1973.

Jarvis, J. H. Post-mastectomy breast phantoms. *Journal of nervous and mental disease*, 1967, *144*. 266–272.

Jason, L. A. Self-monitoring in the treatment of nose squeezing and daydreaming. *Psychological reports*, 1976, *38*, 235–238.

Jelliffe, D. B., and Jelliffe, E. F. P. Human milk, nutrition, and the world resource crisis. *Science*, 1975, *188*, 557–561.

Jensen, A. R. How much can we boost IQ and scholastic achievement? *Harvard educational review*, 1969, *39*, 1–123.

Jensen, A. R. Can we and should we study race differences? In C. L. Brace, G. R. Gamble, and J. R. Bond (Eds.), *Race and intelligence.* Anthropological studies (No. 8). Washington, D.C.: American Anthropological Association, 1971.

Jones, E. How to tell your friends from geniuses. *The Saturday review*, 1957, *40*, 9–11; 39–40.

Jones, K. L., Smith. D.W., Ulleland, C. N., and Streissguth, A. P. Pattern of malformation in offspring of chronic alcoholic mothers. *Lancet*, 1973, *1*(814), 1267–1271.

Jourard, S. [M.] An exploratory study of body-accessibility. *British journal of social and clinical psychology*, 1966, *5*, 221–231.

Joyce, J. *Ulysses.* New York: Random House, 1934.

Kagan, J. S. Inadequate evidence and illogical conclusions. In *Environment, heredity and intelligence.* Harvard educational review reprint series, Vol. 39, (No. 2), 1969.

Kamin, L. J. *The science and politics of I.Q.* New York: Wiley, 1974.

Kamiya, J. Conscious control of brain waves. *Psychology today*, 1968, *1*, 58–60.

Kangas, J., and Bradway, K. Intelligence at middle age: A thirty-eight year follow-up. *Developmental psychology*, 1971, *5*, 333–337.

Kantor, J. R. *Principles of psychology.* Vol. 1. New York: Knopf. 1924.

Kantor, J. R. *Principles of psychology.* Vol. 2, New York: Knopf, 1926.

Kantor, J. R. *A survey of the science of psychology.* Chicago: Principia Press, 1933.

Kantor, J. R. *An objective psychology of grammar.* Science Series (No. 1). Bloomington: Indiana University Publications, 1936.

Kantor, J. R. Toward a scientific analysis of motivation. *Psychological record*, 1942, *5*, 225–275.

Kantor, J. R. *Problems of physiological psychology.* Chicago: Principia Press, 1947.

Kantor, J. R. *The logic of modern science.* Chicago: Principia Press, 1953.

Kantor, J. R. *The scientific evolution of psychology.* Vol. 1. Chicago: Principia Press, 1963.

Kantor, J. R. *The scientific evolution of psychology.* Vol 2. Chicago: Principia Press, 1969.

Kantor, J. R. *The aim and progress of psychology and other sciences.* Chicago: Principia Press, 1971.

Kantor, J. R. *Psychological linguistics.* Chicago: Principia Press, 1977.

Kantor, J. R., and Smith, N. W. *The science of psychology: An interbehavioral survey.* Chicago: Principia Press, 1975.

Karacan, I. The effect of exciting presleep events on dream reporting and penile tumescence during sleep. Unpublished doctoral dissertation, Downstate Medical Center, Department of Psychiatry, State University of New York (New York).

Karacan, I., Williams, R. L., Thornby, J. I., and Salis, P. J. Sleep-related penile tumescence as a function of age. *American journal of psychiatry*, 1975, *132*, 932–937.

Karelitz, W., Karelitz. R. F., and Rosenfeld, L. S. Infants' vocalizations and their significance. *Mental retardation*, 1965, *3*, 439–446.

Karen, R. L. *An introduction to behavior theory and its applications.* New York: Harper & Row, 1974.

Kaufman, B. N. *Son-rise,* New York: Harper & Row, 1976.

Kaufman, B. N. *To love is to be happy with.* New York: Coward, McCann, and Geoghegan, 1977. (a)

Kaufman, B. [N.] Personal communication, November 13, 1977. (b)

Keller, F. S. *Learning: Reinforcement theory.* New York: Doubleday, 1954.

Kellogg, W. N., and Kellogg, L. A. *The ape and the child.* New York: McGraw-Hill, 1933.

Kemph, J. P., Zegans, L. S., Kooi, K. A., and Waggoner, R. W. The emotionally disturbed child with a convulsive disorder. *Psychosomatic medicine*, 1963, *25*(5), 441–449.

Kennedy, W. A. *Child psychology* (2nd. ed.). Englewood Cliffs, N.J.: Prentice-Hall, 1975.

Kety, S. New perspectives in psychopharmacology. In A. Koestler and J. R. Smythies (Eds.), *Beyond reductionism.* London: Hutchinson, 1969.

Kierkegaard, S. *The journals* (A. Dnu, Ed. and trans.). New York: Oxford University Press, 1938.

Kiki, A. M. *Kiki: Ten thousand years in a lifetime.* New York: Praeger, 1968.

Kilbride, R. L., and Leibowitz, H. W. The Ponzo illusion among the Baganda of Uganda. *Annals of the New York Academy of Sciences*, 1977, *285*, 408–417.

Kimble, G. A. Basic tenets of behaviorism. In G. A. Kimble (Ed.), *Foundations of conditioning and learning.* New York: Appleton-Century-Crofts, 1967.

Klaus M. H., and Kennell, J. H. *Maternal–infant bonding.* St. Louis: Mosby, 1976.

Kline, N. S., and Gerard, D. L. Taxonomy of mental disease. *Journal of general psychology*, 1953, *49*, 201–207.

Kluckhohn, C. *Mirror for man.* New York: Fawcett, 1960.

Kohler, W. *The mentality of apes,* New York: Harcourt Brace, 1927.

Kolb, L. C. *The painful phantom.* Springfield, Ill.: Thomas, 1954.

Kolb, L. C., Frank, L. M., and Watson, E. J. Treatment of the acute painful phantom limb. *Proceedings of the staff meetings of the Mayo Clinic*, 1952, *27*, 110–118.

Korn, J. H., and Moyer, K. E. Habituation of the startle response and of heart rate in the rat. *Canadian journal of psychology*, 1966, *20*, 183–190.

Kozar, A. J. Anticipatory heart rate in rope climbing. *Ergonomics*, 1964, *7*, 311–315.

Kroeber, T. *Ishi in two worlds:* A biography of the last wild Indian in North America. Berkeley: University of California Press, 1961.

Krout, M. H. *Introduction to social psychology.* New York: Harper, 1942.

Kuo, Z. Y. *The dynamics of behavior development.* New York: Random House, 1967.

Laing, R. D. and Esterson, A. *Sanity, madness and the family.* New York: Basic Books, 1971.

Lairy, G. C., and Salzarulo, P. (Eds.). *The experimental study of human sleep: Methodological problems.* New York: Elsevier, 1975.

Landis, D., and Hunt, W. A. *The startle pattern.* New York: Farrar and Rinehart, 1939.

Langman, J. *Medical embryology* (3rd ed.). Baltimore: Williams and Wilkins, 1975.

La Piere, R. *The Freudian ethic.* New York: Duell, Sloan and Pearce, 1959.

Lay, C. H., and Paivio, A. The effects of task difficulty and anxiety on hesitation in speech. *Canadian journal of behavioral science,* 1969, *1,* 25–37.

Leboyer, F. *Birth without violence.* New York: Knopf, 1975.

Leboyer, F. *Loving hands.* New York: Knopf, 1976.

Leibowitz, H. W., and Pick, H. Cross-cultural and educational aspects of the Ponzo illusion. *Perception and psychophysics,* 1972, *12,* 403–432.

Lenneberg, E. H. Language in the light of evolution. In T. A. Sebeok (Ed.), *Animal communication: Techniques of study and results of research.* Bloomington: Indiana University Press, 1968.

Leonard, W. E. *The locomotive god.* New York: Century, 1927.

Levinson, E. J. The modification of intelligence by training in the verbalization of word definitions and simple concepts. *Child development,* 1971, *42,* 1361–1380.

Lewin, K. Environmental forces in child behavior and development. In C. Murchison (Ed.), *A handbook of child psychology.* Worcester, Mass.: Clark University Press, 1931.

Lewis, M. M. *Language, thought, and personality in infancy and childhood.* New York: Basic Books, 1963.

Lieberman, O. H., Klatt, D. H., and Wilson, W. H. Vocal tract limitations on the vowel repertoires of rhesus monkey and other nonhuman primates. *Science,* 1969, *164,* 1185–1187.

Liebert, R. M., Neale, J. M., and Davidson, E. S. *The early window: Effects of television on children and youth.* New York: Pergamon Press, 1973.

Liebert, R. M., and Poulos, R. W. Television and personality development: The socializing effects of an entertainment medium. In A. Davids (Ed.), *Child personality and psychopathology.* New York: Wiley, 1975.

Lief, A. *The commonsense psychiatry of Dr. Adolf Meyer.* New York: McGraw-Hill, 1948.

Liley, A. W. The foetus as a personality. *Australian and New Zealand journal of psychiatry,* 1972, *6,* 99–105.

Limber, J. Language in child and chimp? *American psychologist,* 1977, *32,* 280–295.

Lindsley, O. R. Direct measurement and prosthesis of retarded behavior. *Journal of education,* 1964, *141,* 62–81.

Lipsitt, L. P., and Kaye, H. Conditioned sucking in the human newborn. *Psychonomic science,* 1964, *1,* 29–30.

Livingston, S. Etiologic factors in adult convulsions. *New England journal of medicine,* 1956, *254,* 1211.

Lombroso, C. T., and Pinchas, L. Breatholding spells (cyanotic and pallid infantile syncope). *Pediatrics,* 1967, *39*(4), 563–581.

Lown, B. Verbal conditioning of angina pectoris during exercise testing. *American journal of cardiology,* 1977, *40,* 630–634.

Lown, B., and Verrier, R. L. Neural activity and ventricular fibrillation. *New England journal of medicine,* 1976, *294,* 1165–1170.

Lown, B., Verrier, R. L., and Rabinowitz, S. H. Neural and psychologic mechanisms and the problem of sudden cardiac death. *American journal of cardiology,* 1977, *39,* 890–902.

Lynch, J., and Paskewitz, D. On the mechanisms of the feedback control of human brain wave activity. *Journal of nervous and mental disease*, 1971, *153*, 205–217.

Lynch, J. J., Paskewitz, D. A., Gimbel, K. S., and Thomas, S. A. Psychological aspects of cardiac arrhythmia. *American heart journal*, 1977, *93*, 645–657.

McCall, R. B., Applebaum, M. I., and Hogarty, P. S. Developmental changes in mental performance. *Monographs of the Society for Research in Child Development*, 1973, *38*, 1–84.

MacCorquodale, K. On Chomsky's review of Skinner's *Verbal behavior. Journal of the experimental analysis of behavior*, 1970, *13*, 83–99.

McCurdy, H. G. The childhood pattern of genius. *Journal of the Elisha Mitchell Scientific Society*, 1957, *73*, 448–462.

McGaugh, J. L., and Herz, M. J. (Eds.). *Memory consolidation*. San Francisco: Albion, 1976.

McKearney, J. W. Maintenance of responding under a fixed-interval schedule of electric shock-presentation. *Science*, 1968, *160*, 1249–1251.

McKearney, J. W. Fixed-interval schedules of electric shock presentation: Extinction and recovery of performance under different shock intensities and fixed-interval durations. *Journal of the experimental analysis of behavior*, 1969, *12*, 301–313.

McKearney, J. W. Responding under fixed-ratio and multiple fixed-interval fixed-ratio schedules of electric shock presentation. *Journal of the experimental analysis of behavior*, 1970, *14*, 1–6.

McKearney, J. W. Maintenance and suppression of responding under schedules of electric shock presentation. *Journal of the experimental analysis of behavior*, 1972, *17*, 425–432.

McKearney, J. W. Methamphetamine effects on responding under a multiple schedule of shock presentation. *Pharmacology, biochemistry, and behavior*, 1973, *1*, 547–550.

McKearney, J. W. Book review: *Behavioral pharmacology*, [S. D. Glick and J. Goldfarb (Eds.), St. Louis: Mosby, 1976]. *Brain research bulletin*, 1976, *1*, 609–611. (a)

McKearney, J. W. Punishment of responding under schedules of stimulus–shock termination: Effects of d-amphetamine and pentobarbital. *Journal of the experimental analysis of behavior*, 1976, *26*, 281–287. (b)

McKearney, J. W. Asking questions about behavior. *Perspectives in biology and medicine*, 1977, *21*, 109–119.

McKearney, J. W. Interrelations among prior experience and current conditions in the determination of behavior and the effects of drugs. In T. Thompson and P. B. Dews (Eds.), *Advances in behavioral pharmacology*. Vol. 2. New York: Academic Press, 1978.

McKearney, J. W., and Barrett, J. E. Punished behavior: Increases in responding after d-amphetamine. *Psychopharmacologia* (Berlin), 1975, *41*, 23–26.

MacLean, P. The triune brain, emotion, and scientific bias. In F. O. Schmitt (Ed.), *The neurosciences: Second study program*. New York: Rockefeller University Press, 1970.

McNeil, E. B. *The concept of human development*. Belmont, Calif.: Wadsworth, 1966.

Mahan, H. C. *The interactional psychology of J. R. Kantor: An introduction*. San Marcos, Calif.: Project Socrates Press, 1968.

Mahoney, M. J. The sensitive scientist in empirical humanism. *American psychologist,* 1975, *30,* 864–867.

Maier, N. R. F. Reasoning and learning. *Psychological review,* 1931, *38,* 332–346.

Mairet, P. (Ed.). *Alfred Adler: Problems of neurosis.* London: Kegan Paul, Trench, Trubner, 1929.

Marek, G. R. *Beethoven: Biography of a genius.* New York: Funk and Wagnalls, 1969.

Marks, I., and Lader, M. Anxiety states (anxiety neurosis): A review. *Journal of nervous and mental disease,* 1973, *156,* 3–18.

Mathis, J. L. A sophisticated version of voodoo death: Report of a case. *Psychosomatic medicine,* 1964, *26,* 104–107.

May, R. *Love and will.* New York: Norton, 1969.

Mead, M. Margaret Mead answers. *Redbook,* 1966, *126,* p. 32.

Medawar, P. B., and Medawar, J. B. *The life science: Current ideas in biology.* New York: Harper & Row, 1977.

Mencken, H. L. *The American language: An inquiry into the development of English in the United States.* New York: Knopf, 1937.

Mendelson, J., Solomon, P., and Lindemann, E. Hallucinations of poliomyelitis patients during treatment in a respirator. *Journal of nervous and mental disease,* 1958, *126,* 421–428.

Menninger, K. A. Totemic aspects of contemporary attitudes toward animals. In G. B. Wilbur and W. Muensterberger (Eds.), *Psychoanalysis and cultures: Essays in honor of Geza Roheim.* New York: International Universities Press, 1951.

Menninger, K. Psychiatrists use dangerous words. *Saturday evening post,* April 15, 1964, 12–14.

Mercer, J. R. The lethal label. *Psychology today,* 1972, *7,* 44–47; 95–97.

Mercer, J. R. *Labeling the mentally retarded.* Berkeley: University of California Press, 1973.

Mercer, J. R., and Brown, W. C. Racial differences in I.Q.: Fact or artifact. In C. Senna (Ed.), *The fallacy of I.Q.* New York: Third Press, 1973.

Meyer, A. *Psychobiology: A science of man.* Springfield, Ill.: Thomas, 1957.

Milkovich, L., and Van den Berg, B. J. Effects of prenatal meprobamate and chlordizaepoxide hydrochloride on human embryonic and fetal development. *New England journal of medicine,* 1974, *291,* 1268–1271.

Miller, D. B. Dog control. *Science,* 1974, *86,* 394.

Mills, J. *Experimental social psychology.* New York: Macmillan, 1969.

Montagu, A. *The direction of human development.* New York: Harper, 1955.

Montagu, A. *The biosocial nature of man.* New York: Grove Press, 1956.

Montagu, A. *Touching: The human significance of the skin.* New York: Columbia University Press, 1971.

Montagu, J. D., and Coles, E. M. Mechanism and measurement of the galvanic skin response. *Psychological bulletin,* 1966, *65,* 261–279.

Moore, O. K. *Black excellence.* Pittsburgh: The Responsive Environments Foundation, 1974.

Moore, O. K. *Discontinuity and deontics.* Pittsburgh: The Responsive Environments Foundation, 1977.

Moore, O. K. *Black excellence.* Film available from International Communications,

244 Thorn St., Sewickley, PA 15143.

Moore, O. K. *Reaction to black excellence.* Film available from International Communications, 244 Thorn St., Sewickley, PA 15143

Moore, O. K., and Anderson, A. R. *Early reading and writing.* I: Skills. Pt. 2: Teaching methods. Pt. 3: Development. Pittsburgh: The Responsive Environments Foundation, 1960.

Moore, O. K., and Anderson, A. R. Some principles for the design of clarifying educational environments. In D. A. Goslin (Ed.), *Handbook of socialization theory and research.* Chicago: Rand McNally, 1969.

Moos, R. H. Conceptualizations of human environments. *American psychologist,* 1973, *28,* 652–665.

Morgan, J. J. B. The overcoming of distraction and other resistances. *Archives of psychology,* 1916, *5*(35), 1–84.

Morgan, M. J. *Molyneux's question: Vision, touch, and the philosophy of perception.* London: Cambridge University Press, 1977.

Morishima, A., and Brown, L. F. A case report on the artistic talent of an autistic idiot savant. *Mental retardation,* 1977, *15,* 33–36.

Morris, C. G. *Psychology: An introduction.* New York: Appleton-Century-Crofts, 1973.

Morris, J. *Conundrum.* New York: Harcourt Brace Jovanovich, 1974.

Morse, W. H., McKearney, J. W., and Kelleher, R. T. Control of behavior by noxious stimuli. In L. L. Iverson, S. D. Iverson, and S. H. Snyder (Eds.), *Handbook of psychopharmacology.* Vol. 7. New York: Plenum Press, 1977.

Mowrer, O. H. Speech development in the young child. I. The autism theory of speech development and some clinical applications. *Journal of speech and hearing disorders,* 1952, *17,* 263–268.

Moyer, K. E. Startle response: Habituation over trials and days, and sex and strain differences. *Journal of comparative and physiological psychology,* 1963, *56,* 863–865.

Muravchik, M. The child abusers: The story of one family. *Saturday review world,* 1972, *55,* 28–30.

Murooka, H. Lullaby from the womb. Capitol stereo cassette 4XT-11421.

Murphy. J. V., Miller, R. E., and Finocchio, D. V. Spontaneous recovery of an avoidance response over an extended time interval in the monkey. *Journal of genetic psychology,* 1956, *89,* 119–125.

Mussen, P. H. *The psychological development of the child.* Englewood Cliffs, N.J.: Prentice-Hall, 1963.

Neary, J. A scientist's variations on a disturbing racial theme. *Life,* 1970, *68*(22), 58B–65.

Neumann, E., and Blanton, R. The early history of electrodermal research. *Psychophysiology,* 1969, *6,* 453.

Nissen, H. W. The nature of drive as innate determinant of behavior organization. *Nebraska symposium on motivation,* 1953, *2,* 281–321.

Nock, A. J. "Thoughts on Utopia," *Atlantic Monthly,* 1935, *156,* 24.

Nowlin, J., Troyer, W. Jr., Collins, W., Silverman, G., Nichols, C., McIntosh, H., Estes, E., and Bogdonoff, M. The association of nocturnal angina pectoris with dreaming. *Annals of internal medicine,* 1965, *63,* 1040–1046.

O'Brien, J. Observer of the human comedy. *Saturday review,* 1966, *49,* 26–27.

Onions, C. T. (Ed.). *The Oxford dictionary of English Etymology.* New York: Oxford

University Press, 1966.

Patterson, F. Conversations with a gorilla. *National geographic,* 1978, *154,* 438–465. (a)

Patterson, F. G. The gestures of a gorilla: Language acquisition in another pongid. *Brain and language,* 1978, *5,* 72–97. (b)

Patterson, F. Intraspecific communications. *Gorilla,* 1978, *1*(2), 3. (c)

Paulson, M. J., and Blake, P. R. The physically abused child: A focus on prevention. *Child welfare,* 1969, *48,* 86–95.

Pavlov, I. P. *Conditioned reflexes: an investigation of the physiological activity of the cerebral cortex* (G. V. Anrep, trans. and Ed.). London: Oxford University Press, 1927.

Peters, R. S. *The concept of motivation.* London: Routledge and Kegan Paul, 1958.

Podgorny, P., and Shepard, R. N. Functional representations common to visual perception and imagination. *Journal of experimental psychology,* 1978, *4*(1), 21–35.

Poincaré, H. *The foundations of science.* Lancaster, Pa.: Science Press, 1946.

Potter, M. C. Meaning in visual search. *Science,* 1971, *187,* 965–966.

Premack, A. J. *Why chimps can read.* New York: Harper and Row, 1976.

Premack, D. Language in chimpanzee? *Science,* 1971, *172,* 808–822.

Premack, D. Teaching language to an ape. *Scientific American,* 1972, *227,* 92–99.

Price, D. B. Miraculous restoration of lost body parts: Relationship to the phantom limb phenomenon and to limb-burial superstitions and practices. In W. D. Hand (Ed.), *American folk medicine: A symposium.* Berkeley: University of California Press, 1976. (a)

Price, D. B. Phantom limb phenomenon in patients with leprosy. *Journal of nervous and mental disease,* 1976, *163,* 108–116. (b)

Pronko, N. H. An effective classroom demonstration of operant conditioning in the pigeon. *Psychological record,* 1960, *7,* 285–296.

Pronko, N. H. *Textbook of abnormal psychology.* Baltimore: Williams and Wilkins, 1963.

Pronko, N. H. *Panorama of psychology* (2nd. ed.). Monterey, Calif.: Brooks/Cole, 1973.

Rachlin, H. A review of M. J. Mahoney's *Cognition and behavior modification. Journal of applied behavior analysis,* 1977, *10,* 369–374.

Ratner, S., Altman, J., and Wheeler, J. E. (Eds.). *John Dewey and Arthur F. Bentley: A philosophical correspondence, 1932–1951.* New Brunswick, N.J.: Rutgers University Press, 1964.

Ray, R. D., Upson, J. D., and Henderson, B. J. A systems approach to behavior. III: Organismic pace and complexity in time–space fields. *Psychological record,* 1977, *27,* 649–682.

Reik, T. *Of love and lust.* New York: Farrar, Straus & Cudahy, 1949.

Reisner, R. *Graffiti: Selected scrawls from bathroom walls.* New York: Canyon Books, 1967.

Reisner, R. *Graffiti: Two thousand years of wall writing.* New York: Cowles, 1971.

Rheingold, H. L., Gewirtz, J. L., and Ross, H. W. Social conditioning of vocalizations in the infant. *Journal of comparative and physiological psychology,* 1959, *52,* 68–73.

Rice, R. D. Premature infants respond to sensory stimulation. *APA monitor,* 1975, *6,* 8–9.

Richards, M. P. M. (Ed.). *The integration of a child into a social world.* London:

Cambridge University Press, 1974.

Riegel, K. F. *Psychology of development and history.* New York: Plenum Press, 1976.

Riegel, K. F., and Meacham, J. A. *The developing individual in a changing world.* Vol. 1: *Historical and cultural issues;* Vol. 2: *Social and environmental issues.* Chicago: Aldine, 1976.

Riegel, K. F., and Rosenwald, G. C. (Eds.). *Structure and transformation: Developmental and historical aspects.* New York: Wiley, 1975.

Riesman, D., Glazer, N., and Denney, R. *The lonely crowd.* New York: Doubleday, 1953.

Riesman, D. Personal communication, February 28, 1978.

Rogers, C. R. Some new challenges. *American psychologist,* 1973, *28,* 379–387.

Rogers-Warren, A., and Warren, S. F. *Ecological perspectives in behavior analysis.* Baltimore: University Park Press, 1977.

Rosenblatt, G., Hartmann, E., and Zwilling, G. R. Cardiac irritability during sleep and dreaming. *Journal of psychosomatic research,* 1973, *17,* 129–134.

Rosenzweig, S. Babies are taught to cry: A hypothesis. *Mental hygiene,* 1954, *38*(1), 81–84.

Rumbaugh, D., Gill, T. V., and Von Glaserfeld, E. Reading and sentence completion by a chimpanzee (Pan). *Science, 182,* 731–733.

Russek, H. I. Emotional stress and coronary heart disease in American physicians. *American journal of medical science,* 1960, *240,* 711–720.

Sakabe, N., Arayama, T., and Suzuki, T. Human fetal evoked response to acoustic stimulation. *Acta oto-laryngologica, supplementum,* 1969, *252,* 29–36.

Salk, L. The effects of the normal heartbeat sound on the behavior of the new-born infant: Implications for mental health. *World mental health,* 1960, *12,* 1–8.

Salk, L. The importance of the heartbeat rhythm to human nature: Theoretical, clinical, and experimental observations. *Proceedings of the Third World Congress of Psychiatry.* Toronto: University of Toronto Press, 1961.

Salk, L. Mother's heartbeat as an imprinting stimulus. *Transactions of the New York Academy of Sciences,* 1962, Series 2, *24*(7), 753–763.

Sanford, R. N. The effects of abstinence from food upon imaginal processes: A preliminary experiment. *Journal of psychology,* 1936, *2,* 129–136.

Sanford, R. N. The effects of abstinence from food upon imaginal processes: A further experiment. *Journal of psychology,* 1937, *3,* 145–159.

Sapir, E. Speech as a personality trait. *American journal of sociology,* 1926–1927, *32,* 892–905.

Sartre, J. P. *L'etre et le néant* [Being and Nothingness]· Paris: Librarie Gallimard, 1948.

Schaie, K. W. Translations in gerontology—from lab to life: Intellectual functioning. *American psychologist,* 1974, *29,* 802–807.

Schaie, K. W., and Labouvie-Vief, G. Generational versus ontogenetic components of change in adult cognitive behavior: A fourteen-year cross-sequential study. *Developmental psychology,* 1974, *10,* 305–320.

Scheff, T. J. The role of the mentally ill and the dynamics of mental disorder: A research framework. In S. P. Spitzer and N. K. Denzin (Eds.), *The mental patient.* New York: McGraw-Hill, 1968.

Schiffer, I. *Charisma: A psychoanalytic look at mass society.* New York: Free Press, 1973.

Schuster, D. H., and Schuster, L. Study of stress and sex ratio in humans. *Proceedings of the seventy-seventh annual convention of the American Psychological Association*, 1969, 335–336. (a)

Schuster, D. H., and Schuster, L. Theory of stress and sex ratio. *Proceedings of the seventy-seventh annual convention of the American Psychological Association*, 1969, 223–224. (b)

Schuster, D. H., and Schuster, L. Speculative mechanisms affecting sex ratio. *Journal of Genetic Psychology*, 1972, *121*, 245–254.

Segal, E. M., and Lachman, R. Higher mental processes. In M. H. Marx, and F. E. Goodson (Eds.), *Theories in contemporary psychology* (2nd. ed.). New York: Macmillan, 1976.

Seitz, P. F. D. Psychocutaneous conditioning during the first two weeks of life. *Psychosomatic medicine*, 1950, *12*, 187–188.

Selye, H. *The stress of life.* New York: McGraw-Hill, 1956.

Selye, H. The evolution of the stress concept. *American scientist*, 1973, *61*, 692–699.

Senden, M. V. *Space and sight.* New York: Free Press, 1960.

Shapiro, D., Tursky, B., Gershon, E., and Stern, M. Effects of feedback and reinforcement on the control of human systolic blood pressure. *Science*, 1969, *163*, 588–589.

Shaw, G. B. The doctor's dilemma. In the *AYOT St. Lawrence edition of the collected works of G. B. Shaw.* New York: Wise, 1930. (Originally published 1906.)

Shepard, R. N. Externalization of mental images and the act of creation. In B. S. Randhawa and W. E. Coffman (Eds.), *Visual learning, thinking, and communication.* New York: Academic Press, 1978.

Shepard, R. N., and Podgorny, P. Cognitive processes that resemble perceptual processes. In W. K. Estes (Ed.). *Handbook of learning and cognitive processes.* Hillsdale, N.J.: Lawrence Erlbaum Associates, 1978.

Sherwood, S. Self-induced epilepsy (collected cases). *Archives of neurology*, 1962, *6*, 49.

Shields, J. *Monozygotic twins brought up apart and brought up together.* London: Oxford University Press, 1962.

Shoham, S. Psychopathy as social stigma. *Corrective psychiatry and journal of social therapy*, 1967, *13*, 21–41.

Shotter, J. The development of personal powers. In M. P. M. Richards (Ed.), *The integration of a child into a social world.* Cambridge, England: Cambridge University Press, 1974.

Sidman, M. *Tactics of experimental research.* New York: Basic Books, 1960.

Sievers, W. D. *Freud on Broadway.* New York: Hermitage House, 1955.

Singer, J. L., and McCraven, V. G. Some characteristics of adult daydreaming. *Journal of psychology*, 1961, *51*, 151–164.

Skeels, H. Early status of children with contrasting early life experiences. *Monographs of the Society for Research in Child Development*, 1966, *31* (Serial No. 3, 105).

Skinner, B. F. *The behavior of organisms.* New York: Appleton-Century, 1938.

Skinner, B. F. *Science and human behavior.* New York: Macmillan, 1953.

Skinner, B. F. *Verbal behavior.* New York: Appleton-Century-Crofts, 1957.

Skinner, B. F. *Cumulative record.* New York: Appleton-Century-Crofts, 1959.

Skinner, B. F. *Contingencies of reinforcement: A theoretical analysis.* New York:

Appleton-Century-Crofts, 1969.

Skinner, B. F. *Beyond freedom and dignity.* New York: Knopf, 1971.

Skinner, B. F. *About behaviorism.* New York: Knopf, 1974.

Skinner, B. F. A science of behavior. In M. H. Marx, and F. E. Goodson, *Theories in contemporary psychology* (2nd ed.). New York: Macmillan, 1976.

Skinner, B. F. *Reflections on behaviorism and society.* Englewood Cliffs, N.J.: Prentice-Hall, 1978.

Skorpen, E. The whole man. *Main currents in modern thought,* 1965, *22,* 10–16.

Slater, P. *The pursuit of loneliness.* Boston: Beacon Press, 1970.

Smith, N. W., and Shaw, N. E. An analysis of common-place behaviors: Volitional acts. *Psychological record,* 1979, *29,* 179–186.

Smoking and pregnancy. Reprinted from *The health consequences of smoking: A report of the surgeon-general.* Washington, D.C.: U. S. Department of Health, Education and Welfare, 1971.

Snyder, F. W., and Pronko, N. H. *Vision with spatial inversion.* Wichita, Kan.: University of Wichita Press, 1952.

Snyder, R. G. The sex ratio of offspring of pilots of high-performance military aircraft. *Human biology,* 1961, *33,* 1–10.

Sommer, R. Toward a psychology of natural behavior. *APA monitor,* January, 1977, 1, 7.

Sontag, L. W., Baker, C. T., and Nelson, V. L. Personality as a determinant of performance. *American Journal of orthopsychiatry,* 1955, *25,* 555–562.

Sontag, L. W., Baker, C. T., and Nelson, V. L. Mental growth and personality development: A longitudinal study. *Monographs of the Society for Research in Child Development,* 1958, *23*(68), 13–143.

Southard, E. E. *The open mind.* New York: Normandie House, 1938.

Spelt, D. K. The conditioning of the human fetus *in utero. Journal of experimental psychology,* 1948,, *38,* 338–346.

Spinetta, J. J., and Rigler, D. The child-abusing parent: A psychological review. *Psychological bulletin,* 1972, *77,* 296–304.

Standley, K., Soule, A. B., III, Copans, S. A., and Duchowny, M. S. Local-regional anesthesia during childbirth: Effect on newborn behaviors. *Science,* 1974, *186,* 634–635.

Stanley, J. C. Intellectual precocity. *Journal of special education,* 1975, *9,* 29–44.

Steele, B. F., and Pollock, C. B. A psychiatric study of parents who abuse infants and small children. In R. E. Helfer and C. H. Kempe (Eds.), *The battered child.* Chicago: University of Chicago Press, 1968.

Stone, M. Interview with Lili Kraus who studied with Kodaly and Bartok. *Clavier,* 1968, *7,* 22–23; 36.

Story, S. *Rodin.* New York: University Press, 1949.

Stratton, G. M. Some preliminary experiments in vision without inversion of the retinal image. *Psychological review,* 1896, *3,* 611–617.

Stratton, G. M. Vision without inversion of the retinal image. *Psychological review,* 1897, *4,* 341–360; 463–481.

Sullivan, H. S. The illusion of personal individuality. *Psychiatry: Journal for the study of interpersonal processes,* 1950, *13,* 317–332.

Sullivan, H. S. *Schizophrenia as a human process.* New York: Norton, 1962.

Suzuki, S. *Nurtured by love.* New York: Exposition press, 1969.

Suzuki, S. Any child can be tone deaf. Matsumoto, Japan: Talent Education Research Society, no date.

Szasz, T. [S.] The problem of psychiatric nosology. *American journal of psychiatry, 1957, 114,* 405–413.

Szasz, T. S. *The myth of mental illness.* New York: Hoeber-Harper, 1961.

Szasz, T. S. *Ideology and insanity.* New York: Doubleday, 1970.

Szasz, T. [S.] *Schizophrenia: The sacred symbol of psychiatry.* New York: Basic Books, 1976.

Szigeti, J. Personal communicaton, December 13, 1975.

Taylor, N. B., and Taylor, A. E. (Eds.). *Stedman's medical dictionary* (19th ed.). Baltimore: Williams and Wilkins, 1957.

Tedeschi, J. T. Prediction, control, and the multi-environment problem. *Psychological record, 1966, 16,* 409–418.

Terman, L. M. *The measurement of intelligence.* Cambridge, Mass.: Riverside Press, 1916.

Terman, L. M. *The intelligence of school children.* Boston: Houghton Mifflin, 1919. (a)

Terman, L. M. The vocabulary test as a measure of intelligence. *Journal of educational psychology, 1919, 9,* 452–466. (b)

Terman, L. M., and Merrill, M. A. *Measuring intelligence.* Boston: Houghton Mifflin, 1937.

Thackray, R. I., and Orne, M. T. A comparison of physiological indices in detection of deception. *Psychophysiology, 1968, 4,* 329–339.

Thigpen, C. H., and Cleckley, H. M. *The three faces of Eve.* New York: McGraw-Hill, 1957.

Thurman, S. K. Environmental maintenance of retarded behavior: A behavioral perspective. *Education, 1976, 97*(2), 121–125.

Time, "Pianist: View from the inside." October 14, 1966, p. 50.

Timmermans, C. *How to teach your baby to swim.* New York: Stein & Day, 1975.

Timmermans, C. Personal communication, October 17, 1976.

Toulmin, S. *Foresight and understanding.* New York: Harper & Row, 1961.

Tripp, C. A. *The homosexual matrix.* New York: McGraw-Hill, 1975.

Trotter, R. J. Leboyer's babies. *Science news, 1977, 111,* 59.

Ullman, A. D. The experimental production and analysis of a "compulsive eating symptom" in rats. *Journal of comparative and physiological psychology, 1951, 44,* 575–581.

Užgiris, I. C. Plasticity and structure. In I. C. Užgiris and F. Weizmann (Eds.). *The structuring of experience.* New York: Plenum Press, 1977.

Van Buren, A. Dear Abby. *Wichita eagle,* June 4, 1970, 6b.

Varon, E. J. The development of Alfred Binet's psychology. *Psychological monographs, 1936, 46*(3), 128.

Vaught, G. M., Simpson, W. E., and Ryder, R. *Perceptual and motor skills, 1968, 26,* 848.

Vinacke, W. E. *The psychology of thinking* (2nd ed.). New York: McGraw-Hill, 1974.

von Helmholtz, S. *Physiological optics* (Vol. 3). (J. P. S. Southall, Ed.). Optical Society of America, 1925. (Originally published, 1866.)

Wade, N. Bottle-feeding: Adverse effects of a Western technology. *Science, 1974, 184,* 45–48.

Wade, N. IQ and heredity: Suspicion of fraud beclouds classic experiment. *Science,* 1976, *194,* 916–919.

Wagman, M. Sex differences in types of daydreams. *Journal of personality and social psychology,* 1967, *7,* 329–332.

Walker, E. L. Personal communication, March 9, 1979.

Washburn, S. L. Human behavior and the behavior of other animals. *American psychologist,* 1978, *33,* 405–418.

Watson, D. O. *Talk with your hands.* Watson Publications, 1964.

Watson, J. B. *Behavior: An introduction to comparative psychology.* New York: Holt, 1914.

Weaver, P. D., and McPherson, M. W. Gains in children's vocabulary scores during the last three decades. *Psychological record,* 1976, *26,* 519–522.

Weigel, J. A. *B. F. Skinner.* Boston: Twayne, 1977.

Weigert, E. *The courage to love.* New Haven, Conn.: Yale University Press, 1970.

Weintraub, D. J., and Walker, E. L. *Perception.* Belmont, Calif.: Brooks/Cole, 1966.

Weisberg, P. Social and nonsocial conditioning of infant vocalizations. *Child development,* 1963, *34,* 377–388.

Weisman, A. D., and Hackett, T. P. Psychosis after eye surgery. *New England journal of medicine,* 1958, *258,* 1284–1289.

Wesman, A. G. Intelligent testing. *American psychologist,* 1968, 23, 267–274.

Wesman, A. G. *Selected writings of Alexander G. Wesman.* New York: Psychological Corporation, 1975.

Westermeyer, J. A comparison of amok and other homicide in Laos. *American journal of psychiatry,* 1972, *129*(6), 703–709.

Wheaton, J. L. Fact and fancy in sensory deprivation studies (Review 5–59), *Aeromedical reviews,* August 1959.

White, B. L., Kaban, B., Shapiro, B., and Attanucci, J. Competence and experience. In I. C. Užgiris and F. Weizmann (Eds.), *The structuring of experience.* New York: Plenum Press, 1977.

Whitehead, A. N. *The concept of nature.* Ann Arbor: University of Michigan Press, 1957.

Willems, E. P., and Raush, H. L. *Naturalistic viewpoints in psychological research.* New York: Holt, Rinehart and Winston, 1969.

Williams, D. I. Ethology and human behavior. *Bulletin of the British psychological society,* 1971, *24,* 17–22.

Williams, G. W., and Degenhardt, E. T. Paruresis: A survey of a disorder of micturition. *Journal of general psychology,* 1954, *51,* 19–29.

Williams. R. J. *Biochemical individuality.* New York: Wiley, 1963.

Williams, R. L. Scientific racism and IQ: The silent mugging of the black community. *Psychology today,* 1974, 7, 32–41, 92.

Williamson, G., and Payne, W. J. A. *An introduction to animal husbandry in the tropics.* London: Longmans, Green, 1959.

Wilmer, H. A. "Murder, you know." *Psychiatric quarterly,* 1969, *43,* 1–34.

Wittels, I., and Bornstein, P. E. A note on stress and sex determination. *Journal of genetic psychology,* 1974, *124,* 333–334.

Wohlsetter, A. Technology, prediction and disorder. *Bulletin of atomic scientists,* 1964, *20,* 11–15.

Wolf, S., and Wolff, H. G. *Human gastric function: An experimental study of a man and his stomach.* New York: Oxford University Press, 1943.

Wolff, H. G. *Stress and disease.* Springfield, Ill.: Thomas, 1953.

Wolman, B. B. *Dictionary of behavioral sciences,* New York: Van Nostrand Reinhold, 1973.

Woodger, J. H. *Biological principles.* London: Kegan Paul, Trench, Trubner, 1929.

Woodger, J. H. *Physics, psychology and medicine.* Cambridge, England: University Press, 1956.

Woodworth, R. S. *Psychology* (4th ed.). New York: Holt, 1940.

Wright, J. *The English dialect dictionary.* 6 vols. New York: Putnam's, 1898–1905.

Young, P. T. *Motivation of behavior.* New York: Wiley, 1936.

Young, P. T. *Emotion in man and animal.* Huntington, N.Y.: Krieger, 1973.

Zelazo, P. R. From reflexive to instrumental behavior. In L. Lipsitt (Ed.), *Developmental psychobiology: The significance of infancy.* Hillsdale, N.J.: Lawrence Erlbaum Associates, 1976.

Zelazo, P. R., Zelazo, N. A., and Kolb, S. "Walking" in the newborn. *Science,* 1972, *176,* 314–315. (a)

Zelazo, P. R., Zelazo, N. A., and Kolb, S. Newborn walking. *Science,* 1972, *177,* 1057–1060. (b)

Zelson, C., Rubio, E., and Wasserman, E. Neonatal narcotic addiction: 10-year observation. *Pediatrics,* 1971, *48,* 178–189.

Zeigarnik, B. Uber das Behalten von unerledigten Handlungen. *Psychologische Forschung,* 1927, *9,* 1–85.

Zemp, J. W., and Middaugh, L. D. Some effects of prenatal exposure to d-amphetamine sulfate and phenobarbital on developmental neurochemistry and on behavior. *Addictive diseases,* 1975, *2,* 307–331.

Indexes

Name Index

Abbot, Charles Greeley, 46–47, 310
Abrams, S., 434
Adler, A., 254
Aeschylus, 259
Alexander, F., 241–242
Alexander, L., 261
Alland, A., 293
Allen, J. P. B., 481
Allport, F. H., 351, 360–363, 369–370
Allport, G. W., 250
Altman, J., 388, 502
Anderson, A. R., 60
Anderson, M., 212
Anson, B. J., 206
Apgar, V., 120
Applebaum, M. I., 302–305, 306
Arayama, T., 90–93
Aristotle, 86, 259, 382
Arnheim, R., 349
Attanucci, J., 152–154
Azrin, N. H., 444

Bach, J. S., 197, 259
Baer, D. M., 203–204, 217, 227, 268, 331, 333
Bakal, D. A., 434, 435
Bakker, C. B., 213–214, 335
Baltes, P. B., 312
Balzac, Honoré de, 212–213
Bandura, A., 34, 40, 158–163
Barker, R. G., 34, 38–40, 55, 228–230
Barrett, J. E., 55
Barrington, B. L., 425
Barry, M. J. Jr., 450
Basmajian, J., 439
Bates, M., 176
Beecher, H. K., 254–255
Beethoven, van, L., 48, 59, 196, 197, 259
Bentley, A. F., 15, 388, 390, 502
Bergum, B. O., 346
Berlyne, D. E., 398, 399, 400
Bernstein, L., 59, 60
Bexton, W. H., 412, 413
Bijou, S., 138–139, 334
Billings, J., 197
Binet, A., 283
Binswanger, L., 209
Birch, H. G., 401
Birren, J. E., 310
Blake, P. R., 150
Blanton, R., 433
Bloodstein, O., 443
Blum, J. E., 310, 314
Blum, J. M., 285
Blumberg, M. L., 149
Bonaparte, Napoleon, 220

Bond, J. R., 293
Bornstein, P. E., 442
Bosanquet, C., 144, 146
Bourne, J. E., 381
Bowers, A. M., 237
Bowers, F., 483
Bowes, W. A., Jr., 98
Brace, C. L., 293, 294
Brackbill, Y., 98
Bradway, K., 309–310
Bressler, B., 396, 397
Briggs, J., 180
Brill, A. A., 146, 171, 240
Bronner, A. F., 237
Bronsema, G., 61
Brook, D., 59
Brophy, B., 58
Brown, L. F., 329–331
Brown, W. C., 284, 290
Browning, Robert, 46
Brunswick, E., 39
Bryant, William C., 46
Buck, R., 438, 439
Buffon, de G. L. L., 476
Burt, C., 295–297, 323
Butts, J. D., 83

Caesar, Julius, 220
Cameron, N., 16, 227, 256, 262, 265–268, 272, 275
Campbell, G., 371–372
Cannon, W. B., 456
Capote, T., 59
Carlyle, T., 59
Carmichael, L., 363–365, 367
Carnegie, A., 259
Carr, J. E., 456
Carroll, L., 477
Carter, J. W. Jr., 255–256
Caruso, E., 259
Casals, P., 69
Cassatt, Mary, 107
Cattell, P., 300–301, 314
Ceasar, J., 68
Charles, D. C., 307–309
Cherry, L., 441
Chomsky, N., 480, 481, 482, 483, 494
Clarke, A., 297
Cleaver, E., 214–215, 216
Cleckley, H. M., 257
Clement, J. D., 82–83
Cohen, S. J., 396, 397
Cohn, R. H., 492
Coles, E. M., 433
Collier, B., 46, 47
Colson, C., 215, 216
Conway, A., 98
Conway, J., 297
Cook, C. A., 67, 69
Cooper, L. A., 417, 418
Copans, S. A., 98

Corliss, R., 59
Craik, K. H., 34, 40
Curtiss, S., 154–157
Cushing, H., 30

Daley, D. D., 450
Darlington, C. D., 198
Darwin, C., 259, 283
Daube, J. R., 450, 451
Davidson, E. S., 160, 164–165
Davis, D. M., 408, 409
Davis, K., 122
Day, W. F., 419
Debussy, C., 259
DeForest, I., 210
Degenhardt, E. T., 11
Dement, W. C., 404, 406, 407
Demming, J. A., 311
Denney, R., 207–209
Descartes, R., 259
Dewey, J., 15, 459
Dickens, C., 259, 474
Dobbs, J. W., 83
Dodd, B. J., 480
Dominowski, R. L., 381
Donaldson, G., 313
Donat, A., 214
Dostoevsky, F. M., 259, 448, 449, 450
Duchowny, M. S., 98
Dunbar, E., 81
Duncker, K., 402, 403

Ebbinghaus, H., 51–53
Edison, T. A., 259
Edwards, A., 408, 409
Ehrlich, P., 259
Ehrlich, V., 462
Einstein, A., 13, 33, 259, 330
Eisdorfer, C., 310, 314
Ekstrand, B. R., 381
Emerson, R. W., 416
Emery, R. D., 269
Epstein, A. W., 406
Erikson, E. H., 258
Esterson, A., 279
Evans, P., 296

Faraday, M., 259
Farb, P., 467, 468, 482, 490
Faulkner, W., 259, 422
Finocchio, D. V., 50
Fisher, C., 408, 409
Fisher, G. H., 555–556
Fitzgerald, W., 259
Flamm, L. E., 346
Flanagan, B., 444
Fouts, R., 487, 488, 489, 490, 493
Fox, G., 274–275
Frank, L. M., 394
Frederiksen, W., 34, 40

Freud, S., 146, 232–242, 405, 456
Friedlander, S., 456
Fromm-Reichmann, F., 209

Galdston, R., 151
Galton, F., 283, 287
Gamalian, I., 69
Gamble, G. R., 293
Garber, H., 318–323, 334, 336
Gardner, B. T., 485, 486, 488, 489, 493
Gardner, R. A., 485, 488, 493
Gerard, D. L., 250–251
Gershon, E., 438
Gesell, A., 86, 89
Gewirtz, J. L., 479
Gibson, J. J., 393
Gill, T. V., 490
Gillie, O., 296
Gimbel, K. S., 455
Glazer, N., 207–209
Goddard, H. H., 244, 284, 286, 287
Goethe, von, Johann Wolfgang, 46
Goldiamond, I., 444
Goldstein, S., 454
Goleman, D., 249
Gonick, M. R., 229
Goodall, J., 400, 401, 403
Goode, D. M., 205
Gorer, G., 191
Gottlieb, G., 144
Greenberg, G., 123–124
Greene, G., 258–259
Greene, W. A., 454
Griffiths, B., 178
Groddeck, G., 234
Guthrie, G. M., 97
Guthrie, H. A., 97

Haber, W. B., 396
Hackett, T. P., 410, 411
Haire, D., 99, 110
Haley, A., 59
Hall, C. S., 405
Hansen, C., 269
Hanson, N. R., 5, 42, 346, 352–355, 379
Hardin, G., 245
Harris, W. H., 4, 47, 476
Hart, J., 215–216
Hartmann, E., 454
Harvey, W. P., 452, 453
Hauri, P., 407
Hazlitt, W., 220
Healy, W., 237
Hearnshaw, L. S., 297
Hearst, P., 192
Hebb, D. O., 412, 413

Subject Index